Foundations of Biopsychology

Visit the *Foundations of Biopsychology, second edition* Companion Website at **www.pearsoned.co.uk/wickens** to find valuable **student** learning material including:

- Learning objectives for each chapter
- Multiple choice questions to help test your learning
- Essay writing guide
- Internet search guide
- Mind Maps material focusing on the various parts of the brain

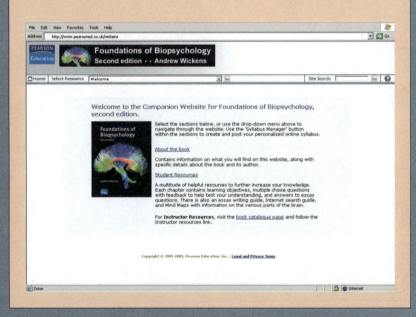

Front cover image: Coloured 3-dimensional MRI scan of the white matter pathways of the brain, side view.

White matter is composed of myelin-coated nerve cell fibres that carry information between nerve cells in the cerebrum of the brain (top half of image) and the brain stem (bottom centre). This image was created by an MRI scanner sensitised to the movement of water around the brain. Blue represents neural pathways from the top to the bottom of the brain, green represents pathways from the front (left) to the back (right), and red shows pathways between the right and left hemispheres of the brain.

Foundations of Biopsychology

Second edition

Andrew Wickens

PEARSON

Prentice Hall

Harlow, England • London • New York • Boston • San Francisco • Toronto
Sydney • Tokyo • Singapore • Hong Kong • Seoul • Taipei • New Delhi
Cape Town • Madrid • Mexico City • Amsterdam • Munich • Paris • Milan

Pearson Education Limited
Edinburgh Gate
Harlow
Essex CM20 2JE
England

and Associated Companies throughout the world

Visit us on the World Wide Web at:
www.pearsoned.co.uk

First published 2000
Second edition published 2005

ISBN 0 131 97138 7

British Library Cataloguing-in-Publication Data

A catalogue record for this book is available from the British Library

Library of Congress Cataloging-in-Publication Data
Wickens, Andrew P.
    Foundations of biopsychology / Andrew Wickens.—2nd ed.
        p. cm.
    Includes bibliographical references and index.
    ISBN 0-273-68694-1 (pbk.)
        1. Psychobiology.   I. Title.

    QP360.W525 2004
    152—dc22   2004053151

10 9 8 7 6 5 4 3 2 1
09 08 07 06 05

Typeset in 10.25/13.5pt Sabon by 35
Printed and bound by Ashford Colour Press, Gosport, Hants

The publisher's policy is to use paper manufactured from sustainable forests.

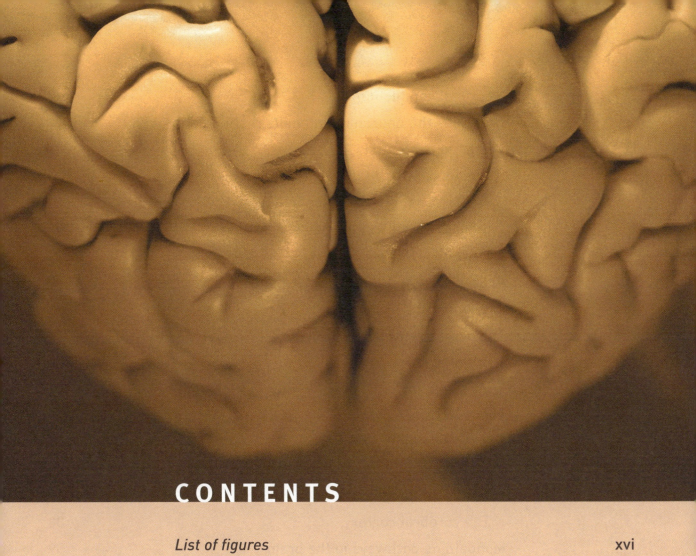

CONTENTS

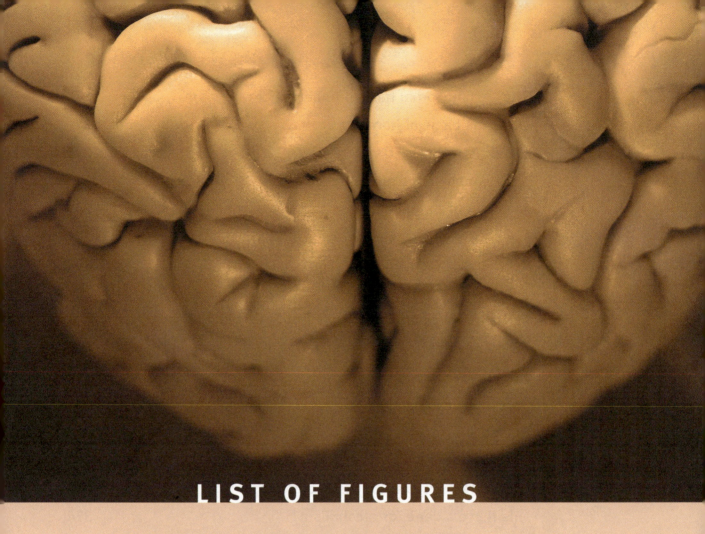

LIST OF FIGURES

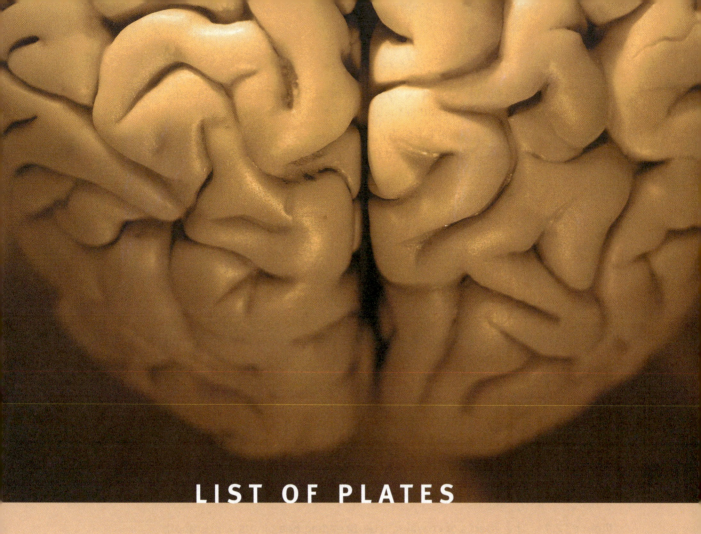

LIST OF PLATES

Supporting resources

Visit **www.pearsoned.co.uk/wickens** to find valuable online resources

Companion Website for students
- Learning objectives for each chapter
- Multiple choice questions to help test your learning
- Essay writing guide
- Internet search guide
- Mind Maps material focusing on the various parts of the brain

For instructors
- PowerPoint slides that can be downloaded and used as OHTs
- Seminar ideas that provide suggestions for questions and areas of discussion

Also: The regularly maintained Companion Website provides the following features:

- Search tool to help locate specific items of content
- E-mail results and profile tools to send results of quizzes to instructors
- Online help and support to assist with website usage and troubleshooting

For more information please contact your local Pearson Education sales representative or visit **www.pearsoned.co.uk/wickens**

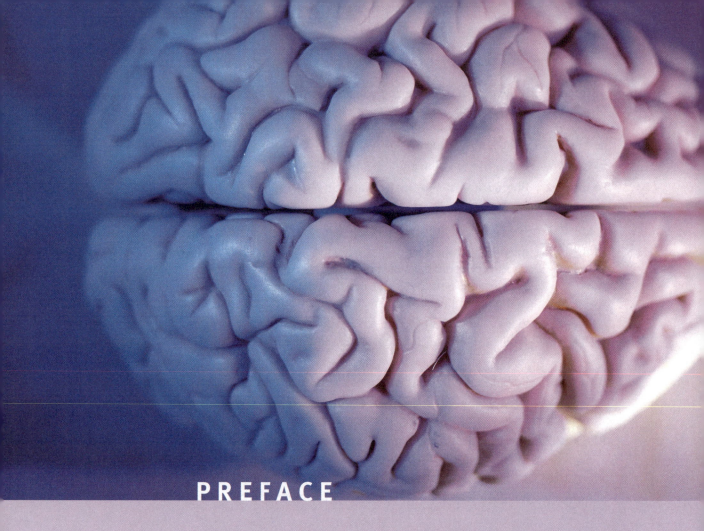

PREFACE

The human brain is the most complex living object known in the universe. Although an average adult brain only weighs about a kilogram and a half, it contains in the region of a billion nerve cells, and an unimaginable number of connections (or synapses) between them – tiny gaps constantly awash with neurotransmitters and chemicals, where the main information processing of the brain takes place. Somehow, the neural and chemical melee of our brain activity gives rise to the human mind with its remarkable capacity for behaviour, thought and consciousness. How it achieves this remarkable feat is still largely a mystery, and the conundrum taxes the ingenuity of psychologists, neuroscientists and philosophers alike. Nonetheless, the number of fascinating scientific discoveries about the brain increases with every year. The aim of this book is to make this ever-growing knowledge accessible and entertaining to the interested student who may not have any previous knowledge of biological psychology. It is also hoped that the book will take you on a journey that will fascinate, surprise and give you a greater insight into your behaviour and that of others.

This is the second edition of *Foundations of Biopsychology*, which updates much of the subject matter from the book first published in 2000. Moreover, this new edition has a number of new features, that greatly improves upon the old edition. Most noticeable is the inclusion of colour diagrams and pictures which gives the book greater visual appeal. It is sometimes said that a picture is worth a thousand words and, if this is true, then the new figures will greatly help you to grasp the subject with much more immediacy. Another feature is the brand new set of special interest boxes, which are designed to stimulate thought and show what a fascinating subject biological psychology is. The book also contains new chapter summaries and a comprehensive glossary. But, perhaps most importantly, this book now comes with a companion website, that is designed primarily to encourage independent learning. This website includes multiple choice questions for each chapter, useful website addresses, detailed information on how to research and write essays, and a mindmaps section that describes various areas of the brain and their functions. For a student who is keen to learn more about biological psychology, this will be a valuable learning resource.

Despite all these improvements, I still believe the most important feature of *Foundations of Biopsychology* is that it is comprehensive, yet easy to read! At the time of writing the first edition, I had been lecturing in biopsychology and neuroscience for over a decade, and knew that the secret of being a good teacher was to make the subject informative, entertaining and simple to follow. These also became the guiding principles I tried to follow in writing my book, whilst at the same time keeping it academically rigorous. The feedback I have received from students who have read the first edition has led me to believe that I was successful in my endeavour. Thus, I am even more secure in my belief now that this is a book which provides an enjoyable introduction to biopsychology, and with sufficient information for it to be used as an university text for a semester-based course. However, just as important, I hope it will also be of interest to anybody who wants to know more about the brain, and how it produces behaviour.

Biological psychology is the study of how the brain produces behaviour, and it is one of the most demanding subjects of all. Indeed, a good knowledge of biological psychology requires more than a passing understanding of many other disciplines including anatomy, physiology, biochemistry, pharmacology, genetics, and psychology. Thus, one might be excused for finding a simpler subject to study. But, by doing this, one would miss out on a subject that has no equal when it comes to providing such powerful and insightful explanations of human nature. The Nobel Prize laureate, Gerald Edelman, called the subject 'the most important one imaginable' because, in his view, 'at its end, we shall know how the mind works, what governs our nature and how we know the world'. This is only one of the benefits, because as our knowledge progresses, it will lead to far more successful treatments for a wide range of medical, behavioural and psychological problems. Without doubt, the scope and potential for biopsychology is enormous. And, it would be a shame if anyone interested in human behaviour was not part of it.

Inevitably, writing a book of this size will reflect the author's interests and biases. There are many areas that merit inclusion, but which have been omitted due to lack of space (this includes, for example, sensory systems other than vision, pain, and recovery from brain damage). On the other hand, unlike some texts, this book contains a final chapter on genetics which introduces some of the remarkable new developments taking place in molecular biology, that are likely to have a profound effect on biopsychology in the coming years. But, most of all, I hope this book will get across some of the excitement and wonder I feel when contemplating the brain – as well as providing an enjoyable and educational introduction to the biological basis of behaviour. If this book helps you to pass an exam in biopsychology that is great. But, if it has stimulated you to explore beyond its pages, and develop an ongoing fascination with the brain, then this book will have been an even greater success. I like to think that for some of its readers, *Foundations of Biopsychology* will do just that.

Andrew Wickens
October 2004

GUIDED TOUR OF THE BOOK

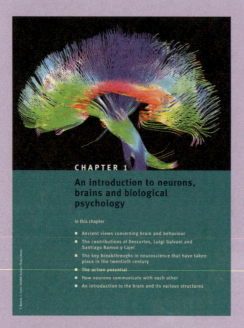

Each chapter opens with a **list of the main themes and issues** that are about to be explored.

An **Introduction** clearly outlines the scope of the chapter and introduces the themes for discussion.

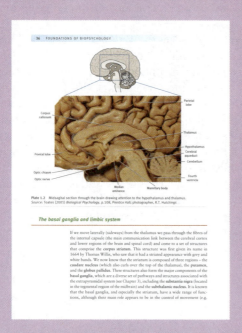

Coloured figures and photographs illustrate key topics, and processes visually to reinforce learning.

Special interest boxes throughout the text stimulate thought by bringing biological psychology to life through fascinating discussions of real-life examples.

A **Summary** at the end of each chapter helps you to recap and review the main topics discussed.

Essay Questions enable you to test your understanding and help track your progress. Each question is accompanied by a list of **Helpful internet search terms** for you to input when researching for your answer on the Web.

Each chapter is supported by suggested **Further Reading**, directing you to further information sources.

A comprehensive **Glossary** at the end of the book defines the key terms related to biological psychology.

GUIDED TOUR OF THE WEBSITE

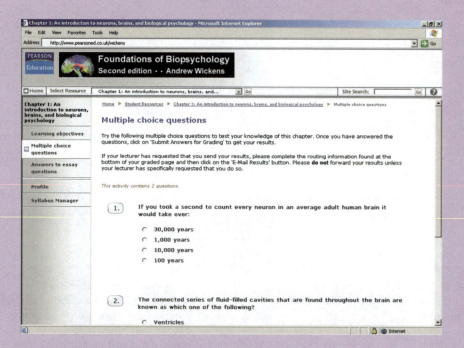

Multiple choice questions to test your learning.

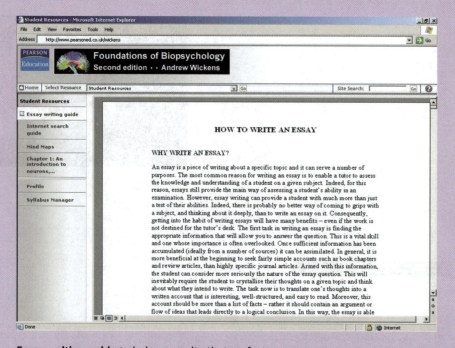

Essay writing guide to help you write that perfect essay.

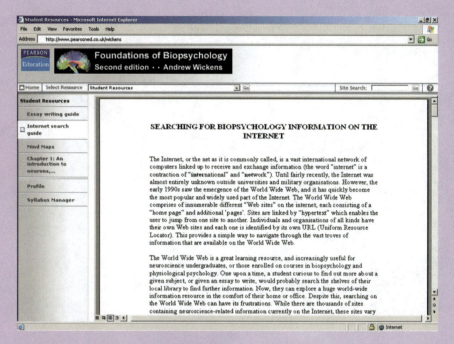

Internet search guide to help you efficiently navigate the Web.

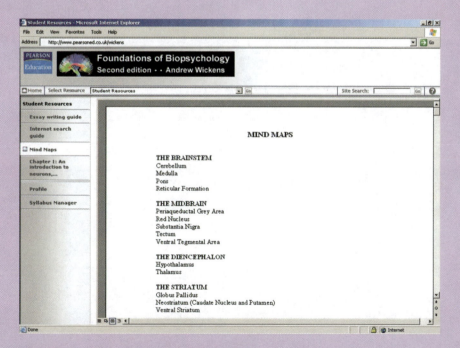

Mind Maps to aid your exploration of the brain.

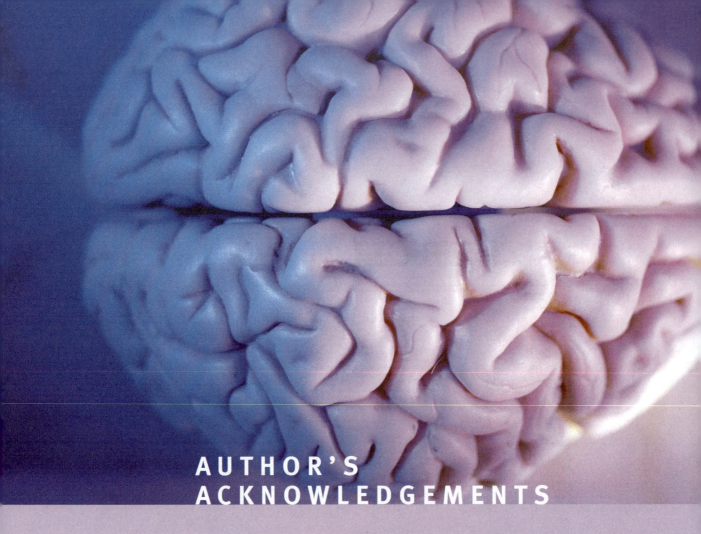

AUTHOR'S ACKNOWLEDGEMENTS

There are many people to whom the author owes gratitude for the development and publication of this book. In particular, I am thankful to my editor, Morten Fuglevand, who is the main instigator behind this new edition. His support, enthusiasm and belief in the book made my task an easier and much more enjoyable one. I would also like to thank Sarah Wild who has assisted me in many ways – not least for taking care of copyright issues, and helping track down the pictures and plates that now adorn the pages of the book. Others who also deserve credit are Alex Whyte who copy-edited the scripts, Sally and Mark Spedding of Outbox who drew the artwork, and Kevin Ancient who was responsible for the book's layout and design of its cover. I am sure there are also many others at Pearson Education who I have failed to name, yet have made important contributions to these pages. Finally, I should also like to mention two work colleagues – Mike Stone and Andrew Churchill – who unwittingly gave me ideas for two of the special interest boxes.

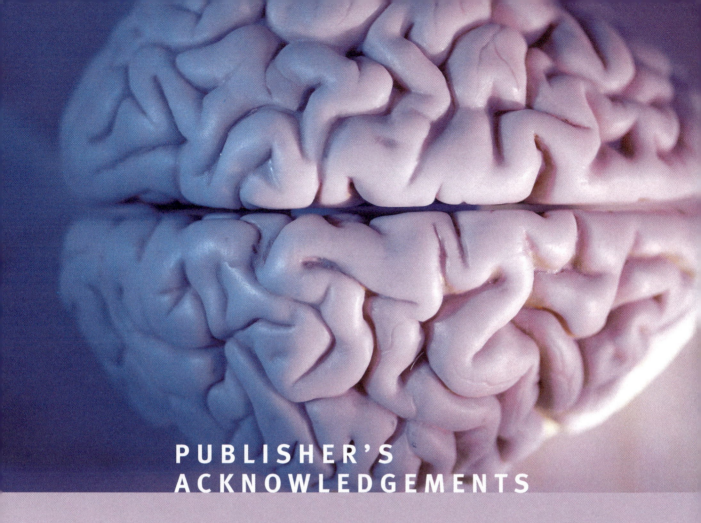

PUBLISHER'S ACKNOWLEDGEMENTS

We are grateful to the following for permission to reproduce copyright material:

Fig. 1.3 from *Franz Joseph Gall, Inventor of Phrenology and His Collection*, (Ackerknecht and Vallois, 1956), reprinted with permission; Plates 1.1, 1.2, 1.3a from *Biological Psychology*, (Toates, F. 2001) with permission from Pearson Education and Ralph T. Hutchings; Plate 1.3b reprinted by permission of Omikron/Photo Researchers Inc; Fig. 1.19, from *Physiology of Behaviour,* 7th edition (Carlson, Neil R, 1998). Published by Allyn and Bacon, Boston, MA. Copyright © 2001 Pearson Education. Reprinted by permission of the publisher; Plate 2.1 from *The Journal of Neuroscience*, August 1991, Vol. 11(8), p.2392, figure 7 (Corbetta *et al.* 1991). Copyright © 1991 by the Society for Neuroscience; Figs. 2.3, 2.8, 3.8, 4.3, 8.3, 8.8, 8.17 from *Biopsychology*, 3rd edition (Pinel, John P.J. 1997) Published by Allyn and Bacon, Boston, MA. Copyright © 1997 by Pearson Education. Reprinted by permission of the publisher; Fig. 2.4 from *Proceedings of the Royal Society of London*. 166, 80–111 (Dowling, J.E. and Boycott, B.B., 1966). Used with permission of the Royal Society of London; Fig. 2.7 from The Open University, course SD286, Module C7; Figs. 2.9 and 2.11 from *Eye, Brain and Vision*, (Hubel, D.H. 1995), with permission from the author; Figs. 2.10, 3.5(a)&(b), 3.7 from *Elements of Physiological Psychology* (Schneider, A.M. and Tarshis, B. 1995), © 1995 The McGraw-Hill Companies, Inc; Fig. 2.17 from *Images of Mind* (Michael I. Posner and Marcus E. Raichle 1997). Copyright © 1994, 1997 by Scientific American Library. Reprinted by permission of Henry Holt and Company, LLC; Fig. 3.2 from *Human Anatomy and Physiology*, (Carola, *et al.* 1990), with permission from John Hagan; Plate 3.1a&b, with thanks to Daniel P. Perl, MD, Mount Sinai School of Medicine; Plate 3.1c with thanks to Alfred Pasieka/Science Photo Library; Plates 3.2 and 10.1 from *Physiology of Behaviour*, 8th edition, (Carlson 2004), published by Allyn and Bacon, Boston, MA. Copyright © 2004 by Pearson Education. Reprinted with permission from the publisher; Fig. 3.6 from *Neuroanatomy through Clinical Cases*, (Blumenfeld 2002). Used with permission of Sinauer Associates Inc; Plate 4.2 from *Biopsychology* 5th edition (Pinel, John P.J. 2003). Published by Allyn and Bacon, Boston, MA. Copyright © 2001 by Pearson Education. Reprinted by permission of the publisher and The Jackson Laboratory; Figs. 5.1, 5.6, 5.9, 8.9 from *Neuroscience: Exploring the Brain* (Bear, M.F., Connors, B.W., Paradiso, M.A. 1996). Copyright © 1996 Lippincott, Williams and Wilkins; Plate 5.1 from *Neurophysiology and Emotion*, (Glass, D.C. 1967) © Russell Sage Foundation. Reprinted with permission from the Russell Sage Foundation and The Rockefeller University Press; Fig. 5.5 from *Cognitive Neuroscience and Neuropsychology*, 2nd edition (Banich, Marie, T.) Copyright © 2004 by Houghton Mifflin Company. Used with permission; Plate 5.11 reprinted with permission from the Warren Anatomical Museum; Fig. 5.12 from Freeman, W. (1949) *Proceedings of the Royal Society of Medicine*; Plate 6.1 reprinted with permission from the Stanford Center for Narcolepsy; Plate 6.3 from Alfred Pasieka/Science Photo Library; Figs. 6.5, 7.1 from *Physiology of Behaviour* 6th Edition (Carlson, Neil R. 1998). Published by Allyn and Bacon, Boston, M.A. Copyright © 1998 by Pearson Education. Reprinted by permission of publisher; Plate 7.1 reprinted with permission from Reptile Conservation International, photograph by P. DeVries; Fig. 7.4 from *Evolution and Human Behaviour*, vol. 22 (Professor J.T. Manning 2001). Reproduced by permission of Professor Manning; Plate 8.1 from Simon Fraser/MRC Unit, Newcastle General Hospital/Science Photo Library; Fig. 8.2 from *Brain Mechanisms and Intelligence* (Lashley, K.S. 1963), with permission from Dover Publications, Inc; Fig. 8.6 from 'Brain changes in response to experience', *Scientific American* (Rosenzweig, M.R., Bennett, E.L., and Diamond, M.C. 1972) © by W.H. Freeman and Company. Used with permission; Fig. 8.14 from *Brain, Mind and Behaviour*, (Floyd Bloom, *et al.* 1985) © 1985 by Educational Broadcasting Corp. Used with permission; Fig. 8.15 from *Nature*, 297, (Morris, R.G.M. *et al.* 1982) reprinted with permission from Macmillan Magazines Limited; Fig. 8.16 from 'Navigation-related structural change in the hippocampi of taxi drivers' from *Proceedings of the National Academy of Sciences* (Maguire, E.A. *et al.* 2000). Copyright © 2000 National Academy of Sciences; Fig. 9.1 from *Biological Psychology*, 3rd edition (Rosenzweig *et al.* 2002). Used with permission of Sinauer Associates, Inc; Plate 9.2, photograph of the Beatles © Bettmann/CORBIS, photograph of the MRI brain scanner from the British Neuroscience Association; Plate 9.3 from Wellcome Dept. of Cognitive Neurology/Science Photo Library; Fig. 9.4 from *Fundamentals of Human Neuropsychology*, (Kolb and Whishaw 1985) © by W.H. Freeman and Company. Used with permission; Fig. 9.7 from *Neuroscience*, (Purves, D. *et al.* 1997), used by permission of Sinauer Associates; Plate 10.1, with thanks to the National Institute of Health; Plate 10.2 from National Institute of Health/Science Photo Library; Fig. 11.5 from *Physiological Psychology*, (Graham, R.B. 1990), with permission from the author; Plate 11.1a © Copyright Dan Piraro. Reprinted with special permission of North America Syndicate; Plate 11.1b from *Neuron*, (Mobbs *et al.* 2003) Copyright 2003, with permission from Elsevier; Table 12.1 from *Behavioural Genetics*, 3rd edition (Robert Plomin, *et al.*) © 1980, 1990, 1997, by W.H. Freeman and Company. Used with permission; Plate 12.1 from Biophoto Associates/Science Photo Library; Plate 12.2 from A. Barrington/Science Photo Library; Plate 12.3 © Bettmann/COBIS; Fig. 12.4 from *Biological Science 2 3rd edition*, (R. Soper, N.P.O. Green, G.W. Stout , D.J. Taylor 1997). Used by permission of Cambridge University Press.

In some instances we have been unable to trace the owners of copyright material, and we would appreciate any information that would enable us to do so.

CHAPTER 1

An introduction to neurons, brains and biological psychology

In this chapter

- Ancient views concerning brain and behaviour

- The contributions of Descartes, Luigi Galvani and Santiago Ramon y Cajel

- The key breakthroughs in neuroscience that have taken place in the twentieth century

- The action potential

- How neurons communicate with each other

- An introduction to the brain and its various structures

INTRODUCTION

An isolated human brain is a pinkish-grey mass of tissue which at first sight is not dissimilar in appearance to a giant walnut. If held in the palm of one's hand, it is deceptively firm and heavy (an adult brain weighs about three and a half pounds or 1.5 kilograms) and greasy to touch. It may not appear to be the most complex object in the universe, but it probably is. Indeed, when holding a brain in our hands, or viewing it from a distance, it is difficult not to be moved by what we have in our presence. This structure once housed the mind of a human being – memories, thoughts and emotions; wishes, aspirations and disappointments – and the person's capability for consciousness, reflection and free will. Moreover, this organ has enabled the human race to become the most dominant species on Earth with all of its many artistic, scientific, medical and technological achievements. But what exactly is it that is so special about the human brain? Part of the answer is undoubtedly its great complexity. Like any other part of the body, the brain is composed of highly specialised cells, the most important being **neurons**, whose function is to communicate with each other using a mechanism that is not dissimilar to an electrical on–off switch. It has been estimated that our brain contains in the region of a billion neurons (1,000,000,000,000) – a figure so great that if you took a second to count each one it would take over 30,000 years (Gilling and Brightwell 1982). However, what makes the human brain really complex is the way its neurons are connected. Neurons rarely form connections with each other on a one-to-one basis, but rather they have a large number of axon terminals which project to many other neurons. Moreover, the average neuron has around 10,000 synapses (actually, a small gap between axon terminal and recipient terminal). This means that for 1 billion neurons there may be 100 trillion synaptic connections in the human brain, and it is at these sites where the remarkable capacity for information processing takes place. This figure is truly astronomical – in fact, Richard Thompson (e.g. Thompson 1993) has gone so far to say that the number of possible synaptic connections among cells in the human brain is greater than the number of atomic particles that constitute the entire universe. If you don't fully understand this logic, don't worry, nor does the author of this book – but it is certainly a lot of connections!

One might be forgiven for thinking that the brain is so complex that it defies comprehension. But, I hope this book will show otherwise. The study of the brain is one of the most rapidly expanding areas in modern science today, and part of this development is a quest to understand how its physical and chemical structure gives rise to human behaviour. In addition, brain research has many practical benefits for us all, including greater insights into the causes of a great variety of human afflictions, such as mental illness and degenerative diseases, along with the prospect of much more effective treatments. The brain may be complex, but it is increasingly giving up its secrets to scientific progress. Arguably, there is no other discipline that can give us greater insight into ourselves, as well as having the potential to change people's lives for the better.

What is biological psychology?

To understand what is meant by biological psychology it is helpful first to put the word 'psychology' under the spotlight. The term derives from the Greek words *psyche* meaning 'mind' and *logos* meaning 'reason'. Thus, 'psychology' literally means the reasoning (or study) of the mind. However, few psychologists would unreservedly accept this definition today. The study of psychology first emerged in the eighteenth century as a branch of philosophy concerned with explaining the processes of thought by using the technique of introspection (i.e. self-reflection). The problem with this method, however, is that no matter how skilled the practitioner, it is subjective and its findings cannot be verified by others. Because of this, a more experimental approach to psycholgy began to emerge in the late nineteenth century that focused on mental phenomena, and perhaps more importantly on behaviour that could be observed and measured (James 1890, Watson 1913). The emphasis on experimentation and measurement has continued to the present day and many psychologists would probably now describe psychology as *the scientific or experimental study of behaviour and mental life*.

Psychology has now developed into a wide-ranging discipline and is concerned with understanding behaviour and mental processes from a variety of perspectives. As the name suggests, biological psychology is the branch of science that attempts to explain behaviour in terms of biology, and since the most important structure controlling behaviour is the brain, biological psychology is therefore *the study of the brain and how it causes or relates to behaviour*. Implicit in this definition is the assumption that every thought, feeling and behaviour must have a physical or neural basis in the brain. In fact, this is the same as saying that the mind is the product of the brain's electrical and neurochemical activity. Although there are some philosophical grounds for criticising this viewpoint (Gregory 1981) it must nevertheless be the case that mind and brain are inextricably linked, and this is the main assumption on which biological psychology is based.

To link the brain with behaviour, however, is a daunting task. Indeed, any attempt to do this requires a good understanding of the brain itself, and traditionally the two areas most relevant to the biological psychologist in this respect have been **neuroanatomy** (the study of how the various parts of the brain are connected) and **neurophysiology** (the study of how neurons 'work'). However, in the last few decades the study of brain function has expanded greatly and attracted the interest of specialists from many other disciplines, including those from **biochemistry, molecular biology, endocrinology, pharmacology** and **psychiatry**. Not all scientists working in these fields are necessarily interested in behaviour, although those who are have an important contribution to make to biological psychology. Consequently, in recent years, psychologists interested in the brain have had to become acquainted with many other areas of biological science that lie outside the traditional domains of anatomy, physiology and psychology.

A number of different names have been used to describe the study of brain and behaviour, and for the first-time student these terms can be confusing. For most of the twentieth century, the study of brain and behaviour was called **physiological psychology** because its investigators typically used 'physiological' techniques such as **lesioning** (the removal of various parts of the brain) and **stimulation** (both electrical and chemical) as their main experimental tools. This approach was often complemented by examining human subjects who had suffered brain damage from accidents, stroke, etc., and this area was known as **clinical neuropsychology**. Although these terms are still used today, there is a growing realisation that they do not adequately cover many of the newer techniques being used to examine brain function. Because of this, others have argued for broader terms such as 'biological psychology' or 'behavioural neuroscience' to describe these areas of research (Davis *et al.* 1988, Dewsbury 1991). Whatever the arguments for and against these terms, they roughly mean the same thing – they are trying to give an appropriate name to the scientific discipline that attempts to relate the biology of the brain to behaviour.

Ancient historical beginnings

Among the first people to realise that the brain was the organ of the mind (and thus behaviour) were the Ancient Greeks. For instance, Plato (429–348 BC) proposed that the brain was the organ of reasoning – although others disagreed, including his pupil Aristotle, who believed that the heart served this function and that the brain merely served to cool the blood. In most of the ancient world, the human body was sacred and autopsies were prohibited (the first drawings of the human brain were not undertaken prior to Leonardo da Vinci around 1480), though the Greeks were aware of the basic shape of the brain, mainly through animal dissection, and of its **ventricles** – a series of connected fluid-filled cavities that could be seen when the brain was sliced open (Figure 1.1). Because the ventricles stood out visually as one of the main features of the brain, it is perhaps not surprising that these structures were used to formulate theories about how the brain worked.

One of the first writers to propose a theory of brain function based on the ventricles was Galen (AD 130–200), who was the most important physician of the Roman Empire. Galen believed that the heart was the crucial organ of the body because it contained the *vital spirit* that gave the spark of life to the person. This vital spirit was also seen as providing the 'substance' of the mind, and it was transported to a large group of blood vessels at the base of the brain called the *rete mirabile* ('wonderful net'). Here the vital spirit was mixed with air that had been inhaled through the nose, and transformed into *animated spirit* that was stored in the ventricles. When needed, the vital spirit was then seen as being able to enter nerves that passed into the body, where it moved muscles and produced behaviour. Galen knew that the brain had four main ventricles (the first two,

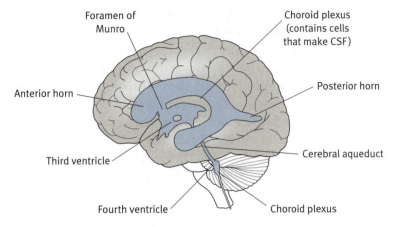

Figure 1.1   Lateral view of the ventricles of the brain

now called the lateral ventricles, form a symmetrical pair inside the cerebral cortex, which then feed into the third ventricle, located in the mid-part of the brain that joins with the fourth ventricle in the brain stem) although he did not ascribe them different functions.

However, others who followed Galen expanded these ideas, and in the fourth century AD, Nemesius, the Bishop of Emesa, hypothesised that the lateral ventricles were the site of sensory and mental impressions, the third ventricle was the site of reason and the fourth ventricle was the site of memory. This theory was to become the most popular in the brain's written history as it remained unchallenged for nearly 1,500 years. In fact, it only began to be challenged in 1543 when Vesalius showed that the human brain does not actually contain a *rete mirabile*. It seems that Galen, who had not been allowed to perform human dissection in Rome, had inferred its human existence by observing it in animals.

René Descartes

René Descartes (1596–1650) was a famous French philosopher who, more than any other individual, was responsible for the demise of the intellectual assumptions of the Middle Ages, and helped to usher in a new age of reason. His importance in psychology lies largely with his attempt at resolving the mind–body problem. Descartes believed, as did Plato, that mind and body were two entirely different things (a theory known as dualism) with the body composed of physical matter and the mind or soul being non-physical and independent of the material world. A problem with this position, however, lies in trying to explain how the non-material mind can control the physical workings of the body. In his attempt to provide an answer, Descartes proposed the **pineal gland** to be the site where mind and body interacted. Descartes chose the pineal gland since it was a single structure in the brain (most other brain areas are paired) and because, in his view, the soul had to be a single indivisible entity. Moreover, it helped that the pineal gland was located close to the third ventricle, and partly bathed by the cerebrospinal fluid, where it was in a prime position to influence the animated spirits of the brain. Thus, for Descartes, the pineal gland provided an ideal site where the soul could act upon the body (Mazzolini 1991).

Despite this, Descartes also realised that a great deal of behaviour was mechanical and did not require mental intervention. In fact, it was during a visit to the Royal Gardens in Paris as a young man that he probably began to develop this idea. The gardens exhibited mechanical statues that moved and danced whenever they were approached (this movement was caused by hydraulic pressure-sensitive plates hidden under the ground) and this experience led Descartes to reason that the human body might also work along similar mechanical principles. From this premise, he developed the concept of the automatic **reflex**, which occurs, for example, when a limb is quickly moved away from a hot source such as a fire. To explain this response, Descartes hypothesised that a sensory nerve composed of a hollow tube containing *vital spirit* conveyed the message of heat to the ventricles of the brain, which in turn directed animal spirit to flow out through the nerves from the brain, back to the muscles of the affected limb thereby causing its withdrawal. The important point was that this behaviour was reflexive: the mind was not involved (although it felt pain and was aware of what had happened) and therefore not a *cause* of behaviour.

Prior to Descartes, it had generally been accepted that the soul controlled all the actions of the human body. But Descartes showed that the human body worked according to mechanical principles – not unlike the mechanism of a watch – and did not need a soul to make it operate once it had been put into motion. More controversially, Descartes not only proposed that functions such as digestion and respiration were reflexive, but also a number of mental functions, including sensory impressions, emotions and memory. He based this idea partly on his observation that animals (which he believed had no soul) were also capable of sensory processing along with emotion and memory. Thus, if these did not need the involvement of a soul (or mind), why not the same in humans? In other words, these behaviours could be seen as reflexive responses that belonged to the world of physical phenomena. The one exception, according to Descartes, was reasoning and pure thought, which he believed was the exclusive property of the soul and unique to humans – a view that was also in accordance with the religious teachings of the time.

Descartes' theory was to help to lay the foundations for the modern development of physiology and psychology. Although it continued to be a dualist theory of the mind that had existed since antiquity, it helped to shift the focus more on to the problem of how reflexes may operate in human behaviour and mental processing, without fear of contradicting religious dogma. In addition, it encouraged others to speculate more deeply on the localisation of different functions in the brain. But, perhaps most important, Descartes' work provided a great impetus for experimental research, and not least because some of his ideas could be tested. For example, as we have seen, Descartes believed that the nervous system controlling reflexes was a hydraulic system consisting of hollow tubes through which fluids (or animal spirits) flowed from the ventricles to the muscles. If this idea was correct then it followed that muscles should increase in volume as they 'swelled' with animal spirit during contraction. When investigators tested this theory, however, by flexing a person's arm in a container of water, no increase in its level was found.

The discovery of 'animal' electricity

In 1791, the idea of animal spirit as the cause of nervous activity was challenged by the Italian Luigi Galvani, who undertook a series of experiments on amputated frog legs that included the exposed ends of their severed nerves. Galvani found that he could induce the frog's leg to twitch in a number of ways – as was indeed shown in one famous case where, during a thunderstorm, he connected a nerve stump to a long metallic wire that pointed to the sky and obtained strong muscular contractions in the detached leg. He also found that he could produce similar movements when he suspended the frog's leg between two different metals. Although he did not know it at the time, Galvani had shown that when dissimilar metals make contact through a salt solution an electrical current is produced (this was, in fact, the first demonstration of the battery later formally invented by Volta in 1800). These discoveries led Galvani to conclude that nerves are capable of conducting electricity and their 'invisible spirit' must be electrical in nature. Some 50 years after Galvani published his work, various ways of measuring electrical currents were discovered and, when these were applied to nervous tissue, electrical activity was indeed observed. Thus, the twitching frog's legs marked the end to hydraulic theories of nervous action and the start of a new chapter in understanding how nerve cells work (Piccolino 1997).

The discovery of the nerve cell

Although Galvani had shown that nervous energy was electrical, there was still much to learn about how nerves worked. For example, in the eighteenth century there was no real idea of what nerves looked like (other than they had long thin projections), and many believed that nerves were joined together in much the same way as blood vessels are interconnected (i.e. through a system of connecting tubes). These beliefs persisted despite the invention of the microscope in 1665 by Robert Hooke, (who was the first to coin the word 'cell'), and the subsequent work of Anton Von Leeuwenhoek who used it to examine biological tissue. Unfortunately, the early microscopes did not reveal neural structure in great detail, and it was not until around 1830 when better kinds of lenses were developed that they were able to provide stronger and clearer magnification. Even so,

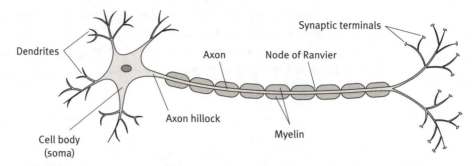

Figure 1.2   The main components of a typical brain neuron

there was the problem of how to prepare the tissue for microscopic work so that nerve cells could be distinguished from other types of material. Although, by the 1800s, histologists had found new ways to stain nerve tissue, their methods stained all neurons indiscriminately. This meant that the only way to visualise a neuron was to remove it from the morass in which it was embedded. Not surprisingly, with neurons being far too small to be seen with the naked eye, this proved extremely difficult and was only occasionally or partially successful.

In 1875, however, a major breakthrough occurred when the Italian anatomist Camillo Golgi (1843–1926) discovered a new stain that allowed individual nerve cells to be observed. By serendipity, he had found that exposing nervous tissue to silver nitrate caused nerve cells to turn black, enabling them to stand out in bold relief and be clearly seen under a microscope. But, even more importantly, Golgi's technique only stained around 2 per cent of the cells in any given slice of nervous tissue. This was a great advantage as it made individual neurons, and all their various components such as **dendrites** and **axons** (Figure 1.2), much more clearly observable. This method soon proved indispensable for examining the wide variety of cells in the brain. Indeed, much of the basic terminology that we now use to describe nerve cells were introduced by anatomists around this time (*circa* 1880).

The person who put the Golgi stain to its greatest use, however, was the Spaniard Santiago Ramon y Cajel (1852–1934), who described the neural anatomy of almost every part of the brain using this technique. He also showed that the brain contains a great variety of cells with many different characteristics. Although some cells had short axons that projected to cells within the same structure (now known as **interneurons**), others had long axons that often formed bundles (or pathways) that projected to distant brain regions. Ramon y Cajel also showed that the brain was not a random jumble of nerve cells as had previously been believed, but a highly organised structure with different regions and nuclei (groups of cell bodies). In other words, the gross structure of the human brain was highly predictable. Santiago Ramon y Cajel even helped to explain how neurons worked. For example, his observations led him to realise that neurons received input via their dendrites and they, in turn, projected information along their cable-like pathways, called **axons** (see Figure 1.5). Thus, he was one of the first to understand how information might travel throughout the neural circuits of the brain.

Ramon y Cajel's most important contribution to neuroanatomy was probably his discovery that nerve cells were separate and individual units. Previously, it had been believed that nerve cells were joined together in a network of tubes which allowed the direct passage of information from cell to cell (in fact, Golgi himself was a strong advocate of this 'reticular' theory). However, Ramon y Cajel showed that nerve cells do not join in this way – rather, the axon terminals end very close to the neurons (or dendrites) to which they project, but do not touch. In other words, each neuron is an individual unit separated from its neighbour by a very small gap (these gaps were called **synapses** in 1897 by Charles Sherrington). This discovery raised many new questions, not least the problem of how nerve cells sent information across the synapse, and how this was able to generate a new electrical signal in the postsynaptic neuron.

Following Golgi's discovery many other staining techniques were developed that enabled investigators to examine nerve cells in more detail. For example, some techniques were able to selectively stain cell bodies (the **soma**), whereas others stained the axons (or rather their **myelin** covering) allowing neural pathways in the brain to be traced. In other instances, staining techniques were combined with lesioning methods to provide useful information (e.g. neural pathways can be traced by staining degenerating axons that arise from a structure that has been experimentally destroyed). By the turn of the century the study of neuroanatomy had become an established discipline (Shepherd 1991). Moreover, this subject provided one of the foundation stones on which physiological psychology was based, for without knowledge of brain structure and organisation, very little can be said about how it produces behaviour.

The rise and fall of phrenology: do you need your head examined?

Franz Joseph Gall (1758–1828) is regarded as the founder of phrenology, although he did not approve of the term or wanted to be associated with the phrenological movement. Nonetheless, he was the first to propose that it was possible to measure a person's character by examining the shape and surface of that person's skull. Gall first became interested in this possibility as a 9-year-old schoolboy, when he noted a classmate with bulging eyes who was gifted in being able to remember verbatim long passages of script. This observation led Gall to reason that the ability for verbal memory lay in the frontal region of the brain behind the eyes. Later, as a young doctor, Gall examined the cranial features of a wide variety of people, including criminals, the insane, peasants, great writers, artists and statesman. His technique involved feeling the contours of the head for a cranial prominence, assuming that it represented a well-developed area of the brain below. By 1792, Gall had discovered several regions (or 'organs') of the brain where he believed distinct faculties resided. These included, for example, the faculty of murder and the inclination to steal. Gall was to eventually identify 27 cranial regions that he believed corresponded to a discrete mental trait.

Gall's work attracted much controversy. Indeed, it was clear to many investigators, even in the nineteenth century, that differences in the shape of the skull were unrelated to underlying

The rise and fall of phrenology: do you need your head examined? continued.

brain tissue – a fact that invalidated phrenology. It was also impossible to measure the bumps of the skull precisely, which meant that Gall's observations could not be proved or disproved. Gall also used highly suspect data at times to support his theories. For example, he localised

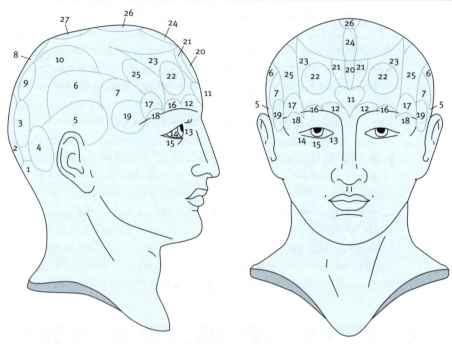

Gall's Faculties of Mind

Faculties shared by humans and animals

1. Reproductive instinct
2. Love of one's offspring
3. Affection or friendship
4. Instinct of self-defence, or courage
5. Destructiveness, carnivorous instinct, or tendency to murder
6. Cunning
7. Desire to possess things
8. Pride
9. Vanity or ambition

10. Circumspection or forethought
11. Memory for facts and things
12. Sense of place
13. Memory for people
14. Memory for words
15. Sense of language
16. Sense of colour
17. Sense of sounds, gift of music
18. Sense of numbers
19. Mechanical or architectural sense

Distinctly human faculties

20. Wisdom
21. Sense of metaphysics
22. Satire and wit
23. Poetic talent

24. Kindness and benevolence
25. Mimicry
26. Religious sentiment
27. Firmness of purpose

Figure 1.3   Gal's system of organology as seen from right and frontal views. *Source*: Ackerknecht and Vallois (1956) *Franz Joseph Gall, Inventor of Phrenology and His Collection*

The rise and fall of phrenology: do you need your head examined? continued.

'destructiveness' to a region above the ear, because it was the largest part of the cranium in carnivores – and a prominence had been found there in a student who was 'so fond of torturing animals that he became a surgeon'. Even had the methods been sound, Gall's classification of psychological functions such as faith, self-love and veneration were impossible to define or quantify. Despite a lack of scientific support, however, phrenology became extremely popular in the nineteenth century. Entrepreneurs such as the Fowler brothers promoted phrenology as a tool for self-improvement, and a large number of respectable phrenological societies were formed. It was also not unusual for people to seek the advice of a phrenologist to hire employees, select a marriage partner, or diagnose an illness – while social reformers proposed that phrenology could be used to rehabilitate criminals, or even select better members of Parliament! Even after phrenology had long been discredited, many were still keen to get their 'bumps' examined, in an attempt to find out more about themselves.

Although phrenology was discredited, Gall's impact on brain research was in some ways positive. For example, prior to the nineteenth century, dualist concepts of brain function held sway that viewed thoughts and emotions as arising from the mind and not necessarily the brain. However, Gall held that the brain was the physical organ of mind that governed all mental faculties and feelings. This was a step forward and allowed scientists more freedom to explore the physiology of the brain. Gall's idea that the cerebral cortex contains different areas with localised functions was another important advance. In fact, he was not entirely wrong, as regions of the cerebrum were later discovered that were specifically involved in language and movement. Also, as this book will show, it is now known that a range of mental functions can be localised to selected areas of the cerebral hemispheres.

The discovery of chemical transmission

One of the most important questions that followed from Ramon y Cajel's work concerned the nature of the message that passed across the synapse from the **presynaptic** (or projecting neuron) to the **postsynaptic** (recipient) neuron. From the time of Galvani, it was known that neurons were electrical in nature, but what about synapses? Did an electrical current jump across the tiny synaptic gap, or was there some other form of communication? As early as 1877 it had been suggested that chemical transmission might be the answer, and in 1905 it was found that the application of adrenaline to nervous tissue produced effects similar to electrical stimulation. However, the crucial experiment that proved chemical transmission was performed by Otto Loewi in 1921. This experiment has now become part of pharmacological folklore. On the night of Easter Saturday (1921) Loewi awoke from a sleep and wrote down the details of an experiment that he had just dreamed about. He then went back to sleep, but upon waking next morning was unable to decipher the notes he had written.

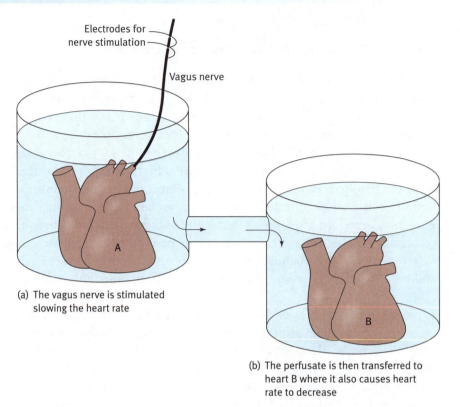

(a) The vagus nerve is stimulated slowing the heart rate

(b) The perfusate is then transferred to heart B where it also causes heart rate to decrease

Figure 1.4   Loewi's experimental set-up showing that nerves send messages by releasing chemical substances

The following morning he awoke at 3 o'clock with the idea back in his mind, and this time went straight to the laboratory to perform an experiment. Two hours later, the chemical transmission of the nervous impulse across the synapse (Figure 1.4) had essentially been proved (Finger 1994).

In his experiment, Loewi used frog hearts, which are similar to our own in that they are supplied by two different peripheral nerves: the sympathetic, which excites the heart and makes it beat more rapidly; and the parasympathetic (also called the vagus nerve), which slows it down. Loewi used two hearts: one with the sympathetic and vagus nerves intact, and the other with the nerves removed. He then placed the intact heart in a fluid bath and stimulated its vagus nerve causing its beat to slow down. Loewi collected the fluid surrounding this heart and applied it to the second one – and found that its beat also began to slow down. The results could only mean one thing: the fluid contained a substance that had been secreted by the stimulated vagus nerve projecting to the heart. Later analyses by Sir Henry Dale and his colleagues showed this chemical to be acetylcholine, now known as an important neurotransmitter in the peripheral and central nervous systems.

It is now well established that neurons communicate with each other, across the synapse, by releasing chemical transmitters (Figure 1.5). The series of events that produce this transmission can be described as follows: (1) the axon terminals of the presynaptic neuron receive an electrical impulse called an **action potential** (this will be discussed later), and in response they secrete a **neurotransmitter** that (2) passes across the synapse, and (3) acts on the postsynaptic neuron at sites

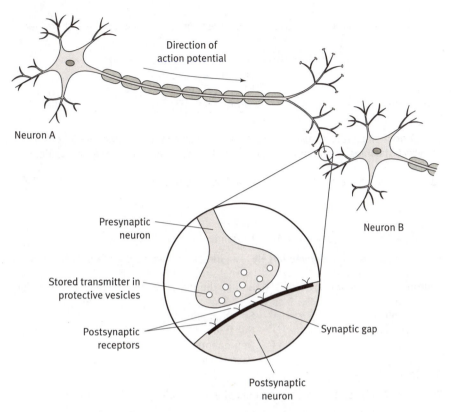

An action potential passes down the axon of Neuron A and when it reaches the axon terminals it causes the synaptic vesicles to fuse with the membrane thereby spilling transmitter into the synaptic gap. This then crosses the short space where it can bind to postsynaptic receptors.

Figure 1.5   Chemical transmission at the synapse

called **receptors** (protein molecules that allow binding of a particular transmitter). Receptor activation then acts (4) to increase or decrease the resting electrical voltage of the neuron. If this neuron is excited past a certain level at its axon hillock, it then (5) generates an electrical signal that is passed down its own axon leading to neurotransmitter release, and the whole process begins again.

It is not an easy task to identify neurotransmitters and by the 1970s only six had been proven to exist in the brain: **noradrenaline, dopamine, serotonin, GABA, acetylcholine** and **glutamate**. (These will be discussed in much more detail later in this book.) However, since then, many new chemicals have been detected, including other types of neurotransmitters, and also a range of **neuromodulators** whose role is to 'modulate' the effect of transmitters. In addition, it has been found that some neurons are able to release gases, such as nitric oxide, into the synapse. Along with these discoveries, it has also been realised that neurons do not release a single type of neurotransmitter as had been once thought (this was known as **Dale's Law**), but rather they can secrete several different substances together. Considering that any given nerve cell may receive input from literally thousands of others releasing a variety of neurotransmitters (Table 1.1) and modulators, it can be seen that the nature of the chemical information crossing the synapse is very complex indeed.

Table 1.1   Some of the neurotransmitters most commonly found in the central nervous system

Monoamines (each contains a NH$_3$ group in its chemical structure)

Acetylcholine (Ach)	Histamine
Adenosine	Noradrenaline
Adrenaline	Serotonin (5-HT)
Dopamine (DA)	

Note: Adrenaline, dopamine and noradrenaline also contain a catechol nucleus and are sometimes referred to as **catecholamines**. Serotonin contains an indole nucleus and is sometimes referred to as an **indolamine**.

All the above monoamines are synthesised by enzymes in the vicinity of the axon endings.

Amino acids

Aspartate	Glycine
Gamma-aminobutyric acid (GABA)	Glutamate

Note: All the above are derived largely from dietary (non-essential) forms of amino acids.

Neuropeptides (initially synthesised through the transcription of a gene in the nucleus and translation of messenger RNA)

β-endorphin	Somatostatin
Cholecystokin	Substance P
Dynorphin	Neuropeptide Y
Enkephalins	Vasopressin
Oxytocin	

Note: β-endorphins, dynorphins and enkephalins are all opioid-like substances.

The discovery of synaptic chemical transmission by Loewi provides one of the pivotal points in the history of biological science – not least because it raised the possibility of modifying brain function (and behaviour) by the use of drugs that affect the action of neurotransmitters. Indeed, this possibility has been realised with the development of drugs, including those that can be used to treat organic brain disorders, such as Parkinson's disease (see Chapter 3), and various types of mental illness, such as depression or schizophrenia (see Chapter 10). Many of the drugs that work on the brain do so by either mimicking the action of a neurotransmitter at its receptor site (this type of drug is known as an **agonist**) or by blocking its receptor (this is known as an **antagonist**) (see Figure 1.6). In addition, histochemical advances have allowed neurotransmitters in nerve endings to be visualised, enabling chemical pathways in the brain to be traced and mapped.

Neuronal conduction

By the early part of the twentieth century, biologists knew that neurons were capable of generating electrical currents, but did not know the finer details of how this energy was created or conducted. The main difficulty lies in trying to

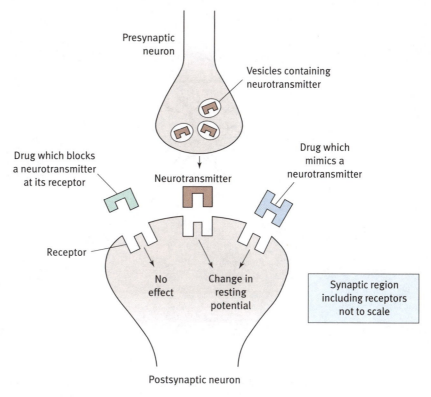

Figure 1.6   Agonist and antagonist effects on receptors

record from the neuron or following its proposed electrical discharge along the axon. Although biologists had at their disposal recording electrodes with very fine tips, along with oscilloscopes and amplifiers that could greatly magnify tiny electrical charges, neurons were too small to enable this type of work to take place. That was until 1936, when John Z. Young, working in Oxford, discovered a neuron, located in the body of the squid, which had an axon about 1 mm in diameter (about 100 to 1,000 times larger than a typical mammalian axon). Not only was this axon large enough to allow the insertion of a stimulating or recording electrode, but it could be removed from the squid and kept alive for several hours, thus allowing the neuron's electrical and chemical properties to be examined in detail.

Practically everything we now know about how neurons work (i.e. how they generate electrical impulses and conduct this current along the axon to cause transmitter release) has been derived from research on the giant squid axon. Because it is believed that all nerve cells, no matter what their size or type of animal they come from, work according to the same principles, the giant squid neuron has thus provided an invaluable means of examining neuronal function. The use of this technique was pioneered by two English researchers, Alan Hodgkin and Andrew Huxley, who published their main findings in 1952. These two scientists not only developed a technique that enabled recording electrodes to be positioned inside the neuron without causing damage, but they also found a way of removing cytoplasm from the axon to enable its chemical composition

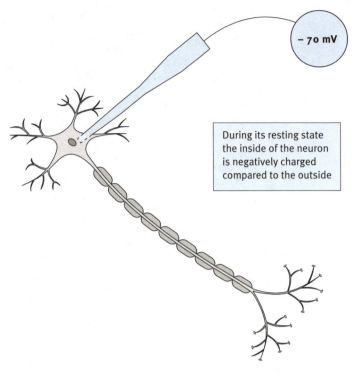

During its resting state the inside of the neuron is negatively charged compared to the outside

Figure 1.7 Measurement of the resting potential of the nerve fibre using a microelectrode

to be examined. This innovation was crucially important in allowing Hodgkin and Huxley to work out how the neuron produced an electrical impulse.

One of the most striking features of the giant squid axon is its **resting potential** (Figure 1.7). If a recording electrode is placed inside the neuron (when it is at rest), and its voltage is compared with an electrode just outside, a small but consistent difference between the two electrodes is found. Crucially, this voltage difference is always around –70 millivolts (mV) with the interior of the neuron being negative compared with its outside (this difference is roughly one-tenth of a volt or about 5 per cent as much energy as exists in a torch battery). This may not appear to be very much, but it is actually a huge energy difference for a tiny nerve cell to maintain – and it is this voltage differential that holds the key to understanding how it can generate electrical current in the form of action potentials.

To explain why the resting potential of –70 mV occurs, it is necessary to understand the nature of the chemical environment that exists in and outside of the cell. One of the most important discoveries made by Hodgkin and Huxley was that the intracellular and extracellular environments are very different in terms of ion concentrations. An ion is simply an electrically charged atom (or particle) that has lost or gained an electron, which gives it a positive or negative charge. As any school pupil knows, an atom is composed of a nucleus (containing positively charged protons and neutrons) orbited by negatively charged electrons. In the atom's normal state, the opposite charges of the protons and electrons cancel themselves out, making it neutral. However, if the atom loses an electron, it will then have one less negative charge, and consequently becomes a positively charged ion called a cation (alternatively if the atom gains an extra electron it

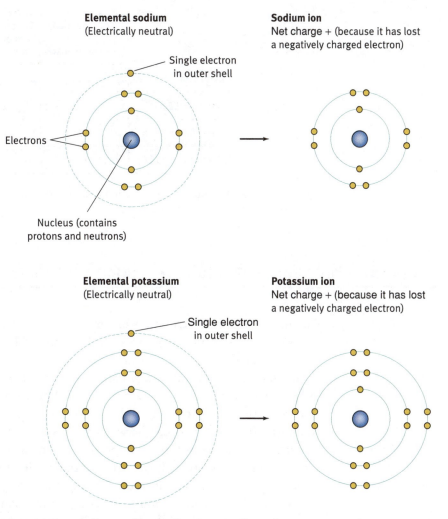

Figure 1.8   How sodium and potassium ions are formed

becomes a negatively charged ion called an anion). Although only a few types of ion exist in the body, they play a crucial role in neural function. These ions include sodium (Na^+) and potassium (K^+), which have lost an electron and are positively charged (Figure 1.8); and chloride (Cl^-) and organic anions (A^-), which have gained an electron and are negatively charged.

One of Hodgkin and Huxley's most important discoveries was that the distributions of ions differed significantly between the interior and exterior of the cell when in its resting state. For example, sodium ions (Na^+) were found to be more highly concentrated outside the cell than inside it (a ratio of around 14:1), as were negative chloride ions (a ratio of around 25:1). In contrast, potassium ions (K^+) were found predominantly inside the cell (a ratio of around 28:1), as were the organic anions (mainly negatively charged proteins or products of the cell's metabolism, which are confined to the inside of the neuron). In fact, when the charges are added up, the relative distributions of the ions explain why the resting potential inside the neuron is negative (dominated by the electrical charges of the anions and potassium), and its outside is positive (dominated by the electrical charges of sodium and chloride) – see Figure 1.9.

	Concentration of ions in axoplasm (mM)	Concentration of ions outside the cell (mM)
Potassium (K⁺)	400	10
Sodium (Na⁺)	50	450
Chloride (Cl⁻)	40	560
Organic anions (A⁻)	345	0

Figure 1.9   The concentration of the four important ions inside and outside the axon expressed in millimoles (mM) per litre (l)

How does the neuron maintain its resting potential?

Due to the uneven distribution of ions, a state of tension exists between the inside and outside of the nerve cell. This occurs because positively charged ions are strongly attracted to negative ones, or vice versa (a force known as the **electrostatic gradient**), and high concentrations of ions are attracted to areas of low concentration, or vice versa (a force known as the **diffusion gradient**). Consequently, when an unequal distribution of electrical charges and different concentrations of ions occur between the inside and outside of the cell, both electrical and diffusion forces are produced. This means that the extracellular sodium ions will be strongly attracted to the inside of the nerve cell by electrostatic and diffusion forces (produced by the cell's negative resting potential and its relative lack of sodium ions), and the intracellular potassium ions will be attracted to the outside of the neuron, albeit more weakly, by diffusion forces.

If this is the case, then why don't ions simply travel down their electrostatic and diffusion gradients to correct the ionic imbalance and cancel out the negative resting potential in the neuron? The secret lies in the cytoplasmic membrane (the nerve cell's semi-permeable outer coating), which contains different types of **ion channel** – tiny pores that allow certain ions to pass in and out (see Keynes 1979). In fact, the neural membrane is about 100 times more permeable to potassium ions than sodium because it has more channels for potassium than for sodium. This means that while potassium ions can move in and out of the cell with relative ease, sodium ions are effectively barred entry – despite the strong electrical and diffusion gradients working to force them into the neuron. Despite this, the membrane barrier is not total and some sodium ions pass into the neuron through potassium channels.

This brings us to another important question: if ions are in constant motion (particularly potassium) how can the resting potential of –70 mV be maintained? Clearly, if physical forces were simply left to operate, then the flow of potassium to the outside of the cell would reduce and eventually neutralise the resting potential – and the flow of sodium to the inside, even at a slow rate of infiltration, would do the same. The answer is that the neuron creates and maintains the intra- and extracellular balance of ions by a complex protein molecule in its membrane called a **sodium–potassium pump** that forces out approximately three sodium ions for every two potassium ions it takes back in. These pumps require considerable energy and it has been estimated that up to 20 per cent of the cell's energy is spent on this process (Dudel 1978). Such is the importance of maintaining the negative resting potential for, without it, the neuron would be unable to generate action potentials.

The action potential

It was known over a century ago that the nerve impulse is a brief pulse of electrical excitation that passes down the axon; but how does the neuron produce this electrical excitation? By using the giant squid axon, Hodgkin and Huxley were able to show that the electrical pulse was caused by sudden movements of ions across the neural membrane. The initial event for this process begins when the resting potential in the neuron is made more positive by neurotransmitters crossing the synapse to bind with its receptors.

The neuron is like a tiny biological battery with the negative pole (–70 mV) inside the cell and the positive one outside, and it goes to great lengths with the sodium–potassium pump to maintain this polarity. This, however, also makes the neuron potentially unstable – not least because of the forces produced by the electrostatic and diffusion gradients that are trying to push sodium ions into the cell. Furthermore, each neuron is also under constant bombardment from a variety of neurotransmitters that act to briefly open ion channels, which also cause fluctuations in its resting potential. Indeed, some neurotransmitters make the resting potential more positive (i.e. by increasing the cell's permeability to positive ions), whereas others make the inside of the cell more negative (i.e. by increasing the influx of negative ions). In fact, a neuron may have thousands of neurotransmitter molecules impinging upon it at any moment, and the net result (or '**summation**') of this stimulation may produce a significant change in the cell's resting potential. If all this stimulation causes the voltage inside the cell to become more positive, this is called an **excitatory postsynaptic potential** (EPSP), and if the cell becomes more negative it is called an **inhibitory postsynaptic potential** (IPSP).

The change in resting potential produced by the flow of ions into the cell following neurotransmitter stimulation normally begins in the dendrites, and the voltage change (i.e. an EPSP or IPSP) spreads down into the cell body. But how does a change in resting potential lead to an action potential? The answer lies with a special part of the neuron called the **axon hillock** located at the junction between the cell body and axon (see Figure 1.2). Like the rest of the neurons, this area normally shows a resting potential of around –70 mV. But if the voltage increases at this site by about +15 mV (this is called the **threshold potential**) then a rapid sequence of events occurs that causes an action potential (or nerve impulse) to be produced.

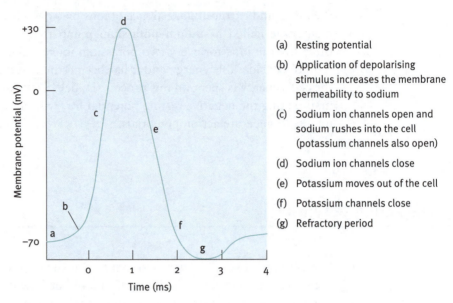

(a) Resting potential

(b) Application of depolarising stimulus increases the membrane permeability to sodium

(c) Sodium ion channels open and sodium rushes into the cell (potassium channels also open)

(d) Sodium ion channels close

(e) Potassium moves out of the cell

(f) Potassium channels close

(g) Refractory period

Figure 1.10 Voltage changes and ion movements that accompany the action potential

If a recording electrode is placed into the axon hillock during this event, it will reveal a sudden increase in voltage from about –55 mV (its threshold value) to about +30 mV which occurs in less than one-thousandth of a second or millisecond (ms)! This huge reversal in polarity (from negative to positive) does not last long, however, and within 4 or 5 ms, the resting potential at the axon hillock will return to –70 mV (although in doing so, it momentarily drops to –80 mV, which produces the **refractory period**). This is the beginning of a process that will result in electrical flow being passed down the axon in the form of a nerve impulse (Figure 1.10).

Thus, the axon hillock is the region of the neuron where the integration of excitatory and inhibitory postsynaptic potentials takes place, and determines whether an action potential will be generated. It can be seen that this response is 'all-or-nothing' as the neuron either fires or doesn't (e.g. there is no in-between). However, once the action potential is formed it has to pass down the axon, and here lies a problem: axons are long, spindly projections, and if the action potential moved passively down the fibre, it would decay almost immediately. Thus, the axon must have some way of *actively* moving the action potential down its length. The secret of how it does this lies with a fatty sheath called **myelin** which covers the axon and is not dissimilar to the rubber coating that surrounds an electrical cable. Unlike an electrical cable, however, the myelin contains short gaps called **nodes of Ranvier**, and it is here that the renewal of the action potential takes place. In short, at each node, the action potential is amplified back to its original intensity, which means that it essentially 'jumps' down the axon. This process is called **saltatory conduction** and explains why the action potential can travel long distances without becoming weakened. This process is also highly efficient with action potentials reaching speeds of over 220 miles per hour in some myelinated neurons.

The ionic basis of the action potential

How does the neuron bring about the sudden change in depolarisation to generate an action potential? The answer lies mainly with the sodium and potassium ions. As already seen, large numbers of sodium ions are found in the extracellular fluid, and these are attracted to the inside of the cell by electrical forces (positive ions are attracted to negative ions) and concentration forces (high concentrations of ions are attracted to low concentrations). Yet the cell's membrane acts as a barrier to sodium, and if any of its ions manage to infiltrate into the neuron they are quickly removed by the sodium–potassium pump. This balance is changed dramatically, however, if the inside of the cell reaches −55 mV (the threshold potential). When this occurs, the membrane suddenly opens its sodium channels and, as if a door is thrown open, sodium ions rush into the cell propelled by electrostatic and concentration forces. It has been estimated that up to 100,000,000 ions per second can pass through a channel (although the channels only remain open for a fraction of this time), and it is this large influx of sodium current into the cell that transforms its negative resting potential into a positive depolarisation.

At the peak of this sodium flow (1 or 2 ms after the ion channels have opened) the permeability of the membrane changes again as the neuron closes its sodium channels and opens its potassium channels. Because the inside of the cell is positively charged at this point due to the sodium influx, the potassium ions are propelled out by electrostatic forces. This not only causes the cell's resting potential to become negative again, but it briefly drops to about −80 mV, producing the refractory period. It is only after the occurrence of this event (some 2–3 ms after the start of the action potential) that the resting potential returns to normal (−70 mV) with the sodium–potassium pump coming back into play to correct the ion balance. This entire sequence of events takes around 4–5 ms, and occurs so quickly that most neurons can produce well over 100 action potentials per second.

A similar pattern of ions rushing in and out of the cell also occurs along the axon's length. As we have seen, the axon is wrapped in myelin, and its membrane is only exposed at gaps called the nodes of Ranvier. When the action potential is generated at the axon hillock, the electrical discharge begins to travel passively down the axon. When it reaches the first node, the increased voltage in the axon acts to open a large number of sodium channels causing an influx of positive ions, which, in effect, generates a new action potential. In this way, the action potential is conducted down the full length of the axon (Stevens 1979).

Neurotransmitter release

When the action potential reaches the end of the axon, it passes through a large number of axon branches ending in swollen boutons called synaptic terminals. Stored within these terminals are large numbers of **synaptic vesicles**, each containing a few hundred molecules of neurotransmitter. When the action potential arrives at the terminal it stimulates the influx of calcium ions (*note*: not sodium), which causes **exocytosis**, in which the synaptic vesicles fuse with the presynaptic membrane, spilling their contents into the synaptic gap. In fact, vesicles are continually fusing with the axon terminal membrane, which results in the ongoing secretion of small amounts of neurotransmitter – although the action potential greatly speeds up this process, enabling a much greater amount of neurotransmitter to be released.

The synaptic gap is a tiny fluid-filled space that measures about 0.00002 mm across. On one side of this gap is the presynaptic neuron, where the axon endings terminate, and on the opposite side is the postsynaptic neuron. When neurotransmitter is released, it diffuses across the synapse, binding to receptors on the postsynaptic neuron (note that the presynaptic neuron may also contain receptors – see Chapter 10). The receptor and its neurotransmitter have sometimes been compared to a lock and key. In the same way that it takes a specific key to turn a lock, a given neurotransmitter will only bind to its own type of receptor. Once this binding occurs, changes in the conformation of the receptor will initiate a series of events leading to the opening of certain ion channels – with the subsequent ion flow then contributing to a change in the cell's internal voltage.

Once the neurotransmitter has bound to the receptor it is quickly deactivated and broken down, otherwise it would continue to exert an effect and block the receptor from receiving further input. A number of mechanisms have evolved to fulfil this requirement. One is **monoamine oxidase** – an enzyme found in axon terminals and synapses – which breaks down excess neurotransmitter. Indeed, some antidepressant drugs such as Marsilid work by inhibiting this enzyme (see Chapter 10). In addition, some transmitters, such as noradrenaline, dopamine and serotonin, are removed from the synapse by means of a **re-uptake pump** that directs them back into the axon terminals. Indeed, certain drugs that block this re-uptake process for either noradrenaline (e.g. Imipramine), or serotonin (e.g. Prozac) are also successful in the treatment of depression (Snyder 1986).

Chemical events in the postsynaptic cell

As we have seen, once a neurotransmitter has bound to its receptor, it induces a change in the permeability of the neural membrane to various ions, contributing to an alteration of the resting potential. But how does the act of the neurotransmitter attaching itself to the receptor lead to the opening of ion channels? In fact, there are two different type of mechanism: one involving the direct opening of the ion channel (**ionotropic receptors**), and the other using an indirect process that requires the involvement of intracellular chemicals known as second messengers (**metabotropic receptors**). In the first example, the receptor and ion channel form part of the same unit so that occupancy of the receptor causes a direct change in the shape of the ion channel (this is sometimes called a ligand-activated channel). An example of this type of ion channel is the

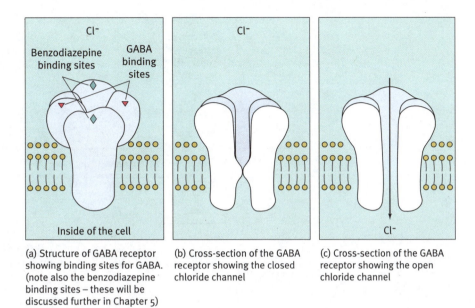

(a) Structure of GABA receptor showing binding sites for GABA. (note also the benzodiazepine binding sites – these will be discussed further in Chapter 5)

(b) Cross-section of the GABA receptor showing the closed chloride channel

(c) Cross-section of the GABA receptor showing the open chloride channel

Figure 1.11   The GABA receptor

GABA-A receptor complex (Figure 1.11), consisting of five elongated protein molecules arranged in the shape of a cylinder that pass through the membrane. These proteins are tightly held together, but if GABA binds to a receptor site on the surface of this complex, they briefly change their shape creating a channel that allows ions (in this case negative chloride ions) to flow into the cell. Another example of a ligand-activated channel is the cholinergic nicotinic receptor found at the neuromuscular junction (see Chapter 3).

However, not all receptors are located on their own individual ion channels. In fact, some receptors are located away from the ion channel(s) they control. In this case, the binding of a transmitter at its receptor induces the opening of ion channels via a sequence of chemical steps between the two sites. This type of receptor (metabotropic) is attached to **G-proteins** located just inside the cell. When a neurotransmitter binds to the receptor, it alters the configuration of the G-protein, setting into motion a series of chemical events, one of which is the increased activity of an enzyme called **adenylate cyclase,** which converts ATP (a substance the cell uses to provide energy) into **cyclic AMP** (cAMP). Cyclic AMP (Figure 1.12) is known as a **second messenger** (the first messenger is the neuro-transmitter), and it diffuses through the cytoplasm where, by a process called protein phosphorylation, it can open ion channels by altering the shape of certain proteins in their structure. It should be noted that cAMP can affect many different proteins in the neuron, and not just those associated with ion channels. In addition, there are also other types of second messengers, although their details need not concern us here.

Second messengers may at first sight appear to be a complex way of opening ion channels, but this process actually gives the cell far greater adaptability. For example, activation of ionotropic receptors (such as GABA-A) typically results in the rapid depolarisation of the cell in as little as 2 to 10 ms (which may be ideally suited for a rapid response such as a muscle contraction or the encoding

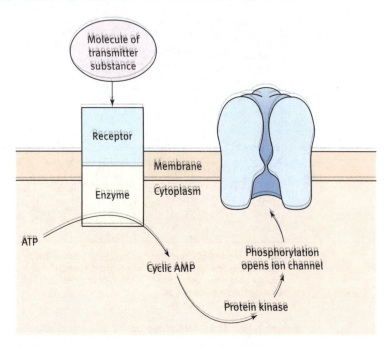

Figure 1.12   Diagram showing the main steps in the cAMP second messenger system

of a pain response), but it shows little variation. In contrast, the slower action of second messenger systems can take from 20 ms to over 10 seconds, and involve many different types of ion channel. In addition, second messengers may be involved in changing the sensitivity of receptors to neurotransmission. Both these types of response are useful when the neuron needs to adapt to new events, and it should be no surprise that second messengers have been implicated in the cellular basis of learning and memory (see Chapter 8).

Glial cells

It may come as a surprise to find out that neurons are not the most common type of cell in the brain. This distinction goes to the glial cells, which are around 10 times more numerous than neurons. Rudolf Virchow in 1846 was the first to show this type of cell in the brain, which he called 'nevroglie' (nerve glue) because they appeared to stick the neurons together. We now know the brain and spinal cord to contain several types of glial cell, with a wide range of functions that are vital to neural functioning.

The most abundant type of glial cell in the brain (accounting for nearly half of its tissue volume) is the **astrocyte** – so called because of its star shape with many spindly extensions. Astrocytes provide structural support, with their interweaving extensions acting as scaffolding to hold neurons in place. In addition, the end feet of their extensions cling to the outer surface of capillaries in the brain and form the **blood–brain barrier**. In the body, capillaries are 'leaky' because the cells that make up their walls contain gaps that allow substances in and out of the blood. But the walls of the capillaries in the brain are tightly compacted, and their outer surface is covered by astrocyte extensions. Although this tight binding allows small molecules, such as oxygen and carbon dioxide to pass into the brain, it bars the entry of larger molecules and toxins. This feature has to be taken into consideration when developing drugs to treat brain disorders. For example, the neurotransmitter dopamine, which would be expected to have a beneficial effect in treating Parkinson's disease, does not cross the blood–brain barrier. Thus, doctors tend to prescribe L-dopa, which can enter the brain, where it is then converted to dopamine.

Astrocytes also have many other important functions. For example, they control the ionic composition of the extracellular fluid, help to break down neurotransmitters in the synaptic cleft, and release growth factors (proteins that are involved in the growth and repair of nerve cells). Astrocytes can also help to increase the brain's activity by dilating blood vessels, enabling greater amounts of oxygen and glucose to reach the neurons. They also contribute to the healing of brain tissue by forming scar material, although they can give rise to tumours (gliomas) if they proliferate abnormally.

Another type of glial cell is the **oligodendrocyte**, which is much smaller than the astrocyte and has fewer extensions (Greek *oligos* means 'few'). This type of glial cell has a very specific function: it provides the myelin that covers the axons of many nerve fibres in the brain and spinal cord. Myelination occurs because the extensions of numerous oligodendrocytes wrap themselves around the axon, thereby producing an insulated covering. However, outside the central nervous system, myelin is produced by the **Schwann cells**. A third type of glia is the microglial cell, and as the name suggests these cells are very small. Microglial cells are scattered throughout the brain and provide its main immune defence. In response to injury or infection, microglials migrate in large numbers to the sites of injury, where they can engulf invading microorganisms and help to remove debris from injured or dead cells.

What happened to Einstein's brain?

Albert Einstein was one of the greatest intellectual figures of the twentieth century. In one year alone (1905) at the age of 26, while working in the Swiss Patent Office in Bern, he published five papers that were to profoundly alter the development of physics, and change for ever the way humans understand their universe. Einstein died in 1955 at the age of 76 years from a ruptured aorta, and within 7 hours of his death, his brain had been perfused with a 10 per cent formalin solution by injection into the internal carotid artery (to enable its fixation) and removed by pathologist Thomas Harvey. After being stored in formalin for several months, the brain was carefully photographed, and measurements were taken of its cerebral structure. The cerebral hemispheres were then cut into around 240 blocks of about 10 cm^3, embedded in celloidin (similar to wax) and stored in alcohol. However, close examination of the brain by Thomas Harvey revealed nothing unusual.

What happened to Einstein's brain? continued.

It appears that Einstein's brain was soon forgotten and stored in two large jars that remained in Dr Harvey's office for the next 20 years or so. In 1978, the whereabouts of the brain was 'rediscovered' by journalist Steven Levy, who brought it to the attention of the media. The discovery was of interest to Marian Diamond and her colleagues working at the University of California. In the early 1960s, Diamond had shown that rats living in enriched environments had more glial cells per neuron in their cerebral cortices than those raised in impoverished environments – indicating that active cortical neurons required greater metabolic assistance from the supporting glial cells. Later work by Diamond also showed that the prefrontal cortex of humans has more glial cells per neuron compared with the inferior parietal lobe – a finding that implied that the prefrontal area was more active and highly evolved in humans than in other brain regions. However, when Diamond examined the brain of Einstein, she found that he had significantly more glial cells in the left parietal cortex than in the frontal regions (Diamond *et al.* 1985).

Further examination of Einstein's brain by Sandra Witelson revealed other unique features. Most striking was an absence of a region called the parietal operculum (Figure 1.13) – a ridge (or gyrus) in the parietal cortex normally located between the Sylvian fissure and the postcentral sulcus. Consequently, the Sylvian fissure and postcentral gyrus were partially

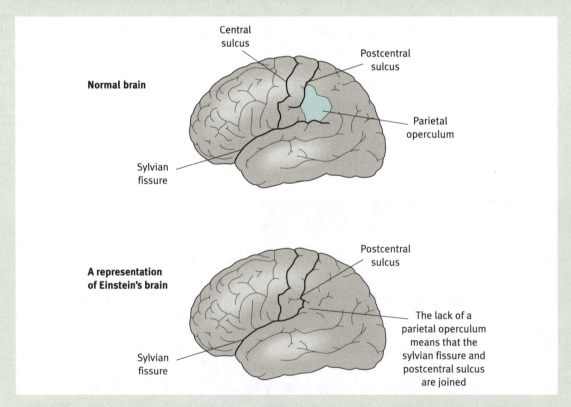

Figure 1.13   The location of the parietal operculum in a normal brain, and the joining of the Sylvian fissure and postcentral sulcus in a representation of Einstein's brain

What happened to Einstein's brain? continued.

joined in Einstein's brain – a feature that Witelson was unable to find in over 90 control brains. It appeared that the areas on either side of these sulci (i.e. the inferior parietal lobes) were enlarged to compensate for the loss. In fact, Witelson also found that the parietal lobes were 1 cm wider (15 per cent) in Einstein's brain compared with controls, and that this enlargement was symmetrical, occurring in both right and left hemispheres. Because most people have a relatively large right parietal cortex compared with the left, this meant that Einstein's left parietal lobe was particularly larger than normal (Witelson *et al.* 1999).

One can only speculate the extent to which Einstein's unique brain anatomy contributed to his ideas and, in particular, to the theory of relativity. However, the inferior parietal lobes are known to be involved in visuospatial cognition (particularly the generation and manipulation of three-dimensional spatial images), mathematical ability and imagery of movement – and these seem to be characteristic of Einstein's thoughts. Indeed, Einstein once said that written and spoken words did not seem to play any role in his mechanism of thought – rather the essential features were 'a combinatory play of certain signs and more or less clear images' (Einstein 1954). Interestingly, enlarged inferior parietal cortices have also been reported for other famous thinkers, including the mathematician Gauss and the physicist Siljestrom.

An introduction to the structure of the nervous system

The complete network of all nerve cells in the human body is divided into two systems: the **central nervous system** (CNS) and **peripheral nervous system** (PNS). The CNS is composed of the brain and spinal cord, and perhaps can be best described simply as the body's life control and decision centre. In contrast, the PNS is a sensory (input) motor (output) system that acts as an intermediary between the environment/body and the CNS, and has two main divisions: the **somatic nervous system** and the **autonomic nervous system** (see Figure 1.14).

The main function of the somatic nervous system is to convey sensory information to and from the CNS. This not only includes sense information (touch, pressure, temperature, pain, etc.) from the skin, muscles, bones and joints, but also visual and auditory input, which goes directly to the brain from the eyes and ears. In addition, the somatic nervous system is composed of motor nerve fibres that conduct impulses from the CNS to the skeletal muscles, and is often referred to as the voluntary nervous system as it allows us to consciously control our muscles for movement and behaviour. We shall discuss the role of this system in more detail when we examine motor behaviour in Chapter 3.

In contrast, the autonomic nervous system consists of nerve pathways that regulate the involuntary activity of smooth muscles that control vital bodily functions such as heart rate, blood pressure, kidney function and breathing. The autonomic nervous system is composed of two divisions: the **sympathetic nervous**

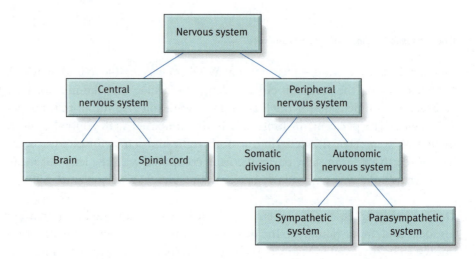

Figure 1.14   Overall organisation of the nervous system

system (SNS) and the **parasympathetic nervous system** (PNS), which tend to have opposite functions. For example, the SNS may prepare an organism for a **flight or fight response** by increasing heart rate and respiration, dilating the pupil of the eye, inhibiting digestion, and diverting blood from the skin to the skeletal muscles (which is the reason that the skin may go white after a sudden fright). It can also cause the adrenal gland to release adrenaline and noradrenaline. In short, this system helps to prepare the body to cope with an actual (or potential) emergency or stressful situation. In contrast, the PNS reverses or normalises the effects of sympathetic activity, and generally acts to conserve energy or maintain resting body function. As we shall see later, the autonomic nervous system plays an important role in emotion (Chapter 5), feeding (Chapter 4) and sexual behaviour (Chapter 6).

The endocrine system

The endocrine system is another important communication system and consists of a number of glands scattered throughout the body that secrete chemicals called **hormones** (from the Greek *hormon* meaning to excite) into the blood. More than 50 different hormones may be circulating through the body at any one time, and these are secreted from a number of organs – for example, the thyroid (in the neck), the thymus (in the upper chest), the adrenal glands (located just above the kidneys), and the gonads, including the testes and the ovaries. All of these organs are under the chemical control of a single pea-sized master gland located on the underside of the brain called the **pituitary gland**, which is attached to the **hypothalamus** (Figure 1.15). The pituitary actually consists of two glands:

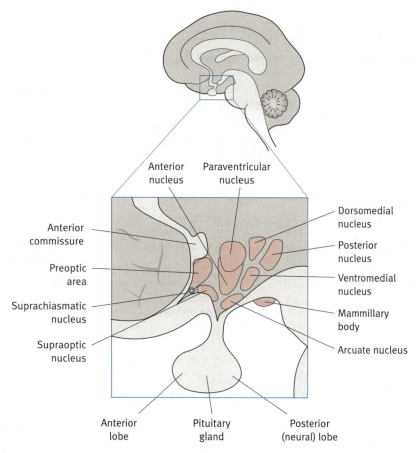

Figure 1.15   The hypothalamus and pituitary gland

the anterior pituitary (connected to the hypothalamus via a complex series of blood vessels) and the posterior pituitary (which has neural connections with the hypothalamus). The anterior pituitary releases into the blood a number of hormones involved in the metabolic control of the body, including adrenocorticotropin (ACTH), which acts on the adrenal gland, whereas the posterior part releases just two – antidiuretic hormone (vasopressin) and oxytocin.

The control of hormonal release by the pituitary gland works on the basis of **negative feedback**; that is, when blood levels of a given hormone begin to rise (i.e. cortisol), the pituitary gland will detect this change and act to decrease the output of its controlling tropic hormone (ACTH). In practice, things are generally more complex than this as the brain will also receive feedback about hormone levels and their effects on the body, and it will therefore also help to regulate the pituitary gland's response via the hypothalamus. Nevertheless, the principle remains the same: negative feedback occurs when the hormone (or its biological response) feeds back into a control centre to turn the system off. Indeed, the combination of the hypothalamus and the pituitary gland working together means that the control exerted over hormone secretion is complex and finely tuned (Table 1.2).

Table 1.2 Summary of the main hormone systems in the human body

Endocrine gland	Hormone(s)	Main actions
Adrenal cortex	Glucocorticoids (including cortisol and cortisone)	Adapts the body to long-term stress
Adrenal medulla	Adrenaline (Epinephrine)	Increases sympathetic arousal and stimulates the breakdown of glycogen
Ovaries	Oestrogen and progesterone	Female sexual development and control of the menstrual cycle
Pancreas gland	Insulin and glucagon	Involved in regulation of blood sugar
Pineal gland	Melatonin	Control of circadian rhythms
Pituitary gland (anterior part)	Vasopressin and oxytocin	Control of water balance and female sexual behaviour
Pituitary gland (posterior part)	Master control of other endocrine glands. Also produces growth hormone and prolactin	Wide range of functions. Growth and protein synthesis. Milk production
Testes	Testosterone	Male sexual development and behaviour
Thyroid gland	Thyroxine and triiodothyronine	Increases metabolic rate

Both the endocrine and nervous systems provide an important means of communication in the body. The nervous system allows for very rapid responses that require immediate action, whereas the endocrine system responds more slowly and may take minutes or even hours to reach its target, whilst typically having a much longer duration of action. Despite this, both systems work towards integrated functioning in many types of behaviour.

The central nervous system

The central nervous system (CNS), and in particular the brain, is the main control centre of the body. It exerts executive control over the peripheral nervous system and endocrine glands, and is the organ of behaviour, emotion, memory and consciousness. As an important prerequisite for understanding how the brain is able to influence behaviour, it is necessary to have a clear picture of its anatomy, including the location of its main regions and the way in which they are connected. However, for the first-time student, trying to establish a picture of how the brain is organised can be a daunting challenge. One difficulty is the terminology as many Greek and Latin terms are used to describe parts of the central nervous system (some areas are also named after people such as Broca and Wernicke) and, at first, these may appear unfamiliar and awkward to remember. An added problem lies with trying to visualise the shape of the structures, where they are located in the brain, and how they fit together. Indeed, the morphology of the brain will provide a complex terrain for most readers of this book, and it might be best to seek out only a few major landmarks in your first attempts at navigation through this strange world.

The evolution of the human brain has taken place over a period of at least 70 million years (if we take the first primates as its starting point) and, as this has occurred, newer structures have developed and taken over the roles of older ones. This does not mean that these older regions have become redundant; they have been incorporated into the neural circuits of the brain and still have vital roles to play. Indeed, the brain functions as a collective entity, but evolution has resulted in the brain showing a hierarchy of function with its newer structures becoming involved in more complex behaviours. Another feature of this evolutionary development is **cephalisation**, that is, the massive increase in size of the brain in relation to the rest of the body. This trend is most noticeable in the forebrain, including the cerebral cortex, which has become so large and complex in humans that it has become a highly convoluted structure (not dissimilar to a screwed-up piece of newspaper) which gives the external surface of brain its highly distinctive, wrinkly appearance.

To complete this chapter we shall describe the various regions and structures of the CNS. If the next few pages prove difficult, don't worry, as most of these areas will be discussed again in the remaining chapters of this book – and will hopefully become more familiar!

The spinal cord

The spinal cord is an extension of the brain that forms a cylinder of nervous tissue running down the back. Its main function is to distribute motor neurons to the their targets (e.g. muscles and glands) and to return internal and external sensory information to the brain. The spinal cord is also capable of producing certain types of behaviour by itself, including simple spinal reflexes (such as the knee jerk response) or more complex patterns of rhythmical activity (the postural components of walking).

The most striking visual feature of the spinal cord is its grey and white nervous matter. The grey tissue forms a butterfly shape in the centre of the spinal cord and is composed of nerve cell bodies: these are either motor neurons, which send their axons out to innervate the smooth and skeletal muscle of the body, or neurons that receive information from the sensory axons that enter the spinal cord. The grey matter also contains a large number of interneurons between sensory input and motor output that allow complex reflexes to take place (see Chapter 3). In contrast, the white matter, which surrounds the grey material, is composed mainly of long myelinated axon fibres (although it also contains some unmyelinated axons), which form the ascending and descending

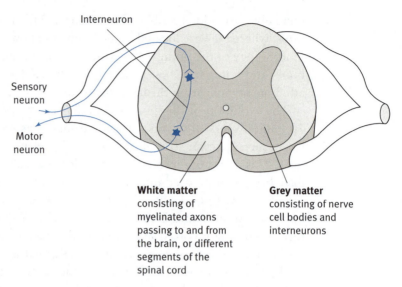

Figure 1.16   Cross-section of spinal cord with spinal nerves attached

pathways of the spinal cord. More specifically, the ascending axon fibres are derived mainly from the cell bodies that receive sensory input in the grey matter – and the descending axons arise largely from the brain and terminate in the grey matter, where they synapse with motor neurons.

Axons enter and leave the grey matter of the spinal cord via spinal nerves that contain many bundles of nerve fibres. There are 31 pairs of spinal nerves along the entire length of the spinal cord (Figure 1.16), and each one serves either the right or left side of the body. A spinal nerve is made up of two branches called roots that enter or leave the grey matter. The dorsal (back) root of each spinal nerve provides the pathway that relays sensory information into the spinal cord, whereas the ventral (front) root is the motor pathway that controls the muscles (including those of the autonomic nervous system). The spinal cord also contains cerebrospinal fluid, which is connected with the brain's ventricles. A sample of this spinal fluid can be a very useful diagnostic tool in determining various brain disorders.

The brainstem

As the spinal cord enters the brain it enlarges and forms the **brainstem** (Figure 1.17). The oldest part of the brainstem is the **medulla** ('long marrow'), which contains various nuclei (most of which are vital for life, including those controlling cardiac function and respiration) as well as a profusion of ascending and descending nerve pathways. If the brain is cut above the medulla, basic heart rate and breathing can be maintained, but damage to the medulla itself is inevitably fatal. The next region is the **pons** (from the Latin for 'bridge'), which

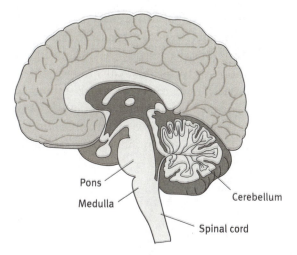

Pons

Medulla

Cerebellum

Spinal cord

Figure 1.17   The main brainstem regions of the human brain

appears as a significant enlargement of the medulla. This area also contains many nuclei, although its increased size is largely due to the many ascending and descending fibre tracts that cross from one side of the brain to the other at this point. The pons is also the main junction between the **cerebellum** ('little

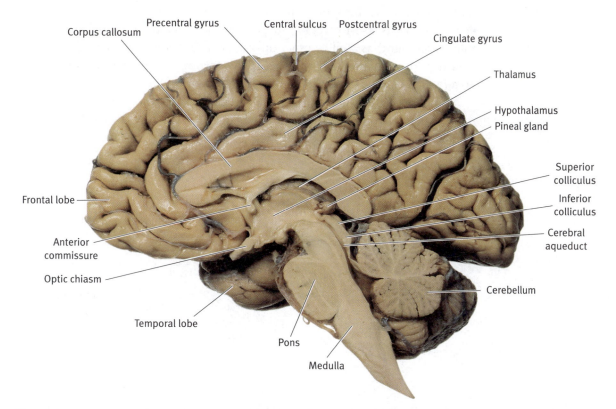

Corpus callosum

Precentral gyrus

Central sulcus   Postcentral gyrus

Cingulate gyrus

Thalamus

Hypothalamus

Pineal gland

Superior colliculus

Inferior colliculus

Frontal lobe

Cerebral aqueduct

Anterior commissure

Optic chiasm

Cerebellum

Temporal lobe

Pons

Medulla

Plate 1.1   Midsagital section through the brain. *Source*: Toates (2001) *Biological Psychology*, p.111, Prentice Hall; photographer, R.T. Hutchings

brain'), spinal cord, and the rest of the brain. The cerebellum with its distinctive wrinkled appearance is involved in coordinating the muscular activity required for smooth automated movement. For example, the cerebellum allows us to automatically move our legs and adjust our posture while walking, or enables us to throw a ball without having to think of the necessary postural adjustments. Although people with cerebellar damage can still perform these actions they are typically 'robotic' and awkward. The cerebellum is also involved in attentional processes and some types of learning, including classical conditioning.

The midbrain

The midbrain (Figure 1.18) is the name give to the region that sits on top of the brainstem and is divided into two areas: the **tectum** ('roof') and the **tegmentum** ('covering'). The tectum contains two pairs of nuclei, called colliculi (derived from Latin, meaning 'small hills'), which protrude from its upper surface. The **superior colliculi** are involved in visual processing and control visual reflexes such as blinking and orientation (see Chapter 2), whereas the **inferior colliculi** serve a similar function for auditory processing. The tegmentum is less easy to define as it consists of several important nuclei (including the **red nucleus** and **substantia nigra**) as well as more diffuse areas including the **ventral tegmental area** (see also Chapter 11) and the upper portions of the **periaqueductal grey area** (which contains opiate receptors and is involved in pain processing).

Also coursing through the centre of the brainstem and into the midbrain is the **reticular activating system,** a tubular net-like structure containing a diffuse

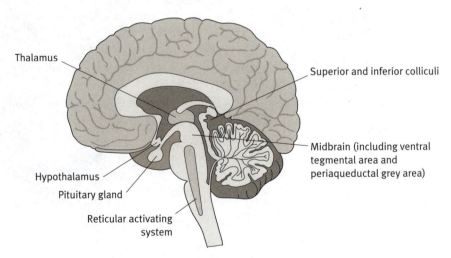

Figure 1.18   Midbrain (mesencephalon) structures of the human CNS (including the hypothalamus and the thalamus of the diencephalon)

interconnected mass of neurons in which over 90 nuclear groups are embedded, including the **locus coeruleus** and the **raphe nuclei**. The reticular activating system serves many essential functions although one of its most important is to control the level of arousal in the cerebral cortex. For example, stimulation of the reticular formation arouses a resting animal and makes an awake animal more alert. In contrast, destruction of reticular structures results in coma. It should come as no surprise to find that the reticular system is involved in sleep (Chapter 6).

The forebrain

Thalamus and hypothalamus

Up to this point, the brain can be likened to a neural tube that has evolved and enlarged from the spinal cord. In general, this part of the brain is concerned with vital life functions or fairly primitive behaviours. However, with the development of the forebrain, we now see the brain 'mushrooming out' so that it not only covers and surrounds much of the older 'tubular' brain, but also adds complexity with the addition of many new structures. Moreover, with this development comes much more advanced behaviours.

The forebrain has two main regions: the diencephalon (or 'interbrain') and telencephalon ('endbrain'). The former contains two main structures: the **thalamus** and the **hypothalamus** (see Plate 1.2). The thalamus (from the Greek for 'inner chamber') is a large egg-shaped structure that contains many different areas, most of which act as relay stations between the cerebral cortex and the rest of the brain. For example, the thalamus contains the **lateral geniculate bodies,** which pass visual information on to the **visual cortex,** and the **medial geniculate nuclei,** which sends input to the **auditory cortex.** The pineal gland (which Descartes believed was the site of the soul) is attached to an old part of the thalamus called the epithalamus.

Located just underneath the thalamus is a small structure called the hypothalamus (*hypo* meaning 'below'), which is part of the limbic system (see later). The hypothalamus is a very old structure with many different regions that show a striking similarity between humans and lower animals. Although, in humans, it is only about the size of a grape, it has been implicated in a wide range of behaviours including feeding (Chapter 4), emotion and aggression (Chapter 5), biological rhythms (Chapter 6), sexual behaviour (Chapter 7) and reinforcement (Chapter 11). To perform many of its functions, the hypothalamus is continually monitoring the internal milieu of the body, and using this information to make the appropriate behavioural or motivational adjustments. The hypothalamus is also the primary centre for control of the autonomic nervous system, and helps to regulate the release of hormones from the pituitary gland (see Figure 1.15).

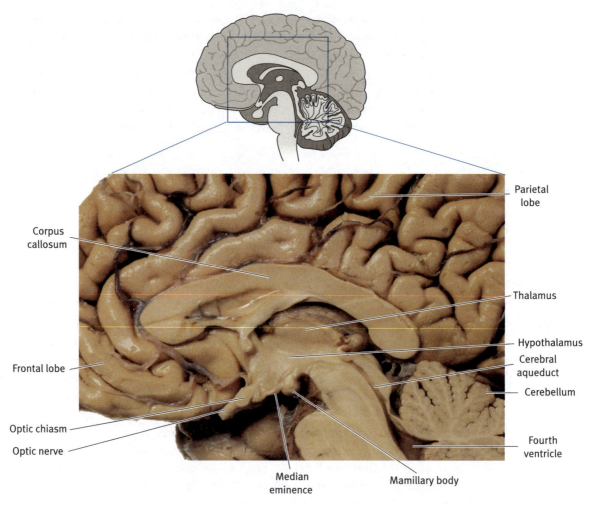

Corpus
callosum

Frontal lobe

Optic chiasm

Optic nerve

Parietal
lobe

Thalamus

Hypothalamus

Cerebral
aqueduct

Cerebellum

Fourth
ventricle

Median
eminence

Mamillary body

Plate 1.2   Midsagital section through the brain drawing attention to the hypothalamus and thalamus.
Source: Toates (2001) *Biological Psychology*, p.108, Prentice Hall; photographer, R.T. Hutchings

The basal ganglia and limbic system

If we move laterally (sideways) from the thalamus we pass through the fibres of the internal capsule (the main communication link between the cerebral cortex and lower regions of the brain and spinal cord) and come to a set of structures that comprise the **corpus striatum**. This structure was first given its name in 1664 by Thomas Willis, who saw that it had a striated appearance with grey and white bands. We now know that the striatum is composed of three regions – the **caudate nucleus** (which also curls over the top of the thalamus), the **putamen**, and the **globus pallidus**. These structures also form the major components of the **basal ganglia,** which are a diverse set of pathways and structures associated with the extrapyramidal system (see Chapter 3), including the **substantia nigra** (located in the tegmental region of the midbrain) and the **subthalamic nucleus**. It is known that the basal ganglia, and especially the striatum, have a wide range of functions, although their main role appears to be in the control of movement (e.g.

(a) The major components of the limbic system

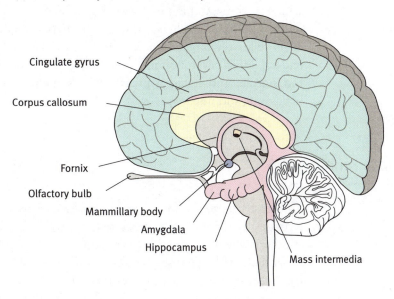

Cingulate gyrus

Corpus callosum

Fornix

Olfactory bulb

Mammillary body

Amygdala

Hippocampus

Mass intermedia

(b) The location of the basal ganglia in the human brain

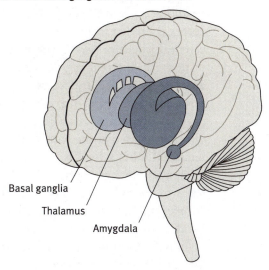

Basal ganglia

Thalamus

Amygdala

Figure 1.19   Location and main regions of the limbic system and basal ganglia. *Source:* Neil R. Carlson, *Physiology of Behavior*, 6th edition. Copyright © 2001 Pearson Education

Parkinson's disease is due to the degeneration of a pathway from the substantia nigra to the striatum that uses the neurotransmitter **dopamine** (see Chapter 3).

The **limbic system** (see Figure 1.19) also contains a number of interconnected structures which, on first sight, form a ring around the central core of the brain (containing the thalamus and striatum). The word *limbus* comes from the Latin word for 'border' and was given to this region of the brain in 1878 by Paul Broca, who viewed it as a lobe that separated the older brainstem with more recent cerebral cortex. This region contains a number of nuclei including the amygdala (found in the medial-anterior aspects of the temporal lobe), and evolutionary 'old' cortex that includes the cingulate gyrus (located above the corpus callosum) and the hippocampus. Another striking feature of the limbic system is the **fornix**, which is a long arching pathway that connects the hippocampus with the **mammillary bodies**, which lie close to the hypothalamus and brainstem. Because of its relatively large size in lower animals, Broca believed that the limbic lobe had an olfactory function. In humans, however, this categorisation is much too simple, and it has a greater involvement in visceral function, emotional behaviour and memory.

The cerebral cortex

The most striking feature of the human brain is undoubtedly the two symmetrical wrinkled cerebral hemispheres that form the cerebral cortex – a remarkable structure which is estimated to contain more than 100,000 km of axons receiving around 3×10^{14} synapses. The cerebral cortex also has a deceptive appearance: it is only around 2–3 millimetres thick, but is highly folded (like a piece of paper that has been screwed up), which allows it to fit inside the small confines of the skull. In fact, if the cerebral cortex was flattened out its total surface area would be about 2.5 sq ft (75 cm^2) (Nolte 1999). Consequently, about two-thirds of the cortex is hidden from view in sulci (or fissures), which are the gaps between the cerebral ridges or 'gyri'. The main sulci also make good surface landmarks to distinguish different regions of the cerebral cortex. For example, all the cortex anterior to the central sulcus comprises the **frontal lobe**, whereas the tissue posterior to it, up to the parieto-occipital sulcus, forms the **parietal lobe**. The parieto-occipital sulcus also separates the parietal lobe from the **occipital lobe**, which is located at the back of the cerebral cortex. The other main region is the **temporal lobe**, which is separated from the frontal and parietal lobes by the sylvian fissure (see Figure 1.20). Moreover, within these main lobes are smaller areas of specialisation. For example, in 1909, Brodmann divided the cerebral cortex into 52 different regions based on anatomical differences (now known as **Brodmann's areas**) and showed that this cortical organisation was similar in all mammals. Although not all investigators agree on this classification, it nevertheless gives some insight into the complexity of the cerebral cortex.

The cerebral cortex serves a wide range of functions. For instance, it includes areas of sensory cortex that are specialised for receiving visual, auditory and somatosensory (touch) input, and it also provides the motor cortex that sends fibres down into the pyramidal tract to enable voluntary movement. However, over 80 per cent of the cerebral cortex in humans serves an association function and is involved in learning, memory and language – abilities that underpin our ability to plan and see the consequences of our actions and to engage in various forms of abstract thought. The right and left hemispheres also tend to show different types of cognition, with the left cortex being dominant for language (this occurs in about 98 per cent of individuals) and the right being more specialised for spatial and perceptual processing (such as face recognition). The two cerebral hemispheres communicate with each other by a huge fibre bundle called the **corpus callosum**, which contains around 300 million axons.

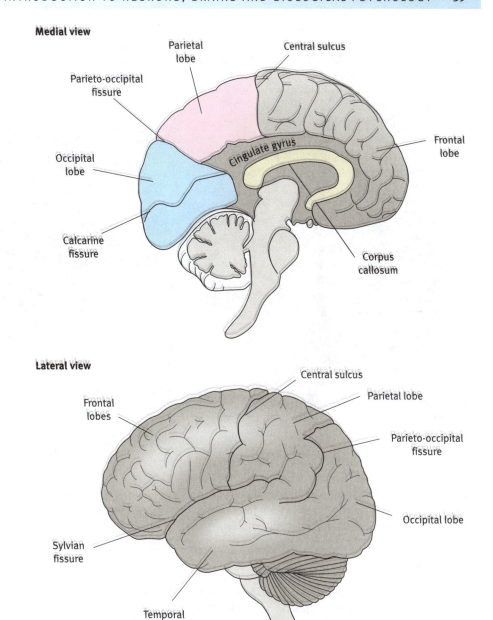

Figure 1.20 The main lobes of the cerebral cortex

Monoamine pathways in the brain

Examining the main regions of the brain provides one way of understanding its anatomy, but there are other ways of gaining important insights into its underlying structure. In particular, the brain has a number of neurotransmitter systems that are crucial to its function. The ability to trace chemical pathways in the brain was first developed in the early 1950s, when it was found that cells of the

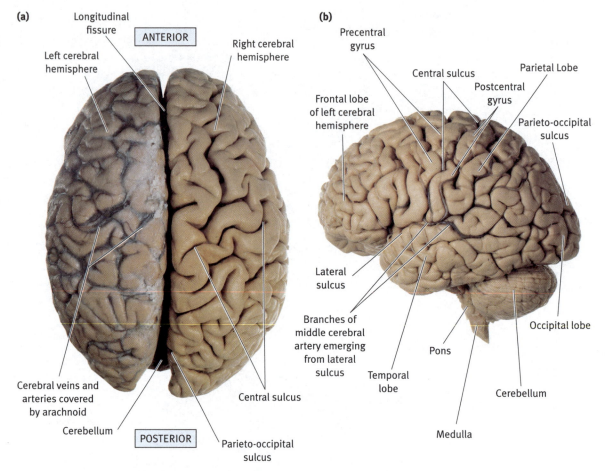

(a)

Longitudinal fissure

ANTERIOR

Left cerebral hemisphere

Right cerebral hemisphere

Cerebral veins and arteries covered by arachnoid

Cerebellum

POSTERIOR

Central sulcus

Parieto-occipital sulcus

(b)

Precentral gyrus

Central sulcus

Parietal Lobe

Postcentral gyrus

Frontal lobe of left cerebral hemisphere

Parieto-occipital sulcus

Lateral sulcus

Branches of middle cerebral artery emerging from lateral sulcus

Temporal lobe

Pons

Occipital lobe

Cerebellum

Medulla

Plate 1.3 The brain highlighting some sulci and gyri: (a) superior view, (b) lateral view. *Source*: Toates (2001) *Biological Psychology*, p.110, Prentice Hall; photographer for a), R.T. Hutchings; source of photograph b) Omikron/Photo Researchers, Inc.

adrenal gland would fluoresce if treated with formalin and exposed to ultraviolet light. This occurred because the cells contained monoamines (primarily adrenaline), which reacted with the formalin to produce fluorescent chemicals. This simple discovery was to be crucial, because some of the most important neurotransmitter systems in the brain also contain monoamines – and this technique provided a way of being able to identify their location. The first use of this method to map neurotransmitter pathways in the brain was undertaken in 1964 by Dahlstrom and Fuxe, who were able to distinguish between noradrenaline (NA) and dopamine (DA) – both of which fluoresced as green – and serotonin (5-HT), which fluoresced as yellow. This research also showed that neurons containing either NA, DA or 5-HT all arose from fairly small areas of the upper brainstem or midbrain, and that their axons formed large diffuse pathways that projected to many regions of the forebrain.

The origin of most NA neurons in the brain is a small nucleus in the pontine region of the upper brainstem called the **locus coeruleus**. Remarkably, in humans, this structure contains only around 24,000 neurons, yet they project with their multiple axon branches to millions of cells throughout the brain, including the cerebral cortex, limbic system and thalamus. In fact, no other brain nucleus has such widespread projections (Foote 1987). The function of this system is not fully understood although it is probably linked to attention and arousal. The **raphe nuclei** (also situated in the pontine region) are a 5-HT counterpart to the locus coeruleus. There are two main raphe nuclei – the dorsal and the median – and they account for about 80 per cent of forebrain 5-HT. Similar to the locus coeruleus, the raphe nuclei contain relatively few neurons, but they give rise to many bifurcating axons with widespread projections. Although the destination of the 5-HT axons typically overlap with the NA axons (particularly in the limbic system), there are some places (notably the basal ganglia) where the 5-HT input predominates. It is difficult to describe precisely the function of the 5-HT system, although it has been shown to be involved in sleep, arousal, mood and emotion.

The DA pathways (Figure 1.22) show some important differences to the NA and 5-HT systems. Not only are there more DA-containing neurons in the brain than for NA and 5-HT (e.g. there are about 40,000 DA cells in total), but they give rise to four pathways that have different projections. The pathway that has attracted most attention (largely because of its involvement in Parkinson's disease) is the nigral–striatal pathway, which projects from the **substantia nigra** to the **striatum** (see Chapter 3). The substantia nigra is embedded in a region of the midbrain called the **ventral tegmental area**, which is also the origin of the three remaining DA pathways. Two of these – the mesocortical and mesolimbic pathways – have long axons that project to the frontal cortex and limbic system respectively (these have been implicated in schizophrenia and reward). The fourth pathway projects to the hypothalamus and controls the release of the hormone prolactin.

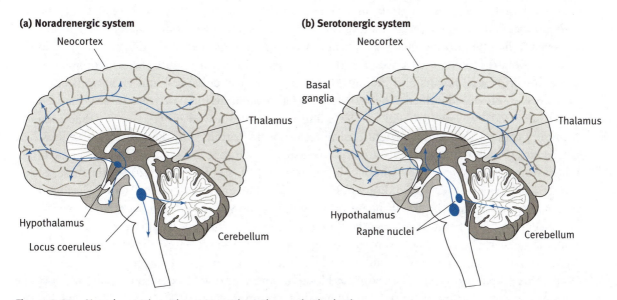

Figure 1.21   Noradrenergic and serotonergic pathways in the brain

Dopaminergic system

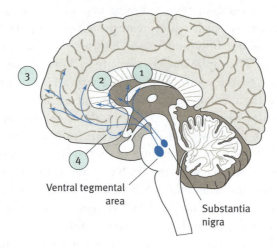

1. Nigral-striatal pathway
2. Mesolimbic pathway
3. Mesofrontal pathway
4. Pathway to the hypothalamus (the tuberoinfundibular tract)

Ventral tegmental area

Substantia nigra

Figure 1.22   Dopaminergic pathways in the brain

Summary

The study of the brain has a long history which stretches back over 2,000 years. One of the earliest theories of brain function was formulated by the Roman physician **Galen** (AD 130–200), who believed that *animated spirit* (analogous to the soul) resided in the ventricles. Later, each ventricle was given a different mental function, and this theory was to remain highly influential for over 1,500 years, partly because it was compatible with Christian beliefs about the immortality and non-material nature of the soul. The first break with this tradition begun with the French philosopher **Descartes** (1596–1650), who argued that much of our behaviour is not 'self-willed' by the soul, but is 'mechanical' and reflexive. The gradual acceptance of this view enabled the neural reflex to become a legitimate subject for scientific study that was largely free from religious interference. Approximately 150 years later, in 1791, the Italian **Luigi Galvani** discovered that the 'force' in nervous tissue was not *animated spirit* but electricity, thereby refuting Galen's doctrine. Although the microscope had been invented in 1665 by **Robert Hooke**, it was not until the late nineteenth century, with the development of more powerful instruments and biological staining, that the nerve cell and its various components were clearly identified. The first stain that allowed individual neurons to be visualised was discovered by **Camilo Golgi** in 1875, and this soon allowed others, such as **Santiago Ramon y Cajel**, to draw the structure of different brain regions and their interconnections. It was also shown that nerve cells are not physically joined, but are separated by small gaps, which were termed synapses by **Charles Sherrington** in 1897. At first the nature of the message that crossed the synapse was not known. However, on Easter Sunday in 1921, an experiment undertaken in the early hours of the morning by **Otto Loewi** showed that synaptic transmission occurred by a chemical process. Despite this, how neurons generated electrical impulses remained uncertain. In 1936, **John Z. Young** discovered a giant neuron in the body of the squid which was about 1 mm in diameter and could be implanted with a recording electrode. It was this preparation that allowed **Alan Hodgkin** and **Andrew Huxley** to describe the formation and propagation of the action potential (nerve impulse) in 1952.

Summary continued.

To understand how an action potential is generated, it is important to realise that the voltage inside a nerve cell, when it is at rest, is negative compared with the outside. In fact, it is about -70 mV, which is known as the **resting potential**. The reason for the voltage difference lies with the distribution of **ions** (atoms that have lost or gained an electron, making them positively or negatively charged), which are found inside and outside the neuron. More specifically, the inside of the neuron contains a large number of negatively charged anions, along with positive **potassium** (K^+) ions, and the extracellular fluid contains a high concentration of positive **sodium** (Na^+) ions. This also creates a state of tension with Na^+ ions being strongly attracted to the inside of the cell by chemical and electrostatic forces. However, the **neural membrane** forms a partial barrier that stops the flow of ions in and out of the cell, and a Na^+/K^+ **pump** further helps to maintain this uneven distribution of ions. The neuron is also being bombarded by neural inputs reaching its dendrites and soma, and if these are sufficient to increase the resting potential at the axon hillock by about $+15$ mV, this results in the membrane opening its **sodium channels**, thus enabling Na^+ ions to rush into the cell. This, in turn, increases the voltage in the neuron to about $+30$ mV in less than a thousandth of a second. This is the start of the **action potential,** which then passes down the axon by the process of **salutary conduction** until it reaches the axon ending, where the fusing of synaptic vesicles with the membrane takes place (**exocytosis**), and **neurotransmitter** is spilled into the synaptic cleft.

The adult brain is believed to contain around one billion neurons, and about 10 times more glial cells. It begins as an extension of the spinal cord called the **brainstem**. This is composed of the **medulla**, which then enlarges to become the **pons**. Running through much of the brainstem is the **reticular system** (known to govern arousal and sleep), while at the back of the pons lies the **cerebellum** (involved in movement). Sitting above the pons, at the end of the brainstem, is the **midbrain** consisting of the **tectum, tegmentum** and **periaqueductal grey area**. The midbrain has an array of functions including sensory processing, movement and emotion. The rest of the brain is known as the **forebrain**. This includes the **thalamus**, which is situated centrally and acts as a relay station for information going to the cerebral cortex, and the **hypothalamus**, which controls the **pituitary gland** (the master gland of the hormone system) and autonomic nervous system. The rest of the forebrain is made up of a number of complex structures and pathways that include the **basal ganglia**, which partially surround the thalamus and contain the **caudate nucleus, putamen, globus pallidis** and **substantia nigra** (the latter is actually located in the tegmentum). Traditionally, the basal ganglia have been associated with movement. Another important forebrain region is the **limbic system**, which is closely associated with old parts of the cerebral cortex and includes the **cingulate gyrus, hippocampus, fornix, amygdala** and **hypothalamus**. Traditionally, these structures have been implicated in emotion. Finally, the most striking feature of the human brain is the phylogenically recent **cerebral cortex** with its distinctive array of ridges (gyri) and fissures (sulci). The cerebral cortex has four main lobes – **occipital, parietal, temporal** and **frontal** – and is involved in a wide range of higher cognitive functions including thought, language, memory, vision and movement. The two cerebral hemispheres are also joined by a huge fibre bundle called the **corpus callosum**.

Essay questions

1. Trace the history of ideas from antiquity to the present day about the workings of nerve cells. How has animated spirit been replaced by action potentials and chemical messengers?

    Helpful Internet search terms: *History of the brain. History of neuroscience. History of neurobiology. Pioneers of brain research. Ancient ideas about the brain.*

2. Explain the formation of the action potential, its propagation down the axon, and its contribution to producing exocytosis of neurotransmitter release.

    Helpful Internet search terms: *How do neurons work? Action potential. Neurons. Ions and the resting potential. Propagation of the action potential. Exocytosis.*

3. What happens when neurotransmitters are released into the synapse? With reference to both ionotropic and metabotropic receptors, explain how neurotransmitters produce excitatory or inhibitory potentials in the postsynaptic neuron.

    Helpful Internet search terms: *Neurotransmitter release. Neurotransmitter receptors. Ionotropic receptors. Second messengers. Ion channels. Excitatory and inhibitory postsynaptic potentials.*

4. Describe the main structures of the brainstem, midbrain and forebrain including basal ganglia, limbic system and cerebral cortex. What functions and behaviours are these regions known to control?

    Helpful Internet search terms: *The human brain. Functions of the basal ganglia. Neuroanatomy of the brain. Limbic system and behaviour. Cerebral cortex.*

Further reading

Afifi, A.K. and Bergman, R.A. (1998) *Functional Neuroanatomy*. New York: McGraw-Hill. A well-illustrated textbook that covers the neuroanatomy of the brain along with discussion of the clinical and functional relevance of key neuroanatomical structures.

Blumenfeld, H. (2002) *Neuroanatomy through Clinical Cases*. Sunderland, MA: Sinauer. A comprehensive and interesting textbook which uses clinical examples to help the student to learn more about the neuroanatomy and behavioural functions of the brain.

Carlson, N.R. (2004) *Physiology of Behavior*. Boston: Allyn & Bacon. First published in 1977 and now in its eighth edition. A classic textbook that keeps getting better and better.

Changeux, J.-P. (1997) *Neuronal Man: The Biology of Mind*. Princeton, NJ: Princeton University Press. A non-specialist and thought-provoking book that attempts to show how the functioning of the human mind is ultimately explainable by an understanding of the brain.

Clark, D.L. and Boutros, N.N. (1999) *The Brain and Behavior: An Introduction to Behavioral Neuroanatomy*. Oxford: Blackwell. Easy to read and an ideal introduction to behavioural neuroanatomy for first-time students.

Diamond, M.C., Scheibel, A.B. and Elson, L.M. (1986) *The Human Brain Colouring Book*. London: HarperCollins. This book contains detailed diagrams designed to be 'coloured-in' to help to illustrate the structure and function of the brain. Lots of fun and a godsend for students who find the various parts of the brain and their inter-relationships difficult to visualise.

Finger, S. (2000) *Minds Behind the Brain*. Oxford: Oxford University Press. A brilliant and captivating history of brain research from ancient times, with individual chapters on its greatest pioneers.

Guyton, A.C. (1991) *Basic Neuroscience*: *Anatomy and Physiology*. Philadelphia: Saunders. Mainly covers neuroanatomy and neurophysiology without losing sight of their relevance for behaviour.

Kolb, B. and Whishaw, I.Q. (2001) *An Introduction to Brain and Behavior*. New York: Worth. Another excellent textbook covering brain and behaviour with a greater emphasis on clinical neuropsychology than that provided by Carlson or Pinel.

Levitan, I.B. and Kaczmarek, L.K. (1991) *The Neuron*. Oxford: Oxford University Press. For students who wish to learn more about the cellular structure, electrical properties, and molecular biology of neurons.

Nicholls, J.G., Martin, A.R., Wallace, B.G and Fuchs, P.A. (2001) *From Neuron to Brain* (4th edn). Sunderland, MA: Sinauer. A book which focuses on the biological workings of the nervous system. Although it contains relatively little on behaviour, sensory and motor systems are discussed in detail.

Pinel, J.P. (2003) *Biopsychology*. Boston: Allyn & Bacon. Another classic textbook on biopsychology, on a par with Carlson.

Toates, F. (2001) *Biological Psychology*. Harlow: Prentice Hall. A comprehensive and engaging introduction to biological psychology with an emphasis on comparative and evolutionary aspects of behaviour.

See website at www.pearsoned.co.uk/wickens for further resources including multiple choice questions.

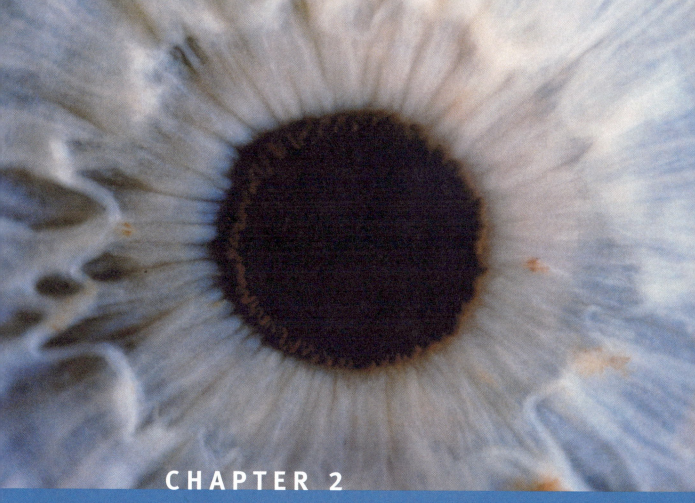

CHAPTER 2

The visual system

In this chapter

- The structure of the eye and the retina
- Visual pathways from the retina to the visual cortex
- The concept of receptive fields
- How the visual cortex processes orientation, form and depth
- The role of the visual association cortex
- Theories of colour vision
- Subcortical structures involved in vision including the superior colliculus
- Blindsight

INTRODUCTION

Most people would say that vision (the ability to detect changes in light) is our most important sense. Certainly, vision provides us with highly detailed information about the form and pattern of the world in which we live. Consider for one moment what our visual system can do: we are able to detect shapes, follow movement, differentiate colours and judge distances – we can focus on nearby objects one second and see far into the distance the next – and if an object should unexpectedly appear in the corner of our eye, we reflexively turn our gaze to it in a fraction of a second. Because these automatic skills are continually at work, it may be tempting to think of the visual system as serving to provide a faithful recording of our visual world. The visual system is, however, much more sophisticated than this – not least, because what we *perceive* is different to what the eyes *see*. In fact, what we perceive is a construction of reality that is manufactured by the brain (see Figure 2.1). Thus, our ability to process visual information is extremely complex, and this is further borne out by the fact that about one-third of the human brain is devoted to visual analysis and perception. Although the visual system and brain mechanisms of visual perception have been extensively studied, a greater understanding of how the brain 'sees' still remains one of the central challenges of modern biological psychology.

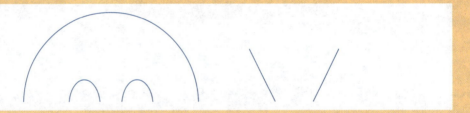

Figure 2.1   A jumble of lines – until you realise that there is a picture there! (See answer at foot of page.)

What is light?

The stimulus for activating the visual system is light, which is a form of electromagnetic radiation generated by the oscillation of electrically charged particles called photons. There are many forms of electromagnetic radiation, (including gamma rays, ultraviolet light and radio waves), all moving at the same speed of 186,000 miles per second (or 300,000 km per second) – and one might wonder why something travelling this fast does not hurt us! What distinguishes each form of electromagnetic radiation is its wavelength (see Figure 2.2) and light is no exception. In fact, light is simply a narrow band of the electromagnetic

Answer: Back view of a washer-woman kneeling down with her bucket!

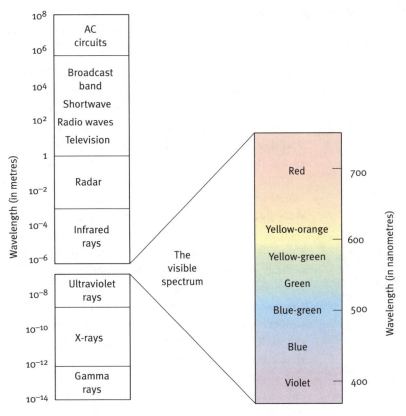

Figure 2.2   The total electromagnetic spectrum

spectrum that has a wavelength ranging from about 380 to 760 nanometres (nm) (a nanometre is one American billionth of a metre or 10 – 9). Put another way, our visual system detects only a very small portion of the electromagnetic spectrum surrounding us.

The two most important qualities that we *perceive* from light are its colour and its brightness. Colour is a function of the light's wavelength. For example, the shortest wavelength detectable by the human eye is around 380 nm and this produces the sensation of violet. As the wavelength of the light increases, so the sensation of colour changes (e.g. approximating to violet, blue, green, yellow and red). The brightness of a colour, however, is not related to its wavelength, but rather by the amplitude (or height) of its oscillation – and this is proportional to the density of photons in the wave. Thus, the more photons there are in the wave, the brighter will the light appear to be.

Of course, we rarely see just pure shades of light since most of our visual world is made up of objects that are reflecting a wide range of different wavelengths. In fact, we only see an object if the light striking its surface is partially absorbed. Indeed, if an object was to absorb all the light hitting its surface it would appear to be black, and if the same object reflected all the light, then it would appear as a mirror surface of the light source. Therefore, it is the patterns of reflection and absorption (along with the many wavelengths they create) that allow us to see the shapes and surfaces of objects.

The structure of the eye

The eye is the organ for sight and its main function is to detect changes in light intensity and transmit this information via the optic nerve to the brain. The human eye can be likened to a camera since both are basically darkened chambers with a small aperture at the front (to let in light); a focusing mechanism; and a plate to receive the projected image at the back (Figure 2.3). In the case of a camera it is the photographic film that records the image and, with the eye, it is the photoreceptors located on the back of the retina that have the same function. Unlike the camera, however, the eye's photoreceptors have to transduce light into neural information to enable it to be processed by the brain.

If an eye was removed from its socket you would find that it has a spherical shape, and for most part is covered in a tough white tissue called the **sclera** (which we often see as the 'white of the eye'). The sclera does not completely cover the surface, however, and it has a small round window called the **cornea** that enables light to enter the eye. The cornea gives the eye most of its focusing power, and once light has passed through this transparent layer, it travels through the **aqueous humour** to reach the **pupil**. The pupil is an aperture (gap) that controls the amount of light entering the next chamber of the eye, and its size is controlled by a ring of muscles called the **iris** (this also gives the eye its colour). The iris not only acts to enlarge the pupil if one moves from bright light into the dark, it also does so if one experiences an arousing or threatening stimulus. Behind the pupil is the **lens**, whose function is to bring visual images into sharp focus by acting as a fine adjustment to the cornea. This process,

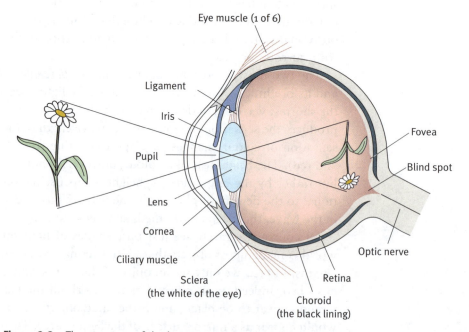

Figure 2.3 The structure of the human eye. *Source*: John P.J. Pinel, *Biopsychology*, 3rd edition. Copyright © 1997 by Pearson Education

known as accommodation, is controlled by the **cillary muscles**, which act to change the shape of the lens, either by 'bending' it (enabling vision of nearby objects) or by making it 'flatter' (allowing vision of distant objects). After the lens, light passes through a clear gelatinous substance called the **vitreous humour**, which helps to maintain the shape of the eye, before it reaches the **retina**.

The structure of the retina

The neural processing of visual information begins with photoreceptors, called **rods** and **cones**, which are located at the back of the retina. There are approximately 120 million rods and 6 million cones in each eye – and each has a different distribution on the retina with rods being mainly found in its periphery and cones located in the centre (or **fovea**). The rods and cones are also capable of dealing with different types of light. The rods are sensitive to dim light and are used mainly for night vision, whereas the cones function best in bright light and provide us with vision of high acuity (i.e. they allow us to see fine detail) and colour. Thus, although the cones are heavily outnumbered by rods in the retina, they nonetheless provide us with our most detailed visual information.

Although the retina is only about 250 micrometres (μm) thick (about the size of a razor blade edge) it contains several layers of cells. The rods and cones are located at the back of the retina, and light has to pass through the overlying cell layers to reach them. This arrangement appears to be somewhat odd as one might expect the overlying cells to interfere with the projection of the light onto the retina, but no visual disturbance seems to occur. One function of the rods and cones is to transduce light into neural information and pass this to the next layer of cells, known as the **bipolar cells**. These cells, in turn, project to the **ganglion cells**, whose cell bodies are found in the outer layer of the retina and whose axons then travel on its surface to form the optic nerve, which goes to the brain. The retina also contains **horizontal cells**, which project laterally (i.e. sideways) and interconnect the photoreceptors and **amacrine cells**, which link the bipolar and ganglion cells in much the same way. Although the function of these two types of cell is not well understood, it is known that they modify the neural information being passed through the retina. Thus, a great deal of neural processing takes place at the retina before it reaches the optic nerve (Figure 2.4).

There are approximately 800,000 axons in each optic nerve and, as we have seen, over 120 million photoreceptors (rods and cones) in the retina (Figure 2.5). This means that a 'convergence' of neural input must take place between the photoreceptors and each ganglion cell. In fact, the degree of convergence depends largely on the location of the photoreceptor in the retina. In the periphery, several hundred photoreceptors (rods) may converge onto a single ganglion cell, but this figure diminishes towards the centre of the retina, and, in the fovea, there is a much closer correspondence between photoreceptor and ganglion cell (i.e. it may receive input from just a few cones). This relationship helps to

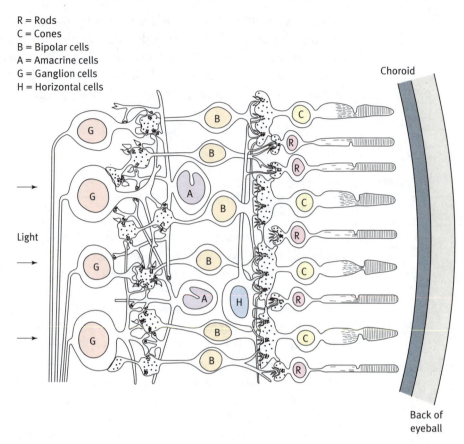

R = Rods
C = Cones
B = Bipolar cells
A = Amacrine cells
G = Ganglion cells
H = Horizontal cells

Figure 2.4   The neural structure of the human retina. *Source*: Adapted from J.E. Dowling and B.B. Boycott, *Proceedings of the Royal Society of London* (1966), **166**, 80–111

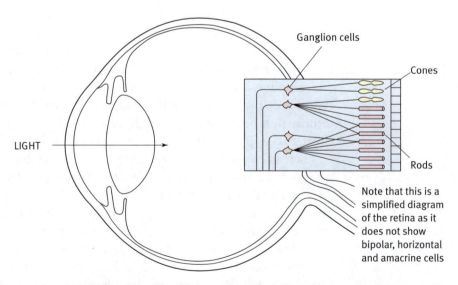

Figure 2.5   The convergence of input from cones and rods onto retinal ganglion cells

explain the better acuity of foveal vision compared with peripheral rod vision. In contrast, because large numbers of rods send information to a single ganglion cell, this 'extra' stimulation means that it is more likely to fire – and this helps to explain why rods are better at detecting changes in dim light.

The visual pathways to the brain

The axons of the ganglion cells form the optic nerve, which leaves the retina at the 'blind spot' and travels along the lower surface of the brain until it reaches the front of the pituitary stalk. At this point, the optic nerves from each retina converge and form the **optic chiasm**, where some (but not all) of the axons pass to the opposite side of the brain. More precisely, the pattern of crossing is as follows: the axons arising from the nasal side of the retina (which includes most of the fovea) cross to the opposite (contralateral) side of the brain, while the fibres from the rest of the retina continue on the same (ipsilateral) side. Although no synapses occur in the optic chiasm (i.e. axons pass straight through) the fibres that leave the chiasm are referred to as the optic tract. Each tract then enters the brain, where about 80 per cent of axons terminate in the **dorsal lateral geniculate nucleus** located in the thalamus. The remainder of the optic tract branches away to various subcortical structures, including the **superior colliculus** and **tectum**.

Each of the two dorsal lateral geniculate nuclei contains six layers of cells and receives information from both eyes (i.e. both crossed and uncrossed input). At this stage, the visual information is segregated with each cell layer receiving input from a single eye (see later). The axons arising from the geniculate layers then form a pathway called the **optic radiations**, which projects ipsilaterally (same side) to the **primary visual cortex** – a region which is located in the **occipital lobe** and the most posterior part of the cerebral cortex. In the human brain the visual cortex is about 1.5 mm in thickness and, similar to the rest of the cerebral cortex, is composed of six main layers. The axons from the lateral geniculate nucleus terminate in its fourth layer, which is subdivided into sub-lamina (4A, 4B, 4Cα and 4Cβ). Layer 4B contains numerous myelinated axon collaterals and is called the **stria of Gennari,** which gives the visual cortex its striped or striated appearance (this part of the brain is also sometimes known as the **striate cortex**). Layer 4 of the visual cortex is also the first site where input from both eyes converges, enabling binocular analysis to take place.

The visual cortex (Figure 2.6) is organised topographically – that is, if two adjacent points are stimulated on the retina, causing different ganglion cells to fire, then adjacent areas in the visual cortex will also be activated. In effect, this means that the layout of the photoreceptors in the retina is mapped out in the visual cortex. Despite this, the organisation of the visual cortex is heavily biased to processing foveal information. Although the fovea forms only a small part of the retina (less than half a millimetre in diameter), about 25 per cent

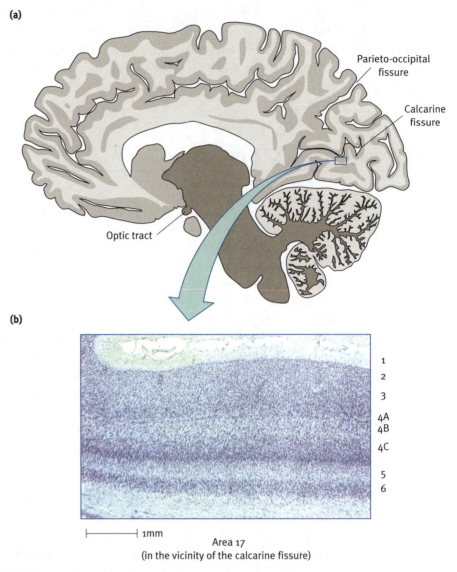

(a)

Parieto-occipital fissure

Calcarine fissure

Optic tract

(b)

1
2
3
4A
4B
4C
5
6

├───────┤ 1mm

Area 17
(in the vicinity of the calcarine fissure)

Figure 2.6 Primary visual cortex. a) Myelin-stained section of the brain showing the visual cortex (seen below the parieto-occipital fissure); b) Insert showing cresyl violet staining of the primary visual cortex, showing different layers, which gives rise to the name striate cortex

of the visual cortex is devoted to analysing its input. It can also be seen from Figure 2.7 that because axons from the nasal halves of each retina cross to the other side of the brain, each hemisphere receives information from the opposite side of the visual scene. In other words, if a person looks straight ahead, the left visual cortex receives information from the right half of the visual field; and the right visual cortex obtains input from the left. Thus, although each visual cortex receives input from *both* eyes, the right visual cortex only processes information from the left side of its world; and the left visual cortex only processes information from the right side of its world. (You will need to study Figure 2.7 carefully to understand this point!)

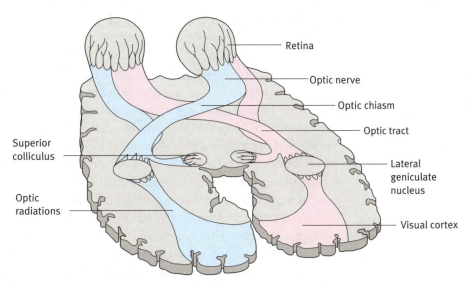

Figure 2.7   The primary visual pathways from retina to cortex. *Source*: The Open University, Course SD286, Module C7

Once information has been encoded by the visual cortex it is then passed to the adjacent **prestriate cortex** at which point it can take a number of routes through the brain. In fact, there are at least 30 other areas of the cortex, scattered throughout the occipital, parietal and temporal lobes, that are known to have at least some involvement in further visual processing (Plate 2.1 gives an idea of the distribution of these areas). These include separate cortical regions for colour and movement, along with other areas involved in reading, object recognition and spatial awareness.

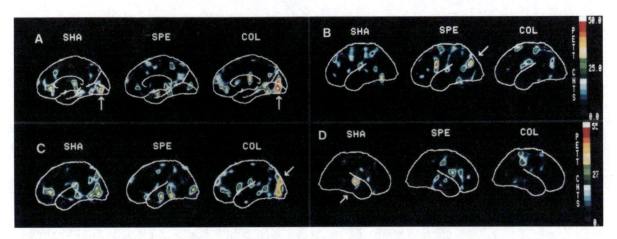

Plate 2.1   Computer-generated drawings of PET scans from an experiment that involved discriminating the shape, colour and speed of a visual stimulus under conditions of selective and divided attention. The subject's task was to compare the first stimulus with a second presented 1500 ms later, and to report if they were the same or different. Frames A shows attention to shape and colour; B shows attention to speed; C shows attention to colour; and D shows attention to shape. Abbreviations: SHA, shape; SPE, speed of movement; COL, colour. *Source*: Corbetta *et al*. Selective and divided attention during visual discriminations of shape, color, and speed, figure 7, in *The Journal of Neuroscience*, August 1991, Vol 11(8), p.2392. Copyright 1991 by the Society for Neuroscience

The receptive fields of retinal ganglion cells

As we have seen, a single ganglion cell arising from the retina receives information from a population of receptor cells (rods and cones) located at the back of the retina. The sensory detection area covered by a group of photoreceptors that converge onto an individual ganglion cell and contribute to its neural activity provides its **receptive field** – and the examination of these fields has given researchers a powerful means of understanding how the visual system encodes information. To identify a ganglion cell's receptive field, however, is no easy task. First, a microelectrode is inserted into the retina or optic nerve of an anaesthetised animal; and, secondly, the eye is then presented with a moving visual stimulus projected either directly into the retina or onto a screen facing the animal until the electrode picks up the neural activity of the visual input. This search may take hours, but once identified the characteristics of the receptive field can be mapped in fine detail.

Much of what we know about the receptive fields of retinal ganglion cells is due to the work of Stephen Kuffler, who pioneered this type of research in the 1950s working with cats (e.g. Kuffler 1953). One of Kuffler's first discoveries was that ganglion cells are not 'silent'. Rather, they are continually generating action potentials with a background firing rate of around five impulses per second. But Kuffler was more interested in discovering how ganglion cells respond to different types of stimuli, and to do this he explored their receptive fields with a fine spot of light. Using this technique, he found that the receptive field of each ganglion cell was circular in shape and they varied in size across the retina, with those in the fovea being small and those in the periphery being much larger.

There was, however, another important characteristic of ganglion receptive fields: they contained two 'zones' – a circular central area and an outer region that surrounded it. These areas also produced different types of neural activity in response to retinal visual stimulation. For example, in some ganglion cells, a spot of light shone directly into the central region of its receptive field greatly increased the background firing rate (an 'on' response), whereas light projected into its surround reduced it (an 'off' response). In other cells, the effect was reversed, with illumination of the centre producing an 'off' response and stimulation of the surround an 'on' response.

When a light was shone over the whole receptive field, Kuffler found that the 'on' and 'off' responses tended to cancel each other. Moreover, the extent of this antagonistic effect depended on the relative proportions of the on–off regions that were stimulated (see Figure 2.8). For example, if a spot of light was progressively made larger in the centre of an 'on'-centre receptive field, the firing rate of the cell increased until the centre was completely filled – at which point the response began to decline as the light encroached into the off-surround. As the surround became increasingly illuminated, however, it cancelled out the cell's on-response, returning it to its baseline level of firing. In other words, the ganglion cell shows a graded response to a light stimulus projecting on its receptive field.

Responses of an on-centre cell

There is an 'on' response when a spot of light is shone anywhere in the centre of the field

There is an 'off' response when a spot of light is shone anywhere in the periphery of the field

Responses of an off-centre cell

There is an 'off' response when a spot of light is shone anywhere in the centre of the field

There is an 'on' response when a spot of light is shone anywhere in the periphery of the field

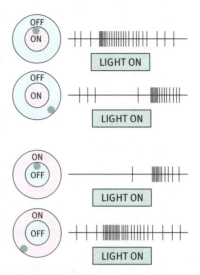

Figure 2.8 The receptive fields of an on-centre and off-centre ganglion cell. *Source*: John P.J. Pinel, *Biopsychology*, 3rd edition. Copyright © 1997 by Pearson Education

Receptive fields in the visual cortex

In the late 1950s and early 1960s, David Hubel and Tortsten Wiesel began to examine the receptive fields of neurons located in the lateral geniculate nucleus and visual cortex (see Hubel 1982, Wiesel 1982). Their approach was similar to Kuffler's – they presented anaesthetised cats (who wore special contact lenses) with various types of visual stimuli and recorded the resulting activity of single neurons in the brain. Because the lateral geniculate nucleus and visual cortex contain huge numbers of tiny microscopic cells, it took Hubel and Wiesel several years before they perfected a technique of being able to visually stimulate groups of retinal cells while simultaneously recording from individual neurons in the brain. Their work provided crucial insights into the cortical processing of vision, and they won the Nobel Prize for Physiology and Medicine in 1981 (see Barlow 1982).

Hubel and Wiesel first examined the receptive fields of neurons located in the dorsal lateral geniculate nucleus, and found that they had similar characteristics to those obtained from retinal ganglion cells. In other words, the receptive field of all the neurons in the visual pathway from retina to visual cortex showed the same basic type of concentric on–off response as found by Kuffler. However, when Hubel and Wiesel recorded from cells in the visual cortex, they discovered that their receptive fields were very different. The visual cortex contains six layers of cells, and receives input from the lateral geniculate nucleus in its fourth layer. When Hubel and Wiesel recorded from neurons at this level, they found that maximal responses were not produced by a circular spot of light, but by a series of spots arranged in a straight line. Thus, cells in this layer of the visual cortex only showed increased activity when the stimulus presented to their receptive field

Simple cell responses

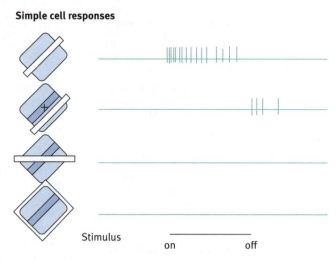

Stimulus

on off

Figure 2.9 The response of simple cortical cells to different orientations of stimuli (lines) placed in their visual fields. *Source*: D.H. Hubel (1995) *Eye, Brain and Vision*, p.73

(on the retina) was a straight line. Nonetheless, these neurons still had antagonistic on–off regions like the receptive fields of ganglion cells, although they were now oblong in shape rather than round. Also, as might be expected, these brain cells tended to fire maximally when the line was located in a very specific orientation on the retina that corresponded to the 'on' region of the receptive field. Hubel and Wiesel named these **simple cells** (see Figure 2.9).

Why do simple cells have oblong-shaped receptive fields? The answer lies with the way simple cells receive input from the lateral geniculate nucleus. In short, it appears that each simple cell receives input from an array of lateral geniculate neurons, which are 'wired' in such a way as to receive converging input from oblong groups of retinal ganglion cells. The result (in theory at least) is that a line falling on the retina may stimulate many photoreceptors, but only exert an effect on a single cell in the cortex. Thus, there is convergence of input from arrays of cells feeding into 'higher' individual neurons (see Figure 2.10).

Complex and hypercomplex cells

Simple cells are not the only type of cell in the visual cortex. When Hubel and Wiesel moved their recording electrodes from the place where simple cells are located to other layers of the visual cortex, they found two other types of cell, which they called **complex** and **hypercomplex**. Complex cells are actually the most common type of cell in the visual cortex and are similar to simple cells – except that they respond maximally when a line falls anywhere in their elongated receptive field, providing it is in the correct orientation. That is, the line stimulus does not have to be precisely located in the centre of the receptive field as long as it is parallel with it. Complex cells are also much more

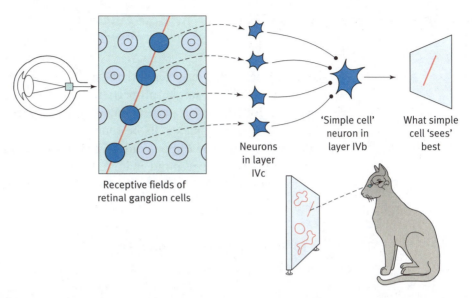

Figure 2.10   An illustration of how simple cells may be 'wired' from geniculate neurons. *Source*: A.M. Schneider and B. Tarshis, *Elements of Physiological Psychology*. Copyright © 1995 by McGraw-Hill, Inc.

sensitive to movement than simple cells as they often fire maximally when a stimulus (usually a line) is moved into the appropriate region of the receptive field from a particular direction (Figure 2.11).

Hypercomplex cells are similar to complex cells, except that they have an extra inhibitory area at the ends of their receptive field. This means that they respond best when the line is not only in a specific orientation, but also of a certain length. In fact, if the line is too long and extends into, or out of, the inhibitory part of the receptive field, then the firing rate of the cell declines. Some hypercomplex cells also respond maximally to two line segments meeting at a particular point, suggesting that they may also act as angle detectors.

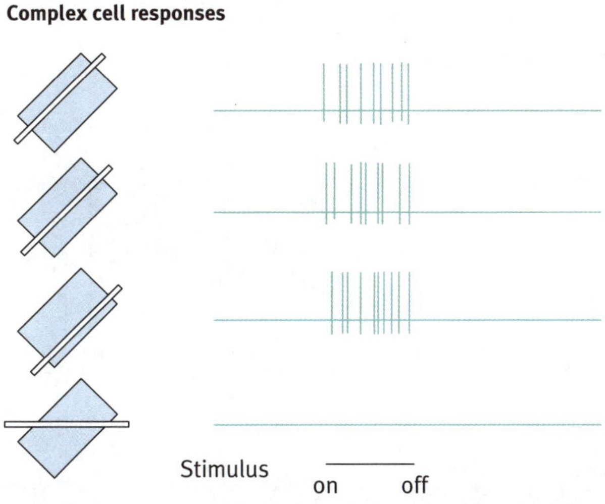

Complex cell responses

Stimulus   ⎯⎯⎯⎯
        on   off

Figure 2.11   The response of complex cortical cells to different orientations of stimuli (lines) placed in their visual fields. *Source*: D.H. Hubel (1995) *Eye, Brain and Vision*, p.75

The arrangement of cells in the primary visual cortex

Hubel and Wiesel also discovered that the visual cortex comprises columns in which all the cells share similar properties. For example, if a recording electrode is lowered into the cortex, perpendicular to its surface, not only will simple, complex and hypercomplex cells be found, but the centres of their respective receptive fields will also be approximately the same. In other words, all neurons in a particular column respond maximally to the same stimulus orientation within their receptive field. Thus, if a simple cell is found to respond best to a

(a) The main cell layers of the visual cortex

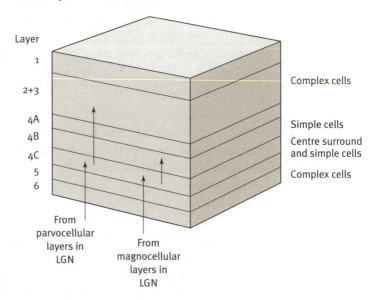

(b) The orientation sensitivity of neurons in the visual cortex

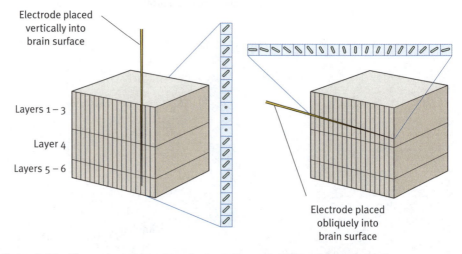

Figure 2.12   The main cell layers and orientation sensitivity of neurons in the visual cortex

vertical line, the complex and hypercomplex cells in the same column will also respond preferentially to vertical lines.

As the recording electrode is moved sideways from one column to the next, another interesting feature of the visual cortex is observed. In short, the preferred axis of orientation of the lines rotates in a clockwise manner with each 0.05 mm of sideways movement producing a rotation of 10 degrees. In other words, if the cells in one column are all 'tuned' to vertical stimuli, the cells in the next column will respond best to lines 10 degrees from vertical, and so on (see Figure 2.12). Moreover, there are enough columns in a 2-mm length of cortex to detect every possible line orientation across 360 degrees; and although the cells in each 360-degree unit respond to many different receptor field orientations, all derive from the same part of the retina, showing that each block of orientation cells is involved with processing visual information from the same part of the world (Hubel 1988).

The columns of the visual cortex are also organised on the basis of ocular dominance. Although we have two eyes, we have only one visual world, indicating that convergence of visual input takes place somewhere in the visual system. This first point of convergence occurs in the visual cortex. Indeed, it has been found that many cells in the visual cortex have binocular receptive fields (i.e. they respond to information from both eyes), although most show a preference for one of the eyes – that is, they will fire more strongly when the 'favoured' eye is stimulated. The organisation of ocular dominance in the visual cortex follows a pattern similar to that found for orientation. That is, if an electrode in lowered into a cortical column, all of its cells (i.e. simple, complex and hypercomplex) will respond best to input from the same eye. Also, as the electrode is moved laterally, the right-eye and left-eye preference alternates, with each band alternating approximately every millimetre. As can be seen in Figure 2.13, orientation and ocular columns are arranged in functional units in the visual cortex called **hypercolumns** (Mecacci 1991).

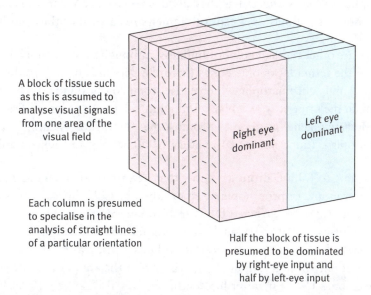

A block of tissue such as this is assumed to analyse visual signals from one area of the visual field

Right eye dominant

Left eye dominant

Each column is presumed to specialise in the analysis of straight lines of a particular orientation

Half the block of tissue is presumed to be dominated by right-eye input and half by left-eye input

Figure 2.13   An example of a hypercolumn (including ocular dominance and orientation columns)

John Dalton and colour blindness

John Dalton (1766–1844), the British chemist, is one of the fathers of modern physical science who is famous for developing the atomic theory – essentially the idea that matter is composed of atoms with different weights, and whose combination and rearrangement forms the basis of all chemical reactions. But Dalton made contributions to many other subjects, including the first detailed account of colour blindness in 1794. It is said that Dalton first realised he had a colour defect when he wore a scarlet robe to receive his PhD degree, thinking it was dark blue. When Dalton tested his vision further by viewing light being passed through a prism, he discovered that while most people could distinguish six colours, he could see just two – blue/violet and yellow. Dalton also found his brother to have the same affliction, and was to find a similar defect in 28 other people, who were all male. Dalton believed that his colour blindness was due to a blue colouring in the vitreous humour of his eyes – and instructed that after his death, his eye should be dissected and examined to prove the hypothesis. However, no blue colouring was found.

We now know that most types of colour blindness are inherited and caused by a faulty gene that makes the photopigments (or opsins) in the cones. The most common type of colour blindness – which occurs in about 8 per cent of males and 0.6 per cent of females – is where the person cannot distinguish between red and green. In fact, there are two forms of this deficit: **deuteranopia**, where the person lacks the photopigment for green, and **protanopia**, where the red pigment is missing, and in both cases those individuals tend to see their world painted in shades of blue, yellow and grey. The reason why red–green colour blindness predominantly affects males is because both the protan and deuteran genes are located on the X chromosome – of which men have one and women two. Thus, women are rarely red–green blind because if one of their X chromosomes is defective, the other, normal one, will compensate. This also means that red–green colour blindness is handed down from a colour-blind male through his daughters (who are normally unaffected) to his male grandchildren. Indeed, his sons will be unaffected as they always receive his Y chromosome and not his defective X chromosome. About 8 per cent of women are carriers of these faulty genes.

There are other types of colour blindness, although they are much rarer and include **tritanopia**, where the retina lacks blue cones (here the person is unable to distinguish between blue and yellow) and **achromatopia**, which causes total colour blindness (here the person sees the world in much the same way as a black and white television picture). Tritanopia is not sex-linked as the defective gene occurs on chromosome 7 and thus occurs equally in males and females. Tritanopia is found in about 1 in every 1,000 people, and achromatopia in 1 in every 100,000.

Returning to John Dalton, we know that he suffered from a red–green colour defect, but was it deuteranopia or protanopia? Remarkably, in 1995, investigators from London and Oxford (Hunt *et al.* 1995) extracted DNA from small samples of Dalton's eyes, which had been kept in the possession of the Manchester Literary and Philosophical Society, and discovered that they lacked the pigment for green. In other words, Dalton was a deuteranope. Dalton would have not only been undoubtedly gratified that the answer to his visual defect had finally been solved some 150 years after his death, but it is also poignant that his atomic theory provides the basis for the chemistry that made its analysis possible.

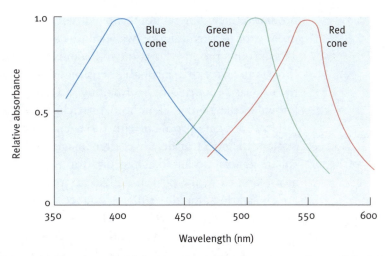

Figure 2.14   The absorbance of light by rods and the three types of cone ('blue', 'green' and 'red') in the human retina

Introduction to colour vision

The processing of colour begins with the cones in the retina, which are specialised to respond to certain wavelengths of light. Our cones detect light wavelengths from around 400 nm, producing the sensation of blue, through to about 550 nm, causing the sensation of green–yellow, and then to around 650 nm, which enables the detection of red. Obviously, we detect all these different wavelengths because the light energy reaching our eyes is transduced by the cones into neural impulses. But this raises a further question: how can we see a spectrum of different colours when we have only one type of photoreceptor for colour (i.e. the cone)?

The answer is that there are three different types of cone (Figure 2.14): the first absorbs light maximally at short wavelengths of around 445 nm (blue), the second absorbs light at medium wavelengths of around 535 nm (green), and the third absorbs light at long wavelengths of around 570 nm (red). Despite this, cones show considerable overlap in their detection of wavelengths. For example, light in wavelengths of 600 nm will not only induce the greatest response from the red cones, but will also produce a weaker response in the green cones. Thus, red-sensitive cones do not respond exclusively to long wavelengths of light – they just respond better – and the same principle holds for the other two cones.

Theories of colour vision

The idea that our eyes contain different receptors for wavelengths of light was first developed by the British physicist Thomas Young in 1802 – long before cones were discovered. He made his claim on the basis that any colour can be produced (including white) if three different types of light are mixed in the right proportion – providing the wavelengths are far enough apart from each other. Thus, Young proposed that the retina must also contain three different receptors for colour, with their probable sensitivities being for blue, green and red. This theory was supported by Hermann von Helmholtz in the 1850s and it became known as the Young–Helmholtz or **trichromatic theory** of colour vision.

However, one problem with the trichromatic theory was that it could not explain the effect of negative after-images. For example, if one stares at a red square against a white background for a few minutes, and then suddenly look at a blank card, the person will see a green after-image of the square. Altern-atively, staring at a blue square produces a yellow after-image, and staring at a black one produces a white effect. A similar type of relationship also exists for colour blindness. For example, the most common form of colour blindness is for red–green, followed by the rarer blue–yellow form (there is no such thing as red–blue or green–yellow blindness). Thus, the colours red–green and blue–yellow are linked in a way that cannot be explained by the trichromatic theory.

In 1870, the German physiologist Ewald Hering proposed an alternative explanation of colour vision. Although agreeing with Young and Helmholtz that the colour spectrum could be created by mixing three primary colours, Hering did not accept that yellow was derived from a mixture of red and green (as the trichromatic theory held), but rather that it was a primary colour along with red, green and blue. With four primary colours (instead of three) Hering saw that the visual system now only required two types of colour detector – one responding to red or green, and the other to blue or yellow. Because each type of detector was hypothesised to produce two different colour sensations, which also acted to oppose each other (red–green, yellow–blue and black–white), the theory was called the **opponent theory** of colour vision.

Which theory is correct?

As we have seen, there is evidence to support the trichromatic theory – namely, the fact that there are three types of cones in the retina that respond to different light wavelengths. Moreover, we now know that each cone contains one of three slightly different proteins called **opsins** that have light-absorbing properties corresponding to blue, green and red. These are, of course, the three primary colours predicted by the trichromatic theory, and this would appear to provide convincing support for the Young–Helmholtz position.

But, things are not so simple – particularly as ganglion cells have been found that increase their activity in response to one colour, and decrease activity in response to another. These are called **opponent neurons** and are of two types: those that produce opposite responses to red and green; and those responding similarly to blue and yellow. For example, one type of cell is excited by the colour of red and inhibited by green (R^+, G^-) or vice versa (R^-, G^+); and the other type of cell is excited by the colour of blue and inhibited by yellow (B^+, Y^-) or vice versa (B^-, Y^+). Thus, the optic nerve contains the type of cells predicted by the opponent-process theory (DeValois and DeValois 1988). These opponent cells also have concentric receptive fields, as described by Kuffler – except that, in this case, the centres and surrounds are colour-sensitive. But the opponent principle remains the same. For example, a ganglion cell might be excited by green and inhibited by red in the centre of its receptive field, while showing the opposite response in the surrounding ring. Similarly, a ganglion cell may show the same response to blue and yellow. There is also a third type of ganglion cell which does not respond to colour in this way, but instead responds to differences in brightness.

Thus, both the trichromatic and opponent theories appear to be correct. If this is the case then the fundamental problem is how do the three types of cone located in the retina (red, green and blue) combine to form the two types of opponent cell (corresponding to red–green and blue–yellow) in the optic nerve? Or put simply: where does yellow come from?

The answer to this problem must lie with the neural 'wiring' that occurs between the cones and the ganglion cells. Indeed, assuming this is the case, then the red–green opponent cell is easy to explain as it must receive input from both the red and the green cones. Thus, if the input from the red cones were excitatory, and input from the green cones inhibitory, then this would explain the R^+, G^- opponent cell. Similarly, a reversed system could account for the R^-, G^+ opponent cell. But, using the same logic, how can the blue–yellow opponent cell be explained when there is no cone for yellow?

The best explanation is that the blue–yellow opponent cell receives input from three sources: the blue, green, and red receptors. In this scheme, the input to blue part of the opponent cell is simple as there is a corresponding cone for blue. In contrast, the yellow part of the opponent cell is derived from both red and green receptor input (see Figure 2.15). That is, we see yellow not because

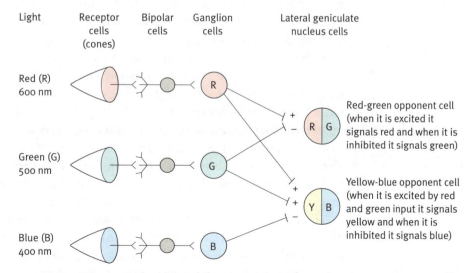

Figure 2.15   Colour coding in the retina as predicted by the opponent-process theory of colour vision

we have a specific photoreceptor for yellow, but because it is 'made up' from inputs arriving from the red and green cones. Thus, when we detect the light wavelength corresponding to yellow (which falls between the red and green bands) this stimulates both red and green cones equally – and it this dual activation that causes the yellow part of the yellow–blue ganglion cell to produce its excitation (or inhibition).

In order for ganglion cells to show opponent red–green and blue–yellow responses, the 'wiring' of the neural pathways linking the cones with opponent ganglion neurons must take place in the retina. It is believed that this function is served by the retinal horizontal cells, which link the cones with the bipolar cells, or by the multi-branched connections of the bipolar cells that synapse with the ganglion cells.

A closer look at the lateral geniculate nucleus

In the human brain, the lateral geniculate nucleus (the word *geniculate* means 'bent like a knee') consists of six layers of cells that are distinguished by their neural input and shape. For example, each layer receives input from one eye only – with layers 1, 4 and 6 receiving axons from the nasal part of the opposite (contralateral) eye, and layers 2, 3 and 5 getting projections from the outer part of the same-sided (ipsilateral) eye. Although it is difficult to picture (see Figure 2.7), this means that each lateral geniculate nucleus receives information from the opposite side of the visual world. In addition, the upper four layers of the lateral geniculate nucleus contain small neurons (called **parvocellular cells**) that are sensitive to colour (in fact they show the same opponent red–green and blue–yellow responses as found with ganglion cells), while the lower two layers have neurons (called **magnocellular cells**) that respond to light of any wavelength (i.e. they do not respond to colour).

There are also other important differences between these two types of cell. For example, the parvocellular neurons have small receptive fields, indicating they are involved in the detection of fine visual details, whereas the magnocellular neurons have larger receptive fields suggesting that they are better at detecting the broader outline of shapes. In addition, parvocellular cells tend to give a sustained response to an unchanging stimulus, whereas magnocellular neurons respond rapidly but briefly to a constant stimulus. These findings suggest that parvocellular cells are better suited to analysing stationary objects, whereas magnocellular neurons respond best to movement.

These ideas have been largely confirmed by examining the visual capabilities of monkeys after selective lesioning of the lateral geniculate nucleus. For example, damage to the magnocellular layers has little effect on visual acuity or colour vision, but impairs the monkey's ability to see moving stimuli. In contrast, damage to the parvocellular layers has little effect on motion perception, but reduces fine pattern vision and abolishes colour perception. These findings show that parvocellular cells are essential for high-resolution vision, which enables the detailed analysis of shape, size and colour of objects to take place, whereas the magnocellular cells process information that is vital for analysing the movement of objects in space (Livingstone and Hubel 1988).

Surprisingly, the retina provides only about 20 per cent of the total input to the lateral geniculate nucleus, and the rest derives mainly from the visual cortex and, to a lesser extent, the brainstem. Even more puzzling is the fact that this input does not appear to significantly alter the nature of the visual responses recorded from the lateral geniculate nucleus. Thus, there is still much to learn about the role of this structure in visual processing.

Colour processing in the cortex

It is only within the last 25 years or so that scientists have begun to understand how cells in the visual cortex process colour. Before then, colour-sensitive cells in the visual cortex had been detected, but their location seemed to occur at random and this made it difficult to study them in a systematic way. However, in 1978, a way of identifying colour-processing cells became possible when it was found that if the visual cortex was stained with a mitochondrial enzyme called cytochrome oxidase (**mitochondria** are tiny structures that produce energy inside cells) then darkened clusters of cells called **cytochrome blobs** were produced. These appeared as peg-like columns scattered throughout the visual cortex, and when David Hubel and Margaret Livingstone recorded from cells located within them, it was found that they were sensitive to colour. Moreover, their responses were similar to those obtained from the parvocellular cells of the lateral geniculate nucleus (i.e. they had concentric receptive fields that responded to red–green and blue–yellow).

It might be expected, therefore, that the colour-processing parvocellular cells projecting to the visual cortex only terminate on neurons located in the blobs. However, this is not entirely the case. Although most of the parvocellular axons entering the visual cortex pass into the blob regions, some project to areas between the blobs (called, appropriately enough, interblobs). The magnocellular cells (which are colour-blind) also send some of their axons into the blobs – perhaps to provide information about brightness or contrast.

The modular structure of the visual cortex

The discovery of cytochrome blobs also led to a revision of ideas concerning the structure of the visual cortex. As we have seen (e.g. Figure 2.12), the visual cortex is organised into hypercolumns with blocks of orientation columns (made

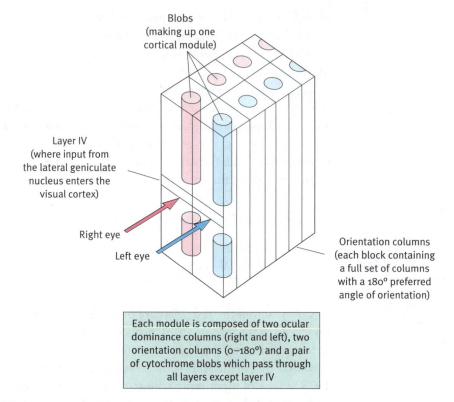

Blobs
(making up one
cortical module)

Layer IV
(where input from
the lateral geniculate
nucleus enters the
visual cortex)

Right eye

Left eye

Orientation columns
(each block containing
a full set of columns
with a 180° preferred
angle of orientation)

Each module is composed of two ocular
dominance columns (right and left), two
orientation columns (o–180°) and a pair
of cytochrome blobs which pass through
all layers except layer IV

Figure 2.16   Hubel and Livingstone's model of the modular structure of the visual cortex

up of simple, complex and hypercomplex cells), and ocular dominance columns (comprising neurons with a preference for input from one of the eyes). Into this columnar unit we can now place the colour-processing blobs. One term that has been used to describe this complex is the **cortical module** (see Figure 2.16). A cortical module consists of two ocular dominance units (each receiving input from each eye), along with two colour-processing blobs that pass through all the layers with the exception of the fourth. Each module also contains the full range (in fact twice over) of orientation columns that cover every orientation across 180 degrees. Thus, it can be seen that each cortical module has many important functions, including the analysis of pattern, colour, luminance, movement and depth.

It is estimated that the visual cortex contains around 2,500 cortical modules, with each one containing in the region of 150,000 neurons, and measuring approximately $1 \times 1 \times 2$ mm. Each module is also responsible for analysing information from the same (small) part of the visual field, as shown by the fact that removal of a cortical module causes a blind spot on the retina. Furthermore, while each module receives around 10,000 neural inputs, each sends out a staggering 50,000 axonal projections to other cortical structures (and subcortical areas) to enable more advanced visual analysis. This would appear to show that visual processing gets even more complex as we go further into the brain.

Visual processing at higher levels

The modules of the visual cortex provide the first stage of processing following the relay of information from the eyes and lateral geniculate nucleus – but it is unlikely that our perception of the visual world takes place at this point. Each module only sees what is happening in its own small part of the visual field and, therefore, if we are to perceive the totality of our visual scene, it must be that information from the cortical modules is integrated elsewhere in the brain. The most likely sites for this integration are the adjacent areas of visual association cortex and/or the areas that span out from these extrastriate regions into the temporal and parietal lobes.

Because the visual cortex is the first region to receive input from the lateral geniculate nucleus, it is sometimes called visual area 1 (V1). The next stage of visual processing takes place in the prestriate region (V2), which is a band of tissue some 6 to 8 mm wide that surrounds the V1 cortex. When the V2 area is stained it reveals three types of 'stripe' – thick, thin and pale – and these contain cells that receive different types of input from the V1 area. In short, the thick stripes receive information about depth perception; the thin stripes get colour information from the blobs; and the pale stripes obtain input from the extrablob areas involved in orientation, form and motion vision. Thus, the prestriate area maintains the segregation of visual input that first takes place in the cortical modules of the V1 region.

However, at this point the three streams of visual information diverge and travel into different areas of the brain. It is known that more than 30 different cortical areas are involved in visual function (Van Essen *et al.* 1992), which makes it difficult to follow the pathways with precision. However, it is clear that one major pathway (the dorsal route) turns into the parietal lobe; and another turns down (the ventral route) to pass through the temporal cortex (Figure 2.17). These have also been shown to be involved in different types of processing, with

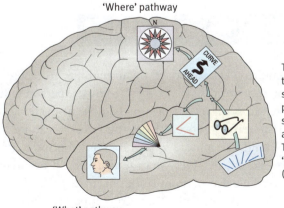

'Where' pathway

'What' pathway

The 'what' and 'where' pathways in the visual system include areas specialised for processing depth perception (symbolised by a pair of spectacles), form (an angle), colour, and direction (the curve ahead sign). The result is object recognition (the 'what' pathway) or object location (the 'where' pathway).

Figure 2.17   The spatial-visual (dorsal route) and object recognition (ventral route) pathways in the brain. *Source*: M.I. Posner and M.E. Raichle (1997) *Images of Mind*, p.15

the dorsal pathway primarily concerned with *where* visual information is located, and the ventral route with the *recognition* of objects (Ungerleider and Mishkin 1982).

Evidence showing that the parietal cortex is involved in the spatial aspects of vision – including the analysis of motion and the understanding of the positional relationships of objects in the visual world – has come from **Balint's syndrome**, where people suffer bilateral damage to the region bordering the occipital and parietal lobes. Although people with this syndrome can perceive and recognise objects, they will often show misdirected movement when they try to reach for them (**optic ataxia**). In addition, they will often have difficulty fixing their gaze on objects, or following their movement (**ocular apraxia**). Interestingly, a person with Balint's syndrome may also demonstrate **simultanagnosia** – an inability to see two objects at once (e.g. if presented with a pen and a toothbrush they might only be able to see one object at a time – not both together).

In contrast, the temporal lobe pathway has been shown to be involved in high-resolution pattern vision, object recognition and colour processing. One consequence of its damage can be visual **agnosia** – an inability to recognise a stimulus or object visually, despite being able to recognise it through other sensory modalities. There are many different types of agnosia (see box) but one of the most interesting is an inability to recognise faces (**prosopagnosia**). For example, Damasio *et al.* (1990) reported the case of a 60-year-old woman (with normal visual acuity) who suffered a bilateral stroke to the border of the occipital and temporal lobes and was unable to recognise the faces of her husband or daughter, despite being able to identify them by their voices. Curiously, people with prosopagnosia are often able to recognise the age and gender of the face, and even its emotional expression, despite not being able to recognise the person to whom it belongs (Tranel *et al.* 1988). A number of mammals have also been shown to have brain regions involved in face recognition. For example, in sheep, cells have been found in the temporal cortex that respond selectively to the faces of horned sheep, unhorned sheep, sheepdogs and wolves (Kendrick and Baldwin 1987).

Visual agnosia: seeing without recognising

Visual agnosia is a rare condition characterised by an inability to recognise familiar objects, although the sense of vision remains essentially intact. Thus, a person with agnosia may have difficulty recognising the features of an object – or be able to perceive the features but not know what the object is. The term 'agnosia' (from the Greek meaning 'lack of knowledge') was first used by Sigmund Freud, but a more important contribution to its understanding was made by Lissauer, who proposed, in 1890, that agnosia could be divided into two types: apperceptive and associative. This distinction was partly made on his idea that visual recognition must involve two processes: perceptual integration (apperception), in which sensory data is organised into a 'whole', and association, where the percept is linked with stored knowledge so that its meaning can be established.

Visual agnosia: seeing without recognising continued.

An example of apperceptive agnosia is the case of Dr P, the character after which Oliver Sacks named his book *The Man who Mistook his Wife for a Hat*. Dr P was a well-educated music teacher who was unable to recognise the faces of his students by sight, although he could identify them when they spoke. He was also impaired at recognising a wide range of objects. For example, when Sacks gave Dr P a glove, he recognised that it had five appendages and guessed it was a cloth container such as a purse. Nonetheless, despite prompting, he was unable to recognise it as a glove. Similarly, when Sacks presented him with a red rose, Dr P described its basic shape as 'a convoluted red form with linear green attachment', but was unable to recognise it until he was asked to smell it. But perhaps the most striking example of his deficit came at the end of his examination when Dr P, looking for his hat, tried to pick up the head of his wife!

In apperceptive agnosia, basic vision is intact, but the person cannot combine the visual elements into a meaningful percept. Thus, although they can see lines, edges, colour, motion, etc., the apperceptive agnostic has trouble 'seeing objects'. This can be demonstrated by getting the person to copy simple letters, shapes and line drawings. Although the task can be attempted, people with apperceptive agnosia are often unable to make even the most rudimentary approx-imation of the shape they are asked to draw. They are also impaired at matching simple shapes. This form of agnosia appears to be associated with damage to the association or extra-striate areas of the visual cortex and adjoining regions of the parietal cortex.

Associative agnosia is a less severe deficit. For example, copying a line drawing is relatively easy for individuals with associative agnosia, although they may be unable to recognise what they have drawn. Alternatively, they may draw the object from memory. Thus, those people can 'see' objects, but they don't know what they are. The extent of this deficit can vary greatly. In some cases, the associative agnostics will not be able to determine the meaning or function of a previously known stimulus, although in other instances they may be able to extract enough information to recognise its main category (e.g. mammal, insect, or bird), but be unable to assess its other attributes (e.g. whether it is tame or dangerous). The brain sites responsible for associative agnosia are found from the occipital–temporal lobe border, through the ventral part of the temporal lobe, to its most anterior regions.

Subcortical visual systems

The pathway from the retina to the occipital cortex, and beyond, is not the only visual system in the brain. In fact, about 20 per cent of the ganglion cells branch away from the optic nerve before reaching the lateral geniculate nucleus and pass to subcortical regions, including the midbrain tectum (located at the top of the brainstem). In many lower species such as fish, reptiles and birds, the tectum provides the main site for visual analysis – and in primates this region, which is dominated by the superior colliculus, still remains functionally important. The main role of the superior colliculus is the control of orientation, especially when the eyes need to be oriented towards stimuli appearing in the visual field. The superior colliculus also helps to coordinate **saccadic eye movements** – sudden automatic and rapid movements of the eyes that allow us to explore changing visual scenes and continually to bring new images onto the fovea.

The superior colliculus also sends some of its axons to the secondary visual areas of the occipital lobe. Evidence that this pathway may make an important contribution to human vision was provided by patient DB, who had much of his right visual (striate) cortex surgically removed for medical reasons. It has long been known that damage to the visual pathways from retina to visual cortex produces blindness in the visual field opposite to the side of the brain where the lesion has occurred – and DB was no exception as he appeared to be initially blind in his left visual field. Despite this, DB was able to point to the position of markers on a wall; decide whether a stick was horizontal or vertical; and distinguish between the letters 'X' and 'O' – although protesting that he could not see what he was doing! This type of residual form of vision has since been found in other subjects with visual cortex damage and been called **blindsight** (Weiskrantz *et al.* 1974).

Although not all investigators are convinced that the superior colliculus is responsible for blindsight (another possibility is that it is caused by stray light passing from the blind visual field into the sighted one thereby giving a clue to the target's location – Campion *et al.* 1983), it is nevertheless clear that the two visual systems (e.g. the geniculate-striate and superior-collicular) have evolved to serve different functions. Indeed, this was shown by Schneider (1967), who found that lesions of the striate cortex in hamsters impaired the performance of simple visual discrimination tasks, whereas removal of the superior colliculus produced an inability to localise the spatial location of objects. For example, these animals could not locate a sunflower seed given to them unless it touched their whiskers. In humans, it is probably the case that the striate system is primarily involved in conscious visual recognition, whereas the superior-colliculi system is more concerned with unconscious aspects of spatial analysis.

Another important subcortical area is the nearby pretectum, which is involved in producing pupil reflexes. For example, if bright light is suddenly shone into the eye, the pupil will automatically constrict. This reflex occurs because some retinal ganglion cells pass to the pretectum, which controls the **Edinger–Westphal nucleus** – the origin of parasympathetic fibres going back to the eye – whose function causes contraction of the pupillary constrictor muscles in the iris. A further subcortical structure also receiving visual input is the **suprachiasmatic nucleus** located in the hypothalamus. This tiny structure is involved in generating and synchronising circadian rhythms, and will be discussed in Chapter 6.

Summary

Vision, or our ability to detect different wavelengths and intensities of light, is our most important sense, and it has been estimated that around one-third of the human brain is devoted to its analysis and perception. Our visual processing begins with the eyes. Light passes through the transparent **cornea**, into the **aqueous humour**, and then to the **pupil**, which is the aperture (controlled by the **iris**, which gives the eyes their colour) that regulates the amount of light entering the eye. Just behind the pupil lies the **lens**, whose function is to bring visual images into clear focus onto the **retina** and whose shape is controlled by the **cillary muscles**. Light then passes through the main chamber of the eye containing **vitreous humour** and is projected onto the retina containing the photoreceptors of the eye. There are two types of photoreceptor: the **rods**, which are found predominantly in its periphery and are involved in the detection of light intensity, and the **cones**, which are found in the **fovea** and are involved in detailed (acute) vision and colour detection. There are three main types of cone, roughly sensitive to blue, green and red wavelengths of light. It is estimated that each retina has in the region of 120 million rods and 6 million cones. From the retina, information from the rods and cones passes to the **bipolar cells** and then to the **ganglion cells**, which make up the optic nerve. There are approximately 800,000 axons in each optic nerve, which passes underneath the brain before appearing to join in the **optic chiasm**. In fact, the optic chiasm is a crossing-over point where about two-thirds of axons from each eye (or more accurately the nasal side of the retina) cross to the opposite side of the brain. The axons continue into the brain, where most (about 80 per cent) terminate in the **dorsal lateral geniculate nucleus** of the thalamus. From here, neurons project via the optic radiations to the **primary visual cortex** (sometimes called the striate cortex) situated in the occipital lobe. From the visual cortex two main routes appear to be involved in visual processing – the **dorsal pathway** extending into the **parietal lobe** concerned with determining '*where*' in space visual information is located, and the **ventral pathway** which passes down into the **temporal lobe**, and is primarily concerned with **object recognition**.

The nature of the information processed by the visual system was examined by **Stephen Kuffler** in the 1950s, who recorded the electrical activity of **ganglion cells** in the cat optic nerve by passing a small spot of light across their **receptive fields** (in effect, the visual fields of the photoreceptors located in the retina from which the ganglion cells received their sensory input). He found that the receptive fields of ganglion cells were concentric, consisting of a circular central area surrounded by a ring. These zones also produced different types of neural activity in response to visual stimulation. For example, in some cells, light shone in the central region increased its rate of firing (an 'on' response) whereas light falling in the surround inhibited firing (an 'off' response). In other cells, the situation was reversed with stimulation of the centre producing an 'off' response, and stimulation of the surround producing an 'on' response. This work was extended in the 1960s by **Hubel** and **Wiesel**, who used a similar technique to examine cells in the **visual cortex**. This research showed that the visual cortex contained three types of cell – **simple**, **complex** and **hypercomplex** – which had elongated receptive fields and were more sensitive to lines than to spots of light. Hubel and Wiesel also showed that the visual cortex contained **columns**, with each one containing six layers and

Summary continued.

having simple, complex and hypercomplex cells that fired to lines of the same orientation. Moreover, the axis of the lines rotated in a clockwise manner by about 10 degrees in adjacent columns – which meant in effect that approximately each 2 mm of visual cortex contained enough columns to detect every possible line orientation over 360 degrees. Further research also showed that the visual cortex is actually made up of **modules** which not only contain a block of **orientation columns** that cover all line angles over 360 degrees, but also two blocks of **ocular dominance columns**, which have a preference for input from each of the eyes, and a pair of **cytochome blobs**, which are responsible for colour processing. It is believed that the human primary visual cortex may contain around 2,500 of these modules, with each one dealing with a small part of the visual world at the retinal level. After the occipital lobe, visual processing appears to take two routes through the brain: one involving the temporal lobe concerned with object recognition, and the other involving the parietal lobe concerned with where objects are located in space.

Essay questions

1. Trace the anatomical structure of the visual system from retina to the brain including its striate cortex and subcortical projections.

   Helpful Internet search terms: *Visual system. The retina. Optic chiasm. Lateral geniculate nucleus. The visual cortex. Superior colliculus.*

2. Electrical recording of single cells in the optic nerve and striate cortex has provided scientists with a powerful means of understanding their role in visual processing. Discuss.

   Helpful Internet search terms: *Receptive fields. Single cell recording in visual system. Kuffler and the optic nerve. Hubel and Wiesel. Simple, complex and hypercomplex cells.*

3. How is the brain capable of 'seeing' a spectrum of fine colour, when the eye contains only three different types of colour detector?

   Helpful Internet search terms: *Cones in the retina. Colour blindness. Trichromatic theory. Opponent theory of colour vision. Colour and the visual cortex.*

4. What evidence supports the existence of dorsal ('*where' is it?*') and ventral ('*what is it?*') visual systems in the cerebral cortex?

   Helpful Internet search terms: *Two cortical visual pathways. Ventral visual pathway. Dorsal visual pathway. Visual processing in temporal lobes. Visual and spatial processing in parietal lobes.*

Further reading

Bruce, V., Green, P.R. and Georgeson, M.A. (1996) *Visual Perception: Physiology, Psychology and Ecology* (3rd edn). Hove: Psychology Press. A comprehensive textbook that covers the physiology of the visual system and its involvement in visual processing and perception.

Farah, M.J. (1999) *Visual Agnosia*. London: MIT Press. Describes how brain damage can result in disorders of object recognition, and the implications of this for understanding visual processing.

Gregory, R.L. (1998) *Eye and Brain*. Oxford: Oxford University Press. A classic book first published in 1966 – and now greatly extended – which provides an essential introduction to perception and visual illusions.

Gross, C.G. (1999) *Brain, Vision, Memory: Tales in the History of Neuroscience*. Cambridge, MA: MIT Press. Although not exclusively about vision, this book will be of interest to students who want to know more about the history of visual research.

Hubel, D.H. (1988) *Eye, Brain and Vision*. New York: Scientific American Library. A beautifully illustrated text, written by a Nobel Laureate, which provides a readable account of how we have come to understand the organisation and function of the visual system.

Milner, A.D. and Goodale, M.A. (1995) *The Visual Brain in Action*. Oxford: Oxford University Press. A book that examines the two main pathways beyond the striate cortex – the dorsal and ventral streams – that underlie vision for action and perception.

Palmer, S.E. (1999) *Vision Science: Photons to Phenomenology*. Cambridge, MA: MIT Press. A textbook devoted to the science of vision that covers all the major topics from early neural processing in the eye to high-level functions such as memory, imagery and awareness.

Zeki, S. (1993) *A Vision of the Brain*. London: Blackwell. A book which outlines how the visual system works and its implications for understanding cortical function.

See website at www.pearsoned.co.uk/wickens for further resources including multiple choice questions.

CHAPTER 3

The control of movement

In this chapter

- The structure of muscles and the neuromuscular junction
- Monosynaptic and polysynaptic spinal reflexes
- Pyramidal and extrapyramidal systems of the brain
- The functions of motor cortex, cerebellum and basal ganglia
- Parkinson's disease and the development of L-dopa therapy
- Huntington's chorea

INTRODUCTION

The human brain processes an enormous amount of sensory information – gathering and analysing input from the external environment and receiving feedback from the internal state of its own body. But no matter how much information is analysed, it is of little use unless it can be acted upon. Indeed, one characteristic of all animals, from the simplest to the most complex, is the ability to produce movement – whether to control and maintain the automated functions of the body (such as respiration, heart rate, digestion) or to carry out more complex and purposeful behaviour. Attempting to understand the neural basis of movement – or, more precisely, how the brain controls the action of muscles in the body – is a considerable challenge. As the brain has evolved, the control of movement has become hierarchically organised with increasing levels of complexity from simple reflexes in the spinal cord to more complex and intricate patterns of behaviour produced by higher brain areas. Nonetheless, the motor system functions as a whole, with higher regions working through and influencing the actions of the lower ones. By trying to explain how this system works we are not only gaining insight into the brain's remarkable ability to integrate a wide range of neural information, but we are also getting close to understanding what causes human behaviour. In addition, a number of crippling and distressing disorders such as Parkinson's disease and Huntington's chorea affect the motor systems of the brain, and it is imperative that we understand their causes, and neural basis, to enable more effective treatments to be developed.

Muscles

There would be no movement without muscles. The body contains three different types of muscle: **skeletal** (muscles attached to the bones); **smooth** (muscle found in the walls of hollow internal structures such as blood vessels); and **cardiac** (muscle forming the bulk of the heart). In this chapter we shall be mainly concerned with the action of skeletal muscle (also called striated muscle because of its striped appearance), which is under the control of the somatic nervous system. The human body contains over 600 different types of striated muscle, which makes up about 50 per cent of its weight and is responsible for posture and voluntary movement. In contrast, the smooth and cardiac muscles are controlled by the autonomic nervous system (and certain hormones) and govern the involuntary functioning of the body's organs. Although smooth and cardiac muscle can function in the absence of neural input (e.g. the heart has its own pacemaker cells that produce contractions), this does not occur with skeletal muscle, which requires neural innervation to allow it to contract and produce movement.

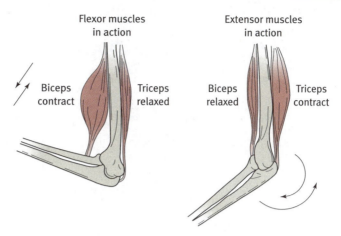

Flexor muscles in action

Extensor muscles in action

Biceps contract

Triceps relaxed

Biceps relaxed

Triceps contract

Figure 3.1   The flexor and extensor muscles of the upper arm

One of the most important functions of skeletal muscle is to bend the joints that allow the limbs to move, and to do this it has to be attached, via tendons, to a pair of bones. In fact, regardless of how complex a skeletal movement may be, these muscles work only one way: by contraction or pulling on a joint. Consequently, joints are controlled by two sets of muscles whose effects oppose or antagonise each other. For example, the arm consists of the upper bone (the humerus) and the lower bones (the ulna and the radius), which are connected at the elbow joint. The biceps (the flexor muscles) connects the upper and lower bones at the *front* of the joint, and when it contracts the elbow is made to bend. In contrast, the triceps (the extensor muscles) run along the *back* of the upper arm bone, and its contraction causes the limb to straighten (Figure 3.1). In practice, the flexor and extensor muscles are finely coordinated with the contraction of one muscle being counterbalanced by the relaxation of the other. Thus, even the simple movement of the elbow requires the integrated action of different muscles, and this principle holds true for all other types of joint and movement.

The fine structure of muscle

If a skeletal muscle (Figure 3.2) is examined closely it will be found to consist of a large mass of long, thin **muscle fibres**, each of which is a living cell which contains several nuclei and is enclosed by its own outer membrane (called the sarcolemma). The length of muscle cells can vary enormously, with the largest being over 30 cm in length (the sartorius muscle of the thigh) and the smallest less than 1 mm (the stapedius muscle in the inner ear). However, no matter its size, packed tightly within each individual muscle fibre are hundreds (sometime thousands) of long cylindrical structures called **myofibrils** that run the entire

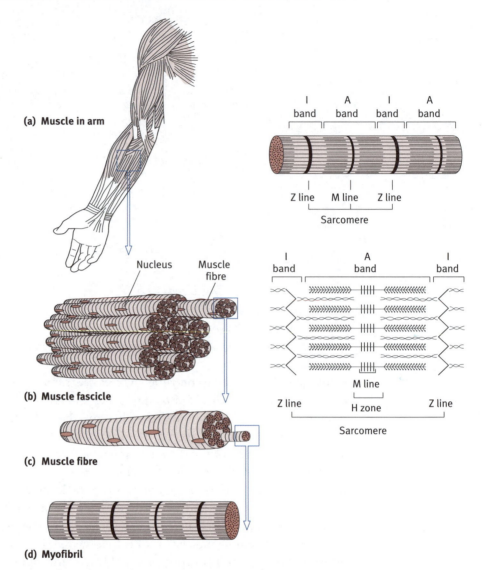

Figure 3.2 The anatomy of a skeletal muscle. *Source*: R. Carola, J.P. Harley and C.R. Noback (1990), *Human Anatomy and Physiology*, published by Random House, Inc.

length of the cell. These make up about 80 per cent of the muscle cell's volume and are the components that allow it to contract in response to a neural impulse. When examined microscopically, the myofibrils can be seen to be made up of a repeated array of short segments called **sarcomeres** that contain very fine filaments made predominantly from **actin** or **myosin**. It is the sarcomere, or more precisely its two darkened ends (called Z lines), that gives the muscle its striated appearance – and it is the movement of the actin and myosin filaments that provides it with the ability to contract.

How then do the actin and myosin filaments interact to produce muscle contraction? The simple answer is that they are made to slide over each other – and by doing this the myosin filaments (which are attached to the Z lines) pull the two ends of the sarcomere inwards. The secret of this movement lies with the myosin and actin. These proteins not only lie sandwiched between each other, but also have different shapes – the myosin filaments being thick with protruding hooks, and the actin filaments being thin with a twisted knobbly appearance. When an action potential arrives at the muscle fibre, it causes a rotation in the shape of the myosin's hook. This catches the actin filaments and forces them to slide along its surface. This, in turn, contracts the sarcomere, thereby shortening the myofibril, and contributing to the contraction of the muscle fibre. The combined activity of large numbers of muscle fibres causes the contraction of the skeletal muscle.

The neural innervation of muscle

Skeletal muscles are stimulated by motor neurons derived from the ventral horn of the spinal cord, or in some cases the brain via its cranial nerves. Each individual muscle is served by at least one motor neuron (sometimes called an alpha motor neuron), which typically gives rise to hundreds of multibranching axonal endings that innervate a large number of its muscle fibres. Thus, when the motor neuron fires, it causes all of its target muscle fibres to contract at the same time. The number of fibres innervated by a single axon varies depending on the type of muscle. For example, the ocular muscles of the eye receive about one motor axon for every 10 muscle fibres; some muscles of the hand may have a motor neuron for every 100 muscle cells, and this figure may rise to 2,000 for the large muscles of the trunk and leg. In general, muscles with low ratios are involved in fine and dextrous movement, and those with high ratios are involved in less flexible responses.

The gap (or synapse) that lies between the axon endings of the motor neuron and the muscle fibre is called the **neuromuscular junction**, and the neurotransmitter used at this site is **acetylcholine**. When acetylcholine is released by the motor neuron, it crosses the synapse, and comes into contact with part of the muscle fibre called the **motor endplate**. This form of synaptic transmission is both fast and reliable as the release of acetylcholine nearly always causes an action potential in the muscle fibre (this is in contrast to most neurons, which typically require the summation of many neural inputs before they can generate an action potential). The reliability of the muscle fibre to respond to acetylcholine is largely due to the large folded surface area of the motor endplate, which is packed full of cholinergic receptors. Because neuromuscular junctions are larger and more accessible than synapses in the CNS, much of what we known about synaptic transmission has actually been derived from research involving this site. Moreover, an understanding of the neuromuscular junction has a broader significance since certain diseases (e.g. myasthenia gravis) affect this area – as do a number of deadly poisons such as curare and bungarotoxin, which are found in the venom of various snakes such as cobras.

Muscle spindles

Deep within the layers of most skeletal muscles (squashed between the muscle fibres) are long thin fibrous capsules called **muscle spindles**. Although a muscle spindle receives neural input from a **gamma motor neuron**, which causes it to contract, this has negligible effect on the main contraction of the muscle in which it is embedded. Rather, the main role of the muscle spindle is to provide sensory information to neurons in the spinal cord about the stretch of the muscle and, for this reason, they are sometimes called stretch receptors.

The importance of stretch receptors can be seen when a heavy weight is placed in a person's hand. At first the arm will begin to drop from the elbow, and the bicep muscles of the upper arm will be forced to stretch. As this movement occurs, however, the muscle spindles in the biceps will also become extended, causing them to relay information about the stretching to the spinal cord. This input then causes the alpha motor neurons that project to the biceps to fire, producing their contraction and helping them to resist the stretch. Thus, in this way, the biceps makes a reflexive movement to the force of the weight. In fact, a basic prerequisite for smooth movement throughout the body is the ability to adjust muscle tone very quickly to sudden shifts in weight. The stretch reflex is vital in this respect and essential for maintaining muscle tone and posture. It must also occur very rapidly, which explains why the stretch reflex is controlled by the spinal cord and not by the brain.

The best-known example of the stretch reflex is the **patellar tendon reflex** (knee jerk), which is used by doctors to assess the condition of the nervous system. When the doctor strikes the tendon of the patient's knee, this causes the extensor muscle running along the thigh (the quadriceps) to be stretched. The sudden stretching of the quadriceps causes the muscle spindles to pass this information to motor neurons in the spinal cord, which then react by sending action potentials down their axons back to the stretched muscle. The result is a compensatory muscle contraction and sudden leg extension. This type of reflex is also called a **monosynaptic stretch reflex** (Figure 3.3) because only one synapse

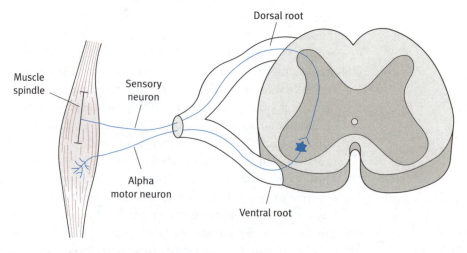

Figure 3.3   The spinal monosynaptic reflex

(located in the spinal cord) is encountered along the route from receptor (muscle spindle) to effector (leg muscle). Thus, the sensory neuron from the muscle spindle directly synapses with the motor neuron controlling the movement.

The polysynaptic reflex

In fact, most spinal reflexes are polysynaptic which means they involve more than one synapse. An example of a polysynaptic reflex is where a person painfully stubs his big toe, causing him to suddenly withdraw his foot from the hard surface. This is also known as a **flexion reflex**. In this situation, pain receptors in the toe send input to the spinal cord via a sensory neuron that synapses with several **interneurons** located entirely within the grey matter of the spinal cord. At this point, the neural input takes several routes through the spinal cord, but the end result is a complex and coordinated response involving several muscles. This reflex is slower than the monosynaptic reflex because the involvement of an interneuron means that at least two synapses will have to be crossed before the motor neuron is activated.

Most of the information that is passed to our motor neurons controlling skeletal muscle is actually derived from interneurons in the spinal cord. These interneurons not only receive axons from sensory neurons, including those from muscle spindles and pain receptors, but they also obtain input from other segments of the spinal cord and brain. In fact, interneurons are known to be involved in a wide variety of reflexes that help to coordinate movement. For example, if you step on something sharp not only will the leg be withdrawn from the painful stimulus, but the opposite leg will be prepared to support the weight suddenly shifted to it. This is known as the **crossed extensor reflex** and is important in maintaining balance. Polysynaptic reflexes (Figure 3.4) can also

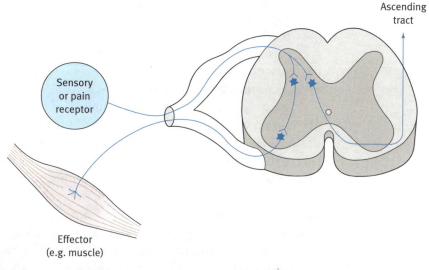

Figure 3.4   The spinal polysynaptic reflex

produce rhythmical movement of the limbs. For example, the vigorous scratching movements produced by a dog in response to a flea are caused by circuits of interneurons (called central pattern generators) located in the spinal cord that generate rhythmical movement of the legs. Similar spinal mechanisms may also be involved in much of our own movement, including walking, running and swimming (Grillner 1996).

The control of movement by the brain

By far the most important organ responsible for body movement is the brain. A large number of brain structures contribute to movement, and these are hierarchically organised so that the lower areas tend to control simple reflexes, while higher regions govern more complex behaviours. Four main regions of the brain are especially important in the control of movement, and these are the **brainstem**, the **cerebellum**, the **basal ganglia** and the **motor cortex**. Although the function of these structures is quite different, they are capable of functioning as an integrated unit. Indeed, most purposeful human behaviour will depend on the simultaneous coordination of numerous motor pathways that involve all of these regions.

All brain regions involved in movement are connected to the motor neurons of the spinal cord via one of two major pathways: the **pyramidal system** (Figure 3.5(a)) and the **extrapyramidal system** (Figure 3.5(b)). The cell bodies of the pyramidal system originate in the cerebral cortex (mainly from the motor cortex and adjacent areas) and form the **corticospinal tract** – a massive bundle of axons that passes down into the spinal cord. Before reaching the spinal cord, however, most of these axons (about 85 per cent) will cross to the contralateral (opposite) side of the brainstem, in a region called the pyramidal decussation (from which the pyramidal system gets its name). Although the uncrossed axons also continue down to the spinal cord, most will pass to the opposite side when they reach the spinal segment in which they terminate. Thus, the pyramidal system is almost completely contralateral – the right motor cortex controlling movement on the left side of the body, and vice versa. Only about 2–3 per cent of corticospinal fibres remain uncrossed.

The extrapyramidal system is composed of the motor regions and pathways of the brain whose output does not contribute to the pyramidal system. It is also distinct from the pyramidal system as its fibres do not cross over to the opposite side of the spinal cord (i.e. the pathways pass down the same side of the body). One of the most important sites contributing to this system is the brainstem, which is the origin of several descending tracts to the spinal cord including the **reticulospinal** tract (originating from a number of reticular nuclei); the **rubrospinal** tract (originating from the red nucleus); and the **vestibulospinal** tract (originating from the vestibular nuclei). The first two of these tracts are also influenced by axons from the cerebral cortex, showing that higher-order or

(a) The pyramidal system

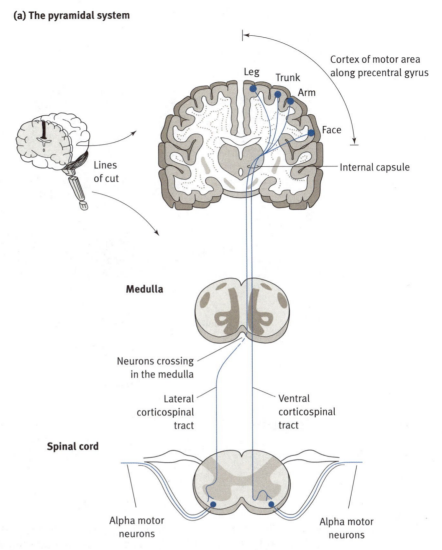

Cortex of motor area
along precentral gyrus

Leg Trunk
Arm

Face

Lines
of cut

Internal capsule

Medulla

Neurons crossing
in the medulla

Lateral
corticospinal
tract

Ventral
corticospinal
tract

Spinal cord

Alpha motor
neurons

Alpha motor
neurons

Figure 3.5(a)   The pyramidal neural system of the brain and spinal cord. *Source*:
A.M. Schneider and B. Tarshis, *Elements of Physiological Psychology*. Copyright ©
1995 by McGraw-Hill, Inc.

conscious information may have some control over basic reflexes. Two other
important areas that belong to the extrapyramidal system are the **basal ganglia**
and the **cerebellum**. Both these structures give rise to complex and multisynaptic pathways, which although having no direct link with the spinal cord are
nevertheless integrated with other movement areas including the brainstem,
thalamus and motor areas of the cerebral cortex.

Traditionally, the extrapyramidal system has been associated with postural,
reflexive and stereotypical forms of movement, and the pyramidal system
with voluntary movement. However, most researchers now believe that this
division is far too simple. For example, some fibres from the extrapyramidal
system go to the thalamus, where they can influence pathways going to the
pyramidal regions of the motor cortex. In turn, the motor cortex innervates

(b) The extrapyramidal system

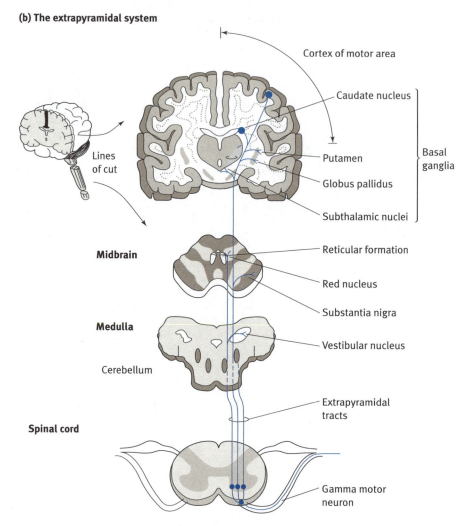

Figure 3.5(b) The extrapyramidal neural system of the brain and spinal cord. *Source*: A.M. Schneider and B. Tarshis, *Elements of Physiological Psychology*. Copyright © 1995 by McGraw-Hill, Inc.

many extrapyramidal structures (such as the striatum) and some of its fibres even project into the descending tracts used by the extrapyramidal system to pass information to the spinal cord. Thus, both systems are intricately interconnected.

Gilles de la Tourette syndrome

In 1885, Georges Gilles de la Tourette, a French doctor working in Paris and an associate of the famous neurologist Charcot, described a remarkable condition in which people exhibited sudden involuntary movements (i.e. tics), vocal utterances including swearing, and impulsive ritualised behaviours. Although Tourette was the first to recognise it as a clinical disorder, it

Gilles de la Tourette syndrome continued.

is certain that a number of previously famous historical figures also suffered from the condition. Perhaps the most convincing case is the eighteenth-century writer Dr Samuel Johnson, who was noted for his various motor tics, facial grimacing, sudden loud vocalisations, shoulder shrugging, and bizarre rituals when going through doorways. It is also possible that Mozart was another with Tourette's syndrome as he was hyperactive and given to sudden impulses that included mimicry, coarse behaviour and swearing. As these two cases show, Tourette's syndrome is not a bar to creativity. This has also been shown by Sacks (1986), who describes 'Witty Ticcy Ray', a weekend jazz drummer renowned for his sudden and tic-like wild improvisations, but who reverts back to taking medication during the working week in order to become his 'sober, solid, square' self.

Tourette's syndrome is rare, occurring in around three–five people in every 10,000, and being some three–four times more frequent in males, although it is possible that as many as one in 200 show a partial expression of the disorder. It also appears to be a genetic condition with a concordance rate of around 50–70 per cent for identical twins compared with just 10–25 per cent for non-identical twins. The course of Tourette's syndrome varies from person to person, but typically begins between the ages of 4 and 8 years, and is often fully expressed by the age of 15. The first symptoms are often facial tics, including eye-blinking, with symptoms gradually progressing down the body with head-jerking and grimacing, body-twisting, and foot-stamping. These movements can be accompanied by a wide variety of vocalisations including grunting, sniffing, shouting and throat-clearing sounds. Despite this, the symptoms are highly variable and can disappear for weeks or months at a time. Although Tourette's syndrome is generally a lifelong disorder, it is not a degenerative condition and does not impair intelligence.

The disorder has been shown to be linked with abnormalities of the striatum and its pathways to the cerebral cortex. For example, MRI studies have shown that people with Tourette's syndrome have a smaller caudate nucleus, which does not show the normal asymmetry in size (most people have a caudate that is slightly larger on the left – Hyde *et al.* 1995). Other studies have measured brain activity during the production of tic movements using PET (Stern *et al.* 2000) and this has shown most brain activity to take place in the striatum, premotor cortex, primary motor cortex and speech areas of the frontal cortex. In short, this indicates that Tourette's syndrome is due to excessive activity in the neural loops that connect the striatum with those areas of the cerebral cortex that are involved in movement and speech. There is also evidence for increased dopaminergic activity in Tourette's syndrome. For example, not only are dopamine antagonists such as Haloperidol the first choice for treatment, but the uptake pumps that removes dopamine from the synapse have been found to be increased in number in the striatum – a finding that may be an attempt by the brain to compensate for excessive dopamine release (Singer *et al.* 1991).

Sadly, Gilles de la Tourette had a tragic ending to his life. In 1893, while sitting in his office, he was shot by a young woman who believed she was under his hypnotic influence. He was shot three times, with one bullet inflicting a serious brain injury from which he never fully recovered, and he died 11 years later in 1904.

The brainstem

The brainstem is responsible for a wide range of reflexive motor functions including respiration and cardiovascular function, eye movements and postural adjustment. It also stores the complex patterns of reflexes that produce many types of species-typical behaviour (i.e. behaviour unique to that species), including those involved in aggression and mating. However, by itself, the brainstem is unable to attach meaning to any given motor act. For example, as Leonard (1998) has pointed out, an animal with a brainstem that has been severed from the rest of the brain will be able to walk and show no deficit in locomotion, until it encounters an obstacle such as a wall, at which point it will bump into it and continue to produce stereotypical walking movements. Thus, without the rest of the brain to guide behaviour, the brainstem's walking reflex becomes a purposeless act.

The brainstem contains a number of tracts that pass directly into the spinal cord and are involved in specific types of movement. For example, the vestibulo-spinal tract (arising from the vestibular nuclei) helps to maintain the balance and stability of the head as the body moves through space, while the tectospinal tract (arising from the superior colliculi) is involved in producing reflexive neck movements to visual stimuli. Two other important pathways descending from the brainstem are the pontine reticulospinal tract and medullary reticulospinal tract, which work in tandem to control the flexor and extensor muscle movements that help the body to maintain a standing posture in response to gravity. Although the brainstem can be regarded as an autonomous unit for motor behaviour, it also receives 'higher-order' projections from other brain areas that influence its control of reflexes.

The brainstem is the origin for most of the 12 **cranial nerves** (nerves that directly leave and enter the brain and not spinal cord), including the oculomotor, trochlear and abducens nerves, which control the movement of the eye, and the facial nerve, which governs facial expression. Indeed, inflammation or damage to this latter nerve may produce **Bell's palsy**, characterised by paralysis of facial muscles on the affected side, with drooping of the lower eyelid and sagging at the corner of the mouth, which makes it difficult to eat or speak normally.

The cerebellum

The cerebellum (meaning 'little brain') is one of the largest and most intricate structures in the human brain. By weight it makes up about 10 per cent of the human brain's mass and contains more than 50 per cent of its neurons. It is also one of the more visually striking brain regions, located towards the back of the brainstem with its surface containing many small fissures and ridges, similar to the cerebral cortex, which provide it with a much larger surface area than would otherwise be the case (e.g. an 'unfolded' human cerebellum measures about 120 cm by 17 cm). Indeed, it is possible that the neural complexity of the cerebellum gives it a capacity for information processing that is comparable with that of the cerebral cortex.

The neural structure of the cerebellum is highly organised with an outer surface of tightly packed grey cell bodies called the cerebellar cortex. The main type of neuron in the outer layer of the cerebellar cortex is the **Purkinje cells,** recognisable by their flask-shaped cell bodies and extensive array of dendrites. The dendrites of the Purkinje cells receive two main types of input. One type is derived from so-called **parallel fibres,** which are bifurcating (split) axons from **granule cells.** In fact, granule cells are the smallest, often densely packed and by far the most numerous type of neuron in the brain and they form a thick layer beneath the Purkinje cells. The granule cells receive imput from **mossy fibres,** which enter the cerebellum from the **pontine nuclei** located in the upper brain- stem. Another type of input to the cerebellar cortex comes from climbing fibres – so called because they 'climb around' the dendrites of the Purkinje cells – and these originate from brainstem neurons of the **inferior olive.** In turn, the Purkinje cells send their axons inwards (forming white matter) to a group of three struc- tures enclosed within the cerebellum, collectively known as the **deep cerebellar nuclei.** More specifically, these are call the dentate, interposed and fastigial nuclei. The dentate nucleus sends its main input to the premotor and prefrontal areas of the cerebral cortex (via a relay in the thalamus) and is involved pri- marily in motor planning, while the interposed and fastigial nuclei have more prominent descending projections that pass through the brainstem to the spinal cord and are involved in the actual execution of movement (see Figure 3.6).

The cerebellum also receives a wide range of other movement-related information. For example, it receives information from the spinal cord (enabling it to keep track of the position of the limbs); the vestibular system (which pro- vides information about balance); and the cerebral cortex, which relays motor and sensory information (also backed up by direct information from the senses via cranial nerves). In fact, the cortical input, which derives mainly from the motor cortex and adjacent areas, including the somatosensory cortex in humans, provides a massive input to the cerebellum and contains about 20 million axons – which is about 20 times more than the number of axons making up the pyramidal tracts. This is called the corticopontocerebellar pathway as it first projects to the pontine nuclei before being passed on to the cerebellum.

The functions of the cerebellum

One way of understanding what the cerebellum does is to examine the effects of its damage. In humans, cerebellar damage reduces the fluidity of voluntary movement and makes it appear mechanical and robot-like. This is most notice- able in tasks that require a series of rapid movements – as occurs during danc- ing, playing sports, or playing a musical instrument. Although a person with damage to the cerebellum may make individual movements, he will probably

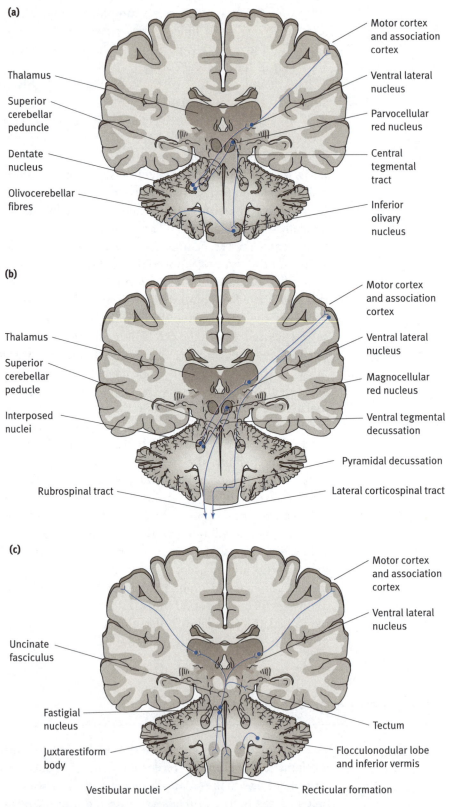

(a)

Thalamus

Superior cerebellar peduncle

Dentate nucleus

Olivocerebellar fibres

Motor cortex and association cortex

Ventral lateral nucleus

Parvocellular red nucleus

Central tegmental tract

Inferior olivary nucleus

(b)

Thalamus

Superior cerebellar peducle

Interposed nuclei

Rubrospinal tract

Motor cortex and association cortex

Ventral lateral nucleus

Magnocellular red nucleus

Ventral tegmental decussation

Pyramidal decussation

Lateral corticospinal tract

(c)

Uncinate fasciculus

Fastigial nucleus

Juxtarestiform body

Vestibular nuclei

Motor cortex and association cortex

Ventral lateral nucleus

Tectum

Flocculonodular lobe and inferior vermis

Recticular formation

Figure 3.6 The afferent and efferent projections of the cerebellum. *Source*: Blumenfeld (2002) *Neuroanatomy through Clinical Cases*, p.662

not be able to link them together into a continuous smooth sequence. For example, imagine you are to throw a baseball with your right hand: if you act out this movement you will probably shift your body weight to the right, stretch out your left arm for balance, and move your head towards the throwing arm. A person with cerebellar damage, however, will tend to throw the ball without making these other adjustments to their body. This action is also likely to be jerky and the arm may show an 'intentional' tremor that disappears once the movement has ceased (this is different to the 'resting tremor' seen in Parkinson's disease, which disappears during movement).

Thus, the cerebellum regulates the fluidity of movement enabling it to be smooth, quick and free of tremor – and it is believed that it does this by assessing the rate of movement required for a particular action and calculating the time necessary for the body or limb to reach its intended position. The primary function of the cerebellum is therefore to correct errors in ongoing movement (Leonard 1998). It is also relevant to note that the cerebellum is involved in other motor functions. For example, damage to the cerebellum impairs the regulation of saccadic eye movements leading to attentional deficits, and causes **dysarthria** – an inability to make fine articulatory movements of the vocal system, resulting in slurred speech. In addition, there is evidence that the cerebellum is involved in motor learning, including classical conditioning and the acquisition of new skills that become automatic (as occurs when learning to play a musical instrument).

The basal ganglia

The basal ganglia (Figure 3.7) is the name given to a group of interconnected extrapyramidal structures and pathways that lie buried beneath the folds of the cerebral hemispheres on each side of the brain. These include the **caudate nucleus** and **putamen** (together known as the **striatum**), **globus pallidus**, **subthalamus** and **substantia nigra**. To understand the anatomy of the basal ganglia it is perhaps best to view them primarily as part of a circuit that is connected to the cerebral cortex. Most regions of the cerebral cortex involved in movement – including primary motor cortex, premotor cortex, supplementary cortex and association areas of the parietal lobe – project to the striatum, especially the putamen. In turn, the striatum sends a substantial part of its output to the globus pallidus, whose axons pass to the **ventral lateral thalamus**. This region of the thalamus then conveys input from the basal ganglia to the entire frontal cortex, although information for motor control travels mainly to the premotor cortex, supplementary motor area and primary motor cortex.

The striatum and cerebral cortex, therefore, form part of a large multi-synaptic loop that connects these two brain regions. Indeed, emerging evidence suggests that this loop may be composed of hundreds of 'mini-circuits' that are involved in a vast range of behaviours. Other basal ganglia outputs also travel

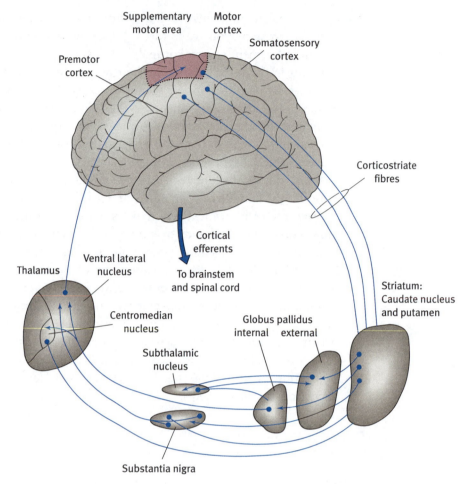

Figure 3.7   The anatomical structures and connectivity of the basal ganglia. *Source*: A.M. Schneider and B. Tarshis, *Elements of Physiological Psychology*. Copyright © 1995 by McGraw-Hill, Inc.

to thalamic nuclei. These include the **intralaminar nuclei** (centromedian and parafiscicular), which project back to the striatum, and the **mediodorsal nucleus**, which is involved primarily in influencing limbic pathways. The striatum also projects directly back to the substantia nigra, which provides a route to the brainstem and descending reticulospinal tract.

It is also worth noting that the striatum and globus pallidus extend ventrally (i.e. downwards) to form the ventral striatum and pallidum. Also embedded in this region are a number of structures including the **nucleus accumbens, basal nucleus of Meynert** and **substantia innominata**. The ventral striatum receives limbic input from the cingulate cortex, along with information from the temporal lobe and frontal cortex. In turn, the ventral striatum completes the loop by returning information to the frontal and cingulate cortices by the **mediodorsal nucleus** of the thalamus. This pathway is particularly important in emotion, motivation and reward rather than movement (see Chapter 11).

The functions of the basal ganglia

The basal ganglia have long been regarded as part of the brain's motor control system, especially as damage to their structures causes a range of movement disorders – including slowness of movement (**hypokinesia**), rigidity, resting tremor, tics and **dystonia**, in which the person exhibits abnormal or distorted positions of the limbs, trunk or face. Damage to the striatum can also cause depression and slowness of thought (sometimes known as subcortical dementia), showing that it is not simply a movement centre. Nonetheless, it is clear that the basal ganglia are importantly involved in movement and interact closely with the motor cortex in performing this function. In fact, the basal ganglia are essential for human movement, although it is interesting to note that they have no direct projections to the spinal cord, nor do they receive direct sensory information from the periphery. Consequently, their main function, it would seem, is to modulate activity in other areas of the brain.

This theory is supported from cellular recording studies showing that striatal neurons generally do not become active until *after* a movement has begun to be initiated by the motor areas of the cerebral cortex (Alexander *et al.* 1986). The basal ganglia, therefore, do not initiate movement (this is left to the cerebral cortex), but rather, once an action has begun, they back up the motor plan of the cerebral cortex with automatic adjustments. Evidence shows that the basal ganglia may do this by generating the right amount of force for a particular movement to occur by acting on dual pathways to the globus pallidus – which are not dissimilar in function to the accelerator and brake pedals in a car (Mink 1999). This idea is supported by the fact that people with some types of basal ganglia damage produce movement that contains too much force (e.g. Huntington's disease), while other types of damage cause a poverty of movement with insufficient force (e.g. Parkinson's disease). Experimental evidence also supports this theory. For example, Keele and Ivry (1991) gave people with basal ganglia damage a task in which they had to exert appropriate amounts of force to maintain the length of a line presented on a television screen, with another one of set length. The results showed that subjects with basal ganglia damage were poor at performing this task as they generated too much or too little force, resulting in a line that was too short or too long. Thus, the basal ganglia can be likened to a volume control whose output determines whether a movement will be weak or strong.

Another way in which the basal ganglia may help to improve the fluency of movement is by making 'large' postural adjustments to the body, leaving the motor regions of the cerebral cortex 'free' to produce voluntary and precise movement. That is, the basal ganglia may be responsible for making gross body movements, whereas the cerebral cortex controls more precise movements such as those of the fingers, hands and face. In support of this idea, it has been shown that people with basal ganglia damage (e.g. Parkinson's disease) often show gross postural dysfunction and have difficulty making 'large' movements of the limbs. It has also been shown that the basal ganglia have an important influence over the control of slow movements. For example, when monkeys move their arms slowly, neural activity increases in the putamen, but this does not occur when they move their arms quickly (DeLong 1974).

Parkinson's disease

In 1817, a London doctor called James Parkinson first described the condition that he called shaking palsy (shaking paralysis) that today bears his name. Parkinson's disease is now known to be a degenerative disorder of the brain which afflicts around one in every 200 people over the age of 50. The main symptoms are slowness of movement (**bradykinesia**), difficulty in initiating movement (**akinesia**) and increased muscle tone (**rigidity**). There also tends to be a persistent resting tremor of the hands, and a loss of facial muscle tone, which gives the face a blank expression. As the disorder progresses there is gradual deterioration of gait and posture so that patients may be unable to walk, move their arms, or even hold up their head – and if left untreated, the disease will often lead to invalidity within 15 to 20 years. In the later stages, there are often signs of dementia, or a general impairment of intellectual and cognitive functioning.

The underlying cause of Parkinson's disease was first identified in 1960 by Ehringer and Hornykiewicz, who found a dramatic loss of the neurotransmitter **dopamine** (about one-tenth of normal) in the striatum of Parkinsonian patients. Later, it was shown that this dopamine is derived from axons innervating the striatum from the substantia nigra (Anden *et al.* 1964), and that the disease was due to degeneration of this pathway (called the **nigral–striatal pathway**). Indeed, postmortem examination of the substantia nigra in Parkinson's disease shows a loss of pigmented cells (see Plate 3.1), and the inclusion of **Lewy bodies** – structures within the cytoplasm of the remaining neurons that contain a core surrounded by filamentous material. Remarkably, the symptoms of Parkinson's disease do not begin to manifest themselves until dopamine levels in the striatum have fallen by about 80–90 per cent, and they are likely to fall even further, becoming almost non-existent in the later stages of the disease (Langston 1990).

The treatment of Parkinson's disease

The discovery that Parkinson's disease was caused by dopamine depletion had important implications. Clearly, if the disease was due to a lack of dopamine, it followed that if a way could be found of replenishing it in the brain, then a treatment for the disorder might be achieved. Unfortunately, injections of dopamine were unsatisfactory because it was unable to cross the blood–brain barrier. However, in 1967 it was discovered that large oral doses of the dopamine precursor L-**dopa** had dramatic effects on relieving Parkinson's symptoms (Cotzias

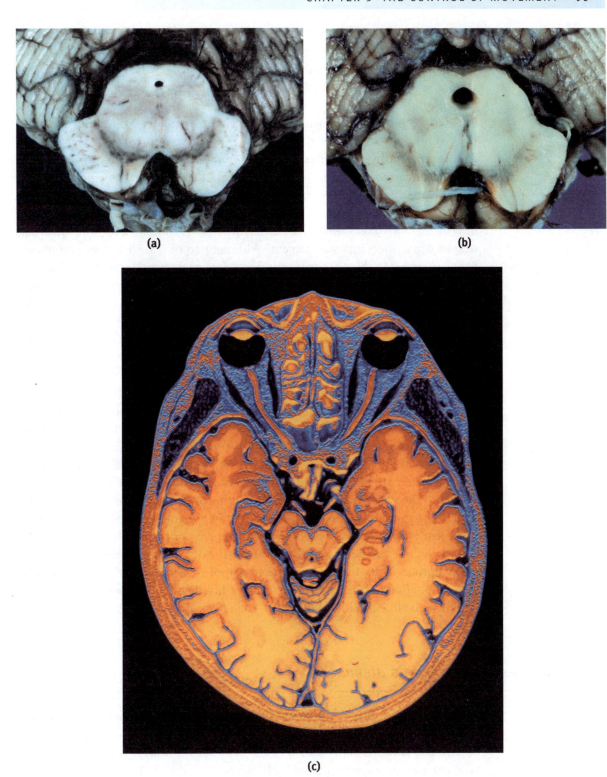

Plate 3.1   a) and b) depict horizontal sections of midbrain including the darkly pigmented substantia nigra from a healthy brain (a) and one with Parkinson's disease (b). Note how the latter is less pigmented indicating degeneration. c) depicts a horizontal MRI scan at the level of the midbrain. Note how both substantia nigra can clearly be seen in the midbrain region. *Source*: a) and b) Daniel P. Perl, MD, Mount Sinai School of Medicine, New York; c) Alfred Pasieka/Science Photo Library

et al. 1967). A proportion of this drug was able to pass into the brain before being broken down, and it was taken up by neurons in the striatum to produce more dopamine. Although the exact mechanism by which this occurs is not clear, the discovery provided a dramatic turning point in the management of Parkinson's disease.

It has been found that around 75 per cent of patients with Parkinson's disease will show some degree of improvement with levodopa (L-dopa) treatment, and in some cases the effects can be immediate and dramatic. Generally, however, treatment is started with low doses of L-dopa and then increased over several months, which produces a gradual improvement over time. Slowness of movement and rigidity are often the first symptoms to respond, with tremor improving with continued treatment (Bradley 1989). In addition, disorders of gait often show marked benefit. Although some Parkinson symptoms are likely to remain, their severity and incidence may be sufficiently reduced to enable the person to return to work and achieve some degree of independence. Thus, L-dopa gives many Parkinson patients a significantly improved quality of life.

Although the initial anti-Parkinsonian effects of L-dopa are generally stable and predictable, after some 3–5 years of treatment many patients begin to experience fluctuations in their symptoms. Initially, this may manifest itself as a 'wearing-off' of the L-dopa just before the next dose is due – an effect that may require a higher amount being administered, thereby increasing the likelihood of side-effects such as nausea, sickness and even psychosis. Later, the patient may begin to develop 'on–off' responses to the drug in which sudden periods of tremors, freezing or rigidity alternate with periods of mobility in an unpredictable pattern. There is no satisfactory explanation for this effect, and it could be due to the way the brain adapts to continued L-dopa administration, or the underlying progression of the disease. Another serious side-effect of long-term treatment is **dyskinesia** – involuntary movements of the hands, limbs and face. Although these can be lessened by reducing the dosage of L-dopa, this may cause the symptoms of Parkinson's disease to reappear. Because of this problem, doctors often advise patients to take 'L-dopa holidays' in the hope that this will minimise the likelihood of long-term side-effects.

The causes of Parkinson's disease

The reason why degeneration of the substantia nigra occurs in Parkinson's disease is not fully understood. Parkinson's disease does not appear to be inherited and this is supported by evidence showing that it is rare for identical twins to both develop the disorder (Johnson *et al.* 1990). Although this need not necessarily rule out the possibility of genetic influences (Golbe *et al.* 1990), most researchers have nevertheless sought to find alternative explanations for the disease. Some of the earliest evidence implicated viral infections. For example, a severe Parkisonism syndrome occurred in many patients who survived the epidemic of **encephalitis lethargica** that occurred throughout the world in the years 1915 to 1926. In its early stages this illness resembled influenza, but in some cases it led to its victims falling into a prolonged stupor, which was known as 'sleeping sickness'. This illness claimed many lives (the mortality was about 40 per cent) and over half of the people who survived developed Parkinsonism. Postmortem examination of the victims showed that degeneration of the substantia nigra had occurred. Remarkably, a few patients who had spent over 30 years in somnolence caused by this sickness were given L-dopa treatment in the 1960s and they 'awoke' from their plight – albeit for a short period of time (the story is told in the film *Awakenings*, based on the book of the same name by Oliver Sacks). Although this raises the possibility that Parkinson's disease could have a similar cause (e.g. a virus), there is no evidence to show that this is indeed the case.

More recently attention has focused on environmental toxins as the cause of Parkinson's disease. In 1982, several people in northern California developed severe Parkinson-like symptoms after using an illegal drug that was used as a heroin substitute. This drug produced and supplied by the same dealer, and on closer analysis found to contain a chemical called MPTP, which happens to be a selective neurotoxin for the substantia nigra. In fact, it provided brain researchers with a powerful means by which to mimic the effects of Parkinson's disease in laboratory animals. For example, injections of MPTP in monkeys were found to cause slow movement, rigidity, tremor and impaired posture, along with a marked loss of dopaminergic neurons in the substantia nigra. Curiously, these types of deficit do not occur in rodents, whose substantia nigra neurons, unlike humans and primates, do not contain melanin pigments. This has led to the suspicion that the pigments contained in the cells of the substantia nigra may be an important factor in the development of Parkinson's disease.

How then does MPTP cause degeneration of the substantia nigra? The answer is that it bonds to an enzyme called monoamine oxidase B (MAO-B) found in the cells of the substantia nigra, which then converts MPTP into the toxic **free radical** MPP^+. Free radicals are highly reactive chemicals that have lost an electron and are normally formed by the breakdown of oxygen. Although they only exist for a few millionths of a second, free radicals inflict considerable damage on biological tissue. Moreover, it appears that MPP^+ in the substantia nigra is highly reactive with melanin, and this generates a cascade of free radicals that causes damage to the cell (Youdin and Riederer 1997).

This finding may well have relevance for understanding the cause of Parkinson's disease. Indeed, the neurons of the substantia nigra produce a number of free radicals as a result of 'normal' metabolic processes, and are also exposed to them when dopamine is broken down in the synaptic cleft. Although the substantia nigra contains special enzymes to protect itself against free radicals, it may be that they become deficient in people with Parkinson's disease. Alternatively, there may be chemicals in the environment that resemble MPP^+ and contribute to substantia nigra degeneration. In fact, substances related to MPTP are present in many foods (Singer and Ramsey 1990), and the chemical structure of MPP^+ is similar to the pesticide paraquat (see Snyder and D'Amato 1986).

The research on MPTP has also led to new treatments for Parkinson's disease. As we have seen, MPTP is harmless by itself, but becomes very toxic when it is converted into MPP^+ by monoamine oxidase. It follows, therefore, that drugs which inhibit monoamine oxidase should help to prevent the damage caused by MPTP. Indeed, monoamine oxidase inhibitors have been shown to protect the substantia nigra in monkeys treated with high amounts of MPTP (Langston *et al.* 1984). These findings also have relevance for humans. For example, the MAO-B inhibitor selegrine (**deprenyl**) has been shown to delay the need for L-dopa therapy in Parkinson patients (Shoulson and the Parkinson Study Group 1989) as well as significantly improving their symptoms (Tetrud and Langston 1989). In fact, deprenyl appears to slow down the progression of Parkinson's disease, and for this reason it is now standard therapy for patients along with L-dopa. Moreover, because deprenyl inhibits MAO from breaking down dopamine, it has the extra benefit of allowing this neurotransmitter to stay in the synapse for longer, thus assisting the action of L-dopa.

New prospects for Parkinson's disease

In recent years, attempts have been made to treat Parkinson's disease by the direct transplantation of tissue into the brain to replenish the 'lost' dopamine, or help to build new neural connections. This technique was first undertaken in the early 1980s by Swedish surgeons (Backlund *et al.* 1985, Lindvall *et al.* 1987) who used tissue from the patient's own adrenal glands which produces small amounts of dopamine (the precursor to adrenaline), and placed it into the caudate or putamen. Unfortunately, the benefits of this procedure were modest, with improvements generally lasting no longer than six months. A more promising technique, however, involved the use of foetal tissue. By the 1980s, animal researchers had shown that it was possible to take tissue from the foetal mesencephalon (which includes the substantia nigra) and implant it into the striatum – where it developed into dopaminergic neurons that formed new connections with the host cells. This use of this technique in Parkinson's disease was controversial as it required foetal tissue from human embryos, but nevertheless was first used to treat patients in the early 1990s. Although the grafts survive well in the brain, the results of this procedure were highly variable. In general, 'mild to moderate' relief from Parkinson's disease has been obtained – although in no case has it provided a full reversal of symptoms (Lindvall 1991).

The technique of foetal transplantation, however, is likely to be superseded in the near future by the use of neural grafts composed of stem cells – essentially 'blank' cells, which are taken from the embryo at a very early age and have the potential to turn into virtually any tissue in the human body, including nerve cells. Already it has been shown that stem cells can be turned into fully functional dopamine neurons. For example, Bjorklund *et al.* (2002) lesioned the substantia nigra in rats, and found that the behavioural deficits of this operation could be overcome within nine weeks by the transplantation of embryonic stem cells into the striatum. Moreover, MRI showed that the restoration of behaviour was accompanied by blood flow

New prospects for Parkinson's disease continued.

returning to the parts of the brain that had been damaged by the lesion. These findings are very exciting. Not only can stem cells be kept alive indefinitely, but scientists believe that they have the potential to treat a wide range of diseases and some day may even be a source of organs for transplant. A cure for Parkinson's disease may at last be on the horizon.

Another exciting development in Parkinson's disease is deep brain stimulation (DBS). In the past, if patients with severe Parkinson symptoms had not responded to L-dopa they were sometimes given brain surgery, including lesions of the globus pallidus, subthalamic nucleus or thalamus. However, now they can be given DBS, which uses implanted electrodes to deliver continuous high-frequency stimulation to these brain areas, which then blocks the signals that cause the disabling motor symptoms of the disease. The electrodes are connected to a pulse generator that is placed in the upper chest and is programmed externally. In addition, the patient can turn the generator off and on using a special magnet (it is normally turned off at night). Research shows that DBS results in a 40–60 per cent improvement in symptoms, which is superior to foetal transplantation or surgery. Thus, DBS is currently the most effective surgical treatment for Parkinson's disease and is also associated with fewer complications and side-effects.

Huntington's chorea

Another disorder of the basal ganglia is **Huntington's chorea**, first described by George Huntington in 1872 (the word *chorea* means 'dance' and refers to the complex twisting and involuntary tic-like movements that characterise the disease). Huntington's chorea is an inherited condition that results in progressive degeneration of the striatum and associated strutures, and is invariably fatal. It is caused by a mutated gene located on chromosome 4, which follows an autosomal mode of inheritance – that is, if a person inherits the gene, the disorder will develop (see also Chapter 12). In effect, this means that if one parent carries the gene, then there will be a 50 per cent probability that it will be transmitted to the offspring. Huntington's chorea doesn't normally manifest itself until after the age of 40. Unfortunately, by this time, a Huntington's carrier (not knowing whether the mutated gene is carried or not) is likely to have had children, thus putting them at risk of inheriting the disorder. Until recently there was no way of knowing whether one was a carrier or not, although new developments in genetic testing have now enabled the Huntington's gene to be identified from a simple blood test. However, whether prospective carriers want to know if they have an incurable, fatal and extremely distressing disorder that causes mental and physical degeneration is another matter. Indeed, only a small percentage of people (12–15 per cent) take up the offer of the test (Harper 1991).

Huntington's chorea is a rare disorder that affects about one person in every 20,000, although there can be pockets of high prevalence in certain places. The initial symptoms often include facial twitching and excessive fidgeting. As the disorder progresses these symptoms develop into rapid and complex flailing movements of the arms and upper parts of the body. The chorea movements are difficult to describe but once seen are seldom forgotten. The body writhes and jerks incessantly, making purposeful behaviour such as walking or holding an object almost impossible. Muscle tone may also be difficult to maintain, resulting in collapse. Other symtoms of the disorder, especially in its later stages, include changes in personality, and a decline of intellectual function leading to dementia, psychosis and slurred speech. Eventually, the victim becomes bedridden with death occurring on average some 10 to 20 years after the disorder's onset. One well-known person to die from the disease was the American folk singer Woody Guthrie.

Brain changes in Huntington's chorea

The most conspicuous change that takes place in the brain of those with Huntington's chorea (Plate 3.2) is cell loss in the caudate nucleus and putamen (striatum). However, by the later stages of the disorder this degeneration may have spread to other areas resulting in the generalised shrinkage of the brain, which can be up to 20 per cent in severe cases. The striatum is the first region to show neural degeneration, and its atrophy continues throughout the disease. At the time of death, up to 95 per cent of its neurons may have been destroyed. As the striatum degenerates, significant cell loss in other areas of the brain also takes place – particularly in pathways and structures of the basal ganglia (e.g. globus pallidus and thalamus) along with the cerebellum and cerebral cortex.

Unfortunately, the neurochemical deficit in Huntington's chorea is not as straightforward as that for Parkinson's disease. The most obvious neurochemical change in Huntington's chorea is a depletion of the inhibitory neurotransmitter **GABA** (and its synthesising enzymes), whose levels in the striatum may decline by up to 80 per cent. In addition, there is also a marked fall in acetylcholine, which may be reduced by 50 per cent. However, the nigral–striatal pathway tends to be preserved in Huntington's chorea and dopamine levels in the striatum may be increased up to 70 per cent. In fact, this increase in dopaminergic activity is probably caused by the loss of GABA neurons in the striatum, as some of these cells project back to the substantia nigra, where they act to inhibit the dopamine neurons. With the loss of this inhibitory control, the substantia nigra neurons become excited and release dopamine into the striatum. This may then contribute to the abnormal movements that characterise Huntington's chorea. Indeed, evidence for this idea comes from work showing that drugs which increase dopamine (such as L-dopa) exacerbate the symptoms of Huntington's disease, whereas drugs that block or reduce dopaminergic activity (such as haloperidol or chlorpromazine) can help to reduce its symptoms.

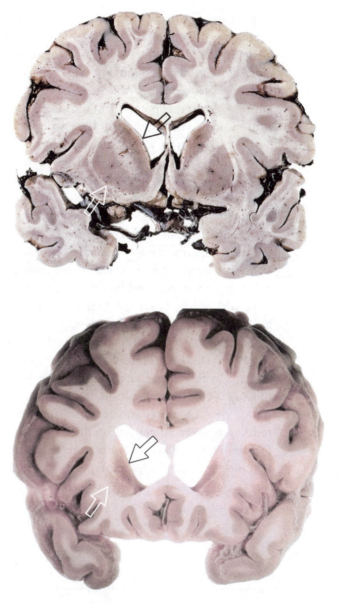

Plate 3.2 The pathological changes in Huntington's disease. The arrows point to the caudate nucleus which shows marked degeneration in the Huntington's brain. *Source*: Carlson (2004) *Physiology of Behavior* (8th edn), p.267, Allyn and Bacon

How does the Huntington's gene cause the disease?

An important question concerns the function of the gene that causes Huntington's chorea. In short, what is the 'normal' role of this gene and how does its mutation cause the cascade of degenerative changes in the brain? Because all genes produce proteins – large complex molecules that serve a huge range of biological functions – Huntington's disease must be the result of a faulty protein appearing in the brain. It is also known that the faulty gene in Huntington's disease contains a large number of extra DNA segments (or trinucleotide repeats) that contain the bases CAG, which are responsible for producing the amino acid glutamine (this topic is discussed in more detail in Chapter 12). Thus, the faulty protein in Huntington's disease contains more glutamine, which presumably changes its shape and function, but how this faulty protein causes brain degeneration in later life is not clear. Perhaps it interferes with the metabolism of the cell in some important way, or makes the neuron more vulnerable to toxic chemicals such as glutamate (see below). To make matters more confusing, the normal function of this protein (which has been named **huntingtin**) has not been established either. Moreover, huntingtin, whether normal or defective, occurs throughout the brain in neurons and glial cells, and it is not known why the striatum is particularly vulnerable to its dysfunction.

One neurotransmitter that has been implicated in the pathology of Huntington's disease is **glutamate**. This is an excitatory transmitter contained in fibres projecting from the cerebral cortex to the striatum, and is believed to be neurotoxic if released in abnormally high amounts. For example, quinolinic acid, which acts to stimulate glutamate receptors, produces a similar type of neural degeneration to that found in Huntington's chorea if injected into the striatum of experimental animals (Beal *et al.* 1986). The possibility exists, therefore, that the Huntington gene might somehow alter the glutamate system, perhaps by increasing its release, or by enhancing the sensitivity of its receptors, to cause neural degeneration. This possibility is supported by the finding that some types of glutamate receptor (particularly the NMDA variety) can be reduced by over 90 per cent in the striatum of people with Huntington's chorea (Young *et al.* 1988). Attempts are currently underway to develop new drugs that block glutamate receptors to see if they help to retard the progression of the disease.

The motor areas of the cerebral cortex

In 1870, Gustav Fritsch and Eduard Hitzig, working not in a laboratory but on a table in the bedroom of Hitzig's house in Berlin, were the first to show that electrical stimulation of certain regions of the cerebral cortex in dogs produced a wide range of movement on the opposite of the body. In fact, what they had discovered was the **primary motor cortex** – an area in humans that is located in the precentral gyrus, which forms a posterior part of the frontal cortex. Later work by Wilder Penfield in the 1950s mapped this region in awake humans using electrical stimulation that was used primarily to identify epileptic tissue in patients prior to its removal. This work showed that the body's representation in the motor cortex was topographically organised – that is, the layout of this cerebral region contained a point-to-point map of the body. For example, if the motor cortex was stimulated along its length, from top to bottom, it produced movement of the feet, legs, body, arms and then head (see Figure 3.8).

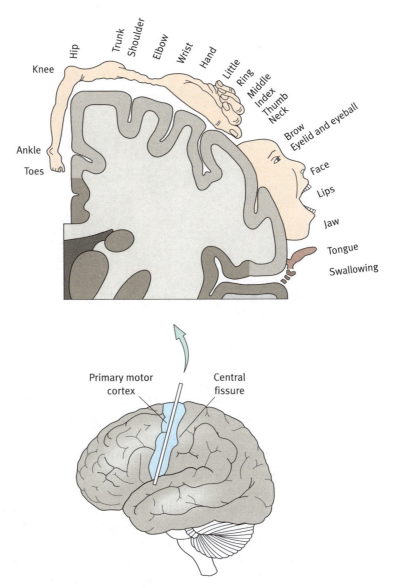

Figure 3.8 Topographic representation of the human motor cortex. *Source*: From John P.J. Pinel, *Biopsychology*, 3rd edition. Copyright © 1997 by Pearson Education

Moreover, the amount of motor cortex given over to each part of the body was related to the precision of its movement. For example, a large proportion of the motor cortex is responsible for controlling the small muscles of the face (particularly the mouth region) and the hands (particularly fingers and thumb), but little of its area moves the trunk and legs. Interestingly, Penfield also showed that his subjects were unaware of the movements produced by the electrical stimulation and had no memory of them afterwards (Penfield and Rasmussen 1950).

The motor cortex is also surrounded by other areas that have an important bearing on its function (Figure 3.9). For example, immediately anterior to the motor cortex, on the superior (topmost) part of the frontal lobe, is the

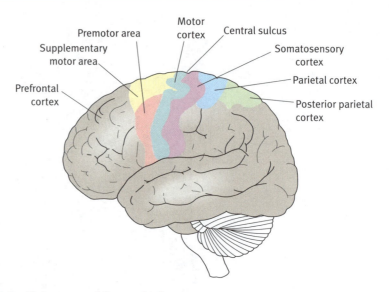

Figure 3.9 Motor areas of the cerebral cortex

supplementary motor cortex, and below and lateral to this region is the **premotor area** (both designated as Brodmann's area 6). Moving further forward we come to the **prefrontal cortex**, whereas just posterior to the primary motor cortex, on the other side of the central sulcus, is the **primary somatosensory cortex**, which receives somatosensory input (touch, temperature and body position) from the body. This latter area of the brain is also arranged in a topographical fashion similar to the motor cortex, and is important for movement that requires continuous sensory feedback.

As we have seen on pages 91–92, the most important input to the motor areas of the frontal lobes derives from the striatum, via the globus pallidus and thalamus. In turn, these regions project back to the striatum, as well as other areas of the cortex – particularly the parietal lobe. However, the movement areas of the cortex have another very important projection – namely the corticospinal tract – which projects directly down into the grey matter of the spinal cord. Because some 85 per cent of fibres in the corticospinal tract cross (or decussate) in the pyramidal region of the medulla, this pathway is sometimes referred to as the **pyramidal system**. The majority of axons that cross to the opposite side of the brainstem form the **lateral corticospinal tract** and they primarily activate the motor neurons that move the limbs such as arm, hand, leg and foot. In contrast, the axons that remain on the original side form the **ventral corticospinal tract** and primarily move the trunk of the body. Thus, the neurons of the cortical motor areas in the right hemisphere control the trunk on the right side of the body, but the limbs on the left side – and vice versa for the left hemisphere. The primary motor cortex contributes about 50 per cent of all corticospinal tract fibres, with the remainder arising from the premotor and supplementary motor areas and areas of the parietal lobes. Interestingly, about 3 per cent of corticospinal axons are derived from giant pyramid-shaped cells, called **Berz cells**, which are the largest neurons in the human nervous system.

The function of the primary motor cortex

The anatomical location of the primary motor cortex puts it in an ideal position to be accessed by conscious thought from the frontal and parietal lobes, and therefore to be involved in the production of voluntary movement. Moreover, because the primary motor cortex is the main point of departure for neurons entering the corticospinal tract, we might expect damage to this region of the brain to produce serious movement deficits and paralysis. However, damage to the primary motor cortex in humans produces less disability than might be expected. Although large lesions of the primary motor cortex may produce muscle weakness, which impairs precise and skilled movement, it does not produce paralysis. Thus, damage to this area of the brain is more likely to impair the ability to isolate movement to a single muscle or limb (e.g. the patient cannot flex the elbow without moving the shoulder), or may reduce the speed, accuracy and force of a person's movement. This is particularly noticeable in the fingers and hands. Indeed, precision grip is almost always lost after motor cortex damage, and finger movements become slow and uncoordinated (Leonard 1998). Clearly, therefore, lesions of the primary motor cortex do not eliminate voluntary movement – presumably because other areas of the cerebral cortex contribute to the corticospinal tract, or because alternative neural pathways back up the cortical input to the spinal cord.

Similar movement deficits occur in monkeys following lesions of the primary motor cortex and corticospinal tracts. For example, Lawrence and Kuypers (1968) lesioned the corticospinal tracts in the brainstem region of the pyramids in monkeys and found that, within a day of the operation, the animals could stand upright, hold the bars of their cage, and move about. Recovery continued to progress, so that after six weeks the monkeys were able to run, climb and reach for food. Despite this, their manual dexterity was very poor. Although they could reach for objects and grasp them, they were unable to manipulate their fingers to enable them to pick up small pieces of food. Furthermore, if food was held in their hands, they were unable to release their grasp. In fact, they were often observed using their mouth to pry their hands open. Curiously, however, they had no difficulty releasing their grip when climbing the bars of their cage, which suggests that this behaviour is controlled by a different pathway or brain region.

The contribution of other cortical areas to movement

As we have seen, the primary motor cortex is involved in producing fine movements of the body, particularly of the hands. But skilled movements require much more than being able to finely move the right set of muscles – it also requires the coordination, sequencing and timing of muscle movements. For example, merely having the ability to perform a series of simple muscle movements is clearly insufficient if we want to play the piano, or throw a baseball in a high-speed curved trajectory towards a small target. In fact, such motor tasks depend on a plan of action, that is, an internal representation of the intended movement which not only contains a series of motor plans for action, but the desired goal of this activity. Thus, in the case of playing the piano, the motor program should contain information about which fingers will move, the order in which they will hit the keys, their direction on the keyboard, and the timing between digit movements. Moreover, these movements will automatically be regulated by the sound of the music that is played. Such skills depend not only on the primary motor cortex but also on a number of other regions localised primarily in the frontal and parietal lobes.

One such area is the **somatosensory cortex**, which lies on the other side of the central sulcus from the primary motor cortex, and receives tactile (touch) information from the body including proprioceptive feedback from the muscles and tendons. Not only is the somatosensory cortex topographically organised in a similar way to the primary motor cortex, but there is a close relationship between the two areas. For example, each main area in the primary motor cortex receives continuous sensory feedback from the corresponding area in the somatosensory cortex. Thus, when your thumb moves across this page to turn it, the sensation from the contact of the thumb is immediately sent to the somatosensory cortex, which then informs the primary motor cortex of the effects of its movement. The importance of sensory information for movement can be seen in the case of **Friederich's ataxia**, a rare genetic condition which causes degeneration of the dorsal columns of the spinal cord, which convey fine touch and pressure to the brain. These people are unable to shift their body weight properly when walking and, consequently, have an unsteady gait, with legs apart, which often gives the impression that they are drunk. Another possible effect of somatosensory damage is **asomatognosia** – the loss of knowledge about one's own body when the eyes are closed (see the case of the 'disembodied lady' in Sacks 1985).

One of the main regions of the brain that plays a role in planning and initiating movements is the **supplementary motor area**, which is located on the medial surface of the frontal lobe just anterior to the primary motor cortex. When this area was stimulated by Penfield he discovered that it gave rise to complex postural movements, such as a raised hand before the face with head and eyes turned towards the hand (Penfield and Rasmussen 1950). Moreover, stimulation of this area also elicits an urge to make a movement, or the feeling of anticipating a movement (Bradshaw and Mattingly 1995). Indeed, it is now clear that this brain area is crucial for initiating movements and sequencing them in their right order. This has also been shown in humans by the use of functional brain imaging techniques such as **positron emission tomography**, which can measure the blood flow through many regions of the brain during the performance of various movements. For example, when subjects are given the simple task of keeping a spring compressed between two fingers, it is found that blood flow increases markedly in the hand area of the contralateral motor cortex and adjacent somatosensory cortex. However, when the complexity of the task is increased so that the subject has to perform a 16-sequence set of movements, the area of blood flow then extends anteriorly into the supplementary motor cortex. Thus, the supplementary motor area is specifically involved in complex movements (Roland *et al.* 1980, Roland 1984).

An interesting finding regarding the supplementary motor cortex is that this area also becomes active when subjects are asked to rehearse these movements in their mind and not actually perform the task. Although blood flow increases by only about 20 per cent under these conditions, it does not increase in the primary motor cortex. This not only offers strong support for the idea that the supplementary motor cortex is involved in planning, but also suggests that the *decision* to act, at least in this case, is more likely to lie in the supplementary motor area rather than the primary motor cortex.

Another area involved in movement is the **premotor area**, which lies laterally to the supplementary motor area and has reciprocal connections with this region. The premotor area also appears to be involved in the temporal sequencing of movement, and research with monkeys shows that it contains neurons that fire in response to specific actions such as 'grasping with the hand' or 'holding' movements. It therefore appears to be similar in function to the supplementary motor area. However, there do appear to be some significant differences between the two regions – notably the premotor cortex appears to become activated more in response to *external* stimuli, whereas activation of the supplementary motor area depends more on *internal* events (Bradshaw and Mattingly 1995).

There are two other important cortical areas involved in movement. Damage to the posterior part of the **parietal cortex** also produces movement dysfunction, which includes an inability to reach accurately for objects, or place a limb in a certain position. The parietal lobe appears to play a crucial role in attention, and also provides a spatial map of the world that allows it to identify where a body or limb movement is in space. In fact, severe damage to the posterior parietal lobe, especially on the right side, can produce **sensory neglect**, where the person ignores personal space on the side of the world opposite to the lesion. Such people are not blind – rather, this 'visual space' does not appear to reach conscious awareness. The parietal lobes are also extensively interconnected with the anterior **frontal cortex**, which, in humans, is believed to be important for abstract thought, decision-making, and the anticipation of the consequences of action. These 'prefrontal' areas, along with the posterior parietal cortex, perhaps represent the highest levels of the motor control hierarchy.

Summary

Movement is the result of muscle contractions, and muscles are controlled by the nervous system. The body contains three types of muscle – **smooth, cardiac** and **striated** – with the latter being responsible for movement of the skeleton and posture. There are over 600 striated muscles in the human body, which make up around 50 per cent of its weight. Muscles are made from bundles of long thin **muscle cells** (fibres) that contain large numbers of cylindrical structures called **myofibrils**. In turn, myofibrils contain sliding filaments of **actin** or **myosin**, which give the myofibril, and ultimately the muscle fibre, its ability to contract. All skeletal muscles are innervated by **alpha motor neurons**, whose cell bodies are located in the ventral horn of the spinal cord. The synapse that lies between the alpha motor neuron and muscle cell is called the **neuromuscular junction**, which uses the transmitter **acetylcholine** (ACH). When ACH binds to the **motor endplate** located on muscle fibres, it sets into motion a series of chemical events in the cell that pulls the actin and myosin filaments together, thus contracting the muscle. Although the spinal cord is capable of producing both **monosynaptic** and **polysynaptic** reflexes, the most important structure for controlling movement is the brain. There are a number of motor pathways that descend into the spinal cord from the brain, and these derive either from the **pyramidal system** or **extrapyramidal system**. The pyramidal system originates in the cerebral cortex (mainly the motor cortex and surrounding areas) and its axons enter the **corticospinal tract**. About 85 per cent of these fibres cross to the contralateral (opposite) side of the brain in a region of the brainstem called the **pyramids** before passing into the spinal cord. (Most of the remaining fibres also cross to the other side of the spinal cord when they reach the spinal segment in which they terminate.) The extrapyramidal system contains all the motor regions and pathways not belonging to the pyramidal system, and includes the **reticulospinal tract** (originating from a number of reticular nuclei), the **rubrospinal tract** (originating from the red nucleus) and **vestibulospinal tract** (originating from the vestibular nuclei). All of these pathways pass from the brain into the spinal cord without crossing over to its contralateral side.

A number of brain areas are crucially involved in producing movement. One such structure is the **cerebellum** ('little brain'), which is highly intricate in terms of its neural circuitry. The cerebellum is believed to be important for coordinating movement by controlling both the force and timing of muscular contractions and reflexes, especially for rapid and well-learned actions. Thus, the cerebellum regulates the fluidity of movement enabling it to be smooth, quick, and free of tremor. The cerebellum is helped in this respect by the **basal ganglia** – a set of interconnected structures that includes the **striatum** (caudate nucleus and putamen), **globus pallidus** and **substantia nigra**. The role of the basal ganglia is not well understood, although they probably help to make smooth postural adjustments of the body, especially in regards to voluntary movement. Indeed, in support of this idea is the fact that people with basal ganglia damage (e.g. **Parkinson's disease**) often show gross postural dysfunction and have difficulty initiating voluntary movement. A number of regions in the cerebral cortex are also involved in producing movement including the **frontal cortex, premotor cortex, supplementary motor cortex** and **primary motor cortex** which is the main source of fibres projecting into the **corticospinal tract**. The primary motor cortex lies adjacent to the **somatosensory cortex** (which receives sensory information from the periphery) and both are **topographically organised** (i.e. they contain a point-to-point representation of the body). The motor areas of the cerebral cortex appear to be especially important for the learning, planning and initiation of voluntary movement.

Essay questions

1. From processes operating at the neuromuscular junction, to the movement of actin and myosin in the myofibrils, explain how impulses in alpha motor neurons ultimately cause muscle contraction.

   Helpful Internet search terms: *Neuromuscular junction. Muscle contraction. Muscle cells. Alpha motor neurons. Myofibrils. Skeletal muscle.*

2. Describe the brain structures and anatomical pathways that make up the extrapyramidal and pyramidal motor systems. What are the main functions of these two systems?

   Helpful Internet search terms: *Extrapyramidal system. Pyramidal system. Cerebellum. Basal ganglia. Motor cortex. Corticospinal tract.*

3. What is known about the neuropathology of Parkinson's disease? What treatments can be used to treat this disorder?

   Helpful Internet search terms: *Parkinson's disease. Nigral–striatal pathway. Parkinson's and dopamine. Treatment for Parkinson's. L-dopa and deprenyl. Deep brain stimulation for Parkinson's.*

4. What regions in the cerebral cortex are known to be involved in movement? How do these areas contribute to the production of motor behaviour?

   Helpful Internet search terms: *Primary motor cortex. Somatosensory cortex. Frontal cortex and voluntary movement. Cortical control of movement. Motor function in cerebral cortex and basal ganglia.*

Further reading

Asanuma, H. (1989) *The Motor Cortex*. New York: Raven Press. A summary of research that has attempted to understand the organisation and function of the motor cortex.

Berthoz, A. (2000) *The Brain's Sense of Movement*. Cambridge, MA: Harvard University Press. Provides new insights and theories into how the brain is able to maintain balance and coordinate movement.

Harper, P.S. (1996) *Huntington's Disease*. London: W.B. Saunders. A multidisciplinary book covering (among other things) molecular biology, clinical neurology, pathology, and psychiatric aspects of this degenerative disease.

Latash, M.L. (1998) *Neurophysiological Basis of Movement*. Champaign, IL: Human Kinetics Publishers. A comprehensive textbook, covering all levels of the motor system from muscle contraction to brain function, that attempts to explain the production of voluntary movement.

Leonard, C.T. (1998) *The Neuroscience of Human Movement*. St Louis: Mosby. A very readable account that covers the role of the central nervous system and its pathways in the control of movement.

Porter, R. and Lemon, R. (1995) *Corticospinal Function and Voluntary Movement*. Oxford: Oxford University Press. A comprehensive analysis of how the cerebral cortex controls the performance of skilled voluntary movement.

Quinn, N.P. and Jenner, P.G. (eds) (1989) *Disorders of Movement*. San Diego: Academic Press. Written by various experts, this covers the clinical, pharmacological and physiological characteristics of a range of movement disorders, and includes a large section on Parkinson's disease.

Rosenbaum, J. (1991) *Human Motor Control*. San Diego: Academic Press. A user-friendly introduction to how cognitive processes are involved in the sequencing of movement with relevance to many areas of interest, including dance, physical education and robotics.

Zigmond, M.J., Bloom, F.E., Landis, S.C., Roberts, J.L. and Squire, L.R. (eds) (1999) *Fundamental Neuroscience*. San Diego: Academic Press. Although this is a monumental textbook on neuroscience, the eight chapters on motor systems, including separate ones on the basal ganglia and the cerebellum, are excellent.

See website at www.pearsoned.co.uk/wickens for further resources including multiple choice questions.

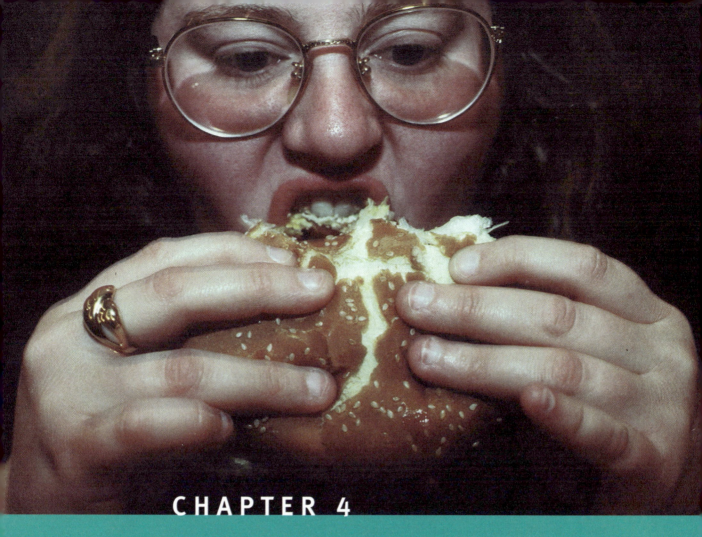

CHAPTER 4

Hunger and eating behaviour

In this chapter

- The concept of homeostasis
- The different bodily states of absorption and fasting
- The glucostatic theory of hunger
- The dual set-point model of hunger and eating
- The effects of hypothalamic lesions on feeding behaviour
- The effects of learning and cognitive factors on eating
- The causes of obesity
- Anorexia nervosa and bulimia

INTRODUCTION

Hunger is a compelling motive and the need to eat (along with sleep) is probably the most important determinant that shapes our daily routines and activities. Clearly, our basic reliance on food for energy and sustenance is shared with all other animals and essential for the maintenance of life. For humans, however, eating behaviour is much more complex than this. One only has to consider the wide variety of food-related information in our world – including magazine articles, TV programmes, advertisements for food and restaurants, diets and obesity clinics – to realise how important the subject of eating is to human existence. The complexity of this behaviour is also seen when we examine the brain mechanisms underlying hunger and eating. Traditionally, hunger has often been explained as a basic physiological response to declining levels of nutrients, with important roles for peripheral mechanisms (i.e. stomach and liver), which send their information to eating areas in the brainstem and hypothalamus. However, it is becoming increasingly clear that our eating behaviour is not so simple. Rather, eating and hunger are the products of a highly complex biological system with a multitude of interacting factors (both physiological and cognitive), involving many levels of the brain, and not determined by any simple nutrient deficiency or peripheral response. Indeed, this is shown by the fact that we typically eat not in response to hunger, but in *anticipation* of it. Eating is also associated with a number of disorders – including obesity, anorexia and bulimia – that can require both medical and psychological intervention, and this further highlights the importance of learning more about the biological basis of this behaviour.

Homeostasis

Hunger has often been viewed as a homeostatic process – that is, dependent on a feedback mechanism to the brain signalling a deficiency of some nutrient below a given set point. To understand the concept of **homeostasis** it is important to realise that, in order to survive, all animals have to maintain the physiological balance of their bodies within very fine limits. For example, human beings are warm-blooded and have to keep their body temperature at about 37 °C regardless of whether they live in the Antarctic or the tropics. A change in core body temperature of just a few degrees will alter the rate of chemical reactions taking place in our cells, and may lead to organ failure and death. Thus, it is essential that the body is able to regulate its temperature within a narrow margin (i.e. homeostasis). In this instance, the body must have a means of detecting temperature change and, in response to this, be able to produce a physiological adjustment (e.g. increased perspiration or shivering) to correct any change when it deviates too far from 37 °C.

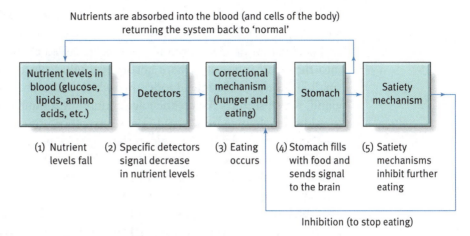

Figure 4.1   A hypothetical outline of a homeostatic system that controls eating

This example illustrates several important features of homeostatic systems. First, there must be a set point or optimal level that the system tries to maintain. Secondly, there must be receptors (i.e. thermoreceptors) in the body that are able to detect the changes taking place. Thirdly, there must be a control centre (normally in the brain) that is continually informed of the body state and decides on the action to be taken. In fact, most control systems work by a process of negative feedback – that is, they *switch off* their compensatory response when the correct level of the variable (e.g. temperature, amount of hormone circulating around the body) has been achieved (Figure 4.1).

It is easy to imagine that hunger must also be a homeostatic process. Put simply, it is reasonable to assume that hunger occurs when the brain detects an energy deficit or decline in the level of a vital nutrient (such as glucose) below a given set point. In turn, eating is the response by which the energy or nutrient source is replenished, and this will eventually provide the negative feedback mechanism that terminates the hunger. However, as we shall see, eating does not fit easily into this type of simple energy- or nutrient-deficient model. This is not to say that there are no homeostatic mechanisms at work in the underlying biology of hunger – rather, they do not appear to function as the main determinants of eating behaviour.

The process of digestion

Food is a collection of proteins, fats and carbohydrates (along with a small amount of essential vitamins and minerals), and digestion is the process by which these foodstuffs are broken down into simple molecules so that they can be absorbed into the blood and used by the body. The process of digestion begins in the mouth, where food is broken up and mixed with saliva, which turns starch-like substances into sugars. The food is then swallowed and enters the stomach, where it is mixed with gastric juices containing hydrochloric acid and pepsin that produce a semifluid mixture called **chyme**. This is then emptied into the small intestine, where absorption takes place. The upper part of the small intestine is called the **duodenum**, which contains a duct from the **pancreas gland**, which secretes pancreatic juice containing a number of digestive enzymes. In addition, the pancreas gland releases two hormones – **insulin** and **glucagon** (see later) – that play a vital role in the digestive process. The remainder of the small intestine (which is about 600 cm in length) absorbs the chyme's nutrients. From here, emulsified fats are absorbed into the lymphatic system, where they will eventually reach the blood – and, other nutrients such as glucose are absorbed into veins that pass directly to the liver via the hepatic portal system. As we shall see, excess glucose is transformed into **glycogen** and principally stored in the liver – although small amounts are also stored in muscle.

Absorption and fasting

It is commonplace to eat a large meal that contains more energy than is immediately needed by the body. In fact, if all the glucose in a large meal was absorbed straight into the bloodstream, it would probably have fatal consequences. Thus, the body needs to quickly store the nutrients following absorption – and then be able to release them gradually, or the energy derived from their transformation, in the intervening periods between feeding. These two bodily states are known respectively as the **absorptive** and the **post-absorptive phases** and are controlled by different physiological processes (Figure 4.2).

The absorptive phase of metabolism begins during a meal. When a person starts to eat, **insulin** is released even before glucose enters the bloodstream. This early release occurs because of neural impulses arriving at the pancreas gland from the parasympathetic vagus nerve, and is triggered largely by taste stimulation in the mouth – although other stimuli associated with eating can also cause the release of insulin. The main function of insulin is to allow glucose to enter the cells of the body, where it is used to produce energy, although an exception are the cells of the brain, which do not require insulin for glucose uptake. Indeed, without insulin the body cells are starved of glucose, even though there could be high levels of glucose in the blood. Thus, with the help of insulin, cells utilise the body's newly acquired blood glucose for their own immediate energy needs. Insulin also has three other important ways of controlling the level of blood glucose during absorption: (1) it helps to convert excess blood glucose into glycogen, which is stored by the liver and muscles; (2) it facilitates the transport of amino acids into cells, allowing protein synthesis to occur; and (3) it facilitates the transport of fats into adipose cells enabling fat storage. In short, insulin allows excess levels of blood nutrients to become quickly stored in the tissues of the body.

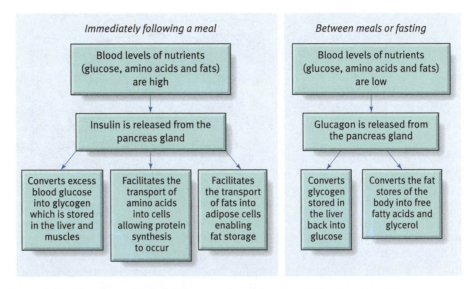

Figure 4.2   Flowchart of metabolic events that take place following absorption (immediately following a meal) and post-absorption (between meals)

Once nutrients have been absorbed into the blood the post-absorptive phase of metabolism takes over. The main signal for this phase to begin is probably a drop in blood glucose being detected by the brain. This results in an increased sympathetic stimulation of the pancreas gland, which halts insulin secretion and instead causes **glucagon** to be released. In the short term, the effect of glucagon is opposite to insulin as it causes the liver to convert its glycogen back into glucose. However, if the fasting period is prolonged (e.g. more than a few hours), glucagon will also begin to break down the body's fat stores into fatty acids, which can also be used by body cells for energy. In addition, glycerol will be converted back into glucose by the liver. This latter process is particularly important for the brain as it cannot utilise fatty acids for energy and has to rely on glucose provided by the liver during the post-absorptive period.

What causes hunger?

A deceptively simple question is: what causes hunger? One possibility is that hunger is associated with movements of the stomach. For example, we tend to feel 'full' when the stomach is distended, and often attribute hunger pangs to the contractions produced by an empty stomach. An experimental test of this idea was undertaken in 1912 by W.B. Cannon, who persuaded his research student A.L. Washburn to swallow a balloon that was inflated in his stomach. The balloon was then connected by a tube to a water-filled glass U-tube, and when a stomach contraction occurred, it caused an increase in the water level

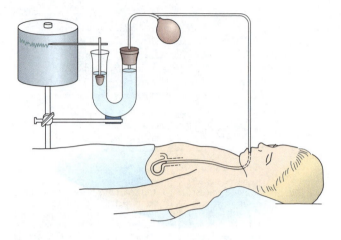

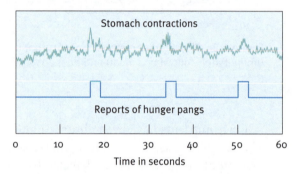

Figure 4.3 The type of experimental set-up used by Cannon and Washburn (1912). *Source*: John P.J. Pinel, *Biopsychology*, 3rd edition. Copyright © 1997 by Pearson Education

that resulted in an upward mark on a moving piece of paper (see Figure 4.3). It was found that Washburn's reported hunger pangs were nearly always accompanied by stomach contractions (Cannon and Washburn 1912). Further support linking an empty stomach with hunger was also obtained in a study where a patient had accidentally swallowed acid, which caused his oesophagus to fuse shut. This person could only be fed by passing wet food through a tube that had been surgically implanted into the stomach. This tube also enabled researchers to observe the internal activity of the stomach directly, which confirmed that contractions were often associated with feelings of hunger (Carlson 1912).

Despite this, it soon became clear that the gastric theory of hunger was far too simple. For example, while the first bite of food would normally terminate stomach contractions, it did not immediately stop appetite. Moreover, in patients who had undergone surgical removal of the stomach (often due to cancer) – which required their oesophagus to be connected directly to the duodenum – normal sensations of hunger were experienced. In fact, although these patients tended to eat smaller meals, they nevertheless showed proper regulation of food intake (Wangensteen and Carlson 1931). The gastric theory was also weakened by animal studies showing that the severing of neural connections between stomach and brain had little effect on food intake (Morgan and Morgan 1940).

The chemical signals of hunger

There are a number of feedback signals from the body that inform the brain of the need to eat, or to cease this behaviour. Although neural input from organs such as the stomach may contribute to this feedback – together with the sight and smell of food even before it gets to the gut – most investigators believe that chemical messengers in the blood also have an important role. Convincing evidence that blood-borne chemicals play a role in signalling satiety has come from a study where hungry and food-deprived rats were given blood trans-fusions from satiated and well-fed ones (Davis *et al*. 1969). Clearly, if the blood contains a substance that signals whether an animal has eaten, then the trans-fusion of blood from a well-fed rat should stop hunger in a food-deprived rat. This is exactly what was found. For example, when the hungry rats were given blood transfusions from satiated animals and presented with food, they ate very little. This effect could not be explained by the transfusion itself, because it was found that hunger was suppressed only when well-fed rats donated the blood. In fact, to be most effective, the blood had to be taken from the donors 45 minutes after their meal, which is about the time it takes for appreciable amounts of nutrients and hormones to accumulate in the blood after eating.

But what chemical in the blood influences eating behaviour? Many theorists have focused on blood glucose as being the main agent, although a strong case can also be made for fats or amino acids. More recently, there has been a growing awareness that certain hormones released by the gut and gastrointestinal tract (e.g. cholecystokinin) also have an important role in the regulation of hunger. However, it is almost certainly the case that no single messenger is responsible for producing hunger. Rather, there are many chemical agents and types of neural signal that convey nutritional information to the brain. Nonetheless, the substance that has attracted the most attention for its role in producing hunger and satiety is glucose – and it is to this agent we shall now turn.

The glucostatic theory of hunger

The basic idea behind the **glucostatic** theory of hunger is simple: if there is a drop in blood glucose reaching the cells of the body the individual gets hungry; and if there is an increase in glucose the individual becomes satiated. However, one problem with this theory is that the level of glucose in the blood varies little in normal circumstances, and this is particularly true for the brain, where even a small drop in glucose can quickly lead to unconsciousness. In addition, people with **diabetes**, who are unable to produce insulin, typically have very high levels of blood glucose as it cannot be taken-up by their cells, yet they are often ravenously hungry. Clearly, if glucose is a signal for eating and satiety then there must be a more complex mechanism. One possibility is that the brain contains special glucostats that measure the rate at which glucose is being metabolised to provide energy. This idea was first proposed in 1955 by Jean Mayer, who speculated that the CNS may contain cells that compared the difference between levels of arterial blood glucose entering the brain and the venous blood leaving it. Thus, a difference between the two values would indicate that sugar was being quickly removed from the blood as it passed through the brain – and hunger would result.

Soon after Mayer proposed the idea of glucoreceptors in the brain, his theory received experimental support (Mayer and Marshall 1956). Mayer reasoned that if glucoreceptors existed, then they would be identified by injecting animals with a compound called gold thioglucose – a substance that mimics glucose but is neurotoxic. In effect, this substance should attach itself to the cells containing the glucoreceptors (wherever they may be) and cause their death. Indeed, after injecting mice with gold thioglucose, it was found that they began to eat huge quantities of food and soon became obese. Moreover, when their brains were examined, damage to the **ventromedial hypothalamus** was found. Presumably, therefore, this was the region that contained the glucostats.

How glucoreceptors control feeding

Although it has been shown that the ventromedial hypothalamus contains cells that detect glucose, their role in eating behaviour is not well understood. For example, if these cells are involved in controlling food intake, then infusions of glucose into the ventromedial hypothalamus would be expected to reduce food intake in hungry animals – but this does not occur (Epstein *et al.* 1975). Moreover, the electrical response of ventromedial hypothalamic neurons to glucose is very brief, which is also not consistent with a role in suppressing hunger. In fact, most researchers now believe that the liver is the most important site for the glucoreceptors. Some of the strongest evidence for this idea has come from studies where glucose has been injected into different areas of the body (e.g. Russek 1971). For example, when glucose is injected into the jugular vein, which carries blood away from the brain into the general circulation, it has little effect on eating behaviour. However, when glucose is injected into the hepatic portal vein – the main blood vessel from the intestines to the liver – hungry animals stop eating. These findings should perhaps not surprise us: the liver is the first organ of the body to receive nutrients from the small intestine and clearly occupies an ideal position to monitor food intake. Moreover, the liver sends information regarding glucose levels in the blood to the brain via the hepatic branch of the **vagus nerve**, because if this pathway is cut, then disruption of eating behaviour occurs in hungry animals.

Further evidence linking the liver with glucose detection has been provided by Stricker *et al.* (1977), who injected rats with insulin, which lowered blood glucose and caused hunger. Following this, the animals were given the sugar fructose. Although this type of sugar is metabolised by the liver, it cannot be used, or detected, by the brain as it is too large to cross the **blood–brain barrier**. Thus, these animals had relatively low glucose levels in the brain, but a satiated liver. Clearly, if glucose receptors in the brain have an important role in hunger, these animals should have eaten when presented with food. But this did not happen. Thus, it is the liver that appears to provide the brain with its most important satiety signal.

A brain area known to be in receipt of information from the liver is the ventromedial hypothalamus. Indeed, the vast majority of hypothalamic cells, which contain glucose receptors, decrease their firing rate to glucose infusions into the hepatic portal vein (Shimizu *et al.* 1983). Thus, this area of the hypothalamus is an important site that monitors glucose levels in the liver. However, the role of the hypothalamus in the termination of feeding is certainly more complex than this. For example, as mentioned, if the vagus nerve is cut, eating behaviour is disrupted with loss of food intake, but this occurs only in the short term. In fact, vagotomised animals eventually resume normal eating patterns, indicating that other mechanisms must compensate for the loss of the liver. Thus, we can conclude that either the liver is not the only site detecting levels of glucose in the blood, or that the brain has access to other types of nutrient information that control hunger and satiety.

Other chemical messengers

In addition to glucose it is likely that fluctuations in the metabolism of fats (or lipids) also play an important role in producing hunger and satiety. Indeed, during the fasting phase, when hunger actually occurs, glucagon is released by the pancreas gland, which not only promotes the formation of glucose from glycogen stores in the liver, but also causes lipid cells to release fatty acids and glycerol into the blood. Thus, one might predict that lipids also play a vital role in hunger. Indeed, this has been supported by Friedman *et al.* (1986), who injected rats with either methyl palmoxirate, which interfered with the metabolism of fatty acids into energy, or 2-deoxyglucose, which interfered with the cell's utilisation of glucose. It was found that when each drug was given alone there was little effect on the animal's food intake, but if both were given together, then eating markedly increased. Thus, signals conveying information about the availability of *both* glucose and lipids appear to be important in the control of hunger.

Hormones involved in the storage or breakdown of foodstuffs may also play a role in providing the brain with information concerning the energy status of the body. Perhaps the most obvious candidate in this respect is insulin, which causes the uptake of glucose into cells and leads to the synthesis of lipids. Until fairly recently, it was believed that insulin did not pass into the brain – but now it is known that small amounts of hormone can cross the blood–brain barrier by a specialised transport system, and that insulin receptors are found in the brain, including the hypothalamus. Indeed, small quantities of insulin injected into the brain have been shown to reduce food intake and body weight (Bruning *et al.* 2000), and mice with a genetic deletion of neuronal insulin receptors overeat and become obese (Elchebly *et al.* 1999). Despite this, it is not yet certain whether insulin acts as a satiety signal, because it is also known that fat individuals secrete more insulin than leaner ones. Hence, it is possible that insulin receptors in the brain are involved in weight control and not hunger *per se* (Woods *et al.* 1998).

There are many other hormones that could signal satiety, and perhaps the most likely are those released by the gut and intestines. In fact, over two dozen hormones have been identified in the gastrointestinal system and although they act primarily locally at sites where they are released, they can nevertheless be carried in the blood. Moreover, many of these substances have also been found in the brain, where they act as neurotransmitters or modulators. The gut hormone that has been most strongly implicated in hunger and feeding is **cholecystokinin** (CCK), which is released by cells of the duodenum to help to break down fats into small particles. In addition, CCK also acts on the stomach to control the rate at which it empties its contents into the duodenum. Because levels of CCK increase immediately after a meal, they could provide the brain with a signal of satiety – especially concerning the level of fat passing through the duodenum. In accordance with this idea, a number of studies have found that injections of CCK in hungry animals quickly stops them eating (Smith and Gibbs 1994).

Despite this, the role of cholecystokinin in feeding behaviour has been controversial because it causes nausea in humans, and it has been proposed that this effect might account for its actions on inhibiting feeding behaviour in animals. It is also uncertain whether peripheral CCK reaches the brain. For example, cutting the vagus nerve reduces or eliminates the satiety-inducing effect of CCK injections, which indicates a peripheral site of action. Despite this, CCK is found in many neurons throughout the brain – and injections of this substance into the brain can suppress feeding, which points to a possible central action. Thus, wherever its main site of action, it is probable that CCK has at least some role in producing satiety. Of particular interest is the finding that injections of CCK when coupled with mild gastric distension produce a large decrease in meal size. This suggest that CCK may interact with many other physiological parameters to produce its effects. It should also be noted that many other hormones involved in digestion (e.g. somatostatin, vasoactive intestinal polypeptide, gastric inhibitory peptide to name a few) could be playing a similar role in feeding behaviour.

New developments in diabetes mellitus

The word *diabetes* was first used in the second century AD by Aretaeus, who took it from the Greek for 'siphon' or 'to pass through', which refers to the frequent urination that is a feature of the disorder. Later, in the seventeenth century, Thomas Willis added the Latin *mellitus*, meaning 'honey sweet', because the urine of a diabetic has a high sugar content. It is now known that diabetes mellitus is due to the pancreas gland producing insufficient insulin – or the available insulin does not function correctly. Without insulin, the cells of the body cannot take up glucose, and its level in the blood becomes abnormally high. In addition to increased urination, diabetes causes persistent hunger and thirst. Despite this, the untreated diabetic will lose weight as the body is forced to rely on its protein and fat stores for energy.

There are two type of diabetes. Type I diabetes normally occurs before the age of 16, and has a sudden onset. This form of diabetes arises when the insulin-producing cells of the pancreas gland are damaged or destroyed by an autoimmune response (i.e. the body's immune system recognises the cells as 'foreign' and attacks them), or are infected with a virus. The result is a potentially life-threatening disease with the immediate risk of hyperglycaemia or ketosis (the accumulation of fatty acids in the blood). Consequently, type I diabetes requires regular insulin injections. Type II diabetes occurs when the pancreas gland fails to produce enough insulin – or when there is a receptor abnormality for this hormone. This usually occurs in people over the age of 40 who are overweight (for some reason, obesity causes the insulin receptor to become less sensitive to insulin), and has a more gradual onset. It is also the most common form of the illness and accounts for about 90 per cent of all diabetes cases. In most patients, the glucose levels in the blood can be controlled by diet or exercise.

Diabetes is associated with a wide range of health problem including atherosclerosis, strokes, heart attacks, accelerated ageing and blindness. It has been estimated that 1.4 million people in the UK have diabetes, with possibly up to a million undiagnosed. Moreover, estimates suggest that diabetes costs the National Health Service at least £12 billion every year, which makes up around 8 per cent of the total hospital expenditure. Diabetes is the fourth leading cause of death in most developed countries, and its incidence is increasing at an alarming rate. For example, between 1995 and 2025, it is estimated that the number of people in the developed world with diabetes will increase from 51 to 72 million, due partly to an ageing population, but also as a result of obesity, a diet high in saturated fats and a sedentary lifestyle (Low 1999).

Research is now underway to treat type I diabetes by using transplants of pancreatic cells. In this procedure, islet cells are extracted from the pancreas of a deceased donor and infused into the recipient's liver via the hepatic portal vein. Remarkably, islet cells grow well in the liver and attach themselves to blood vessels, where they release insulin. This procedure normally takes less than a hour to complete and requires only a local anaesthetic. About 1 million islet cells are needed for an adult (usually two pancreas glands are required to provide this number of cells), and some recipients may need a second transfusion before they can safely stop using insulin. Sadly, because the supply of human islet cells is severely limited, this technique can only be used to treat a very small fraction of people with diabetes. Perhaps, one day, human stem cells (see Chapter 3) will provide a supply of islet cells for this procedure.

Where are the control centres for feeding behaviour?

For over a hundred years, it has been recognised that damage to the hypothalamus in humans, particularly caused by tumours to the nearby pituitary gland, is associated with eating dysfunction and obesity. This was confirmed experimentally by Hetherington and Ranson during the late 1930s when they showed that lesions to the ventromedial hypothalamus (VMH) in rats caused excessive eating (**hyperphagia**) and weight gain (see Plate 4.1). And, as we have seen above, Jean Mayer also showed that this was the hypothalamic area that contained glucoreceptors and appeared to be involved in feeding. But the VMH was not the only area to be linked with feeding behaviour. In 1951, Anand and Brobeck made the dramatic discovery that lesions to the **lateral hypothalamus** (LH) caused profound **aphagia**, where the animal stopped eating and drinking. In fact, these animals would die of starvation even though food and water were freely available.

The importance of the hypothalamus in feeding was also confirmed by studies using electrical stimulation. For example, stimulation of the LH produced voracious eating in animals that had been previously satiated (Delgado and Anand 1953), whereas stimulation of the VMH inhibited eating in hungry animals (Smith 1956). These findings, along with the lesion data, strongly suggested that the hypothalamus was involved in the initiation and termination of feeding. In 1954, a theory based on this notion was proposed by Eliot Stellar, who argued that the VMH acted as the brain's satiety centre, and the LH as its hunger centre (Stellar 1954).

This theory, which became known as the **dual-centre set-point theory** (Figure 4.4), viewed the VMH and LH nuclei as the main control centres that governed hunger and feeding. Indeed, both these structures appeared to be in an ideal position to integrate information from other brain regions, and were known to receive feedback from peripheral organs such as the gut and liver, or blood-borne hormones. Importantly, it was also hypothesised that the VMH and LH interacted with each other. Put simply, the theory held that when the

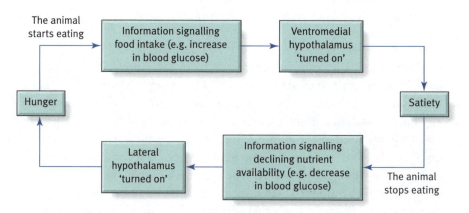

Figure 4.4   The dual-centre set-point model of feeding

VMH was activated by neural or hormonal information signalling food intake, it acted to inhibit the LH feeding centre, and satiation was the result. In contrast, when the LH was activated by signals specifying declining nutrient availability, it acted to inhibit the VMH, thus causing hunger. Not only was this theory simple to understand but it also fitted nicely into a homeostatic framework of feeding. The only problem (it seemed at the time) was to identify the signals and the receptors that initiated hunger and satiety, and to determine how they were integrated in the hypothalamus.

A closer look at ventromedial hypothalamic lesions

It soon become clear that the dual-centre set-point model was not as convincing as it first appeared. For example, the VMH had been viewed as the satiety centre because its lesioning led experimental animals to become ravenously hungry and seemingly unable to stop feeding. However, on closer inspection, it was apparent that this was not the case. Although the VMH-lesioned animal does indeed become a voracious eater and may even double its weight within a few weeks, this period of rapid weight gain does not last, and the food intake drops off with the animal returning to patterns of normal feeding. In other words, the animal undergoes a dynamic phase of weight gain, followed by a static phase where it maintains its new weight, and shows a normal satiety response to eating (Figure 4.5). In terms of the dual-centre set-point model this finding is awkward because these animals clearly become satiated despite having no VMH.

Rather than being impaired in the processing of satiety messages, it is now believed that the VMH lesion actually causes the animal to adopt a new 'set point' for its body weight. For example, if a VMH-lesioned rat in the static phase is force-fed, its weight can be made to increase even further. But if this animal is returned to normal feeding, its weight will also return to the one that existed in the static phase. Similarly, if a VMH-lesioned rat has been made to lose weight by being starved, and then allowed free access to food, it will soon regain its static phase weight. Thus, animals without a VMH appear to be regulating their body weight at a new higher level.

There are other interesting characteristics of VMH-lesioned animals. For example, once these animals have stabilised their weight, they are very finicky and prefer to eat palatable food (e.g. food with extra fat or sugar) rather than their normal 'dry' diet of laboratory chow. In fact, if these animals are given food that is slightly stale, or made to taste bitter by the addition of quinine, they eat less than controls. Thus, animals with VMH lesions show exaggerated reactions to palatability. These animals also appear to be 'lazy' and will show a marked decrease in eating if required to perform a task such as pressing a lever in an operant box to obtain food. Again, these findings do not square well with the idea that the VMH is the brain's satiety centre.

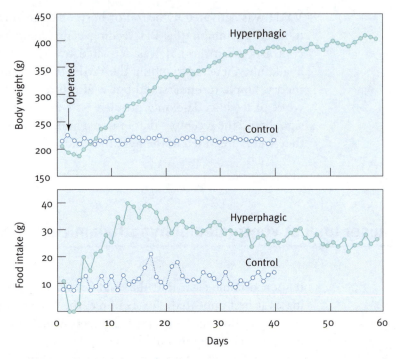

Figure 4.5 The effects of ventromedial hypothalamic lesions on body weight and food intake. *Source*: Adapted from P. Teitelbaum, *Journal of Comparative and Physiological Psychology* (1955), **48**, 156–63

There are a number of reasons why VMH lesions lead to increased eating and weight gain. Perhaps the most important is the fact that these animals release more insulin than controls, which causes more glucose to enter the cells of the body and increase fat storage. It is also possible that damage to the VMH directly disrupts the fibres arising from the paraventricular nucleus of the hypothalamus, which are known to synapse on brainstem nuclei that regulate the parasympathetic vagus nerve. Because this nerve both innervates and receives afferents from the pancreas gland and liver, it is therefore possible that the VMH lesion exerts its effects by disrupting parasympathetic regulation.

A closer look at lateral hypothalamic lesions

As we have seen, lesions of the LH cause the animal to stop eating (aphagia) and drinking (adipsia), and this was used as evidence to support the dual-centre set-point model in which the LH acts as a control centre for the initiation of feeding. However, on closer inspection, this theory also soon ran into difficulties. Perhaps the most problematic finding was that the aphagia and adipsia

Plate 4.1   A hyperphagic rat with a lesion of the ventromedial hypothalamus. *Source*: Graham (1990) *Physiological Psychology*, p.451, Wadsworth

produced by the LH lesion are not permanent. In fact, it was found that a few animals would spontaneously eat and drink about a week after their lesion, and if others were force-fed and given good care and attention, they too would return to normal feeding behaviour. Thus, just as VMH lesions do not totally abolish all inhibition of eating, LH lesions do not permanently stop eating and drinking. Presumably, therefore, other areas of the brain must take over, or be involved, in this behaviour.

It also became clear that LH lesions produced a wide range of other impairments. For example, lesioned animals generally did not move around, right themselves when placed on their sides, or respond to touch and visual stimulation. Moreover, these animals appeared grossly under-aroused – an idea that gained further support when it was found that a mild pinch to the tail could induce LH-lesioned rats to start eating (Antelman *et al.* 1975). In fact, it now appears that many of these deficits are not caused by the destruction of LH

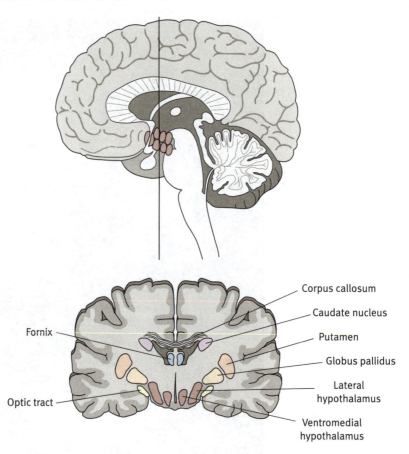

Figure 4.6 The location of the ventromedial and lateral hypothalamus in the human brain

neurons, but are due to the severing of axons from other brain areas that pass through the hypothalamus *en route* to somewhere else. One pathway that goes through the LH is the **nigral–striatal pathway**, which links the substantia nigra with the striatum, and is known to be involved in attention and movement. Indeed, damage to this pathway causes aphagia and weight loss that closely resembles the effects of LH damage (Ungerstedt 1971).

Despite this, it appears that the LH still contributes to feeding behaviour. During the 1970s it became possible to produce chemical lesions of the LH with drugs such as kainic acid and ibotenic acid, which destroy cell bodies without damaging fibres of passage. When these drugs were injected into the LH, they caused a decrease in food intake and body weight, but no deficits in motor or sensory function (Winn *et al.* 1984). Thus, these later deficits appeared to be due to the nigral–striatal pathway. Moreover, it has been shown that, in monkeys, LH neurons become activated within 150–200 ms of a food stimulus being shown, but no response occurs to a neutral stimulus (Rolls *et al.* 1979).

Further evidence linking the LH with eating behaviour has come from the discovery of **neuropeptide Y (NPY)**. This substance was first identified in the CNS in the early 1980s, and despite being closely related to peptides in the pancreas gland and gut, is now recognised as the most abundant neuropeptide in the brain, with a wide range of functions. Of particular interest is the discovery that NPY receptors are found in the hypothalamus, including the paraventricular nucleus (PVN) and the LH. Moreover, when injected directly into the ventricles of the brain, close to the hypothalamus, NPY produces a powerful and prolonged increase in food intake. Indeed, these animals not only appear to be ravenously hungry, but will work frantically hard to obtain food reward. Attempts have been made to identify the sites in the hypothalamus which mediate these effects, and one of the most important areas is the PVN. For example, infusions of NPY into the PVN produce a number of metabolic changes in the body, including increased insulin secretion, decreased breakdown of fats in adipose tissue, and a drop in body temperature. In short, these animals show decreased energy expenditure along with increased storage of glucose and fats – and these changes appear to be linked with overeating and obesity. Injections of NPY into the LH also promote eating behaviour, indicating that it may be another part of the feeding circuit involving the PVN.

Although the PVN and the LH are clearly involved in feeding behaviour, it is probably misleading to regard these areas as simple 'control centres' as they are individual components of highly complex neural systems. For example, the LH projects to various midbrain and brainstem regions, and receives input from many forebrain areas including the striatum, amygdala, and orbitofrontal cortex. All of these brain structures are probably components of a central feeding system (Rolls 1994) and this implies that these brain regions may be able to compensate for each other if one is damaged. This shows the difficulty of tying down a brain region to a particular function. Indeed, this is particularly true for the LH, which has also been shown to be involved in a wide range of motivational behaviour including aggression, sexual behaviour and reinforcement.

Non-homeostatic mechanisms of eating

Do we really eat, or become hungry, because of a decline in blood glucose (or some other nutrient variable) acting on the hypothalamus? In fact, we do not have to look far to see that eating behaviour is not as homeostatically controlled as traditional physiological psychologists would like us to believe. Indeed, one of the most important factors that determines whether or not we feel hungry is *not* blood sugar level, stomach rumblings, or something happening in the hypothalamus – it is our wristwatch! This is shown by the fact that people tend to eat at fixed times of the day, and we often become hungry in anticipation of a meal that is about to take place. Other animals behave in a similar way. For example, as early as 1927, Richter showed that rats, given one meal a day, quickly came to anticipate their feeding time with increased running in activity wheels. The importance of learning in feeding behaviour was also demonstrated by Weingarten (1983), who presented a light and tone to rats every time they were given a meal of evaporated milk. The animals were fed this way six times every day over a period of 11 days, following which they were given unlimited access to food to produce satiation. Although these animals were not hungry, they still began to eat when the light and tone were presented. Clearly, these rats were not consuming food to restore an energy deficit – they were eating because they had been conditioned to do so.

The effects of learning also influence the choice of foods we eat. For example, few of us would find squid cooked in its own ink, fried grasshoppers or sheep eyes very appetising – yet these are eaten as delicacies in other parts of the world. This shows that we learn what we like to eat, and the same principle applies to other animals. Indeed, if a wild rat discovers a new food it will typically eat only a small amount – and then only consume more on its next encounter if it has experienced no adverse effects from it. However, if the food causes illness, the rat will develop an aversion to it. This is a highly specialised type of learning, and occurs even if the delay between eating and illness is 24 hours or more. This is known as the **Garcia effect,** and is of great adaptive benefit to the animal.

Another important factor in feeding behaviour is the *anticipated pleasurable* effect of eating. For example, hunger can often be elicited by a highly palatable food such as a dessert – even after the person has eaten a very large meal. This shows that it is the incentive value of the food, and not its nutrient value, that causes hunger. Again, the same phenomenon occurs in animals. For example, adding a small amount of sugar to standard laboratory rat food tends to produce a large increase in its consumption and a rise in the animal's body weight. The addition of bitter-tasting quinine has the opposite effect.

It should came as no surprise to find out that an effective way of increasing food intake in laboratory animals is to feed them a highly varied diet. For example, rats given bread and chocolate along with their normal chow increased their food intake by 60 per cent, and showed a 49 per cent increase in weight gain after only 120 days of feeding (Rogers and Blundell 1980). This effect is probably caused by **sensory-specific satiety** – the tendency to get 'bored' with a given food if it is consumed over a long period of time. Laboratory rats are highly susceptible to this effect because they are normally only given a diet of dry chow and water. Thus, the introduction of new food into their cages significantly increases the rat's 'pleasure' of eating. The same principle applies to humans. It has been found that if subjects are given a free meal (e.g. cheese and crackers) and are then unexpectedly given a second course of something different (e.g. bananas) they will eat much more of the new food compared with a second helping of the first (Rolls *et al.* 1981). In other words, the second portion of food now becomes much more appetising than the first.

All this evidence shows that a variety of factors play an important role in shaping feeding behaviour, and although it is tempting to explain it in terms of homeostatic mechanisms, eating behaviour is far too complex for this type of explanation to offer more than just a partial account of hunger and satiety. Indeed, learning, anticipation, attitudes, social factors and a host of other psychological variables appear to provide a better predictor of feeding behaviour than physiological factors such as blood glucose levels or stomach contractions.

This should not surprise us. As the brain has evolved, so has the complexity of the behaviour it produces, and there is no reason to believe that feeding is any different.

Eating disorders

Most of us take eating for granted and do not generally consider it as a behaviour that can go wrong. Evidence, however, shows otherwise. Obesity, anorexia nervosa and bulimia, for example, are all disorders where abnormal feeding behaviour occurs with serious repercussions for health and psychological well-being. Increasingly, attempts are being made to understand these conditions and find successful treatments for them.

Anorexia nervosa and bulimia

The term 'anorexia' means loss of appetite and was first used by the English physician Sir William Gull in 1873. Although the term has remained, it is not an accurate description of the disorder as people with anorexia still experience hunger. Rather, anorexics are obsessed with being thin and have a fear of becoming fat. Thus, they eat tiny amounts of food, and this may be accompanied by self-induced vomiting, excessive exercise, or the drinking of large amounts of water to suppress appetite. The result is often a dramatic loss of body weight, which is 60–70 per cent of what is 'normal' for height and age. Although anorexia is most common in teenage girls, about one in 10 cases occurs in males. It is also a common disorder affecting around one teenager in every 200, and reaching a peak incidence of one in 100 among adolescents between 16 and 18. The effects on health are serious and include loss of menstruation, lowered blood pressure, sleep disturbances, and metabolic abnormalities with excess secretion of cortisol from the adrenal glands and decreased thyroid function. Sadly, about 2–5 per cent of anorexics will die from complications arising from their illness (a famous case being Karen Carpenter in 1983).

The neuranatomical and biochemical causes of anorexia are poorly understood, although an involvement for the hypothalamus is suspected. Evidence linking this brain region with anorexia has come from the finding that as many as 25 per cent of anorexic females show loss of menstruation and low levels of reproductive hormones (which are controlled by the hypothalamus) before significant weight loss occurs. These individuals may also not resume menstruation once their weights return to normal. In addition, the high cortisol levels often found in anorexic individuals may be a result of increased secretion of corticotropin-releasing factor (CRH), which is under the control of the hypothalamic–pituitary axis. People with anorexia may also show decreased levels of noradrenergic metabolites in their urine and

Anorexia nervosa and bulimia continued.

cerebrospinal fluid (CSF), which may partly represent the breakdown of noradrenaline in the brain. It is interesting to note that injections of noradrenaline into the hypothalamus cause animals to eat, and a low level would presumably have the oposite effect. Despite all these abnormalities, it is difficult to establish whether they are causal factors in anorexia, or simply a response to the body's starvation.

Another eating disorder, **bulimia**, is characterised by bouts of binge eating where individuals consume large amounts of food in a short space of time. In fact, bulimics may gorge themselves with thousands of calories, especially if eating highly palatable sweet and carbohydrate-rich food, in bouts lasting an hour or so. This is then followed by self-induced vomiting, or the use of laxatives to purge themselves of the food they have just eaten. Although about 40 per cent of anorexics practise binge eating, many people with bulimia do not develop anorexia. Thus, bulimia qualifies as an eating disorder in its own right. Although the causes of bulimia are poorly understood, some bulimic individuals show reduced levels of the serotonergic metabolite 5-HIAA, and the dopaminergic metabolite HVA, in their CSF. Both metabolites are likely to derive from the brain and reflect central serotonergic and dopaminergic dysfunction. It has been speculated that reduced serotonergic function might contribute to the blunted satiety responses in bulimic patients, while low levels of dopamine might play a role in their addiction-like craving for food (Jimerson *et al.* 1992). In this respect, it is interseting to note that antidepressants which block the re-uptake of serotonin have been shown to be of use in the treatment of bulimia.

Obesity

Obesity can be defined as body weight that is 10 to 20 per cent more than is ideal for the person's height and due to the excessive accumulation of fat. Put another way, a body fat content of 20–25 per cent in men, and 25–30 per cent in women, is considered normal for adults, and anything above these values is obese. It has been estimated that approximately 2–5 per cent of children in Great Britain are obese, and this figure increases with age so that by the age of 50, about 20 per cent of the population will suffer from obesity. Over 2,000 years ago, the health risks of obesity were noted by Hippocrates, who wrote that 'persons who are naturally very fat are apt to die earlier than those who are slender', and modern evidence supports this claim. Indeed, obesity is associated with a range of health problems including heart disease, stroke, certain cancers and diabetes (to name a few) and, if this wasn't enough, obese people are also often perceived as being gluttonous, lazy or simply lacking in will-power – although, in most cases, these attributes are either unfair or totally untrue.

A body cell that stores fat is called an adipocyte, and in an average person there are around 25 billion of these cells which are found predominantly in the subcutaneous layer below the skin (especially the abdomen, buttocks and thighs) and around the kidneys and heart. The number of adipocytes in the human body is fixed by early adulthood, which means that people put on weight because their fat cells get larger. Clinically, obesity is classified as either hypertrophic (adult onset) or hyperplastic (lifelong). Adult-onset obesity tends to occur in individuals who are average in weight until they reach middle age, when they develop excess amounts of fat ('middle-age spread'), which is mainly associated with an imbalance between caloric intake and utilisation. In contrast, individuals with lifelong obesity tend to be obese as children, and put on extra weight during adolescence, with excess fat being distributed all over the body. A range of metabolic, hormonal, genetic, developmental and learning factors can be associated with this condition, showing that obesity is not a single disorder or has any simple cause or explanation.

There are many reasons why people become obese, but probably the most important single factor is genetic inheritance. For example, it has been shown that children with two obese parents have approximately a 70 per cent chance of being overweight compared with 40 per cent for children with one obese parent and 10 per cent when neither parent is obese (Logue 1986). Other studies have shown that identical twins are not only more likely to be similar in weight and obesity compared with fraternal twins, but also have very similar weights (often within 1 kg of each other) across the life span. An examination of such studies has suggested a concordance (heritability) rate of about 60–70 per cent for identical twins and 30–40 per cent for non-identical twins (Plomin *et al.* 1997). However, one potential confounding factor with these studies is that a similar environment for family members or twins may have contributed to the effects. One way around this difficulty is to study adoptees who are separated from their biological parents early in life. This type of study was undertaken by Stunkard *et al.* (1986), who examined 504 adoptees and their biological and adoptive parents. The results showed that the weight of the adoptees most closely resembled the weights of their biological parents (particularly the mothers) and not the adoptive parents.

It is a remarakable fact that, during each decade of life, the average adult eats around 10 million calories, yet gains only a few pounds. From this, it can be calculated that the calories eaten are 99.83 per cent of the calories burned. However, it also follows that someone whose metabolic rate is only 99.5 per cent efficient will gain weight at triple the normal rate. This type of 'metabolic efficiency' also appears to be genetic. For example, Bouchard *et al.* (1990) isolated 12 pairs of identical twins who had no history of weight problems and overfed them daily by 1,000 calories over a period of 100 days. In effect, the subjects consumed an extra 84,000 calories above their normal intake. Although the results showed that the average weight gain was 8 kg, there was a high variability between the different sets of twins, but not within each pair. For example, one pair gained 4 kg and another pair gained 12 kg! These results show that people vary in the way they gain weight, and this is due to the metabolism of the individual, which is largely inherited. In another study, Bouchard *et al.* (1994) took seven pairs of identical male twins and fed them a restricted diet, accompanied by a forced exercise regime over a period of 93 days.

Overall the total energy deficit was 58,000 calories below normal, and average weight loss was 5 kg. Again, the results showed marked differences between the twins in terms of weight lost – but highly consistent changes within each twin pair.

Although genetic influences on metabolism make an important contribution to obesity, one should not discount the importance of lifestyle factors. For example, childhood is an important time in setting body weight, and over-eating at this stage may lead to a predisposition towards obesity in later life. Cultural mores also play a role in the development of obesity, and one factor may include the widespread belief that healthy eating requires three large meals a day. In fact, it has been shown that after the age of 30 years, the human body reduces its energy expenditure by about 12 calories per year, and since a decline in the efficiency of metabolism also occurs with ageing, it is likely that weight gain will occur unless the meal intake is reduced. The widespread prevalence of high-fat diets and low levels of physical activity are also important contributors to obesity. To complicate matters further, genetic factors also appear to predispose some individuals to eating high-fat foods or having reduced levels of exercise (Weinsier *et al*. 1998).

The discovery of leptin

As we have seen, the body must have a mechanism that is at least partly genetically determined which allows it to maintain a stable weight despite great fluctuations in food intake. Until recently, however, the means by which the body accomplished this feat was unknown. Nonetheless, it has long been known that certain genes have an important influence on body weight in experimental animals. Indeed, this was shown as early as 1950 when a genetic mutation spontaneously occurred in a colony of mice being housed in a laboratory at Bar Harbor, USA, which caused them to become extremely obese and weigh up to three times heavier than normal. Because these animals carried two copies of the, so called, *ob* (or obese) gene they became known as *ob/ob* mice. Not only did these mice eat large amounts of food and show increased levels of insulin, but they also had a lower body temperature indicating a slower metabolism. Moreover, they also had a greater susceptibility to diabetes, just as occurs with many obese people. The crucial question was: how could this genetic mutation set in motion the biological events that caused these changes?

In the early 1970s, it became clear that the *ob/ob* mice became obese because they lacked a certain satiety signal that was released in the blood. This discovery was made by Coleman (1973), who joined *ob/ob* mice with normal lean ones in a parabiotic preparation. In this technique, two mice are surgically joined along flank incisions running from forelimb to hindlimb, which enables vascular networks to develop between the two animals, but not neural connections.

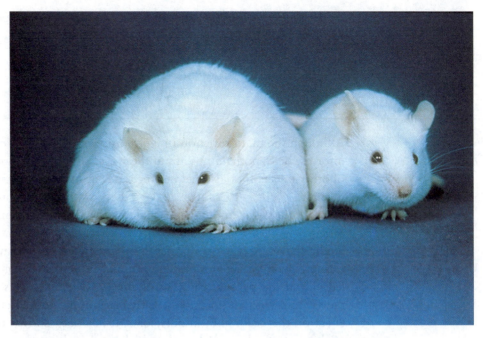

Plate 4.2   An *ob/ob* mouse and a control mouse. *Source*: Pinel (2003) *Biopsychology* (5th edn), p.319, Allyn & Bacon. Reprinted with permission from The Jackson Laboratory and the publisher

The results of this procedure showed that the *ob/ob* mice began to eat less and lose weight – a finding that implied that something in the blood of the lean mice was acting on their obese counterparts to make them less fat. In other words, it appeared as if the blood of the normal mouse carried a weight-regulating substance that was encoded by the normal *ob* gene, and absent in the *ob/ob* mice (Plate 4.2).

But what could this substance be? In order to answer this question, the *ob* gene was localised to chromosome 6 in 1986, and cloned in the early 1990s (Zhang *et al*. 1994). The sequencing of this gene showed that it produced a protein called **leptin** (from the Greek *leptos* meaning 'thin') and that this substance was missing in *ob/ob* mice. Moreover, in normal animals, leptin was secreted into the blood by adipocytes and was able to enter the CSF, where it appeared to gain access to the brain. Moreover, when leptin was injected into *ob/ob* mice it led to a marked decrease in food intake and body weight. In fact, a daily injection of leptin over the course of two weeks caused the mice to lose 30 per cent of their body weight (Halaas *et al*. 1995). In short, the *ob/ob* mice overeat and are obese because they do not produce the protein leptin.

Soon after the discovery of leptin, attempts were made to discover the receptor for this substance in the brain. As might be predicted, receptors for leptin have been found in the hypothalamus, including its arcuate, paraventricular, ventromedial and dorsal nuclei. In addition, leptin receptors have curiously been found in the choroid plexus – a vascular site sticking into the ventricles which is responsible for making CSF – and in some peripheral sites, including the liver and kidneys.

Leptin and obesity

Although the main function of leptin appears to be as a feedback signal which informs the hypothalamus about the stores of fat in the body – it has a number of other effects that also help to regulate eating and body weight. For example, if leptin is given to rats each day, they eat the same number of meals, but consume less – a finding that suggests that leptin is sensitising the brain to satiety signals from the stomach, which causes them to stop eating sooner. Studies have also shown that leptin interacts with other substances involved in eating behaviour. For example, if animals are given a combined small dose of leptin and the peptide cholecystokinin (CCK), they eat significantly less than they would with an injection of either hormone alone. Leptin also has a direct effect on the brain and, in particular, it has been shown to act on the **arcuate nucleus** of the hypothalamus (which has projections to the paraventricular nucleus and lateral hypothalamus), where it inhibits the secretion of **neuropeptide Y**. As we have seen on page 127, when this neuropeptide is injected into the hypothalamus, it produces a powerful and prolonged increase in food intake. Consequently, animals who are deficient in leptin produce greater levels of neuropeptide Y, and this is likely to be an important contributor to overeating

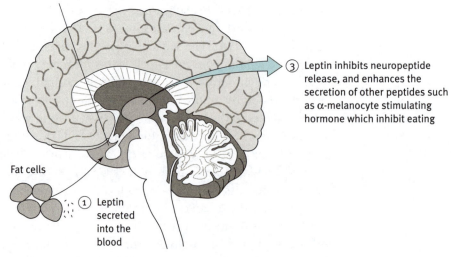

② Leptin binds to receptors in the arcuate hypothalamus. Its neurons project to the lateral hypothalamus and paraventricular nuclei

③ Leptin inhibits neuropeptide release, and enhances the secretion of other peptides such as α-melanocyte stimulating hormone which inhibit eating

Fat cells

① Leptin secreted into the blood

Figure 4.7   How leptin is believed to influence feeding and body weight

and weight gain (Schwartz and Seeley 1997). Leptin also enhances the release of other substances in the hypothalamus, including α-melanocyte-stimulating hormone and corticotropin-releasing hormone, which are believed to help to suppress hunger.

The discovery of leptin has raised many questions concerning its potential role in human obesity. For example, are obese humans like *ob/ob* mice and have a mutation in their *ob* gene? And, do obese people produce low levels of leptin? The answer to both questions is 'No'. So far only a handful of people have been found with a mutation in their *ob* genes, and although they suffer from obesity, they do not represent the vast majority of people who are over-weight. In fact, because leptin is secreted into the blood by fat cells in amounts directly proportional to the level of body adipose mass, obese people tend to have higher levels of leptin in contrast to *ob/ob* mice, which have lower levels. Thus, if leptin plays a role in human obesity, the most likely mechanism would be a reduced sensitivity to this hormone, rather than decreased secretion. Nonetheless, attempts have also been made to treat obesity with injections of leptin, although in most cases this treatment has produced negligible effects (Heymsfield *et al.* 1999).

Other genes and eating behaviour

The *ob* gene is not the only one that has been linked with eating disorders and obesity. In fact, a number of single gene mutations have been found in rats and mice that produce obesity, and four of these genes have been identified and cloned, allowing their function to be better understood (Pomp 1999). In addition, researchers are increasingly using transgenic animals to study obesity and eating disorders, These are animals (normally mice) in which certain genes have either been 'knocked out' or inserted during embryonic development (see Chapter 12). This work has already targeted and modified a number of genes – including those that affect levels of brown adipose tissue, glucocorticoid receptors, growth hormone and insulin-stimulated glucose intake – that have caused excess accumulation of fat in transgenic animals (Morin and Eckel 1997). However, many more genes are probably involved in obesity. In fact, a technique called quantitative trait locus mapping, which is based on cross-breeding studies of inbred strains of rats and mice, has identified 55 regions in the genome where there are genes that affect body fat (Bouchard 1995). Although most of these genes have not been precisely identified, or their func-tion established, researchers nonetheless know that many of these genes also exist in humans, and are probably involved in determining body weight and obesity. Trying to piece together how all these genes act to alter metabolism and body weight is one of the great challenges of molecular biology and neuroscience.

Summary

Although eating is an essential behaviour and is vital for the maintenance of life, it is affected by many variables, both biological and psychological. Traditionally, physiological accounts of eating and hunger have viewed it as a **homeostatic process** in which the body attempts to maintain its various levels of nutrients (i.e. glucose, fats, proteins, vitamins, etc.) within fine limits. However, it is also clear that psychological factors play an important role in eating, as shown by the fact that we often feel hungry in anticipation of food, rather than passively reacting to a decline in nutrient levels. The process of digestion begins in the **mouth**, where food is first chewed and mixed with saliva, then passed to the **stomach**, where it is broken down into **chyme** by gastric juices. The chyme is emptied into the **small intestine**, where absorption takes place, with most nutrients entering the general circulation by the **villi** and entering the **hepatic portal vein** (which passes to the **liver**), although emulsified fats are absorbed into the lymphatic vessels. During a meal, the **pancreas gland** releases **insulin**, which allows glucose to enter the cells of the body (although the cells of the brain do not need insulin for this function). However, in the periods between eating (the post-absorptive phase) the pancreas gland secretes **glucagon**, which helps to convert **glycogen** (stored in the liver) into glucose, and stores of fatty acids into glycerol. A large number of peripheral mechanisms are believed to play a role in keeping the brain informed of the nutrient status of the body. These include neural signals from the **vagus nerve**, which conveys stretch information from the stomach and glucoreceptors in the liver – along with various hormones secreted into the blood including **cholecystokinin** and **leptin**.

Many brain areas are involved in eating behaviour, but most attention has focused on the hypothalamus. In particular, lesions of the **lateral hypothalamus** (LH) have been shown to produce **aphagia** (cessation of eating) while damage to the **ventromedial hypothalamus** (VMH) causes **hyperphagia** (excessive eating and weight gain). These observations led to the formulation of the **dual-centre set-point theory** in the 1950s, which postulated that stimulation of the LH induced eating, while stimulation of the VMH produced satiety. This theory is now regarded as incorrect. Although the LH appears to have a role in food intake, so do many other regions of the hypothalamus, including the **paraventricular nucleus** (PVN) – as is shown by marked increases in eating following injections of **neuropeptide Y** into this region. Moreover, the severe sensory and motor deficits in aphagia following LH lesioning are now known to be largely due to damage of fibres of passage that belong to the **nigral–striatal pathway**, which passes through this area. The weight of evidence also shows that the VMH is much more important in regulating the body's weight than acting as a 'satiety centre'. The discovery in the early 1990s of **leptin**, which is a hormone secreted by fat cells in the body, has provided new insights into the regulation of body weight and eating behaviour. For example, it has been shown that the more fat an individual has stored, the more leptin is released. Leptin provides the brain with a feedback signal concerning the size of its fat stores. However, leptin may also influence appetite. For example, high numbers of leptin receptors are found in the **arcuate nucleus** of the hypothalamus, which has projections to both the LH and PVN – areas where leptin is known to inhibit the secretion of neuropeptide Y, which is an important regulator of food intake and hunger.

Essay questions

1. What are the main roles of insulin and glycogen? What types of neural and chemical feedback from the body does the brain rely on to govern food intake?

   Helpful Internet search terms: *Insulin and glycogen. Feedback signals in hunger. The digestive system. Hunger and eating. Glucostatic hypothesis.*

2. Critically evaluate the roles of the lateral hypothalamus and ventromedial hypothalamus in hunger and satiety. What other brain sites are known to be involved in eating behaviour?

   Helpful Internet search terms: *Dual-centre set-point model of eating. Hypothalamus and hunger. Neural control of eating. Neuropeptides and food intake. Brainstem and hunger.*

3. Can eating be explained in terms of a homeostatic model? What evidence shows that non-homeostatic mechanisms also contribute to feeding?

   Helpful Internet search terms: *Homeostasis and hunger. Sensory-specific satiety. Regulation of food intake. Classical conditioning of food intake. Factors influencing eating behaviour.*

4. How has the discovery of leptin transformed our understanding of eating behaviour and the maintenance of body weight?

   Helpful Internet search terms: *Leptin. Leptin and obesity. Leptin and hunger. Hypothalamus and body weight. Neuropeptide Y and body weight.*

Further reading

Bouchard, C. (ed.) (1994) *The Genetics of Obesity.* Boca Raton, FL: CRC Press. A technical compilation of evidence, written by experts in their field, regarding the role of genetic factors in the aetiology of obesity.

Bouchard, C. and Bray, G.A. (eds) (1996) *Regulation of Body Weight: Biological and Behavioural Mechanisms.* New York: John Wiley. A comprehensive account that covers animal models, aetiology, physiological mechanisms and social factors in obesity.

Bray, G.A., Bouchard, C. and James, P.T. (1998) *Handbook of Obesity.* New York: Dekker. A massive tome, 1012 pages, 49 chapters and 88 authors. A very comprehensive overview of present research into obesity.

Broch, H. (2001) *The Golden Cage: The Enigma of Anorexia Nervosa.* Cambridge, MA: Harvard University Press. First published in 1978, and although dated in some respects, this still provides a vivid insight into the mind of an anorexic and her pursuit of thinness.

Bromwell, K.D. and Fairburn, C.G. (eds) (2001) *Eating Disorders and Obesity: A Comprehensive Handbook.* New York: Guilford Press. Contains a wealth of information including the aetiology of obesity, the role of leptin and the treatment of eating disorders.

Legg, C.R. and Booth, D. (1994) *Appetite: Neural and Behavioral Basis*. Oxford: Oxford University Press. Examines the psychology and neurobiology of appetite in relation to food, drugs, sex and gambling in an attempt to find common denominators between them.

Smith, G.P. (ed.) (1998) *Satiation: From Gut to Brain*. New York: Oxford University Press. A detailed but readable account of the physiological and hormonal mechanisms underlying satiety.

See website at www.pearsoned.co.uk/wickens for further resources including multiple choice questions.

CHAPTER 5

Emotional states

In this chapter

INTRODUCTION

The term 'emotion' is derived from the Latin *emovere* meaning to move or to disturb. The word is highly appropriate as emotions do indeed move us into action and signal that something significant is happening to us. They also create a feeling – love, elation, happiness, fear, anger, joy, surprise, and irritation, to name a few – that colour our perception and add richness to our personal world. Emotions are an essential part of human life and it is hard to imagine the dull and grey world that would exist without them. However, as Charles Darwin pointed out over 125 years ago, many of our emotions can also be recognised in other animals – a fact that shows they must have evolved to serve very important functions. Although the study of emotional behaviour is plagued with a number of conceptual difficulties, most would agree that an emotion has four components: (1) a cognitive appraisal of an arousing event; (2) physiological changes in the viscera or main organs of the body; (3) an increased readiness to act; and (4) a subjective sense of feeling. Since all of these responses involve the brain, emotion is an important topic in biological psychology. However, trying to explain how the neural machinery of the brain can give rise to the sensation of emotion presents a unique challenge. But it is also one with many potential benefits as emotional disturbances can result in anxiety and stress, which underpin other behavioural conditions and illnesses. By understanding the biological psychology of emotion, we not only gain a far deeper insight into human nature, but are also in a stronger position to help those with emotional and behavioural problems.

The autonomic nervous system and emotion

The term 'autonomic' means 'self-governing' and this aptly describes the autonomic nervous system (ANS) which operates, for most part, beyond voluntary or conscious control (see also Chapter 1). The ANS consists of motor nerves that control the activity of the internal organs of the body – as well as certain hormonal glands, including the adrenal glands, which releases **adrenaline** – and comprises two main divisions (Figure 5.1): the **sympathetic nervous system** (SNS) and **parasympathetic nervous system** (PNS). The first of these acts mainly to mobilise the body's resources in response to emergency or stressful situations. In the 1920s, the famous physiologist Walter Cannon called the pattern of responses produced by the SNS the '**flight or fight' response** because it prepares the body for danger should it occur. For example, activity in the SNS increases heart rate and blood pressure, and acts to shunt blood away from the skin to the muscles, where it may be needed for vigorous exercise (this is the reason why skin may go pale after a shock). Among its many other functions, the SNS promotes deeper and faster breathing, while inhibiting digestion and

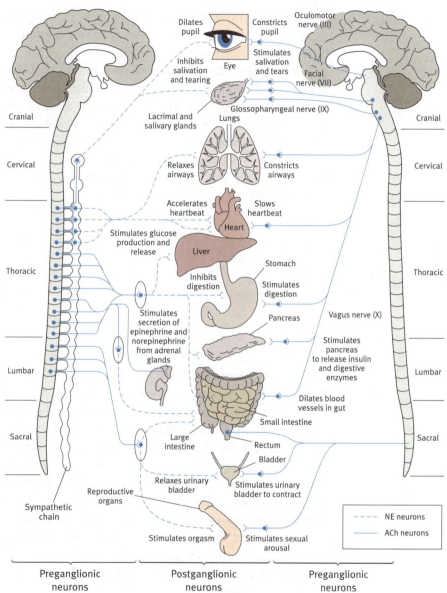

Figure 5.1   Sympathetic and parasympathetic divisions of the autonomic nervous system and the organs they innervate. *Source*: M.F. Bear, B.W. Connors and M.A. Paradiso, *Neuroscience: Exploring the Brain*. Copyright © 1996 by Lippincott Williams & Wilkins

increasing perspiration. These are all adaptive reactions that help to prepare the body for sudden energy output.

In contrast, the PNS promotes relaxation and functions mainly during normal and non-stressful conditions. Thus, this system is most active when the body is at rest, during which time it is mainly concerned with control of the digestive system and conserving body energy. Although the SNS and PNS innervate the same body organs and are often regarded as having opposite effects, in practice these two systems generally work together to control the function of a given organ.

What does this have to do with emotion? The simple answer is that when we experience a significant emotional reaction, a number of bodily changes take place that involve the ANS. For example, if we are frightened we may experience a rapid heartbeat, increased respiration, trembling, a dry mouth, sweaty hands and a sinking feeling in the stomach. These sensations are part of the flight–fight response due to the activation of the SNS. Although these effects may not occur in all emotions, it is generally the case that arousal produced by the ANS is an important component of *most* emotional states. Thus, it is fair to say that the ANS underpins both the expression and experience of emotion. However, as we shall see below, there is much more to this relationship than first meets the eye.

Major theories of emotion

The James–Lange theory of emotion

At first sight, identifying the cause of an emotion appears to be straightforward. For example, a barking dog runs towards us and we prepare to flee – or we are attacked by a mugger and have to defend ourselves. In both cases, the cause of the bodily changes that produce the emotion seems to be obvious: we perceive the event, and if judged to be threatening, the ANS is activated, which also causes an emotion to be produced. However, around the turn of the century the American philosopher William James and the Danish physiologist Carl Lange suggested an alternative theory. Instead of accepting that we run because we are afraid (as the above example suggests), they proposed that we are afraid because we run. In other words, it is the action (or physical response) that comes before the sensation (or perception) of emotion. Put another way, the sensation of an emotion only occurs once we have received feedback about the changes taking place in our body.

This theory is known as the James–Lange theory of emotion (Figure 5.2) and can be briefly summarised as follows: a stimulus is processed by the appropriate part of the brain (such as the visual or auditory cortex), which assesses its relevance. If the stimulus is emotionally significant, the information is passed to the ANS, which sets into motion components of the flight–fight response. This bodily arousal is then detected by the conscious part of the brain, which tries to interpret the nature of the emotional state it is experiencing. If this theory is correct, then it follows that an emotion only becomes a conscious state once it has been produced first in the periphery. One problem with this idea is that different emotions (e.g. love and hate) 'feel' very different. Thus, the implication is that each emotion must have its own constellation of physiological changes that accompany it. Also, it is the pattern of peripheral body responses that tells

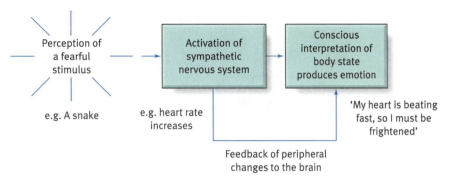

Figure 5.2   The James–Lange theory of emotion

the brain the emotion it is experiencing. In support of the theory, James argued that it was impossible to feel an emotion without experiencing the body response that accompanies it. He also pointed out that people can sometimes feel anxious, angry or depressed without knowing why, which suggests that bodily states can be independent of cognitive or conscious analysis.

The Cannon–Bard theory of emotion

The James–Lange theory, which emphasised the importance of peripheral physiological events in emotion, remained in vogue until 1915, when Walter Cannon compiled a large body of evidence against it. For example, Cannon surgically removed the entire SNS in a cat, and found that while this abolished signs of physical arousal, the animals still showed anger, fear and pleasure. Cannon also noted that the same was equally true of animals that had undergone transaction of the spinal cord, which stopped all visceral input travelling to, and from, the brain. Both these findings provided evidence against the James–Lange theory. Moreover, Cannon's work indicated that emotions were 'experienced' before many parts of the body, such as smooth muscle and endocrine glands, had time to react to autonomic stimulation. Thus, in his view, the feeling of emotion was not dependent on physiological changes in the body. Even if the ANS was involved, Cannon believed that visceral feedback was neither variable nor sensitive enough to provide a basis for each of the wide range of emotions that humans are able to experience (Cannon 1927).

Further evidence against the James–Lange theory came from studies in which human subjects were injected with adrenaline to produce physiological reactions resembling excitement and strong fear (i.e. heart palpitations, trembling, tightness in the throat and drying of the mouth). Despite these bodily changes, the injection procedure did not cause the subjects to experience fear or any other strong emotion. In fact, subjects were able to interpret their bodily reactions without perceiving them as emotional – a finding that was also contrary to the James–Lange theory (Cannon 1927).

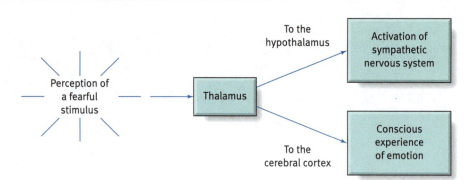

Figure 5.3   The Cannon–Bard theory of emotion

In Cannon's view, it was the brain that decided whether to produce an emotional response to a given stimulus. More specifically, he proposed that emotional events have two separate effects on the brain: they stimulate the ANS to produce physiological arousal thereby preparing the body for possible threat and, at the same time, produce the sensation of emotion in the cortex. Thus, the state of autonomic arousal and the cognitive interpretation of the emotional event were seen as occurring together (see Figure 5.3). Cannon also believed that emotional events affected the SNS indiscriminately by causing general arousal. That is, he did not accept that each emotion had its own individual pattern of body activity as the James–Lange theory maintained, but rather the ANS responded in exactly the same way to all types of emotion (Cannon 1927).

Cannon's theory was developed in the 1930s by the work of Philip Bard, who attempted to identify the areas of the brain that were responsible for producing emotion. One structure implicated in emotional behaviour was the **cerebral cortex**. However, when Bard removed the cortex of cats, he found that they became highly emotional and aggressive – often responding with pronounced reactions (e.g. arching their backs, hissing, snarling) to the slightest provocation (Bard 1934). This behaviour also showed all the usual autonomic features associated with emotion such as increased heart rate and blood pressure. However, the emotional response was not entirely normal as it was never directed towards the threatening stimulus, and it stopped as soon as the threat was removed (Bard called it sham rage). This suggested that the cerebral cortex did not produce emotional behaviour but rather directed it to the appropriate situation.

Bard's discovery was important because it indicated that the cerebral cortex normally acted to inhibit emotion and aggression. This was also in accordance with several other observations. For example, surgeons and dentists had long known that some patients show a strong emotional response – crying, laughter and aggression – during the early stages of anaesthesia, when the cortex is beginning to be inhibited. Furthermore, it had been shown in some cases of hemiplegia (i.e. paralysis of one side of the body due to cortical damage) that although the muscles of the face might be paralysed, they sometimes produced an involuntary reaction (e.g. a smile) in response to an emotion (e.g. happiness). Thus, it appeared that areas below the level of the cerebral cortex were more importantly involved in producing emotional behaviour.

Further work by Bard showed that sham rage could be elicited by brain lesions all the way down to the level of the **hypothalamus**. However, if the hypothalamus was removed, the rage did not occur, although some uncoordinated components of the behaviour were still observed. Thus, the hypothalamus was the critical structure associated with emotional behaviour. On this evidence, Bard concluded that the control of rage behaviour lay in the antagonistic relationship between the cerebral cortex and the hypothalamus. In short, although an intact cortex was necessary for receiving sensory stimulation and directing the emotional response properly, the coordinated pattern of emotional behaviour – including reflex movements and visceral responses – depended on the integrity of the hypothalamus.

Hypothalamic stimulation and aggression

Around the same time as Philip Bard was examining the behavioural effects of decortication, Walter Hess, working in Switzerland, was pioneering the technique of electrically stimulating the brain in freely moving animals (he examined the functions of many brain regions using this method and won a Nobel prize for his work in 1949). When Hess stimulated the hypothalamus, he found that it caused the ANS to be activated. More specifically, stimulating the posterior hypothalamic nuclei caused strong sympathetic activation, while stimulation of more anterior regions resulted in parasympathetic activity. In addition, Hess found that stimulation of the **medial hypothalamus** elicited a full-blown rage with sympathetic arousal, in which the cat arched its back with raised fur, hissed, and struck out aggressively towards a threatening object with unsheathed claws (Plate 5.1). Thus, unlike the rage produced by decortication, Hess showed that stimulation of the hypothalamus elicited an aggressive and threatening attack that was directed specifically *towards* an object.

These findings lent further support to the Cannon–Bard theory of emotion. Despite its small size, the hypothalamus was obviously involved in the control of the ANS, which was responsible for producing the body state associated with emotion. Moreover, it was also clear that stimulation of the hypothalamus caused certain types of species-specific emotional behaviour to be elicited. Thus, in terms of the Cannon–Bard model, it made sense to view the hypothalamus as an 'emotional' centre that received input from the sensory areas of the cerebral cortex and translated this into behaviour. Cannon also believed that the hypothalamus had a pathway that went back to the cerebral cortex, which informed the conscious part of the brain about the emotion it was experiencing.

Plate 5.1   Stimulation of the medial hypothalamus produces affective aggression. *Source*: Photograph depicting the neural aggression in cats. In *Neurophysiology and Emotion*, ed. Glass, Daniel C. © 1967 Russell Sage Foundation, 112 East 64th Street, New York, NY10021. Reprinted with permission

The Schachter–Singer theory of emotion

The cognitive-arousal theory

A study that cast doubt on certain aspects of the Cannon–Bard theory was undertaken by Schachter and Singer (1962). These researchers injected subjects with adrenaline to mimic the effects of sympathetic stimulation and cause physiological arousal. Some subjects were given accurate information about the physiological effects of the injection, while others were not informed of the drug's action. Individuals from both groups were then put into a room that, unknown to them, contained an actor who had been instructed to behave in a happy and euphoric manner, or be irritated and surly. Later, the subjects were questioned about their own emotional state following the social interaction. The results showed that the informed group experienced little emotional change in response to the situation, but the uninformed subjects reported much stronger feelings of euphoria or anger that closely matched the 'emotion' of the confederate.

What does this study tell us about emotion? Firstly, it supports the idea that the same type of physiological arousal can underlie different emotions as proposed by Cannon and Bard. But it also shows that this arousal provides important feedback that enables individuals to interpret what is happening to themselves. In other words, a bodily sensation such as a rapid heartbeat may serve as a signal to trigger emotion, although it is up to the person (i.e. the

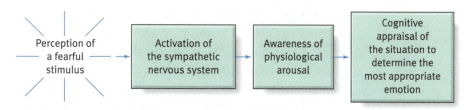

Figure 5.4   The Schachter–Singer theory of emotion

interpretation provided by the cerebral cortex) to decide what type of emotion he or she is experiencing. Thus, Schachter and Singer's experiment also lends some degree of support to the James–Lange theory, which views visceral responses as being the important determinants of emotion. But theory is only partially supported, as Schachter and Singer also show that one type of physiological arousal can produce different types of emotion. In short, the key to understanding different emotions lies with the cognitive interpretation of the event, including analysis of both internal body state and external situation (Figure 5.4).

What causes the body to produce an emotional physiological reaction in the first place? A consideration of this matter leads to the conclusion that the bodily changes must have been set in motion by the brain. In other words, the brain must have analysed the emotional situation on an unconscious level before activating the sympathetic system. Thus, the conscious interpretation of an emotion, as shown by Schachter and Singer, is only the final stage of the appraisal, and a significant amount of processing must occur before this takes place.

Does the same pattern of arousal underlie all emotions?

One of the main features of the Cannon–Bard theory of emotion, and supported by the findings of Schachter and Singer, is that there is one basic state of physiological arousal that underpins all emotion. However, not all researchers accept the *non-specificity* of arousal in emotion. For example, Ax (1953) measured 14 different physiological responses in a experiment that was designed to realistically invoke fear and anger. Essentially, subjects believed they were participating in a study measuring hypertension – although, unknown to them, the experimenter had enlisted the help of a confederate. This person either pretended to be an inept laboratory technician whose incompetence 'made real' the possibility of subjects receiving an electric shock from faulty equipment to elicit fear – or acted abusively to invoke anger. Although self-reports obtained from the subjects following the study confirmed that the confederate had been convincing and evoked the appropriate emotions, Ax nevertheless found that seven of the physiological measures were significantly different between the two emotional states. For example, he found that the increases in pulse rate and blood pressure were much greater when invoked by fear than by anger. In a similar vein, Funkenstein (1955) showed that while the adrenal glands respond to fear by releasing adrenaline, they react to anger by secreting noradrenaline.

More recently, Paul Ekman and his colleagues have provided evidence that distinct patterns of autonomic activity accompany different emotions (Ekman *et al.* 1983). These investigators asked subjects to make a facial expression for each of six emotions (anger, fear, sadness, happiness, surprise and disgust), or to imagine re-enacting a past emotional experience, during which a number of physiological variables were recorded. The results showed that a different pattern of autonomic arousal accompanied each emotion. For example, increased heart rate was found in response to anger and fear, but increased body temperature occurred only as a response to anger. Interestingly, a similar pattern of responses was also obtained from members of the Minangkabau tribe of western Sumatra, showing that these physiological changes may be universal (Levenson *et al.* 1992). However, this area of research is fraught with problems of interpretation, not least because of the difficulty in knowing whether the physiological differences are due to the nature of the emotion itself, or due to its severity (i.e. anger may produce a more severe emotion than imagined fear). On balance, it is probably the case that not all emotions are associated with the same type of autonomic arousal as the Cannon–Bard theory maintains – although this does not mean that each emotion has its own individual pattern of physiological activity, as held by the James–Lange theory. Thus, even if autonomic activity helps to differentiate some emotions, it is unlikely that it differentiates *all* emotions.

The facial feedback hypothesis

To further complicate matters, it is possible that feedback from other parts of the body that are not controlled by the ANS, such as the skeletal muscles, may also contribute to the sensation of emotion. For example, there is evidence that our facial expression may be an important determinant of how we feel. One way this can be tested is to ask subjects to perform movements of the face that correspond to a particular emotion, without letting them know what they are mimicking. Thus, subjects may be asked to follow a set of instructions such as 'pull your eyebrows down and together, raise your upper eyelids and tighten your lower eyelids, narrow your lips and press them together' (Ekman and Friesen 1978). In this case, the facial expression will resemble anger although this should not be obvious to the subject. Alternatively, subjects may be asked to clench a pen between their teeth to mimic a smile, or hold a pen between the lips to simulate a frown.

Experiments using these types of procedure have found that the acted facial expression can influence the subject's emotion. For example, when subjects were asked to judge a series of cartoons, those who had been biting a pen between their teeth (i.e. 'smiling') rated them as funnier compared with those who were 'frowning' (Strack *et al.* 1988). Alternatively, when subjects performed either happy, angry or neutral movements of the face while watching neutral or emotionally charged slides, they reported feeling happier when making a happy face, and angrier when making an angry expression (Rutlidge and Hupka 1985).

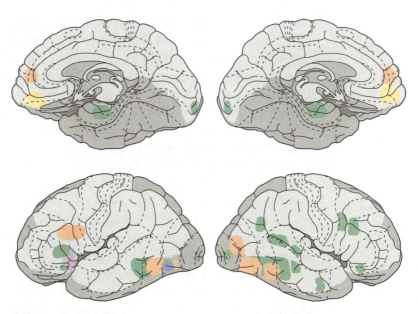

Figure 5.5 Patterns of activation obtained from fMRI scans for different brain regions after subjects viewed black and white photographs of neutral faces or emotional ones (e.g. sad, frightened, happy or angry). The regions in green depict brain regions that exhibit more activity in response to neutral faces. The other regions depict more activity in response to faces showing a given emotion: red represents angry; purple represents frightened; yellow represents happy; and blue represents sad. *Source*: Banich, Marie T., *Cognitive Neuroscience and Neuropsychology*, second edition. Copyright © 2004 by Houghton Mifflin Company. Used with permission

Perhaps these findings should not surprise us. The brain is an extremely complex organ which uses all of the information at its disposal to interpret what is happening to it. Indeed, recent studies have shown that the brain uses specialised regions to identify different emotional expressions in people (see Figure 5.5). Thus, it is probably the case that the experience of emotion can occur as a result of cognitive appraisal (and unconscious processing) in the absence of visceral feedback. Nonetheless, it may also be that bodily feedback, whether from the ANS or from the skeletal muscles, is helpful in allowing the brain to produce a more appropriate and subtle emotional response. Indeed, such feedback may be an important factor in 'colouring' our emotional state and creating a 'harmony' between our conscious and unconscious being.

Introduction to the limbic system

As we have seen, the hypothalamus is an important structure in the production of emotions, but this structure is actually part of a much larger brain region called the **limbic system**. The existence of the limbic system was first recognised in 1878 by Paul Broca, who identified a group of interconnected structures lying underneath the cerebral cortex. These structures formed a border between the cortex and the upper brainstem and, for this reason, Broca called it the limbic lobe (from the Latin word *limbus* meaning 'border'). This region is now called the limbic system and includes a number of different structures such as the **cingulate cortex**, **hippocampus**, **amygdala** and **septum**. Although Broca was interested in the functions of the limbic lobe, he seems to have given little thought to its possible role in emotion. Instead, he and other researchers tended to emphasise its importance in olfaction, and it become widely known as the rhinencephalon ('nose brain').

In 1937, the neurologist James Papez highlighted the involvement of the limbic system in emotion. His ideas were largely based on the work of Cannon and Bard, who had made the distinction between the behavioural expression of emotion (requiring the hypothalamus), and the subjective 'feeling' of emotion (which was believed to occur in the cerebral cortex). In agreement with this theory, Papez viewed the hypothalamus as being responsible for the bodily expression of emotion via its control of the SNS. However, he visualised the circuit for the 'feeling' of emotion as being more complex. Papez believed that the neural basis for experiencing emotion began in the hypothalamus, but information was then passed upwards to the **anterior thalamus** (via the mammillary bodies) and in to the cingulate cortex. At this point, Papez believed that the pathway split into two: one route going to the **frontal cortex**, where the emotion was made conscious, and the other back to the hypothalamus via a multi-synaptic route involving the hippocampus and **fornix** (Figure 5.6). In this

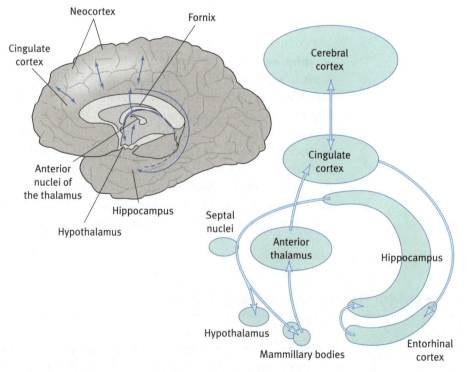

Figure 5.6 The main structures of the Papez circuit. *Source*: M.F. Bear, B.W. Connors and M.A. Paradiso, *Neuroscience: Exploring the Brain*, p.438, fig. 16.4 Copyright © 1996 by Lippincott Williams & Wilkins

scheme, the hypothalamus and cerebral cortex were part of a large neural circuit whose function was to link the behavioural expression of emotion with its subjective feeling.

The importance of the limbic system was further emphasised in 1952 by Paul MacLean, who proposed that it formed one of three major divisions of the brain. The three divisions in his view were, (1) the reptilian brain, responsible for vital life functions and stereotyped action; (2) the old mammalian or 'limbic' brain, involved in emotional behaviour; and (3) the new mammalian brain, or neo-cortex, concerned with higher cognition. MacLean also saw the limbic system and cerebral cortex interacting together, with the former being responsible for what we 'feel', and the latter being responsible for what we 'know'. This view was also consistent with the James–Lange theory of emotion.

The Kluver–Bucy syndrome

Some of the most striking evidence for the involvement of the limbic system in emotional behaviour came in the late 1930s when Heinrich Kluver and Paul Bucy found that bilateral removal of the temporal lobes, which included the amygdala and parts of the hippocampus, had a dramatic effect on reducing fear in rhesus monkeys. Normally these animals are highly aggressive, but Kluver and Bucy found that they became docile and showed no signs of fear or rage following lesioning. These monkeys also exhibited a number of other bizarre behaviours. For example, they were hypersexual, as shown by frequent masturbation and indiscriminate attempts to mate with other male and female monkeys. They were also obsessed with touching everything they saw, and did not seem to recognise objects unless they were able to pick them up and put them in their mouths. Kluver and Bucy called this phenomenon 'psychic blindness' (Kluver and Bucy 1938).

The amygdala

One problem with the work of Kluver and Bucy was that their lesions had destroyed a large brain area (the temporal lobes) that included parts of the cerebral cortex and limbic system. Thus, they set about trying to identify more precisely the part of the temporal lobe that was responsible for the taming effect they had observed. Their research showed that one brain region was particularly important – the amygdala. This structure is located in the anterior tip of the temporal lobe and contains two main regions: the phylogenetically 'old' **corticomedial nuclei** and the 'newer' **basolateral nuclei**. Both these nuclei

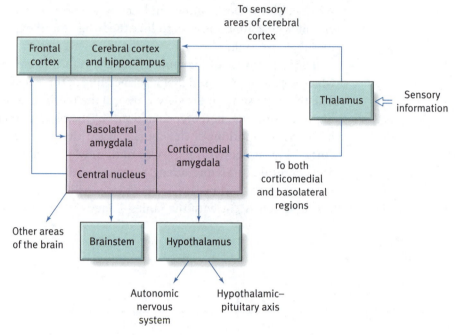

Figure 5.7 The main anatomical connections of the amygdala

receive extensive input from the cerebral cortex, including areas involved in sensory and memory processing. In turn, the corticomedial amygdala projects directly to the hypothalamus, whereas the basolateral nuclei have more diffuse projections that first pass to the **central nucleus of the amygdala** before they are sent to many regions of the brain – including a pathway to the frontal cortex. The site of the amygdala suggests that it occupies a pivotal link in the circuitry of neural pathways involved in emotion (Figure 5.7).

Despite this, not all researchers were able to replicate Kluver and Bucy's findings. For example, Bard and Mountcastle (1948) found that removal of the amygdala produced animals that exhibited *increased* rage and emotion, and this has been confirmed on occasion by others. Why lesions of the amygdala can produce such contrasting effects is not clear. One reason may lie with its structural complexity (the amygdala contains 22 separate nuclei) and it is possible that researchers have produced different patterns of damage. Indeed, slight variations in the size and location of lesions is likely to produce discrepant results as the amygdala has both excitatory and inhibitory effects on emotion and aggression, and the regions involved in these behaviours all lie in close proximity. However, it is also the case that the animal's previous learning may have a significant bearing on how the amygdala lesion manifests itself. For example, Rosvold *et al.* (1954) lesioned the amygdala in the most dominant and aggressive monkey of a group of eight, and found that this animal quickly dropped to the bottom of the dominance hierarchy. However, when a similar lesion was made in the third most dominant monkey, there was no decline in aggressive behaviour or status. A possible explanation is that the effects of the amygdala lesion are dependent upon the monkey's previous experience. For example, the aggressive monkey may have learned to become successful at fighting, and the amygdala lesion possibly interfered with this behaviour more than it did in the less experienced animal.

The effects of amygdala stimulation in humans

The case of Julia S

Some of the most dramatic evidence showing that the amygdala is involved in emotional and aggressive behaviour has come from its stimulation in humans. The use of electrodes to stimulate areas of the brain is more common than many people realise, as it is used by neurosurgeons in the surgical treatment of epilepsy. Prior to removing areas of epileptic tissue, a surgeon needs to determine that the surgery will not have debilitating effects on language and movement, and to do this they can stimulate the brain areas in question with a gentle electrical current. Since the brain contains no pain or touch receptors, electrodes can be placed in an awake patient without discomfort, providing the scalp has been anaesthetised. The surgeon can therefore stimulate the brain and observe its behavioural consequences (e.g. making sure it does not cause limb movements or arrest language) or ask the patient about its mental effects. Perhaps the best-known use of this technique was undertaken by Wilder Penfield, who used it to map out the human motor cortex in the 1950s. He also found that if such stimulation was applied to other areas of the cerebral cortex it could produce various feelings and memory 'flashbacks'.

The amygdala is a site in the brain, along with the adjacent hippocampus, where abnormal neural activity can result in temporal lobe epilepsy (sometimes called a complex partial seizure). This type of epilepsy does not always elicit an external fit, but may produce a semi-unconscious state sometimes called an 'absence', accompanied by odd automated behaviour (e.g. the individuals may repeatedly button and unbutton their clothes, or drum their fingers on a table). In addition, this type of epilepsy can be associated with visual and olfactory hallucinations, feelings of *déjà vu*, and occasionally behavioural disorders, including episodes of aggression and fear. One patient who exhibited signs of this disorder was Julia S, who, at the time of her operation, was a 22-year-old woman with a history of violent behaviour. Julia had begun to experience epileptic seizures consisting of brief lapses of consciousness, lip-smacking and chewing at the age of 10. In between seizures, Julia often had severe temper tantrums and on numerous occasions exhibited violent behaviour. The most serious attack occurred when Julia was 18 years old and watching a cinema movie with her parents. She began to feel unwell and visited the wash room, where she looked into a mirror and perceived herself as 'shrivelled, disfigured and evil'. At this point, another girl accidentally brushed against her, and Julia, who was holding a knife, turned around and stabbed her in the heart (fortunately the victim survived).

Julia was examined by the Boston neurosurgeon Vernon Mark, who implanted electrodes into her temporal lobes and found that her seizures were originating from the amygdala. In his first operation, Mark lesioned Julia's left amygdala. Unfortunately, this produced little behavioural improvement and led Mark to perform a second operation in which he lesioned the right amygdala. However, prior to this operation, Mark decided to stimulate Julia's remaining amygdala with a 'stimo-ceiver', which not only allowed the implanted electrodes to generate current from a radio transmitter, but also do this without her knowledge (Julia and her parents had agreed to this procedure beforehand). Although Mark stimulated a number of her electrodes, there was only one that elicited rage behaviour, and he stimulated this particular electrode on two occasions. On the first occasion Julia was sitting on her bed. Following stimulation, she began to show facial grimacing and lip retraction, which resembled a primate threat display. Then, suddenly, she lurched and attacked the wall with her fists. On the second occasion, Julia's right amygdala was stimulated while she was singing and playing a guitar. After 5 seconds of stimulation she stopped, stared blankly ahead, and was unresponsive to questioning by her psychiatrist. This was followed by a sudden and powerful swing of the guitar, which narrowly missed the psychiatrist and smashed against the wall (Mark and Ervin 1970).

These results show that electrical stimulation of the amygdala can produce violent behaviour in humans, although it must also be pointed out that such stimulation does not cause aggression in most individuals. In fact, a feeling of fear and anxiety is much more likely when the amygdala is stimulated to detect epileptic tissue (see also next section). Whatever the ethics of Julia's demonstration, the second operation proved to be a great success. Mark destroyed a small amount of tissue that was located at the tip of the electrode that had caused the aggression, and shortly afterwards Julia experienced no rage attacks or temporal lobe seizures – and this has continued to the present day.

The amygdala and fear

All higher animals show fear in response to threatening situations, and this can also be demonstrated in the laboratory. For example, one way to produce fear is through **classical conditioning**, in which an animal (typically a rat) is presented with a stimulus such as a light or tone, which is followed by an electric shock. After a few paired trials, the rat will typically begin to exhibit fear in response to the stimulus (e.g. it will freeze, show increased blood pressure and heart rate, and will startle easily). In other words, the animal will show a conditioned emotional response that can be quantified using behavioural and physiological measurements.

This type of fear conditioning has also been used to examine the functional role of the amygdala. For example, Bruce Kapp and his colleagues performed an experiment where they presented rabbits with two tones, one of which was always followed by an electric shock, and one that had no punishing consequence. During the conditioning, Kapp also recorded the electrical activity from cells in the central nucleus of the amygdala. The results showed that, prior to training, the neurons in the amygdala failed to respond to the tones – although after learning, they fired to the shock-related tone, but not to the harmless stimulus. Kapp also found that the rabbit's heart rate developed a 'fearful' anticipatory response to the tone that was associated with shock, but not to the one that was neutral. However, this physiological response was abolished by lesions of the central nucleus of the amygdala, indicating that this area was a crucial part of the system in which fear is expressed by the sympathetic nervous system (Kapp *et al.* 1979, 1984).

This conclusion is supported by experiments that have examined the amygdala using electrical stimulation. As might be expected this procedure often produces behaviours associated with fear. For example, stimulation of the amygdala in animals may cause a sharp increase in respiration, heart rate and vigilance. Moreover, certain amygdala sites elicit 'fearful' escape behaviour or aggression. Indeed, in cases where the amygdala has been electrically stimulated in humans to identify epileptic tissue prior to surgery, patients typically exhibit changes in autonomic nervous activity and frequently report feeling fear and anxiety. In some instances this feeling may be so intense that the patient emits a terrifying scream and acts as if he or she is in the grips of the most extreme terror (Gloor 1990).

Neural circuits for learned fear

The classical conditioning technique can also be used to examine the pathways that connect the amygdala with other brain areas involved in producing fear. At first sight, it might be expected that the amygdala would receive its main sensory input from the cerebral cortex. Indeed, it is known that auditory information (e.g. a tone signalling an electric shock) goes to the **auditory cortex**, which, in turn, has neural connections with the amygdala. Thus, this route is the obvious one for auditory information to reach the amygdala. However, Joseph LeDoux has shown that there is another pathway (Figure 5.8). He lesioned the auditory cortex and found that animals were still able to learn a fearful conditioned emotional response (CER) involving tone stimuli. However, lesions made to subcortical structures involved in the early stages of auditory processing such as the **inferior colliculi** and **auditory thalamus** abolished conditioned fear responding. Thus, auditory input does not have to reach the cerebral cortex before it is received by the amygdala. Instead, there is a more important subcortical route. These two routes to the amygdala have been called the 'high' and 'low' roads (LeDoux 1998).

This finding perhaps should not surprise us. Animals and humans require a quick alarm mechanism to respond to a potentially dangerous stimulus, and this is what subcortical input to the amygdala allows. In fact, it appears that the thalamus activates the amygdala at around the same time as it activates the cortex – an arrangement that probably enables fear responses to begin in the amygdala before we are completely aware of what is happening to us. Indeed, failing to respond to danger for most animals is likely to prove fatal and it is thus better

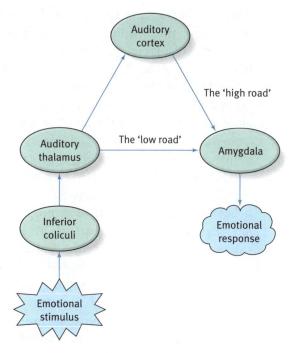

Figure 5.8 The 'low' and 'high' roads to the amygdala

to be safe than sorry. Thus, the subcortical route to the amygdala allows for this quick 'react first – think later' response to take place (LeDoux 1994).

Nevertheless, the cortical route to the amygdala is still important because it enables us to form a more accurate representation of the fear-provoking stimulus. Cortical analysis also allows us to consciously interpret what is happening to us, and make decisions based on knowledge and previous experience. Interestingly, the amygdala also receives input from the hippocampus that appears to alert it to dangerous environments. For example, Phillips and LeDoux (1992) found that lesions to the hippocampus had no effect on a rat's ability to learn a conditioned emotional response (CER). But when these animals were later placed in the apparatus in which they had been conditioned, they showed no fearful responses (unlike normal animals). This example shows that frightening events can be complex and require simultaneous analysis of many different aspects of the situation.

LeDoux and his colleagues have also examined the output pathways from the amygdala involved in producing fearful responses. To do this they lesioned various structures 'downstream' from the central nucleus of the amygdala (which, as we have seen above, is involved in activating the ANS), and determined the extent to which these lesions interfered with the behavioural expression of a CER. The results showed that at least two pathways were involved, with lesions of the **lateral hypothalamus** interfering with conditioned changes in blood pressure, and damage to the **periaqueductal grey matter** (located at the top of the brainstem) disrupting the expression of the freezing response. Other pathways from the amygdala are involved in producing startle responses and controlling the release of 'fear' hormones.

(a) The anatomical location of the amygdala

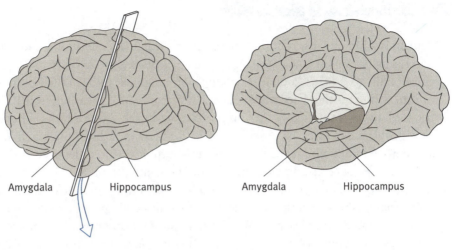

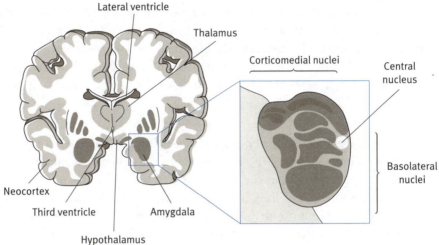

(b) Proposed neural circuits for learned fear

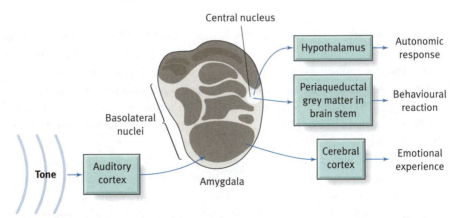

Figure 5.9   The different outputs of the amygdala for the behavioural expression of fear.
Source: M.F. Bear, B.W. Connors and M.A. Paradiso, *Neuroscience: Exploring the Brain.*
Copyright © 1996 by Lippincott Williams & Wilkins

Autism and the amygdala

Autism is a lifelong disorder that manifests itself in early childhood and was first described by Leo Kanner in 1943. One of the main signs of autism is an inability to communicate and relate emotionally to others. Autistic individuals often appear to be in their own world and unaware of others (in fact the word autism is derived from *autos* meaning 'self'). Thus, many autistic people have great difficulty learning to engage in the give and take of everyday interaction. This problem can often be observed in the first few months of life when an autistic baby may avoid eye contact with its parents, and resist attention and affection. Although the child may passively accept hugs and cuddling, he or she generally prefers to be alone. This type of un-responsiveness often continues into adulthood and severely affects the person's ability to form relationships. Another characteristic of autism is poor use of language. About half of autistic children never learn to speak and are mute throughout life. Those who do speak often use language in unusual ways, with some being unable to combine words into sentences, and others just using single words. Others repeat the same phrase no matter what the situation. The tone of voice may also be 'flat' and 'robot-like', and be accompanied by inappropriate facial movements and gestures. Despite this, some autistic people have unique skills. Like the person played by Dustin Hoffman in the movie *Rainman*, some can memorise entire television shows, pages of the phone book, or the scores of every major league baseball game for the past 20 years.

The prevalence of autism is about 30–40 per 100,000 children, and it is about four times more common in boys than in girls. The cause of autism is unknown, although genetic factors are believed to be important as the condition is at least 50 times more frequent in the siblings of affected persons than in the general population. Twin studies also show a concordance rate of around 60 per cent for identical twins, in contrast to fraternal twins, where there is no con-cordance. Despite this, many researchers now believe the disorder could have its origins in early pregnancy. Not only is there an increased frequency of complications in pregnancy and childbirth in mothers who give birth to autistic children, but there is some evidence that foetal exposure to toxins, metabolic disorders or viral infections can also cause autism.

It is now generally accepted that autism is caused by abnormalities in certain brain structures. Indeed, postmortem studies have shown that some autistic brains have a smaller brainstem with the near absence of the facial nucleus (which controls facial expression) and superior olive, which is a relay for auditory input (Rodier 2000). In addition, magnetic resonance imaging (MRI) studies have shown that the temporal, parietal and occipital lobes are often bigger in autistic brains, which may reflect immature development (Piven 1997). Despite this, the corpus callosum has been reported as being smaller (Egaas *et al.* 1995). Perhaps the most interesting finding concerns the amygdala. This brain region is involved not only in anxiety, but also in the recognition of faces. Indeed, when 'normal' subjects are given a face recogni-tion task, they show increased activity in the amygdala and adjacent temporal lobes. In autism, however, the amygdala is not only larger in size, but it has also been found to have no involvement in face recognition, as shown by functional MRI (Pierce *et al.* 2001). In autism, this function appears to be taken over by other 'aberrant' brain sites.

The frontal lobes

Another brain structure that has extensive connections with the limbic system, and which has been implicated in emotion, is the frontal lobes. In humans, the frontal lobes make up about one-third of the entire cerebral cortex and are generally viewed as being important for abstract thinking and self-awareness. The anterior (front) part of the lobe is often referred to as the **prefrontal cortex** and is divided into a **dorsolateral area** and an **orbitofrontal region**. Of particular interest is the orbitofrontal region, which lies at the base of the frontal lobes and gets its name because it lies just above the orbits (the bones that form the eye sockets). This region receives input from the amygdala via the **dorsolateral thalamus** and projects, in turn, to several regions of the limbic system including the cingulate cortex, hippocampus, lateral hypothalamus and amygdala (Figure 5.10).

Some of the earliest evidence linking the frontal lobes with emotion was reported in 1868 by Harlow, who described the case of Phineas Gage, a railroad foreman who in 1848 suffered a horrifying accident where an explosion shot an iron rod (measuring 100 cm long and 2.5 cm in diameter, and weighing almost 6 kg) like a bullet through his cheek and out of the top of his skull (landing some 30 metres away!). Remarkably, not only did Gage regain consciousness soon after the accident, and was able to talk with his companions who led him away from the scene for medical assistance, but, at first sight at least, the injury appeared to have little effect on his behaviour. In the weeks and months following the accident, however, Gage began to show marked changes in his personality. He had been described as 'the most efficient and capable' employee in the company, but after the injury he started to lose interest in work. He became rude and disrespectful to fellow workers and paid little attention to advice from others, particularly if it

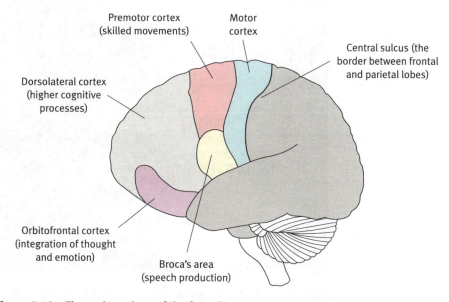

Figure 5.10   The main regions of the frontal cortex

conflicted with his own desires. He also experienced great difficulty in planning an action and carrying it through to its conclusion, and was particularly inept at successfully carrying out tasks that required responsibility. However, this seemed not to bother him as he became emotionally apathetic and childish. Phineas Gage was fired from his position of foreman and never again regained full employment, although he was to find various types of temporary work until his death from a severe epileptic fit 11 years later (Macmillan 1996).

It is not known for certain what parts of his brain were damaged by the accident because no autopsy was performed at the time of Gage's death. However, John Harlow (the physician who first reported Gage's case) was permitted to exhume the body several years later, and he estimated from the skull that damage had occurred mainly to the left anterior part of the frontal lobes, including the orbitofrontal cortex. The skull was in fact preserved in a museum at Harvard Medical School and was recently re-examined using magnetic resonance imaging (Damasio *et al.* 1994). This new analysis indicated that the rod severely damaged the frontal lobes of both hemispheres, with damage being especially marked in the left orbitofrontal cortex (Figure 5.11).

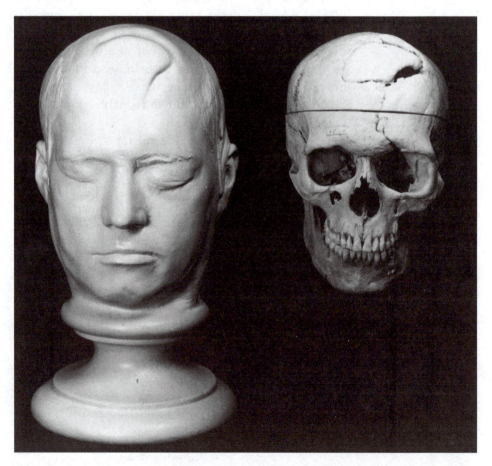

Figure 5.11 Death mask and skull (showing exterior damage) of Phineas Gage. *Source*: The Warren Anatomical Museum, Harvard Medical School

Frontal lobe surgery

In the years following Gage's accident a number of other clinical cases were reported that linked the frontal cortex with behavioural and personality change. However, there was a general reluctance to view the frontal cortex as being involved in emotion. That was until 1935, when John Fulton and Carlyle Jacobsen accidentally found that frontal lobe lesions had a calming effect on chimpanzees. This finding was to have far-reaching consequences. On hearing about this work, the Portuguese neurologist Egas Moniz had the idea that similar lesions could be used to treat emotionally disturbed patients. Indeed, within a few months, Moniz had persuaded neurosurgeon Almeider Lima to help him to perform the operation on one of his patients, thus producing the first prefrontal lobotomy. The operation, which involved severing the main connections between the frontal lobes and the rest of the brain with cutting devices called leucotomes, was so successful that it soon became widely used by other doctors. Moniz also won a Nobel prize in 1949 for his work – although, tragically, this was not before he had been shot and made paraplegic by one of his lobotomised patients.

A number of surgical operations involving different brain areas evolved from Moniz's work. One procedure, called transorbital lobotomy, could even be performed in the physician's surgery without hospitalisation. This involved a leucotome that was positioned beneath the upper eyelid and driven through the bottom of the cranium into the brain by a mallet! This instrument was then swept back and forth so that it severed the white matter connecting the orbitofrontal cortex and subcortical areas (Figure 5.12). This technique, which became known as 'ice-pick' **psychosurgery**, was performed on thousands of patients in the United States in the 1940s. One reason for its popularity was that

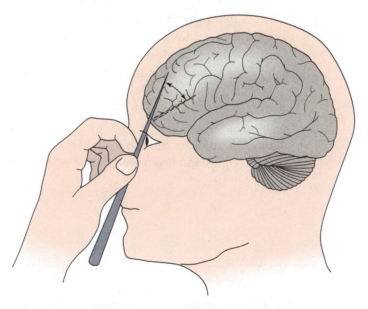

Figure 5.12 'Ice-pick' surgery. *Source*: Adapted from W. Freeman, *Proceedings of the Royal Society of Medicine*, 1949, 42 (suppl.), 8–12

it left no obvious scar. However, many other types of surgical lesioning were developed around this time (i.e. before the advent of modern drug therapy) and it has been estimated that 50,000 patients received psychosurgery during the 1940s and 1950s in the USA alone (Culliton 1976).

Psychosurgery – that is, the use of brain lesions to treat psychiatric illness in the absence of any identifiable brain damage – is still performed today, although, in the UK, less than 100 such operations are carried out each year (Lader and Herrington 1990). Nonetheless, in the past, lobotomy was often successful in reducing the patient's emotional suffering – particularly in cases of depression, anxiety, obsessions and compulsions. Unfortunately, these operations also tended to produce a variety of other problems. For example, lobotomised patients were often found to have difficulty solving problems and following instructions. In addition, emotions tended to be flattened, which often led to patients having no social inhibitions, and little concern about the consequences of their actions. Thus, in some respects, these patients were like Phineas Gage. Despite this, the use of psychosurgery still has its advocates (Ballantine *et al.* 1987) and it may be that, in some cases, the drawbacks of surgery are preferable to its disadvantages. However, not everyone agrees (Breggin 1993).

What, then, is the role of the orbitofrontal cortex in emotional behaviour? An interesting study bearing on this question was undertaken by Eslinger and Damasio (1985), who described a 35-year-old man (known simply by the initials EVR) who had extensive bilateral damage to the orbitofrontal cortex caused by a tumour (which was successfully removed). Following his operation, Eslinger and Damasio tested EVR and found that he had superior intelligence on IQ tests and above normal comprehension of complex social and political issues. He was also capable of sound social judgement when given hypothetical 'moral dilemma' situations that required him to make a decision about whether a certain behaviour in a given situation was right or wrong. He provided convincing and sensible answers to these type of problems and justified them with reasoned logic. However, his own behaviour did not follow the same rules when he was confronted with real-life problems, and this often resulted in disastrous consequences at work or in his personal relationships. In fact, he was described by acquaintances as irresponsible, disorganised, obsessive and lazy. He was also extremely detached and showed very little emotion (Damasio 1994). Thus, the orbitofrontal cortex may not be necessarily involved in making judgements about situational events – but, rather, it translates these judgements into appropriate feelings and behaviours in the real world.

Anxiety

Fear is an important reaction because it protects us from dangerous and potentially life-threatening situations. Although fear tends not to be an everyday occurrence, most of us experience a related emotion called **anxiety**. Anxiety is usually distinguished from fear by the lack of an immediate external threat – that is, anxiety comes from within us, and fear from outside (LeDoux 1998). For example, the sight of a snake in long grass may elicit fear, but the anticipation that the grass may be harbouring a snake causes anxiety. Thus, anxiety can also be viewed as fearful anticipation which typically occurs in situations that are not inherently dangerous. Both anxiety and fear share a similar biological basis, with increased activation of the SNS, although the physiological arousal tends to be less intense but more prolonged in anxiety. For most of us, this is no bad thing as anxiety helps to increase apprehension and caution while acting as a brake against excessive or careless behaviour. Thus, anxiety is a useful albeit unpleasant necessity of life. Unfortunately, for some people, anxiety can be so intense that it loses its adaptive function and causes mental dysfunction and general ill health.

Anxiety becomes a clinical disorder when it occurs for no good reason, or is more intense than is justified by the perceived threat. In clinical practice, anxiety disorders are common and it has been estimated that around 15 per cent of the population will suffer from an anxiety disorder at some time in their lives. These disorders can take many forms. Phobias or irrational fears are the most common type of anxiety problem with a prevalence of about 13.5 per cent in the population, followed by obsessive–compulsive disorder (2.5 per cent) and panic disorders (2.5 per cent) (Holmes 1991). However, these figures probably represent just the tip of the iceberg as many of us also suffer periods of anxiety from the pressures of modern life. Indeed, it is thought that as many as 30 per cent of patients seen in general practice have problems that are due in some way to anxiety (Beaumont 1991). Thus, anxiety has a significant bearing upon our health and well-being.

Obsessive–compulsive disorder

Obsessive–compulsive disorder (OCD) is a condition characterised by the intrusion of thoughts (obsessions) that lead to patterns of strange and ritualistic behaviour (compulsions). The most common type of compulsion is hand-washing, accompanied by obsessive thoughts about dirt and contamination. This may be so severe that the person washes his or her hands over a hundred times each day, and uses paper towels when touching objects. A compulsion to check lights, doors, locks or electric switches over and over before leaving the house is another frequent manifestation of OCD. In other cases, OCD may take the form of strange doorway rituals. For example, Rapoport (1989) reports the case of a man who had to take 74 steps in a specific zigzag pattern before he could enter his front door. There are others who engage in rituals that involve rolling about on the grass and touching various trees before entering doors. This behaviour is often embarrassing for the individual, and the obsessive thoughts can also be repugnant. Yet the thoughts remain persistent and the person is compelled to perform them at whatever cost. OCD is classified as an anxiety disorder because of the severe anxiety that is felt if the intrusive thoughts are not acted upon. The disorder

Obsessive–compulsive disorder continued.

is also surprisingly common. It is estimated that more than 2 per cent of the population suffer from OCD, making it more common than schizophrenia, manic depression or panic disorder.

Clinical trials in recent years have shown that drugs that affect the neurotransmitter serotonin (5-HT) can significantly improve the symptoms of OCD. The first of these drugs to be discovered (in the early 1980s) was the 5-HT uptake blocker, clomipramine. This was followed by drugs with a similar action, including fluoxetine (Prozac) and fluvoxamine. Large-scale studies have shown that at least 60 per cent of patients show a significant improvement with these drugs – especially if combined with behavioural therapy. The discovery of clomipramine was also important since it indicated that OCD could be due to 5-HT dysfunction. However, the nature of this dysfunction remains unclear. Although some people with OCD have higher levels of the 5-HT metabolite 5-HIAA in their CSF, indicating overactivity of 5-HT in the brain, this is not always found. The fact that drug treatment often requires several weeks to become effective suggest that changes in the sensitivity of certain 5-HT receptors may be a more important causal factor.

Although much remains to be learned about the role of 5-HT in OCD, there is strong evidence that the anatomical basis of the disorder involves the basal ganglia and frontal cortex. For example, studies using positron emission tomography (PET) have shown that resting blood flow and glucose metabolism are abnormally increased in the frontal orbital cortex and caudate nucleus. Moreover, when OCD patients are exposed to phobic stimulation (e.g. skin contact with dirty objects), blood flow increases even more in the orbital cortex and caudate nucleus – along with the putamen, thalamus and anterior cingulate cortex (Baxter 1995). As we saw in the previous chapter, the striatum has long been implicated in movement, and the frontal cortex in emotion and planning. Thus, the involvement, and dysfunction, of these two brain regions in OCD makes a great deal of sense, especially as they both receive 5-HT innervation from the raphe nuclei.

Anxiolytic drugs

Humans have always used drugs to help them to cope with the stresses of life. Alcohol, opium and barbiturates are just some of the substances that have been used to sedate and reduce anxiety. However, in the early 1960s a new class of drugs was developed that reduced anxiety without producing sedation. These were the **benzodiazepines** (BZPs), which included diazepam (Valium) and chlordiazepoxide (Librium), and within a decade of their introduction they had become the most heavily prescribed type of drug in the world. The extent of their popularity can be gauged by annual prescription figures for the UK, which slowly rose from the early 1960s to reach 18 million prescriptions in 1972, and

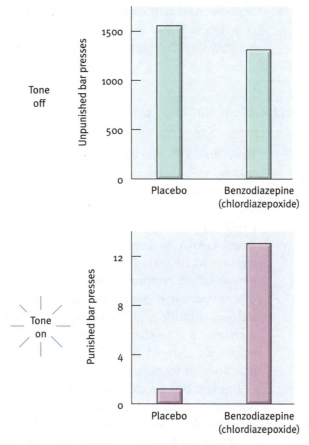

Figure 5.13   The effects that benzodiazepines have on punished responding (as recorded by the number of bar presses) in the Gellar conflict test

to over 30 million by 1979 (Beaumont 1991). Although there has since been a decline in their use, there are still around 1.2 million long-term BZP users in the UK and several million worldwide (Ashton 1992). Because of their addictive potential, BZPs are now more commonly used as short-term hypnotics (sleeping tablets) than for the relief of anxiety.

BZPs also appear to reduce anxiety in animals. One way this can be tested is to examine the effects of these drugs in a conflict test (Gellar 1962). In this situation, a rat is first trained to press a lever in an operant box for food reward. Following conditioning, a hungry rat is put back into the box, but this time whenever a tone is 'on', a lever press delivers food accompanied by a mild electric shock. Drug-free rats quickly become very 'anxious' during the tone presentation, and despite their hunger will typically stop pressing the lever. However, if these animals are given a BZP they often continue to work the lever as before (Figure 5.13). Since BZPs neither increase hunger nor suppress pain, it appears that they are acting on the conflict itself, thereby making the animal less 'anxious' about being punished. Similar results can also be obtained with barbiturates and alcohol, except that these drugs also cause sedation and a depression of responding in both unpunished (tone-off) and punished (tone-on) conditions. This does not occur with BZPs (except at very high doses), indicating that they exert a genuine anxiolytic effect.

The neurochemical basis of anxiety

How do BZPs work? Until relatively recently, their pharmacological action was not fully understood. However, in 1977 a breakthrough occurred when it was found that BZPs have their own specific receptor (Squires and Braestrup 1977). That is, certain neurons in the brain have receptors that are highly selective for BZPs. In fact, the BZP receptor turned out to be a site on the much larger **GABA-A** receptor that is typically found on postsynaptic neurons. As we saw in Chapter 1, (see page 23), the GABA-A receptor is an example of an ionotropic receptor consisting of five elongated proteins arranged in a shape of a cylinder that passes through the neuron's membrane. These proteins form a closed chloride channel. However, when GABA binds to the receptor, it causes a change in the shape of the proteins forming the ion channel that allows negatively charged chloride ions to flow into the neuron, where they produce inhibition of its resting potential.

It might be expected that BZP receptors act in a similar fashion – namely, by opening the chloride channels. In fact, research shows that BZPs do not open the chloride channel by themselves – rather, they facilitate the effects of GABA. That is, if the BZP receptor is stimulated along with the GABA-A receptor, there is greater neural inhibition (i.e. the chloride ion channel remains open for a longer period) than if the GABA-A receptor is stimulated by itself. This facilitatory action is known as 'alloseric modulation'. Both alcohol and barbiturates have a similar effect on GABA-A receptors by an alloseric mechanism.

BZP receptors are found throughout the brain, with highest numbers located in the basal ganglia, cerebellum, cerebral cortex and limbic system (especially the amygdala). This distribution helps to explain the muscle relaxant, cognitive and emotional effects, respectively, of the BZPs. But why should the brain have receptors for BZPs in the first place? The obvious answer is that the brain presumably makes its own kind of BZP that acts on the receptor. Indeed, a number of endogenous substances have been found in the brain that bind to BZP receptors including a class of drugs called the β-carbolines, and a peptide called diazepam-binding inhibitor. However, these substances increase anxiety rather than reduce it! In other words, the substances produced by the brain do not appear to function as anxiolytics.

The function of the BZP receptor has been found to be very complex. While BZPs such as diazepam facilitate the action of GABA, other substances (such as RO 19-4603) which act on the same receptor have been shown to decrease GABA's ability to open chloride channels. A drug that produces an effect on a receptor opposite the main one is called an **inverse agonist**. In fact, the BZP receptor was the first one to be found in the CNS where this type of bidirectional effect was shown to occur. To make matters more complex, there are other substances such as flumazenil that are true antagonists at the BZP receptor, (i.e. they block the effects of agonists and inverse agonists). This shows that the role of endogenous 'BZPs' in the brain may be potentially very complex, with some substances having anxiogenic (anxiety-inducing) effects, and others acting as anxiolytics.

New developments

Because of the addictive potential and side-effects associated with the use of BZPs, attempts have been made in recent years to develop alternative drugs for the treatment of anxiety. One such substance is **buspirone** (BuSpar), first introduced into clinical practice in 1986. This drug has been shown to be as effective as diazepam in the treatment of anxiety, but with fewer side-effects. Buspirone does not cause sedation or muscle relaxation, or interact with alcohol – and, more importantly, it does not cause dependence or withdrawal symptoms. For example, in one study, patients underwent BZP or buspirone treatment for six months, after which they were switched to placebo. The results showed that 80 per cent of the BZP group suffered side-effects, including the recurrence of original symptoms, which required them to resort to 'reserve' medication – while none of the buspirone group reported withdrawal symptoms or a need for extra drug treatment (Rickells *et al.* 1988).

Interestingly, buspirone is structurally unrelated to the BZPs, and does not bind to BZP or GABA receptors. Although buspirone has a complex pharmacological action that includes blocking both dopamine D-2 and noradrenergic alpha-2 receptors (see Chapter 11), it appears to produce its main anxiolytic effect by having an agonist effect on serotonergic 5-HT_{1A} receptors. These receptors are found in high concentrations postsynaptically in the hippocampus, amygdala and dorsal raphe, and when stimulated they act to reduce neuronal excitability in these structures. Indeed, because buspirone inhibits dorsal raphe neurons, this also results in a reduction of serotonin release throughout the brain, including the striatum and cerebral cortex. The discovery of buspirone has led drug companies to search for new 5-HT_{1A} agonists, which are known collectively as second-generation anxiolytics.

Unfortunately, buspirone has a slower onset of action than the BZPs and it may take up to two weeks before it has an anxiolytic effect, which limits its usefulness in treating sudden or short-term anxiety. Moreover, buspirone is not effective in alleviating anxiety associated with BZP withdrawal. Despite this, the discovery of buspirone, along with the fact that at least seven different types of serotonin receptor are now known to exist, has led to optimism that more efficient anxiolytic serotonergic drugs can be developed. Indeed, as well as the 5-HT_{1A} agonists, drugs that antagonise 5-HT_{1C}, 5-HT_2 and 5-HT_3 receptors have also been found to have anxiolytic effects, and these are currently being tested for this purpose.

Summary

Emotions are an important determinant of behaviour. They create a feeling that signals that something significant is happening to us, and often propel us into action. When we experience a significant emotion, a number of bodily changes take place which resemble the **flight–fight response**, which is governed by the **sympathetic division** of the **autonomic nervous system** (ANS). These changes may include, for example, a rapid heartbeat, increased respiration, dilated pupils and sweaty palms. The relationship between the physiological response and the subjective experience of the emotional event is still a matter of some conjecture. The **James–Lange theory** holds that each type of emotion is asociated with a specific set of physiological changes that are put into motion before they are experienced as an emotion. In contrast, the **Cannon–Bard theory** not only proposes that we are capable of experiencing an emotion before the accompanying bodily changes take place, but that all emotions produce the same physiological response. **The Schachter–Singer theory** also proposes that there is only one basic physiological response, but we determine the nature of our emotion by combining a cognitive appraisal of both our body state and environmental situation. None of the above theories is wholly convincing – partly because some emotions appear to differ slightly in terms of physiological response, and partly because emotions also appear to be appraised at an unconscious level before they reach consciousness.

The **hypothalamus** has been shown to be an important brain stucture in the regulation of the autonomic nervous system and emotional behaviour. For example, in the 1930s, Philip Bard showed that lesions of the hypothalamus eliminated rage (e.g. hissing and snarling) in cats, whereas lesions of the **cerebral cortex** tended to elicit this type of behaviour. These results indicate that the cerebral cortex inhibits the hypothalamus in its expression of emotional behaviour. The hypothalamus is also part of a brain region known as the **limbic system**, which contains a number of other structures that contribute to emotional behaviour. Of particular importance is the **amygdala**. For example, in the late 1930s, **Kluver** and **Bucy** showed that lesions of the amygdala had a dramatic effect on reducing aggression and fear in rhesus monkeys. Electrical stimulation of this structure has also been shown to induce fear and aggression in humans (e.g. the case of Julia). Both subcortical (unconscious) and cortical (conscious) pathways have been shown to influence neural activity in the amygdala, with the former providing a quick 'alarm' response. The frontal lobes are another region known to affect emotion. This was most dramatically seen in the case of **Phineas Gage**, a railway worker, who in 1848 suffered a horrifying accident when a 100-cm long iron rod was blown through the front of his brain. Although Gage was regarded as an exemplary worker, in the years after the accident he was described as 'gross, profane, coarse and vulgar, to such a degree that his society was intolerable to decent people'. Lesions of the frontal lobe and its pathways (**psychosurgery**) have also been used to treat severe forms of mental illness, including depression and obsessions. More recently, a number of drugs have been developed to treat emotional problems, including the benzodiazepines for anxiety.

Essay questions

1. Critically evaluate the main theories that have been used to explain emotion. What do you think is the best theory and why?

    Helpful Internet search terms: *Theories of emotion. James–Lange theory. Cannon–Bard theory. Schachter–Singer theory. Cognitive appraisal of emotion.*

2. In what ways has the limbic system been shown to be involved in emotional behaviour?

    Helpful Internet search terms: *Limbic system and emotion. Hypothalamus and emotion. Amygdala and emotion. Kluver–Bucy syndrome. Emotion and the hippocampus.*

3. What are the main functions of the frontal lobes? Using evidence from human data, show how this region of the brain contributes to emotion.

    Helpful Internet search terms: *Frontal lobes and emotion. Phineas Gage. Frontal lobe damage in humans. Anatomy of frontal lobes. Frontal lobotomy for depression. Orbitofrontal cortex.*

4. What is known about the neurobiological basis of anxiety? What types of drug have been used to treat this disorder?

    Helpful Internet search terms: *Amygdala and fear. Anxiety disorders. Benzodiazepines and anxiety. Drugs for anxiety. Hippocampus and anxiety. Brain and anxiety.*

Further reading

Aggleton, J. (ed.) (2000) *The Amygdala: A Functional Analysis*. Oxford: Oxford University Press. Although this is a wide-ranging account of the amygdala and not limited to emotion, it contains much of relevance to this chapter.

Borod, J.C. (2000) *The Neuropsychology of Emotion*. Oxford: Oxford University Press. A comprehensive review of the psychology and neurobiology of emotion with an emphasis on how this knowledge can be used to understand emotional disorders.

Damasio, A.R. (1994) *Descartes' Error: Emotion, Reason and the Human Brain*. New York: Putnam & Sons. Drawing on his experience with brain-damaged patients, the author shows how emotions and feelings contribute to reason and adapative social behaviour.

Davidson, R.J., Scherer, K.R. and Goldsmith, H.H. (eds) (2003) *Handbook of Affective Sciences*. Oxford: Oxford University Press. Consisting of 59 chapters written by various experts, and over a thousand pages in length, this is a comprehensive and surprisingly lucid overview of research into the psychobiology of emotion.

LeDoux, J. (1998) *The Emotional Brain*. London: Weidenfeld & Nicolson. A well-written account, based partly on LeDoux's own research, that explores the brain mechanisms underlying emotion.

Panksepp, J. (1998) *Affective Neuroscience: The Foundation of Human and Animal Emotions*. Oxford: Oxford University Press. An account that shows the similarity between human and animal emotions, and how they can be understood in terms of the neurochemistry and neurobiology of the brain.

Pert, C.B. (1997) *Molecules of Emotion*. London: Simon & Schuster. A very readable account of how opiate receptors were discovered in 1972, and how our emotions are determined by a variety of neurochemicals in the brain.

Plutchik, R. (1994) *The Psychology and Biology of Emotion*. New York: Harper & Row. A wide-ranging textbook that covers topics such as general theories of emotion, neurophysiology of facial expression, evolutionary influences and brain function.

Rolls, E.T. (1999) *The Brain and Emotion*. Oxford: Oxford University Press. An examination of the brain mechanisms involved in emotion and motivated behaviours such as hunger, thirst, sexual behaviour and addiction.

Sapolsky, R.M. (1994) *Why Zebras Don't Get Ulcers*. New York: Freeman. A beautifully written and engrossing account of the body's stress response and its importance for physical and psychological well-being.

See website at www.pearsoned.co.uk/wickens for further resources including multiple choice questions.

CHAPTER 6

Sleep and circadian rhythms

In this chapter

- EEG brain waves associated with waking and sleep states
- The characteristics of slow-wave and REM sleep
- The functions of sleep
- The effects of sleep deprivation
- The neurological basis of sleep
- Circadian rhythms
- The role of the suprachiasmatic nucleus
- The pineal gland and melatonin

INTRODUCTION

The urge to sleep is extremely powerful. We spend around one-third of our lives asleep – that is, roughly 25 years of an average life in a state of inertia where normal consciousness is suspended. Sleep occurs in all mammals (and probably all vertebrates as well), which indicates that whatever it does, sleep must serve a very important purpose. Indeed, the instinct to sleep is never far away. We crave sleep if deprived of it, and animal studies have shown that sleep deprivation, if prolonged, can have fatal consequences. Thus, sleep is an essential behaviour. But why do we sleep? At first sight, it appears to be a form of rest or recuperation, but on closer inspection it is clear that sleep is more than the brain, or body, at rest. In fact, as we shall see, sleep is an integrated neural state consisting of several distinct stages that are under the control of various brainstem nuclei. Consequently, sleep is not a passive winding down in response to tiredness, but a series of different arousal states that are actively produced by the brain. Why the brain takes the trouble to produce sleep is an enigma. Indeed, one leading sleep researcher (Horne 1988) has gone so far as to say that after 50 years of research, all we can conclude about the function of sleep is that it overcomes sleepiness! Clearly, there is much more to sleep than this, although proving it is not easy. We also have the tantalising puzzle of dreaming, which accompanies certain stages of sleep, to add further interest to the mystery.

What is sleep?

It is tempting to think of sleep as a resting state that is opposite to being awake – and, until the 1950s, most researchers believed that this was the case. However, in 1953 a different view emerged with the work of Eugene Aserinsky and Nathaniel Kleitman, who were the first to examine sleep in humans using an **electroencephalogram** (**EEG**). This machine, invented by the German psychiatrist Hans Berger in 1929, records electrical brain activity by means of electrodes placed on the scalp. The electrodes detect the very small voltages of neurons firing beneath the skull and meninges, and this is amplified to increase the tiny electrical signals many thousands of times. The neural activity is then recorded on a polygraph consisting of a moving strip of paper and marker pens for each electrode placement.

It might be expected that this procedure, with each electrode recording voltage charges from many tens of thousands of neurons, would produce a random and disorganised mess of activity. But, as Berger found, this was not the case. Instead, he showed that the electrical activity of the brain (or rather the cerebral cortex) was wave-like, indicating that large numbers of neurons were firing together in a synchronised pattern. Moreover, Berger identified two different

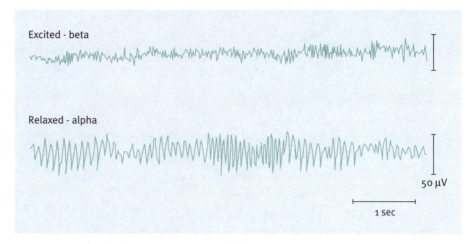

Excited - beta

Relaxed - alpha

50 µV

1 sec

Figure 6.1   Alpha and beta EEG waves

types of activity that occurred during waking, which he called **alpha** and **beta waves** (Figure 6.1). Beta waves – the more common – were characterised by low-amplitude and very irregular (desynchronised) waves that varied between 13 and 30 cycles (Hz) or 'beats' per second. This pattern occurred when subjects were aroused, or engaged in some mental activity. During periods of rest and relaxation, however, the waves slowed down (8–12 Hz) producing a more synchronised 'high-amplitude' pattern of alpha waves.

When Aserinsky and Kleitman examined brain activity during sleep they discovered other types of EEG activity. In fact, they found that distinct types of EEG activity were associated with different forms of sleep, which they called **slow-wave sleep (SWS)** and **rapid eye movement (REM) sleep**. SWS was characterised by EEG activity whose 'beat' was much slower than that normally found during the awake state, and four distinct stages (stages 1–4) could be distinguished. In contrast, REM sleep was identified by EEG activity that resembled more closely the type of brain waves found during waking. As its name suggests, this type of sleep was accompanied by eye movements that could be seen darting about under the eyelids (Aserinsky and Kleitman 1953).

The characteristics of slow-wave sleep

When we fall asleep we normally enter SWS, characterised by the presence of slower brain waves than those normally found in waking. For example, the onset of sleep (stage 1) is identified by **theta waves**, which are slightly slower (4–7 Hz) than the alpha waves (8–12 Hz), which occur when we are relaxed and awake. Although the first signs of theta waves signify the transition between waking and sleep, if the person is wakened during this stage he or she typically reports being drowsy rather than asleep. As sleep becomes deeper, however, stage 2 sleep is reached in which the person is 'properly' asleep. This stage is also

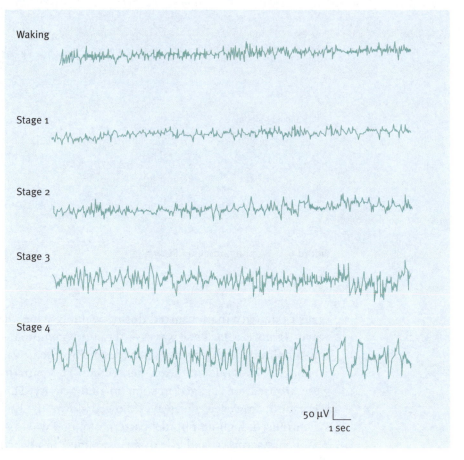

Waking

Stage 1

Stage 2

Stage 3

Stage 4

50 μV

1 sec

Figure 6.2   The stages of sleep as recorded from the EEG

characterised by theta activity, but this time it is frequently interrupted with 0.5-second bursts of 12–15 Hz activity called sleep spindles. In stage 3, the number of sleep spindles declines and the EEG shows the first signs of very slow (1–4 Hz) high-amplitude waves called **delta waves**. Finally, stage 4 is reached, which is the deepest sleep state and the most difficult to be wakened from. This stage is similar to the previous one, except that delta waves predominate and make up at least 50 per cent of the brain waves (Figure 6.2).

A number of changes also take place in the brain and body during SWS. For example, the energy consumption of the brain as measured by cerebral blood flow gradually declines, falling to about 25 per cent of its waking value by the fourth stage of sleep. Thus, the brain appears to slow down and become more restful. Similarly, the body shows signs of resting with reduced muscle tone and inactivity. Indeed, during SWS, the person may only change his or her body position every 10 or 20 minutes. This is accompanied by increased activity in the parasympathetic nervous system, which decreases heart rate, blood pressure, respiration and body temperature, although activity of the gastrointestinal system may increase.

The characteristics of REM sleep

After about 90 minutes of SWS, an abrupt and dramatic change takes place in the brain's electrical activity. The EEG pattern suddenly enters a highly desynchronised state in which the brain waves are faster and smaller (i.e. they have less amplitude) than before. These waves are actually very similar to the desynchronised beta waves that occur during arousal and waking. Moreover, if oxygen consumption and blood flow are measured in the cerebral cortex at this point, they are also found to be similar to when the person is awake. At this point, the person is in REM sleep – and it appears that the brain has now decided to leave its slow-wave resting state behind.

When REM sleep occurs, a new set of physiological changes begin in the body. For example, there is a general loss of muscle tone with the body becoming effectively paralysed, apart from periodic (or phasic) 'twitches' involving facial and eye muscles, along with the fingers and toes. Indeed, because the activity of the body and brain are so different (i.e. the brain appears to be awake, but the body is unresponsive) this form of sleep was called 'paradoxical' by Jouvet in 1967. In addition, REM sleep causes increased activation of the sympathetic nervous system with periods of cardiac acceleration, increased blood pressure and irregular changes in breathing. In males there is also often penile erections, and in females increased vaginal blood flow. With the exception of the reduced muscle tone, it can hardly be said that the body is resting during this phase of sleep!

Perhaps the most important feature of REM sleep is that this is the main stage where we dream. For example, Dement and Kleitman (1957) found that when people were wakened up during REM sleep, 80 per cent of them reported dreaming – although only 20 per cent of them did so in SWS. Indeed, this probably explains the lack of muscle tone in REM sleep, as it acts as a brake to stop the dreamer acting out the dream. These two forms of sleep are also associated with different types of dreaming. While REM sleep produces dreams that typically follow a narrative, or story line, with vivid or intense situations which, on waking, often appear bizarre or illogical, SWS dreams often involve repetition of ideas that do not progress (Hobson 1989). Indeed, night terrors in children, or nightmares where the person feels 'trapped', are more likely to occur in SWS. However, dreams are quickly forgotten and subjects who are wakened only minutes after the end of a REM episode rarely remember them. It is probable that all people dream, but because they are quickly forgotten some people claim that they never dream.

The sleep cycle

What happens after we have gone through the stages of SWS and a subsequent period of REM sleep? The simple answer is that we go into SWS again (unless we wake up). In fact, periods of SWS and REM sleep occur in repeating cycles throughout the night (Figure 6.3). The first four stages of SWS normally last for

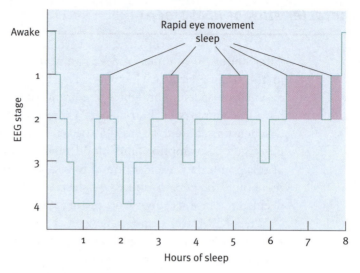

Figure 6.3 The sequence of EEG stages during an average night's sleep

about 90 minutes, and are followed by a period of REM sleep. This is called a **sleep cycle** and because people sleep on average for around 6–8 hours per night, this means that most of us will undergo four or five sleep cycles during this time. It appears that all mammals show this cycle, although its length varies considerably between species, with SWS generally taking up a much larger proportion of the cycle than REM sleep. Indeed, this is also true for humans, who spend around 80 per cent of sleeping time in SWS and the remainder in REM sleep.

In humans, the relative proportions of SWS and REM in each cycle changes as the sleep progresses. For example, although the REM periods will roughly occur at regular 90-minute intervals, the actual amount of time spent in REM sleep will tend to increase – from about 20 minutes during the first REM period to around 40 minutes in the last. This means that as sleep continues, the time spent in SWS gradually becomes less. In fact, the pattern is even more complex than this because SWS also gets shallower, with stages 3 and 4 dropping out of the cycle. Thus, by the time the last sleep cycle occurs just before waking, it may consist entirely of stage 2 SWS (stage 1 is a transitional stage that occurs only when the person starts to fall asleep).

Why do we sleep?

As far as we know, all mammals, birds and reptiles sleep, although only mammals and some birds apparently show REM activity. However, even the simplest creatures have a rest–activity cycle that, in most instances, like sleep, follows a **circadian rhythm** (from the Latin words *circa* meaning 'about' and *dies* for 'day'). Thus, cycles of rest and activity are a universal feature of life, and it appears that sleep is a variation on this basic requirement. But why do we have cycles of rest and activity – or sleep? From an evolutionary perspective it is certain that sleep must have bestowed some advantage to the animals that engaged in it, otherwise it would never have evolved. It is also clear that, for whatever reason, each species has evolved its own distinctive pattern of sleep. For example, giant sloths sleep for about 20 hours each day; cats for about 14 hours; humans around 8 hours; and horses around 3 hours. But why have animals developed these different sleep patterns and what is it telling us about the functions of sleep? Surprisingly, there is no satisfactory answer to this question.

Most theories that explain the reasons for sleep fall into one of two categories: those that highlight the importance of body restoration, and those that emphasise evolutionary adaptation. The first theory suggests that the body needs regular periods in which to rest and recuperate. The implication is that being awake impairs the functioning of the body in some way, and sleep acts to restore it to its optimal state. This theory makes sense, not least because the body does appear to be in a more restful state when it is in SWS. But if sleep is restorative, what exactly is it restoring? Sadly, this theory flounders on the fact that no one has clearly identified a specific physiological process that is restored by sleep. For example, if the function of sleep was to repair the daily effects of wear and tear, then one might predict that heavy exercise would increase the duration of sleep. But, in general, this does not occur. A number of studies have examined this issue and most have concluded that subjects show little increase in sleep following increased mental activity or heavy exercise (Horne 1988). Indeed, we only need to look at the animal world to see problems with this theory. For example, the giant sloth sleeps around 20 hours a day, and clearly is not the most active of animals!

In contrast, adaptive theories of sleep function propose that sleeping has evolved to enhance the survival of the species. For example, it has been suggested that predatory animals such as lions have evolved a rest pattern that allows them to sleep for long uninterrupted periods because they have little threat from other predators. Smaller animals or grazing animals such as zebras, however, need to be more vigilant, and thus they tend to sleep for shorter periods of time (e.g. a zebra sleeps only about 2 or 3 hours a day). Other types of evolutionary pressure may also be involved in determining sleep patterns. For example, some species have possibly evolved their sleeping patterns in an adaptive response to conserve energy rather than to avoid danger. Or perhaps the patterns of sleep are determined by the amount of time the animal has to spend searching for food and eating. Indeed, it would be surprising if sleep has not been modified by evolutionary pressures in this way. However, there is one major problem with adaptation theories: animals simply have to sleep! Perhaps this can best be illustrated by the case of the bottlenose dolphin, which continually has to break the surface of the water to breathe. Remarkably, these animals 'sleep' with one eye closed at a time – that is, the two sides of the brain take turns to sleep and one hemisphere always remains awake to guide behaviour. Thus, it is difficult not to agree that sleep must provide some vital need – and restoration (or something similar) must presumably take place.

Evidence supporting the restorative hypothesis has come from the finding that, in humans, a huge increase in **growth hormone** release occurs during the first few hours of sleep. In fact, the surge of growth hormone is directly linked to the onset of sleep since it does not occur during sleep deprivation. The main role of this hormone in children is to promote growth, and in adults it stimulates the formation of cells and increases protein metabolism. These are, of course, exactly the type of effects that one would expect if sleep was providing a restorative function. Despite this, the restorative role of growth hormone in sleep remains controversial. For example, protein synthesis requires both a steady release of amino acids into the blood and insulin to allow them to be taken up into cells – yet neither of these things occurs at night when levels of insulin and amino acids are low. In fact, some researchers have suggested that growth hormone may help to spare the use of protein as an energy source, thus stimulating the breakdown of fat (Horne 1988). Put another way, the release of growth hormone may have nothing to do with reconstitution! However, there is still room for doubt over this conclusion (e.g. see Adam and Oswald 1977, Hodgson 1991), especially regarding the repair of brain tissue (Dorociak 1990).

Sleep across the life span

Another way to consider the possible function of sleep is to examine how sleep patterns change across the life span (Figure 6.4). Although everybody knows that newborn infants sleep a great deal (i.e. they generally sleep for around 16 to 17 hours a day), it is less widely known that much of this is REM sleep.

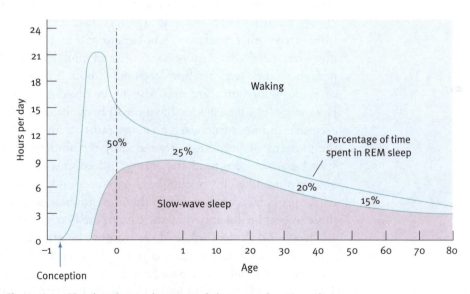

Figure 6.4 The duration and pattern of sleep as a function of age

In fact, about 50 per cent of a newborn infant's sleep is made up of REM sleep, and this proportion is even greater in premature infants (i.e. babies born after 30 weeks of gestation), who spend about 80 per cent of their sleep in this state. Interestingly, however, there is no motor paralysis at this early stage. Instead there are spasmodic movements of the hands, feet and facial muscles, and occasionally the facial expressions associated with crying, anger and rejection (the first smile that the infant makes is normally made during REM sleep). However, as the infant develops, the percentage of time spent in REM sleep decreases, falling from 50 per cent at three months to 33 per cent at eight months, and stabilising at about 25 per cent at one year of age (this is roughly the same proportion of REM sleep as occurs in young adults).

There are also other differences between a young infant's sleep and that of an adult. For example, an infant's full sleep cycle takes approximately an hour, compared with 90 minutes for an adult. Moreover, there is a tendency for babies to enter their first REM episode immediately upon falling asleep, unlike adults, who enter this stage about 90 minutes after sleep onset. It is also interesting to note that after the first eight months of life children sleep for around 14–15 hours a day (i.e. they are awake for an extra three hours each day) and that the 'lost' sleep is almost exclusively REM sleep (Hobson 1989).

The fact that a high amount of REM sleep occurs in the first year of life, and during foetal development, has led some researchers to argue that this type of sleep must have an important role in neural development and maturation of the CNS. For example, Roffwarg et al. (1966) proposed that REM sleep plays a role in the development of the nervous system, which is not unlike that of physical exercise in the formation of muscles. Just as muscles require activity to develop properly, so Roffwarg argued that the CNS requires exposure to sensory stimulation at certain critical stages of development. This is seen, for example, in the case of kittens reared in total darkness from birth, which show impaired vision and degeneration of cells in the visual cortex. Thus, REM sleep may serve a similar role by ensuring that the cerebral cortex receives a type of 'stimulation' that is crucial to the development of nerve cells during a critical period. In support of this theory, it has been shown that REM sleep deprivation in rats, starting some 11 or 12 days after birth, is associated with a reduction in size of the cerebral cortex (Mirmiran 1986). The problem with this theory, however, is that it does not explain why REM sleep continues after the brain has fully developed. An alternative theory is that REM sleep is necessary for the storage of information in the brain to allow learning and memory to take place. Indeed, it is generally accepted that we learn more during our first year of life than at any other time in our life span, and perhaps this is reflected in the time we spend in REM sleep.

The maturation of the sleep cycle normally occurs by early adolescence, at which point the young adult will probably sleep between six and eight hours each night, with about a quarter of this time spent in REM sleep. However, as ageing takes place, the characteristics of the sleep cycle also changes. Not only does the amount of time spent sleeping fall to approximately four–six hours by the age of 50 – but, even more dramatic is the decline in SWS, particularly stages 3 and 4, which, by the age of 60 years, is typically only 50 per cent of what it was at the age of 20. This decline appears to start relatively early (perhaps even in the late 20s) and its gradual loss means that by the age of 90, stages 3 and 4 SWS have virtually disappeared (a similar loss also occurs in other mammals). No one knows for certain why this decline occurs although it may be related to diminished cognitive abilities that can accompany the ageing process. Support for this idea comes from the finding that there is a marked reduction of SWS in people with Alzheimer's disease. In contrast to the decline of SWS in normal ageing, periods of REM sleep are well maintained into extreme old age.

Sleep habits in famous people

'Early to bed, early to rise, makes a man healthy, wealthy and wise' is a saying that many people would agree with. But is it really true? In fact, there are many notable individuals whose sleeping habits do not, or did not, follow this advice. For example, Napoleon needed little sleep. Apparently, he went to bed about midnight and slept for about two hours, at which point he got up and worked until 5 am, when he then went back to bed for another two hours. In fact, Napoleon is quoted as saying that five hours sleep is enough for a man, six for a woman and seven for a fool. Few would accept Napoleon's sexist views today – but, nevertheless, there is little doubt that he was not alone in his sleep habits. For example, Winston Churchill worked until 3 or 4 am and was up again by 8 am (although he generally took a two-hour nap in the afternoon), and it is known that Margaret Thatcher only needed a few hours sleep each night. On the other hand, there are others who needed much longer. For example, Albert Einstein enjoyed spending 10 hours a night in bed, where he 'discovered' crucial aspects of his relativity theory (Borbely 1986).

What, then, are the norms for patterns of sleeping in human beings? According to Empson (1993), surveys have shown that adults sleep an average of $7\frac{1}{2}$ hours with a standard deviation of about 1 hour. This means that about two-thirds of the population can be expected to sleep between $6\frac{1}{2}$ and $8\frac{1}{2}$ hours per night – and that another 16 per cent regularly sleep over $8\frac{1}{2}$ hours with a further 16 per cent sleeping under $6\frac{1}{2}$ hours. However, healthy individuals who regularly sleep less than five hours (and in some cases as little as two hours each night) represent a sizeable minority. For example, Jones and Oswald (1968) verified in a sleep laboratory the cases of two middle-aged Australian men who claimed that they needed only two–three hours sleep per night. Interestingly, not only did their sleep contain relatively more deep SWS (stages 3 and 4) but it also had more REM sleep, which occurred soon after the onset of sleep. Perhaps the shortest 'healthy' sleeper examined by sleep researchers is the case of Miss M, a 70-year-old retired nurse who slept for only about an hour each day (Meddis 1977). Although this lack of sleep is unusual there are other individuals for which similar sleep patterns have been reported.

Despite this, it is probably the case that all people sleep. There have been some claims to the contrary, although these have not stood up to close scrutiny. For example, Oswald and Adam (1980) reported the case of a man who claimed that he had not slept for 10 years following a car accident. When examined for several nights in a sleep laboratory it was found that he

Sleep habits in famous people continued.

remained awake for the first few nights. However, by the fifth day he became sleepy and fell asleep and snored loudly until his wife woke him two and a half hours later. According to Oswald this was a clear case of a short sleeper who attempted to make profit out of his alleged disability (he had been awarded £12,000 at the insurance company's expense). It is perhaps fair to say that on the basis of this, and other reports, no healthy person has yet been found who does not require at least a small amount of sleep.

The effects of sleep deprivation

Another approach that can be taken to understand the function of sleep is to examine the effects of its deprivation. The reasoning behind this procedure is simple: a change in behaviour or decrease in performance caused by keeping an individual awake can be attributed to the lack of sleep. Unfortunately, sleep deprivation in humans has not been so easy to interpret, because it appears to have relatively little consistent effect other than make the person feel very sleepy. A famous example of sleep deprivation is the case of Peter Tripp, a disc jockey who attempted to stay awake for 200 hours as a publicity stunt to raise money for charity. He made radio broadcasts from a glass booth in New York's Times Square in full view of the public, and was constantly attended in order to prevent sleeping. However, it was only during the last days of his deprivation that Tripp began to experience difficulties. The first signs were slurred speech followed by night-time auditory hallucinations and paranoia. By the end of his ordeal he believed that he was being drugged and refused to cooperate with his helpers (Dement 1976). However, it had taken about a week's sleep deprivation to produce these effects, and if there was any implication it was that prolonged sleep deprivation could have adverse effects for mental health.

However, this conclusion was put into doubt by the case of a 17-year-old college student from San Diego called Randy Gardner, who, in 1965, challenged the world sleep deprivation record of 260 hours (10 days and 20 hours), which was, at the time, the world record in the *Guinness Book of Records*. Gardner was constantly under the scrutiny of two observers and, for the last five days, was closely followed by William Dement and George Gulevich from Stanford University. During his attempt, Gardner experienced a number of difficulties including fatigue, irritability and memory problems. By the seventh day his EEG no longer showed the normal patterns of alpha waves associated with being awake. But, these symptoms showed considerable fluctuation – and on the last night he went to an amusement arcade for several hours where he played William Dement at a penny basketball game (about 100 games were played) and won every single game! After breaking the world record, Gardner gave a coherent and impeccable account of himself at a national press conference.

He then slept for 15 hours, followed by another night's sleep of 10½ hours, after which he showed no adverse effects from the ordeal.

The cases of Peter Tripp and Randy Gardner have not provided much illuminating evidence about the functions of sleep, and other deprivation studies do not fare much better. For example, Horne (1978) has reviewed over 50 studies in which humans have been deprived of sleep for varying lengths of time, and found that the main effect appears to be on the performance of complex mental or physiological tasks requiring a steady degree of concentration. Changes in personality, such as those experienced by Peter Tripp (i.e. confusion and suspicion), are also found, although they are not inevitable. Nevertheless, all things considered, the results from these studies do *not* provide convincing evidence that sleep is a vital process. This conclusion is also partially supported by the case of a 33-year-old man called YH who, as a young man in the Israeli army, suffered a shrapnel injury to the brain which abolished his capacity for REM sleep (Lavie *et al.* 1984). When YH was examined in a laboratory, he showed no REM sleep whatsoever on three of his eight nights, and on the remaining five nights the average time spent in REM sleep was found to be 6 minutes. But this did not seem to produce any ill-effects. In fact, after the injury YH completed high school, graduated at law school, and became a successful lawyer (Lavie 1996).

It might come as a surprise, therefore, to discover that the brain attempts to make up for lost sleep after periods of deprivation. For example, a person who is deprived of sleep for 24 hours will usually make up the 'sleep debt' in a day or two (although the recovery of sleep may not be complete if the deprivation is more prolonged). Moreover, the brain appears particularly intent on recovering its REM sleep. For example, if subjects are deprived of REM sleep (by being wakened up every time they enter this phase of sleep) they will typically show an increase of REM sleep next time they sleep which is about 50 per cent above normal. In fact, if subjects are deprived of REM sleep for several days, the 'rebound' effect may be as high as 90 per cent when they return to sleeping, with increased REM sleep recovery continuing for several more days afterwards.

Sleep deprivation in animals

Although sleep deprivation in humans does not appear to produce any obvious life-threatening effect, the same cannot be said of animals. One way of producing sleep loss in experimental animals is to use a carousel apparatus (Figure 6.5), which consists of two chambers in a Plexiglas cylinder that share a rotating turntable as a floor. A rat is placed in each chamber (with food and water) and both are attached to electrodes that record EEG and body temperature. One rat is to be deprived of sleep and the other its control. When EEG recordings show that the designated deprived rat is beginning to sleep, the floor automatically begins to rotate, thus forcing the 'dozing' rat to walk backwards or fall into a shallow pool of water. But during the periods when the deprived rat is awake, and the floor is motionless, the control animal can snatch periods of sleep. In

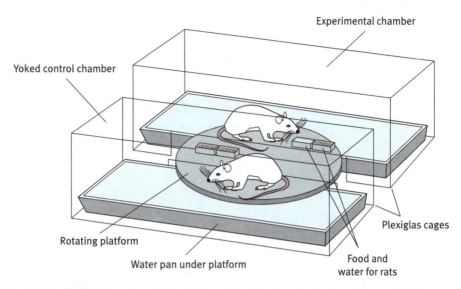

Figure 6.5   The sleep carousel apparatus as used by Rechtschaffen. *Source*: Neil R. Carlson, *Physiology of Behavior*, 6th edition. Copyright © 1998 by Pearson Education

this way the control animal gets exactly the same amount of exercise as the deprived rat, but gains more sleep.

This procedure is very successful at producing sleep deprivation. For example, in one study it reduced the amount of sleep by 87 per cent in the deprived condition and by 31 per cent in the control. But most striking were the consequences of the forced deprivation. Although no effects were observed in the first seven to 10 days (which coincidentally is the limit in most human experiments), the deprived rats showed marked deterioration after this period. For example, they began to look ill and stopped grooming, giving their fur a matted and dishevelled appearance. The rats also started to lose weight despite eating significantly more, and their body temperature declined. With continued sleep deprivation, the animals died within two to three weeks of the ordeal (Rechtschaffen *et al.* 1983).

What was the cause of death in these animals? Surprisingly, there is no clear-cut answer to this question. When various body organs (such as brain, liver, spleen, stomach, thyroid and thymus) were examined there was no difference between the two groups of animals. There was, however, an increase in the size of the adrenal glands and release of cortisol in the final few days before death in the deprived rats. This was also accompanied by a marked drop in body temperature at the same time. Because of this, it was initially hypothesised that sleep-deprived animals were dying because they could not maintain their body temperature, but when these rats were kept warm with increased external heating, they still died. Thus, the cause of death is not known, although it is probably linked to some form of metabolic dyscontrol in which the brain can no longer adequately control the metabolism (or chemical reactions) of the body. Interestingly, if the animals were removed from the apparatus when near death and allowed to sleep, they quickly recovered and showed huge increases in REM sleep, which was sometimes 10 times greater than normal.

Despite these dramatic findings, it is not clear how far they can be extrapolated to human behaviour. For example, a human in a sleep deprivation study knows that he or she is being observed and can terminate the proceedings at any time. In contrast, the rat has no control over the situation and no way of 'knowing' if the situation is going to end. Thus, the stress placed on the animal is much more severe, and this may also be an important factor in producing the deleterious effects of sleep deprivation.

Brain mechanisms of sleep

Until the late 1930s it was widely believed that sleep was a passive process that occurred in response to sensory deprivation. In short, the idea was simple: deprive the brain of sensory input and the animal will fall asleep. In humans, the onset of sleep was therefore attributed to the gradual decay in the level of stimulation that occurs over the course of the day. One of the first to test this idea experimentally was Frederic Bremer (1937), who made a complete cut in the upper brainstem of cats (called a *cerveau isolé* preparation), which deprived most of the sensory input getting to the higher reaches of the brain (Figure 6.6). If the passive theory was correct then this lesion should produce sleep. Indeed, this appeared to be the case as the lesioned animals were always drowsy, and EEG activity recorded from the cerebral cortex showed a continuous sleep pattern.

However, Bremer soon discovered a problem with his theory. When he made another cut – this time at the base of the brainstem where it joined the spinal

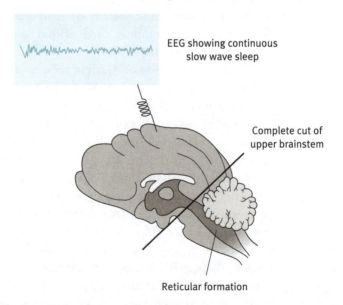

EEG showing continuous
slow wave sleep

Complete cut of
upper brainstem

Reticular formation

Figure 6.6 The *cerveau isolé* preparation

cord (called *encéphale isolé*) – he found to his surprise that the cycles of sleep and waking were not affected (Figure 6.7). In fact, these animals were hyper-vigilant and showed increased wakefulness, despite being deprived of much sensory input (the only difference between the *cerveau* and *encéphale isolé* preparations being that the former received input from the trigeminal nerve, which provided sensory information from the head and face). Rather than sleep being a passive response to external stimulation, these findings indicated that it was an active process, with the mechanism for producing sleep and wakefulness located somewhere between the two transections in the brainstem. This theory turned out to be the correct one.

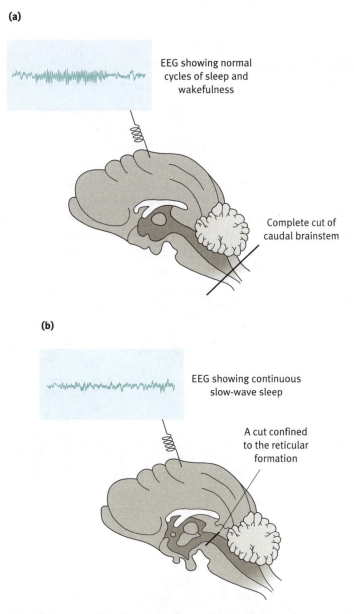

(a)

EEG showing normal cycles of sleep and wakefulness

Complete cut of caudal brainstem

(b)

EEG showing continuous slow-wave sleep

A cut confined to the reticular formation

Figure 6.7   Two other types of brainstem lesion and their effect on sleep

The brainstem is a long tubular structure that enters the brain from the spinal cord, and the inner core of this structure, called the **reticular formation**, is now known to be a crucial site in the production of sleep. For example, lesions restricted to just the upper part of the reticular formation, but which spared the nearby ascending sensory pathways to the cortex (see Figure 6.7(a)), produced EEG activity characteristic of deep sleep (Lindsley *et al.* 1949). Thus, the lack of sensory input to the cortex could not explain this effect. But, even more importantly, electrical stimulation of the reticular formation, without sensory activation, was found to produce cortical arousal (Moruzzi and Magoun 1949). In short, these findings indicated that it was the brainstem, or rather the inner part of it called the reticular formation, that was the critical site in the active control of sleep and wakefulness.

The reticular activating system

The reticular formation (*reticulum* means 'net') is made up of a diffuse group of neurons (mainly interneurons) whose axons criss-cross through the medial part of the brainstem from the spinal cord up to the thalamus. It was once thought that the reticular formation was simply a random mass of neurons without any organisation, but this view is incorrect as it is now known to contain large numbers of different centres and pathways. Indeed, as seen in previous chapters, the reticular formation is involved in a wide range of functions, including autonomic activity, motor reflexes and sensory analysis, and receives input from many other brain structures. Certain parts of the reticular formation also have another very important characteristic: they are capable of generating their own rhythms of electrical activity. Many of these regions send their axons out into a diffuse pathway, called the **ascending reticular activating system** (Figure 6.8), that projects extensively to the thalamus and cerebral cortex. This is this system that is largely responsible for causing the wave-like patterns of neural activity

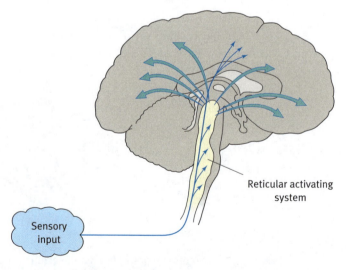

Figure 6.8   The ascending reticular system

in the cerebral cortex (as measured by the EEG) that correlate with sleep and wakefulness.

But what areas of the reticular formation are involved in the production of sleep? In 1959 it was found that injections of anaesthetic into certain areas of the reticular formation awakened sleeping cats and caused a desynchronised EEG that was characteristic of waking (Magni *et al.* 1959). This indicated that there were specific areas in the brainstem where neural stimulation, rather than inhibition, was needed to produce sleep. In other words, the reticular formation contained sleep centres which, if activated, caused sleep. The next important question was: where exactly were they?

What areas of the brainstem are involved in sleep?

The first attempts to identify specific regions of the reticular formation that were involved in sleep took place in the early 1960s. A leading pioneer was the Frenchman Michel Jouvet, who found that electrical stimulation of the **pontine formation** located in the Pons area of the upper brainstem in cats could sometimes induce REM sleep, providing the animal was already well into its non-REM sleep phase. Jouvet also found that the rapid eye movements of the sleeping animal occurred when a sequential pattern of EEG activity, known as **ponto-geniculo-occipital** (PGO) **waves**, arose in the pontine region, and passed to the occipital cortex, via the midbrain and thalamus. Both these findings showed that the pontine region of the brainstem was involved in the production of REM sleep, and was confirmed when Jouvet found that bilateral damage of this area produced a marked decrease in the amount of REM sleep that lasted from five to 10 days (Jouvet 1967).

The pontine formation (the word *pons* is derived from the Latin word for 'bridge' and refers to its position, which connects the two sides of the cerebellum) lies above the medulla and below the midbrain (see Plate 1.1). It is also an anatomically complex area with a great variety of fibre tracts and nuclei associated with a wide range of functions. The next step was to locate more precisely the regions in the pontine area where sleep was produced, and here Jouvet's search was assisted by the new development of histofluorescent techniques in the 1960s that allowed visualisation of certain neurotransmitters in the brain along with their pathways. Two transmitters that were mapped out in this way were **noradrenaline** and **serotonin**. Although fibres containing these neurochemicals were found to innervate large areas of the brain, including the cerebral cortex, their site of origin was traced back to small structures in the pontine formation. The site of noradrenaline-containing fibres was found to be the **locus coeruleus** and the site of serotonin fibres was the **raphe** nuclei.

These new histological techniques enabled the raphe and locus coeruleus to be lesioned with a reasonable degree of precision. In 1966, Jouvet destroyed the raphe in cats, and found that this caused insomnia that lasted for some three–four days after the operation (Jouvet and Renault 1966). Although there was some partial recovery of sleep after this period, it never exceeded 2½ hours each day (cats normally sleep about 14 hours a day). The raphe was further linked with sleep when it was found that drugs such as p-chlorphenylalanine, which blocked the synthesis of serotonin, also produced insomnia, and that this effect was reversed with serotonergic-enhancing drugs. Thus, lesioning and pharmacological studies pointed to the raphe as a sleep-promoting area.

Another area that was implicated in sleep by Jouvet was the locus coeruleus. For example, in the 1960s, Jouvet found that lesions of the dorsolateral pons, which included the locus coeruleus, abolished REM sleep. In addition, Jouvet found that damage to the ventral part of this nucleus eliminated the appearance of muscle paralysis (atonia), which, as we have seen above, occurs in REM sleep. Electrical or noradrenergic stimulation of the locus coeruleus also produced an 'aroused' EEG pattern that, in some ways, resembled the brain waves found in REM sleep (Jouvet 1967).

The proposed involvement of the raphe and locus coeruleus in sleep led Jouvet to propose a theory that linked these two structures together. Put simply, he suggested that the onset of sleep (and SWS) was controlled by serotonergic fibres, and REM sleep was caused by noradrenergic activity. Put another way, activity in the raphe was seen as producing SWS by inhibiting cortical arousal through its influence over the reticular formation, including the locus coeruleus. In turn, the locus coeruleus was believed to have the capacity to switch off raphe activity, thereby causing cortical arousal and REM sleep. In this way, activity in the two transmitter systems could alternate back and forth throughout the night to produce slow-wave and REM sleep (Jouvet 1967). Further support for this idea came from the discovery that raphe lesions (which produced insomnia) led to increased activity in noradrenergic neurons, and lesions of the locus coeruleus enhanced raphe activity. Thus, a reciprocal relationship existed between the two structures.

The reciprocal interaction model of REM sleep

Although the idea of the raphe and locus coeruleus interacting together to produce slow-wave and REM sleep is attractive, there is now evidence that it is far too simple, and is fundamentally incorrect. For example, a number of studies have shown that the crucial area of the pontine region involved in the production of REM sleep is not the locus coeruleus but is located ventrally (below) in a medial area of the pontine region called the **gigantocellular tegmental field** (GTF). For example, lesions of this region disrupt REM sleep while leaving SWS intact (Hobson 1988). In addition, the GTF has been shown to be the origin of PGO waves, which precede the occurrence of rapid eye movements and other physiological changes in REM sleep. But perhaps the best evidence linking this area of the brain with sleep comes from the finding that GTF neurons receive cholinergic projections from two nearby lateral brainstem areas called the **laterodorsal tegmental nucleus** (LTN) and the **pedunclopontine tegmental nucleus** (PTN), and that cholinergic agonists such as carbachol and oxotremorine when injected into the GTF dramatically increase REM sleep (McCarley *et al.* 1995). Despite this, lesions of the GTF do not abolish REM sleep completely – and the

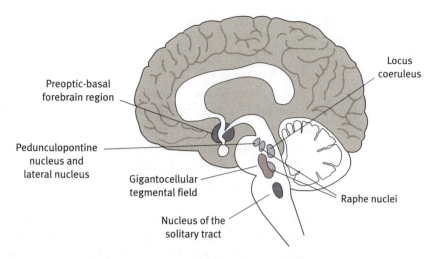

Preoptic-basal
forebrain region

Locus
coeruleus

Pedunculopontine
nucleus and
lateral nucleus

Gigantocellular
tegmental field

Raphe nuclei

Nucleus of the
solitary tract

Figure 6.9 Some of the most important brain regions involved in the regulation of sleep

LTN and PTN, which also have ascending cholinergic projections that go to the thalamus and cerebral cortex, are also believed to be involved in producing REM sleep. To make things more complex, the raphe and locus coeruleus both project to the LTN and PTN, and serotonin and noradrenaline have been shown to suppress the activity of these nuclei (Figure 6.9).

Research that has recorded the activity of neurons in the pontine region during sleep and wakefulness has also produced results that are inconsistent with Jouvet's theory. For example, neural activity in the raphe and locus coeruleus is at its highest during waking, is diminished during SWS, and becomes almost non-existent during REM sleep (Hobson *et al*. 1975). In contrast, neural activity increases in the GTF (and nearby structures) during REM sleep (Table 6.1). Clearly, this is not the pattern of activity one would predict from Jouvet's theory, and to accommodate these new findings, the reciprocal interaction model was proposed by McCarley and Hobson (1975). This theory views the raphe and locus coeruleus as structures that terminate REM sleep by their inhibition of cholinergic neurons in the LTN and PTN. In turn, when the cholinergic neurons in the LTN and PTN are 'turned on' they stimulate the production of REM sleep by activating neurons in the GTF, while inhibiting the raphe and locus coeruleus (see McCarley 1995).

Table 6.1 Response rates of neurons in three brainstem areas importantly involved in sleep

	Waking	SWS	REM Sleep
Locus coeruleus	Slow and steady activity (about 3 spikes per second)	Decreased	Nearly zero
Dorsal raphe	Slow and steady activity (about 3 spikes per second)	Decreased	Nearly zero
Gigantocellular tegmental field	Very slow activity (a spike every few seconds)	Increased	Fast (about 10 spikes per second)

The neurobiology of slow-wave sleep

The neurobiology of SWS is less well understood, although a number of brain areas have been identified that have a role in producing this state. Interestingly, this work has tended to highlight areas outside the brainstem. Of particular importance in this respect is the basal forebrain, which includes the hypothalamus. This area was first recognised as having a role in sleep in the 1920s by Constantin von Economo, who examined the brains of people who had died from sleeping sickness (*encephalitis lethargica*). This was an illness that mysteriously appeared in 1917, and which over the next 10 years was to cause the deaths of over 5 million people (see Sacks 1990, Cheyette and Cummings 1995). Although the illness had varying effects, in about one-third of cases it caused patients to fall asleep for extended periods from which they could not be wakened (in fact, many died in this state). When von Economo examined the brains of these victims he found damage located in the posterior part of the hypothalamus. Subsequent animal work has indeed shown that large posterior hypothalamic lesions produce a prolonged sleep-like state (Nauta 1946) whereas lesions in the preoptic-anterior hypothalamus cause severe insomnia (McGinty and Sterman 1968). These findings show that the hypothalamus is an important sleep centre – an idea which makes a great deal of sense considering that sleep follows a circadian rhythm, and that the hypothalamus contains a 'clock' for the generation of internal circadian rhythms (see below). The hypothelamus also contains some neurons that are sensitive to the temperature as they become more active when the body is warm – and it is interesting to note that one often feels more sleepy when warm and comfortable.

Another area implicated in SWS is the thalamus. Although Walter Hess, in his pioneering work that examined electrical stimulation in freely moving animals, had drawn attention to the role of the thalamus in sleep in the 1940s, more recently this structure has been implicated in a very rare condition known as fatal familial insomnia. The first account of this condition was provided by Lugaresi *et al.* (1986), who described the case of a 53-year-old man who began to have problems falling asleep, which soon led to total insomnia and heightened autonomic arousal. He died nine months later. Moreover, his father and two sisters had died in the same manner. Remarkably, in all four cases, postmortem brain examination revealed severe degeneration of the anterior part of the thalamus. These findings have been confirmed in others, and it is now known that familial insomnia is an inherited disease and is always fatal (Lavie 1996).

The brainstem may also be involved in SWS. For example, a structure that lies just below the raphe, called the **nucleus of the solitary tract** (NST), has been implicated in sleep since stimulation of this region produces EEG patterns of slow-wave activity. In addition, single unit recordings show that about half of the neurons in this nucleus are more active in SWS than in wakefulness. Despite this, lesions to the NST do not appear to disrupt sleep. Interestingly, this area receives information from the stomach, liver, duodenum and tongue, and this may help to explain why a large meal often facilitates sleep.

Narcolepsy

Narcolepsy is a disorder in which people suffer frequent, intense attacks of sleep that usually last from 5 to 30 minutes, thereby making them prone to falling asleep at dangerous or inappropriate times. Although the narcoleptic will often sleep poorly at night, which exacerbates their daytime sleepiness, the condition is more than a sleep deficit. For example, narcoleptics may show sleep paralysis, where they cannot move or speak for several minutes in the transition between waking and sleep, and this may be followed by vivid and frightening dreams known as hypnagogic hallucinations. Another feature is cataplexy – a sudden loss of muscle tone that causes the body to collapse without loss of consciousness. About a third of narcoleptics experience at least one cataplexic attack each day, and they can also be triggered by strong emotions such as laughter, anger and sexual arousal. An examination of the EEG shows that narcolepsy occurs when the person goes directly into REM sleep, unlike a normal person, who enters a period of SWS first. Thus, narcolepsy is due to the sudden intrusion of REM sleep into wakefulness, and cataplexy to the inhibition of the motor systems that is associated with this state.

A major advance in narcolepsy research occurred in the early 1970s when scientists found that some strains of dogs showed sudden motor inhibition (cataplexy) and short latencies to REM sleep onset (Plate 6.1). These consequently provided an ideal animal model of narcolepsy. In fact, canine narcolepsy turned out to be a recessive genetic condition, which meant that the dog had to inherit a copy of the mutant gene from both its parents. The brains of these dogs also contained increased numbers of cholinergic receptors in the pons, and noradrenergic alpha 2 receptors in the locus coeruleus. But human narcolepsy is not a recessive condition, or even strongly genetic. For example, most narcoleptics do not have any first-degree relatives with the disorder, and identical twins are no more likely to share the condition than unrelated strangers.

Nonetheless, scientists set out to identify the gene that caused the canine narcolepsy and after a 10-year search they located it on chromosome 12 (Lin *et al.* 1999). Curiously, the only gene known to lie within this region was called *Hcrtr2*, which was responsible for making a receptor for a class of neuropeptides called **orexins** that had been associated with eating. But the lack of this receptor turned out to be crucial for narcolepsy. For example, when knockout mice without the orexin gene were created, they exhibited increased REM sleep and episodes of cataplexy (Chemelli *et al.* 1999). This indicated that orexin dysfunction might also be involved in human narcolepsy. Indeed, this was soon confirmed when it was found that narcoleptics had a 93 per cent reduction of orexin neurons in the hypothalamus compared with controls (Thannickal *et al.* 2000). These hypothalamic orexin neurons are now known to be important in the regulation of sleep. They not only project to the brainstem including the raphe, locus coeruleus and nearby pontine regions, but injections of orexins into these regions enhance REM sleep and cause changes in muscle tone (Siegel *et al.* 2001). Thus, as von Economo showed some 70 years ago when examining *encephalitis lethargica*, the hypothalamus is a crucial structure in the regulation of sleep.

Plate 6.1   Narcoleptic dogs. *Source*: Courtesy of the Stanford Center for Narcolepsy

Circadian rhythms

Almost without exception, all land animals coordinate their behaviour with the daily cycles of light and dark that dominate living on Earth. The most conspicuous daily rhythm of all is the sleep–wake cycle, but less obvious is the fact that nearly every physiological and biochemical activity in the body also has an unique circadian rhythm. For example, body temperature fluctuates by about 2 °C during the 24-hour day, reaching its peak in the late afternoon and dropping to its lowest value in the early hours of the morning. Hormones are also released in circadian patterns. For instance, peak levels of **melatonin** are released late in the evening, and **growth hormone** in the early part of the night. In contrast, most **cortisol** and **testosterone** is released in the morning around waking, and **adrenaline** in late afternoon. Even birth and death appear to follow a circadian rhythm with approximately one-third of natural births occurring around 3 am, whereas death is more likely at 5 am (Groves and Rebec 1992).

At first sight the existence of circadian body rhythms may not appear to be too surprising. After all, it is easy to imagine that they are directly caused by the world around us – possibly by the alternating periods of light and dark, which, somehow, affect the biological processes of the body. But this is not the case. In fact, instead of being passive responders to events around us, we have our own internal clocks that time and control the body's rhythms. And we are not alone as nearly every life-form has its own time-keeping mechanisms. For example, in 1729, the French astronomer DeMarian was intrigued when he noted that his heliotrope plant opened its leaves during the day and shut them at night. To examine this further, he shut his plant away in a dark cupboard and found that it continued to open and shut its leaves in time with the light and dark cycles outside. Thus, the leaf rhythm of the plant was controlled by its own innate mechanism. Similar circadian patterns have been found in creatures as simple as single-celled algae (Palmer 1975).

In 1832, the Swiss botanist de Candolle performed an experiment similar to the one by DeMarian, but this time he noted something odd – when placed in the dark, his plant opened and shut its leaves every 22 hours, not every 24 hours. The plant therefore appeared to have an internal 'clock' that did not have a very accurate timing mechanism. In fact, this was the first demonstration of a 'free-running' rhythm – that is, a rhythm which was running at a speed that didn't quite match the outside world. Cut off from the normal cues of the environment, the plant was relying on its own, less than precise, timing mechanism. This also suggested that the plant was keeping accurate time (i.e. entraining itself to the rhythms of the outside world) by 'resetting' its clock by using external time cues such as periods of light and dark, temperature or humidity. Indeed, these stimuli are now known to be important regulators of circadian rhythms and are collectively called **zeitgebers** (from the German for 'time-givers').

Free-running rhythms in humans

What evidence is there that humans have internal biological clocks with their own time-keeping mechanism? To show that such clocks exist it is necessary to prove that circadian rhythms can still operate in the absence of time cues. However, the problem with human subjects is that it is extremely difficult to separate them from this type of information. Even in the confines of a laboratory, there are many subtle time cues, such as the sound of the outside world or people coming and going, that provide information about the time of day. How then can one cut off all time cues from a human subject? One of the most ideal or isolated environments for this type of study is an underground cave, and caves have been used on occasion as 'laboratories' to examine free-running circadian rhythms in humans.

Perhaps the most famous isolation experiment was performed by the French geologist Michel Siffre, who, in 1972, lived for six months in a carefully prepared cave 100 feet below the ground in Texas (Siffre 1975). During his time underground, Siffre was cut off from all forms of time information from the outside world, and the temperature of his cave was maintained at 70 °F. Although linked to the surface by a telephone that was manned at all times, his conversations were kept to a bare minimum. He had a stockpile of food (the same type as used on the Apollo 16 space mission) and water (780 one-gallon jugs), and he phoned the surface when he wanted to sleep so that researchers could switch off the lights. When Siffre went to bed he attached himself to equipment that enabled his body sleep cycles to be recorded, as well as his heart rate, blood pressure and muscle activity. He also saved his beard cuttings, recorded his body temperature several times a day, and sent his urine samples to the surface for analysis.

Not surprisingly, the experience took its toll on Siffre, who, by the 80th day of his isolation, was experiencing depression and failing memory (at this point the experiment was to continue for another 100 days). Moreover, long after the confinement had ended, Siffre complained of 'psychological wounds' from the ordeal that he did not 'understand'. But, from the scientific point of view the study was a success. One of its main findings was that the body appeared to have two internal clocks that ran at different speeds. For example, Siffre's sleep–waking cycle tended to free-run between 25 and 32 hours, which meant that he went to sleep at a later time each day (or, put another way, his 'days' were longer than normal). In fact, Siffre was on his 151st sleep–wake cycle by the last (179th) day of the experiment, so that he had psychologic-ally 'lost' 28 days. However, Siffre's temperature rhythm was more stable and ran consistently on a 25-hour cycle with little fluctuation. This meant in effect that his temperature cycle went in and out of synchronisation with the sleep–wake cycle. In fact, this is an unusual situation since we normally go to sleep when our body temperature is beginning to drop. Thus, there appeared to be at least two oscillators governing circadian rhythms: one was a relatively stable and controlled temperature (this has sometimes been called the X pace-maker), and the other was more variable and controlled sleep and arousal (the Y pacemaker).

The neural basis of circadian rhythms

If the sleep–wake cycle is under the control of a circadian pacemaker, then where in the body does it exist? One of the first scientists to address this question was Carl Richter, who, beginning in the 1950s, focused his attention on the endocrine glands of the body. However, removing the main endocrine glands had little effect on altering the circadian rhythms of laboratory animals, and Richter there-fore turned to the brain. He made lesions to many different brain structures and examined their effects on circadian patterns of locomotor activity. Only one structure appeared to disrupt circadian behaviour – the ventral hypothalamus, but partly because this region was so small, and anatomically complex, he was unable to go further with his investigation.

However, in 1972, two independent groups of researchers (Stephan and Zucker 1972, Moore and Eichler 1972) found a small cluster of neurons in the front part of the ventral hypothalamus, called the **suprachiasmatic nucleus** (SCN), where damage caused disruption to a variety of circadian rhythms, including the release of corticosterone, drinking behaviour and locomotor activity. Further research soon showed that damage to the SCN affected other circadian rhythms, including the sleep–wake cycle. Although the SCN lesion did not change the length of time spent sleeping, or the relative proportion of REM sleep and SWS, it altered the sleep pattern, which occurred more randomly during the 24-hour day. In short, lesions of the SCN abolished the circadian rhythmicity of sleep.

Why did it take so long to discover the SCN? For one reason, it is extremely small. In humans, each nuclei comprises approximately 10,000 neurons, which are confined in a space of about 0.3 mm^3. The SCN also contains some of the smallest neurons to be found in the human brain, and they can only be identified with specialised staining techniques. In rodent brains the size of this nucleus is even smaller, therefore it is hardly surprising that Richter, with his relatively crude lesioning techniques, was unable to narrow his search down to this tiny structure.

The suprachiasmatic nucleus and circadian rhythms

If a region of the brain is to qualify as a circadian pacemaker it must have three properties: (1) it receives information from the senses (particularly helpful would be visual information concerning day and night) to account for the fact that circadian rhythms can be reset by zeitgebers; (2) it has an intrinsic rhythm of its own so circadian rhythms can be free-running; and (3) it has output to other regions of the brain that are involved in circadian types of behaviour, such as the sleep–wake cycle. The SCN fulfils all these criteria thus confirming its role as a circadian pacemaker.

To begin with, the anatomical location of the SCN strongly supports an involvement in detecting visual information. For example, the SCN lies just above the **optic chiasm**, where the nerve fibres from each eye cross to the contralateral side of the brain. Branching off from the optic nerve, near the chiasm, is a tiny pathway called the retinohypothalamic tract, which goes to the SCN. When this pathway is lesioned, it is found that light and dark cues are no longer able to reset the circadian 'clock', although animals still have normal vision (Rusak 1977). Thus, the SCN is in an ideal position to receive rudimentary visual information acting as a zeitgeber to reset its rhythms.

It has also been shown that the SCN generates its own rhythmical activity. For example, it is possible to keep slices of brain tissue that contain the SCN in a saline bath, and then record the electrical activity of its neurons. This work has shown that the SCN neurons display discharge rates of electrical activity

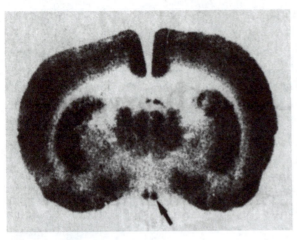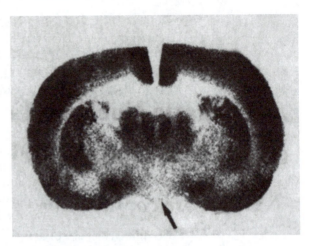

Plate 6.2   Increased metabolic activity of the suprachiasmatic nucleus during the day compared with night using 2-deoxyglucose. *Source*: Schwartz and Gainer (1977) *Science*, 197, 1089–91 (in Carlson, 2004, *Physiology of Behavior*, Allyn & Bacon)

that are synchronised to the light–dark cycle that the animal experienced when alive (Bos and Mirmiran 1990). Similar types of neural activity have also been shown in the intact animal. For example, Schwartz and Gainer (1977) injected rats with **2-deoxyglucose** (an inert radioactive form of glucose), which is taken up and accumulates into neurons. Because the most active neurons use more 2-deoxyglucose, this substance provides a way of measuring regional differences in brain activity. Using this technique it was found that the SCN took up significantly more 2-deoxyglucose during the day compared with night (Plate 6.2). Thus, the SCN shows a circadian rhythmicity in its neural activity.

But how does the SCN produce the circadian changes that take place in the rest of the body? Although the neurons of the SCN project to a large number of brain structures, including other regions of the hypothalamus, pituitary gland and brainstem, the most important pathway is to the **pineal gland**. This structure has long intrigued researchers (see Chapter 1), although it was not until the early 1960s that it was found to be an endocrine gland that secretes the hormone **melatonin**. In most animals, the secretion of melatonin is directly under the control of light. That is, light suppresses melatonin release whereas darkness has a stimulatory effect on its secretion. This effect is controlled by a pathway called the **superior cervical ganglion**, which passes from the SCN to the pineal gland. During darkness, the fibres of the superior cervical ganglion release noradrenaline onto pineal cells, which then transforms serotonin (by increasing the activity of an enzyme called N-acetyltransferase) into melatonin. However, during periods of light this process is terminated. Most animals are very sensitive to the effect of light on melatonin secretion, and in rats the light from a candle flame is even sufficient to inhibit its release. Although it takes much higher intensities of light to suppress melatonin in humans, it nevertheless still shows a circadian pattern of release with most being secreted during the late part of the evening and little during the day (Lewy *et al.* 1980).

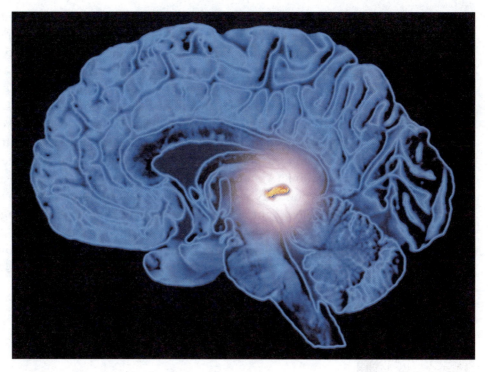

Plate 6.3 The pineal gland. *Source*: Alfred Pasieka/Science Photo Library

The functions of melatonin

In animals, melatonin is involved in a wide range of functions, including the synchronisation of circadian rhythms as well as seasonal patterns of behaviour including changes in body weight, coat colour and reproductive activity. Thus, not only does melatonin have a circadian function, but in many animals it also regulates the changing response of the body to light over the year. Although seasonal changes in behaviour are less obvious in humans, there is little doubt that melatonin has an important effect on circadian rhythms. In humans, very little melatonin is produced during the day, but it shows a sudden rise in the late evening, with high levels being produced throughout the night, until it drops again around awaking. As might be expected, the most important effect of melatonin is to induce sleepiness, perhaps because it lowers body temperature thereby causing a reduction of arousal. It is also interesting to note that as we get older, the pineal gland shows signs of calcification and produces less melatonin – which may be one reason why elderly people sleep less and are more prone to suffer from insomnia. However, melatonin has other functions and it helps to orchestrate the activity of other hormone systems in the body, enabling them to synchronise their activity with the sleep–wake cycle. As an example, melatonin promotes a significant increase in the release of growth hormone, which occurs early in the sleep cycle.

There are instances where our circadian rhythms fall out of synchronisation with the outside world. One example is jet lag, where a person may fly across several time zones. Indeed, when arriving in a new country the person may feel listless and have difficulty in sleeping at the appropriate time. The solution to this problem is to get the internal clock readjusted to the external environment as quickly as possible, and this can be done by the administration of melatonin. Indeed, if one takes melatonin during the early evening at one's arrival destination (or in some cases the day before the journey), it is often possible to effectively shift the body's circadian rhythm into phase with the new prevailing time conditions (Arendt *et al.* 1987). Melatonin has also been shown to help to synchronise circadian rhythms and improve the sleep of some blind people, who cannot use light as a zeitgeber (Skene *et al.* 1999). Changes in light may also benefit those who are employed in shift work or at night. In particular, people are more likely to adapt better to their working conditions if strong artificial light is used, while their bedroom is kept as dark as possible (Eastman *et al.* 1995).

Summary

We spend about one-third of our lives asleep (roughly 25 years of an average life). Yet, remarkably, no one is absolutely sure why we do it! This is all the more confusing when one considers that all mammals (and probably all vertebrates) show patterns of sleep. Despite the uncertainty, it is likely that sleep either produces some form of tissue restoration that helps to combat the wear and tear of living, or it helps to maintain the plasticity of the brain. The experimental investigation of sleep began with the invention of the **electroencephalograph** (EEG) by Hans Berger in 1929, which allowed the electrical rhythms of the brain to be measured. In 1954, Kleitman and Aserinsky showed that the brain has two sleep states – **slow-wave sleep** (SWS) and **rapid eye movement** (REM) **sleep**. There are four stages of SWS, with EEG waves 'slowing down' from 8 to 1 Hz, and these are accompanied by a physiological relaxation of the body. The SWS cycle takes about 90 minutes to complete and is followed by a period of REM sleep characterised by much faster and desynchronised EEG rhythms (similar to when we are awake), accompanied by muscle twitches, eye movements and general loss of body tone. It is also the stage of sleep in which we **dream**. The four consecutive stages of SWS followed by REM sleep is called a **sleep cycle**. There are normally around four–five sleep cycles in an average night's sleep. As sleep progresses through the night, the REM sleep periods tend to get longer, and SWS periods get shorter, with stages 3 and 4 showing the greatest reduction.

Sleep is an active process (and not a passive response to sensory deprivation as once believed) that is predominantly controlled by various regions in the **brainstem** that influence the electrical activity of the **cerebral cortex** through their action on the ascending **reticular activating system**. In the 1960s, Michael Jouvet appeared to show that the **locus coeruleus** (the main source of fibres that provide **noradrenaline** to the forebrain) was responsible for producing

Summary continued.

many of the manifestations of REM sleep – and that the **raphe** (the main source of fibres that provide **serotonin** to the forebrain) was involved in producing SWS. This view is no longer accepted although their involvement in sleep cannot be ruled out. A more important region for producing REM sleep is now believed to be the **gigantocellular tegmental field** (GTF), which sends acetylcholine-containing fibres into the forebrain. This site is also the origin of **PGO waves,** which are known to precede REM sleep. In turn, the GTF receives cholinergic projections from two nearby brainstem areas: the **laterodorsal tegmental nucleus** (LTN) and **pedunclopontine tegmental nucleus** (PTN). The neurobiology of SWS is less well understood although one crucial area is the **anterior-preoptic hypothalamus,** where damage causes severe insomnia. This area is also the source of neurons, which project to the brainstem. The medial and lateral hypothalamus further contain **orexin** neurons, which also pass down into the brainstem and are involved in sleep and **narcolepsy.** The hypothalamus also contains the **suprachiasmatic nucleus,** which governs certain **circadian rhythms,** partly though its influence on the **pineal gland,** which releases the hormone **melatonin.**

Essay questions

1. Describe the different types of EEG brain wave and behaviour that occur during a sleep cycle. How does a sleep cycle change during the course of a night?

    Helpful Interned search terms: *The sleep cycle. EEG brain waves and sleep. Slow-wave sleep. Rapid eye movement sleep. Behaviour in sleep.*

2. What brain regions and neurochemical systems are known to be involved in the regulation of sleep?

    Helpful Interned search terms: *Neural basis of sleep. Neurobiology of sleep. Gigantocellular tegmental field. Hypothalamus and sleep. Reticular formation. Neurochemistry of sleep.*

3. What are the functions of slow-wave sleep (SWS) and rapid eye movement (REM) sleep?

    Helpful Interned search terms: *Functions of sleep. Functions of REM sleep. Functions of slow-wave sleep. Restoration and sleep. Adaptive theories of sleep. Why do we sleep? Sleep deprivation.*

4. What is known about the neurobiology and endocrinology of circadian rhythms?

    Helpful Interned search terms: *Circadian rhythms. Suprachiasmatic nucleus. Melatonin. Pineal gland. Circadian clocks in the brain. Circadian rhythms in depression. Neurobiology of circadian rhythms.*

Further reading

Carkadon, M.A. (ed.) (1993) *Encyclopaedia of Sleep and Dreaming*. New York: Macmillan. Over 700 pages with hundreds of interesting entries (e.g. 'Dreams of the Blind', 'Short Sleepers in History and Legend') that summarise the many medical, biological and psychological facets of sleep.

Dement, W.C. (1972) *Some Must Watch While Some Must Sleep*. New York: Norton. An excellent short introduction to the topic of sleep research written by one of the pioneers in the field.

Dunlap, J.C., Loros, J.J. and DeCoursey, P.J. (2003) *Chronobiology*. Basingstoke: Freeman. A much needed textbook which provides a thorough overview of biological rhythms from molecular mechanisms to physiological systems in humans and other animals.

Empson, J. (2001) *Sleep and Dreaming*. New York: Harvester Wheatsheaf. A concise and easy to follow account which includes information on the electrophysiology and neurophysiology of sleep, along with sleep disorders.

Hobson, J.A. (1989) *Sleep*. New York: Scientific American Library. A beautifully illustrated book that covers everything from the evolution of sleeping patterns to the biochemistry of the brain during sleep, and the interpretation of dreams.

Horne, J. (1988) *Why We Sleep: The Functions of Sleep in Humans and Other Mammals*. Oxford: Oxford University Press. A book that attempts to evaluate the biological reasons why humans and other mammals have to sleep.

Jouvet, M. (1999) *The Paradox of Sleep*. Cambridge, MA: MIT Press. A short and readable book in which the author takes the reader on a scientific tour of sleep and dream research, concluding with his own ideas on the function of dreaming.

Lavie, P. (1996) *The Enchanted World of Sleep*. New Haven, CT: Yale University Press. A highly enjoyable and thought-provoking overview of what we know about sleep and dreaming, including an examination of the brain centres involved in sleep regulation.

Moorcroft, W.H. (1993) *Sleep, Dreaming, and Sleep Disorders: An Introduction*. Lanham, MD: University Press of America. A book that is suitable for psychology undergraduates and provides a broad account of sleep, including its characteristics, functions, physiology and disorders.

Schwartz, W.J. (ed.) (1997) *Sleep Science: Integrating Basic Research and Clinical Practice*. Basel: Karger. A highly technical account aimed at scientists and clinicians interested in linking the neurobiology of sleep with its associated disorders.

See website at www.pearsoned.co.uk/wickens for further resources including multiple choice questions.

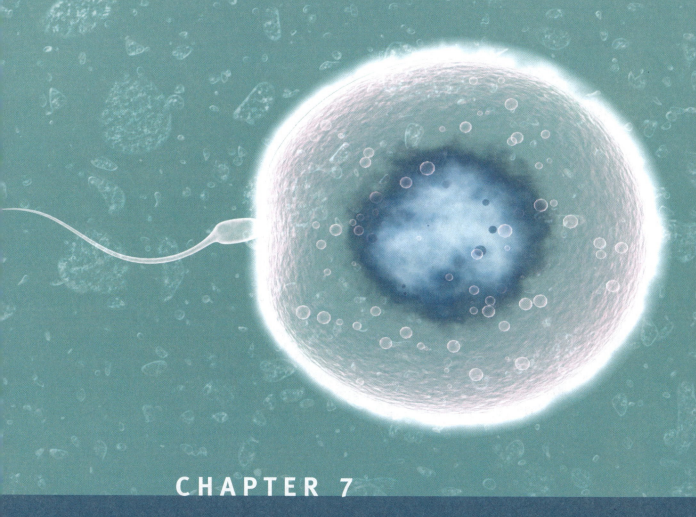

CHAPTER 7

Sexual development and behaviour

In this chapter

INTRODUCTION

Although sexual behaviour satisfies no vital tissue need, nor is it necessary for individual survival, from an evolutionary perspective it is crucial as, without it, we would not produce offspring or continue the survival of the species. The drive to engage in sexual activity is therefore, not surprisingly, a powerful one. It is also a behaviour with many manifestations. Not only has evolution gone to the great trouble of developing two different sexes, but it also requires that they come together in courtship to engage in sexual intercourse. In addition, most higher animals provide their offspring with some form of parental assistance to ensure that they reach a stage where they can look after themselves. It is easy to take all this behaviour for granted, but it must have taken millions of years to evolve, and be largely programmed into the brain. Understanding the biological basis of sexual identity, and how the brain controls sexual behaviour, presents a major challenge, especially when it comes to understanding human sexuality, which goes far beyond the act of procreation. But the challenge is an important one, especially as the well-being of individuals, couples, families and even entire societies can depend on matters that are fundamentally sexual (Haas and Haas 1993). The most important sexual organ of the body is the brain, and for this reason the biological psychologist has an important role to play in attempting to explain the causes of this complex behaviour and provide insights into its dysfunction.

Why have sex?

The obvious answer to this question is that it is enjoyable! But as true as this answer is, we must ask why sexual behaviour has evolved in the first place. At first sight the answer appears to be simple: sexual behaviour is necessary for the continuation of the species. However this is not an entirely satisfactory answer because reproduction without sex (asexual reproduction) is also possible (see Plate 7.1 for an interesting example). Indeed, many plants produce seeds that are clones of themselves, and most single-celled organisms (e.g. bacteria) replicate by dividing into two. Some other creatures also reproduce asexually. For example, female greenfly give birth to 'virgin' young for several generations, and there are even some vertebrates that reproduce without sex (e.g. the whiptail lizard and a type of fish called the Amazon molly are all-female). Since these forms of life can reproduce successfully, why go to the bother of inventing sexual reproduction? Sex is all the more puzzling when one considers that it is not without its risks: it can cause harmful genetic mutations, result in sexually transmitted diseases, and prove behaviourally hazardous during courtship and copulation. Yet sexual behaviour is the norm in nature. Why?

The main reason for the evolutionary development of sex probably lies with the great variety of gene combinations it produces compared with asexual reproduction. With sexual reproduction, each parent passes on a unique set of

Plate 7.1   Pseudosex in parthenogenic lizards. The desert grassland whiptail lizard (*canemidophorus uniparens*) is an all-female species. These reptiles reproduce by parthenogenesis: eggs undergo a chromosome doubling after meiosis and develop into lizards without being fertilised. However, ovulation is enhanced by mating rituals that imitate the behaviour of a closely related species that reproduce sexually. *Source*: Photo by P. DeVries

genes to each of its progeny, which guarantees that the offspring will be different to either of its parents, or to its brothers and sisters (unless it has an identical twin). Indeed, a couple can produce an almost infinite number of genetically discrete offspring. This constant shuffling of genes, and the large number of different individuals it creates, produces 'variation' in the population, which is of great evolutionary advantage to the species. For example, if we were all genetically identical, or even close to being the same, we would be equally vulnerable to the same diseases, environmental catastrophes or other threats to our survival. But a species with many genetically different individuals is much more likely to survive. Variability between individuals also means that some will become better suited to their environments than others, and these will be more likely to survive and pass on their genes. In this way, the survival of the 'fittest' ensures that a species is able to adapt optimally to its own ecological niche. Thus, sexual reproduction greatly assists the process of evolution.

Sexual development and differentiation

Nearly every cell in the human body contains 23 pairs of **chromosomes**, which carry the 30,000 or so **genes** that we inherited from our parents at the moment of conception. One exception to this rule are the **gametes** (sperm and ova), which have only 23 single chromosomes. In fact, it is only when the sperm and ova come together during fertilisation that all the chromosomes become paired and a new genetic entity is created. Remarkably, we all start life as this single microscopic cell. But even more astonishing is the fact that encoded in our first set of chromosomes are the genetic instructions that will ultimately turn the egg into an adult human being containing more than 100 million million cells. There is another surprising fact: males and females differ in terms of only one single chromosome! Thus, all genetically normal humans, regardless of their sex, share 22 pairs of chromosomes and only one pair is different. These are the sex chromosomes and they exist in two forms: X and Y. Put simply, if a fertilised egg inherits two X chromosomes (XX) it will become female, and if it receives X and Y chromosomes (XY) it will be male. Because males carry both types of chromosome, it is the father that determines the genetic sex of the fertilised egg.

Although the egg receives its full set of chromosomes at conception, it is not until the sixth week of foetal development that the first sex differences begin to emerge. Up to this point, males and females are identical and have the potential to develop into either sex as the embryo contains the precursor tissue for making both types of **gonads** (i.e. testes or ovaries). This precursor gonadal tissue is connected to two tubular duct structures: the **Wolffian duct** has the potential to develop into the male reproductive system, and the **Müllerian duct** is capable of developing into the female one. However, only one of these ducts will develop to determine the sex of the foetus. The event that initiates this change occurs in the sixth week of gestation, when the Y chromosome produces a chemical called **testis-determining factor**, which causes the foetal gonadal tissue to develop into **testes**. There is no female equivalent of this substance and in its absence the gonadal tissue remains undeveloped until it starts to develop into **ovaries** at about 12 weeks of gestation.

The differentiation of gonadal tissue into testes or ovaries is the first stage of sexual development in which a difference between the sexes can be observed. It also marks the point where the genetic influence on foetal sexual development effectively ends and hormonal influences take over. The testes and ovaries have a critical role to play at this stage because they produce the male or female hormones that set in motion the changes that ultimately produce the sex of the individual. In the case of a male, the testes produce two hormones called **testosterone** and **Müllerian duct-inhibiting substance**. The first of these acts to masculinise the sex organs by developing the Wolffian duct system into the internal male sex organs, including vas deferens, seminal vesicles and prostrate – while the second prevents the (female) Müllerian system from forming. In contrast, the ovaries do not secrete sex hormones at this stage. Nevertheless, the lack of hormonal stimulation still exerts an important effect as it causes the Wolffian system to degenerate and the Müllerian system to develop into the female internal sex organs, including the uterus and fallopian tubes.

The external genital anatomy (penis and vagina) start to appear at about 8–12 weeks of gestation, and the same principles of hormonal organisation hold for internal development. That is, the release of testosterone by the testes causes the male sex organs such as the seminal vesicles and prostate to be formed, and its absence results in the development of the female genitalia. With the differentiation of the external genitalia the foetus can be seen to be either male or female.

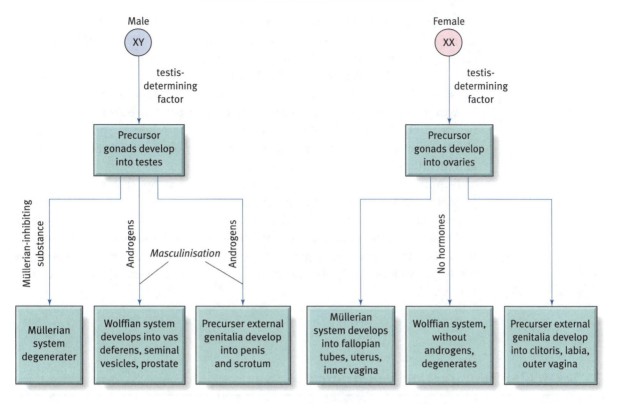

Figure 7.1   The hormonal control of embryonic sexual differentiation. *Source*: Adapted from Neil R. Carlson, *Physiology of Behavior*, 6th edition. Copyright © 1998 by Pearson Education

The adrenogenital syndrome

As we have seen, the normal sexual development of the foetus depends on the differentiation of the gonads into testes or ovaries to provide the necessary hormonal environment for the internal and external sex organs to develop. But what if something goes wrong? What happens, for example, if the female foetus is exposed to high levels of testosterone (say, around the sixth week of gestation) when differentiation of the sex organs is normally taking place? In fact, this type of event occurs in a condition called congenital **adrenal hyperplasia**, in which the foetal adrenal glands (which normally produce insignificant amounts of male steroids or **androgens**) secrete excessive levels of these hormones. A similar situation can also occur when the mother uses androgenic drugs such as **anabolic steroids** during the early stages of pregnancy. In both cases, the consequences of high androgen exposure is the masculinisation of the female genitalia.

The effects of androgens on early female development was first shown by researchers in the 1940s, when it was found that if pregnant rhesus monkeys were injected with testosterone, the female offspring were born with a small penis and well-formed scrotum. In other words, the treatment produced an animal with gonads (testes or ovaries) that matched their sex chromosomes, but with a genital appearance of the opposite sex (i.e. **pseudo-hermaphrodite**). A similar situation can also occur with humans. For example, newborn females with congenital adrenal hyperplasia often have an enlarged clitoris and partially fused labia (although in most cases the internal sexual organs are normal because the adrenal androgens are released too late in development to stimulate the development of the Wolffian system). If identified at birth, the external genitals can be surgically corrected and drug therapy used to reduce androgen levels. However, in some cases, the genitals may be so masculinised that the sex of the newborn child is misidentified. Contrary to what might be predicted, these children are often happily reared as boys, with problems of sexual development and identification only emerging during adolescence.

Females who have experienced prenatal adrenal hyperplasia also have a greater tendency to show masculine behavioural characteristics. For example, young female monkeys exposed to prenatal androgens are more aggressive and tend to exhibit male-type sexual behaviour as adults. Similarly, in humans there is evidence that young girls with andrenogenital syndrome are likely to be tomboys, and as adults be more inclined to being bisexual or lesbian (see below).

Testicular feminisation syndrome

Although increased amounts of androgens in foetal development have little effect on changing the sexual appearance of males, a decrease in the levels of these hormones, or a reduced sensitivity to them, can produce feminine effects. One such condition is **testicular feminisation syndrome**, which occurs when testosterone, and other androgens, have no biological action on body tissues. In this situation, the foetus has normal levels of male sex hormones, but the androgen receptors in the tissues are insensitive to their effects. The consequence is that the male develops external female genitalia (e.g. labia and clitoris) and the infant appears to be female at birth. However, because the testes still continue to produce Mullerian duct-inhibiting substance, which causes the internal female sexual organs to degenerate, the foetus does not develop a uterus or fallopian tubes. The result is a male **pseudo-hermaphrodite** (a male with testes but with the genital appearance of a female).

A newborn baby with testicular feminisation syndrome looks like a girl, and will often be mistaken for one unless the testes have descended into the labia. Consequently, these children are normally raised as females and their condition is not recognised until the lack of menstruation in puberty becomes suspicious. In fact, during adolescence the individual may develop feminine breasts because some of their testosterone is metabolised into oestrogen. Thus, these 'genetic males' appear to be girls, and their sexual behaviour is also typically that of a female – although, without internal sexual organs, they obviously cannot produce children. In fact, in many cases of testicular feminisation, physicians recommend that the child should be raised as a girl, since neither surgery nor hormonal treatment can create a functioning penis or alter the feminine appearance of the body (Masters *et al.* 1995). This does not generally present a problem, however, as these individuals typically regard themselves as female anyway.

Genetic syndromes

We normally inherit 23 pairs of chromosomes including a pair of sex chromosomes (XX or XY). But there can be occasions when this inheritance does not occur. One such condition is **Turner's syndrome**, which occurs in about one in 2,500 live births, where the egg is fertilised by a sperm that has lost its sex chromosome. Thus, the individual inherits only one X chromosome (X_0). Because the Y chromosome is missing, the gonads do not differentiate into testes and the male sex organs fail to develop. Instead, poorly developed ovaries are formed, which results in the development of a girl. Indeed, at birth these infants have normal external genitalia and appear to be normal females. However, when they reach puberty, they do not undergo an adolescent growth spurt, begin menstruation or develop breasts, due to their non-functional ovaries, There can also be webbing of the neck and heart abnormalities. Interestingly, the male version of Turner's syndrome (Y_0) does not exist, since embryos with this combination do not survive.

There are also genetic conditions where females inherit extra copies of the X chromosome including triple (XXX), tetra (XXXX) and even penta (XXXXX) inheritance. The triple X female appears 'normal' but, as an adult, is normally beset with menstrual cycle irregularities and a premature menopause. Despite this, they are fertile and give birth to normal offspring. In cases where tetra and penta inheritance occurs there is a much greater likelihood of problems with sexual development, and a chance of mental retardation.

Another sex-related genetic condition is **Klinefelter's syndrome**, where males inherit an extra X chromosome (XXY). This disorder, which occurs in about one in every 500 live births, increases the feminine characteristics of the individual, although this is not usually noticed until adulthood. The main problem with the extra X chromosome is that it causes abnormal development of the testes with reduced release of androgens. This results in adult males tending to be very tall with poor muscular definition and enlarged breasts. In addition, they are often infertile with low sexual desire or impotence, which may be accompanied by mild mental retardation.

Males can also be born with an extra copy of the Y chromosome (XYY). This is one of the most controversial of genetic syndromes because it has been associated with individuals who are mentally retarded or have criminal and violent tendencies. These males also tend to be very tall and have low IQs. Although XYY inheritance occurs in only about one in 1,000 births, some surveys have shown that these individuals may make up 2–3 per cent of the inmates of mental or penal institutions (Emery and Mueller 1992). However, because this genetic abnormality normally only comes to light when individuals are institutionalised, it may be that the incidence of XYY inheritance is much higher in the general population than estimates currently show. Indeed, it is now known that some XYY individuals are neither delinquent nor mentally retarded, which shows that this condition is not inevitably linked with behavioural problems. Thus, there may be many other males who have this genetic abnormality, but appear to be normal.

The organisational effects of hormones on behaviour

Prenatal androgen secretion exerts a development effect not only on the internal and external reproductive organs but also on the brain, where it helps to organise the nervous system for later male or female behaviour. This was shown in a study by Phoenix *et al.* (1959) that looked at female sexual behaviour in guinea pigs that had been exposed to high testosterone levels during foetal development. Around the time of ovulation, an adult female guinea pig will often show **lordosis**, essentially a mating position that includes raising the hind quarters and moving the tail to one side, thus signalling sexual receptivity for a male. In fact, lordosis is under hormonal control and can be induced by giving the female a priming dose of oestrogen for a few days, followed by an injection of progesterone – a procedure that mimics the hormonal state of ovulation and makes the guinea pig sexually receptive a few hours later. However, when Phoenix *et al.* (1959) attempted to induce lordosis by hormone injections in females that had been given testosterone during early development, the behaviour did not occur. In other words, the early exposure to testosterone had abolished this adult form of female sexual behaviour.

This example shows that sex hormones, such as testosterone, exert two main types of effect. During early development, they have an **organisational effect** on the animal that determines its sex, and helps to organise the structure of the brain for later adult behaviour. But once development is complete, the sex hormones start to produce **activational effects** where they can stimulate certain behaviours such as lordosis. These two effects are not exclusive, however, because whether a hormone is able to exert an activational effect on behaviour is largely dependent on the way the brain has been 'organised' during development.

What is the situation regarding males? As might be expected, male rats do not normally show lordosis behaviour when given injections of oestrogen and progesterone. But if males rats are castrated at birth (in rats this is a period when sex hormones have a particularly important effect on development) they do show lordosis if they are administered female sex hormones. These animals also show reduced levels of male-related sexual behaviour as adults, even if given testosterone. Thus, the neural circuits governing sexual responses in rats are organised early in development, although the adult sexual behaviour is not produced until later.

Because androgens clearly influence the sexual behaviour of rodents, there have been attempts to discover if early exposure to high levels of these hormones in humans, or primates, produces similar effects. Although the behaviour of higher animals is more complex, it nevertheless appears that a hormonal influence is at work. For example, Goy *et al.* (1988) examined the behaviour of female monkeys given prenatal androgens, and found that they engaged in more rough-and-tumble play than normal. A similar finding was also reported by Money and Ehrhardt (1996) in human females who had been exposed to high levels of testosterone as a result of adrenogenital syndrome (see above). These girls also showed a greater tendency to play with toys that were normally preferred by boys.

But what about sexual behaviour as adults? Interestingly, Money *et al.* (1984) questioned 30 young adult women who had a history of adrenogenital syndrome. When asked to describe their sexual orientation, 37 per cent described themselves as bisexual or homosexual; 40 per cent were exclusively heterosexual; and 23 per cent refused to disclose their sexuality. In short, these findings indicate that high prenatal androgen levels in females may bias the person towards bisexuality or homosexuality. However, since there appear to be more heterosexual women than bisexual or homosexual ones in this group, this effect is far from inevitable.

Adult sexual development

At birth, normal human males and females are physically similar (apart from the differences in sexual anatomy) and they remain so until puberty, when secondary sexual characteristics begin to develop. This is the final stage of sexual development and it transforms the young person into an adult capable of reproduction. One of the most striking changes that takes place during this period is the adolescent growth spurt, which results in both sexes growing taller. In males, this is influenced by the maturation of the testes, and testosterone production, which increases skeletal and muscle mass, along with the growth of body and pubic hair, a deepening of the voice, and the ability to ejaculate. In females, the release of sex hormones helps to promote a fuller figure along with enlarged breasts and wider hips. Approximately two years after the start of puberty in the female the first signs of menstruation occur, which marks the point where, in theory, pregnancy becomes possible, although it normally takes another year before the release of mature ova finally occurs.

The onset of puberty is put into motion by the release of sex hormones from the gonads – namely, the testes, which produce testosterone, and ovaries, which produce oestrogen and progesterone. Furthermore, at this point, both testes and ovaries come under the control of the **hypothalamus** and adjoining **pituitary gland** (Figure 7.2). To be more precise, the release of sex hormones begins with the hypothalamus, which secretes **gonadotropin-releasing hormone** (GnRH), which diffuses through the hypophyseal portal blood vessels to the anterior part of the pituitary. In turn, GnRH stimulates the anterior pituitary gland to secrete two hormones called **luteinising hormone** (LH) and **follicle-stimulating hormone** (FSH). Both these hormones are released into the bloodstream, where they are transported to the gonads. They also have different functions: in males, the

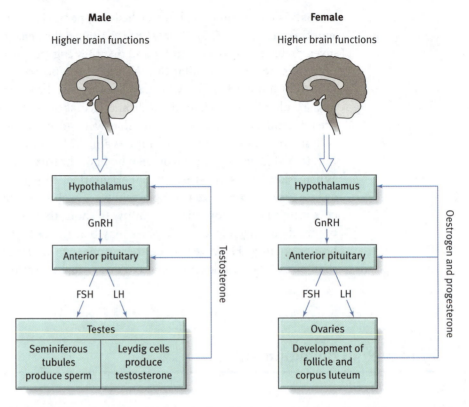

Figure 7.2 Flowchart showing how the hypothalamic–pituitary system influences activity of the testes and ovaries

release of LH causes the **Leydig cells** of the testes to manufacture testosterone, whereas in the female the same hormone is a trigger for ovulation (see next section). In contrast, FSH in males stimulates the production of sperm, while in females it prepares the ovary for ovulation. Although both LSH and FSH play an important role in the development of puberty, they also influence gonadal functioning throughout much of life.

The menstrual cycle

For most species, the female is only sexually receptive and able to conceive during a specific period known as **oestrus**, when ovulation usually occurs. However, human females along with certain other primates are an exception to this rule because they can be sexually receptive at any point in their reproductive cycle and not just during ovulation. The human reproductive cycle is called a **menstrual cycle** (from *mensis* meaning 'month') and it also differs from the oestrus cycle because of menstruation – that is, the process by which the lining of the uterus is discarded at the end of the cycle (Figure 7.3). Despite this, oestrus and menstrual cycles show some similarities and are both under the control of hormones released by the pituitary gland.

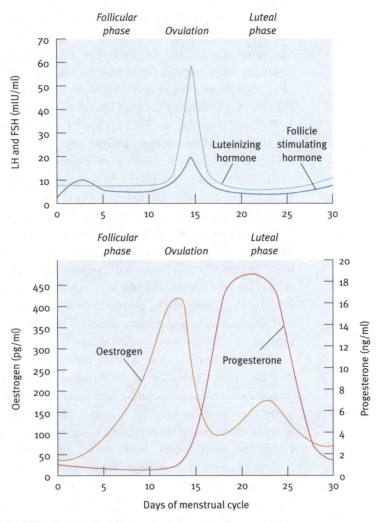

Figure 7.3   The menstrual cycle

The menstrual cycle has three main phases, known as follicular, ovulatory and luteal. By convention, the first day of the menstrual cycle begins with menstruation (which usually lasts for a few days) and this marks the start of the follicular phase. During this period, the hypothalamus secretes GnRH, which causes the pituitary gland to release FSH and LH. It is the former that exerts the most important effect at this stage because it stimulates the development of a follicle – a protective sac that surrounds the ovum or unfertilised egg – in the ovary. In turn, the follicle is responsible for releasing oestrogen. Although as many as 20 follicles may start to develop at the beginning of each cycle, only one usually reaches maturity, and this will secrete increasing amounts of oestrogen until a level is reached (usually around the 12th day of the cycle) which is sufficient to turn off the pituitary gland's release of FSH. At this point the pituitary begins to secrete large amounts of LH instead.

By this stage of the cycle, the follicle has grown large enough to form a large bulge in the lining of the ovary. But the sudden surge in circulating LH now causes the walls of the follicle and ovary to rupture, releasing the mature egg into the upper sections of the fallopian tubes – a process known as **ovulation**. At this point the egg can be fertilised by a male sperm. However, the time-frame for this event is relatively short since the egg is viable for only about 12–24 hours, and most sperm exist in the female reproductive tract for only about a day, although some 'super' sperm may survive up to 72 hours. Thus, there is a period of around three days in every menstrual cycle when pregnancy can take place as the egg moves down the fallopian tube into the uterus.

Following ovulation, the ruptured follicle in the ovary forms a yellow mass of tissue called the **corpus luteum** and it begins to secrete large amounts of progesterone (and to a lesser extent oestrogen), which initiates the luteal phase of the menstrual cycle. The main function of progesterone ('pro-gestation') is to build up the lining of the uterus with blood and nourishment for the implantation of the egg should it be fertilised. The increase in progesterone also turns off GnRH release from the hypothalamus, producing a rapid decline in LH and FSH. If fertilisation of the egg occurs, then the level of progesterone remains high and the womb's lining will continue to develop; but if fertilisation does not take place, the corpus luteum will shrink and reduce its secretion of hormones. Because the lining of the uterus cannot be maintained without progesterone, it will fall away causing menstruation. The total amount of blood lost is usually around 30 millilitres or a twentieth of a pint.

On average, most women have menstrual cycles that last 28 days (although they can range from 20 to 40 days) and they continue until the menopause. This means that a non child-bearing female can expect to undergo around 400 menstrual cycles in her life. It is also of interest to note that birth-control pills prevent pregnancy by interfering with the normal development of the menstrual cycle. The most widely used contraceptive pill is the combination pill, which contains oestrogen and progesterone and works in two ways: the increased level of oestrogen suppresses the release of FSH thereby blocking the development of the follicle; while the increased level of progesterone inhibits the secretion of LH thus making sure that ova will not be released by the ovary.

Index and ring fingers: do they provide an insight into your sexual development and behaviour?

Take a look at your hands. To an educated observer they may give more away about your personal self than you may first realise. It has been known for over a century that males tend to have ring fingers (the 4th digit) that are slightly longer than their index fingers (the 2nd digit), while females are more likely to have digits of the same length. The full significance of this sex difference in 2D : 4D ratio, however, was not fully appreciated until recently. In 1998, John Manning and his colleagues measured the lengths of the index and ring fingers in 800 males and females ranging from 2 to 25 years, and confirmed that males had a lower 2D : 4D ratio compared with females on both hands. This difference also occurred in all age groups indicating that it arose early in development. In fact, digit ratios are established by the 13th week of foetal development, and governed by the same genes (called Homeobox or *Hox*) that control the formation of our testes and ovaries. Finger growth also occurs when the foetus is exposed to high levels of testosterone. The implication, therefore, is that this hormone may be responsible for the sex differences in the 2D : 4D ratio. Indeed, Manning supported this theory

Index and ring fingers: do they provide an insight into your sexual development and behaviour? continued.

by finding a significant relationship between digit ratio and sex hormones in his sample of subjects, with higher levels of testosterone and increased sperm counts being associated with a lower 2D : 4D ratio (most common in males), and higher levels of luteinising hormone and oestrogen being related to higher 2D : 4D ratios (most common in females).

As we have seen in this chapter, there is compelling evidence that sex hormones exert organisational effects upon the CNS before or shortly after birth, which helps to masculinise or feminise certain brain structures and functions. Although it is not viable to measure hormonal levels *in utero* during early development, our digit ratios may provide an alternative means of obtaining this information – especially for the latter part of the first trimester, which is a critical time for sexual differentiation of the body and brain. Thus, a low 2D : 4D ratio (ring finger longer than index) may act as a marker for a uterine environment that is high in testosterone and low in oestrogen. Conversely, a high 2D : 4D ratio (index longer than ring finger) may be a marker for a uterine environment low in testosterone and high in oestrogen.

If this is the case, then one might expected to find a wide range of behavioural differences between individuals with high and low digit ratios. In fact, a number of remarkable differences have been discovered. For example, a low 2D : 4D ratio was found in a group of 88 British homosexual men compared with controls, indicating that homosexuality may be caused by exposure to high androgen levels before birth. A low 2D : 4D ratio, however, has also been found to be associated with other male traits, including better spatial ability, left-handedness and a predisposition towards autism. Remarkably, a low 2D : 4D ratio has also been found in professional soccer players (Figure 7.4) – the ratio was even greater for internationals – and in élite musicians from a British symphony orchestra. There are a number of reasons why a low 2D : 4D ratio may exist in these two groups. Perhaps improved visuo-spatial ability in soccer players, and increased competitiveness in musicians, both known to be influenced by testosterone, have contributed to the men excelling in these disciplines. Whatever the explanation, it shows that exposure to sex hormones early in development has a significant bearing on our later behaviour as adults (Manning 2002).

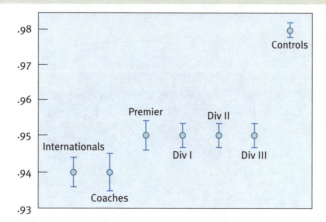

Figure 7.4   Digit ratios of professional soccer players. *Source*: Professor John T. Manning (2001), *Evolution and Human Behaviour*, vol 22, pp.61–9. Reproduced by permission of Professor Manning

Sexual differentiation of the nervous system

As might be expected, there are certain differences between males and females in the anatomy of their nervous systems. One difference occurs in a small group of motor neurons in the lower half of the spinal cord called the **bulbocavernosus nucleus,** which in male rats controls the reflexes of the penis during copulation. This structure shows a difference between the sexes, with adult males containing around 200 neurons in their nucleus and females typically having less than 70. Although this nucleus is present in both sexes, it atrophies early in female development due to the lack of androgen stimulation. Indeed, females given testosterone during a critical period of development will show an increased number of bulbocavernosus neurons in adulthood, whereas male rats deprived of androgens will develop a nucleus that resembles the female one. Humans also have bulbocavernosus motor neurons although they are found in a spinal structure called **Onuf's nucleus.** Again, there is a difference between the sexes, which is known to result from around the 26th week of gestation when the male foetus produces high amounts of androgens (Forger and Breedlove 1986).

There are also some neuroanatomical differences between male and females in terms of their brain structure. One of the first studies to demonstrate this was undertaken by Raisman and Field (1973), who examined the **preoptic area** of the hypothalamus in rats. These researchers found that the female preoptic area contained significantly more synapses than that of the male. However, when males were castrated soon after birth the number of synapses increased to female levels. Alternatively, testosterone given to young females resulted in a decrease of synapses to male levels. This was proof that early androgen exposure could

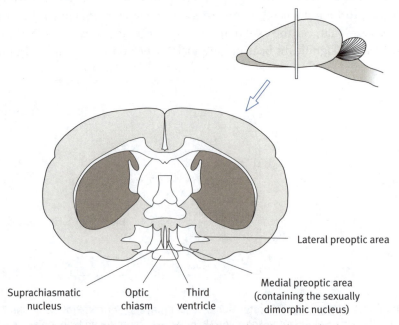

Lateral preoptic area

Suprachiasmatic nucleus

Optic chiasm

Third ventricle

Medial preoptic area (containing the sexually dimorphic nucleus)

Figure 7.5   The location of the sexually dimorphic nucleus in the rat brain

alter the neural structure of certain sites in the brain known to be associated with sexual behaviour.

Following this, another important discovery was made: a small nucleus was found embedded in the preoptic area of rats that was three to five times larger in males than in females (Gorski *et al.* 1978). This nucleus was called the **sexually dimorphic nucleus** (Figure 7.5) and its size was shown to be directly linked with early androgen stimulation. For example, males castrated at birth showed much smaller dimorphic nuclei, whereas females given androgens at birth had a much larger nucleus. In fact, the size of the sexually dimorphic nuclei could only be altered during a critical stage that corresponded to the first 10 days after birth. If male rats were castrated after this period, or females given androgens as adults, this had no effect on the size of the nucleus.

Human sex differences in brain structure

What about the humans? The preoptic area of the hypothalamus is much more complex in the human brain, and instead of having just one dimorphic nucleus, we actually have four! These are known as the **interstitial nuclei of the anterior hypothalamus** (INAH 1–4). Interestingly, Allen *et al.* (1989) have shown that while the INAH-1 and INAH-4 do not show any size difference between the sexes, the remaining two nuclei (particularly INAH-3) are much larger in males. Controversially, there is some evidence that INAH-3 may be influencing our sexual orientation since it has also been shown to be significantly smaller in homosexual men than in heterosexual men (LeVay 1993), although this finding has not always been replicated (Byne *et al.* 2001). Another brain structure which has been claimed to show a difference between homosexual and hetero-sexual men is the suprachiasmatic nucleus. This is also located near the preoptic part of the hypothalamus and is known to be involved in the production of circadian rhythms. This small nucleus is larger in homosexual men compared with heterosexual males and females (Swaab and Hofman 1990).

A third area where differences have been found between males and females is a structure called the **bed nucleus of the stria terminalis** (BNST), which is found on a pathway (the stria terminalis) that connects the amygdala with the hypoth-alamus. The size of this nucleus is larger in males than in females (Zhou *et al.* 1995). Interestingly, while it is the same size in male heterosexuals and homo-sexuals, it was found to be significantly smaller in male transsexuals. These are men who feel as if they are women trapped in male bodies, and some may go to great lengths to change their gender by having hormone therapy, or sex change operations. Although little is known about the functions of the BNST it would appear to be involved in determining the sexual identity of the person.

There are grounds for believing that both the hypothalamus and amygdala may have important roles to play in sexual behaviour and orientation. But there are other regions of the brain not so obviously linked with sexual behaviour where differences have been found between the sexes. One such structure is the **corpus callosum,** which is the huge bundle of white matter that connects the two cerebral hemispheres. In 1982 it was reported that the posterior part of the corpus callosum, called the **splenium,** which joins the occipital and parietal regions, was significantly larger in females than in males (Lacoste-Utamsing and Holloway 1982). Unfortunately, subsequent research has provided a more confused picture with one study confirming these results (Clarke 1990), one showing increased splenium size in right-handed but not left-handed women (Witelson 1989), and one reporting no sex differences whatsoever (Byne *et al.* 1988). But even if the corpus callosum is the same size in males and females, this is still a significant finding because men on average have brains that are approximately 15 per cent bigger than those of women. This means, therefore, that females have a *relatively* bigger corpus callosum than men (LeVay 1993). More recently, women have also been shown to have a relatively larger **anterior commissure**, which interconnects parts of the right and left temporal lobes (Allen and Gorski 1992).

It would appear, therefore, that the two cerebral hemispheres are more richly connected in women – a finding that may help to explain why there are some differences between the sexes in their cognitive skills (see also Chapter 9). Indeed, PET and MRI research that has examined the cerebral cortex in mental performance have shown that the two hemispheres of the female brain share more functions than those of a male. In other words, mental functioning in a male tends to be more lateralised towards a single hemisphere, whereas it is spread more evenly in a female. This probably explains why males who suffer a stroke to the left cortex are more likely to show serious language deficits compared with a female, who has a greater degree of function across both hemisphere (Breedlove 1994).

The activational effects of hormones on sexual behaviour

So far, we have looked at some of the ways that sex hormones can influence foetal and pubertal development, and examined differences in the morphology of spinal cord and brain between males and females. But long after these hormones have shaped sexual differentiation, 'organised' the CNS, and produced secondary sex characteristics, they still continue to exert 'activational' effects on behaviour. This is seen, for example, in the case of lordosis (described above), which is dependent on the way the nervous system has been organised by androgens during development, and on the activating level of certain hormones circulating in the body as an adult. The same principle holds true in some instances for male reproductive behaviour. For example, if an adult male rat is castrated, it shows a marked decline in sexual activity and little interest in a receptive female. Reproductive interest is restored, however, by testosterone administration, which appears to show that this hormone is necessary for producing sexual motivation and activity (Becker *et al.* 1993).

For humans and primates, the relationship between testosterone and sexual activity is not so straightforward. For example, male primates are typically able to maintain sexual behaviour for some years after castration, although it does eventually produce a decrease in activity and interest. In humans, the situation appears to be similar with a gradual waning of sexual motivation. However, there is also great variability between individuals with some castrated men quickly becoming impotent, while others show relatively normal sexual function for years, or even decades, after the operation (Money and Ehrhardt 1996). Indeed, historical accounts of eunuchs who were employed as harem guards, or young men castrated for their opera singing abilities, point to a similar conclusion (Heriot 1955). Furthermore, many reliable reports show that castrated men are capable of both erections and orgasms (Kinsey *et al.* 1948). Thus, it would appear that a loss of testosterone is not crucial for male sexual activity, although with time a lack of androgenic stimulation may well lead to a decline in this behaviour. In other words, there is much more to male (and female) sexual behaviour than just the simple effects of hormones.

Despite this, testosterone is still capable of producing activational effects on sexual behaviour. For example, when hypogonadal men with abnormally low levels of testosterone are given hormone replacement therapy, they typically report increases in sexual activity, along with increased frequencies of sexual thoughts and fantasies (Davidson *et al.* 1979). This effect may not be specific to males since the adrenal glands in women also produce small amounts of testosterone, and females who have injections of this hormone also often report a heightened sexual desire (Michael 1980).

The effects of testosterone on aggressive behaviour

Numerous studies have also shown a positive relationship between testosterone levels and aggression in many species. Indeed, in the majority of animals, including humans, the male is generally regarded as the more aggressive sex – and, aggression is most often seen around puberty, which coincides with the stage when androgen levels are at their highest. One of the earliest studies to show the effects of androgens on aggression was undertaken by Allee *et al.* (1939), who injected testosterone into low-ranking hens and found that they increased their aggressive behaviour, which enabled them to rise in the group's status hierarchy, sometimes to top position. In addition, their comb size increased (a male characteristic), some began crowing (rare in hens), and a few started courting other hens. More recently, similar findings have been found in female rhesus monkeys given regular testosterone injections over an eight-month period. In fact, these monkeys became so aggressive that they replaced the males in the top position of the social hierarchy (Joslyn 1973).

Similarly, a reduction of testosterone is known to decrease aggressive behaviour in a large number of species. Indeed, for thousands of years, humans have castrated domestic animals to control aggression and make them more manageable, and this has also been shown in numerous experimental studies. The effects of castration on aggression can normally be reversed by the administration of testosterone, although this is often dependent on the earlier organisation of the nervous system. That is, if the animal is castrated early in life and given testosterone as an adult, there is often little enhancement of aggression.

However, the relationship between testosterone and aggression in humans is not straightforward. Although males throughout the world engage in more violent behaviour than females, numerous studies have shown that high levels of testosterone do not necessarily correlate with aggressive behaviour. For example, Archer (1994) examined 10 studies in which aggressive and non-aggressive groups were compared (e.g. prisoners or young offenders with matched control groups), and although only one study failed to find a difference in circulating androgens, the overall correlation between aggression and testosterone was in the region of +0.3. This is far from a perfect positive relationship, which is represented by the value of +1.0. A comparable finding was obtained by Dabbs and Morris (1990), who measured testosterone in 4,462 US military veterans, and found that those with levels in the top 10 per cent were also the ones that had previously shown greater amounts of antisocial behaviour including assault. But although this relationship was significant, it was again relatively small. Moreover, the tendency towards aggressive behaviour was also found to be more pronounced in the men from lower socio-economic groups – a finding that suggests that this type of environment may help to increase the expression of antisocial and aggressive behaviours.

Although the environment may be an important determinant of aggressive behaviour, there is also evidence that it may contribute to testosterone levels. As we have seen above, a number of species live in social groups with dominance hierarchies, and in some cases the highest-ranked individuals are those with greater levels of testosterone. At first sight this suggests that the most dominant individuals are also the most aggressive, presumably because of their high testosterone levels. This, however, is not necessarily the case. For example, Rose *et al.* (1975) found that, before it was placed into a new social group, a monkey's testo-sterone level did not correlate with the rank it would later attain in the group. In fact, once the social groups were established and dominance ranking stabilised, a significant rise in testosterone (as much as ten fold) could often be found in the dominant male. This indicates that it is the success in achieving dominance through aggressive encounters that determines the level of testosterone. In short, victory increases levels of androgens, while defeat reduces them. Indeed, subsequent studies have shown that a defeated monkey may show a fall in testosterone of some 10–15 per cent within 24 hours, and this level can remain depressed for several weeks (Monaghan and Glickman 1992).

Similar findings have also been reported for humans. For example, testosterone in athletes rises shortly before their sporting events, and levels remain high in the winner one or two hours after the competition. Similar increases in testosterone have also been found in chess players, or laboratory contests of reaction time (Mazur and Booth 1998). It would appear that competition is the key variable, since testosterone levels are greater during a judo competition than during an equally energetic session of exercise. Remarkably, even direct participation in a competition may not always be necessary for the testosterone effect to occur. For example, prior to the 1994 World Cup soccer final between Brazil and Italy, testosterone samples were taken from both sets of fans. The results showed that testosterone levels rose in 11 of the 12 'winning' Brazilian fans by an average of 27.6 per cent, and decreased by 26.7 per cent in the nine Italian fans (Fielden *et al.* 1994). All of these findings show that it is far too simple to equate testosterone with aggression. Rather, levels of testosterone in humans appears to be more closely linked with success or failure in competition, and in the pursuit of dominance, than aggressiveness *per se*.

Pheromones: do they play a role in human attraction?

Pheromones are chemicals that act as odour signals secreted by an animal to convey information – normally for attraction, repulsion, or about sexual condition – to other members of the same species. It is often overlooked by humans, who get much of their information about the world from sight and sound, that many other animals rely heavily on this type of information to guide communication and social interaction. In fact, most mammals have a special structure in their nostrils called a **vomeronasal organ** (VNO), which has evolved to detect a wide range of pheromone signals. This organ plays a crucial role in the male sexual behaviour of the golden hamster, for example. If a male hamster is anaesthetised and placed in a lordosis position, other males will give it a cursory examination. But if the hindquarters of this hamster are smeared with a vaginal discharge, then the males will try to mate with it! The vaginal pheromone responsible for producing this behaviour has been isolated and called *aphrodism* (see Agosta 1992), and it requires an intact VNO in male hamsters for it to produce its stimulatory effect on the mating response.

Pheromones also play an important part in female sexual behaviour. For example, if groups of female mice are housed together, their oestrus cycles will lengthen and eventually stop. This is called the **Lee–Boot effect** and it may have evolved to help to conserve reproductive energy in the absence of males when ovulation is unlikely to lead to pregnancy. However, if the urine of a male is introduced into the female group, they will start cycling again and go into oestrus more frequently (the **Whitten effect**). The presence of an unfamiliar male can even terminate the pregnancy of a recently impregnated female (the **Bruce effect**). This effect is likely to be advantageous for the female because the new male, by taking over his predecessor's territory, has shown himself to be more 'fit' and have 'stronger' genes, which will produce healthier offspring. Both the Whitten and Bruce effects are caused by pheromones that are found in the urine of intact adult males. The urine of a castrated male has no effect, showing that this pheromone requires the presence of testosterone.

But what about human behaviour? Although humans have a VNO, it is not well developed, and the weight of evidence suggests that it is non-functional (Doty 2001). Despite this, pheromones still influence human behaviour. For example, when groups of women live together, their menstrual cycles will tend to become synchronised. The chemical responsible

Pheromones: do they play a role in human attraction? continued.

for this effect may derive from the armpits. When an extract from this region of the body was swabbed on the upper lips of a group of women three times each week, their menstrual cycles began to synchronise with the cycle of the donor (Russell *et al.* 1980). Pheromones may also play a role in human sexual attraction. In one study, males were asked to wear a T-shirt in bed for two consecutive nights, and to give a blood sample that enabled the genes governing their immune system to be determined (Wedekind *et al.* 1995). When these shirts were smelled by women, it was found that they preferred the ones that had been worn by males with the most genetically dissimilar immune systems to their own. In fact, this preference would be highly beneficial for the offspring since a greater mix of different immunity genes would give them greater protection to a wider range of diseases. Thus, humans may be more susceptible to the effects of pheromones than is generally recognised.

The neural control of sexual behaviour

As we have seen, higher animals are less dependent on their sex hormones to control reproductive behaviour, and this is particularly true for humans, who show the most complex and varied sexual activity of all. This is undoubtedly due to the greater complexity of our brains, especially the cerebral cortex, which enables human sexual behaviour to become less instinctual and more influenced by cognition and experience. Despite this, we still share much of the neural circuitry underlying sexual behaviour with other animals. In fact, many of the basic reflexes that form an integral part of our sexual behaviour are controlled by the spinal cord. Indeed, stimulation of the genitals in animals is able to elicit sexual responses such as penile erections, pelvic thrusting and ejaculation even when the brain is severed from the spinal cord (Hart 1967). Similar responses have also been observed in paraplegic men. For example, Money (1960) in a study of paraplegic males with broken spinal cords that had severed the neural pathways between brain and sex organs, found that 65 per cent of the sample were capable of achieving a complete erection; 20 per cent managed a partial erection; and 20 per cent were able to engage in coitus. Furthermore, many of these men were able to ejaculate, although they did not 'sense' the orgasm mentally. Thus, even in a species as advanced as humans, erection and ejaculation can take place without a brain!

Despite this, the brain remains the most important structure that governs sexual behaviour, and one structure with a vital role to play in this respect is the hypothalamus. This tiny region not only influences the release of LH and FSH from the pituitary gland, which controls the secretion of sex hormones from the gonads, but it also exerts important control over the autonomic nervous system. Moreover, some regions of the hypothalamus are more important than others in controlling sexual behaviour. A crucial area is the **medial preoptic area**, with lesions of this region eliminating copulatory behaviour in male rats, and producing an impairment that is not corrected with testosterone treatment (Heimir and Larsson 1967). In contrast, electrical or androgen stimulation of the same region facilitates sexual behaviour in male rats, even if they have been castrated (Davidson 1980). This region of the brain in the male also contains a high concentration of androgen receptors (about five times more than that found in females), which shows that it is particularly sensitive to the effects of testosterone. As mentioned above, the preoptic area is also the site of the sexually dimorphic nucleus, which is far bigger in male brains, and whose size is also dependent on circulating androgen levels (Gorski *et al.* 1978).

An area of the brain that has been implicated in female sexual behaviour is the **ventromedial hypothalamus** (VMH). This area contains high numbers of oestrogen and progesterone receptors and is crucial for inducing lordosis behaviour (see above). Indeed, direct implants of oestrogens into the VMH produce lordosis behaviour, whereas lesions of this structure abolish the response and stop the female from becoming sexually active, even when she is given oestrogen and progesterone. Thus, one function of the VMH is to monitor gonadal hormone concentrations, and at the right time (i.e. ovulation) produce lordosis. It appears to do this by activating a pathway that projects to the **periaqueductal grey** region of the midbrain, which in turn projects to the **reticular formation** located in the medulla. From here, a multisynaptic pathway passes down to the grey matter of the spinal cord, which controls many of the basic reflexes required for the lordosis response.

Another structure involved in the control of sexual behaviour is the **amygdala**. For example, it has long been known that lesions of this structure in monkeys produce hypersexuality, with indiscriminate attempts at mating with almost any other animal or object in the environment (Kluver and Bucy 1938). More recently, the amygdala has been shown to receive olfactory information from the vomeronasal organ in the nose, which detects pheromones – that is, chemicals released by animals of the same species, which affect reproductive behaviour. Indeed, lesions of the amygdala have been shown to abolish penile erections to receptive females in oestrus, which may involve pheromones (Kondo *et al.* 1997). The amygdala also projects to the medial preoptic area of the hypothalamus, which, as we have seen above, is also involved in male sexual behaviour.

It is probable that the cerebral cortex plays a vital, if not the most important, role in many aspects of human sexual behaviour. Although this is difficult to prove conclusively, animal studies have confirmed the importance of the cerebral cortex. For example, Beach (1940) found a decrease in male copulation in rats following cortical damage, with lesions involving 60 per cent of the cortex abolishing copulatory behaviour completely. However, similar cortical damage did not have any effect on female sexual activity! The main reason for this difference probably lies with the motor act of copulation. Indeed, lordosis is a relatively simple and passive behaviour that is under the control of the VMH, but the male sexual response is more complex and requires a much greater degree of motor coordination. Thus, the male's sexual response may depend more on neural circuits in the cerebral cortex (particularly its motor areas) than for the female.

The biological basis of homosexuality

One of the most controversial topics in biological psychology, and a subject associated with many predjudices, is homosexuality. At the heart of the debate is a simple question: are some people biologically predisposed to become homosexuals, or is their sexual orientation a learned behaviour influenced by such factors as childhood experiences, parental relationships or adolescent sexual encounters? This type of question is relevant not only to homosexuality but also to understanding the development of sexual orientation in all of us. Although there are many uncertainties, one thing is reasonably clear: heterosexuals and homosexuals do not show any differences in levels of their circulating hormones. Moreover, altering the levels of sex hormones has no bearing on sexual preference. For example, castration may reduce the frequency of sexual behaviour, but it does not change sexual orientation. Similarly, injections of testosterone can help to increase sexual desire in both sexes, but it does not change their sexual preference (Money and Ehrhardt 1996).

The question of whether there is hormonal influence at work during foetal development, however, is less easy to answer. As we saw earlier (page 205), the high percentage of homosexuals in women with adrenogenital syndrome appears to be in accordance with the idea that early hormonal exposure can have a bearing on later sexual preference. In the case of men, however, the nature of the hormonal influence remains uncertain. For example, some researchers have proposed that male homosexuality is in part due to increased levels of testosterone occurring prenatally, particularly in the latter part of the first trimester (see box on digit ratio, pp.212–13). However, others believe that low levels of testosterone may be more instrumental in determining homosexuality in men (Ellis and Ames 1987). Indeed, in support of this latter view is the finding that male laboratory animals exposed to low levels of testosterone early in life show a greater preference for their own sex as adults (Adkins-Regan 1989).

Another way of examining whether a biological factor is involved in the causation of homosexuality is to determine the extent to which genetic factors play a role in shaping this behaviour. This can be done, for example, by comparing the incidence of homosexuality in identical twins, who share the same genes, with fraternal twins, who share 50 per cent of their genes. One study that examined male homosexuality in this way found a concordance rate of 52 per cent for identical twins and 22 per cent for non-identical twins (Bailey and Pillard 1991). Similar findings (48 per cent compared with 16 per cent) have also been found for lesbians (Bailey *et al.* 1993). These results suggest that genetic influences may have a bearing on the development of homosexuality, although it is not marked, and environmental factors may be just as important. Indeed, supporting this latter view is the fact that there are many cases of identical twins where one is homosexual and the other heterosexual (Byne 1994).

Brain structure and homosexuality

If there is a biological basis to homosexuality then one would expect to find a biological difference, somewhere in the brain, between heterosexuals and homosexuals. In the early 1990s a difference of this type was discovered by Simon LeVay, who examined the interstitial nuclei of the anterior hypothalamus. As mentioned previously, there are four of these nuclei (INAH 1-4) located in the medial preoptic area of the hypothalamus, with INAH-2 and INAH-3 being much larger in the male. Although LeVay confirmed these findings, he also examined the INAH nuclei in homosexual men and found that one of them (INAH-3) was more than twice as large in heterosexuals as in homosexuals (Figure 7.6). In

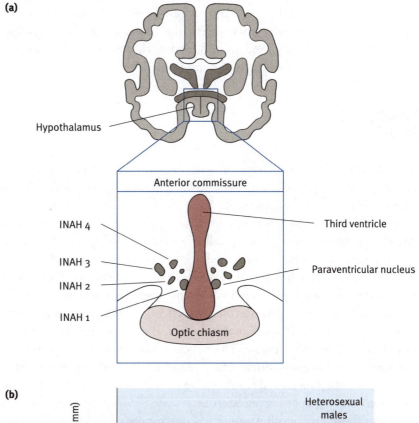

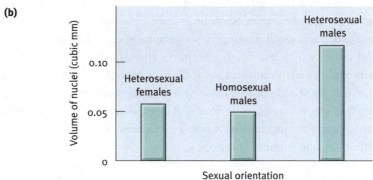

Figure 7.6   (a) The size of INAH-3 in heterosexual men and women, and in homosexual men; (b) the location of the INAH nuclei in the human brain

fact, its size in homosexual men was similar to that found in heterosexual women. This discovery led LeVay to suggest that homosexuality may, in part, be due to the 'feminisation' of the NIHA-3 nucleus (LeVay 1993).

The significance of this work remains unclear. For example, although LeVay examined a relatively large sample of homosexual men at postmortem ($N = 19$), all had died from AIDS, which raises the possibility that the small INAH-3 size may be partly linked to illness (although a large INAH-3 was importantly also found in six heterosexual men who had also died of AIDS). More worryingly, not all researchers have confirmed LeVay's findings (Byne *et al.* 2001). But even if LeVay's findings are reliable, they raise more questions than answers. For example, are the changes in the size of INAH-3 due to genetic or environmental causes? If there is a hormonal involvement, does this act prenatally or post-natally? Perhaps most importantly: is the size of the INAH-3 a *cause* of homo-sexuality or simply a *result* of this behaviour? Despite all these uncertainties, LeVay's work offers the prospect of these questions being examined more closely, and the possibility that more will be discovered about the biological basis of sexual orientation.

Summary

Sexual or reproductive behaviour is necessary for the continuation of the species. It is also a complex behaviour that, for most advanced animals, requires the coming together of male and female in sexual intercourse, as well as courtship, territorial ownership and parental assistance. In humans, whether a fertilised egg develops into a **male** or **female** depends on the **sex chromosomes**. Nearly every cell in the human body contains 23 pairs of chromosomes, and the sexes differ in just one: males inheriting one pair of **XY chromosomes**, and females **XX chromosomes**. After around six weeks of gestation, the Y chromosome helps to produce **testis-determining factor**, which causes the foetal gonadal tissue to develop into **testes**. This tissue starts to secrete **testosterone**, which begins the masculinisation process of the foetus. However, without this hormonal influence, the foetus develops ovaries at about 12 weeks of gestation and becomes female. The action of hormones to shape physical sexual development is known as an **organisational effect**. Another type of organisational effect also takes place at puberty, when increased testosterone production results in adult male characteristics, and increased **oestrogen** and **progesterone** released from the ovaries causes adult female charac-teristics. These last two hormones also become secreted in a monthly pattern known as the **menstrual cycle**, which essentially prepares the womb for a fertilised egg (should it occur). The sex hormones also continue to influence behaviour after sexual development has been completed (i.e. these substances now have an **activational effect** on behaviour). In particular, testosterone is known to increase levels of **aggression, dominance** and **sexual libido**. Levels of testosterone can also fluctuate as a result of experience, with success in sporting contests and competition causing higher secretion.

Although male and female brains appear to be very similar, there are now known to be some important differences. For example, two of the **interstitial nuclei of the anterior hypothalamus**

Summary continued.

(INAH-2 and INAH-3) are bigger in male than in female brains – although this relationship does not appear to hold for homosexual men. Another structure that tends to be bigger in male brains is the **bed nucleus of the stria terminalis**, which connects the **amygdala** and **hypothalamus**. In contrast, parts of the **corpus callosum**, especially the **splenium** and **anterior commissure**, appear to be relatively larger in women's brains. This anatomical finding may help to explain why PET studies have shown that the two hemispheres of the female brain tend to share more functions (i.e. are **less lateralised**) than those of a male. The neuroanatomy of sexual behaviour is complex, although the basic reflexes that allow male copulation are controlled by the **spinal cord**. For example, paraplegic men are often capable of coitus with both erection and ejaculation. Despite this, the brain is crucial for all aspects of sexual behaviour. In males, stimulation of the **medial preoptic area** of the hypothalamus facilitates copulatory behaviour, whereas **ventromedial hypothalamus** stimulation in females induces lordosis. This latter behaviour is also dependent on neural circuits involving the **periaqueductal grey area** and **reticular formation**. Another important brain structure is the **amygdala**, which is known to receive olfactory information from the **vomeronasal organ** in the nose, which detects **pheromones**. Indeed, lesions of the amygdala in monkeys can lead to hypersexuality with indiscriminate attempts at mating with other animals or objects.

Essay questions

1. How does sexual differentiation of the embryo take place? In what ways can the genetic and hormonal control of sexual differentiation go wrong?

   Helpful Interned search terms: *Sexual differentiation. Organisational effect of hormones. Sex chromosomes and development. Turner's and Klinefelter's syndrome. Adrenal hyperplasia. Testicular feminisation.*

2. What are the main activational effects of testosterone on adult male behaviour?

   Helpful Interned search terms: *Activational effects of testosterone. Sex hormones and aggression. Testosterone and sexual behaviour. Dominance and testosterone. Sex hormones and mental rotation.*

3. What brain regions are known to be involved in male and female sexual behaviour? What differences are known to exist between male and female brains?

   Helpful Interned search terms: *Hypothalamus and sexual behaviour. Brain regions in male and female sexual behaviour. Brain mapping of sexual arousal. Neural control of sexual behaviour. Sex differences in brain structure.*

4. Does homosexuality have a biological basis?

   Helpful Interned search terms: *Interstitial nuclei. Biological determinants of sexuality. Anterior hypothalamus and sexuality. Causes of homosexuality. Neuroscience of sexuality.*

Further reading

Andreae, S. (1998) *Anatomy of Desire*. London: Little, Brown and Co. Written for the lay person, this entertaining book argues that our sexuality is the result of evolutionary, psychological and cultural forces.

Becker, J.B., Breedlove, S.M. and Crews, D. (eds) (2000) *Behavioral Endocrinology*. Cambridge, MA: MIT Press. A well-written textbook with a number of relevant chapters, including several that cover hormonal influences on sexual behaviour, and others that examine the effects of hormones on brain development and cognition.

Bullough, V.L. (1994) *Science in the Bedroom: A History of Sex Research*. New York: Basic Books. Informative and accessible to the general reader, this covers the historical development of sex research and provides a good overview of current issues.

Ellis, L. and Ebertz, L. (eds) (1998) *Males, Females, and Behavior: Towards Biological Understanding*. Westport, CT: Praeger. A series of nine chapters, written for academics, that examine the genetic, hormonal and neurological factors affecting the behaviour of males and females.

Kohl, J.V. and Francoeur, R.T. (1995) *The Scent of Eros: Mysteries of Odor in Human Sexuality*. This book examines the impact of odours and pheromones on our sexuality and sexual behaviour.

LeVay, S. (1993) *The Sexual Brain*. Cambridge, MA: MIT Press. A lucid and wide-ranging account that examines how brain structure and function can influence sexual behaviour and orientation.

LeVay, S. and Valente, S.M. (2002) *Human Sexuality*. Basingstoke: Palgrave Macmillan. An undergraduate textbook, illustrated in full colour with a CD-ROM, that takes a multidisciplinary approach to understanding human sexuality.

Manning, J.T. (2002) *Digit Ratio: A Pointer to Fertility, Behavior and Health*. New Brunswick: Rutgers University Press. A compelling account that shows how digit ratio, which is determined by early exposure to sex hormones, correlates with a wide variety of traits including testosterone levels, sperm counts, musical genius, sporting prowess and family size!

Money, J. and Ehrhardt, A.K. (1996) *Man and Woman, Boy and Girl*. Northvale: Aronson. An authoritative book that traces the development of gender from conception to maturity, with an emphasis on understanding the interaction between hormonal and environmental influences.

Pease, A. and Pease, B. (2001) *Why Men Don't Listen: Women Can't Read Maps*. London: Orion. Although written for a general audience and contains little about the brain, this is a very entertaining book that is well worth a bedtime read.

 See website at www.pearsoned.co.uk/wickens for further resources including multiple choice questions.

CHAPTER 8

Learning and memory

In this chapter

- The search for the memory (the engram) in the brain
- The effects of experience on the physiology of the brain
- The synaptic basis of learning and memory
- Long-term potentiation
- The role of the medial temporal lobes in human memory
- Diencephalic amnesia, including Korsakoff's disease
- Working memory and cognitive mapping in rats
- The use of primates in memory research

INTRODUCTION

Learning and memory go hand in hand together. Learning can be defined as the acquisition of new information, while memory is the capacity for storing and retrieving this material. Obviously, there can be no learning without memory, although some types of memory can be innate, such as instincts and basic reflexes. However, for all intents and purposes our memory is derived exclusively from learning experiences. It is easy to take our ability to learn and remember for granted, although without that ability we would not be able to recognise our friends, objects, possessions or even ourselves. We would be unable to think, to use language, or even to perceive the world around us. In short, without learning and memory we would be mentally and psychologically dead. Understanding how the brain is able to acquire complex new information, store the memory within its vast arrays of neurons and then retrieve it when necessary presents a considerable challenge to the biological psychologist. Indeed, a complete explanation must require an account of brain function on many different levels – from protein synthesis, synaptic activity and neurotransmitter release to the activation of neural pathways and networks, and interaction of various brain structures. However, the challenge is a very important one. Not only does an understanding of learning and memory provide valuable insights into the functioning of the human brain, but it has the potential to help those with serious memory disorders such as amnesia and dementia. In fact, 5 per cent of people over 65, and 20 per cent of those over 80, suffer from Alzheimer's disease, which makes it one of society's most important and pressing health concerns. This alone means that brain research into learning and memory is going to be a central endeavour in science for many years.

How are memories stored?

Ultimately, learning and memory must involve some relatively permanent change in the structure of the CNS, but what is the nature of this change? Although this question has no simple answer, the explanation must lie with changes taking place in neurons – and there are a number of possible ways this could occur. For example, perhaps long-term memory results in changes taking place in the neuron's structure that involves the creation of new synapses or dendrites – or maybe it involves altering the sensitivity of receptors, and their associated second messenger systems to certain neurotransmitters. Alternatively, learning and memory may set up new patterns of electrical activity in circuits of many thousands, if not millions, of neurons. As we shall see below, all these forms of neuronal change, or 'plasticity', have provided plausible explanations of how the brain encodes and stores new information.

Although the types of change taking place in an individual neuron may be relatively simple, the sheer number of cells that are involved in human learning and memory makes any simplistic account of this phenomenon practically impossible. The human brain contains around 1 billion neurons, with their axon terminals perhaps making over 10 trillion synaptic connections (see Chapter 1). It is at this point of contact between neurons that the most important structural, chemical or electrical changes underlying learning and memory probably take place. Unfortunately, the extremely small size of synapses (they can only be seen with an electron microscope), along with their incredible abundance in the brain, means that even identifying the sites where memory is stored is fraught with great difficulty – let alone identifying the neurochemical and physiological changes that take place.

The work of Karl Lashley

Karl Lashley was one of the first scientists to examine the question of where in the brain memory is located, and he spent most of his research career trying to discover the anatomical site of the memory trace, or what he called the **engram**. When Lashley began his research in the 1920s, psychologists were strongly influenced by the work of the Russian physiologist Ivan Pavlov, who had discovered a form of learning known as **classical conditioning** (see Figure 8.1). This is essentially a simple reflex that occurs when an animal links specific events (or stimuli) with particular responses. For example, Pavlov showed that if he presented food to a hungry dog, it would always produce salivation (this he termed an *unconditioned* or 'unlearned' response). But if he repeatedly paired a tone with the food, the tone alone would also eventually be able to elicit salivation (this is now a *conditioned* response). Since the tone was initially a neutral stimulus that produced no response, then clearly the dog showed evidence of learning. Psychologists were particularly interested in Pavlov's work because they believed that human learning followed the same principles of classical conditioning. Moreover, in anatomical terms, it was easy to regard the stimuli as being processed by the sensory areas of the cerebral cortex, and the response as being produced by its motor regions. Thus, Pavlov and others hypothesised that the neural basis of learning must involve the growth of new connections or pathways that linked the sensory regions of the cerebral cortex with its motor areas.

It was in this intellectual climate that Lashley set about trying to discover the engram. Lashley reasoned that if learning took place in the cerebral cortex, and was the result of new connections being formed between sensory and motor areas, then making a knife cut between these two brain areas following conditioning should impair the memory of the learned response. To test this hypothesis, Lashley trained rats on a variety of maze tasks, and then made fine cuts to the cerebral cortex, after which he tested the animals again. For each rat, Lashley made a cut in a different location. However, to his surprise, he found that no single cut, or combination of cuts, impaired the animal's memory of the

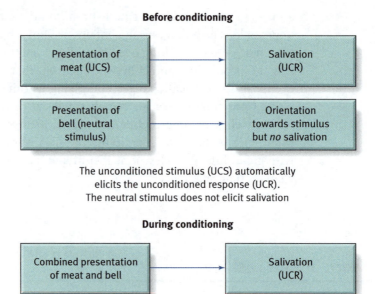

Figure 8.1 An illustration of how classical conditioning occurs

task. That is, the site of the knife cut had no effect on the rat's memory of how to run through the maze. This finding was seemingly at odds with the Pavlovian idea that learning required the formation of new connections in the cerebral cortex.

In a further set of experiments, instead of using knife cuts, Lashley lesioned parts of the cerebral cortex. This time Lashley did find an impairment when the animals were placed back in the maze. In short, he found that the deficit in relearning the task was proportional to the amount of cerebral cortex removed. For example, if a small amount of cortex (around 5 or 10 per cent) was destroyed, the performance loss was scarcely detectable, but if large amounts (50 per cent) were removed, then the memory for the task was lost, and retraining back to previous levels of performance took a large number of trials (see Figure 8.2). Again, as with his previous work, the actual site of damage did not appear to be important. Thus, cortical lesions of equal size produced similar behavioural effects regardless of where they were placed. It was as if memory was stored everywhere – or at no site in particular.

On the basis of these findings Lashley concluded that memories for maze tasks were stored diffusely throughout the cerebral cortex, which he called the principle of **mass action**, and that all parts of the association cortex played an

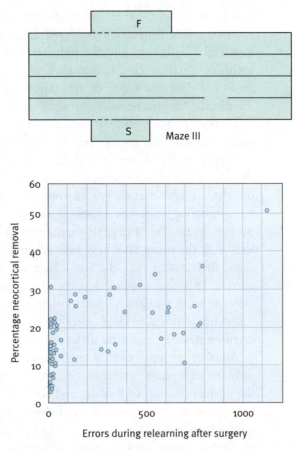

Figure 8.2   The maze used by Lashley along with a graph of his findings showing relearning performance as a function of cortex removal. *Source*: K.S. Lashley, *Brain Mechanisms and Intelligence*. Copyright © 1963 by Dover Publications

equal role in their storage, which he called the principle of **equipotentiality** (Lashley 1950). Although Lashley found that some areas of the cerebral cortex were more important than others in the storage of certain memories (e.g. the visual cortex was particularly important in tasks requiring the discrimination of visual patterns), he nevertheless found that no structure was absolutely crucial. No matter what area of the cortex was removed the animal could eventually relearn the task it was given.

Was Lashley correct?

Lashley was probably correct in his belief that memories are distributed throughout the brain and not localised in one place. Despite this, his conclusion that all parts of the cerebral cortex play an equal role in learning and memory is not widely accepted today. To the contrary, it is clear that certain areas of the cerebral cortex, especially in humans, have specialised and localised functions.

For example, as we shall see in the next chapter, there is strong evidence that the two cerebral hemispheres have different roles, with the left tending to be involved in language and the right more responsible for spatial processing and emotion. Furthermore, within each hemisphere there are also clearly localised areas for different types of specialisation. This suggests that memory is not distributed homogeneously throughout the cortex.

Lashley's choice of task (maze learning) can also be criticised as inappropriate for studying localisation of function. Indeed, rather than requiring the involvement of just one area of the cerebral cortex, it is almost certainly the case that the maze task requires the formation of many 'engrams' spread throughout the cerebral cortex. For example, as the rat runs through the maze, it may be combining different types of sensory information (i.e. vision, olfaction, proprioception, etc.) to perform the task. Thus, although each engram could be localised, the maze task may be so complex and draw upon so many different types of learning that the total memory is essentially stored throughout the cortex. This also implies that the maze task can be learned in many different ways. If so, this might help to explain why an animal can relearn the maze task following removal of large parts of the cortex. The animal simply adopts a new learning strategy based on different cues.

Another criticism of Lashley is his assumption that the cerebral cortex is the only site of learning and memory. Although to some extent this bias was due to the initial influence of Pavlov, and the difficulties in performing lesions to other regions of the brain, it is nevertheless now clear that a large number of subcortical structures also have a role to play in learning and memory. In fact, as we shall see later, some subcortical areas (particularly in the limbic system) have a vital role in learning and the retrieval of memory.

The contribution of Donald Hebb

Donald Hebb (who obtained his PhD at Harvard University under Lashley's guidance in 1936) was more interested in understanding how neurons are able to learn and store information than in identifying the actual locations in the brain where this occurs. To do this, however, Hebb was forced to theorise about the likely mechanisms of neuronal plasticity because at the time there were no experimental techniques available that could meaningfully examine this type of question. Nonetheless, Hebb was aware that neurons formed huge numbers of connections with each other, and on this basis he hypothesised that memory must involve large circuits of neurons distributed throughout the brain. But how could circuits of neurons encode memory? To provide an answer, Hebb proposed that learning resulted in groups of neurons, or **cell assemblies**, reverberating with increased electrical activity that lasted for some time after the event. In effect, this activity 'held' the memory for a limited period and formed the basis for short-term memory.

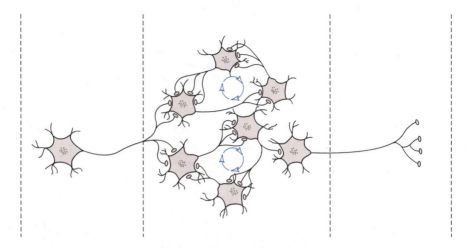

1. Experience activates sensory pathways, which conduct neural impulses to the CNS

2. **Short-term memory:** Hebb hypothesised that the short-term memory of each experience is stored by neural activity reverberating in closed-loop CNS circuits

   Long-term memory: Hebb hypothesised that reverberating activity, if maintained for a sufficiently long time, produces structural changes in synapses and that these changes facilitate subsequent transmission over the same pathways

3. The changed pathways of transmission produced by synaptic facilitation can influence motor output and thus behaviour

Figure 8.3 A hypothetical model of how reverberatory circuits may be set up in neural networks. *Source*: John P.J. Pinel, *Biopsychology*, 3rd edition. Copyright © 1997 by Pearson Education

It was unrealistic, however, to believe that reverberatory circuits were active over very long periods of time. Thus, to explain permanent memory, Hebb took his idea one step further and proposed that if reverberatory circuits maintained their activity long enough, then the result would be a structural change in the neurons making up the cell assembly. And the likeliest site for this change according to Hebb was the synapse (Hebb 1949). Indeed, a synapse that is 'strengthened' as a result of learning is now called a **Hebbian synapse**. Thus, as reverberation gradually produced structural change in cell assemblies, the consolidation of memory would occur (Figure 8.3). Hebb's theory was intuitively appealing since it was compatible with the idea that memory was distributed throughout the brain, yet it also explained how neurons might encode and store memory. Although Hebb had no practical way of testing his theory, recent research has given considerable support to his ideas.

Some of the best evidence to show that electrical activity can be changed in neural circuits after learning has come from the discovery of **long-term potentiation** (LTP), first shown by Timothy Bliss and Terje Lomo in 1973 (Figure 8.4). These scientists found that if they stimulated the perforant pathway which enters the hippocampus from the nearby entorhinal cortex with a series of electrical impulses, and then recorded from the hippocampal cells that received

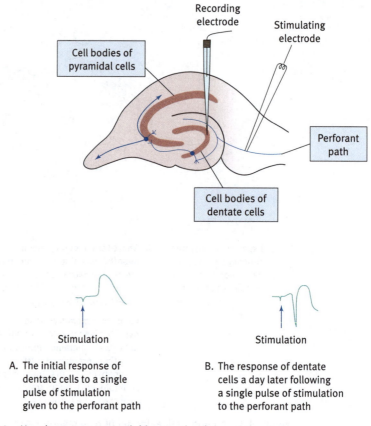

A. The initial response of dentate cells to a single pulse of stimulation given to the perforant path

B. The response of dentate cells a day later following a single pulse of stimulation to the perforant path

Figure 8.4 How long-term potential is examined

this input, the neurons demonstrate a form of 'memory'. That is, they showed increased electrical responses that could last for days after the initial stimulation had occurred. Soon after this discovery, others found that LTP could also be produced in slices of hippocampal tissue kept alive in a saline bath. This was important as it enabled the neural basis of LTP to be studied outside the organism and in much greater detail.

What causes long-term potentiation? It is now known that the first stage in the process involves the release of **glutamate** from the neurons of the perforant path, which crosses the synaptic gap and binds to receptors located on the hippocampal cells. The activation of this receptor causes the entry of calcium ions into the postsynaptic, cell which, in turn, sets in motion a series of chemical reactions involving enzymes called **protein kinases** within the neuron. These enzymes have a number of roles, although one of their main effects in LTP is to increase the conductance at glutamate receptors. In addition, protein kinases are involved in protein synthesis, which may be important in changing the long-term structure of the neuron. LTP also produces changes in the presynaptic neuron. Although the process by which this occurs is not well understood, it appears that the hippocampal cells release a substance (possibly a gas called nitric oxide) that feeds back to the presynaptic cell, causing it to increase glutamate release in response to further stimulation (Figure 8.5).

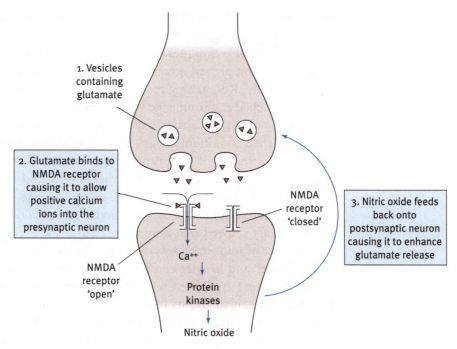

1. Vesicles containing glutamate

2. Glutamate binds to NMDA receptor causing it to allow positive calcium ions into the presynaptic neuron

NMDA receptor 'closed'

3. Nitric oxide feeds back onto postsynaptic neuron causing it to enhance glutamate release

NMDA receptor 'open'

Ca++

Protein kinases

Nitric oxide

Figure 8.5   A hypothetical model of the chemical events underlying long-term potential

Importantly, LTP is not only found in the hippocampus but has been produced in other brain structures including the prefrontal cortex, motor cortex, visual cortex, thalamus, amygdala and cerebellum. Thus, this form of neural plasticity occurs throughout the brain and may underlie many types of learning. Remarkably, LTP has even been shown to occur in human neocortex that was surgically removed to treat a seizure disorder (Chen *et al.* 1996). The occurrence of LTP in the hippocamus is, however, likely to be particularly important. As we shall see later, the hippocampus has a vital role in the consolidation of long-term memory, and its damage causes profound amnesia. It may well be that the LTP set-up in the hippocampus has an important bearing on memory storage elsewhere in the brain.

The effects of experience on the brain

Psychologists have long known that the effects of early experience can have a profound effect on later development. Indeed, Donald Hebb in 1949 noted that the same principle applied to rats. In particular, he was struck by the observation that his own pet rats were superior to laboratory rats when learning to run through a maze. This finding implied that a more enriched home environment had produced a 'brighter' animal. But could such a rat be distinguished from a less intelligent one on the basis of brain structure or neurochemistry? This was the question that Mark Rosenzweig set out to examine in the mid-1950s. The likelihood of finding any difference using the relatively crude histological and neuroanatomical techniques of the time appeared to be improbable, although his findings soon proved otherwise (see Rosenzweig *et al.* 1972).

In one study, Rosenzweig reared rats for various lengths of time in impoverished or enriched environments. In the impoverished condition, the animal lived alone in a small cage located in a quiet room, with as little stimulation as possible. In the enriched condition, groups of 12 rats lived together in a large cage furnished with a variety of toys, runways and objects. Moreover, a new object was placed in the cage each day to add further novelty and stimulation. At the end of a given period – between 30 days and several months – the rats were sacrificed and their brains examined to detect whether any neural changes had taken place.

The results showed that animals reared in the enriched conditions differed in a number of important ways to control rats. For example, the enriched rats had a thicker and heavier cerebral cortex (this was especially marked for the occipital cortex) compared with the impoverished animals. Rosenzweig also found that the enriched rats had greater levels of **acetylcholinesterase (AChE)** – an enzyme that breaks down **acetylcholine** – in their cerebral cortices, which was consistent with the idea that their brains were producing more of this neurotransmitter. The most striking discovery, however, was the difference in the shape of the neurons taken from parts of the cerebral cortex. In particular, animals reared in the enriched environment were found to have more spines on their dendrites, which is an important site for synapses. Thus, this finding indicated that the number of synapses were being increased as a result of experience. Indeed, this prediction, along with evidence showing that dendritic synapses were much larger in the enriched animals, was later confirmed by electron microscopy (Turner and Greenough 1983, 1985). In fact, the enriched rats were shown to have about 9,400 synapses per neuron in their occipital cortex, compared with about 7,600 for deprived animals – an increase of more than 20 per cent (Figure 8.6).

Learning and memory in *Aplysia*

It is one thing to show that dendritic spines and synapse numbers change with experience, but it is quite another to prove that these provide the underlying basis of learning and memory. Although the rat has long been a favoured subject in research, it has limited usefulness for showing how learning produces the structural changes in neurons necessary to provide memory. For this reason, researchers have looked for organisms with simpler nervous systems in an attempt to discover how engrams are formed. The animal that has been most widely used in recent years to examine this question is perhaps a surprising choice: it is a large marine snail found off the coast of California and northern Mexico called *Aplysia* (Figure 8.7). The use of *Aplysia* has been pioneered by Eric Kandel, who was awarded the Nobel Prize for Physiology and Medicine

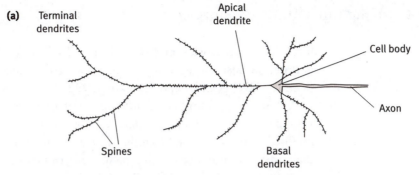

(a)

Terminal
dendrites

Apical
dendrite

Cell body

Axon

Spines

Basal
dendrites

Dendritic spines are tiny projections from the dendrites of a nerve cell that serve
in many of the synaptic contacts between neurons. Rats from an enriched environment
have more of these spines than those from impoverished environments.

(b)

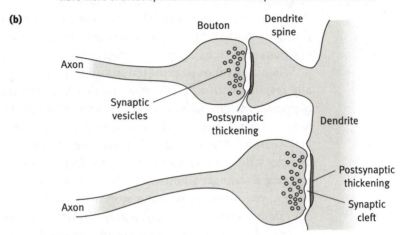

Bouton

Dendrite
spine

Axon

Synaptic
vesicles

Postsynaptic
thickening

Dendrite

Axon

Postsynaptic
thickening

Synaptic
cleft

Synaptic junctions can lie between axon and denditic spine, or axon and dendrite
itself. Neurotransmitter is released from the axon endings and stimulates receptors
on the dendrites. The size of the postsynaptic membrane is believed to be an
indicator of synaptic activity.

Figure 8.6 Some effects of enriched experience on the structure of neurons and their
synaptic connections. *Source*: Rosenzweig *et al.* (1972) Brain changes in response to
experience, *Scientific American*, February

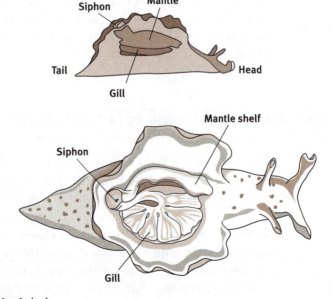

Siphon

Mantle

Tail

Gill

Head

Mantle shelf

Siphon

Gill

Figure 8.7 An *Aplysia*

in 2000 for his work – and there is lttle doubt that it has enabled the synaptic and neural basis of learning and memory to be understood in exquisite detail (Kandel 1979, Kandel and Hawkins 1992).

Aplysia has a number of advantages if one wants to examine how neural systems can learn. Firstly, it has a simple nervous system containing around 20,000 neurons grouped together in several ganglia, which is significantly less than any vertebrate. Secondly, the number of neurons and their location are the same for all individuals. Thirdly, *Aplysia*'s neurons are relatively large and can be studied more easily than those in vertebrates. Finally, *Aplysia* is capable of several types of learning, including habituation, sensitisation and classical conditioning. We shall examine habituation to illustrate some of the neural changes that may underlie learning, although the reader interested in other forms of plasticity shown by *Aplysia* is referred to Kandel *et al.* (1995).

When a novel or unexpected stimulus is presented to an animal, it will typically respond with a defensive or startle reflex, but if the stimulus is found to be harmless, the animal will soon learn to ignore it. This decrease in behavioural responding when a stimulus is repeatedly presented to the organism is known as 'habituation'. Humans also demonstrate habituation – for example, the ticking of a clock that fades away as we try to sleep, or a new but temporary smell when entering a stranger's house. Simple as it may seem, this form of learning must depend on information being stored somewhere in the nervous system – and *Aplysia* has provided us with a very important insight into how this can occur.

Kandel examined the process of habituation in *Aplysia* by measuring its **gill-withdrawal reflex**. *Aplysia* has a large gill (located on its back) that is responsible for extracting oxygen from water and is connected to a siphon, which expels the waste. Both the gill and the siphon are delicate organs and, if touched, *Aplysia* will respond by retracting them into a protective cavity, which it quickly covers with a large fleshy pad called the mantle shelf. However, if a weak stimulus (Kandel used a calibrated jet of water) is applied repeatedly to the siphon, *Aplysia*'s withdrawal response habituates – that is, it becomes less and less pronounced until it ceases to occur. This habituated response may last several minutes following a single training session of 10 stimuli, or as long as three weeks if *Aplysia* is given several training sessions spaced over a number of days.

The neural basis of short-term habituation in Aplysia

To understand how habituation occurs in *Aplysia* it is necessary to identify the neural circuitry that produces the gill-withdrawal reflex. The first stage of this reflex involves the siphon, which contains 24 sensory neurons that act as touch receptors, sensitive to tactile information produced by the water jet. These sensory cells, which use glutamate as their neurotransmitter, then project onto a cluster of six motor neurons that control the retraction of the gill. In reality, the neural circuitry is more complex than this, as the sensory neurons have extra axon endings that project onto excitatory and inhibitory interneurons,

Mechanism of habituation

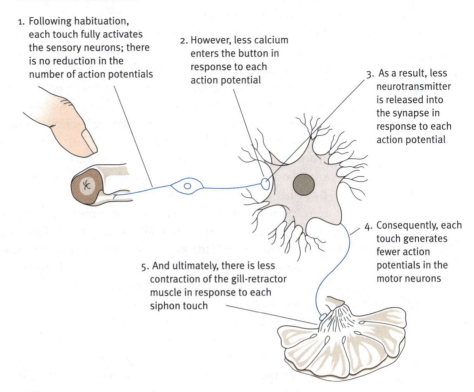

1. Following habituation, each touch fully activates the sensory neurons; there is no reduction in the number of action potentials

2. However, less calcium enters the button in response to each action potential

3. As a result, less neurotransmitter is released into the synapse in response to each action potential

4. Consequently, each touch generates fewer action potentials in the motor neurons

5. And ultimately, there is less contraction of the gill-retractor muscle in response to each siphon touch

Figure 8.8   The neural and biochemical stages underlying habituation of the gill-withdrawal reflex in *Aplysia. Source*: John P.J. Pinel, *Biopsychology*, 3rd edition. Copyright © 1997 by Pearson Education

although we need not discuss these any further here, as they do not play a significant role in habituation. Thus, somewhere in this neural circuit of 24 sensory cells and six motor neurons, habituation takes place. But the question is *where*?

To answer this question, Kandel and his colleagues placed electrodes into the sensory and motor neurons and measured the number of neural impulses that accompanied the habituation of the gill-withdrawal reflex. They found that the sensory neurons in the siphon did not show any decline in activity despite repeated stimulation by the jet of water (i.e. whenever the siphon was stimulated the sensory neurons fired). Thus, changes in the firing of the sensory neurons could not explain the habituation. In contrast, the motor neurons did show a decline in neural activity (i.e. fewer nerve impulses were produced with each siphon stimulation), which correlated with the decline of the gill-withdrawal reflex. There were two possible explanations: either the motor neuron was becoming less able to invoke a response, or changes were taking place at the synapses between the sensory and motor neurons. The first possibility was ruled out when it was found that electrical stimulation of the motor neurons always produced the same amount of muscle contraction – that is, the motor neuron was not becoming 'tired' with repetitive firing. Thus, the cause of habituation appeared to be taking place at the synapse located between the sensory and motor neurons.

But where in the synapse was the important change taking place? There are basically two possibilities: either the sensory neurons were releasing less neurotransmitter each time they fired, or the receptors on the postsynaptic motor neuron were becoming less responsive to the transmitter. In fact, the answer was found to be the former. In short, it was shown that fewer molecules of transmitter were being released from the siphon's sensory neurons with each action potential (Castellucci and Kandel 1974). In turn, the reduced amount of neurotransmitter released into the synapse caused less stimulation of the motor neurons innervating the gill, thus producing habituation.

But what causes the reduction in the release of neurotransmitter? The answer, it appears, is a gradual decrease in the number of calcium ions that enter the axon terminal of the sensory cell. As we saw in Chapter 1, neurotransmitter release occurs through the process of **exocytosis**. That is, when an action potential reaches the axon ending, it causes calcium channels to open, which enables calcium ions to rush into the terminal and propel the synaptic vesicles (containing neurotransmitter) into the presynaptic membrane. This, in turn, causes the neurotransmitter to be released into the synaptic cleft. However, with repeated stimulation of the sensory neuron, it appears that the calcium channels become less effective at opening. The result is a reduced influx of calcium into the synaptic terminal, which causes less neurotransmitter release. Thus, if we want to reduce habituation of the gill-withdrawal reflex to its most basic explanation, it can be blamed on calcium ions!

Kandel's work shows that changes in the effectiveness of synaptic transmission may underlie simple forms of learning. This, however, is not the only way in which habituation can occur. For example, Baily and Chen (1983) examined the terminals of the sensory neurons in long-term habituated *Aplysia* (i.e. where the animal had been trained to exhibit learning that lasted several weeks) and found that they contained fewer synapses. In other words, the sensory neurons had structural alterations that were caused by biochemical processes other than those simply involving calcium channels. As we have seen, changes in the number and structure of synapses have been found in rats reared in enriched conditions. Thus, these types of synaptic change may be a common form of information storage for a wide range of different species.

Brain structures involved in human memory

So far, we have focused our attention on how small systems of neurons may be capable of producing the structural and neurochemical changes that underlie learning and memory. But, of course, our brains contain billions of neurons arranged in various structures and pathways. It is also clear that some of these structures are more important than others in learning and memory. One site we have already mentioned is the cerebral cortex. Across species, learning ability is roughly correlated with the size and complexity of the cerebral cortex, and not surprisingly this structure is most highly evolved in humans. Indeed, the cerebral cortex is the primary site for sensations, perception, voluntary movement, language and cognition, as well as providing a store for our vast bank of memories. The cerebral cortex that covers the surface of the brain is actually **neocortex** – a distinct six-layered tissue that is found only in mammals and which, in humans, contains around 50 subdivisions or cytoarchitectonic areas. Many of these regions are also known to be involved in specialised forms of cognition and memory. However, beneath the neocortex of the temporal lobe is an evolutionary older part of the cerebral cortex called the **archicortex**, which only contains three laminae. This type of cortex is found in all vertebrates, and in humans part of it forms the **hippocampus** (from the Greek word meaning 'seahorse'). Although it is 'older' that the neocortex, the hippocampus has a crucial role in the storage and consolidation of long-term memories, with its damage capable of causing profound memory loss or **amnesia**.

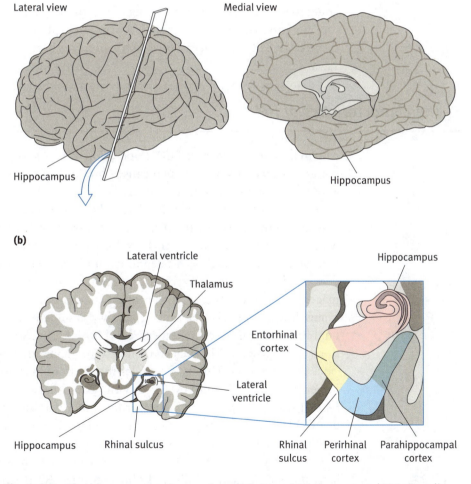

(a)

Lateral view   Medial view

Hippocampus   Hippocampus

(b)

Lateral ventricle

Thalamus

Hippocampus

Entorhinal cortex

Lateral ventricle

Hippocampus   Rhinal sulcus

Rhinal sulcus   Perirhinal cortex   Parahippocampal cortex

Figure 8.9   The hippocampus. *Source*: From M.F. Bear, B.W. Connors and M.A. Paradiso, *Neuroscience: Exploring the Brain*. Copyright © 1996 by Lippincott Williams & Wilkins

The hippocampus was first, properly, identified as being crucial for human memory in the mid-1950s when a Canadian patient, who is simply known by his initals of HM, had this part of his brain removed in a surgical operation. Since then, HM has had more written about him than any other clinical case in the history of psychology. He has also participated in many experimental studies that have examined the characteristics of his amnesia. Despite this, few researchers know his real name and no pictures of him have ever been published.

HM was born in 1926 and had a normal childhood until the age of 9, when he had a bicycle accident that caused him to be unconscious for several minutes. Soon after this, HM began to suffer from seizures that developed in severity to *grand mal* epilepsy by the age of 16. His fits continued throughout early adulthood and by his late twenties were so severe that he could not work despite being prescribed near toxic levels of medication. At this point, in 1953, the neurologist William Scoville identified the **medial temporal lobes**, which included the hippocampus and amygdala, as being the origin of his seizure activity, and he decided to bilaterally remove these areas in an attempt to stop the epilepsy. Similar operations had been performed previously and, although smaller amounts of tissue had been removed, there was little to suggest that the operation was going to have a seriously debilitating effect. In fact, in terms of reducing seizures, the operation was a great success. Unfortunately, it also left HM with a profound memory deficit, the severity of which had never been seen before.

The characteristics of HM

The main consequence of HM's operation was a severe **anterograde amnesia** (*antero* means 'in front'), which caused him to forget the events of his daily life almost as soon as they occurred (Scoville and Milner 1957). For example, if HM meets someone new, he quickly forgets them as soon as they leave his presence, and does not recognise them again if reintroduced (this includes Dr Brenda Milner, who has worked with HM for over 40 years). Similarly, if asked to memorise an item such as a telephone number, HM not only forgets it if he is distracted, but is unable to recall being requested to perform the task in the first place. HM also easily gets lost around his neighbourhood (his family moved to a new house after his operation); he always underestimates his age; and he is unable to recognise a current picture of himself. In short, with only a few exceptions (see below), HM has been unable to permanently remember anything new since his operation. This also includes the death of his parents. For example, his father died in 1967 and HM lived with his mother until she died at the age of 94 in 1981, but when asked whether his father was alive (several years after his death) HM replied that he wasn't sure, and in 1986 when asked where he lived, HM answered that he lived in a house with his mother.

Yet, in many respects, HM appears to be normal since he has a good vocabulary, normal language skills and above-average IQ (Corkin 1984). Moreover, HM shows excellent retention of childhood and adolescent memories, although there is some degree of amnesia for the couple of years preceding his operation (**retrograde amnesia**). HM also has a normal short-term memory and can repeat a string of seven numbers forward and five numbers backwards; he can also repeat sentences and perform mental arithmetic. He can keep a piece of information in his mind for a considerable time if asked to concentrate, which presumably is one reason why he can have meaningful conversations, but if distracted for just a moment then it is forgotten. Poignantly, HM is vaguely aware of his condition and apologetic about his memory loss:

> Right now I am wondering. Have I done or said anything amiss? You see, at this moment everything looks clear to me, but what happened just before? That's what worries me. It's like waking from a dream. I just don't remember.

> *(Milner 1970)*

Despite this, HM sometimes experiences 'islands' of memory. For example, he inaccurately recalled certain aspects of the *Challenger* Space Shuttle disaster several years after the event, and on occasion has remembered that his parents are dead. When asked where he is, he sometimes correctly guesses the Massachusetts Institute of Technology, which is the place where he has been regularly tested over the last 40 years. Nevertheless such memories are highly fragmented and inconsistent. Although HM requires constant supervision and now lives in a nursing home, he remains a great favourite with researchers and clinical staff – in no small part 'because of his endearing nature, his sense of humour and his willingness to be helpful' (see Ogden and Corkin 1991).

Tasks that HM can perform

Although HM probably has the severest anterograde amnesia known to psychology, there are nevertheless some tasks where he shows learning. For example, in 1965, Brenda Milner presented HM with a mirror drawing task, requiring him to trace around the outline of a complex geometric figure that was hidden from direct view, and which could only be observed by using a mirror. Initially, most subjects find this task difficult and frustrating, but within a few trials they become reasonably proficient at it. This is also true of HM; for example, when given 10 trials, he became skilled at drawing around the shape and made progressively fewer errors. He also maintained this skill over the next two days despite claiming not to recognise the apparatus or what to do!

It might be thought that HM's ability to perform mirror drawing is in some way linked to the motor requirements of the task, but there is more to his abilities than this. For example, HM can show learning when given a prompt to help him to recall past information. One example of this is the 'recognition of incomplete pictures' task, where subjects are presented with fragmented drawings, one at a time and in progressively more detail, until they can recognise the picture (Milner *et al.* 1968). Typically, when subjects are given the incomplete pictures again, after a given delay, they recognise the pictures more quickly. HM also demonstrates this ability. For example, when he is given a series of incomplete pictures, and then tested one hour later, he shows a significant improvement on his initial performance. A similar improvement also occurs with verbal material. When HM was shown a word such as 'Define', and later given the prompt 'Def' and asked what word came to mind, he typically gave the correct word (Ogden and Corkin 1991).

These tasks show that HM can retain certain types of information over a period of several hours or days. Despite this, there are some tests in which HM forgets information very quickly. For example, Prisko (1963) presented HM with pairs of tones, coloured lights or patterns of clicks, and found that he had great difficulty judging whether the two stimuli were the same or not. A similar deficit was also shown by Sidman *et al.* (1968), who asked HM to indicate which of eight ellipses matched a sample that had been presented a few seconds earlier. It was found that HM was unable to perform this task if a short delay was interposed between the stimuli. However, when HM was presented with verbal stimuli (three consonants) he had no difficulty identifying the matching stimulus even after a 40-second delay. These results show that HM has a relatively intact ability to store short-term verbal information, which does not extend to non-verbal information.

The fact that HM is able to use verbal information, even if only for a short period of time, has enabled him to perform quite complex tasks. For example, Cohen and Corkin (1981) taught HM a puzzle called the Tower of Hanoi (Figure 8.10), which, in its simplest version, consists of three wooden spindles,

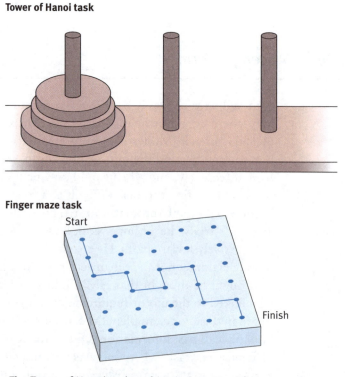

Tower of Hanoi task

Finger maze task

Start

Finish

Figure 8.10 The Tower of Hanoi task and 'stepping-stone' finger maze

with the left-hand spindle holding three discs arranged on top of each other in descending size. The objective is to move the single discs, one step at a time, from the spindle on the left to the spindle on the right without placing a disc on top of a smaller one. The task has to be learned through trial and error and the quickest solution for this puzzle takes seven moves. Remarkably, HM was able to perform a five-disc version of this puzzle (which requires a minimum of 31 moves) in only 32 moves.

Despite this, HM cannot perform the stepping-stone maze (Figure 8.10), which requires a set pathway to be learned through a 10 by 10 maze (this maze is constructed from metal bolts screwed into wood and the subject has to touch the bolts to illustrate the route). Although most subjects find this task relatively easy, HM could not trace the correct pathway after 125 trials. When HM was given a simple 4 by 4 version of the maze, he eventually learned the task, but he took 155 trials. What then is the difference between the Tower of Hanoi and the stepping-stone tasks? The answer appears to be that the former can be performed on the basis of using simple verbal rules, whereas the latter requires learning a pattern of movements that cannot easily be rehearsed in short-term memory.

Theories of medial temporal lobe function

The fact that HM can retain certain types of information over the long term shows that his amnesia is not complete, and that the brain must contain memory systems that are not dependent on the hippocampus. Nonetheless, the hippocampus obviously has a very important role in human learning and memory. But what is its main function? Firstly, it is apparent that the hippocampus is not the actual site of memory storage because HM retains intact memories of his early life. Thus, it is more likely that the hippocampus is involved in the formation or consolidation of new memories. Using Hebbian terminology, this could mean that the hippocampus is responsible for setting up circuits of reveberatory activity that enable structural change in neurons to take place elsewhere in the brain. The discovery of long-term potentiation in hippocampal neurons has provided evidence broadly in line with this idea (see page 234).

But why can HM acquire some types of knowledge and not others? How can we best describe the nature of HM's memory deficit? One idea proposed by Cohen and Squire (1980) is that HM has an impairment of **declarative** but not **procedural** memory. This theory has its roots in the work of the British philosopher Gilbert Ryle, who distinguished between memory arising from 'knowing that' and 'knowing how'. In short, declarative memory is knowledge that we use to think with and talk about – that is, semantic and episodic information that can be 'declared' into consciousness. In contrast, procedural memory is largely non-conscious, non-verbal, and only accessible through the performance of certain behaviours, such as riding a bicycle or typing on a computer keyboard.

Thus, HM's deficit would be one of declarative memory, with procedural or automatic skills remaining intact. A similar idea is the distinction between *explicit* and *implicit* memory. Explicit memory occurs when a subject is required to recollect a specific event or name of an object, whereas implicit memory occurs when a subject performs a task (e.g. how to do the Tower of Hanoi) without being able to recall the learning event. In this respect, HM would appear to be capable of implicit but not explicit memory.

Use it or lose it: what nuns have told us about Alzheimer's disease

The term 'dementia' is derived from the Latin for madness, although it now refers to the deterioration of intellectual functioning that arises as a result of a disease or brain dysfunction. There are more than 60 disorders that can cause dementia, but the most common is Alzheimer's disease, which was first described by the German Alois Alzheimer in 1907. It has been estimated that 5 per cent of the population over 65 suffer from this disorder, and the figure rises to over 20 per cent in those over 80, who are also the fastest-growing age group in the population. There are currently around 750,000 people with Alzheimer's in the UK, and this number will increase in the future. In fact, complications arising from the disease make up the fourth most common form of death in old people. Considering that the average life expectancy is now about 74 years for men, and 79.5 for women, it is perhaps not surprising that Alzheimer's has been called '*one of the most pervasive social health problems of our generation*' (Royal College of Physicians 1981) and '*the disease of the century*' (Thomas 1981).

It is a sad fact that as we get older we lose brain cells, and by the time a healthy person reaches 80 years his or her brain will have shrunk by about 15 per cent. The rate of degeneration, however, tends to be more marked in Alzheimer's disease with brain shrinkage up to 30 per cent. This cell loss is particularly noticeable in the entorhinal cortex and adjacent hippocampus – areas that are involved in memory processing. However, there is great variability in the extent of degeneration, and actual cell loss correlates poorly with the severity of dementia. A more reliable indicator of Alzheimer's disease is microscopic plaques that contain a protein called amyloid, which are typically surrounded by a ring of degenerating axons and are found scattered throughout the cerebral cortex. A second histological feature is neurofibrillary tangles (NFTs), which are twisted tangles of fine filaments that once served as the internal scaffolding of nerve cells. The accumulation of both plaques and NFTs parallels the progressive loss of mental, physical and social functioning that occurs in Alzheimer's victims.

Although genetic factors probably play a role in Alzheimer's disease, the effects of lifestyle and environment are also believed to be important. An ongoing study that has highlighted some of the factors that may contribute to Alzheimer's was started in 1988 by David Snowdon of Kentucky University, who persuaded 678 Notre Dame convent nuns, aged from 75 to 106,

Use it or lose it: what nuns have told us about alzheimer's disease continued.

to allow investigators full access to their convent and medical records, and to undergo rigorous mental and physical testing once a year. Nuns make excellent subjects for narrowing down risk factors in dementia as they are celibate, non-smokers, have similar jobs and income, and receive good health care. But, more importantly, the nuns also agreed to donate their brains at death so that any mental and physical decline with ageing could be correlated with brain pathology. Although this study has provided a number of important findings (for a very readable account see Snowdon's book *Aging with Grace*) one of the most interesting occurred when investigators discovered the autobiographies of 93 sisters that had been written some 60 years earlier just prior to their religious vows. When the language in these diaries was examined it was found that the nuns who had the richest vocabulary, wrote the most complex sentences and expressed the greatest number of ideas were the ones who tended to develop dementia at a later age. Put another way, the nuns who appeared to exercise their brains more as young women were seemingly more protected against Alzheimer's disease later in life.

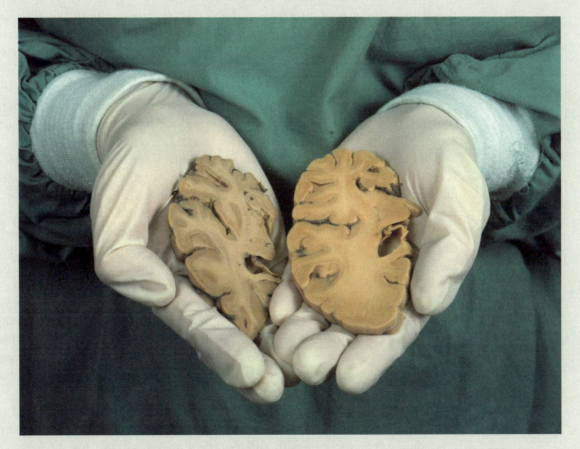

Plate 8.1   Gloved hands comparing a brain segment affected by Alzheimer's disease with a healthy one. The segment affected by Alzheimer's disease is on the left. It appears shrunken, and the fissures are noticeably larger. *Source*: Simon Fraser/MRC Unit, Newcastle General Hospital/Science Photo Library

Diencephalic amnesia

The hippocampus is not the only brain area associated with memory. In fact, the most common form of amnesia seen by clinical neuropsychologists is **Korsakoff's syndrome**, named after the Russian physician Sergi Korsakoff, who first described the condition in 1889. Korsakoff's syndrome is mainly found in alcoholics and develops as a result of thiamine (vitamin B_1) deficiency due to a poor diet and long-term reliance on alcohol. It is also associated with damage to the **diencephalon** region of the brain, which includes the **thalamus** and **hypothalamus**. The first signs of the disorder often appear as **Wernicke's encephalopathy,** characterised by confusion in which the patient may be unable to recognise friends and surroundings, have unsteadiness of balance, and poor motor coordination (ataxia). Although these symptoms can normally be treated with thiamine and glucose injections, this will often be the start of an irreversible illness resulting in the deterioration of memory and personality that is symptomatic of Korsakoff's syndrome.

One of the most striking features of Korsakoff's syndrome is a severe deficit in learning new information. For example, patients with this disorder may take weeks or months to learn the names of their doctors and nurses, or even the location of their hospital beds. This type of deficit has also been shown experimentally. For example, learning a list of paired associate words such as *man–hamster* in which the subject is required to recall the second word upon presentation of the first, may take the Korsakoff patient some 30 or 40 trials in comparison to only three or four trials for a normal subject (Butters 1984).

Another characteristic of Korsakoff's syndrome is **retrograde amnesia**, which is generally most severe for events occurring just prior to the onset of the illness, although the memory loss can also cover much longer periods of time. For example, there are Korsakoff patients who can remember their participation in the Second World War, but are unable to recall the assassination of John Kennedy or the Apollo space missions. This may also result in the patients believing that they are living in the past (e.g. see the case of Mr G in *The Man who Mistook his Wife for a Hat* by Oliver Sacks). Korsakoff patients also tend to make up stories or confabulate if they have gaps in their memory, and can often provide a plausible answer to a question which, upon verification, is found to be totally false. This behaviour may partly be because the patients are embarrassed at their memory loss, but also because they are genuinely confused. This problem is also often exacerbated by amnesiacs' lack of insight into their condition, and their belief that there is nothing wrong with their memory.

The symptons of retrograde amnesia, confabulation and confusion, help to distinguish diencephalic amnesia from temporal lobe damage, since the latter is predominantly associated with anterograde amnesia without loss of personal insight. In addition, while people with diencephalic amnesia take a long time to learn new information, they nevertheless forget at normal rates, unlike those with damage to the medial temporal lobes, who forget very rapidly (Huppert and Piercy 1979).

The neural basis of Korsakoff's syndrome

It has long been known that Korsakoff's disease is associated with damage to the diencephalon, especially the **mammillary bodies** situated in the posterior part of the hypothalamus (Figure 8.11). Indeed, as early as 1928, Gamper examined the brains of 16 Korsakoff patients and showed that they all had degeneration of the mammillary bodies – and a large number of studies have subsequently confirmed this observation. Despite this, the Korsakoff's brain nearly always shows widespread damage at postmortem, which typically includes the brainstem and thalamus. Moreover, the traditional view of mammillary body damage being responsible for the amnesia in Korsakoff's syndrome was challenged in the early 1970s when a study of over 80 brains found five cases where mammillary body damage was not associated with memory decline (Victor *et al.* 1971). There was, however, a structure in which damage was always present, and this was the **dorsomedial thalamus**.

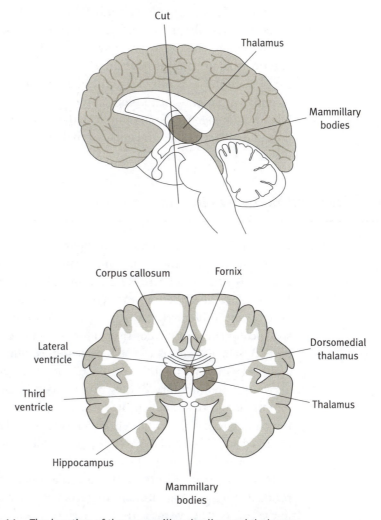

Figure 8.11   The location of the mammillary bodies and thalamus

This finding has complicated our neuroanatomical understanding of Korsakoff's syndrome and raises the possibility that some degree of damage to both the mammillary bodies and thalamus may need to take place before diencephalic amnesia occurs. Evidence broadly in line with this idea has come from a patient known as NA who, at the age of 22, suffered severe amnesia following an injury. The accident happened when NA was busy building a model aeroplane in the company of a friend who was playing behind him with a fencing foil. When NA turned suddenly, he was stabbed through the right nostril, with the foil entering the base of his brain. The initial effect of NA's injury was a retrograde amnesia for the two-year period preceding the injury, and a severe inability to learn new information. Although the retrograde amnesia largely disappeared, the anterograde amnesia persisted. He can still give little verbal information about events since his accident in 1960, although he shows almost normal recall for his life preceding this event.

In 1979 Squire and Moore performed a CAT scan on NA and found that the foil had terminated in the left dorsomedial thalamus. This initial report also indicated that the injury was highly localised, with little damage to other brain structures. However, a later study that used MRI scanning showed the damage to be more widespread and include the mammillary bodies and the mammillothalamic tract – a pathway connecting the mammillary bodies with the anterior thalamus (Squire *et al.* 1989). Which of these regions is most crucial for NA's amnesia is not clear, although it may be that all are important. More recently, a patient with severe anterograde amnesia has been shown to have bilateral damage to the mammillothalamic tract, confirming the importance of the mammillary bodies and anterior thalamus for memory (Malamut *et al.* 1992).

The Papez and Yakovlev circuits

As we have seen, there are two separate regions of the brain where damage results in amnesia: the hippocampus and the diencephalon. These two regions have also been shown to be anatomically connected. For example, in 1937, James Papez described a brain circuit (now called the **Papez circuit**) that connected the limbic system with the cerebral cortex (see also page 150). More specifically this circuit consists of the cingulate gyrus (a part of the cerebral cortex), which projects to the hippocampus, which, in turn, projects via a long arching pathway called the **fornix** to the mammillary bodies. As we have seen above, the mammillary bodies project to the anterior thalamus via the mammillothalamic tract, which, in turn, completes the circuit by sending fibres to the cingulate gyrus. Although Papez originally hypothesised this circuit to be involved in emotional behaviour, one might also expect it to have a crucial involvement in memory.

Indeed, evidence supports the idea that bilateral damage to the Papez circuit produces memory impairment. In particular, investigators have taken an interest in the fornix (the word 'fornix' is derived from the Latin for *arch* and has provided us with the word *fornicate*, because brothels in ancient Rome were often in chambers with arched roofs) since it directly links the hippocampus with the diencephalon. The human fornix is a massive pathway that contains around a million fibres, and several studies have now shown that damage to this structure causes anterograde amnesia. Moreover, in one study that looked at six individuals who had cysts surgically removed from the fornix, the amount of damage correlated with the severity of the memory impairment (McMacken *et al.* 1995). Although some fibres pass into the hippocamus from the fornix (notably cholinergic axons from the medial septal nucleus and nucleus of the diagonal band), the fornical relay of hippocampal information to the diencephalon is likely to be crucial for the formation of long-term memory.

However, the astute student will note that the Papez circuit does not project to the dorsomedial thalamus – which, as we have seen above, has also been implicated in memory (see page 249). In fact, the dorsomedial thalamus is part of a different system, sometimes referred to as the **Yakovlev circuit**, whose focal point appears to be the amygdala. Despite its close proximity to the anterior region of the hippocampus, the amygdala sends many of its fibres to the dorsomedial thalamus, which, in turn, projects to the frontal cortex. The circuit is then completed with the frontal cortex projecting back to the amygdala. Historically, this pathway has not attracted as much attention as the Papez circuit, perhaps because specific damage to the amygdala is more associated with emotion and learning of fear than with amnesia. Despite this, some animal experiments (see later) have shown memory deficits following amygdala lesions. Moreover, it is sometimes overlooked that HM had both the amygdala and hippocampus removed in his operation, which severed both the Papez and the Yakovlev pathways (Figure 8.12). It may be, therefore, that damage to both circuits has to take place, as probably occurs in Korsakoff's disease, before serious amnesia is produced.

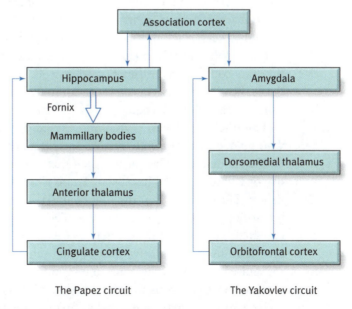

Figure 8.12   The Papez and Yakolev circuits

The evidence from animal studies

If the hippocampus is involved in memory, then presumably its removal should also produce learning deficits in animals. However, following Scoville and Milner's description of HM in 1957, a number of studies showed that hippocampal damage did not always produce this type of impairment. In fact, hippocampal-lesioned rats could perform a number of tasks, including (1) various forms of operant conditioning in a Skinner box; (2) a visual discrimination task in which the animal had to distinguish between a black and white goal box to obtain food reward; and (3) avoiding an electric shock in a situation that required running to a 'safe' location when a warning tone was presented (Douglas 1967). Despite this, there were other tests in which marked deficits were observed. Two such tasks were those that involved working memory and cognitive mapping.

Working memory

In their natural habitat, animals have to forage for food, which requires that they find their way around their environment. Obviously, it helps if the animals can remember where they have just been, to avoid having to go back to the same location. In fact, even simple animals such as bees are surprisingly adept at this skill. In 1976, David Olton designed a task that tested a similar type of memory in rats (Olton and Samuelson 1976). This was the radial arm maze, which consisted of a round platform with arms, containing food at their ends, that radiated out like the spokes of a wheel (Figure 8.13). To gain maximum reward, the rat had to learn to enter each arm once, without revisiting any of the previously entered arms. At first sight, this task appears very demanding as it requires the animal to keep track of where it has been, while remembering where it still has to go (a skill that Olton called 'working memory'). Nevertheless, Olton found that rats could perform this task very well, even when short delays were introduced between arms or when the animals were forced down certain arms in order to abolish fixed sequences of responding (Olton *et al.* 1979).

This ability, however, did not extend to rats with hippocampal lesions, who tended to continually retrace their paths and negotiate the maze in a very inefficient manner. Thus, it was as if these animals were unable to form a memory of where they had just been. There were two possible explanations for this deficit. The first was that the hippocampal-lesioned rat had a deficit of working memory – essentially it could not 'list' the arms it had visited. The second explanation was that the animals were simply getting 'lost' because they were unable to form a cognitive map of their environment – that is, they could not recognise the arms of the maze in relation to the spatial layout of the room. This is somewhat analogous to our getting lost in a new town because we are unable to recognise the main landmarks, or their relative position to each other. To test which theory was correct, Olton and Papas (1979) built a 17-arm maze

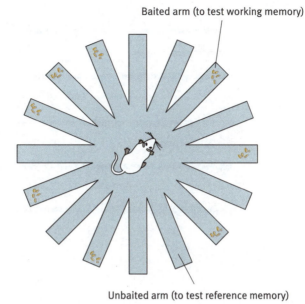

Baited arm (to test working memory)

Unbaited arm (to test reference memory)

Figure 8.13   The radial arm maze (showing working and reference memory components)

containing nine arms that were always empty, and eight arms that always contained food. To negotiate this new maze with optimun efficiency, the animal had now to learn two types of information. The first simply required that the rat did not visit the empty arms. Because these arms always remained empty from trial to trial, Olton argued that this skill required the rat to develop a permanent mental map of the maze, which he called 'reference memory'. The second component of the task, however, required the animal to find the food without revisiting any of the arms. This was essentially the working memory task again, with the rat having to remember where it had just been, and where it had to go.

When Olton tested normal rats in his maze he found that they soon learned to avoid the empty arms, while retrieving food efficiently from the baited ones. That is, they were capable of both reference memory and working memory. Surprisingly, the hippocampal-lesioned animals also learned to avoid the non-baited arms, although they only performed at chance levels when visiting the arms containing food. In other words, the lesioned rats showed reference memory, which Olton believed was evidence of an ability to form a mental map of the radial maze, but were incapable of retaining a working memory.

Cognitive mapping

A different approach to understanding hippocampal function was undertaken by John O'Keefe and his colleagues at the University of London. Instead of examining the effects of hippocampal damage, O'Keefe recorded the electrical activity of individual cells in the hippocampus as rats moved around their environment. His main finding was that some neurons fired only when the animal

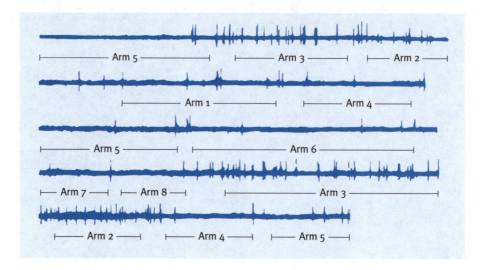

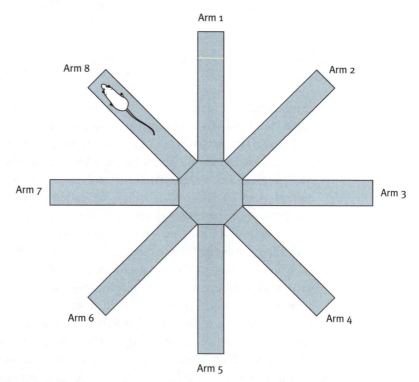

Figure 8.14   The firing of hippocampal place cells as a rat negotiates a radial arm maze.
Source: F.E. Bloom and A. Lazerson (1985) *Brain, Mind and Behaviour*, p.249

was in a certain location. These were neurons that remained quiet until the animal reached a certain point, when suddenly the cell would begin to fire rapidly. As the animal moved away to a new location the neuron would stop firing. However, if the rat returned to the location at a later time, the neuron would 'remember' the site and fire again. O'Keefe called these neurons '**place cells**'.

Further research showed that hippocampal place cells were dependent on the configuration of cues located outside the testing arena (extramaze cues) and not those within its confines. For example, O'Keefe and Conway (1978) trained rats to run a T-maze where one of the arms always contained food. The maze was surrounded by a black curtain that had a distinct cue (a fan, a buzzer, a light and a square card) hanging on each of its four sides. Moreover, this curtain could also be moved around the apparatus, although, of course, the cues always remained in the same place relative to each other. On all trials, the arm containing the food was always pointed towards the corner situated between the light and the card. To make sure that the rats learned the spatial location of the arm, and not a simple right- or left-turning response, the location of the starting position was changed from trial to trial.

Again, the T-maze task showed that the hippocampal place cells only fired when the animal was in a specific location in relation to the cues. If the curtain was moved around, shifting the configuration of the cues with it, the place cell still fired – providing the animal was in the same *relative* position to the cues. That is, it was the animal's position relative to the external cues – and not the actual site in the maze – that was important. The importance of the external cues was further highlighted when they were removed. If any two cues were removed, the place cells still continued to fire; but if more than two cues were removed, the neurons often stopped firing. The important factor, therefore, was the *spatial configuration* of the cues. According to O'Keefe and Nadel (1978) these findings showed that the hippocampus was responsible for forming a cognitive map that enabled the animal to move around its environment successfully.

Some of the best support for the cognitive mapping theory has come from Morris *et al.* (1982), who developed a spatial memory task that required rats to swim a water maze. The 'maze' was in fact a large circular tank of water, made opaque with the addition of milk, that contained a small escape platform hidden just below the surface. Rats were put into the water and allowed to swim around until they 'bumped' into the platform, which they then inevitably climbed onto. Although the rats could not see the platform, and were forced to learn its location by determining its position in relation to the spatial configuration of extramaze cues around the water, Morris found that it took just a few trials for normal animals to swim directly to it, despite being started from different locations. In contrast, the hippocampal-lesioned rats were unable to learn the location of the platform even after 40 days of training.

It is difficult to see how the water maze is testing any behavioural function except spatial memory, and the failure of the hippocampal-lesioned rats to perform this relatively easy task provides strong support for the cognitive mapping theory. However, the performance of animals in the water maze appears to contradict the findings of Olton and Papas, who showed that hippocampus-lesioned rats have intact reference memory in the radial maze, which they argued was dependent on learning the location of extramaze cues. Indeed, successful performance in both the water maze and reference memory component of the radial maze appears to require forming a spatial map of the environment – yet only the former causes a problem for hippocampal-lesioned animals. At present, the reason for this difference remains unclear.

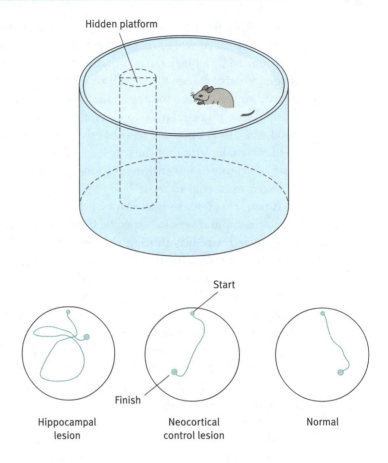

Figure 8.15 The Morris water maze. *Source*: Examples of routes taken after training by rats in water maze taken from R.G.M. Morris *et al.* (1982) *Nature*, **297**, 681–3

Do London taxi drivers have a unique hippocampus?

Whether visiting a friend, or popping out to the shops, finding our way around the environment is something we take for granted. Yet it is truly a remarkable skill that requires both spatial memory and an ability to construct a mental map of our world. One brain area that has been implicated in this ability is the hippocampus. Not only do lesions of this structure impair performance on tests of cognitive mapping and spatial processing, but there is evidence that the size of the hippocampus may also correlate with the ability to perform such tasks. For instance, birds that store food (which requires them to remember the locations of the storage sites) have a larger hippocampus than those that do not horde (Sherry *et al.* 1992). Another example where hippocampal differences are found is in North American voles. For example, the male meadow vole (*Microtus pennsylvanicus*) has a territory several times larger than the female and a much larger hippocampus. In contrast, male and female pine voles (*Microtus pinetorum*), which travel over equal distances, show no significant difference in the size of their hippocampi (Jacobs *et al.* 1990).

Do London taxi drivers have a unique hippocampus? continued.

But can navigational experience have an impact on the structure of the hippocampus in humans? To answer this question, Eleanor Maguire and her colleagues at University College, London, examined the brains of 16 right-handed London taxi drivers by using magnetic resonance imaging. London taxi drivers are an ideal group for this type of study. Most are highly experienced (the men in Maguire's study had been driving taxis for a mean of 14.3 years) and to get a licence they must have passed an examination that tested their ability to navigate some 24,000 streets in the city – a task that takes about two years to learn. It seems that this experience has an effect on the size of the hippocampus. For example, the posterior part of the right hippocampus was significantly larger in both right and left hemispheres of the taxi drivers when compared with controls (Figure 8.16) – although, surprisingly, the anterior part

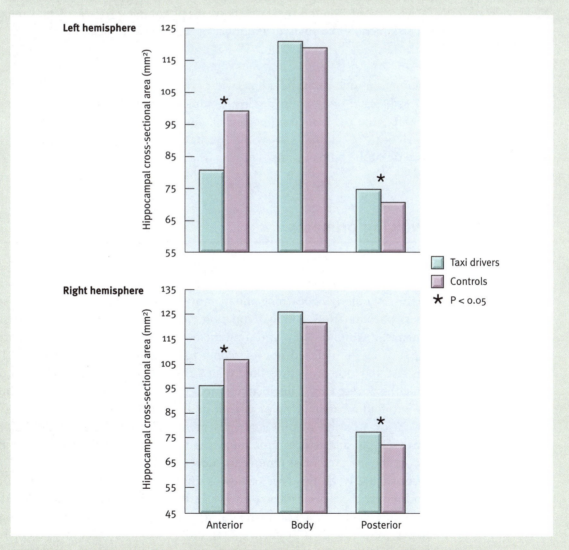

Figure 8.16 The volume of hippocampal tissue (mm²) in London taxi drivers and control subjects. *Source*: E.A. Maguire *et al.* (2000) 'Navigation-related structural change in the hippocampi of taxi drivers' from *Proceedings of the National Academy of Sciences*, 97, 4398–4403

Do London taxi drivers have a unique hippocampus? continued.

of the hippocampus was found to be smaller. There was no difference between the two groups in the medial parts of the hippocampus, or in its overall size (Maguire *et al.* 2000).

The investigators also plotted the volume of the anterior and posterior hippocampus against the number of months each person had spent as a taxi driver. The analysis showed that the volume of the right-sided hippocampus was significantly correlated with the amount of time spent as a taxi driver (there was a positive association for the posterior hippocampus and a negative one for the anterior region) although the left-sided hippocampus did not show this relationship. In other words, it appears that driving a taxi for a long time causes the right posterior hippocampus to become larger. This finding also supports an earlier study by Maguire *et al.* (1997), who asked London taxi drivers to recall complex routes around the city and found that this task increased activity in a number of brain regions including the right hippocampus, but not the left.

These findings raise a number of questions including: what are the functions of the right and left hippocampi? Is it possible that taxi drivers are losing some of their abilities in return for increased knowledge? And is the right-sided hippocampus the actual site that produces and stores cognitive maps? All of these questions show that we have still a long way to go before we understand the plasticity of the human brain – or even that of taxi drivers!

Memory tasks involving primates

Primates provide an alternative way of experimentally investigating the brain mechanisms underlying learning and memory, and one that is likely to represent a closer approximation of human function. Because primates have similar vision to humans, a common way of testing memory deficits is to use discrimination tasks, such as the **delayed non-matching to sample** procedure (Figure 8.17). In this test, the monkey is presented with a tray containing two food wells, one of which is covered by a distinctive object (the sample) that the animal must remove to find a banana chip or peanut underneath. Following this, the tray is removed for a period of time and presented again with two test objects: the original sample and a new unfamiliar object. To obtain the reward on this occasion, the monkey must remove the new object.

Surprisingly, when this type of task is given to primates with lesions of the hippocampus, their performance shows little impairment. For example, after a 10-minute delay on a non-matching to sample task, hippocampal-lesioned monkeys were found to perform at around 75 per cent accuracy, compared with 90 per cent for control animals (Squire and Zola-Morgan 1985, Mahut *et al.* 1982). At first sight this finding is not easily reconciled with the human data, where the hippocampal deficit appears to be much more pronounced. The monkeys' performance on the delayed matching to non-sample task following dorsomedial thalamic lesions, however, appears to be much closer to the human

1. The monkey moves the sample object to obtain food from the well beneath it

2. A screen is lowered in front of the monkey during the delay period

3. The monkey is confronted with the sample object and an unfamiliar object

4. The monkey must remember the sample object and select the unfamiliar object to obtain the food beneath it

Figure 8.17   The delayed matching to non-sample task. *Source*: From John P.J. Pinel, *Biopsychology*, 3rd edition. Copyright © 1997 by Pearson Education

deficit. For example, this type of lesion in primates reduces accuracy to 62 per cent (which is close to chance at 50 per cent) after a 10-minute delay (Zola-Morgan and Squire 1985).

But why do hippocampal lesions produce such a small impairment on this type of task? Or, if we put this another way, why is HM's amnesia so severe? An experiment by Mishkin (1978) may have helped to clarify this issue. Mishkin made lesions to the hippocampus, or amygdala, in macaque monkeys and found that neither had much effect on the non-matching to sample task (both groups performed at about 90 per cent correct after a 2-minute delay). However, when he combined the two lesions, a much more severe impairment was found, with performance falling to near chance (60 per cent) accuracy. This finding is particularly interesting because HM's operation also involved the removal of the amygdala and hippocampus, as well as the surrounding portions of the medial temporal lobe. Thus, the implication of Mishkin's work is that both the hippocampus and the amygdala are important for memory processing. Indeed, as we have already seen, these two structures appear to be part of different memory circuits in the brain (the Papez and Yakovlev circuits). Thus, perhaps both circuits need to be damaged before severe amnesia occurs in both monkeys and humans.

Mishkin's work has also encouraged investigators to look at other types of temporal lobe damage, including the cortical tissue surrounding the hippo-campus. These regions include the **perirhinal cortex** (this area was also damaged by Mishkin's combined hippocampal–amygdala lesion), and the **parahippo-campal gyrus**, which includes the **entorhinal cortex** (see Figure 8.18). In fact, lesions confined to the perirhinal cortex and parahippocampal gyrus (spanning the hippocampus and amygdala) were found to produce a deficit on the non-matching to sample task which was nearly as severe as that for the combined

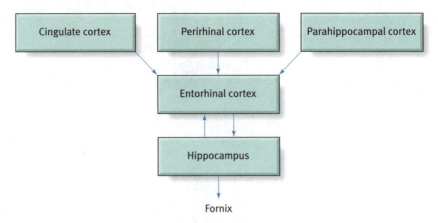

Figure 8.18 Cortical areas immediately adjacent to (and feeding into) the hippocampal formation

hippocampal–amygdala lesion (Zola-Morgan *et al.* 1989). Thus, the medial temporal lobe contains several regions that are collectively important for memory. This is perhaps not surprising as some hippocampal neurons project back into the parahippocampal gyrus (via the **subiculum**), which, in turn, provides an important relay of information to the cerebral cortex. This output from the hippocampus, along with the fibres passing through the fornix (i.e. Papez circuit), are likely to be both crucially involved in memory processing.

Summary

There is no learning without memory, although some memories can be innate such as instincts and basic reflexes. The search for the **engram** (the anatomical site of memory storage) was initiated in the 1920s by Karl Lashley, who made knife cuts, or lesioned, different proportions of the **cerebral cortex** in rats after they had learned to run through mazes. Lashley showed that his animals were always able to relearn the task, even after receiving large lesions, and he concluded that memories for mazes were stored diffusely throughout the cerebral cortex, which he called the principle of **mass action**, and that all parts of the cortex played an equal role in their storage, which he called the principle of **equipotentiality**. His work was supported, in part, by Donald Hebb, who theorised that learning and memory must involve large groups of neurons, or **cell assemblies**, reverberating for some time after the event, which leads to structural change at **synapses**. Evidence of increased electrical activity in neurons after learning has come from the discovery of **long-term potentiation**, while a detailed account of the synaptic changes that accompany **habituation** and **classical conditioning** of the **gill-withdrawal reflex** has come from an examination of *Aplysia*. Research examining the effects of rats reared in enriched environments has also shown that such experience can produce a number of changes in the brain, including increased numbers of **dendritic spines**, which include **synapses,** and higher levels of **acetylcholinesterase** (AChE), which is an enzyme that breaks down the neurotransmitter **acetylcholine.**

Summary continued.

A brain structure that is crucial for learning and memory in humans is the **hippocampus**. This was dramatically shown in the case of **HM**, who underwent bilateral removal of the **medial temporal lobes** in 1953 for treatment of epilepsy. Since the operation HM has suffered from a profound **anterograde amnesia** in which he is unable to lay down permanent **long-term memories**, although he has a relatively normal **short-term memory**. Although HM has a normal recall of events prior to his operation, there is **retrograde amnesia** for the few years leading up to his surgery. Despite this, HM demonstrates learning on some tasks and this has led to the idea that the hippocampus is necessary for **declarative memory** (which can be 'declared' into consciousness), but not **procedural memory** (implicit or 'knowing how' knowledge). Animal studies of the hippocampus have shown it to be involved in **working memory**, **cognitive mapping** and **spatial memory**. Another region of the brain implicated in human amnesia is the **diencephalon**, which includes the **mammillary bodies** and **dorsomedial thalamus**. Damage to both of these areas has been found in **Korsakoff's disease**, which generally occurs as a result of chronic alcohol abuse. The location of brain sites implicated in amnesia points to two main memory pathways in the brain: the **Papez circuit** and the **Yakovlev circuit**. The former includes the hippocampus, fornix, mammillary bodies and cingulate gyrus, and the latter includes the amygdala, dorsomedial thalamus and frontal cortex. It is probable that the most severe forms of amnesia require damage to both these pathways.

Essay questions

1. With reference to neural, synaptic and electrophysiological changes, what would a memory engram in the brain be likely to look like?

   Helpful Internet search terms: *Synaptic changes in memory. Long-term potentiation. Dendritic changes in memory. Learning and memory in* Aplysia. *Hebbian synapses. Phosphorylation of memory. The effects of experience on the brain.*

2. What brain structures and circuits are known to be particularly important for human memory?

   Helpful Internet search terms: *Hippocampus and memory. Papez circuit and memory. Mammillary bodies and Korsakoff's disease. Temporal lobe and memory. Thalamus and memory. Amnesia. Penfield and memory storage.*

3. Discuss the evidence linking the hippocampus with an involvement in cognitive mapping and spatial memory.

   Helpful Internet search terms: *Hippocampus and cognitive mapping. Neurobiology of working memory. Radial arm maze. Place cells. Spatial memory and hippocampus. Lesions of the hippocampus.*

4. What are the main characteristics of HM? What does his memory deficit tell us about the function of the hippocampus and medial temporal lobes?

   Helpful Internet search terms: *Patient HM. Anterograde amnesia. Declarative and procedural memory. Functions of the hippocampus. Explicit and implicit memory in amnesia.*

Further reading

Cohen, N.J. and Eichenbaum, H. (1993) *Memory, Amnesia, and the Hippocampal System*. Cambridge, MA: MIT Press. Written for experts, this attempts to bring together evidence from neuropsychology, neuroscience and cognitive science to explain the role of the hippocampus in memory and amnesia.

Dubai, Y. (1990) *The Neurobiology of Memory*. Oxford: Oxford University Press. A textbook that will appeal to neuroscience students, especially those interested in the molecular and cellular aspects of memory.

Martinez, J.L. and Kesner, R.P. (eds) (1998) *Neurobiology of Learning and Memory*. San Diego: Academic Press. A comprehensive and well-written series of chapters by experts in the field covering learning and memory from a diversity of approaches including genetic, pharmacological and physiological perspectives.

McGaugh, J.L., Weinberger, N.M. and Lynch, G. (1995) *Brain and Memory: Modulation and Mediation of Neuroplasticity*. Oxford: Oxford University Press. A fairly technical and wide-ranging account which examines the processes underlying the formation of new memories and their possible sites of storage.

Parkin, A.J. and Leng, N.R. (1993) *Neuropsychology of the Amnesic Syndrome*. Hove, UK: Lawrence Erlbaum. A concise but well-written introduction to memory disorders, including Korsakoff's syndrome and temporal lobe amnesia.

Rose, S. (2003) *The Making of Memory: From Molecules to Mind*. London: Bantam Books. Winner of the Rhone–Poulenc Science Prize in 1993, this is a highly enjoyable introduction to the molecular and neurobiological basis of memory and amnesia.

Seifert, W. (ed.) (1983) *Neurobiology of the Hippocampus*. London: Academic Press. Although this book is now dated, it nevertheless contains useful chapters by the main protagonists who were involved in examining the role of the hippocampus in working memory, cognitive mapping and spatial processing.

Snowdon, D. (2001) *Aging With Grace*. London: Fourth Estate. An extraordinary book about what nuns have told us about ageing and dementia, with lessons for us all.

Squire, L.R. (1987) *Memory and the Brain*. New York: Oxford University Press. A good introduction, suitable for undergraduates, that attempts to show how memory is organised in the brain using evidence from both experimental research and clinical studies.

Squire, L.R. and Kandel, E.R. (1999) *Memory: From Mind to Molecules*. New York: Scientific American Library. A well-written and richly illustrated text that provides a good overview of research into the neural mechanisms underlying learning and memory.

See website at www.pearsoned.co.uk/wickens for further resources including multiple choice questions.

CHAPTER 9

Language and cognition

In this chapter

- The main areas involved in the production and comprehension of language

- Different types of aphasia

- The Wernicke–Geschwind model of language

- Hemispheric differences and evidence from split-brain studies

- The development of lateralisation

- The causes of dyslexia

- Computerised scanning techniques and their application to understanding language

INTRODUCTION

All animals are capable of communication, but humans are the only ones who use an extremely complex, creative and powerful system of language and writing that enables them to express their thoughts and feelings. Our ability to use language is remarkable in many ways. For example, during a simple conversation we speak about 180 words a minute from a vocabulary of between 60,000 and 120,000 words. This is an impressive figure, but even more important is our ability to utilise an extensive knowledge of intricate linguistic rules, including those that govern the sequencing of words and their form (i.e. grammar). In fact, this rule system provides us with the potential to make an infinite number of word sequences from a limited number of sounds, and without this ability our language would be very simple. The richness and complexity of human language has provided the keystone that underpins cultural evolution, and enables discoveries and knowledge to be written down for prosperity. Language is also much more than communication: it is a system for representing knowledge and a vehicle for thought that lies at the core of human cognition. Indeed, language has been described as the greatest of all human achievements (Ornstein 1988) and the one species-typical behaviour that sets us apart from all other animals (Thompson 1993). Thus, by attempting to understand the neural basis of language, we are getting to the heart of what makes us and our brain truly unique.

Broca's area

Until recently, most of our knowledge concerning the neural basis of language has come from examining language impairments in patients suffering brain injuries caused by stroke or accidents. The first area of the brain to be implicated in language was the frontal lobes, and this was shown as early as the nineteenth century when a number of French doctors, including Jean-Baptiste Boullaud in 1825 and Marc Dax in 1836, found that damage to this part of the cortex often resulted in loss of speech. However, perhaps the most dramatic case was reported in 1861 when Simon Aubertin described the case of a man who had shot away part of his frontal cranium in a failed suicide attempt that exposed his brain. During the course of his examination, Aubertin discovered that if he pressed a spatula against the exposed brain while the man was speaking, the speech was immediately halted. However, when the compression was lessened, speech resumed (Finger 1994).

Despite this, there was a general reluctance by investigators at the time to accept that highly specific functions such as speech could be localised to individual brain regions. This was partly because localisation of function seemed to provide support for phrenology, which, by then, had been acrimoniously discredited, and partly because frontal lobe damage tended to produce other behavioural

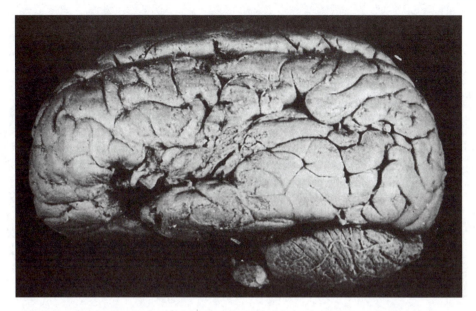

Plate 9.1 The brain of Leborgne (nicknamed 'Tan'). *Source: Hopitaux de Paris*

disabilities as well (see later). Definite proof of a speech centre in the frontal lobes, however, was finally provided by the great French neurologist Paul Broca. One of Broca's patients was a man called Leborgne who had been incapable of speech for 21 years, except for the utterance of 'Tan', which became the name by which he was more widely known. Despite this, Leborgne was intelligent, capable of comprehending spoken and written language, and able to communicate with motor gestures. When Leborgne died in 1861, Broca undertook an autopsy and found a large lesion located towards the back of the frontal lobes in the left hemisphere (Plate 9.1). Broca was the first to show that a localised lesion in the human brain could produce a highly specific language disability.

Following this discovery, Broca performed autopsies on eight other patients who had shown similar types of language deficit, and found that they all had damage to the same area of the frontal lobes. This region has now become known as **Broca's area** and is located just in front of the motor cortex, which controls the muscles of the vocal cord and mouth (Figure 9.1). However, Broca's autopsies seemed to show that similar damage to the right frontal cortex had no effect on speech production or comprehension. Thus, the brain areas involved in language production appeared to be highly localised to the left hemisphere of the frontal cortex.

Broca's aphasia

It is now known that people with damage to Broca's area suffer from a language disturbance known as **Broca's aphasia**. This form of aphasia is characterised by language that is slow, laboured and lacking in grammatical structure. Although

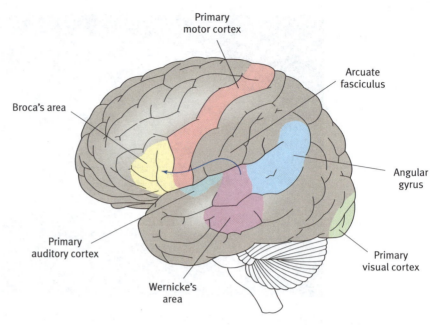

Figure 9.1 The location of the main areas involved in language comprehension and production. *Source*: M.R. Rosenzweig *et al.* (2002) *Biological Psychology*, 3rd edition, p.617

the person may have a considerable vocabulary, the speech tends to be composed of simple nouns, verbs and adjectives – not unlike the type of language one may use to write a telegram. In addition, the speech often lacks the intonation and inflection of normal language, making it sound unnatural. Another characteristic of Broca'a aphasia is a difficulty in finding the 'right word', known as **anomia**, which results in long pauses during speech. To make matters worse, the aphasic is also likely to have articulation difficulties and substitute incorrect sounds into words, making them difficult to understand. Despite this, Broca's aphasics 'know' what they are trying to say, and often become highly frustrated at their inability to make themselves understood. Interestingly, simple automated expressions such as 'hello', or emotional outbursts including swearing, may be spoken without difficulty. Also, in some cases a Broca's aphasic may even be able to sing old and well-learned songs.

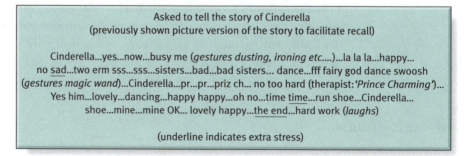

Figure 9.2 Non-fluent Broca-type aphasia. *Source*: Provided by Mandy Galling, Reg RCSLT, Guild Community Healthcare NHS Trust

How then can we best characterise the deficit in Broca's aphasia? One clue comes from the fact that such people will often have difficulty in carrying out a simple command such as being asked to stick out their tongue (**oral apraxia**), yet typically have no problem licking their lips after eating a sugary doughnut. This observation suggests that one deficit in Broca's aphasia is an inability to produce the correct motor movements for the articulation of speech. Indeed, because of this deficit, Broca's aphasia is sometimes known as expressive or **motor aphasia**. Although this explanation makes sense – particularly as Broca's area is adjacent to the part of the motor cortex that controls the movements of the mouth and face – it is not the whole answer as Broca's aphasics can also show impaired comprehension. Although they often give the impression of being able to fully understand verbal speech, it has nevertheless been shown that Broca's aphasics often have problems in comprehending language that is grammatically complex. For example, they may be unable to perform an instruction such as '*Put the cup on top of the fork and place the knife inside the cup*'. Similarly, Broca's aphasics may have problems understanding sentences where there is an atypical word order. Thus, they may be unable to understand who is doing the chasing in '*The boy was chased by the girl*' but have no problem with '*The mouse was chased by the cat*', where world knowledge constraints contribute to the correct interpretation. Thus, Broca's area appears to have a role in understanding grammar as well as being crucially involved in the expression of language.

Wernicke's area

In 1874, a 26-year-old German neurologist called Carl Wernicke described a very different type of aphasia – one that was linked with damage to a region in the left hemisphere some distance from Broca's area. This region, now known as **Wernicke's area**, is located in the temporal lobe adjacent to the **primary auditory cortex**. Unlike Broca's aphasia, damage to Wernicke's area does not interfere with the rhythm and grammar of speech, and people are able to articulate words quickly and fluently (Figure 9.3). Unfortunately, there is one major problem: the speech is largely devoid of meaning. In other words, although the speech may sound 'normal' and grammatically correct, it is devoid of sensible content. To a large degree this is because the language is composed of either inappropriate words (**paraphasias**) or ones that do not exist (**neologisms**). For example, in reply to the question 'Where do you work?' one Wernicke's aphasic was quoted as saying '*Before I was in the one here, I was in the other one. My sister had the department in the other one*' (Geschwind 1972). Alternatively, when Roachford (1974) asked a Wernicke's aphasic to name a picture of an anchor, the patient called it a '*martha argeneth*'; and when Kertesz (1979) asked a patient to name a toothbrush and a pen, the patient responded with '*stoktery*' and '*minkt*'.

Damage to Wernicke's area also produces a profound deficit in language comprehension. While simple sentences and instructions may be understood, there is nearly always a marked inability to comprehend more complex forms

Required to tell the therapist about trip to visit his daughter and a meal out

Claire?...yes...well...I was will...miner...mineral water...of my 'pitch' on stonework 'make' and 'ww' and 'wiker' of 'wenner'. December and London...on 'minter' of 'minder' and 'si' or 'risher'...I was 'madge'

(Targets very difficult to interpret. Items in quotation marks show broad phonological approximation)

Figure 9.3 Fluent Wernicke-type aphasia. *Source*: Provided by Mandy Galling, Reg RCSLT, Guild Community Healthcare NHS Trust

of speech, which makes it extremely difficult to engage in meaningful conversation with Wernicke's aphasics. And, to make matters worse, they may be unaware that they have a speech or comprehension deficit! Thus, a person with Wernicke's aphasia is likely to talk gibberish while being unaware that he or she cannot understand the speech of others. Yet, remarkably, such a person will still follow the non-verbal rules of conversation by pausing and taking turns to speak, and is also sensitive to tone of voice and facial expressions. Reading and writing are also impaired. Indeed, there are Wernicke's aphasics who, if given a book, will go through the motions of reading it aloud only to speak utter nonsense (Springer and Deutsch 1989).

How, then, can we best understand Wernicke's aphasia? One clue comes from its location next to the primary auditory cortex, which indicates that it is probably associated with the translation of auditory information into words. Indeed, for this reason Wernicke's aphasia is sometimes known as **receptive aphasia**. But there is more to Wernicke's aphasia than this. Because of the marked deficit of comprehension, Wernicke's area also appears to be crucially involved in the translation of words into their proper meanings. In other words, Wernicke's area (or, perhaps more accurately, a network of other areas interconnected with it) appears to be specialised for storing the memories of the sounds that make up words, and for these to be used subsequently to evoke conceptual meanings.

Alexia and agraphia

In 1892, the French neurologist Jules Dejerine reported the cases of two patients that had another type of language deficit. Instead of suffering from aphasia, Dejerine found that his patients had great difficulty in reading (**alexia**) and writing (**agraphia**). One of his patients, for example, could speak and comprehend spoken language perfectly well, but was unable to read or write. When a brain autopsy was later undertaken, it revealed damage to the **angular gyrus** – a site that is located between the occipital (visual) cortex and Wenicke's area. The angular gyrus appeared to be in an ideal position to receive visual input and Dejerine concluded that it acted to translate written information into the appropriate mental sounds and meanings.

Dejerine's other patient was unable to read, although he could still write, and this deficit produced some odd patterns of behaviour. For example, although this patient could not read or comprehend written words, he could copy them out correctly, and was able to recognise their meaning when he wrote them. He was also able to recognise the words when the individual letters were spoken out aloud to him (e.g. c-a-t). And, even more remarkably, he even knew how to spell words that he could not read.

A clue to the underlying nature of the deficit came from the finding that this patient was also blind in his right visual field, which indicated that damage had occurred to the left visual cortex (note that the right visual field of both eyes goes to the left hemisphere, and vice versa – see Figure 2.7). Indeed, left visual cortex damage was confirmed at autopsy. But perhaps just as important to explaining the reading deficit was the discovery of damage to the posterior portion of the corpus callosum, which carries visual information between the two hemispheres. This meant that although the person could see words and letters with his intact right visual cortex, he was unable to cross this information over to the angular gyrus in the language-dominant left hemisphere, where, presumably, the 'reading' took place. Consequently, the person could see written words, but was unable to recognise them from their visual characteristics. Nonetheless, the person was still able to copy out written information, and this is probably because of intact connections between right visual cortex and the motor areas that control hand movement. In other words, copying involved an alternative route through the brain that did not utilise the left-sided angular gyrus.

The Wernicke–Geschwind model

Carl Wernicke not only described a type of aphasia that now bears his name, but in 1874 he also formulated a theory that attempted to show how language was processed by the brain. His theory viewed language comprehension and production as dependent on the left hemisphere of the brain, and it involved several regions and interconnected pathways. In particular, he emphasised the importance of a sensory speech centre in the temporal lobe that served as the repository for 'remembered images' (Wernicke's area), which was connected to a frontal area (Broca's area) responsible for storing the 'impressions of action'. In effect, Wernicke had invented what we would now regard as a flow diagram for language in the brain, and his theory was a major stimulus for the discovery and understanding of new forms of aphasia. Indeed, his theory remained influential until elaborated upon by Norman Geschwind in 1972. This more recent combined account is widely known as the **Wernicke–Geschwind model** (Figure 9.4).

The basic idea of the Wernicke–Geschwind model is that when we hear spoken language, the sound is first processed by the auditory cortex, which then passes its input to Wernicke's area, where the sounds are decoded and comprehended. A similar process is also believed to occur for reading, except, in this case, the flow of information is passed from the visual cortex to the angular gyrus, which

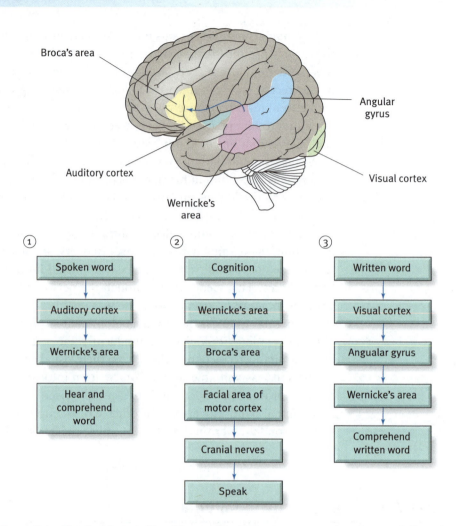

Figure 9.4 The Geschwind–Wernicke model of language processing. *Source*: Kolb and Wishaw (1985) *Fundamentals of Human Neuropsychology*

is believed to translate the visual code into an auditory one before it is passed to Wernicke's area. Thus, Wernicke's area is a pivotal site that combines the streams of visual and auditory verbal input, which then translates this information into thought. Wernicke's area is also believed to play an important role in generating verbal responses, and for this to happen, thought processes have to be translated back into verbal codes. This information is then passed to Broca's area, which provides the articulation centre and contains the programs for the complex coordination of the muscle movements necessary for speech. Thus, the neural code for the verbal response originates in Wernicke's area but is then transferred to Broca's area, where it is transformed into language. Most of this processing is believed to take place in the left hemisphere, although information can also cross to the right hemisphere (and back) via the corpus callosum.

This theory, of course, implies that a pathway exists between Wernicke's area and Broca's area. Although this had not been conclusively discovered by the end of the nineteenth century, Wernicke nevertheless had the foresight to predict the type of aphasia that would occur if this connection was destroyed. In short, he reasoned that it would not affect the comprehension of auditory or written information (because Wernicke's area would be intact) or impair the production of speech (as Broca's area would be intact). What then would be the deficit? According to Wernicke it would be highly specific: this type of aphasia would result in a person being unable to repeat words and sentences fluently.

In fact, Wernicke turned out to be largely correct in his prediction. A pathway between Wernicke's area and Broca's area is now known to exist and is called the **arcuate fasciculus**. Moreover, people with damage to this pathway have no difficulty in understanding language and are capable of producing fluent speech. However, they do suffer from **conduction aphasia**, characterised by an impairment in repeating certain words and sentences. For example, a person with conduction aphasia may be able to repeat concrete words such as 'bicycle' and 'elephant', but often unable to repeat abstract words or non-words such as 'blaynge'. It has been suggested by Geschwind that this occurs because, upon hearing a concrete word, a visual image can be formed, which is then able to pass to Broca's area via a different pathway. In addition, patients with conduction aphasia often find it difficult to read aloud, despite being able to read silently with good comprehension. Sometimes, when given an object to examine, they will typically 'know' what it is, but be unable to name it correctly.

Problems with the Wernicke–Geschwind model

Although the basic tenets of the Wernicke–Geschwind model are generally accepted, it is accurate only up to a point. For example, studies that examine stroke patients have confirmed the essential prediction that Broca'a aphasia is more often associated with a frontal stroke, whereas a posterior stroke is more likely to produce Wernicke's aphasia. Despite this, the effects of such damage are rarely as predictable as the Wernicke–Geschwind model implies. Indeed, people with Wernicke's aphasia nearly always have some degree of speech abnormality, and those with Broca's aphasia show comprehension deficits. Thus, the sharp functional distinctions between regions as implied by the model do not exist.

A similar conclusion was reached in the 1950s by Wilder Penfield, who stimulated various regions of the cerebral cortex with electrical current in order to detect abnormal tissue in human patients who were about to undergo brain surgery for epilepsy because the brain contains no pain receptors, subjects can remain fully conscious during this procedure. Penfield found that stimulation of the cortex could affect language in several ways. For example, it could induce vocalisations (e.g. a sustained utterance such as 'oh . . .'), interfere with the comprehension of language, or disrupt the production of speech. Despite this, the stimulation effects did not always correspond to the brain regions predicted by the Wernicke–Geschwind model. For example, naming difficulties (i.e. 'That is a . . . I know. That is a . . .'), or the misnaming of objects (e.g. saying 'camel' when meaning to say 'comb'), were elicited from widespread regions of the left hemisphere that went beyond the speech zones of either Broca or Wernicke (Penfield and Roberts 1959).

Penfield's observations have been extended by the work of George Ojemann and his colleagues at the University of Washington, who have shown that the extent of the cortical language zones, as identified by stimulation, varies greatly in size and location between individuals (Ojemann 1983). Thus, the brain regions involved in language only approximate those predicted by the Wernicke–Geschwind model, and their exact locations differ greatly between individuals. In fact, Ojemann's mapping work shows that the regions of temporal, parietal and frontal lobes that border the Sylvian fissure (a fissure that extends along the lateral aspect of each hemisphere for about half its length – see Figure 1.20) are all capable of being involved in language comprension and production. Thus, the language regions of the brain are not as clearly localised as the Wernicke–Geschwind model of language implies.

One reason why the identification of brain sites involved in language has proved difficult is because most studies in the past have examined people who had suffered strokes or accidents. Unfortunately, this type of damage tends to be diffuse with widespread bleeding that is rarely located to one specific region. Thus, a stroke or wound may cause more damage than is first apparent. Indeed, this may help to explain the paradoxical finding that long-lasting speech impairments rarely occur in patients who have precise surgical lesions made to their 'language' areas. For example, Penfield reported that the arcuate fasciculus could be removed without producing aphasia, and similar evidence has also been found following surgical removal of Broca's area. Clearly, other brain areas can take over the responsibility for language, and this also probably accounts for the fact that there is often significant recovery of function in the months after a stroke.

It should also be noted that the Wernicke–Geschwind model fails to take into account the role of subcortical regions in language processing. Indeed, both Wernicke's and Broca's areas have reciprocal connections with the thalamus, and damage to this structure can also cause symptons of aphasia, including mild comprehension deficits. In fact, it has been shown that stimulation of the **pulvinar region** of the thalamus can arrest speech (Ojemann 1975), and that damage to the **basal ganglia** (whose output fibres project to the thalamus) can result in language that is slow, arhythmical and monotonous.

The split-brain procedure

Evidence linking the left hemisphere with language goes back to the early part of the nineteenth century, but more recent support for this relationship was dramatically shown in the 1960s when the behaviour of patients who had received a **commissurotomy** was closely examined. This operation, which involved the complete severing of the **corpus callosum** (the massive axon bundle containing over 200 million fibres that connects the two cerebral hemispheres) was performed in a small number of patients who suffered from severe epilepsy. Although commissurotomy had first been performed in the 1940s to control the spread of epileptic seizures, the operation, which effectively split the brain into two halves, appeared to have little effect on behaviour or mental functioning. This led Karl Lashley to remark, tongue in cheek, that the only known function of the corpus callosum was to stop the hemispheres sagging!

In the 1960s, however, a clearer picture of corpus callosum function began to emerge with the work of Roger Sperry and his associate Michael Gazzaniga. These researchers attempted to examine the functions of the two hemispheres by delivering information individually to each cortex. This task is far from straightforward, however, because our visual system delivers information from each eye to both hemispheres (i.e. input from the right visual field of the eye goes to the left hemisphere, and input from the left goes to the right). To overcome this problem, Sperry and Gazzaniga designed a task where they asked split-brain subjects to stare at a point in the middle of a screen, following which they briefly flashed visual stimuli to either side of the fixation point. By doing this, they were able to project stimuli into the right or left visual field of the eyes. The exposure was long enough for subjects to detect the stimulus, but brief enough to make sure that they did not have time to turn their eyes to it. In effect, this meant that stimuli presented to the left visual field passed to the right hemisphere, and stimuli in the right visual field went to the left hemisphere (Figure 9.5).

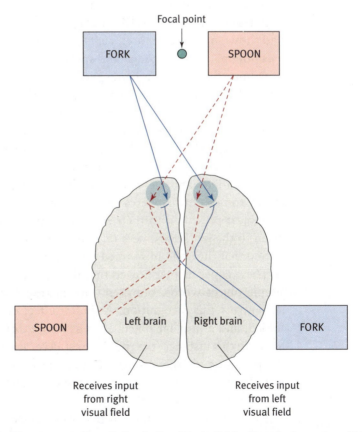

Figure 9.5   The presentation of visual stimuli to individual hemispheres in split-brain subjects. *Source*: Adapted from T.S. Brown and P.M. Wallace (1980) *Physiological Psychology*, p.520

A second task developed by Sperry and Gazzaniga used split-brain patients who were blindfolded and had to identify objects placed in their right or left hands. In humans, the somesthetic pathways which convey the bodily sensations of touch, pressure and pain to the brain, unlike the visual system, completely crosses from one side of the body to the opposite hemisphere of the brain. Thus, when split-brain subjects are blindfolded and asked to hold an object in their right hand, they will be sending information to the left hemisphere only. With these two tasks, Sperry and Gazzaniga thus had a means of examining the specific functions of the two hemispheres (see Sperry 1964, Gazzaniga 1970).

Language and the split-brain

Using these new procedures, it soon became clear that the left hemisphere was crucially involved in language. For example, when a written word was presented to the right visual field so that it reached the left hemisphere, it was found that the split-brain patient had no trouble reading it aloud or understanding its meaning; but when the same word was presented to the right hemisphere, it elicited no verbal response. In fact, subjects often reported that they had seen nothing or only detected a flash of light. These results confirmed what Wernicke had shown nearly a hundred years previously – namely, that the left hemisphere was dominant for language and speech.

Despite this, the right hemisphere was not without its abilities. For example, when an object name was flashed to the right hemisphere (e.g. 'fork'), it was found that the left hand (controlled by the right hemisphere) could correctly select the target from a range of objects hidden behind a screen, although the subjects typically reported that nothing had been seen! However, despite correctly selecting the object, subjects could not describe what they had just picked up in their left hand. In fact, when different object names were flashed simultaneously to both hemispheres (e.g. key-ring) the patients would typically pick up the object presented to their right hemisphere (e.g. ring), but name the object given to the left hemisphere (e.g. key). Moreover, the subjects were astonished to find that they had misnamed the object when it was bought into full view.

These experiments showed that the right hemisphere was able to understand simple object words, but could not name or produce any verbal response to accompany this recognition. A similar effect occurred if the patient was blindfolded, and a familiar object such as a toothbrush was placed in his or her left hand. In this instance, the right hemisphere clearly recognised the object because the person made the gesture of brushing his or her teeth when asked what it was. However, the person was unable to name the toothbrush unless it was placed into his or her right hand.

Although it is now known that in most people the right hemisphere has a very limited ability to read, and virtually no capacity to produce speech, it nonetheless plays an important role in human cognition. For example, when geometric patterns, drawings or faces are presented to the right hemisphere, the left hand is normally able to point to the correct picture in a recognition test. Furthermore, in split-brain subjects, the left hand is generally much better at drawing pictures, learning finger mazes, completing jigsaws and arranging colour blocks to form a specific pattern – even if the person is predominantly right-handed. Thus, the right hemisphere clearly shows a superiority in visuospatial tasks over the language-dominant left hemisphere.

The right hemisphere and emotion

There is also evidence to show that the right hemisphere is predominantly involved in the processing of emotion. For example, studies have found that if a picture of a nude figure is presented to the right hemisphere, the split-brain subject may report that nothing has been seen, while at the same time blushing and showing embarrassment or humour, thereby showing that recognition has taken place. The same degree of emotion, however, is not elicited when the stimulus is projected to the left hemisphere.

In fact, a difference between the two hemispheres in emotion had been suspected before the work of Sperry and Gazzaniga. For example, in the 1950s, Goldstein reported that some patients with injuries to their left hemisphere exhibited feelings of despair, hopelessness and anger – or what he called a **catastrophic-dysphoric reaction** (Goldstein 1952). In contrast, those with right hemisphere damage tended to be placid and indifferent to their injury, even when it led to paralysis. Indeed, in one study that looked at the reactions of 150 people with unilateral brain injury, it was found that 62 per cent of those with left hemispheric damage showed the catastrophic reaction, compared with only 10 per cent with right-sided injuries. Alternatively, 38 per cent of subjects with damage to the right hemisphere were indifferent to their plight, whereas only 11 per cent of the left-sided group showed the same non-emotional response (Rasmussen and Milner 1977). These results suggest that when the left cortex is damaged, the right hemisphere recognises the loss and responds with a strong emotional reaction. But this emotional reaction is nullified when damage occurs to the right hemisphere.

It also appears that the right hemisphere is dominant in the recognition of the emotional tone of language. Speech is much more than just words, as shown by the fact that the tone of what we say may completely change its meaning. For example, the sentence '*you look really nice today*' can sound either complimentary or sarcastic depending on the tone of the expression. In fact, the ability to make or recognise these prosodic or tonal changes (*prosody* refers to the patterns of stress and intonation that are made during speech) is often impaired in people with damage to the right hemisphere. Furthermore, there is evidence that the regions responsible for these deficits are located in the right-sided areas corresponding to the language centres in the left. For example, Elliot Ross has found that individuals with damage to the right-sided Broca's area often produce spoken language that is lacking in prosody, whereas those with lesions of the right-sided equivalent of Wernicke's area are impaired in their ability to comprehend the prosodic nature of speech (Ross 1984).

The independence of the two hemispheres

As we have seen, the two cerebral hemispheres control very different aspects of thought and action, and this can also be demonstrated in situations when the hands of split-brain patients behave in a contradictory manner. For example, in one task where a split-brain patient was required to arrange a group of blocks to make a particular pattern with his right hand (i.e. testing the ability of his left hemisphere), it was found that his left hand (right hemisphere) persistently tried so hard to take over the task that the experimenter actually had to wrestle with the hand to prevent it solving the problem. Thus, if the left hemisphere is given a task that it finds difficult, the right hemisphere will attempt to take over proceedings. A related event can occur when split-brain patients try to read a book while holding it in their left hand. Although the patients may find the book interesting, they often find themselves putting it down. The reason, it appears, is because the right hemisphere (which controls the left hand) cannot read and therefore sees little point in holding the book. Michael Gazzaniga has also described the case of a patient who would sometimes pull his trousers down with one hand only to immediately pull them up with his other hand!

Roger Sperry has argued that the results of split-brain research show that the human brain essentially has two separate minds, with each hemisphere having its own private mental world of sensations, perceptions, memories and ideas (Sperry 1974). In other words, this points to a doubling-up of consciousness. However, not all scientists accept that both hemispheres are conscious. For example, Sir John Eccles, a Nobel Laureate for his work in physiology, believes that the right hemisphere cannot truly think – and what makes us uniquely human are the speech centres in the left hemisphere, which provide the sites where the interaction between mind and brain occurs. This view can be supported, for example, by the great surprise expressed by split-brain patients when they find that their left hand (controlled by the right hemisphere) does something completely unexpected (e.g. put down an interesting book or make a rude gesture). The left hemisphere does not appear to produce these types of unexpected responses, because the subjects are 'aware' or actively control their behaviour. Despite this, it should be pointed out that people who have suffered massive damage to the left hemisphere, or who are aphasic, are not considered to have lost conscious awareness. Thus, although language may alter the nature of our conscious experience, it probably makes more sense to view consciousness as a product of all cortical areas, their connections, and their cognitive processes.

Reading people's minds: imitation and mirror neurons in the frontal cortex

The ability to imitate occurs early in human infants. If an adult sticks out her tongue to a baby, even once in its first week of life, the baby is likely to imitate the gesture (Anisfeld 1996). Yet this behaviour is not as simple as it first seems. If one considers the mental processes underlying this ability, it soon becomes apparent that even the simplest imitation requires the observer to be able to recognise similarities between the model's behaviour and their own, and then be able to recreate the behaviour. This is clearly an exceptional skill for a baby in the first week of life! Although imitation obviously provides an important form of social learning, its role in human development may be more profound. Indeed, many psychologists now believe that imitation allows us to develop empathy – that is, our capacity to put ourselves in the place of others and 'read' their minds. Humans are very good at this. If we see someone cry we are likely to feel sad, and when we observe a person yelling and gesticulating towards us, we are likely to be concerned about his or her anger. In fact, as long ago as 1903, the German psychologist Theodore Lipps theorised that the perception of another individual's emotional expression, or gesture, automatically activates the same emotion in the perceiver. Thus, according to Lipps we don't even have to consciously think about empathy – we do it automatically. Indeed, this is supported by more recent evidence showing that observing a particular action weakly primes the same muscles that are need to perform that action (Fadiga *et al.* 1995).

Imitation is becoming an important subject in biopsychology. Indeed, one of the most astonishing discoveries in recent years has been the identification of neurons in the brain that become activated in response to imitation. These were first discovered in the monkey by Giacomo Rizzolatti and his colleagues at the University of Parma in 1996. Initially, these investigators were interested in understanding the role of the premotor cortex in planning and making movements, and they identified neurons that fired when the monkey performed a specific action with its hand, such as pulling, pushing, tugging, grasping, or picking up a peanut. But, much to the experimenters' surprise, closer examination showed that these cells also became active when the monkey observed another monkey (or even an experimenter) performing the same action. For example, the neurons did not fire at the sight of an object (e.g. peanut) but to the sight of a whole action (e.g. picking up the peanut). Moreover, these cells were highly selective in their firing. They might fire to an experimenter picking a raisin off a tray – but not when the same raisin was taken from a food well. These cells were dubbed 'mirror neurons' (Rizzolatti *et al.* 1996).

Rizzolatti also looked for these neurons in humans by using positron emission tomography (PET; see Rizzolatti *et al.* 2001). In his study, subjects were asked to imitate an experimenter making a grasping movement, or imagine the action taking place. In both tasks, increased neural activity was found in the lateral frontal lobe of the left hemisphere, which included Broca's area. The liklihood of mirror neurons in Broca's area – an area involved in language – raises many new issues, not least the possibility that our capacity to communicate with words may have evolved from the mirror neuron system. Thus, the evolution of imitation was perhaps the precursor to the evolution of language. Indeed, simple observation of others shows that gesturing is closely related to speech. For example, we gesture when speaking on the telephone, and it is known that congenitally blind people gesture, even when speaking to other blind individuals.

The Wada procedure

Another procedure that can be used to measure hemispheric function is the **Wada test,** named after its inventor Juan Wada in the late 1940s. This test was originally designed to help surgeons to locate the main hemisphere for language prior to surgery so that they could avoid causing accidental aphasia (although language is normally dominant for the left hemisphere, there can be exceptions, as we shall see later). The Wada test involves injecting a short-acting anaesthetic called sodium amytal into the carotid arteries (located at the side of the neck), which carry blood from the heart to the brain. Because the right and left arteries feed their own respective hemispheres, it is possible to selectively anaesthetise one side of the brain, which temporarily causes it to lose function, while the other hemisphere remains functionally intact. The effectiveness of the procedure can be quickly confirmed by paralysis of the opposite side of the body.

It is generally found that if sodium amytal is injected into the left or dominant hemisphere, it produces a sudden and complete aphasia that lasts for around 5 minutes. Alternatively, if the anaesthesic is injected into the right or non-dominant hemisphere, language function remains relatively intact and the person will be able to converse and answer questions without difficulty. Indeed, in the vast majority of patients language is found to be localised to the left hemisphere. However, this is not always the case and, in a minority of patients, language may be localised to the right hemisphere, or be equally distributed across both cortices (mixed dominance).

One of the most interesting findings revealed by the Wada test is that the cerebral dominance of language has a tendency to be different, depending on whether the person is right- or left-handed. For example, Rasmussen and Milner (1977) studied 262 patients with the Wada technique and found that 96 per cent of right-handed people had language that was strongly lateralised to the left hemisphere. However, in left-handed subjects this figure dropped to about 70 per cent. Moreover, about 15 per cent of left-handed people were found to have language lateralised to the right hemisphere, and the remaining 15 per cent showed mixed dominance (Figure 9.6). Because it is known that around 90 per cent of people are right-handed, a simple calculation shows that over 90 per cent of the population will have a left hemispheric dominance for language, with the remaining 10 per cent showing a right-sided specialisation or bias.

The development of lateralisation

Although the left hemisphere is normally dominant for the comprehension and production of language, it is also clear that the right hemisphere has the potential to take over these functions in some circumstances. Indeed, when the left hemisphere is damaged during infancy, it is generally found that near-normal language ability is attained by adulthood. For example, Smith and Sugar (1975) described the case of a 5-year-old boy who had almost the whole of his left

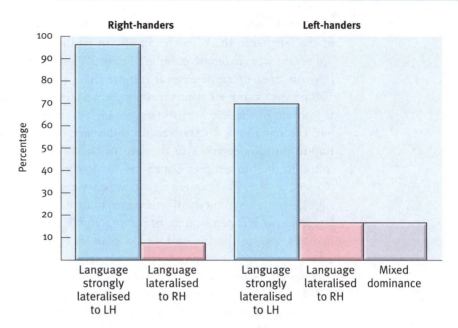

Figure 9.6 The hemispheric lateralisation of language in right- and left-handed subjects

hemisphere removed to treat epilepsy. Prior to the operation, the boy was suffering from 10–12 seizures a day, and paralysed on his right side, indicating widespread damage to the left hemisphere. Further, although his verbal comprehension was normal, his speech production was poor suggesting that this function was also localised on the left side. Following surgery, the boy's progress was monitored and, by the time of early adulthood, he had an above-normal IQ and superior language abilities. In other words, removal of the left hemisphere at an early age does not necessarily impair the development of language. However, this is in marked contrast to when damage occurs in adulthood, as in the case of stroke, which normally produces a severe impairment in speech and writing, and rarely recovers to its original level of function.

How, then, does lateralisation develop and when is it completed? According to Lenneberg (1967), damage to the left hemisphere has little effect on language acquisition if it occurs before the age of 2 years, but causes increasing impairment after this age. According to Lenneberg this shows that both hemispheres are equipotent for language until the age of 2 years, and only then does lateralisation slowly develop (normally in the left hemisphere) until it is completed in puberty. Further support for this idea has come from Eran Zaidel, who has shown that most split-brain subjects have a degree of language ability in the right hemisphere that is approximately the same as that found in a 6-year-old child (Zaidel 1985). The simplest explanation for this finding is that language becomes fully lateralised to the left hemisphere around this time.

However, this theory has declined in popularity over recent years by the discovery that the structure of the two hemispheres, at least in most people, show innate anatomical differences. For example, in 1968, Norman Geschwind and Walter Levitsky drew attention to a region of the cerebral cortex, called the **planum temporale** – which corresponds to part of Wernicke's area along with some of the adjacent auditory cortex – that is normally found to be much larger in the left hemisphere. For example, in adults, the left planum is on average 3.6 centimetres in length compared with 2.7 on the right, and is about one-third larger in area (in some cases it is more than five times as large). Indeed, out of 100 brains examined at postmortem, it was found that 65 had a larger planum temporale in the left hemisphere; in 11 it was larger in the right hemisphere; and the remaining 24 showed no difference (Geschwind and Levitsky 1968). Importantly, differences in the size of the planum temporale have also been found in the human foetus and can be detected by the 31st week of gestation (Chi *et al.* 1977). If anything, it appears that the left planum temporale is slightly more asymmetrical in infants than in adults, being some 57 per cent larger in the left hemisphere of infants and 50 per cent larger in adults. These findings suggest that the size of the planum temporale is not a developmental consequence of left hemisphere use for speech, but rather represents an innate predisposition for the two hemispheres to be different.

If this is the case, and assuming that the planum temporale is involved in language development, how then can we account for the fact that the right hemisphere is able to acquire language? Firstly, it needs to be remembered that language still has to be learned, and this process occurs at a time when the brain is highly adaptable and plastic. Thus, if early developmental problems arise, the plasticity of the right hemisphere has sufficient capacity to take over the control of language. Indeed, like many other types of neural development, the acquisition of language appears to depend on innate capacities that can be modified by experience for a limited period during maturation. Secondly, the role of the planum temporale in language development still remains unclear. For example, as we have seen, a larger planum temporale in the left hemisphere only occurs in around 65 per cent of human brains, whereas the left hemispheric dominance of language is found in over 90 per cent. It has also been found that higher apes tend to show a larger left-sided planum temporale, which casts further doubts on its presumed role in language.

Dyslexia

Although **dyslexia** ('dys' meaning *bad*, 'lexia' meaning *reading*) can be acquired through brain injury, in most cases it is a developmental disorder that first manifests itself when the child begins to read. There are several types of dyslexia, with deficits ranging from mild to severe, and it has been estimated that 3 to 6 per cent of children may have reading problems severe enough to be classified as dyslexic. Despite popular belief, dyslexic children do not lack intelligence, nor are they word 'blind' as they have normal object and picture recognition abilities. In fact, some dyslexics have very high IQs, showing that the problem is specific to reading. In some cases, this may be due to an impairment in relating the characters of written language with the phonological sounds that they represent. In other instances, dyslexia may arise from difficulties in reading words, although individual letters can be recognised (in this type of dyslexia words can often be identified if the letters are read out one by one). In addition, some dyslexics have problems with writing and they may try to write from right to left, or confuse letters with a specific right–left orientation (such as d, b, p or s). Thus, a wide range of impairments can accompany dyslexia, indicating that a large number of brain regions are involved in reading and writing.

What causes dyslexia? One clue comes from evidence showing that reading difficulties often tend to run in families, which implies a genetic component. Indeed, linkage studies have begun to implicate genes on chromosomes 6 and 15 in different aspects of this disorder (Grigorenko *et al.* 1997). Another clue comes from the fact that dyslexia is four–five times more common in males than in females – a finding which implies that the organising effects of testosterone on the developing brain may also have an important role (see later). Indeed, it has been pointed out that males have fewer fibres in the posterior parts of their corpus callosum, which connect the two visual association areas, and this may be a possible factor in the development of the disorder. But what about the rest of the brain? Although it has long been suspected that dyslexia might result from some type of neural mis-wiring, researchers have only recently begun to find differences in brain structure between dyslexic and normal subjects. For example, Galaburda and Kemper (1979) examined the brain of a young dyslexic man who died in a fall, and found abnormalities in the planum temporale. As mentioned above, for most people the planum temporale is larger in the left hemisphere, but in this case it was the same size on both sides of the brain. Even more significant was the discovery that its neurons were immature, and the columnar organisation of its layers had not developed properly. Infact, this pattern was similar to the neural formations known to occur in the sixth week of gestation when the last stages of neural migration take place in the cerebral cortex. In short, it appeared that something had happened at this point in gestation to disrupt normal neural development.

Further postmortem work has confirmed these findings in a small number of other cases (Galaburda *et al.* 1985) although the neural abnormalities, which also include excessive cortical folding (micropolygyria) and clusters of extra cells (ectopias), are much more widespread than initially believed and are found predominantly in the vicinity of the Sylvian fissure and frontal cortex. Although these changes are much more frequently found in the left hemisphere, they can also occur in the right hemisphere (Galaburda 1993). Moreover, there appears to be no one single region that consistently shows these brain abnormalities, indicating that it is wrong to view dyslexia as simply resulting from planum temporale dysfunction.

Brain damage associated with dyslexia has also been found in subcortical sites, including abnormalities in the magnocellular system of the lateral geniculate nucleus (Galaburda and Livingstone 1993). As we saw in Chapter 2, the magnocellular system is part of the visual pathway from eye to brain that encodes information about form, movement and depth – and contrasts with the parvocellular system, which transmits information regarding colour and fine detail. Furthermore, whereas the magnocellular system projects mainly into the dorsal visual pathways encoding information about the 'where' of vision, the parvocellular system contributes more to the ventral visual pathway, which encodes input about stimulus recognition or the 'what' of vision (see Figure 2.17). Galaburda and Livingstone found that neurons in the magnocellular layers of the lateral geniculate nucleus were not only 27 per cent smaller, but were more variable in their size and shape compared with the parvocellular cells, which were normal. The significance of this finding remains with be established, although it has been suggested that the magnocellular abnormality may impair the ability to determine the order in which visual stimuli are presented, or disrupt eye movements, thus confusing the process of visual perception.

Studies using scanning techniques have also examined the brains of people with dyslexia. As mentioned above, for most people, the planum temporale of the left and right hemispheres are asymmetric, with the left hemisphere being larger than the right. However, studies using magnetic resonance imaging (MRI) have shown that dyslexics tend to show symmetric planum temporales – or even reversed asymmetry. For example, Larsen *et al.* (1990) examined 19 dyslexics using MRI and found that 70 per cent of their brains showed symmetry compared with only 30 per cent of the controls. There is also evidence to show that this region of the brain is functionally abnormal in some people with dyslexia. For example, in studies using positron emission tomography (PET) it has been found that normal readers who score most highly on reading tests tend to show increased activation over larger areas of the left angular gyrus (which partially overlaps with the planum temporale). In contrast, the more this area was activated in dyslexics the poorer were their reading scores. In fact, the better reading scores for dsylexics were associated with increased activation of the right hemisphere (Rumsey *et al.* 1999). These results show that dyslexics may be utilising different brain regions to normal when attempting to read.

What causes dyslexia?

Although dyslexia has a tendency to run in families, it does not follow any clear pattern of inheritance. A more consistent finding is that dyslexia occurs more frequently in males and in those who are left-handed. This later finding was confirmed by Norman Geschwind and Peter Behan, who looked at the frequency of dyslexia (along with other developmental disorders) in a random sample of 500 left-handed and 900 right-handed subjects. The results showed that the incidence of dyslexia was 10 times higher in the left-handed group than in the right. An unexpected finding also emerged from the study – left-handed subjects had twice the rate of autoimmune disorders, such as allergies, arthritis and diabetes, than right-handed subjects (Geschwind and Behan 1982).

To account for these findings, Geschwind proposed that increased levels of testosterone during the last trimester of foetal development were acting to slow cortical maturation, particularly in the left hemisphere, which was then increasing the chances of the right hemisphere taking over the function of language. To support his theory, Geschwind pointed out that during foetal growth, the planum temporale normally starts to develop one to two weeks earlier on the right side of the brain, but is then overtaken in size by the later developing left-sided planum. However, this switch may not occur in some people with dyslexia. According to Geschwind, the likeliest explanation is that if too much testosterone is released during this stage of foetal development, then it will slow the growth of the left hemisphere, leading to a smaller planum temporale on this side of the brain. This explanation would account for the fact that dyslexia is more frequent in males (i.e. they produce higher levels of testosterone), and in left-handed subjects (i.e. their right hemisphere has become more dominant). But why is there an increased susceptibility to autoimmune diseases? According to Geschwind, the high level of testosterone not only suppresses the development of the left hemisphere, but also inhibits the formation of the immune system – particularly by slowing down the development of the thymus gland.

Although it is difficult to test directly, the Geschwind theory is very appealing. For example, if embryonic surges of testosterone slow down the development of the left hemisphere, then it can be predicted that males will, generally, have better developed right hemispheres – which would endow them with superior spatial skills. Indeed, it is well established that males tend to outperform females on these types of task. Conversely, with less exposure to testosterone, the female brain will be more likely to develop faster and more evenly. Thus, females would be expected not only to perform better on verbal tasks than males – which is indeed the case (Kimura 1992) – but also show less cerebral dominance for language. In fact, studies that have measured blood flow, or glucose utilisation, during the performance of language tasks by females have again confirmed this hypothesis (i.e. they tend to use both hemispheres to a greater degree than males). But perhaps most convincing is the simple fact that women are much more likely to show better recovery of language function after left hemispheric brain damage, or stroke, compared with men (Kimura and Harshman 1984).

Handedness

The incidence of right-handedness is about 90 per cent, and evidence shows that the majority of humans have had this preference for the last 2 million years or so (see McManus 2002). Like most minority groups, prejudices against left-handers abound. A measure of this bias can be seen by the way the word '*left*' has evolved in Western language. In English the word stems from the Anglo Saxon '*lyft*' meaning 'broken' or 'weak', and similar sentiments are expressed in Latin (where the word left is *sinister*, derived from *sinistrum* meaning 'evil'); French (where the word for left is *gauche* meaning 'clumsy' or 'crooked'); and Italian (where the word 'left' is *mancino*, meaning 'dishonest'). If this is not bad enough, the world of human objects strongly favours right-handers. For example, scissors, knives, coffee pots, power tools, golf clubs and guitars are usually made for people who use their right hand – as indeed is the book you are reading! There are many explanations for why right-handedness has dominated. One idea is that it was better for warriors to hold shields in their left hand to protect the heart, thus enabling the right hand to become more skilled. A female version of this idea proposes that it was more adaptive for mothers to hold babies in their left hand, so they were soothed by the beating of the heart. Both claims are probably unsound because most animals show some

Handedness continued.

form of right–left bias. It is also clear that handedness develops before birth. For example, in a study of 224 foetuses, aged from 4 to 9 months, it was found that 94.6 per cent sucked their right thumb while in the womb (Hepper *et al.* 1991).

A hotly debated question is the issue of whether being left-handed results in a diminished life expectancy. For example, Porac and Coren (1981) reported that 13 per cent of 20-year-olds were left-handed, but only 5 per cent of those in their fifties, and virtually nobody of 80 or above. Another study by the same research group examined the life expectancy of professional baseball players, and found that right-handers lived eight months longer on average than left-handers (Halpern and Coren 1988). The authors explain these results partly as a result of left-handers being more susceptible to accidents (e.g. left-handed drivers are 1.9 times more likely to have traffic crashes, and 3.8 times more prone to die of crash-related injuries) and also because of developmental problems. This latter idea is supported by evidence showing that 18 per cent of twins are left-handed (e.g. almost twice the level found in the population), and that they also show a high incidence of neurological disorders, which may arise from intrauterine crowding and stress during birth. However, the higher mortality of left-handers has not gone unchallenged. To give but one example: Aggleton *et al.* (1994) carried out a survey of 3,599 cricketers and found that while right-handers lived slightly longer than left-handers, the difference was not statistically significant.

Although a higher number of left-handers suffer from disorders such as autism and dyslexia, it is also widely believed that left-handers are more likely to have greater intelligence, and be gifted in art and music. In terms of intelligence, there is little support for these claims. For example, when combining the results of two large-scale studies, it was found that left-handers had an average IQ of 99.5, which was only half a point less than right-handers. In contrast, a survey of 17 professional orchestras in the UK found that 13 per cent of the musicians were left-handed – which was greater than expected by chance (McManus 2002). Although few studies have looked at artists, there is some evidence that right- and left-handers view the world slightly differently. For example, when Canadian and British subjects were asked to indicate whether the face portrait on their coinage pointed to the left or to the right (it points to the right), the left-handers were more accurate. This may be because right-handers tend to draw heads facing left – and left-handers draw heads facing right (see Carlson *et al.* 2004, p. 403).

The development of brain-imaging techniques

Until recently, researchers interested in identifying brain areas involved in language were forced to rely largely on postmortem examination of patients who had previously experienced aphasia or language difficulties. This was far from ideal for a number of reasons, not least because the main source of patients was generally those who had suffered widespread brain damage as a result of stroke or head injury. Not only did this make identifying language regions difficult, but by the time the patient came to autopsy, some recovery of function had often taken place, which made it even more difficult to link pathology with behavioural deficits. Fortunately, we are no longer stuck with this situation because a revolution has taken place over the last two decades in the study of language with the development of non-invasive brain-imaging techniques. These methods allow investigators to 'look' into a living brain and enable them to examine its various structures and areas of damage, or even to observe the brain at work while it is engaged in some mental activity or behaviour.

For most of this century the only way psychologists could visualise the brain in a living person was to make the major blood vessels visible through a procedure known as **cerebral angiography**. This technique involved injecting a radioactive dye into the carotid arteries and observing the perfusion of the dye by taking X-ray photographs of the brain. The pictures produced by this technique were called angiograms, and used to identify vascular damage and the location of tumours as revealed by the displacement of blood vessels. This technique works because X-ray photography is only effective when the internal structures of the body differ in the extent to which they absorb X-rays. Thus, if injected with a dye, the blood vessels and the surrounding brain tissue absorb the X-rays differently, thus allowing the blood vessels to stand out and be visualised.

However, this technique was of little use in examining different brain regions because X-rays only provided an outline of the main vascular pathways and did not visualise the tissue surrounding them. However, in the late 1960s and early 1970s, Allan Cormack (a South African physicist) and Godfrey Hounsfield (a British electrical engineer working for EMI) independently pioneered a system where brain X-rays could be resolved by computers that performed complex mathematical analysis of multiple photographs taken from many different angles. This technique, called **computerised axial tomography** (CAT – see Figure 9.7) involved passing a large number of narrow-beam X-rays through the brain using a ray gun that moved around the person's head. Because the amount of radiation absorbed by the brain was found to vary from region to region using this type of technique (the denser the tissue the more energy it absorbs), the amount of radiation picked up by the detectors could be used to construct

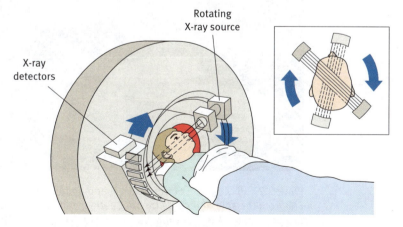

Figure 9.7   The basic procedure of computerised axial tomography. *Source*: From D. Purves *et al.*, *Neuroscience*. Copyright © 1997 by Sinauer Associates Inc.

a three-dimensional image of the brain. Moreover, by adjusting the angles through which the X-rays were sent, a picture of any slice (or plane) of the brain could be reconstructed. Thus, by repeating this procedure, a series of horizontal images of the brain could be obtained from any angle (Plate 9.2).

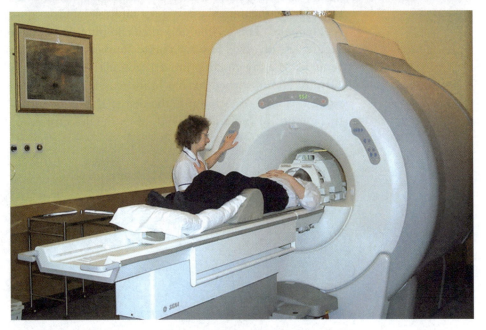

Plate 9.2 Photograph of the Beatles, and an MRI brain scanner. The profits made by EMI from the sale of records by the Beatles, and other artists, helped to pay for the development of the first brain scanners. *Source*: Beatles photograph © Bettmann/Corbis; Brain scanner from *Neuroscience. Science of the Brain* (2003). Published by the British Neuroscience Association

Soon after this breakthrough, a second method of examining brain structure was developed through **magnetic resonance imaging** (MRI), which produces pictures of higher resolution than those provided by CAT scans. MRI does not rely on radiation to create its pictures, but uses radio waves. This type of imaging works on the basis that any atom with an odd electron (such as hydrogen) has an inherent rotation. Passing radio-frequency waves through tissue containing these atoms changes the direction of their rotation, making them spin in a different way. By measuring the energy that is created by this reverberation, it is then possible to construct an image of the brain in much the same way as for CAT. Indeed, because grey matter (cell bodies), white matter (axons), cerebrospinal fluid and bone all differ in terms of their water content, and thus hydrogen, these tissues are easily distinguished by this type of imaging.

Both CAT and MRI scans have greatly facilitated the way in which researchers can judge the location and extent of brain damage. They are effective in identifying tumours and areas of damage produced by strokes – and can identify enlarged ventricles, which is generally an indication of brain atrophy and degeneration. Moreover, the resolution of CAT scans has been improved to such an extent that a relatively small change such as a shrinkage of a single gyrus can now be detected. In the case of MRI, it is possible to detect the loss of myelin around groups of axons, which can be used to diagnose such diseases as multiple sclerosis. Indeed, because of its sensitivity to myelin, MRI has been used to measure the difference in the size of the corpus callosum in people who are right- or left-handed. One study that used this technique has found that the corpus callosum is larger in people who are left-handed (Witelson 1985). In addition, the development of new MRI technologies has now permitted imaging of the brain as it performs various tasks with high resolution (see below).

Functional neuroimaging techniques

Although structural neuroimaging techniques have provided important information about brain morphology and the extent of tissue damage in patients, they contribute little to our understanding of the *functioning* of the brain. Thus, researchers have sought ways of measuring various types of brain activity to provide ongoing pictures of the 'mind' at work. One of the earliest techniques measured the rate of blood flow through the brain. This was based on the assumption that increased perfusion would reflect greater levels of oxygen flowing to that area, signifying increased metabolic and neural activity. Blood flow was measured by asking subjects to inhale a short-acting radioactive gas such as xenon-133 (which does not react with the tissues of the body but simply 'flows' with the blood) and detecting the level of radioactivity emitted by the brain with gamma-ray detectors. This technique was performed in the early 1960s by Niels Lassen and his colleagues (see Lassen *et al.* 1978), who used a camera with 254 detectors, each of which scanned a brain area of about

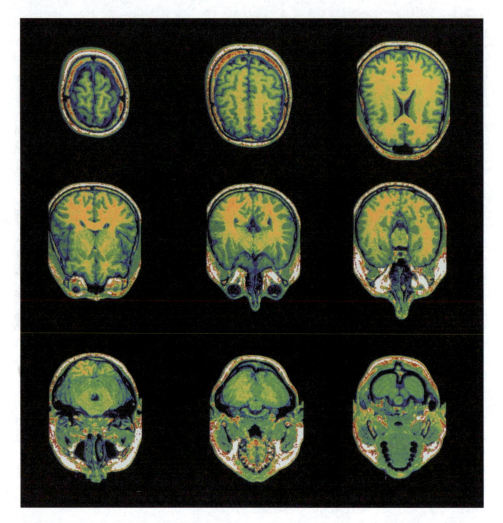

Plate 9.3 Coronal sections of the brain viewed with magnetic functional imaging (MFI). *Source*: Wellcome Dept. of Cognitive Neurology/Science Photo Library

1 square centimetre. This information was then shown on a monitor on which the different levels of blood flow in the brain were represented by different colours (e.g. violet, blue, green, yellow, orange and red).

Although this technique was used as a diagnostic tool to help to detect tumours, stroke and abnormal brain activity, it also enabled scientists to observe the brain when it was engaged in certain tasks. For example, it has been used to examine areas of sensory processing in the brain, and the patterns of activity in motor regions that accompany voluntary movement (Lassen *et al.* 1978). It has also detected differences in people with psychological disorders (e.g. schizophrenics often show reduced blood flow to their prefrontal cortex), and has been used to examine language. For instance, this technique has tended to show a similar activation of both right and left hemispheres in the performance of language tasks (e.g. Larsen *et al.* 1978).

Two drawbacks of the regional blood flow technique are, however, the short life of xenon-133 and other, similar, isotopes, which allows testing for only a few minutes, and the inability to measure perfusion in subcortical structures. A more sophisticated technique that has overcome these limitations is **positron emission tomography** (PET), which was first developed in the early 1970s. Again, this technique works by measuring the level of metabolic activity in the brain, except that the radioactive substance can be anything that is able to emit positrons, including gases (e.g. oxygen) and chemical agents (e.g. glucose and water). These substances are generally taken up into the brain through inhalation or injection into the carotid arteries, where they start to decay and emit positrons. A positron is, in fact, a short-lived particle which travels only a short distance before it collides with an electron. When this happens, the positron is turned into two gamma rays, which travel away from the impact exactly 180 degrees apart. These rays are picked up by an array of gamma-ray detectors, and the sites of the positron–electron collisions are reconstructed by computer, which then generates a continuous high-resolution three-dimensional colour picture of the regions where most decay – or brain activity – is taking place. Thus, by monitoring the brain's use of energy by the emission of positrons, one has a window on its inner workings. For example, PET scanning has provided researchers with many new insights into the neural basis of language comprehension and production (see next section).

More recently, technological advances have allowed scientists to obtain images of functional brain activity using MRI. This technique (e.g. fMRI) measures the amount of oxygen in the blood – and so in some respects is similar to the regional blood flow procedure described above. However, instead of using radioactive isotopes, this method is based on the fact that the concentration of oxygen in the blood affects the magnetic properties of haemoglobin – and this is the change that MRI detects. Not only does this make fMRI much safer than other scanning techniques, but the procedure can be combined with structural images from static MRI, thereby providing very accurate localisation of activity with high resolution.

The application of functional neuroimaging techniques to understanding language

The application of modern scanning techniques to the study of higher mental function and language has produced some unexpected findings. For example, in one study (Posner and Raichle 1994) the amount of blood flowing through the cerebral cortex was measured using PET during the performance of several language-related tasks by college students. To measure brain activity, these investigators used intravenous injections of radioactive water since this affected the two hemispheres simultaneously, enabling the performance of each to be directly compared. In one task, subjects were asked to fixate on a small cross

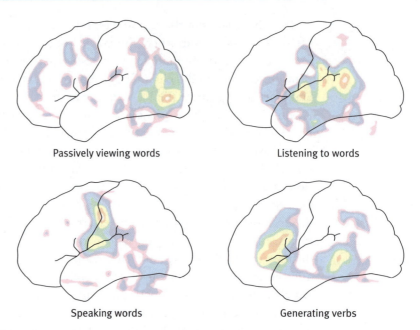

Passively viewing words

Listening to words

Speaking words

Generating verbs

Figure 9.8 The effect of different language tasks on brain activity as revealed by positron emission tomography

(+) shown on a computer monitor, and then to read (or listen via head-phones) to simple nouns that were presented one by one. After this, the subjects were given another exercise where they were asked to read the nouns aloud (or to recite them). Finally, subjects were given a task where they had to provide an appropriate verb to go with the presented noun (e.g. *cake* : eat, *hammer* : hit).

The results from this study (see Figure 9.8) produced a very different pattern of cerebral activation than might have been predicted from the Wernicke-Geschwind model. For example, the passive viewing of the nouns increased activation in both halves of the occipital lobe, although most markedly on the left side, and not elsewhere in the cortex. More surprising, however, were the results from the verbal naming condition (i.e. speaking words), which produced increased activity along the central fissure (which separates the frontal and parietal cortex) of both hemispheres, as well as producing marked activation of the cerebellum. Finally, it was found that the verb-generating task increased activity in several areas of the brain, including the left frontal cortex (just in front of Broca's area), the anterior cingulate cortex, the left posterior temporal lobe (adjacent to Wernicke's area) and the right cerebellum. The most surprising finding, however, was the non-participation of Wernicke's area in all of these reading tasks. Although Wernicke's area was activated when words were spoken to the subject, it was not active when words were read silently or aloud by the subject or when the generation of verbal responses was required. These findings demonstrate that the human brain almost certainly contains a much more complex array of areas dealing with language than the Wernicke–Geschwind model would have us believe.

Summary

Language provides us with a complex, creative, and powerful system of communication, and vehicle for thought, which makes us uniquely human. The first brain region to be linked with language was **Broca's area**, named after **Paul Broca**, who in 1861 performed an autopsy on a patient called Tan who had been unable to produce meaningful speech for over 20 years. This autopsy showed a large area of damage to the posterior part of the left **frontal lobe**, which is now known to be adjacent to the **motor cortex**, which controls the muscles of the face, mouth and vocal cords. People with **Broca's aphasia** generally exhibit language that is slow, laboured and lacking grammatical structure or inflection (i.e. **telegraphic speech**), although verbal comprehension is normally intact. Later, in 1874, **Carl Wernicke** described a second type of aphasia in which his patients appeared to utter grammatically correct speech, although its content was largely devoid of meaning and was accompanied by severe comprehension defects. This deficit is now known as **Wernicke's aphasia** and is associated with damage to a region of the **temporal lobe** that is adjacent to the **primary auditory cortex**. A neural pathway called the **arcuate fasciculus** passes from Wernicke's area to Broca's area, and damage to this route produces a third type of aphasia – **conduction aphasia** – which is characterised by an inability to repeat abstract or non-words. The theory that is most commonly used to explain how the brain processes language is the **Wernicke–Geschwind model**, which proposes that both the primary auditory cortex (for speech) and visual cortex (for reading) project to Wernicke's area, where word recognition and comprehension take place. The translation of mental thoughts into verbal codes is also believed to take place in Wernicke's area, and this information can be passed to Broca's area, which produces the motor output necessary for speech.

It is generally accepted that the **left hemisphere** of the cerebral cortex is predominantly involved in language, and the **right hemisphere** is more concerned with visual-spatial skills and emotion. Evidence supporting this theory was provided by Roger Sperry and his associates in the 1960s when they examined patients who had received a **commissurotomy** or severing of the **corpus callosum**. This is an operation that stops the two hemispheres of the brain from directly communicating with each other. It was found that if a written word was presented to the left hemisphere, split-brain subjects typically had no problem reading it – although they often reported seeing nothing when it was presented to the right. In contrast, the right hemisphere was found to be much better at copying drawings or completing jigsaws. In addition, pictures presented to this hemisphere were more likely to elicit an emotional response (e.g. blushing or arousal) than the left. However, language (or other cognitive functions) is not always lateralised to one side of the brain. For example, around 90 per cent of people are right-handed, which is controlled by the left hemisphere of the brain. Studies using the **Wada test**, where one of the hemispheres is temporarily anaesthetised by an injection of **sodium amytal** into the **carotid artery**, have shown that around 95 per cent of right-handed people have language strongly localised to the left hemisphere. But in left-handed subjects this figure drops to about 70 per cent. Moreover, about 15 per cent of left-handed people have language lateralised to the right hemisphere, and the remaining 15 per cent show mixed dominance. It has been suggested that if high levels of **testosterone** occur during the last trimester of foetal development, this may slow maturation of the left hemisphere, with the right more likely to take over some of its functions.

Essay questions

1. Compare and contrast Broca's aphasia with Wernicke's aphasia. What cortical regions need to be damaged to produce these types of aphasia, and what do they tell us about the brain mechanisms underlying language?

   Helpful Internet search terms: *Broca's and Wernicke's aphasia. Broca's area. Wernicke's area. Planum temporale. Arcuate fasciculus. Wernicke–Geschwind theory of language.*

2. With reference to research involving split-brain patients, describe the different functions of the right and left hemispheres of the brain.

   Helpful Internet search terms: *Split brain. Functions of the left hemisphere. Functions of the right hemisphere. Corpus callosum. Two minds in one brain.*

3. Why does lateralisation of brain function occur? What are some of the potential problems that can arise if language is not fully lateralised in the left hemisphere?

   Helpful Internet search terms: *Lateralisation of the brain. Testosterone and lateralisation. Causes of handedness. Neurobiology of dyslexia. Right hemisphere and autism.*

4. 'Brain scanning technology is providing new insights into our understanding of the brain'. Explain how CAT, MRI, PET and fMRI scanning work, and some of the ways this technology has been used to justify the above statement.

   Helpful Internet search terms: *Regional blood flow in the brain. CAT scans. MRI scans. PET scans. Functional MRI scans. Functional MRI and language.*

Further reading

Altmann, G.T.M. (1987) *The Ascent of Babel*. Oxford: Oxford University Press. A fascinating and wide-ranging exploration of language which attempts to understand the development of the mental processes that are responsible for the production of spoken and written language.

Basso, A. (2003) *Aphasia and its Therapy*. Oxford: Oxford University Press. A book that provides a useful description of the classic aphasia syndromes, neuropsychological models, and forms of therapy.

Calvin, W.H. and Ojemann, G.A. (1994) *Conversations with Neil's Brain: The Neural Nature of Thought and Language*. Boston: Addison-Wesley. A highly enjoyable tour of the brain for the lay person in an attempt to understand the brain mechanisms of thought and language.

Gazzaniga, M.S. (ed.) (2000) *The New Cognitive Neurosciences*. Cambridge, MA: MIT Press. A massive textbook of 1,440 pages with 592 illustrations, with an excellent section on language written by a variety of experts. Includes other sections on motor systems, memory and emotion, which also make appropriate reading for Chapters 3, 5 and 8 in this book.

Loritz, D. (2002) *How the Brain Evolved Language*. Oxford: Oxford University Press. A book that examines the relationship between brain structure and language, and controversially contradicts the idea that human language is innate (e.g. as proposed by Pinker).

McManus, C. (2002) *Right Hand, Left Hand*. London: Weidenfeld & Nicolson. A compelling and diverse book that attempts to understand the asymmetry of the world we live in, including an attempt to explain why most people are right-handed, and why each side of the human brain has different functions.

Obler, L.K. and Gjerlow, K. (1999) *Language and the Brain*. Cambridge: Cambridge University Press. A brief (168 pages) but excellent introduction to the neurobiological basis of language, focusing predominantly on brain-damaged individuals.

Pinker, S. (1994) *The Language Instinct*. New York: William Morrow. A comprehensive and readable account which argues that language is an instinct that is hard-wired into the brain and programmed through the process of evolution.

Plum, F. (ed.) (1988) *Language, Communication and the Brain*. New York: Raven Press. A series of well-written chapters, by various experts, that are of great relevance to biopsychologists interested in the relationship between brain and language.

Posner, M.I. and Raichle, M.E. (1994) *Images of Mind*. New York: Scientific American Library. A clearly written and fascinating account which shows how new scanning techniques, especially PET and fMRI, are revolutionising our knowledge of how the brain is involved in thought and language.

Springer, S.P. and Deutsch, G. (1989) *Left Brain, Right Brain*. New York: Freeman. An award-winning book, perfect for psychology undergraduates, which examines in detail the asymmetry of hemispheric function in human brains.

See website at www.pearsoned.co.uk/wickens for further resources including multiple choice questions.

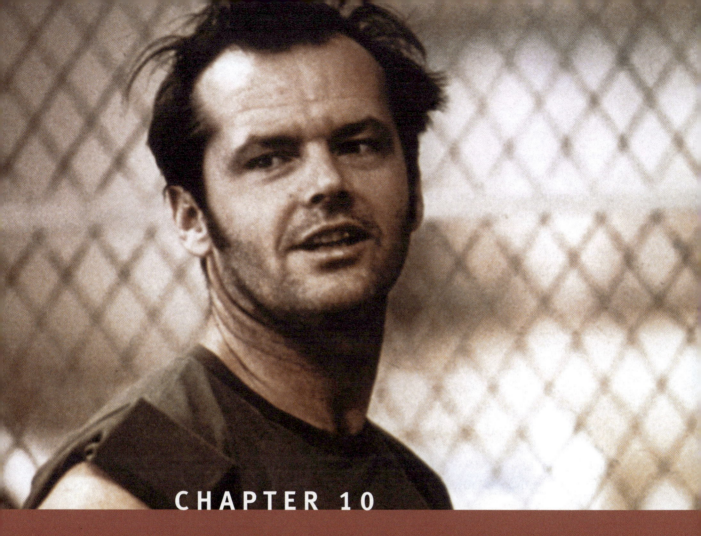

CHAPTER 10

The biological basis of mental illness

In this chapter

- How antidepressant drugs work
- The catecholamine theory of depression
- The role of serotonin in depression
- How antipsychotic drugs work
- The causes of schizophrenia
- The dopaminergic theory of schizophrenia
- Types of brain damage found in schizophrenia
- New developments in schizophrenia

INTRODUCTION

The term 'mental illness' has no precise definition, but is generally used to refer to the more severe disorders treated by psychiatrists. Although mental illnesses can arise through organic injury to the brain – including tumours, infection and diseases of the arteries – in the vast majority of instances they are conditions where the symptoms appear to be largely in the person's mood or thinking, with no sign of structural damage. Because of this, some investigators (e.g. Szasz 1960) have argued that psychiatric disorders are not true illnesses, and should not be treated by medical practitioners. However, this is a controversial view, and a more balanced one holds that mental illnesses arise from a complex interaction of biological, social and personal factors, which may lead to neurochemical or synaptic changes in the brain, even if they cannot be reliably identified. Whatever one's view, it cannot be disputed that the symptoms of mental illness, which can include suicidal depression, mania, illogical and incoherent thought, hallucinations and anxiety, are very real and severely debilitating. Moreover, mental health problems are surprisingly common. In the UK, about one person in eight will consult a doctor for psychological problems in any given year, and about 10 per cent of these patients will be referred to a psychiatrist. This makes mental health problems only surpassed in frequency by common colds, bronchitis and rheumatism (Gregory 1987). Thus, the onus is very much on the biological psychologist to better understand the causes of mental illness and help to develop more effective treatments.

Affective disorders: an introduction

Everyone from time to time feels depressed – or experiences what the *Oxford Dictionary* defines as a state of 'low spirits or vitality' – in response to adversity, loss or perceived misfortune. Indeed, depression, whether it consists of feelings of slight sadness or utter misery, is an emotion known to almost every human being. These feelings play a vital role in human existence, not least because depression along with happiness form part of the mechanism by which our brains register and process information regarding punishment and reward. However, there are some people for whom the feeling of depression has become maladaptive. In such cases, the severity of depression is out of proportion to the event that triggered it, or is long-lasting or very debilitating. It is difficult to say exactly the point at which depression becomes a mental illness, although when it is so severe that the person continually feels suicidal and cannot function properly at work or engage in social relationships, then the problem is clear for all to see. In the most severe cases, depression can result in such apathy that such people are even unable to look after themselves and require extensive hospitalisation.

Although, in everyday language, depression is viewed as a state that is characterised by feelings of sadness or gloom, in most clinical cases there is much more to the disorder. Severe depression normally exhibits a constellation of symptoms, which are often categorised under four headings: emotional, cognitive, motivational and physical. For example, not only is the clinically depressed person likely to feel sad, tearful and miserable (i.e. emotional symptoms), but they may also have many negative thoughts including low self-esteem and a sense of helplessness (i.e. cognitive symptoms). This is also likely to be accompanied by varying degrees of psychomotor retardation, where even the simplest chore can appear to be daunting (i.e. motivational symptoms), and finally there may be a number of physical problems including sleep disturbances and early morning awakening, appetite loss, sexual difficulties, muscle weakness and various aches and pains (i.e. somatic symptoms). When it is so severe, depression is beyond doubt an illness, with the individual losing control over his or her behaviour, and showing impaired interaction with the external world.

Depression is classified as an affective or 'mood' disorder although it is not the only condition that is characterised by emotional extremes. For example, the opposite of depression is mania, which leads to heightened euphoria, exuberance and increased energy. In fact, most people who experience mania also suffer from lengthy bouts of depression (i.e. manic depression), which can occur in a regular or cyclical pattern. Because of this, affective disorders are divided into two categories: **unipolar depression,** in which the person suffers exclusively from prolonged periods of sadness and despondency (although a very rare form of unipolar disorder involves just mania), and **bipolar depression**, where the person undergoes alternating periods of depression and mania. As we shall see later, there is good evidence that these two disorders have a different biological basis. Another type of affective disorder is **dysthymia**, which can be regarded as a milder albeit long-lasting version of unipolar depression.

Mood disorders are the most common form of mental illness. It has been estimated that approximately 10 per cent of men and 20 per cent of women will suffer from at least one bout of unipolar depression in their life – and in about one-fifth of these cases the depression will return or become recurrent. As these figures show, women are more likely to suffer from depression than men, although the reason why this occurs is controversial. Some researchers believe that these figures represent a biological difference in susceptibility to depression, whereas others argue that socialisation factors are more important (e.g. it may be that women are more likely than men to seek help for their problems, or find themselves in menial life situations with reduced opportunities). In contrast, bipolar illness is approximately 10 times less likely than unipolar depression and occurs in males and females equally (Goodwin and Jamison 1990).

The development of antidepressant drugs

Until the mid-1950s, the two main biological treatments for depression were electroconvulsive therapy (ECT) and, in extreme cases, brain surgery. Although ECT was often effective in treating depression (and is still used today) it was not suitable for all types of affective disorder. Thus, there was a need to invent more humane forms of therapy, and the first breakthrough occurred in the early 1950s with the development of a drug called **iproniazid**. This drug was originally used, although not very successfully, as an antibacterial agent in the treatment of tuberculosis. However, it was discovered that iproniazid made a number of patients – some of whom were in a terminal condition – feel much happier and optimistic. In other words, it appeared to exert an antidepressant effect. In 1956, the American psychiatrist Nathan Kline began testing iproniazid on hospitalised patients with various types of mental illness, and found that it significantly reduced depression. Within a year of this work, iproniazid was being marketed as an antidepressant under the trade name of Marsilid, making it the first drug to be available for the treatment of depression.

The advent of antidepressant drugs had a huge impact on the clinical treatment of depression, and provided researchers with a very important experimental tool by which to examine the biological nature of the illness. In short, if researchers could understand how iproniazid (and other antidepressant drugs) worked, then this knowledge might help to explain the neurochemical reasons why depression occurred in the first place. The first clue was provided in 1952 by Albert Zellar, who found that iproniazid exerted its main biochemical effect by inhibiting an enzyme called **monoamine oxidase** (Zellar 1952). This enzyme, located in nerve terminals and the synaptic cleft, is responsible for metabolising and inactivating the excess release of **monoamines** (i.e. neurotransmitters that contain a single amine in their chemical structure and include **noradrenaline, dopamine** and **serotonin**). Thus, when monoamine oxidase was inhibited by iproniazid it elevated levels of these neurotransmitters in the brain. The implication was clear: iproniazid appeared to be producing its antidepressant effect by increasing the level of monoamines in the brain and, presumably, in the process, correcting a deficit that had caused depression (Figure 10.1).

Further evidence to support this theory came from the drug **reserpine**. This drug was first isolated from the Indian snakeroot plant (*Rauwolia serpentina*) in 1951 by the Ciba Drug Company and found to be effective in the treatment of high blood pressure. Unfortunately, reserpine also produced severe and sometimes suicidal depression in about 15 per cent of its patients. What was responsible for this mood-altering effect? In the early 1960s it was found that reserpine depleted the brain of **catecholamines** (neurotransmitters that contain a catechol nucleus in their chemical structure and include the monoamines noradrenaline and dopamine) by making these transmitters 'leak out' from their protective vesicles in the nerve terminals. As a result, these 'free' neurotransmitters were then broken down by monoamine oxidase. Consequently, reserpine produced an opposite neurochemical effect to iproniazid. That is, it depleted the brain of noradrenaline and dopamine, and by doing this it appeared to cause depression (Figure 10.2).

Although monoamine oxidase inhibitors (MAOIs) are still used in clinical practice they are normally only chosen when other treatments for depression have failed. One reason is that these drugs produce a number of side-effects, many of which are caused by their interactions with various foodstuffs which

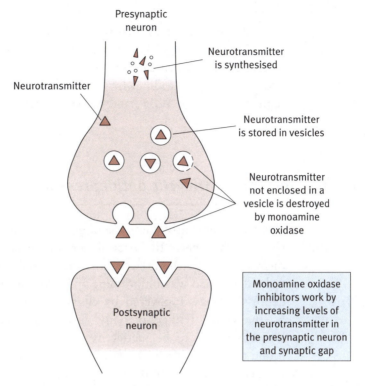

Presynaptic neuron

Neurotransmitter is synthesised

Neurotransmitter

Neurotransmitter is stored in vesicles

Neurotransmitter not enclosed in a vesicle is destroyed by monoamine oxidase

Postsynaptic neuron

Monoamine oxidase inhibitors work by increasing levels of neurotransmitter in the presynaptic neuron and synaptic gap

Figure 10.1   The mechanism by which monoamine oxidase inhibitors exert their pharmacological effects

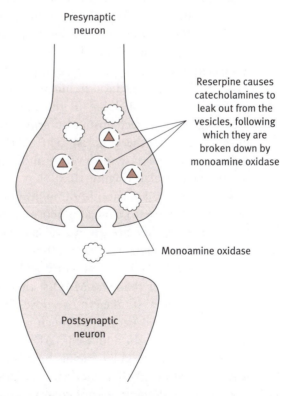

Presynaptic neuron

Reserpine causes catecholamines to leak out from the vesicles, following which they are broken down by monoamine oxidase

Monoamine oxidase

Postsynaptic neuron

Figure 10.2   The mechanism by which reserpine exerts its pharmacological effects

contain **tyramine** (this includes cheese, wine, pickled fish and chocolate). Tyramine is a powerful elevator of blood pressure and is metabolised by the liver. However, MAOIs interfere with this metabolism and result in hypertensive effects, which can lead to severe headache, increased body temperature and intracranial bleeding. In some cases these effects have proved fatal; thus, patients taking MAOIs have to be careful with their diet and avidly avoid certain foods.

The development of the tricyclic antidepressants

The most frequently used type of drug for treating depression (or at least until recently) has been the **tricyclic antidepressants** (TADs), so called because their molecular structure contains a three-ring chain. The first TAD compound to be developed was **imipramine** and, like iproniazid, its usefulness in treating depression was discovered by chance. Imipramine was originally developed by the Geigy Drug Company as an antipsychotic to treat schizophrenia, but was found to be ineffective for its intended purpose. However, it was found to reduce depression (Kuhn 1958) and in the late 1950s imipramine was marketed under the trade name of Tofranil as an alternative antidepressant to Marsilid.

Although imipramine and other TADs were found to elevate levels of monoamines in the brain, their pharmacological mode of action turned out to be very different to the MAOIs. In fact, the TADs produced their effect not by inhibiting monoamine oxidase, but by preventing the re-uptake of monoamines. Re-uptake is the main way by which monoamines are removed from the synaptic cleft once they have been released by the axon terminals of the presynaptic neuron. In effect, the axon terminal 'pumps' excess neurotransmitter back into its terminals, thus helping to regulate the concentration of monoamines in the synapse (this mechanism also provides an efficient way of 'recycling' transmitter back into the vesicles). The TADs block the re-uptake pump, and in doing so they increase the levels of monoamines – particularly noradrenaline – in the synaptic cleft (Figure 10.3).

Following the appearance of imipramine in 1958, more than 20 TADs have been introduced into clinical practice in the UK (Lader and Herrington 1990), and providing they are given over a period of several weeks, are effective at reducing depression in around 70 per cent of patients compared with 35 per cent for placebo (Lickey and Gordon 1991). Although the TADs are generally regarded as safer than the MAOIs, they are not free of side-effects. Notably, they can be lethal if taken in overdose, which is very worrying when considering that depressed people are much more likely to attempt suicide than other groups of people. In addition, TADs may also produce cardiovascular problems, including irregular racing heartbeats and hypotension, where the person may feel faint when suddenly standing up. Other side-effects can include psychomotor slowing, loss of concentration, muscle weakness, dry mouth and blurred vision.

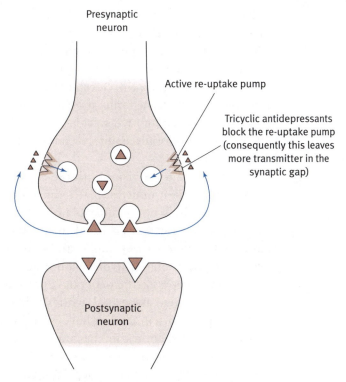

Figure 10.3 The mechanism by which the tricyclic antidepressants exert their pharmacological effects

The monoamine theory of depression

The discovery that reserpine produced depression, and drugs which increased monoamines either by inhibiting monoamine oxidase or by blocking the process of re-uptake had antidepressant effects, led to the development of the **catecholamine theory of depression**. The first person to propose this theory was Joseph Schildkraut, who argued in 1965 that depression was the result of reduced neurotransmission of catecholamines, particularly noradrenaline, at certain synaptic sites in the brain, and that mania was associated with an increased release of this neurotransmitter. Partly as a result of this hypothesis, noradrenaline became one of the most intensively studied neurotransmitters in the brain.

One way of testing the catecholamine theory was to look for biochemical abnormalities in the plasma, urine or cerebrospinal fluid of depressed patients. Indeed, if the catecholamine theory was correct then one would have expected to find a decrease in noradrenaline levels, or its major metabolites, in depressed people. However, most studies were unable to demonstrate this effect. For example, noradrenergic function can be examined by measuring one of its metabolites called **MHPG** (3-methyl-4-hydroxyphenylglycol), which is known to be derived in large part from the brain. Contrary to the predictions of the catecholamine theory, most studies found that there was great variability in the levels of MHPG in depressed people, with some showing low concentrations of MHPG and others showing high levels. Moreover, successful responses to antidepressant medication were frequently associated with decreases in MHPG. Another way of testing the catecholamine theory was to examine the level of neurotransmitters in the brain at postmortem of people who had been severely depressed or had committed suicide. Again, this work showed little evidence of reduced levels of noradrenaline, or its metabolites, in patients with depression (Slaby 1995).

One of the main problems with the catecholamine theory as formulated by Schildkraut is that it underestimates the importance of serotonin, which somewhat confusingly is not a catecholamine but an indolamine. In fact, we now know that serotonin has an equal, if not more important, role in depression than noradrenaline. For example, studies examining the amount of serotonin, or its main metabolite 5-hydroxyindoleacetic acid (**5-HIAA**) in the cerebrospinal fluid of depressed patients have shown that low levels of these neurochemicals are often associated with suicide attempts (Asberg *et al.* 1987). Moreover, postmortem studies have found decreased concentrations of serotonin and its metabolites in the brains of some depressed patients (Ashton 1992). Also, as we shall see later, drugs that selectively block the re-uptake of serotonin are very effective antidepressants.

For this reason, it is more meaningful to talk of the **monoamine theory of depression** (serotonin is both an indolamine and a monoamine) rather than the catecholamine theory. The monoamine theory is much broader in scope than the one proposed by Schildkraut since it 'proposes that depression is due to a deficiency in one or another of three monoamines, namely serotonin, noradrenaline and/or dopamine' (Stahl 1996). Indeed, this theory is supported by the fact that MAOIs increase concentrations of serotonin, noradrenaline and dopamine in the synapse, and that the TADs predominantly block the re-uptake of both noradrenaline and serotonin to varying degrees. In addition, reserpine depletes the concentrations of all these three monoamines in the brain.

The problem of antidepressant time lag

A perplexing problem about the effects of antidepressants is the time course of their action. For example, the inhibition of MAO, or blocking of re-uptake by tricyclic compounds, is known to be almost instantaneous – yet it normally takes around two–three weeks before these drugs begin to alleviate the symptoms of depression. This points to the possibility that it is not the direct or immediate pharmacological action of the antidepressant itself that is causing the improvement in mood, but rather the continuous action of the drug on the brain is causing a secondary or longer-term adaptive change to take place in the monoaminergic neurons.

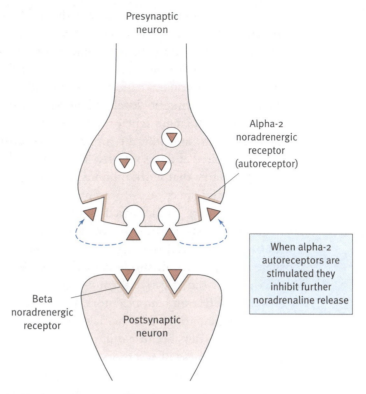

Presynaptic
neuron

Alpha-2
noradrenergic
receptor
(autoreceptor)

When alpha-2
autoreceptors are
stimulated they
inhibit further
noradrenaline release

Beta
noradrenergic
receptor

Postsynaptic
neuron

Figure 10.4   How autoreceptors affect presynaptic transmitter release

One explanation for the time lag of antidepressant action is that the continued exposure to the drug produces changes in the sensitivity, or number, of **autoreceptors** (Figure 10.4). These receptors are normally located near the axon terminals of presynaptic neurons, although in some cases (e.g. in the dorsal raphe) they may be found on cell bodies. Thus, the neuron has receptors for detecting its own transmitter! The reason for autoreceptors is that they offer a mechanism for monitoring the concentration of neurotransmitter in the synapse. That is, when levels get too high they provide feedback enabling the presynaptic neuron to inhibit further release. In this way, autoreceptors regulate the amount of neurotransmitter secreted by the presynaptic neuron. The best-characterised type of autoreceptor is the alpha-2 receptor found on the presynaptic terminals of noradrenergic neurons. These autoreceptors have also been implicated in the time lag of antidepressant treatment, particularly in the case of the TADs.

How, then, are alpha-2 autoreceptors involved in the delayed therapeutic effect of antidepressants? In the first days of treatment, the alpha-2 autoreceptors might be expected to compensate for the initial increase of noradrenaline in the synapse by inhibiting further release of this neurotransmitter. However, with repeated administration of antidepressants over a two–three week period, the alpha-2 autoreceptors are believed to lose their inhibitory capacity, thereby causing more noradrenaline to be released. This may happen in one of two ways: either the autoreceptors lose their sensitivity in response to the constant exposure of increased noradrenaline in the synapse, or the actual number of autoreceptors becomes down-regulated. Whatever the mechanism, the effect is the same – the loss of inhibitory control of the autoreceptors causes the presynaptic neuron to gradually release more noradrenaline over a two–three week period.

But what about the receptors located on the postsynaptic neurons? These are, after all, the main target for the neurotransmitter, and we might expect the increased synaptic levels of noradrenaline to affect these receptors as well. Indeed, the main type of noradrenergic receptor found postsynaptically is **beta receptors**, and like the alpha autoreceptors they also appear to become down-regulated and less sensitive to increased exposure of noradrenaline. Thus, antidepressants that work on noradrenergic systems such as the TADs not only have an initial effect on autoreceptors but also exert a secondary effect on beta receptors (Figure 10.5). Indeed, until a few years ago, this explanation appeared to account so successfully for the time lag of antidepressant therapy that some researchers believed that the desensitisation of beta receptors was a property shared by virtually all antidepressants (e.g. Wilner 1985, p. 256). However, the discovery of the selective serotonergic re-uptake blockers (see below), which have little effect on beta receptors, would appear to cast doubt on this claim.

This explanation of time lag greatly complicates our understanding of affective disorders because it implies that the main cause of depression lies with the responsiveness of receptors, and not with the concentration of neurotransmitters in the synapse. Similarly, it could be that antidepressant treatment is effective because it stabilises the sensitivity of receptors, and not because it raises

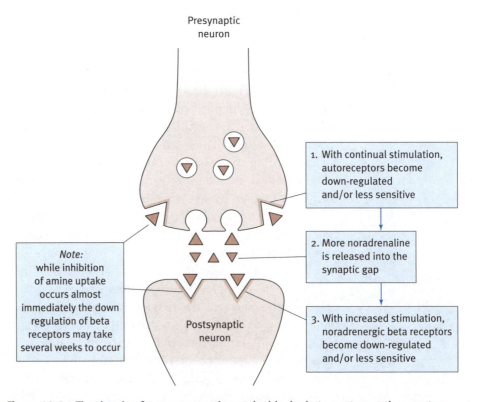

Presynaptic
neuron

1. With continual stimulation, autoreceptors become down-regulated and/or less sensitive

2. More noradrenaline is released into the synaptic gap

Note:
while inhibition of amine uptake occurs almost immediately the down regulation of beta receptors may take several weeks to occur

Postsynaptic
neuron

3. With increased stimulation, noradrenergic beta receptors become down-regulated and/or less sensitive

Figure 10.5 The time lag from presynaptic uptake blockade to postsynaptic receptor down-regulation

neurotransmitter levels. To complicate the picture even further, it is known that desensitisation of receptors occurs through a process known as **phosphorylation,** which involves alterations in the shape of membrane proteins, which is also known to alter ion channels, regulate enzymes, synthesise transmitters and control a diverse number of biological functions in the neuron. This makes it extremely difficult to pin down exactly how antidepressant drugs may be exerting their effects on neural function.

Selective serotonergic re-uptake inhibitors

Although the TADs predominantly block noradrenergic re-uptake, they also have a significant effect on inhibiting the uptake of serotonin. This fact, along with the wide range of side-effects associated with the TADs, has led researchers to seek safer and more selective serotonergic compounds for the treatment of depression. Indeed, a large number of 'second-generation antidepressants' have been developed over the years that are neither MAOIs nor TADs. One drug to emerge from this group was **fluoxetine (Prozac)**. This drug was manufactured by Eli Lilly and Company and first appeared in the USA in 1987. Within a few months Prozac had proved so popular, it was outselling every other antidepressant. Moreover, its pharmacological profile was relatively easy to understand as it blocked the uptake of just one neurotransmitter – serotonin. Since then, a number of other selective serotonergic re-uptake inhibitors (SSRIs) have been introduced into clinical practice including sertraline, paroxetine and citalopram.

Although the SSRIs are not necessarily superior to the TADs in terms of their efficacy in treating depression, they are safer (especially in overdose), tolerated well by the elderly, and have a much broader range of application. Indeed, they have been found to be effective in the treatment of panic disorder, obsessive–compulsive disorder, bulimia and alcohol withdrawal. Thus, serotonergic dysfunction may underlie all these disorders in addition to depression. Despite this, the SSRIs are not totally free of side-effects and can cause nausea, gastrointestinal problems, insomnia, headache and sexual dysfunction. The SSRIs have also gained a reputation for making the patients 'feel good about themselves', bolstering productivity, and increasing self-esteem.

The development of the SSRIs makes a very strong case for the involvement of serotonin in the aetiology of depression, particularly as these drugs have little *direct* effect on noradrenergic receptors. Instead, they appear to produce their main antidepressant effects by acting on serotonergic autoreceptors (especially 5-HT_{1A}) in much the same way as the tricyclics cause the desensitisation of alpha-2 receptors. Does this mean, therefore, that noradrenaline is unimportant in depression after all? The answer to this question is almost certainly 'no'. There is much evidence to support the involvement of noradrenaline in depression, as there is with serotonin, and perhaps the best hypothesis is that both transmitters are involved in mood dysfunction. Indeed, it has been proposed that depression is the result of an imbalance in both noradrenaline and serotonergic systems, rather than being due to a dysfunction in just one. For example, the **permissive hypothesis** (Figure 10.6) proposes that low levels of serotonin 'permit' abnormal levels of noradrenaline to produce depression or mania (e.g. Prange *et al.* 1974). That is, low levels of serotonin result in dysregulation of the noradrenergic system. Thus, by correcting the serotonergic system, one corrects the noradrenergic system. Certainly, there is much evidence to show that both these neurotransmitter systems are closely connected. For example, the locus coeruleus, which is the main source of noradrenergic fibres in the brain, and the raphe,

(a) Noradrenergic system

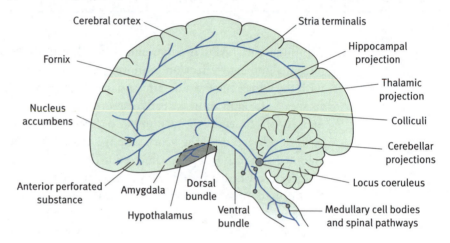

(b) Serotonergic system

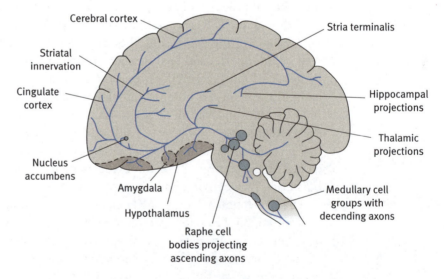

The noradrenergic and serotonergic systems show a great deal of overlap. The locus coeruleus and raphe are also reciprocally connected. The permissive hypothesis proposes that serotonin regulates activity in the noradrenergic system. Thus low levels of serotonin will cause dysregulation of noradrenergic activity.

Figure 10.6   The permissive theory of depression

which is the source of serotonergic fibres, are located close together in the brainstem and anatomically connected. Moreover, their projections show a great deal of overlap and often synapse on the same cells in the forebrain. It has also been shown that while the SSRIs are highly selective for serotonin, the repeated administration of these drugs nevertheless increases noradrenaline (and dopamine) concentrations in certain areas of the brain, including the frontal cortex and striatum (Goodnick and Goldstein 1998). Thus, it seems reasonable to suppose that the stabilisation of one transmitter system by anti-depressants (e.g. serotonin) can help to stabilise the functioning of others (e.g. noradrenaline), or possibly vice versa.

What a yawn becomes an orgasm: a rare side-effect of serotonergic antidepressants

When the selective serotonergic re-uptake inhibitors (SSRIs) first appeared in the late 1980s they were widely seen as being relatively free of side-effects. However, experience has shown they do have side-effects and are more problematic than first realised. One problem is the increased likelihood of sexual dysfunction. For example, the SSRIs have been shown to reduce sexual desire, producing impotence and making it difficult to reach orgasm in both men and woman (anorgasmia). Although the exact incidence of these side-effects is uncertain, some studies suggest that they may occur in more than 40 per cent of patients (Balon 1997). But one of the most unusual side-effects of the serotonergic antidepressants, albeit an extremely rare one, is a spontaneous orgasm when the person yawns! This was first reported by McLean *et al.* (1983), who described two patients (one man and one woman) who experienced an orgasm when they yawned and two other patients (one man and one woman) who had intense sexual desires while yawning. Although the drug in this instance was clomipramine, which is a tricyclic compound, it exerts its main effect by blocking serotonin rather than noradrenaline receptors. In fact, there have been similar reports with fluoxetine (Prozac), sertraline and bupropion. In some cases, however, the orgasm may not be yawn-related. For example, one study reported the case of a woman who experienced a three-hour sudden-onset spontaneous orgasm while shopping. She said the experience was pleasurable but found it socially awkward and stopped taking her medication (Pasick 2000). Although the 'yawning orgasm' is believed to be very rare, it could be more common than is currently thought because patients are too embarrassed to report their experiences.

This brings us to an interesting question: Why do we yawn? Yawning is a surprisingly complex stereotypical reflex behaviour (including a sudden deep inhalation of air, accompanied by an open mouth, tightened cheek muscles, eye closure, and increased heart rate) that occurs in all mammals, and can even be observed in the 12-week-old human foetus. For years, many people assumed that yawning was a response to lowered levels of oxygen. That is, when people become bored or tired, they breathe more slowly, and as carbon dioxide builds up in the blood, the brain produces a yawn to increase oxygen intake. However, Robert Provine has cast serious doubt on this idea by showing that when people breathe air containing different concentrations of oxygen and carbon dioxide, it has no effect on yawning (Provine *et al.*

What a yawn becomes an orgasm: a rare side-effect of serotonergic antidepressants continued.

1987). In another study, Provine found that although physical exercise caused subjects to breath faster, it did not change the level of yawning. Thus, it is difficult to see how yawning can be a response to decreasing oxygen levels.

One of the most curious facts about yawning is that it is highly contagious. Research shows that about 55 per cent of people will yawn within five minutes of seeing someone else yawn – and this effect even occurs in blind people if they hear others yawn. Remarkably, the contagious effect of yawning first manifests itself between the first and second years of life (Provine 1989). This has led to speculation that yawning may be a leftover response from our evolutionary history when it acted to coordinate the social behaviour of the group. Indeed, far from being always associated with sleepiness, yawning also occurs in situations of anxiety, conflict or physical readiness. Thus, yawns may have served as a signal to synchronise the behaviour of the whole group during times of change. However, this is far from certain and yawning remains one of the great mysteries of human nature.

The hypothalamic–pituitary–adrenal axis and depression

Depression is more than just a mental disorder. Indeed, people suffering from severe depression often show a number of hormonal irregularities, including elevated levels of the glucocorticoid cortisol. This is a hormone released by the adrenal gland, which is under direct control of the hypothalamus and anterior pituitary gland (this combined system is known as the **hypothalamic–pituitary–adrenal axis** – see Figure 10.7). To be more precise, the pituitary gland secretes adrenocorticotropic hormone (ACTH) into the bloodstream, which then induces the adrenal cortex to release cortisol. When the level of cortisol reaches a certain point, it then acts as a negative feedback signal to the pituitary gland and hypothalamus, which causes the release of ACTH to be terminated. The main function of cortisol is to maintain the correct chemical balance of the body in the face of change and adversity, and is absolutely vital for life. In particular, cortisol helps to mobilise the body's energy reserves during periods of acute or prolonged stress. In this event, cortisol not only speeds up the body's metabolism for energy needs but also acts to increase blood pressure and depress the activity of the immune system.

It is perhaps not surprising that depressed persons show elevated cortisol levels since depression is obviously a very stressful condition. However, there is more to increased cortisol secretion in depression than this. In fact, in many cases, there appears to be a dysfunction of the hypothalamic–pituitary–adrenal axis. Evidence for this view has come from the **dexamethasone test**. Dexamethasone is a synthetic glucocorticoid and its administration normally produces

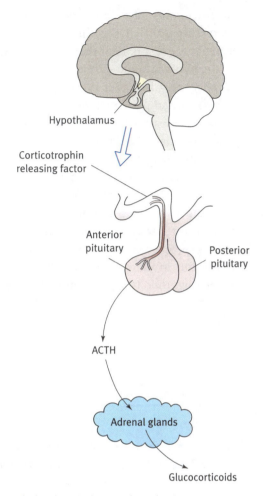

Figure 10.7   The hypothalamic–pituitary–adrenal axis

a suppression of ACTH from the pituitary gland, and subsequent inhibition of cortisol release from the adrenal cortex. Thus, in effect, the dexamethasone 'fools' the hypothalamus into believing that there are high levels of cortisol, which then reacts by turning off the pituitary's secretion of ACTH. However, in many people with clinical depression, the dexamethasone suppression does not occur. One explanation is that depressed people have a reduced number of hypothalamic glucocorticoid receptors that detect cortisol. Fortunately, the loss is reversible since the successful treatment of depression results in the reinstatement of the dexamethasone effect.

One possible reason for the lack of hypothalamic glucocorticoid receptors in depression is that high cortisol levels have led to their down-regulation. However, there is evidence to show that antidepressants may have a more direct way of correcting the functioning of the glucocorticoid receptors in the hypothalamus. For example, Reul *et al.* (1993, 1994) have shown that antidepressants increase the activity of genes involved in the formation of proteins that make up hypothalamic glucocorticoid receptors. These researchers also found that five weeks of treatment with the TAD desipramine produced a 25 per cent increase in the number of glucocorticoid receptors in the hypothalamus, and that this increase paralleled the clinical improvement of depression. Thus, antidepressants may exert part of their effect by helping to restore the normal functioning of the hypothalamic–pituitary–adrenal axis.

There are also other types of hormonal dysfunction in depression. For example, depressed patients tend to secrete more growth hormone than normal, and in some cases there can be an underactive thyroid. In addition, depression is often associated with marked disruption of circadian rhythms, with peaks of hormone release occurring at the wrong time or with reduced amplitude. The desynchronisation of circadian rhythms may cause depressed people to suffer from sleep disturbances, including an early onset of REM sleep, and early morning awakenings. To make matters worse, other circadian rhythms, such as temperature, may fall out of phase with the sleep patterns. For example, in healthy people, the lowest point in body temperature normally occurs at around 6 am, but in depressed people this may occur several hours earlier. It is not surprising, therefore, that many people with depression often feel physically ill in addition to their mental anguish.

Bipolar illness and the discovery of lithium

A person who suffers from bipolar disorder alternates between periods of mania (from the Greek word for 'madness') and depression, generally passing through a period of relative normality on the way. Both types of mood may be so severe that they interfere significantly with normal activities and everyday living. During a manic episode such individuals are excessively energetic. They are usually elated and self-confident, gregarious, flit from one idea or grandiose plan to the next, and show a diminished need to sleep. In addition, these individuals may engage in uninhibited social activity, go on spending sprees, or invent money-making schemes. If the mania persists it may progress in severity, leading to the emergence of delusions and hallucinations. However, at some point, the individuals slow down, their range of interests diminish, and they withdraw into themselves. Although they may feel well at this point, it is likely that this phase will eventually progress into a period of severe depression. The length of time that an individual remains 'normal' between episodes of illness varies from one person to the next. Moreover, some people may have only two or three episodes of illness in their entire life. Whilst others may have four or more episodes per year (referred to as 'rapid cycling'). In a few cases, the cycle of mania and depression may be so regular that the person is able to plan holidays and social events to avoid the difficult periods.

Considerable evidence shows that bipolar illness has a different biological basis compared with unipolar depression. For example, not only is the incidence of bipolar illness much less than that for unipolar depression (i.e. about 1 and 5 per cent respectively), but its age of onset tends to be much earlier and it occurs equally in males and females. In addition, bipolar illness has a far stronger tendency to be inherited. It is found in about 25 per cent of first-degree relatives of manic depressive parents, and the concordance rates for identical and nonidentical twins is about 70 and 15 per cent (the corresponding figures for unipolar depression are 40 and 15 per cent). In fact, evidence suggests that a single dominant gene is responsible for bipolar disorder, although the identification of this gene has yet to be achieved (Spence *et al.* 1995). But perhaps the most convincing evidence showing that bipolar illness is different to unipolar depression is that it is best treated with a drug called **lithium**, and not by standard antidepressants. In fact, treatment with antidepressants may exacerbate bipolar illness by precipitating mania.

Lithium salts were first used in the nineteenth century to treat gout (they were believed to 'dissolve' the uric acid that had accumulated in the joints), although their usefulness in bipolar illness was not reported until 1949. The story begins in the mid-1940s, when an Australian psychiatrist called John Cade hypothesised that mania might be due to a substance that builds up in the body fluids. Cade reasoned that if this was the case it should be possible to induce mania in guinea pigs by injecting them with urine taken from manic patients. The problem with this idea, however, was that urine contained uric acid, and to provide an adequate control group Cade also injected animals with uric acid that had been dissolved with lithium. To his great surprise he found that this combination made the animal very sedated. This effect was caused by the lithium, and when he administered the same substance to bipolar patients he found it quickly stabilised their moods and calmed them down.

Following Cade's report, the use of lithium quickly spread to Europe – particularly through the work of Danish investigator Mogens Schou, although it took longer to be accepted in the USA. The evidence from a large number of clinical trials shows that lithium improves manic depression and reduces the risk of relapse. Although the results of these studies vary, it is probably fair to say that 80 per cent of bipolar patients respond positively to lithium. According to Lickey and Gordon (1991), without lithium the typical bipolar patient has a manic episode about every 14 months, whereas this mood swing occurs only every nine years if lithium is taken. To provide this type of protection, lithium has to be taken on a daily basis, although if the patient is carefully monitored there is little risk of toxicity or serious side-effects.

Seasonal affective disorder

Seasonal rhythms may also be linked with feelings of depression and mania. One rhythmical condition is **seasonal affective disorder**, where people begin to feel low and depressed in winter when the days become gloomier and shorter. Not only do people with seasonal affective disorder suffer from feelings of sadness and despondency, but they tend to be lethargic, sleep a lot, and have carbohydrate cravings that can lead to weight gain. These symptoms typically disappear in spring when the days get longer and brighter – and in some people they are replaced by feelings of elation and increased energy that resembles mania. As might be expected, epidemiological studies tend to show that the incidence of seasonal affect disorder increases as one goes further from the equator, although an exception is Iceland, which has a relatively low incidence of this illness. It has been hypothesised that this could be due to the process of selection, where genes tolerating greater periods of darkness have been favoured (Magnusson and Axelrod 1993).

Seasonal affective disorder can be treated successfully with phototherapy, which involves exposing its sufferers to bright light for several hours each day. For example, one study produced a significant improvement in symptoms when patients were exposed to bright light twice a day: from 5 am to 8 am, and from 5:30 pm to 8:30 pm (Rosenthal *et al.* 1985), although the antidepressant effect was soon lost when the therapy was terminated. More recently, studies have shown that lights placed next to the patient's bed, which gradually increase in intensity thereby stimulating the dawn, are especially effective in treating the disorder (Avery *et al.* 2001).

It has long been suspected that phototherapy is effective because the bright light suppresses the release of the hormone melatonin from the pineal gland. Indeed, most animals are very sensitive to this effect (e.g. the light from a candle flame can even inhibit melatonin release in rats) and light suppression also occurs in humans. Partly because of this, melatonin is released in high amounts during the night (although humans show a 'melatonin surge' during the later part of the evening) and is suppressed during the day. However, this circadian rhythm may be delayed or abnormal in patients with seasonal affective disorder, which means that the release of melatonin is not synchronised properly with patterns of sleep and waking. Thus, it has been suggested that light therapy works because it 'resets' the melatonin rhythm to its normal time course (Lewy *et al.* 1989). Despite this, it has been shown that oral administration of melatonin is not effective in treating seasonal affective disorder, making it likely that other biological mechanisms are also involved.

Schizophrenia: an introduction

About 1 per cent of the population suffer from **schizophrenia** and perhaps another 2 to 3 per cent show borderline symptomology, making it a common form of mental illness. It is also one of the most devastating for its victims. The term 'schizophrenia' was first introduced by Eugen Bleuler in 1911, who derived it from the Greek *schizio* meaning 'split' and *phreno* meaning 'mind'. By adopting this term, Bleuler was trying to emphasise the fragmented or dissociative thought processes that were 'split from reality' as one of the key features of the illness. However, in some respects this is an unfortunate term because it has been confused with a completely different, and rare, condition known as multiple personality syndrome, where the person exhibits two or more different personalities (like Dr Jekyll and Mr Hyde). A person with schizophrenia, however, does not have multiple personalities but has rather a single personality that is overpowered by marked disturbances of mental function and feelings that are out of step with reality.

One of the most striking features of schizophrenia is the occurrence of bizarre delusions, which are beliefs that clearly are contrary to fact. For example, schizophrenics may believe that they are being controlled by others (e.g. messages are being broadcast to them by radio), or are being persecuted (e.g. someone is trying to poison them). In some individuals the whole personality may become deluded so that they believe they are someone else (e.g. Napoleon or Jesus), or have a divine mission to fulfil. These delusions may also be accompanied by auditory hallucinations, which include voices telling the schizophrenic what to do, along with tactile and olfactory disturbances. Even if schizophrenics are free of delusions and hallucinations, the continuity of their thought is often fragmented, making their behaviour or speech incomprehensible or puzzling. Schizophrenics are also likely to have abnormal emotions, including increased excitability, blunted affect, or feelings that most normal people would consider inappropriate. This may result in schizophrenics showing signs of excitement or agitation (i.e. nervously pacing up and down and talking in repetitive rhymes), or being lethargic and catatonic (i.e. long periods without movement).

The clinical picture of schizophrenia just described is stereotypical. In practice there are different types of schizophrenia, each with its own set of symptoms. To help distinguish the symptoms, some investigators have divided them into two basic categories: positive and negative. Positive symptoms are those that appear to reflect overactive brain functions such as hallucinations, delusions, confused thinking and exaggerated emotions. Negative symptoms are those that seem to reflect under-aroused brain functions and include poverty of thought or speech, blunted affect and social withdrawal. Some types of schizophrenia are predominantly characterised by positive symptoms, others by negative symptoms, and some by a mixture of the two (Crow 1980).

The genetics of schizophrenia

Several lines of evidence indicate that genetic inheritance may contribute to the development of schizophrenia. For example, the parents and siblings of schizophrenic patients have a higher risk of developing the illness than second-degree relatives (e.g. nephews, nieces, uncles, aunts). Further support for a genetic effect has come from studies that have examined the rates of schizophrenia in identical and fraternal twins. Identical (or **monozygotic**) twins are those who have been derived from the same fertilised egg and are genetically identical;

fraternal (or **dizygotic**) twins develop from two different eggs and two different sperm. Consequently, fraternal twins share only 50 per cent of their genes with each other, which is the same genetic difference that would be found between any other brother or sister they may have.

The logic of comparing identical and fraternal twins is compelling. All things being equal, one would expect a trait that is strongly genetic to be more concordant (i.e. found in both twins) in groups of identical twins. In fact, if a trait was consistently 100 per cent concordant, this would point to a genetic effect whose expression is not influenced in any significant way by environmental factors. Of course, most human behaviour is shaped by both genetic and environmental influences – and few traits or disorders show perfect concordance. This is particularly true of schizophrenia. For example, twin studies have now been undertaken for over 50 years, and nearly every one has reported that the concordance rate for schizophrenia is higher in identical twins. In general, the concordance for identical twins is around 40–60 per cent, whereas the rate for non-identical twins is 10–20 per cent (Gottesman 1991). Since the prevalence of schizophrenia is around 1 per cent in the population as a whole, this implies that a genetic factor is at work in schizophrenia. Despite this, the genetic influence is not marked (i.e. about 50 per cent), which shows that the environment plays a crucial, if not equal, role in the development of the illness.

One problem with these studies is that identical twins are likely to have been brought up in the same environment and treated alike by parents and friends. Ideally, it would be better to compare identical twins who are reared apart, but, of course, this type of separation rarely occurs. An alternative approach is to look at people born to schizophrenic parents – but adopted at an early age. Thus, if schizophrenia has a genetic basis, we would expect adoptees of schizophrenic parents also to have a higher incidence of this illness. Indeed, this appears to be the case. For example, Kety *et al.* (1968) examined the records of adopted children born in Copenhagen between 1924 and 1947 who were taken away from their parents at an early age. From this group, 33 adoptees were identified as adults who had been diagnosed with schizophrenia. On closer examination it was found that 8.7 per cent of the biological parents, but only 1.9 per cent of the adoptive parents, had histories of mental illness – a difference that was highly significant. Despite this, it remains that the majority of the schizophrenic adoptees did not have schizophrenic parents, showing that the genetic predisposition is not particularly marked.

As yet, no gene for schizophrenia has been discovered, although many potential candidates have been identified on a large number of chromosomes. It is now clear that the illness is not caused by a single dominant or recessive gene, although it is possible that an individual genetic factor could impart a *susceptibility* to develop schizophrenia. In this case, it would need the right combination of genetic and precipitating factors, such as birth complications or later stress, for the disorder to develop. However, it more probable that multiple genes are involved in the emergence of schizophrenia, thus greatly complicating the interaction of inheritance and susceptibility, and the nature of the illness (e.g. see Plomin *et al.* 1997). It has also been found that schizophrenia is more likely to arise in people who have fathers over the age of 50 years (Malaspina *et al.*

2001). This may occur because there is a greater chance of genetic mutations occurring in the cells (called spermatocytes) that produce sperm.

Environmental causes

There are many environmental factors that could increase the susceptibility to schizophrenia, but one that has often been implicated is stress. For example, it has been suggested that because society's values are often contradictory and difficult to tolerate, taking 'refuge' in schizophrenia is one means of escaping from such psychological conflict (some theorists such as Thomas Szasz have even argued that it is society that is sick, and not the schizophrenic). Others, such as R.D. Laing, have pointed to stresses and communication difficulties in the family as important factors in the development of schizophrenia. It is, however, difficult to evaluate these theories. Although the incidence of schizophrenia tends to be higher in lower social classes and large urban areas, where levels of stress might be expected to be higher, it could also be that schizophrenics have drifted down into these positions because of employment and relationship difficulties. In fact, the World Health Organisation has shown that schizophrenia is a worldwide disorder, found in all socio-economic groups and all types of society from industrial to third world (Sartorius *et al.* 1986, Jablensky *et al.* 1992). Thus, it is too simple to lay the blame for schizophrenia on life's stresses – although there is little doubt that stress can affect the course of the illness and increase its severity.

There is also some evidence to show that foetal exposure to viral infections may be an important contributor to schizophrenia. For example, in the northern hemisphere there is a small but significant risk that people with schizophrenia will be born in the winter months (January, February and March). In addition, this effect is more pronounced at higher latitudes and disappears in the tropics (Kendell and Adams 1991). Why, then, should this finding implicate viruses? The answer is that in northern latitudes, viral epidemics are more common in autumn – and for children born in winter, this period also corresponds to the second trimester of pregnancy, which is a crucial time for brain development. Indeed, several studies have shown a clear relationship between schizophrenia and influenza epidemics that occurred during the second trimester of pregnancy. For example, Sham *et al.* (1992) examined the outcome of pregnancies during several influenza outbreaks between 1939 and 1960, and found that there was a greater likelihood of schizophrenia when an influenza outbreak occurred five months before birth. Although this may be the most sensitive period, viral outbreaks occurring at any point during pregnancy may also increase the chances of schizophrenia (Barr *et al.* 1990).

The fact that exposure to other types of viral agents (e.g. rubella and AIDS) can cause brain damage lends support to the influenza theory. Thus, it is tempting to speculate that a virus may produce a toxin that harms the foetus at a critical stage, or the mother's immune system produces a viral antibody that damages the baby. But, even if we assume that the cause of schizophrenia lies in the developing foetus, there are still many unanswered questions. Most notably, schizophrenia does not normally appear until adulthood, so why should the illness take so long to develop if the triggering factor takes place prenatally? Even more difficult to answer is the fact that identical or fraternal twins are not always concordant for the illness. If developing twins sharing the same womb were exposed to the same prenatal insult, then one would expect both to be equally affected.

The Genain quadruplets

The Genain quadruplets are four genetically identical women born in the early 1930s who all developed schizophrenia by their early adulthood (the chances of this happening by chance is around 1 in 2 billion). Because all share identical genes, they provide a unique opportunity to assess the influence of genetic inheritance and environment on the development of schizophrenia. The sisters first came to the notice of the National Institute of Mental Health (NIMH) in the 1950s. To provide the twins with anonymity, researchers invented the name 'Genain' as a pseudonym for 'bad gene', and they also named the sisters (from youngest to oldest) Nora, Iris, Myra and Hester, so that their initials corresponded with NIMH. The quadruplets were described in a book by David Rosenthal (1963), and they have been examined on several occasions since. The last follow-up study took place in 2000 when the sisters were tested on a variety of different tasks – some 39 years after they were first identified (Mirsky *et al.* 2000).

Although all sisters are genetically identical, the symptoms of their schizophrenia differ. For example, Nora was the first to be hospitalised at the age of 22, although she has managed to live in the community most of the time since, and has held down several short-term clerical jobs. Iris was admitted to hospital seven months after Nora, and has been there, intermittently, over the same period. The next to be diagnosed was Hester, at the age of 24. She is regarded as the most severely ill of the four, and has spent much of her life in hospital under constant medication. The least affected is Myra, who was the last to show schizophrenic symptoms. She recovered, has worked steadily in clerical jobs, was married at the age of 26 and had two children. In fact, Myra appears to have functioned normally until the age of 46, when, under stress, she became paranoid and delusional and was hospitalised for two months.

In 1981, all sisters underwent CAT scans of the brain. The results showed that there were no brain atrophy or significant differences between the sisters. Despite this, there were changes in response when the sisters were taken off medication for a short period. For example, Nora and Hester quickly deteriorated, Iris kept reasonably well, and Myra actually improved. On another positive note, the sisters have demonstrated stable performance on a variety of tasks over the last 39 years, showing that cognitive decline is not a degenerative process in schizophrenia. Although the sisters would appear to provide convincing evidence for the idea that schizophrenia is inherited, they also grew up in a highly stressful and impoverished environment. For example, their father was an alcoholic and child molester, and their mother offered little love or support. Thus, in the final analysis it appears as if both heredity and an unfavourable upbringing were important factors in the Genain sisters' development of schizophrenia (see Plate 10.1).

The genain quadruplets continued.

Plate 10.1   The Genain quadruplets at preschool age.

The discovery of antipsychotic drugs

As with the development of antidepressants, the discovery of the first drugs that were effective in treating schizophrenia was fortuitous. In the 1940s the Rhone–Poulenc Drug Company began to develop antihistamine compounds that could be used to treat allergies. However, it was also found that these drugs could enhance anaesthesia and a French surgeon, Henri Laborit, began to examine these effects in more detail. He found that one compound, **chlorpromazine**, produced very marked sedation without loss of consciousness, and since there was a need at the time for new sedative drugs, Laborit recommended chlorpromazine to his colleagues for testing on agitated patients. Although the initial results were disappointing, in 1951 two French psychiatrists, Jean Delay and Pierre Deniker, found that chlorpromazine improved schizophrenia. Even more importantly, it appeared to reduce the symptoms of schizophrenia rather than simply cause sedation. For example, hallucinations and delusions disappeared, with the patient showing more logical thought processes. In addition, agitated patients were calmed, whereas catatonic patients became more active, allowing them to engage more effectively in psychotherapy.

In effect, chlorpromazine was a 'true' antipsychotic drug, and it first became available for this purpose in 1954 under the trade name Thorazine – making it the first drug to be marketed for treating a specific mental illness. In fact, within a few years of its introduction, chlorpromazine had proved so successful in treating schizophrenia that the number of people in mental institutions began to show a marked decline. Chlorpromazine belonged to a class of drugs known as the **phenothiazines**, most of which also showed antischizophrenic properties. However, it soon became clear that they were not the only substances with antipsychotic effects. In the early 1960s, another drug was discovered called **haloperidol**, which belonged to a class of agents known as the **butyrophenomes**, and, if anything, was even more effective at treating schizophrenia. Remarkably, both chlorpromazine and haloperidol have provided the main forms of treatment for schizophrenia over the last 30 or 40 years, and it is only recently that other types of drug have been found that are comparably effective.

Origins of the dopamine theory of schizophrenia

How then do chlorpromazine and haloperidol work to reduce the symptoms of schizophrenia? Beginning in the late 1950s evidence began to show that both drugs exerted their main pharmacological effects by reducing **dopamine** activity in the brain. One of the first lines of evidence to support this theory came from the drug **reserpine**, which (as we have seen earlier) is known to precipitate depression. But reserpine was also found to have antipsychotic effects in schizophrenic patients. In fact, reserpine and chlorpromazine not only calmed patients down but often produced Parkinson-like side-effects such as rigidity and tremor in high doses. This suggested that chlorpromazine and reserpine were having similar neurochemical effects on the brain. Indeed, because it was known that reserpine depleted the brain of catecholamines (noradrenaline and dopamine), this indicated that chlorpromazine must be exerting a similar effect.

This view was reinforced in 1960 when investigators discovered that Parkinson's disease was due to a deficiency of dopamine in the nigral–striatal pathway of the brain (see Chapter 3). Since treatment with reserpine or chlorpromazine could also mimic the symptoms of Parkinson's disease, this was convincing evidence

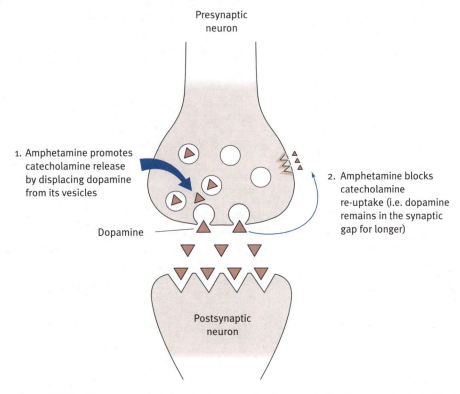

1. Amphetamine promotes catecholamine release by displacing dopamine from its vesicles

2. Amphetamine blocks catecholamine re-uptake (i.e. dopamine remains in the synaptic gap for longer)

Presynaptic neuron

Dopamine

Postsynaptic neuron

Figure 10.8   The mechanism by which amphetamine exerts its pharmacological effects

that they were both reducing dopamine activity in some way. This finding also provided an important clue about the possible underlying biological cause of schizophrenia. Put simply, if reserpine and chlorpromazine were reducing dopamine activity, this implied that schizophrenia was being caused by an excess, or over-activity, of dopamine in the brain. This hypothesis formed the basis for the **dopamine theory of schizophrenia**.

Further support for the involvement of dopamine in schizophrenia came from the drug **amphetamine** (Figure 10.8). Indeed, it has long been known that injections of amphetamine can cause psychotic behaviour in people, including hallucinations, delusions and agitated actions that closely resemble schizophrenia (Connell 1958). Furthermore, amphetamine exerts a specific pharmacological effect by stimulating the release of catecholamines, particularly dopamine, from nerve terminals (Leake 1958). Thus, by the early 1960s, evidence was pointing to excess dopaminergic activity as the cause of schizophrenia.

How do antipsychotic drugs work?

Because both reserpine and chlorpromazine are effective in treating schizophrenia, and since the former is known to deplete the brain of catecholamines, it was logical to suspect that chlorpromazine was having a similar mode of action. However, in 1963, Carlsson and Lindqvist showed this was not the case. For example,

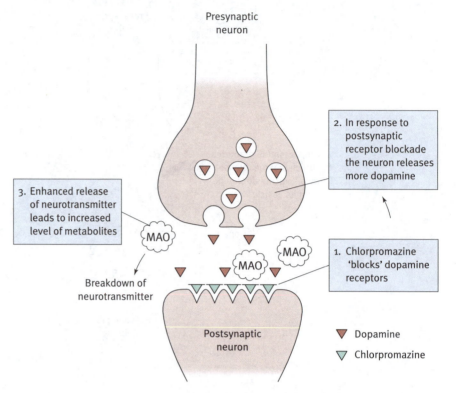

Presynaptic
neuron

2. In response to
postsynaptic
receptor blockade
the neuron releases
more dopamine

3. Enhanced release
of neurotransmitter
leads to increased
level of metabolites

MAO

MAO

MAO

1. Chlorpromazine
'blocks' dopamine
receptors

Breakdown of
neurotransmitter

Postsynaptic
neuron

▼ Dopamine

▽ Chlorpromazine

Figure 10.9 The Carlsson and Lindqvist (1963) theory of how chlorpromazine and haloperidol produce their pharmacological effects

when they injected rats with chlorpromazine (or haloperidol), they found that it did not deplete the brain of catecholamines. In fact, the reverse was true as the level of catecholamine metabolites (i.e. the breakdown products of dopamine and noradrenaline) actually increased – a finding that suggested that chlorpromazine was *increasing* the release of catecholamines, which were then being broken down into metabolites. Clearly, despite similar behavioural effects, reserpine and chlorpromazine were having different neurochemical effects on the brain.

To account for these results, Carlsson and Lindqvist proposed a novel theory by suggesting that chlorpromazine was acting as a 'false' neurotransmitter (Figure 10.9). That is, chlorpromazine was binding to the dopamine receptor, but instead of activating the receptor, the drug was *blocking* it. It was further hypothesised that if dopamine was unable to get to its receptors, the presynaptic neurons would increase their release of dopamine in an attempt to compensate for this deficit (this assumed that the presynaptic neuron received a 'message' from the postsynaptic one that signalled the lack of dopamine stimulation). The net result of this receptor blockade was therefore an increased release of dopamine, which was then broken down in the synaptic cleft. However, in the 1960s, there was no way of directly testing this theory and it remained hypothetical, although many thought it was a convincing explanation for the action of chlorpromazine.

During the early 1970s, new research methods were bought to bear on the problem of identifying receptors in the brain. In particular, one technique called

radioligand binding helped to show that Carlsson and Lindqvist were correct. In this technique, a radioactive tracer is added to a neurochemical or drug that is known to selectively bind to certain receptors. This substance is then washed through specially prepared brain tissue (taken from brain regions known to contain high numbers of the appropriate receptor), leaving behind tissue that emits a small amount of radioactivity. Because this emission is derived from the drug bound to the tissue's receptors, the level of radioactivity allows the number of receptors to be estimated. As might be expected, dopamine was found to bind with high affinity to striatal tissue, which is the largest area of dopamine receptors in the brain (Cresse *et al.* 1976).

Following the development of this technique, the effects of chlorpromazine and haloperidol on displacing radioactive dopamine was examined in a procedure known as **competitive binding**. This procedure rested on the assumption that if these two drugs blocked dopamine receptors, then they would compete with the dopamine if washed through the striatal tissue together. The consequence would be less radioactivity emitted from the dopamine receptor. Indeed, this is what occurred when chlorpromazine was washed through striatal tissue with radioactive dopamine. Moreover, not only did chlorpromazine block the effects of dopamine, but even more impressive was the finding that the clinical potency of a wide range of antischizophrenic drugs correlated with their ability to displace dopamine. In other words, the more effective a given drug was at treating schizophrenia, the better it was at blocking dopamine receptors.

However, there was an exception to this rule, namely haloperidol, which also happened to be a very effective and widely used drug to treat schizophrenia. In fact, in this test, haloperidol was relatively weak at binding (and competing)

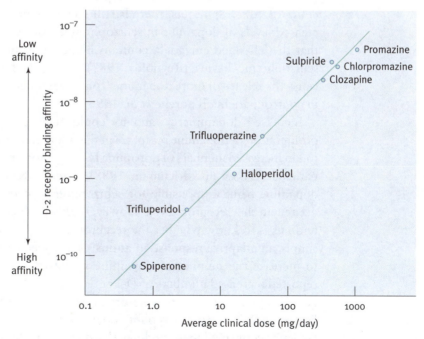

Figure 10.10   Graph showing the correlation between the clinical potencies of antipsychotic drugs and their ability to block the D-2 dopamine receptor

with dopamine receptors. In short, its poor ability to bind with striatal dopamine receptors did not match its potency at treating schizophrenia. Despite this, haloperidol was clearly binding to striatal tissue and other dopaminergic areas in the brain. How then could this puzzling finding be explained? The answer turned out to be that there was more than one dopaminergic receptor in the brain (Kebbian and Calne 1979). In fact, the brain was shown to contain two types of dopamine receptor, which were designated **D-1** and **D-2**. Importantly, it was also found that chlorpromazine binded with equal affinity to both D-1 and D-2 receptors, whereas haloperidol bound only to D-2 receptors. This was an important finding because it not only explained the discrepant results obtained with competitive binding, but it also indicated that antipsychotic drugs worked by blocking D-2 receptors. Extending this idea one step further, it also implicated the D-2 receptor in the aetiology of schizophrenia.

Problems with the dopamine theory

If chlorpromazine and haloperidol work by blocking dopamine receptors, then this could imply that schizophrenia is caused by excess dopaminergic activity. Consequently, one might predict that schizophrenics will have higher levels of dopamine in their brains than normal. However, this appears not to be the case. For example, there is little evidence showing increased levels of dopamine in the brains of schizophrenics at postmortem (Deakin 1988). Moreover, most studies of dopamine metabolites such as **homovanillic acid (HVA)** in cerebrospinal fluid, blood and urine have not found increases in schizophrenic patients (Post *et al.* 1975). Despite this, there is still some doubt about the possibility of increased levels of dopamine in schizophrenia. For example, it has been reported that the left-sided amygdala contains higher dopamine levels than the right in schizophrenic brains (Reynolds 1983), and that injections of amphetamine cause the release of more dopamine from striatal neurons in schizophrenics than in control patients (Laurelle *et al.* 1996).

Increased dopaminergic activity could also occur in schizophrenia by the proliferation of dopamine receptors in the brain. Indeed, a number of studies have found increased numbers of dopamine D-2 receptors in the brains of schizophrenic patients (Jaskiw and Kleinman 1988). Thus, rather than increased levels of dopamine being responsible for schizophrenia, it may be that excess activity occurs at the receptor level. However, the problem with interpreting these findings is to know whether the receptor increase is part of the illness itself, or simply an adaptive response to antipsychotic medication, which is also known to increase the number of dopamine receptors. Although some studies have reported increased numbers of D-2 receptors in schizophrenic patients who had been drug-free for some time before their death (Owen *et al.* 1978), studies that have used PET scanning to count dopamine receptors in medication-free subjects have not confirmed these findings (Farde *et al.* 1990, Pilowsky *et al.* 1994).

Another problem with the dopamine hypothesis is that antipsychotic drugs typically block receptors within a day or two, although it generally takes several weeks before they exert their full clinical effect. Thus, the blockade of dopaminergic receptors is probably not the final mechanism by which these drugs work. Indeed, it is even possible that this long-term change does not involve the dopamine receptors. For example, one expected effect of long-term antipsychotic drug treatment is an increase in the sensitivity of dopamine receptors (or their up-regulation). Consequently, this should lead to a massive exacerbation of symptoms when treatment is stopped. However, this type of withdrawal effect rarely occurs.

Evidence for brain damage

In some people there is evidence of brain damage in schizophrenia, with one of the most common findings being an enlargement of the lateral ventricles which are situated in the two cerebral hemispheres. For example, Weinberger and Wyatt (1982) examined the CAT scans of 80 chronic schizophrenics and found that the size of the ventricles was more than twice that of the controls. This finding indicated that there may be a significant loss of brain tissue in schizophrenia. Despite this, increased ventricle size is not a reliable characteristic of schizophrenia, and appears to be most highly correlated with negative symptomolgy including blunted affect, poverty of speech and loss of drive (Johnstone *et al.* 1978, Andreasen 1988). These also happen to be the types of symptom that respond less favourably to antipsychotic medication (Weinberger *et al.* 1980). Another type of abnormality often found in schizophrenia is reduced blood flow to the frontal lobes (see Plate 10.2).

These findings have led British psychiatrist Timothy Crow to propose that there are two types of schizophrenia (type 1 and 2) each with its own pathology and aetiology (Crow 1985). For example, type 1 schizophrenia is characterised by positive symptoms including hallucinations and delusions, whereas type 2 has a greater incidence of negative symptoms (see Table 10.1). Type 1 schizophrenia is also seen as being associated with dopaminergic dysfunction, whereas type 2 is the result of structural brain damage and neuron loss. In addition, these

---

Table 10.1   A summary of Crow's classification of schizophrenia (types 1 and 2)

Type 1 schizophrenia

Is characterised by positive symptoms including hallucinations, delusions and fragmented thought processes.

Often exhibits a fluctuating course with periods of remission.

Generally shows a good response to antipsychotic medication.

Is believed, in part, to be due to dopaminergic dysfunction (e.g. increased numbers of dopamine receptors).

Type 2 schizophrenia

Is characterised by negative symptoms including flattening of affect, poverty of speech and reduced motor activity.

Often exhibits a chronic course with little improvement.

Generally shows a poor response to antipsychotic medication.

Is believed, in part, to be due to neural loss (as supported by findings showing an increased likelihood of ventricular enlargement and reduced blood flow to the frontal lobes).

two types of schizophrenia have different treatment outcomes. That is, type 1 schizophrenia responds well to drug therapy with the chances of recovery being good, whereas type 2 responds poorly to drug treatment with poor prognosis. The implication of this classification is that schizophrenia is not a single disorder but rather two diseases that differ in important ways.

Despite this, many cases of schizophrenia do not fall neatly into Crow's classification system. For example, in one study that examined the progress of 52 hospitalised schizophrenic patients, it was found that, over a 25-year period, positive symptoms gradually changed into more pronounced negative ones, such as social withdrawal and blunted affect (Pfohl and Winokur 1983). Indeed, most schizophrenics probably show a mixture of positive and negative symptoms. Despite this, some do appear to fall neatly into the type 1 and 2 categories. For example, Andreasen (1985) found that some patients with negative symptoms have no prior history of positive symptoms and remain in this state for the rest of their lives. Alternatively, there are others with positive symptoms who have few negative characteristics and no signs of brain damage.

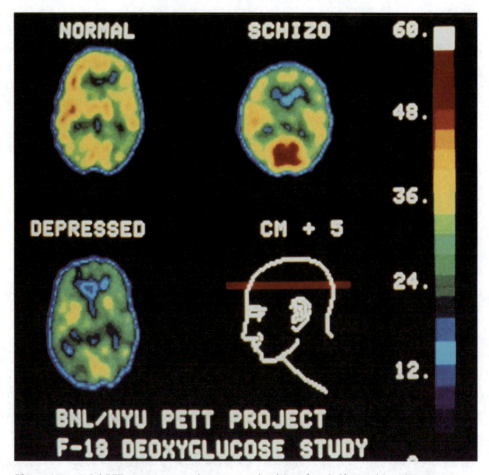

Plate 10.2 Axial PET scans comparing a normal subject (top left), a schizophrenic person (top right), and a person suffering from depression (bottom left). Note the low brain activity (shown by blue) in the frontal part of the schizophrenic brain compared with the high activity (shown by red) in the occipital lobe. *Source*: National Institute of Health/Science Photo Library

Side-effects of antipsychotic drugs

Chlorpromazine and haloperidol are not without their limitations. For example, they are not very effective in treating the negative symptoms of schizophrenia, and are associated with a wide range of side-effects, including tremor, postural rigidity, cramp and an unpleasant feeling of physical restlessness called **akathisia**. Furthermore, because many people with schizophrenia need to take medication for long periods of time, the continued use of these drugs can also have serious health effects. One complication is **tardive dyskinesia**, which produces repetitive and involuntary movements, especially of the face, mouth, lips and tongue. For example, people with tardive dyskinesia may continually flick their tongue out, or suck and smack their lips, which can become a problem more socially debilitating than the schizophrenia itself. Tardive dyskinesia is particularly worrying because, unlike other side-effects, it does not always improve when the drug dose is reduced or halted. Unfortunately, it is common in certain groups of schizophrenic patients, and it has been estimated that tardive dyskinesia may occur in around of 20 per cent of hospitalised patients with chronic forms of the illness who require long-term medication (Stoudemire 1998).

The reason why tardive dyskinesia develops is not well understood. It possibly occurs because the prolonged blockade of dopamine receptors causes them to become supersensitive. But others point out that it normally takes a long time for tardive dyskinesia to develop, and yet dopamine receptors become sensitive within weeks of taking antipsychotic medication. Whatever the explanation, most researchers agree that the disorder arises – along with other side-effects, including tremor, rigidity and akathisia – because antipsychotic drugs act on the

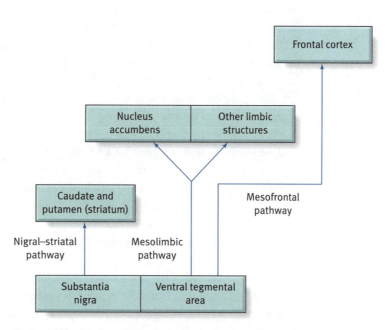

Figure 10.11   A reminder of the main dopaminergic pathways of the brain

striatum. This is unfortunate because the striatum, although the largest dopaminergic area in the brain, is not believed to be directly implicated in schizophrenia. Two dopaminergic pathways that are much more likely to be involved are the **mesolimbic pathway**, which projects to the nucleus accumbens, amygdala and hippocampus and is believed to play an important role in emotion, and the **mesofrontal pathway**, which goes to the frontal cortex and is likely to be involved in higher-order cognition. However, chlorpromazine and haloperidol are largely indiscriminate in their effects on all dopamine systems in the brain.

New drug developments in schizophrenia

Approximately 20 per cent of schizophrenic patients respond poorly to chlorpromazine and haloperidol, which in high dosage are also associated with a number of side-effects. This has led researchers to develop new drugs that are more selective for treating schizophrenia. One such compound is **clozapine**, which was synthesised in 1958 as a tricyclic antidepressant and first used to treat schizophrenia in the early 1970s. It soon developed a reputation for treating chronic forms of the illness (McKenna and Bailey 1993). Unfortunately, it also produced fatal agranulocytosis (lack of white blood cells) in about 2 per cent of patients and was withdrawn from clinical practice. Despite this, clozapine continued to be used experimentally and was found to be as effective as haloperidol. But, perhaps more importantly, it produced improvement, sometimes dramatically, in about 30–50 per cent of patients who did not respond to standard antipsychotic medication (Kane 1992). Clozapine also improved the positive and negative symptoms of schizophrenia, and was associated with a very low incidence of extrapyramidal side-effects, including a notable lack of tardive dyskinesia. Thus, clozapine has been reintroduced, although it is only prescribed to patients who have failed to respond to other antipsychotic medication or who suffered intolerable motor side-effects. In addition, the risk of agranulocytosis means that such patients have to undergo weekly blood monitoring.

Clozapine has also attracted a great deal of interest from psychopharmacologists interested in understanding how it works on the neurochemical systems of the brain. Surprisingly, it has been found to have little effect on dopaminergic D-2 receptors (its binding is short-lived) and has a greater blocking action on D-1 receptors. But, more importantly, clozapine is also a potent antagonist of $5\text{-}HT_2$ receptors and increases serotonin release – an action that is believed to be an important mechanism by which clozapine exerts its effects (Sodhi *et al.* 1995). This is a particularly interesting because certain hallucinogenic drugs, such as lysergic acid diethylamide (LSD), are known to be agonists on $5\text{-}HT_2$ receptors, and researchers have long been intrigued by a possible link between LSD hallucinations and schizophrenia. Another very interesting feature of clozapine is that it selectively blocks dopaminergic activity in the mesolimbic system and has little effect on the nigral–striatal system. Indeed, this action probably explains why it has so few extrapyramidal side-effects. Not surprisingly, clozapine is currently acting as a prototype for newer antipsychotic compounds as well as opening up new ideas concerning the biological basis of schizophrenia.

The last two decades have seen exciting advances taking place in the field of receptor pharmacology with the discovery of another three dopamine receptor subtypes (called D-3, D-4 and D-5). The D-3 and D-4 receptors have generated considerable interest because they are structurally similar to the D-2 receptor. However, unlike the D-2 receptor, the D-3 and D-4 receptors appear to be found predominantly in the limbic system (particularly the nucleus accumbens and hippocampus), which is one of the main brain regions likely to be involved in schizophrenia (Seeman 1995). Perhaps even more intriguing is the finding that chlorpromazine is 10 times less effective in binding at D-4 receptors than at D-2 or D-3, whereas clozapine is 10 times more potent at D-4 receptors than at D-2 or D-3 (Feldman *et al.* 1997). Not only do these findings help to explain why clozapine has a much more selective effect on the mesolimbic system, but they also suggest that our understanding of how antipsychotic drugs work will probably have to undergo major revision in the coming years. It is also of interest that two postmortem studies have found increased numbers of D-3 and D-4 receptors in the brains of schizophrenics. For example, a twofold increase of D-4 receptors was found in the nucleus accumbens (Murray *et al.* 1995), and a similar increase of D-3 receptors was found in the nucleus accumbens and striatum by Gurevich *et al.* (1997).

Summary

Mental health problems are surprisingly common, and it is estimated that one person in eight will consult a doctor each year with a psychological difficulty. The most common mental illness is depression. The first antidepressant to be developed (in the late 1950s) was **Marsilid**, which is a **monoamine oxidase inhibitor** (MAOI). This drug increased levels of **noradrenaline** (NA) and **serotonin** (5-HT) in the synapse by inhibiting their breakdown by monoamine oxidase. The MAOIs were followed in the 1960s by the **tricyclic antidepressants**, which included **impiramine**. These drugs were also shown to increase NA and 5-HT levels, but by a different pharmacological mechanism – namely the blocking of the **re-uptake pump**. These findings led to the **catecholamine theory**, which proposed that depression was due to reduced levels of NA at central synapses. This theory is now known to be far too simple. For example, it normally takes some two–three weeks of drug treatment before the symptoms of depression begin to improve, although their pharmacological action (e.g. inhibiting re-uptake) is immediate. The cause of this delay appears to lie with the neurotransmitter receptors. Put simply, the chronic use of antidepressants reduces the sensitivity of alpha **autoreceptors** located on **presynaptic neurons** which control NA release. In turn, the increased level of NA in the synapse gradually leads to **down-regulation** and **reduced sensitivity** of NA **beta receptors** found on **postsynaptic neurons**. Thus, it is possible that the cause of depression lies more with receptor sensitivity than with neurotransmitter release. In 1987, the first **selective serotonergic re-uptake inhibitor** (SSRI) called **Prozac** was marketed and became the most popular antidepressant in the world. However, this drug has no direct effect on the NAergic system. Thus, it is likely that both NA and 5-HT systems are involved in depression.

Schizophrenia is a serious mental illness characterised by bizarre delusions, hallucinations, fragmented thought processes and inappropriate emotions. This illness can have a strong genetic

Summary continued.

origin, as shown by twin and adoption studies, although environmental factors are also likely to be important. The first successful antipsychotic drug was **chlorpromazine** (**Thorazine**), which became available in 1954 and was followed by **haloperidol** (**Haldol**) in the early 1960s. Both these drugs produced side-effects resembling **Parkinson's disease**, which indicated that they depleted the brain of **dopamine** (DA). This also implied that schizophrenia was due to increased DA activity – a theory supported by the fact that high doses of **amphetamine** (which stimulates DA release) can produce delusions, hallucinations and hyperactivity. However, chlorpromazine and haloperidol do not deplete the brain of DA. In fact, their pharmacological mode of action was not proven until the early 1970s, when they were found to block DA receptors (i.e. they were **dopamine antagonists**). Moreover, their antipsychotic effect correlated positively with their potency at blocking **D-2 receptors**. Some studies have also shown increased numbers of DA receptors in the brains of schizophrenics, although this is not always found, indicating that there are different types of this disorder. A number of recent antipsychotic drugs have been developed, including **clozapine**, which has little effect on D-2 receptors but blocks serotonergic 5-HT$_2$ **receptors**. Clozapine is therefore acting as a prototype for new antipsychotic drugs, as well as opening up new ideas about the biological basis of schizophrenia.

Essay questions

1. What is the monoamine theory of depression? What evidence supports this hypothesis as a cause of affective disorder?

   Helpful Internet search terms: *Monoamine theory of depression. Neurotransmitters and mood. Noradrenaline and depression. Serotonin and depression. Neurobiology of depression.*

2. It generally takes two–three weeks of chronic treatment before an antidepressant begins to have a clinical benefit, yet the drug's pharmacological effect (e.g. its inhibition of MAO, or re-uptake) is usually immediate. What synaptic mechanisms may underlie this time lag?

   Helpful Internet search terms: *Time lag of antidepressant treatment. Synaptic changes and antidepressants. Autoreceptors and depression. Desensitisation of receptors. Mechanisms of antidepressant action.*

3. Provide evidence for and against the dopamine theory of schizophrenia.

   Helpful Internet search terms: *Dopamine and schizophrenia. Mechanism of haloperidol. Dopamine receptors and schizophrenia. Brain changes in schizophrenia. Neurobiology of schizophrenia.*

4. With reference to twin studies, discuss the probable interplay of nature and nurture in the development of schizophrenia.

   Helpful Internet search terms: *Twin studies and schizophrenia. Genetics of schizophrenia. Genain quads. Schizophrenia and stress. Nature nurture of schizophrenia.*

Further reading

Barondes, S.H. (1993) *Molecules and Mental Illness*. New York: Scientific American Library. A well-written and nicely illustrated account that covers the genetics, molecular biology, neuroscience and neuropharmacology of the main psychiatric disorders.

Bloom, F.E. and Kupfer, D.J. (eds) (1995) *Psychopharmacology: The Fourth Generation of Progress*. New York: Raven Press. A massive text of nearly 2,000 pages, with large comprehensive sections on mood disorders (19 chapters), schizophrenia (11 chapters) and anxiety disorders (17 chapters).

Goodwin, F.K. and Jamison, K.R. (1990) *Manic-Depressive Illness*. Oxford: Oxford University Press. A scholarly and comprehensive account that probably covers everything you will need to know about manic depression.

Gottesman, I.I. (1991) *Schizophrenia Genesis*. New York: Freeman. An excellent introduction for undergraduate students that discusses the causes of schizophrenia, including genetic, psychological and environmental influences.

Horton, R. and Katona, C. (eds) (1991) *Biological Aspects of Affective Disorders*. London: Academic Press. Contains a number of relevant chapters including ones on the monoamine hypothesis of depression, postmortem studies of neurotransmitter biochemistry and the genetics of affective disorders.

Lickey, M.E. and Gordon, B. (1991) *Medicine and Mental Illness*. New York: Freeman. A well-written textbook, suitable for undergraduates, looking at the diagnosis, causes and treatment of schizophrenia, depression and anxiety disorders.

Mann, J.J. and Kupfer, D.J. (1993) *Biology of Depressive Disorders*. New York: Plenum. Although a technical account, the first part of the book contains useful information on the involvement of neurochemical systems in depression.

McKenna, P.J. (1994) *Schizophrenia and Related Syndromes*. Oxford: Oxford University Press. Useful overview of many facets of schizophrenia research, including a chapter on the dopamine hypothesis.

Snyder, S.H. (1986) *Drugs and the Brain*. New York: Scientific American Library. A captivating and well-illustrated book which also covers some recreational drugs. The chapters on antidepressant and antipsychotic drugs, however, are worth the price of admission alone – especially for their historical perspective.

Stahl, S.M. (1996) *Essential Psychopharmacology*. Cambridge: Cambridge University Press. This book concentrates primarily on neuropharmacological actions of drugs that are commonly used to treat mental illness.

Torrey, E.F. (1994) *Schizophrenia and Manic-Depressive Disorder*. New York: Basic Books. A fascinating book that reports the findings of a six-year study of 66 pairs of identical twins, which indicates that schizophrenia originates either *in utero* or within the first five years of life, even though the symptoms do not appear until adulthood.

See website at www.pearsoned.co.uk/wickens for further resources including multiple choice questions.

CHAPTER 11

Drugs and addiction

In this chapter

- The neural basis of reinforcement

- The role of dopamine in reward

- The role of opiate systems in the brain

- The concept of addiction

- Biological and psychological factors in drug tolerance and withdrawal

- The pharmacological effects of commonly used 'abused' drugs

INTRODUCTION

Put in simple terms, a drug is any chemical that alters biological function. However, the effects of drugs on biological systems are far from simple, and this applies particularly to substances that act on the brain to influence a person's mood, cognition or behaviour. In the previous chapter we saw how drugs can be used to treat various forms of mental illness, but, of course, they can also be used for other purposes, not least for their intoxicating and pleasurable properties. Human beings have been taking psychoactive agents for thousands of years. Early written records show that opium was used 4,000 years ago, and alcohol use probably goes back over 10,000 years. Moreover, there are few places in the world where drugs are not used for their mind-altering qualities. Humans are drug-taking animals, and one only has to imagine life without alcohol, nicotine and caffeine to realise the truth of this statement. Yet drugs are not without their risks, and there are many substances where the perceived costs of use, either to the well-being of the individual or to society, are deemed too great to permit them to be freely, or legally, available. One of the most serious risks is drug addiction, which is widely seen as one of the biggest difficulties facing our society today. Not surprisingly, this problem, along with the fact that there has been a significant increase in illegal drug use over the last 30 years, has led to great efforts to understand how drugs produce their effects and influence behaviour. Moreover, by understanding why some drugs are addictive, one is gaining insight into the neural basis of pleasure and reinforcement, which are important determinants of behaviour for us all.

The discovery of reward systems in the brain

Many drugs that are seen as highly addictive (including heroin, cocaine, nicotine and alcohol) produce pleasurable effects. But how is pleasure produced by the brain? Part of the answer to this simple but deceptively complex question emerged in the 1950s with the discovery that the brain contains specific neural systems that mediate responses to reward (and punishment). The initial discovery of the brain's reward systems was made accidentally in 1954 when James Olds, and his research student Peter Milner, were examining the unrelated issue of whether electrical stimulation of the reticular formation could facilitate arousal and learning. During this work, Olds and Milner discovered that if they placed rats in a large open box, the animal would show a preference for a certain location or corner where they had been given the stimulation. That is, the animal would return to the site, and remain there, apparently awaiting further stimulation – a response that indicated that the rat was finding the experimental manipulation highly pleasurable.

Olds and Milner were also to have another surprise. When the location of the electrode placements was examined after behavioural testing, they found that the reticular formation had not been stimulated as originally planned, but a region of the brain close to the hypothalamus called the septal area. Thus, they had discovered the rewarding effects of brain stimulation by accident! In fact, had their electrode placements been correctly positioned, they probably would not have discovered the effect, as stimulation of the reticular formation is often aversive to the animal.

But was the electrical stimulation really acting as a reward? There was some doubt as the stimulation also caused the rat to look around and sniff the air, raising the possibility that the procedure might be provoking curiosity or exploration. To examine this further, Olds and Milner trained rats to run through a T-maze, which required them to make either a right or left turn for food reward. The task was designed, however, so that each goal arm had different consequences for the animal. In one of the arms, Olds and Milner gave the rat brain stimulation before the food was reached, while in the other arm, the animal was allowed to eat the food unperturbed. The important question was: what arm would the rat choose (stimulation or food) if given a free choice? The results showed that the rat always chose the arm where it received stimulation, and it even stopped at the stimulation point ignoring the food that was only inches away. Thus, despite being hungry, the animal would wait for the brain stimulation. Clearly, the electrical stimulation was highly rewarding.

Following this discovery, Olds and Milner developed a more efficient procedure of testing the effects of brain stimulation. They placed the rat into an operant box where every bar press (or combination of bar presses) made by the animal triggered a train of electrical impulses to its brain from a lead that hung from the ceiling of the chamber. The animal required little training to perform the task (i.e. it simply had to learn to press the lever) and had full control over the stimulation it received. In turn, the experimenters could estimate the intensity,

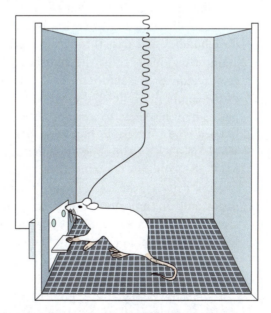

Figure 11.1   Experimental set-up for intracranial self-stimulation

or pleasurability, of the reward by recording the number of bar presses the rat was prepared to make to obtain stimulation. With this technique, Olds and Milner (1954) opened up a new field of research that allowed the neurobiological mechanisms underlying motivation and reinforcement to be understood in far greater detail.

The medial forebrain bundle

One of the first things that researchers sought to discover about self-stimulation was the location of the brain sites from which it could be elicited, and it soon became clear that these regions were spread throughout the brain. Moreover, the sites gave rise to different rates of responding (i.e. bar pressing). For example, Olds and Milner found that high rates of self-stimulation were obtained from the **septum**, **amygdala** and anterior **hypothalamus** (in the region of 500 bar presses per hour), whereas moderate levels of responding (200 bar presses per hour) were elicited from the **hippocampus**, **cingulate gyrus** and **nucleus accumbens**. However, the region that led to the greatest rates of self-stimulation was the **lateral hypothalamus**, which sometimes produced bar-pressing rates in excess of 1,000 presses per hour. In fact, one rat made 2,000 responses per hour for 24 consecutive hours before completely exhausting himself (Olds 1958). Many other brain sites also gave rise to self-stimulation, and there were some where stimulation was aversive (i.e. the animal would try to escape from the situation or refuse to press the bar).

Although a surprisingly large array of brain regions give rise to self-stimulation, it was found that most contribute to a massive multisynaptic pathway called the **medial forebrain bundle** (MFB). This is a collection of over 50 fibre bundles that pass through (or terminate in) the lateral hypothalamus and connect regions such as the **ventral tegmental area** (VTA) and **periaqueductal grey region** of the midbrain with the **limbic system**, **striatum** and **neocortex** of the forebrain. Indeed, the MFB is one of the few pathways in the brain that passes between these two regions (i.e. midbrain and forebrain), and it has been likened to an interstate highway that connects the two coasts of a continent (Graham 1990). Although this analogy is useful, it is a simplification as the MFB also contains many smaller pathways that join adjacent regions, such as the link between the lateral hypothalamus and the septal area. Thus, the MFB is not only an important interstate route allowing communication over a large area but also a series of smaller roads that turn off from the main pathway. For example, the hippocampus receives projections from the ascending fibres of the MFB, which suggests that the reward signal may play an important role in the formation of memories.

As we have seen, the region of the brain that yields the highest rates of responding from self-stimulation is the medial part of the MFB, which contains the lateral hypothalamus. Indeed, rats will respond with extreme vigour to

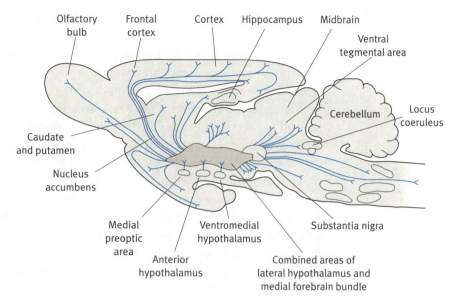

Figure 11.2   The medial forebrain bundle

obtain stimulation from this site, and, in doing so, will ignore basic drives such as hunger, thirst and sleep. Moreover, the animal will respond continuously and often show no satiation until exhausted. This behaviour clearly shows that MFB stimulation is highly pleasurable, and it led Olds and Olds (1963) to propose that neurons in the lateral hypothalamus provided the main substrate of reward for the animal. In short, they proposed that the purpose of the MFB was to collect information about reinforcement from a wide range of brain sites (involved in activities such as eating, drinking, aggression, sexual behaviour and sleep), and to channel this information to the lateral hypothalamus, which provided the most important rewarding and drive-reducing event in reinforcement. Thus, the MFB was seen as the final common path for reward messages from a variety of brain sites, with the lateral hypothalamus being the most important terminus reward for its many converging pathways.

Problems with the medial forebrain bundle hypothesis

It was also clear that stimulation of the MFB produced a variety of motivational behaviours linked with reward or pleasure, including eating, drinking, sexual behaviour, running and escape. Nonetheless, a number of challenges have been made to the hypothesis that the MFB provides the sole substrate of brain stimulation reward. For example, Valenstein and Campbell (1966) found that self-stimulation of the septal area continued, despite massive lesions which destroyed more than 90 per cent of the MFB, including the complete destruction of the lateral hypothalamus. In a similar study, it was found that self-stimulation of the lateral hypothalamus was not significantly reduced following extensive damage to the MFB (Lorens 1966). Both these findings show that neither the lateral hypothalamus nor other portions of the MFB are essential for self-stimulation to occur – a finding that shows that other brain pathways must contribute to reinforcement and reward.

Indeed, it is now clear that a number of regions lying outside the MFB can give rise to self-stimulation. One brain area that has attracted a great deal of attention in this regard is the **medial prefrontal cortex**. Not only do electrodes implanted in the medial prefrontal cortex give rise to significant amounts of self-stimulation, but anatomical and autoradiographic studies show this region to have connections with the limbic system, thalamus and caudate nucleus, rather than the MFB. Self-stimulation produced by the medial prefrontal cortex is also qualitatively different to that produced by the MFB. For example, it is characterised by low response rates, higher current intensities, and increases in the rate of responding that takes place over several weeks of testing. In addition, rats receiving stimulation of the medial prefrontal cortex typically remain immobile in contrast to MFB stimulation (Philips and Fibiger 1989). Further evidence showing the independence of the medial prefrontal cortex has come from lesioning studies. Lesions of the MFB do not significantly alter self-stimulation of the medial prefrontal cortex (Corbett *et al.* 1982), nor is self-stimulation of the MFB affected by massive lesions in the medial prefrontal cortex (Huston and Borbely 1973).

The role of noradrenaline in reward

As well as examining the neuroanatomical basis of reward in the brain, researchers have also looked at the role of its chemical pathways. This approach began in the early 1960s, when investigators began to map out **catecholamine** (**noradrenaline** and **dopamine**) pathways in the brain using **histofluorescence techniques** (see Chapter 1). One of the main findings to emerge from this work was that catecholaminergic pathways coincided with the distribution of sites that gave rise to self-stimulation. Moreover, nearly every catecholaminergic pathway that passed from the midbrain to forebrain was found to travel in the MFB, raising the possibility that they were involved in reward processing. This hypothesis was also supported when it was found that amphetamine (which stimulates the release of catecholamines) increased the injections of rate of responding to rewarding brain stimulation. In contrast, drugs which depleted the brain of catecholamines (e.g. reserpine) or those that blocked catecholamine receptors (e.g. chlorpromazine) reduced self-stimulation from various brain sites.

But what type of catecholamine was more important in reward: noradren-aline or dopamine? This was not an easy question to answer with traditional lesioning approaches because many of the regions that gave rise to self-stimulation received projections from both the noradrenergic and dopaminergic

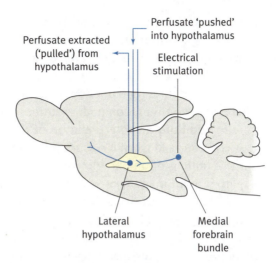

Figure 11.3 The push–pull experimental set-up used by Stein and Wise

systems. Furthermore, many of the drugs that were initially used to examine catecholaminergic function (e.g. amphetamine and reserpine) affected both noradrenaline and dopamine.

Another way of examining whether catecholamines are involved in reinforcement is to measure their levels after self-stimulation. That is, if rewarding brain stimulation is dependent upon the release of catecholamines, it follows that levels of noradrenaline or dopamine should increase following this procedure. This hypothesis was examined by Stein and Wise (1969), who extracted noradrenaline from a number of brain sites known to be implicated in self-stimulation. To do this, these researchers implanted **push–pull cannulae** (essentially double-barrelled tubes) into the brain, through which fluid was introduced ('pushed') to pick up various neurochemicals in the vicinity of the cannula tip, and then withdrawn ('pulled') for collection and chemical analysis. Using this technique, Stein and Wise found that when they stimulated the MFB, a marked increase of noradrenaline was obtained from the lateral hypothalamus and amygdala.

Stein and Wise (1971) also provided further evidence to support the noradrenaline hypothesis. The formation of noradrenaline in neuron terminals is known to involve a number of chemical steps, one of which requires the formation of dopamine, which is converted into noradrenaline by the enzyme dopamine-β-hydroxylase. When Stein and Wise injected their animals with a drug called disulfiram – which inhibited dopamine-β-hydroxylase activity, thereby reducing the release of noradrenaline, but not dopamine – they found that it reduced self-stimulation. However, this behaviour was quickly reinstated following administration of noradrenaline. This indicated that noradrenaline, not dopamine, was the main catecholaminergic mediator of reward.

However, not all evidence supported the noradrenaline hypothesis. For example, lesions of the dorsal bundle (the pathway that arises from the locus coeruleus and provides the most important noradrenergic input to the MFB), which depletes the forebrain of noradrenaline, had little effect on rewarding brain self-stimulation (Clavier and Routtenberg 1975). Moreover, self-stimulation is not readily induced by electrodes placed in the locus coeruleus. In addition, later fluorescence studies that selectively examined noradrenaline-containing fibres (and not dopamine) showed little correlation between the brain sites of self-stimulation and noradrenergic axons (Corbett and Wise 1979).

In addition, the interpretation of the above study by Stein and Wise (1971) was questioned when it was found that disulfiram-treated animals, if aroused by the handling of an experimenter, would respond by a burst of bar pressing if placed in an operant box. This suggested to some researchers (e.g. Roll 1970) that disulfiram caused sedation, and that noradrenaline mediated arousal rather than reward. Indeed, the development of two drugs (called FLA-63 and U-14625), which had a similar action to disulfiram but fewer side-effects, were found to have little effect on self-stimulation, despite depleting the brain of noradrenaline (Olds and Forbes 1981). Indeed, it is now believed by many investigators that noradrenaline is more involved in attention than reward – possibly by screening out irrelevant stimuli, or by preserving attentional selectivity during conditions of high arousal.

The role of dopamine in reward

The role of dopamine in reward has attracted an enormous amount of research. This work originated with the discovery that neuroleptic drugs (such as chlor-promazine and haloperidol), which blocked dopamine receptors, were also very effective in reducing self-stimulation from a number of brain sites, including the MFB. Later, during the 1970s, a number of highly selective D-2 antagonists, including pimozide and spiroperidol, were also developed which produced similar effects when injected into experimental animals. Further support for the involvement of dopamine in reward and pleasurable sensations came from the discovery that the feelings of euphoria produced by amphetamine in humans could be eliminated by drugs that blocked dopaminergic, but not noradrenergic, receptors (Wise and Bozarth 1984).

Dopamine neurons are less widely distributed in the brain than noradrenergic ones. Although it is anatomically more accurate to view dopamine pathways as a unitary system that arises in the midbrain and ascends to various forebrain structures, for our purposes it will be more helpful to divide them into three specific pathways. These are (1) a projection that goes from the ventral tegmental area (VTA) to limbic structures, including the nucleus accumbens, which lies in the ventral part of the striatum; (2) a projection that extends from the VTA to the frontal cortex; and (3) a pathway that passes from the substantia nigra (a dark nucleus that lies embedded in the VTA), which projects to the striatum (see Figure 1.22). Importantly, all of these areas, particularly the VTA, give rise to self-stimulation, which lends further support to the idea that dopamine is crucially involved in reward. In addition, the VTA receives considerable input from the axons of the MFB, which locates it at an important interface between the descending pathways of the forebrain and the ascending dopamine pathways of the midbrain.

If dopamine is involved in mediating reward, then it should be released following self-stimulation. However, because dopamine is quickly broken down after its release, it is difficult to measure accurately, and consequently most researchers use other means to assess its activity. One of the most frequently used techniques is to measure the ratio of DOPAC (one of dopamine's main breakdown products) to dopamine. In short, as the ratio of DOPAC to dopamine increases, the greater the presumed release (or turnover) of dopamine. In support of the dopamine theory of reward, it has been found that the DOPAC ratio increases significantly in both the nucleus accumbens and frontal cortex following bouts of self-stimulation produced by electrodes placed in the ventral tegmental area (Fibiger and Philips 1987). Another way of examining dopaminergic involvement in reward is to use lesioning approaches. For example, Philips and Fibiger (1978) lesioned the ascending dopamine pathways going to the nucleus accumbens and frontal cortex with the highly selective neurotoxin **6-hydroxydopamine**, and found that this operation abolished self-stimulation of the ventral tegmental area (VTA). It has also been shown that microinjections of dopamine antagonists into the nucleus accumbens decrease VTA stimulation rates. Thus, the ascending dopaminergic neurons arising from the VTA – particularly those projecting to the nucleus accumbens – appear to play an important role in reward and reinforcement.

Chemical self-stimulation

Some of the best evidence implicating dopamine in reward has come from experiments where animals are able to self-inject themselves with drugs. Instead of using electrical stimulation, animals can also be made to press a lever to turn on a pump that injects a chemical directly into their body by means of a flexible plastic tube (Weeks 1962). This procedure has proved very useful for examining the addictive potential of drugs as many of the substances that animals self-administer are also those that are abused by humans. Indeed, one class of drug that gives rise to high rates of self-injection are those that increase dopaminergic activity, including amphetamine, which acts to release dopamine from nerve terminals, and cocaine, which is a selective uptake blocker for dopamine (see also, Figure 10.3) and increases the level of this neurotransmitter in the synapse.

In particular, animals will work hard to administer themselves with cocaine. For example, in a study involving monkeys, the rewarding property of cocaine was compared with a number of other drugs by using a progressive ratio procedure in which the animals had to increase their bar presses by 50 every time they received a drug reinforcement (Yanagita 1987). Thus, the task was designed so that the monkey had to work progressively harder for each reward until the demand becomes so great that the responding stops. Clearly, the more reinforcing a drug is, the more responses the animal will be prepared to make. The study showed that four of the six monkeys worked harder for cocaine injections than for any other drug. In fact, one monkey was prepared to press the lever 6,400 times to obtain a single cocaine reinforcement!

In another study (Deneau *et al.* 1969), monkeys were allowed unlimited access to cocaine 24 hours a day – a situation that resulted in such a high rate of self-administration that many suffered from convulsions and died within 30 days. To avoid this problem, the researchers later restricted the maximum intake of cocaine to 1 dose (1.0 mg/kg) per hour. Although this schedule stopped the fatal overdosing, the animals self-administered cocaine around the clock until exhaustion occurred (typically some two–five days into the experiment). However, this cessation was only temporary and the drug administration soon started again. Thus, the monkey's behaviour showed a great deal of fluctuation with sessions of high cocaine intake along with periods of abstinence. Interestingly, a similar type of pattern also occurs with humans who use cocaine in high amounts. Thus, the self administration procedure has relevance for understanding our own drug-taking behaviour.

Cocaine not only blocks the re-uptake of dopamine but also inhibits noradrenaline and serotonin uptake. In addition, it acts as a local anaesthetic and may increase catecholamine receptivity sensitivity. Thus, cocaine has a number of pharmacological effects. Despite this, considerable evidence shows that dopamine is the most important neurotransmitter responsible for the reinforcing actions of cocaine. For example, a number of dopaminergic agonists elicit self-stimulation, and some provide a viable substitute for cocaine in this procedure. Conversely, drugs that selectively block dopaminergic receptors (particularly D-2) abolish the rewarding properties of cocaine in animals (Kuhar *et al.* 1991). This effect also appears to apply to humans. For example, pretreatment with the D-2 antagonist haloperidol has been shown to reduce the 'high' produced by intravenous cocaine, although it does not appear to stop the 'rush' that immediately follows the injection (Sherer *et al.* 1989). It has also been found that haloperidol reduces craving in addicts when they are exposed to cues that are normally associated with cocaine administration (Berger *et al.* 1996). Thus, enhanced dopaminergic activity appears to explain some of the pleasurable sensations of cocaine and cravings associated with its use.

Cocaine's effect on the nucleus accumbens and prefrontal cortex

If cocaine exerts its rewarding effect by blocking the re-uptake of dopamine, thus increasing the amount of this neurotransmitter in the synapse, then this event must take place at some point within the dopamine pathways of the brain.

But where exactly? The answer appears to be the nucleus accumbens. Evidence in support of this idea has come from studies where infusions of dopaminergic-blocking drugs into the nucleus accumbens reduce reward produced by MFB stimulation, and also that caused by intravenous self-administration of cocaine (Philips and Broekkamp 1980). The same effect, however, is not obtained with similar injections into the frontal cortex, or caudate nucleus, showing that the nucleus accumbens is the crucial site for cocaine's rewarding effects. Lending further support to this theory is research showing that cocaine self-administration is weakened by lesions of the nucleus accumbens (Roberts *et al.* 1977) and VTA (Roberts and Koob 1982), but not the prefrontal cortex (Martin-Iversen *et al.* 1986).

Despite this, animals do not bar press to obtain direct infusions of cocaine into the nucleus accumbens, although they will do so for amphetamine and other dopaminergic agonists. The reason for this anomaly is not clear, although it is possible that when cocaine is injected into the nucleus accumbens it produces a local anaesthetic effect. However, this effect does not occur in the medial frontal cortex, where rats will work hard to self-administer cocaine (Goeders and Smith 1983). This indicates that other dopamine pathways are involved in reward, although the nucleus accumbens probably still provides the most important site for producing cocaine's pleasurable and reinforcing effects. Further support for this idea has come from studies that have measured dopamine levels in various brain sites using **microdialysis** following intravenous injections of cocaine. For example, it has been shown that moderate doses of cocaine (1 mg/kg) produce an increase of dopamine in the nucleus accumbens, whereas higher doses (2 mg/kg) produce an increase in the prefrontal cortex, but to a lesser degree than that found in the nucleus accumbens (Fibiger *et al.* 1992).

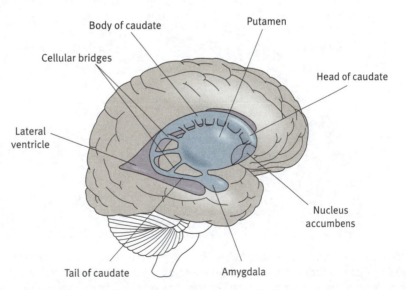

Figure 11.4 The location of the nucleus accumbens in the human brain

Laughter, like cocaine, tickles the nucleus accumbens

If we were unable to laugh, or find jokes funny, life would be immeasurably less enjoyable and rewarding. Laughter is an essential part of our life that occurs in young babies (the first laughter occurs at about 4 months) and all races. Yet, remarkably, no one is sure why we do it. It has been estimated that, on average, we laugh 17 times a day, and in many of these instances we will laugh at mundane comments or ordinary life events. Moreover, we laugh not only in times of happiness but also when we are nervous, embarrassed or disappointed. Laugher is likely to serve several functions. In some cases, it may act to reduce stress and help us to release pent-up negative emotions such as anger or anxiety. This is seen when a well-timed joke eases the tension in a threatening or aggressive situation. Laughter may also have cognitive benefits by allowing people to view a problem or event in a new perspective. For example, sick humour may allow us to confront issues that we would not normally want to contemplate. More importantly, perhaps, laughter helps to strengthen social bonds as it is a sign that we are feeling comfortable and relaxed in our immediate surroundings. Indeed, laughter is a vital component of play, and for some mysterious reason we laugh when being tickled, yet we can't tickle ourselves! Despite this, we should not lose sight of the fact that we laugh because it is pleasurable. One might predict, therefore, that laughter will also stimulate the reward systems of the brain.

This possibility has been examined in a study (Mobbs *et al.* 2003) that used magnetic resonance imaging to photograph the brain activity of 16 young adults who were presented with 42 cartoons that had previously been rated as very funny, and 42 non-funny cartoons (i.e. cartoons with funny visual or written cues omitted – see Plate 11.1). The researchers found that the funniest cartoons activated a number of brain regions, including the nucleus accumbens.

Plate 11.1(a)   An example of a funny cartoon, and the same cartoon with the funny cues omitted. *Source:* © Dan Piraro. Reprinted with special permission of North America Syndicate

Laughter, like cocaine, tickles the nucleus accumbens continued.

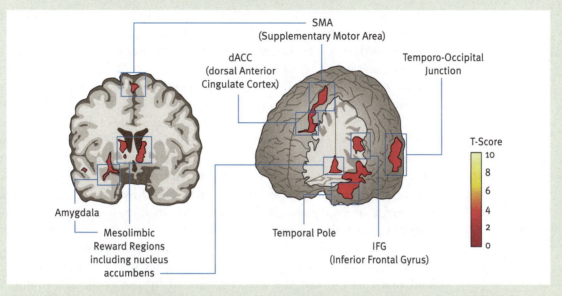

Plate 11.1(b) Functional topography of funny cartoons minus non-funny cartoons. *Source*: Mobbs *et al.* (2003) *Neuron*, **40**, 1041–8, Copyright 2003, with permission from Elsevier

Moreover, the degree of activity in the nucleus accumbens strongly correlated with how funny the subject thought the cartoon was: the extremely funny jokes causing more activation of the accumbens than the less funny ones. Other brain areas stimulated by the funny jokes included the amygdala, which is also believed to be involved in the sensation of pleasure, the left frontal cortex, including Broca's area, which is probably involved in the cognitive interpretation of the cartoon, and the motor cortex, which is responsible for producing the movements of laughter. Evidence for the latter has come from a study that applied electrical stimulation to the surface of the cerebral cortex in a 16-year-old girl to locate areas of epileptic tissue (Fried *et al.* 1998). During this investigation, a small area (about 2 cm by 2 cm) in the left motor cortex was found that always elicited laughter. This laughter was evoked on several trials and a different explanation was offered by the girl each time. Thus, laughter was attributed to the particular object seen during a naming object task ('the horse was funny'), to the content of a paragraph during reading, or to persons present in the room while the patient received the electrical stimulation ('you guys are just so funny . . . standing around').

The finding that funny cartoons activate the same reward circuits in the brain as addicting drugs such as cocaine – and, indeed, other types of reinforcement, such as money, sex and food – undoubtedly helps to explain our unique 'addiction' to humour. But laughter does more than just make us feel good by stimulating our nucleus accumbens. There is evidence that it can reduce feelings of pain, boost the immune system, decrease cortisol levels, and lower blood pressure (Martin 2001). Thus, laughter is not only a sure sign of happiness, but arguably the best medicine of them all.

The reward circuits of the brain revisited

We have seen earlier in this chapter that the highest rates of self-stimulation are produced when electrodes are placed in the MFB. In addition, there is convincing evidence that dopamine plays an important role in reward. Thus, it would make sense to hypothesise that one reason why stimulation of the MFB is reinforcing is because it increases activity in dopamine pathways that originate in the VTA. That is, descending *first-stage* neurons in the MFB project to the VTA, where they activate the *second-stage* dopamine neurons. Evidence to support this idea was provided by Stellar and Corbett (1989), who injected a dopamine antagonist into 56 different sites throughout the brain and found that only one area – the nucleus accumbens – significantly reduced (but not abolished) the rewarding effects of lateral hypothalamic stimulation. Moreover, self-stimulation of the lateral hypothalamus is enhanced by injections of amphetamine into the nucleus accumbens (Spencer and Corbett 1986). In another study, Bielajew and Shizgal (1986) inhibited neuronal activity in the VTA by means of an electrode that used hyperpolarising (negative) current, and found that this blocked the effects of lateral hypothalamic self-stimulation. Thus, the simplest interpretation of all these findings is that fibres travelling 'downwards' through the MFB synapse in the VTA in turn exert an excitatory effect on the ascending dopamine pathways, thereby causing increased dopamine release in forebrain regions such as the nucleus accumbens.

Lesion studies have shown that the nucleus accumbens plays an important role in the motivation for food, water, sex and maternal behaviour. Moreover, the release of dopamine in the nucleus accumbens occurs in response to appetite rewards, and after classical conditioning (Cheng *et al.* 2003). Despite this, whether or not the MFB contributes to this activity is far from certain. Surprisingly, for example, lesions of the nucleus accumbens do not reduce the reinforcing effects of lateral hypothalamic brain stimulation (Johnson and Stellar 1994). Moreover, Gallistel *et al.* (1985) used the technique of **2-deoxyglucose** autoradiography to map out the brain regions activated by self-stimulation of the MFB and found that while the VTA showed significantly increased activity, this did not extend to the ascending dopaminergic pathways. Just as problematical is the finding that huge lesions of the forebrain that destroy most of the dopamine terminals of the nucleus accumbens, septum, striatum and frontal cortex have relatively little effect on reducing lateral hypothalamic stimulation (Colle and Wise 1987). These findings show that the rewarding effects of MFB stimulation do not necessarily require the activation of dopaminergic pathways. Indeed, it has also been shown that self-stimulation of the VTA can still occur after large lesions of its dopamine pathways. This suggests that other chemical pathways are also involved in producing reward at this site, and perhaps they are also influenced by the MFB.

It is difficult to draw any firm conclusions about the nature of the reward systems in the brain. Although most researchers agree that the MFB provides a key biological mechanism in reinforcement, there is little consensus on how this occurs. Similarly, while dopamine pathways and the nucleus accumbens

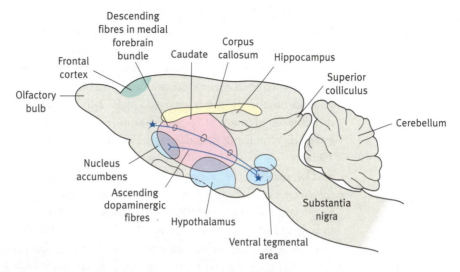

Figure 11.5   Diagram showing how descending fibres of the medial forebrain are able to influence ascending dopaminergic systems which have their cell bodies in the ventral tegmental area. *Source*: R.B. Graham, *Physiological Psychology*. Copyright © 1990 by Wadsworth Inc.

have been identified as important for mediating the pleasurable and reinforcing effects of certain drugs, and have also been implicated in several types of rewarding behaviour, the role of dopamine, particularly in the nucleus accumbens, remains unclear. Perhaps the safest conclusion to draw from this research is that dopamine is not the only reward transmitter, nor are dopaminergic neurons the final common path for reward in the brain. In addition, it can be said with some certainty that the MFB is not the only reward system in the brain. The fact that self-stimulation occurs throughout the brain implies that there are multiple reward systems with different functions. Whether these are interconnected into one large multisynaptic system, or functionally independent, remains to be seen.

The opiates and reward

The term '**opiate**' refers to any substance, natural or synthetic, that has properties similar to opium. These drugs, which include morphine and heroin, are known to be effective painkillers, and have the potential to be highly addictive. In particular, heroin addiction represents a serious threat to society. The number of people addicted to heroin has been rising by about 15 per cent each year over the last decade, and it has been estimated that there are over 150,000 heroin addicts in the UK, with the majority of these injecting the drug. Not only does this practice increase the risk of diseases such as hepatitis and AIDS, but there is always a possibility of a fatal overdose. In many cases, the use of heroin leads to such physical and mental dependence that the addict becomes drawn into a lifestyle structured around buying, dealing and using the drug. To maintain their habit, addicts may turn to crime to obtain funds to buy the drug. It has been estimated that a typical heroin addict in the UK spends over £8,000 on the drug per year (Ashton 2002), and although the exact figure is difficult to calculate, it is clear that millions of pounds worth of goods are stolen every day to fund illegal usage (Institute for the Study of Drug Dependence 1996).

The reasons for taking heroin are complex. Initially, it is normally smoked (*chasing the dragon*) and it may be used for its pleasant sedating qualities. However, tolerance usually builds quickly to these effects, which means that the individual will need to increase the dose. At some point, due to the increasing tolerance, the individual may turn to injecting the drug. This is likely to produce strong feelings of pleasure and a 'rush', which is sometimes described as 'orgasmic' by its users – followed by a long dreamy state that has been described as being wrapped-up in cotton wool. However, tolerance also builds to these effects, and the individual has to increase the dose yet again. Eventually, the dosage may increase to such an extent that the person becomes so physically dependent on the drug that it must be taken regularly simply to stave off the withdrawal symptoms.

Almost nothing was known about how heroin worked on the CNS until the early 1970s, when it was discovered that the brain contained receptors for opiate substances (Pert and Snyder 1973). This implied that opiate substances had a neurotransmitter type role in the brain and led to a frantic search for their identification. The first endorphins (derived from endogenous and morphine) were discovered in Aberdeen by Hans Kosterlitz and his colleagues (Hughes *et al.* 1975), who showed that they were peptides made up of amino acid chains. There are now known to be three families of opiates in the CNS (enkephalins, dynorphins and beta-endorphins), and several types of receptor including mu, delta and kappa. It is the mu receptor which mediates many of the effects of morphine (and therefore heroin) and is heavily localised in the periaqueductal grey area (where it helps to produce analgesia) and in the limbic system, VTA and nucleus accumbens – areas that are closely linked with the dopaminergic reward systems.

These findings suggested that opiate drugs produce their pleasurable effects by acting on the dopamine systems of the brain. Indeed, support for this idea came from the discovery that rats will quickly learn to lever press at high rates to obtain infusions of morphine into the VTA – an effect that is not reliably obtained from other brain areas (Bozarth 1986). Moreover, injections of morphine into the VTA were shown to stimulate the release of dopamine in the nucleus accumbens. This effect appears to occur because morphine acts on mu receptors located on **GABA** interneurons in the VTA. This causes the GABA neurons to become inhibited, with the ascending dopaminergic neurons being released from their usual GABAergic inhibition (Bozarth 1987). Consequently, the dopamine neurons become activated and secrete more neurotransmitter into the nucleus accumbens.

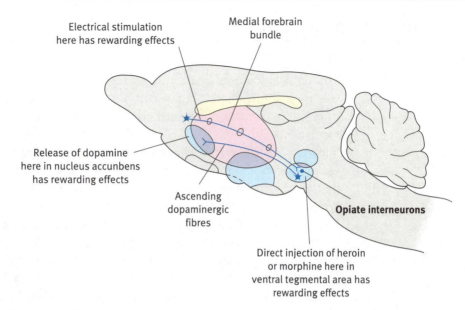

Electrical stimulation
here has rewarding effects

Medial forebrain
bundle

Release of dopamine
here in nucleus accumbens
has rewarding effects

Ascending
dopaminergic
fibres

Opiate interneurons

Direct injection of heroin
or morphine here in
ventral tegmental area has
rewarding effects

Figure 11.6   The role of opiate-containing interneurons in the ventral tegmental area

However, not all evidence is consistent with the idea that the dopaminergic link between the VTA and nucleus accumbens is responsible for producing the rewarding effects of opiates. For example, heroin self-administration is not blocked by dopaminergic antagonists given in doses that block cocaine self-administration (Ettenberg *et al.* 1982). Moreover, large 6-hydrodopamine lesions of the VTA and nucleus accumbens have relatively little effect on the acquisition of heroin self-administration. Indeed, in one study, Pettit *et al.* (1984) trained rats to self-administer cocaine and heroin on alternate days, then they lesioned the nucleus accumbens. Although this lesion completely abolished cocaine self-stimulation, it had little effect on heroin self-administration.

Curiously, although dopamine-depleting lesions of the nucleus accumbens have little effect on blocking opiate reinforcement, heroin self-administration is abolished by kainic acid lesions. This is a neurotoxin that destroys all cell bodies (not just dopaminergic types), but leaves fibres of passage (axons) intact. Moreover, heroin self-administration is abolished by similar lesions of the **ventral pallidum**, an area that receives input from the nucleus accumbens (in turn, the ventral pallidum is known to project to the mediodorsal nucleus of the thalamus and then to the frontal and cingulate cortex – other areas known to be involved in reward). The fact that the nucleus accumbens contains mu receptors, and that animals will self-administer opiates into this structure, indicates that the nucleus accumbens link with the ventral pallidum is important. These results show that neural elements in both the VTA and nucleus accumbens are likely to be responsible for the reinforcing effects of the opiates, and involve both dopaminergic and non-dopaminergic pathways (Koob and Bloom 1988).

What is meant by addiction?

The term 'addiction' (Addictus was actually a citizen of ancient Rome who was forced into slavery because of his debts) first began to be associated with drug use in the late nineteenth century, when the temperance and anti-opium movements used it as a replacement for words such as 'intemperance' and 'inebriety'. Around the same time, alcohol and opiate misuse also began to be viewed not as a moral issue or weakness of character, but as a medical problem that led to the user developing tolerance to the drug, suffering withdrawal symptoms and experiencing strong cravings. It is perhaps not surprising, therefore, that from the outset these were taken as the defining features of addiction. Although most drug workers now prefer the term 'drug dependence' and have expanded the concept to include out-of-control use (e.g. a person can be said to be dependent if he or she takes more drug than originally intended, continues to use despite serious personal risk, or returns to drug abuse after long terms of abstinence), tolerance, withdrawal and craving are still regarded as key features of dependence by the World Health Organisation and the American Psychiatric Association.

Traditionally, alcohol and opiate addiction has been explained in terms of physical dependence. That is, individuals continue drug-taking behaviour in order to avoid the unpleasant effects of withdrawal symptoms. This concept of addiction views tolerance, withdrawal and craving as inevitable consequences of taking particular drugs, which in turn force addicts to behave in certain ways. However, it is now recognised that psychological dependence is a more important determinant of drug-taking. That is, people abuse drugs for a variety of reasons and continue taking them not because of withdrawal symptoms but because of the pleasurable, habitual or comforting effects they produce. This also implies that the causes of addiction lie more with the personality (set) and environment (setting) of the user than with the actual drug itself. A contentious and extreme way of putting this is to say that there is no such thing as addicting drugs – only addictive personalities and situations.

Biological tolerance

Drug tolerance occurs when the body has become so adapted to the presence of a drug that a given amount of that substance will produce less of an effect than when the user first tried it (or, put another way, it requires a higher dose to repeat the initial effect). For example, many of us will remember the highly intoxicating (and probably embarrassing) effect of our first ever alcoholic drink – although with practice this effect gets less and less. Indeed, an alcoholic is often able to drink prodigious amounts of alcohol without becoming sick, somnolent, or inebriated. The opiates are another group of drugs that produce tolerance. In fact, it is possible for a heroin addict, after several months of heavy intravenous use, to be able to self-administer 40 to 50 times the normal lethal dose. The same effect is also seen in monkeys when allowed free access to heroin (Griffiths *et al.* 1980).

When a drug is administered over a long period of time, a number of adaptive biological changes are likely to occur in the body. One type of change that can take place is **pharmacokinetic** (or biodispositional) tolerance. This occurs when a drug's potency is reduced because smaller amounts of it reach the site at which it exerts its pharmacological effect (e.g. receptors). For example, the rate at which a drug is metabolised may be increased, and this takes place with alcohol consumption, when the liver increases its production of certain enzymes such as **alcohol dehydrogenase** that speed up its metabolism of alcohol. Another form of tolerance is **pharmacodynamic** tolerance, which occurs when the efficiency by which a drug carries out its mechanism of action is reduced. For example, if a drug is binding to a neurotransmitter receptor to produce its effect, the neuron may compensate for this increased activity by decreasing the number of receptors (down-regulation). Thus, more drug will be needed to produce the same effect. Another type of pharmacodynamic tolerance is receptor desensitisation, which results from phosphorylation (a change in the shape of proteins) of certain components of the receptor, thereby altering its ability to produce second messengers. Indeed, morphine may produce some of its pharmacodynamic tolerance by inhibiting adenylate cyclase (an enzyme that catalyses ATP into the second messenger cAMP). And, in response to the adenylate cyclase inhibition, the cAMP system becomes up-regulated in many areas of the brain, including the locus coeruleus (see below).

Behavioural tolerance

It may come as a surprise to discover that biological factors do not fully account for tolerance. Behavioural tolerance occurs when there is a reduction in the potency of a drug due to a change in the behaviour of the user – especially in anticipation of the possibility of adverse effects. This can be seen when heavy alcohol consumption produces motor dysfunction that the alcoholic can anticipate and modify. For example, when alcoholics begin to stagger and sway, they may begin to walk with their feet wider apart to maintain better balance. Thus, they adapt their behaviour to reduce the effects of the drug's action. This type of effect has also been demonstrated in animals. For example, in one study, rats were given injections of alcohol, then placed on a moving treadmill that required constant motor coordination (Wenger *et al.* 1981). In this condition, it was found that the rats quickly became tolerant to the effects of alcohol on subsequent days of testing. However, if the rats were given alcohol *after* each trial of treadmill training, they showed no tolerance (motor coordination) to alcohol when it was later given prior to the task. Clearly, learning to maintain coordination under the influence of alcohol was the crucial factor in developing this form of tolerance.

Another important factor contributing to tolerance is the environment in which the drug is taken. This was demonstrated by Le *et al.* (1979), who examined the effects of alcohol on lowering body temperature (hypothermia) in rats.

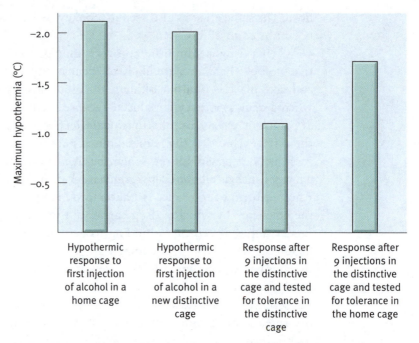

Figure 11.7   The situational specificity of tolerance to the hypothermic effects of alcohol. *Source*: Adapted from A.D. Le *et al.*, *Science* (1979), **206**, 1109–10

As expected, the administration of alcohol led to a decrease in body temperature, which became less severe over subsequent days with repeated injections (i.e. the rats became tolerant to the hypothermic effect of alcohol). However, when the animals were given alcohol in a different room, the tolerant effect was lost and a decrease in body temperature occurred, similar to that found in the first days of the study. In other words, the tolerance was associated with a particular testing room. This finding may have relevance for understanding certain aspects of human drug taking behaviour. For example, Siegel (1984) interviewed 10 heroin users who had been hospitalised for an overdose and found that several had taken the drug in a new environment. The implication, therefore, is that this reduced the addict's tolerance to the drug – similar to the rats described above.

It is clear that learning and environmental factors play an important role in the development of drug tolerance. But how can these effects be explained? According to Siegel the process comes about through Pavlovian conditioning (Siegel 1976). Pavlov was a physiologist who won a Nobel prize in 1904 for his work on digestion, and part of this work involved giving dogs food to elicit salivation. In Pavlovian terminology, the food was viewed as the unconditioned stimulus (UCS), and salivation as the 'unlearned' or unconditioned response (UCR). However, Pavlov also discovered that when he paired the food (UCS) with the sound of a bell (the conditioned stimulus or CS) for several trials, the bell alone would elicit salivation (now the conditioned response or CR). That is, the dog had learned that the bell was associated with food, and it produced salivation in anticipation of being fed.

According to Siegel, drug tolerance can develop through a similar process, although one that differs in some respects from Pavlov's formulation. Consistent with Pavlovian conditioning, Siegel argues that the various environmental cues that regularly accompany the use of the drug (e.g. pubs, washrooms, needles) are acting as conditioned stimuli (CSs), which elicit conditioned responses (CRs). However, instead of viewing the CRs as being similar to the intoxicating effects of the drug (as Pavlovian conditioning would predict), Siegel proposes that they act to reduce the drug's impact on the body. Put another way, the environmental cues associated with drug use will, by themselves, produce a form of tolerance – a reaction that Siegel calls a compensatory conditioned response.

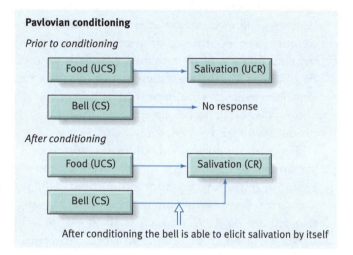

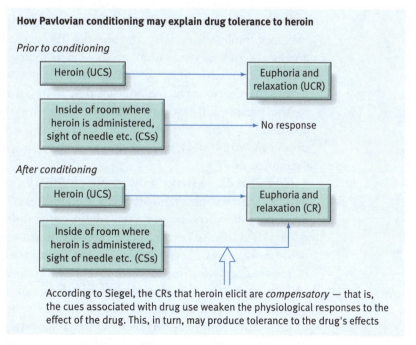

Figure 11.8   The differences between conditioned responses in Pavlovian conditioning and conditioned compensatory responses shown by Siegel

Physical dependence and withdrawal symptons

Physical dependence refers to a state where physiological changes have occurred in the body so that continuation of the drug is necessary for normal functioning, withdrawal symptoms occur when that drug is discontinued. This is otherwise most likely to occur when drug use is abruptly terminated after a long period of time, leading to unpleasant reactions (which are often opposite to the effects produced by the drug) and psychological distress. Some of the most severe withdrawal symptoms are seen following long-term alcohol and opiate use. For example, alcoholics may experience seizures, frightening hallucinations (*delirium tremens*), shaking and anxiety, while heroin addicts can suffer from feelings of illness, muscle aches, hot and cold flushes, pupillary dilation and tremors. The occurrence of withdrawal symptoms is a powerful reason for the continuation of drug-taking, especially as relief from these symptoms can be obtained by the re-administration of the drug. The presence of physical dependence has always been seen as one of the cardinal features of addiction, although it needs to be remembered that not all 'addicting' drugs necessarily produce withdrawal symptoms.

The neurobiological substrates for withdrawal symptoms from opiate use are known to be complex and involve multiple sites throughout the CNS. For example, the abrupt cessation of morphine administration in animals has been shown to decrease dopamine neurotransmission in the nucleus accumbens (Rossetti *et al.* 1992), which is likely to underlie the feelings of dysphoria in the early phase of drug abstinence. However, other areas are responsible for the physical symptoms of withdrawal. For example, Maldonado *et al.* (1992) made rats physically dependent on morphine by the implantation of two morphine pellets. After three days, the experimenters injected an opiate antagonist into several areas of the brain to trigger withdrawal symptoms. These were measured by counting the bouts of wet dog shakes, teeth chattering, mastication, rearing and jumping. The area of the brain that gave rise to the most number of withdrawal symptoms was found to be the locus coeruleus, closely followed by the periaqueductal grey area. Other areas that produced withdrawal symptoms included the nucleus accumbens and medial thalamus.

Considerable evidence now implicates the locus coeruleus in opiate withdrawal. For example, in one study, Rasmussen *et al.* (1990) made rats physically dependent on morphine, and then administered the opiate antagonist naltrexone while simultaneously recording the activity of neurons in the locus coeruleus and behavioural signs of withdrawal. It was found that the withdrawal symptoms increased dramatically after the naltrexone injection, but later decreased in two phases: quickly over 4 hours, then more slowly over 72 hours. Importantly, the neural activity in the locus coeruleus also closely paralleled all these three phases of increasing and decreasing activity. The importance of the locus coeruleus in producing opiate dependence is further supported by evidence showing that lesions of this structure reduce withdrawal symptoms – as does the central administration of clonidine (an alpha-adrenoreceptor agonist), which suppresses neural activity in the locus coeruleus (Koob *et al.* 1992).

However, as with tolerance, there is evidence that environment and psychological factors can also play an important role in producing withdrawal symptoms. This is seen, for example, in cases where heroin users experience strong withdrawal symptoms (such as sweating, nausea and lacrimation) when revisiting an environment where drugs had previously been used or obtained. Indeed, this type of effect may be an important reason why some people re-establish compulsive drug use after quite long periods of abstinence. Conditioning to the positive states produced by drugs has also been observed in experimental animals. For example, stimuli associated with drugs of abuse can cause operant responding in rats and monkeys when presented without the drug. Moreover, when neutral stimuli are paired with naloxone in morphine-dependent animals, the stimuli alone can come to elicit signs of opiate withdrawal (Koob 1999).

The importance of the environment on drug-taking can be seen from studies of servicemen in the Vietnam War. For example, during the late 1960s and early 1970s it was estimated that around 35 per cent of enlisted men were using heroin in Vietnam, with about half of this number showing dependence. In response to these findings, the US army set up treatment centres in Vietnam, although they achieved relatively little success (Zinberg 1984). This situation led to widespread fears that the servicemen would take their opiate problem back home with them. However, surveys found that few servicemen continued taking heroin on return to the USA. Thus, it was the unpleasant and stressful experience of Vietnam that probably led many of the men to use heroin – and when this situation was alleviated, their drug use ended.

Other commonly abused drugs

Virtually all drugs that cause dependence in people are also rewarding for laboratory animals. This can be demonstrated by the fact that animals will self-administer exactly the same type of substances that are potential drugs of abuse for humans. For example, as seen above, animals will work tirelessly to self-administer cocaine and heroin, which are two highly addictive drugs for humans. But, the antipsychotic drug chlorpromazine is not abused by humans, nor is it self-administered by monkeys. Similarly, hallucinogens such as LSD are rarely self-injected by animals, and it is also rare to see dependence to these type of drugs occurring in humans.

Why then are some drugs liable to cause addiction? Part of the answer is that all drugs that have significant dependence liability, including cocaine, heroin, alcohol and nicotine (and to a lesser extent caffeine and cannabis), are known to increase the release of dopamine in the nucleus accumbens. Indeed, this has led some investigators to suggest that dopamine in the nucleus accumbens may be the final common neurotransmitter in drug reinforcement (Bozarth and Wise 1986, Di Chiarra and Imperato 1988). However, although the nucleus accumbens is undoubtedly an important neural substrate for drug use, it is not the only one. For example, we should not forget that opiates can produce their rewarding effects independent of dopamine (as shown by the fact that lesions of the nucleus accumbens fails to stop intravenous heroin administration), and that cocaine is also self-administered into the prefrontal cortex. Thus, although there is a good deal of evidence to show that the nucleus accumbens is crucially involved in the rewarding effects of addictive drugs, it is too simple to regard this as the only mechanism.

Alcohol

In Western society, alcohol is a commonly used drug. It has been estimated that approximately 75 per cent of the population drink alcohol at least occasionally, with 25 per cent of men and 15 per cent of women regularly drinking more than is considered 'safe' (Hughes 1991). Although there are many different types of alcohol, the substance we drink is called ethanol (or ethyl alcohol) and is produced by the distillation and fermentation of sugar. Ethanol is a very small molecule, soluble in both water and fat, which allows it to cross cell membranes and travel freely throughout the body. It is generally agreed that in a fasting individual, 20 to 25 per cent of alcohol in a drink is absorbed from the stomach, and 75 to 80 per cent is absorbed from the small intestine, with peak blood alcohol concentrations occuring some 30 to 60 minutes after ingestion, (although it may take much longer in people who have dined). Although there is considerable individual variation, the average person is able to metabolise approximately 15 ml of alcohol per hour regardless of blood concentration, which is roughly equivalent to a 'standard' drink (half a pint of beer, a glass of wine, or a single shot of spirits).

Alcohol is a depressant of the CNS whose net effect is to depress neural firing. However, unlike most other psychoactive substances, alcohol does not bind directly to receptors or uptake mechanisms, but exerts its main effect by dissolving in the outer membrane of cells. This increases the fluidity of the membrane, which, in turn, alters its function. One type of structure – which is located in the membrane that is particularly affected by alcohol – are the ion channels, which allow the transport of positively and negatively charged particles in and out of the neuron. For example, alcohol has been shown to decrease (1) the influx of calcium into nerve endings, which reduces neurotransmitter release, and (2) the flow of sodium into the dendrites and cell body, thereby inhibiting neural excitability. Alcohol also exerts an important effect on certain receptors that are closely linked with ion channels. For example, alcohol enhances the effects of GABA at its receptor, which leads to an increased flow of negative chloride ions into the cell. This is believed to be an important mechanism by which alcohol causes neural inhibition. In addition, alcohol has the opposite effect on the N-methyl-D-aspartate (NMDA) receptor, which is sensitive to the excitatory neurotransmitter glutamate. For glutamate receptors to be opened, glycine needs to be present. However, alcohol prevents glycine from executing its normal role, resulting in fewer excitatory calcium ions entering the neuron. This adds to the neural inhibition produced by the increased GABAergic activity.

And, if this wasn't complex enough, there is evidence to show that it might not be alcohol *per se* that produces the most important psychoactive effects, but rather some of its metabolites. For example, alcohol is metabolised by the liver to produce acetaldehyde, which has been found to interact with catecholamines (especially dopamine) in the brain to form opiate-like substances called **tetrahydroisoquinolines** (TIQs). Not only do TIQs act on opiate receptors, but they also stimulate the release of dopamine from nerve endings (Hoffman and Cubeddu 1982). The role of the TIQs in producing the psychoactive effects of alcohol, however, is highly controversial (Blum and Payne 1991).

When alcohol is made available to laboratory animals in their home cages they will drink alcohol, but not in quantities that cause intoxication or dependence (McKim 2003). Animals will consume more alcohol if it is self-administered through a cannula direct into the bloodstream, although the consumption tends to be erratic with periods of use and abstinence. These findings imply a complex effect on the reward systems of the brain. Indeed, it has been found that low doses of alcohol cause the release of dopamine in the nucleus accumbens, but not other dopaminergic regions of the brain – an effect that might help to explain the euphorant effects of alcohol in low doses in humans (Imperato and Di Chiarra 1986). It has also been shown that low doses of alcohol increase the firing rate of neurons in the VTA, although high doses have the opposite effect and cause neural inhibition (Feldman *et al.* 1997). Thus, it appears that the systems of the brain are more sensitive to low doses of alcohol than to higher doses. It is also interesting to note that it is possible to breed strains of mice and rats that have a preference for drinking alcohol, and this behaviour is associated with changes to both dopaminergic and serotonergic systems in the brain (see Chapter 12).

Nicotine

Of all addictive substances, nicotine must rank worldwide as the one that causes the most widespread harm to its users. According to the World Health Organisation, there are 1.1 billion smokers in the world, and 6,000 billion cigarettes are smoked every year. Although many developed countries have seen a decline in smoking in recent years (in the UK, the percentage of men smoking cigarettes fell from 65 per cent in 1978 to around 28 per cent in 1992, resulting in approximately equal numbers of men and women now smoking), the practice is on the increase in many poorer countries of the world. Smoking is also common in young people. About 25 per cent of 11-year-olds have tried smoking, and about 30 per cent of 16-year-olds of both sexes are regular smokers (Gossop 2000). Around 450 children will start smoking every day, and as a group they consume over 1,000 million cigarettes yearly (Robson 1999). By learning to smoke, individuals run the risk of a lifetime habit. Around four male smokers out of five, and more than three female smokers out of five, will consume 15 or more cigarettes a day – roughly one per waking hour. No other substance used by humans is used with such remarkable frequency, and no other drug is associated with such a variety of health problems. Every year at least 100,000 people die prematurely in the UK due to the effects of smoking.

A burning cigarette is a miniature chemical factory with its smoke containing well over 4,500 different compounds. However, by far the most important psychoactive ingredient in tobacco is nicotine, which makes up about 2 per cent of its weight. Nicotine is a poison and about 60 mg injected into a vein would be sufficient to kill a person. The average cigarette contains about 8–9 mg of nicotine, but because most of it is burnt off, the typical smoker only absorbs around 1 mg. When heated in a cigarette, nicotine 'rides' on small particles of tar, and when this mixture gets into the lungs, the nicotine is absorbed quickly through the mucus membranes and carried directly to the heart, from where much of the blood goes straight to the brain. Nicotine reaches the brain in about 8 seconds after the smoke is inhaled. It also stays in the brain for a considerable length of time with about 50 per cent of the dose taking 20 to 40 minutes to be redistributed to the body. Incredibly, the average smoker administers about 70,000 separate doses of nicotine to the brain every year.

There are two types of receptor for acetylcholine in the body – muscarinic and nicotinic – and, as the name suggests, nicotine acts (as an agonist) on the latter. Because this type of receptor is found in both the somatic and autonomic nervous systems, as well as the brain, the pharmacological effects of nicotine are complex. For example, nicotinic receptors are found at the neuromuscular junction, where nicotine increases muscle tone and the strength of skeletal reflexes. Nicotine also affects the sympathetic nervous system, where it stimulates heart rate and constricts blood vessels in the skin. But nicotine's most important effect is in the brain. Nicotinic receptors are found in the cerebral cortex – especially on the terminals of the ascending fibres that project from the reticular formation – and this is probably one reason why nicotine increases cortical arousal and makes the person feel more alert. High numbers of nicotinic receptors are also found in the VTA, nucleus accumbens, striatum and substantia nigra. In particular, nicotine has been shown to have an important effect in the nucleus accumbens, where nicotinic receptors are found presynaptically on the axon endings arising from the VTA. These receptors help to control the release of dopamine. Indeed, nicotine has been shown to increase the release of dopamine in the nucleus accumbens at plasma concentrations that are similar to those found in smokers – although to a lesser degree than those that occur with cocaine or heroin (Di Chiarra and Imperato 1988). In addition, it has been found that administration of dopaminergic antagonists, or lesions of the nucleus accumbens, reduce (but not abolish) the effects of nicotine self-stimulation in rats.

LSD and the last trip of Timothy Leary

The person who best epitomises the drug scene of the 1960s is Timothy Leary, who gained notoriety for his attempts to encourage the use of lysergic acid diethylamide (LSD). Described as 'the most dangerous man in America' by President Richard Nixon, Leary claimed to have taken over 5,000 doses of LSD, and coined the phrase 'Turn on, tune in, and drop out'. Leary was a psychology professor at Harvard University who first tried hallucinogenic mushrooms on vacation in Mexico. Upon his return to Harvard in 1960, he tested the effects of LSD on graduate students. Leary believed that LSD offered a way of replacing conventional psychotherapy, and could be used to treat alcoholics and reform convicted criminals. Indeed, many of his subjects reported profound spiritual experiences from their drug use, although others were to suffer bad trips, flashbacks and psychological damage. However bizarre he was on occasion, Leary was sincere in his promotion of LSD as a means of psychological revelation. Nonetheless, Leary (along with colleague Richard Alpert) were the first professors to be fired from Harvard in 1963 – an event that bought them great publicity. The two relocated to a 4,000-acre estate with a 64-room mansion in New York called Millbrook to continue research. However, LSD was made illegal in 1965, and police raids bought an end to Millbrook in 1966. Nonetheless, by this time, *LIFE* magazine had estimated that over a million people had taken LSD, which was seven years sooner than Leary had predicted in 1963.

In 1970, Leary declared himself a candidate for the governor of California, but the campaign was cut short when he was arrested for marijuana possession and sentenced to 20 years (the longest sentence ever imposed for such an offence). When he arrived in prison he was given a standard psychological test used to assign inmates to work placements. Having written the test himself, Leary was able to give the answers that secured him a job in the prison library. In any case, his prison stay was short-lived when he escaped and fled to Algiers. In 1971, he moved to Switzerland, where he lived for 18 months before going to Afghanistan. It was here, in early 1973, that Leary was kidnapped at gun point by American agents, who took him back to the USA, where he spent three more years in jail. During the 1980s, Leary began to embrace the new computer revolution. He formed a software company and marketed a number of successful video games. He died at the age of 75 years from prostrate cancer, surrounded by friends, and his last words were 'why not?' In 1997, some of Leary's ashes were launched into space, along with the ashes of 23 others, including Gene Roddenberry, the creator of *Star Trek*. It is estimated that they orbited the earth every 90 minutes for approximately two years, before they burned up on re-entry. Some would say it was Leary's ultimate trip.

LSD was first synthesised by Albert Hoffman in 1938, who derived it from a fungus called 'ergot' that grows on rye. The mechanism by which LSD acts on the brain is only partially understood. Structurally, LSD is similar to serotonin (5-HT) and has both agonist and antagonist effects on many different types of 5-HT receptor. LSD's potency to cause hallucinations is believed to be largely due to its ability to block $5\text{-}HT_2$ receptors, which are found in high numbers in the neocortex and limbic system. Through an indirect action on this receptor, LSD also leads to increased activity in the locus coeruleus, which may enhance the effects of sensory stimulation. In addition, LSD causes very strong inhibition of the dorsal raphe by inhibiting $5\text{-}HT_{1A}$ receptors located there, which causes a marked reduction of 5-HT release from axon endings in many forebrain areas.

Cannabis

Cannabis is one of the world's most commonly used drugs. There are approximately 300 million users worldwide with about 15 million of these in the UK. This makes cannabis by far the most widely used illegal drug in the UK, and during the 1990s it accounted for around 80 per cent of all drug convictions, and 90 per cent of all seizures by HM Customs and Excise. At the time of writing (January 2004), cannabis has just been reclassified from a class B drug under the Misuse of Drugs Act (1971) to class C, making penalties for its possession less punitive – which, if anything, will increase its use even more. Cannabis is generally derived from the *Cannabis sativa* plant (otherwise known as hemp), which has historically been used to make cloth and paper, and was the most important source of rope until the development of synthetic fibres. Its use as a drug of intoxication is a relatively recent phenomenon, and is said to have been introduced into Western Europe by Napoleon's soldiers returning from their Egyptian campaigns in the late eighteenth century. Curiously, although cannabis had been cultivated for many centuries in Europe, its inebriating effects were largely unknown. This may be because plants with more intoxicating properties grow better in hot, sunny climates.

Smoking cannabis can produce a wide variety of effects, including euphoria, reduction of fatigue and relief of tension. It also increases appetite, slows down the sense of time, relaxes some inhibitions and increases self-confidence. A heightened awareness of colour and aesthetic beauty, and the production of rich and novel mental associations, are also commonly reported. Some users even report that the cannabis experience can be 'psychedelic', resulting in heightened awareness or consciousness-expanding change in perspective and ideas about life – although it is not such a powerful hallucinogenic drug as LSD. There are many psychoactive ingredients in cannabis, but by far the most important is **delta-9-tetrahydrocannabinol** (THC). This substance is highly lipid (fat) soluble and, not unlike alcohol, will become distributed to all areas of the body depending on the rate of blood flow. Blood levels of THC peak within 15 minutes, with only about 1 per cent of the THC entering the brain at peak blood concentrations. The psychogenic effects typically last for 3–4 hours, and in some cases for much longer as the rate of release of THC from the brain into the blood is quite slow (McKim 2003).

Because THC readily dissolves into lipid (one reason why it is able to cross the blood–brain barrier so rapidly) it was once thought that cannabis acted on the brain much like alcohol, that is by seeping into the neural membrane. However, in 1990, the first cannabinoid receptor was discovered (Matsuda *et al.* 1990) and was shown to have a widespread distribution in the brain (Herkenham *et al.* 1991). It is now known that the body contains two types of cannabinoid receptor (CB1 and CB2), with the former being found predominantly in the CNS, and the latter in the periphery, The discovery of cannabinoid receptors also implied that the brain contained its own endogenous cannabis-type substances, and one such agent – called **anadamide**, derived from the Sanskrit word for bliss (Devane *et al.* 1992) – was soon discovered.

Pharmacological research shows that stimulation of cannibinoid receptors in the brain with THC (or other cannabinoid agonists) produces a variety of behavioural effects including hypothermia, analgesia, decreased motor activity and catalepsy. In addition, THC has been shown to increase levels of dopamine in the brain, including the nucleus accumbens (Gardner and Vorel 1998), which presumably underlies its rewarding effects.

The mechanism by which THC increases dopamine release in the nucleus accumbens has yet to be fully elucidated. Although there are relatively few cannabinoid receptors in the VTA, it has been shown that injections of THC cause the excitation of tegmental neurons, including those projecting to the nucleus accumbens. One explanation is that THC inhibits GABAergic inter-neurons in the VTA, which then frees the dopaminergic neurons from their normal inhibition (Szabo *et al.* 2002). As we have seen above, opiates have been shown to stimulate nucleus accumbens release through a similar mechanism. Interestingly, THC's effect on the nucleus accumbens is blocked by injections of the opiate antagonist naloxone, indicating that cannabinoids may be increasing dopamine release through the release of opioids. It has also been shown that drugs which block the cannabanoid CB1 receptor reduce heroin self-administration and lessen dopamine release in the nucleus accumbens (Navarro *et al.* 2001). These findings indicate that the rewarding effects of THC are dependent on opiate–cannabinoid interactions in the brain. Although these remain to be clarified, it is relevant to note that opiate and cannabinoid receptors are structurally similar, have overlapping neuroanatomical distributions in the brain, and both produce their neurochemical effects by inhibiting adenylate cyclase in neurons.

Caffeine

Caffeine belongs to a class of drugs known as the methlyxanthines and is found in some of our most popular beverages and foods, including coffee, tea, fizzy drinks and chocolate. More than 80 per cent of the world's population, regard-less of age, gender, and culture, consume caffeine daily, which makes it by far the most popular drug in the world. It has been estimated that the world uses 120,000 tons of caffeine per annum, with the average cup of coffee containing about 100 mg of caffeine (tea tends to contain less caffeine but its content can be highly variable). In the UK, people consume around 400 mg per person per day, with over half of this being in the form of tea (Nehlig 1999). Although widely perceived as harmless, it has nevertheless been argued that caffeine is the 'model drug of abuse' (Holtzman 1990). For example, caffeine can produce self-administration in laboratory animals, although its use tends to be irregular and the level of responding far less than that maintained by amphetamine or cocaine (McKim 2003). Caffeine can also produce physical dependence, which leads to withdrawal symptoms including headache, fatigue and drowsiness after non-use. Although withdrawal has been reported from consumption of as little as 100 mg per day, it is far more common in people who regularly take 300 mg or more. There is also evidence that tolerance to caffeine can occur, with heavy drinkers of coffee being more resistant to its adverse effects (e.g. jitteriness, nervousness and upset stomach) than non-drinkers.

The means by which caffeine produces its behavioural effects are still not fully understood. One effect of caffeine is as a phosphodiesterase inhibitor. Phosphodiesterase is an enzyme that controls the level of the second messenger cAMP in certain cells (especially those using noradrenaline in the autonomic nervous system) and this inhibition is known to cause cardiac stimulation and bronchodilation. However, very high doses of caffeine are needed to inhibit phosphodiesterase, and it is now widely believed that caffeine is more likely to exert its biological effects by blocking **adenosine** receptors. Adenosine is an inhibitory neurotransmitter, and its receptors are found presynaptically on neurons in the brain, where they inhibit the release of a wide range of neuro-transmitters, including acetylcholine and dopamine. Thus, by blocking adenosine receptors, caffeine enhances the release of these neurotransmitters. However, the effect appears to be biphasic on dopaminergic neurons, with low levels of caffeine increasing neurotransmitter release and higher doses decreasing it (Garrett and Griffiths 1997). Thus, small doses of caffeine may stimulate the dopaminergic reward systems of the brain – a hypothesis that is supported by the finding that caffeine can enhance low-dose cocaine self-administration. Moreover, caffeine can also reinstate the self-administration response that was previously maintained by cocaine (Daly and Fredholm 1998).

Despite this, the acute administration of caffeine does not lead to a release of dopamine in the nucleus accumbens unless very high doses (about five times higher than the mean human daily consumption) are used. In fact, such a high dose also activates many other brain regions (Nehlig 1999). Thus, if caffeine has any effect on the reward systems of the brain, it is probably relatively minor. It may well be that people consume caffeine more for its ability to enhance wakefulness than for its rewarding effects.

Summary

Drug addiction is one of the biggest problems facing society today. The discovery that the brain contains neural systems that mediate responses to **reward** (and **punishment**) was made accidentally by James Olds and his research student Peter Milner in 1954, who demonstrated that rats worked hard (i.e. pressed an operant lever) to obtain electrical **self-stimulation** of the brain. A large array of brain sites give rise to self-stimulation, although most contribute to the **medial forebrain bundle** (MFB) – a large bidirectional multisynaptic pathway that connects regions of the **forebrain** with the **midbrain**. Initially, it was thought that the **lateral hypothalamus** was the final common terminus for reward messages travelling in the MFB. This view has changed, and it is now known that the MFB mediates reward more by its influence on midbrain **dopamine**-containing neurons in the **ventral tegmental area** (VTA), including those that project to the **nucleus accumbens** (located in the **ventral striatum**) and **medial prefrontal cortex**. Evidence supporting the role of dopamine in reward has come from experiments where animals self-administer drugs. For example, rats and monkeys will lever press to receive an injection of **cocaine**, which is a potent blocker of dopamine re-uptake. The **nucleus accumbens** is a critical structure in cocaine's rewarding effects as injections of dopaminergic antagonists into this structure greatly reduce self-stimulation. Further support for the pivotal role of the nucleus accumbens in reward has come from understanding how **opiate** drugs such as **heroin** work in the brain. The rewarding effects of these drugs work by acting on **opiate receptors** that are located on **GABA interneurons** in the VTA. In turn, this reduces the inhibition on tegmental dopaminergic neurons, causing increased dopamine release in the nucleus accumbens. Many other drugs of abuse – including **alcohol**, **nicotine** and **marijuana** – are also known to influence, at least in part, the dopaminergic reward pathways of the brain.

Traditionally, the concept of addiction has been explained in terms of **physical dependence**, with addicts being compelled to continue and increase their drug use in order to avoid the unpleasant effects of **withdrawal symptoms**. However, more recently, it has been recognised that **psychological dependence** is an equally, if not more, important determinant of drug-taking. When a person administers a drug over a long period of time, he or she is likely to show **tolerance** to some of its effects. This tolerance may be **biological** (i.e. the drug is metabolised more quickly, or adaptive changes take place in the nervous system), or it can be **behavioural** (i.e. the tolerance is learned). An example of behavioural tolerance is seen when a rat is administered with an opiate over several weeks in the same test cage, and then injected in a new environment. This procedure restores the initial (non-tolerant) drug effect and can result in overdose. According to Siegal, this form of tolerance occurs because environmental cues produce a **conditioned compensatory response** (similar to a conditioned response in **classical conditioning**) that lessens the effects of the drug. Environmental factors are also known to affect the severity of withdrawal symptons. This was seen, for example, in US servicemen returning from the Vietnam War. It was estimated that about one-third of servicemen used heroin in Vietnam, with many physically addicted to it, although few continued their drug habit when they returned home. This indicates that **set** (personality variables) and **setting** (the environment), as well as the biological effects of the drug on the brain, are all important determinants of drug-taking and addiction.

Essay questions

1. What is the medial forebrain bundle? Discuss evidence for and against its involvement in reward.

    Helpful Internet search terms: *Medial forebrain bundle. Reward pathways in the brain. Stimulation of the MFB. Pleasure centres in the brain. MFB and reward.*

2. Review the evidence showing that the brain's dopamine pathways are critically involved in pleasure and reward.

    Helpful Internet search terms: *Dopamine pathways. Nucleus accumbens. Dopamine and reward. VTA and reward. Effects of DA antagonists on self-stimulation.*

3. What are the differences and similarities in the action of cocaine and heroin on the brain's reward systems? Do all addictive drugs work by causing the release of dopamine in the nucleus accumbens?

    Helpful Internet search terms: *Heroin and nucleus accumbens. Opiates and dopamine. Cocaine and the brain. Nicotine and dopamine. Alcohol and nucleus accumbens. Rewarding self-stimulation.*

4. In what ways have learning and conditioning been shown to be important determinants of drug tolerance?

    Helpful Internet search terms: *Drug tolerance. Conditioned compensatory response. Addiction and tolerance. Classical conditioning of drug action. Neurobiology of addiction.*

Further reading

Engel, J. and Oreland, L. (eds) (1987) *Brain Reward Systems and Abuse*. New York: Raven Press. A book whose authors tend to emphasise the importance of transmitter systems, and receptors, in the reward systems of the brain for understanding drug abuse.

Diaz, J. (1997) *How Drugs Influence Behavior*. New Jersey: Prentice Hall. A concise but well-written account that focuses mainly on drugs of abuse, and how they work on neuropharmacological mechanisms to influence behaviour.

Feldman, R.S., Meyer, J.S. and Quenzer, L.F. (1997) *Principles of Neuropsychopharmacology*. Sunderland, MA: Sinauer. A comprehensive and indispensable textbook that has sections on neurotransmitter systems, drugs of abuse, and clinical disorders.

Goldstein, A. (1993) *Biology of Addiction: From Biology to Drug Policy*. New York: Freeman. This book discusses all the main classes of addictive drugs, how each affects brain chemistry, and how they can lead to physical and behavioural dependence.

Goudie, A.J. and Emmett-Oglesby, M.W. (eds) (1989) *Psychoactive Drugs: Tolerance and Sensitization*. Clifton, NJ: Humana Press. A good coverage of the behavioural and molecular mechanisms that contribute to drug tolerance.

Grilly, D.M. (1998) *Drugs and Human Behavior*. Boston: Allyn & Bacon. A textbook that provides an introduction to psychopharmacology, with an emphasis on how drugs work on the nervous system.

Korenman, S.G. and Barchas, J.D. (eds) (1993) *Biological Basis of Substance Abuse*. Oxford: Oxford University Press. A multidisciplinary approach to drug abuse, including its cell biology, neural basis, neuropharmacology, genetics, behavioural aspects and pharmacological treatment.

Liebman, J.M. and Cooper, S.J. (eds) (1989) *The Neuropharmacological Basis of Reward*. Oxford: Oxford University Press. A series of chapters written by various experts that still provides the best overall coverage of the anatomical, neurochemical and behavioural characteristics of the brain's reward systems.

Lowinson, J.H., Ruiz, P. and Millman, R.B. (1996) *Substance Abuse: A Comprehensive Textbook*. Baltimore: Williams & Wilkins. A large book of over 1,000 pages written by various experts with sections on determinants of substance abuse (eight chapters), and drugs of abuse (17 chapters).

McKim, W.A. (2003) *Drugs and Behavior*. New Jersey: Prentice Hall. An excellent introductory textbook that adopts a multidisciplinary approach to understanding drug use, including a good coverage of animal models of self-administration.

Niesink, R.J.M., Jaspers, R.M.A., Kornet, L.M.W. and van Ree, J.M. (eds) (1999) *Drugs of Abuse and Addiction: Neurobehavioral Toxicology*. Boca Raton, FL: CRC Press. Despite its unusual title, this book contains many chapters of interest, including those on genetic factors, reward systems, molecular mechanisms of addictive substances and new treatment strategies.

Tyler, A. (1995) *Street Drugs*. London: Coronet Books. A highly informative book that offers sane, balanced, impartial advice and information about drugs of abuse. It should be compulsory reading for everyone – not just university students.

See website at www.pearsoned.co.uk/wickens for further resources including multiple choice questions.

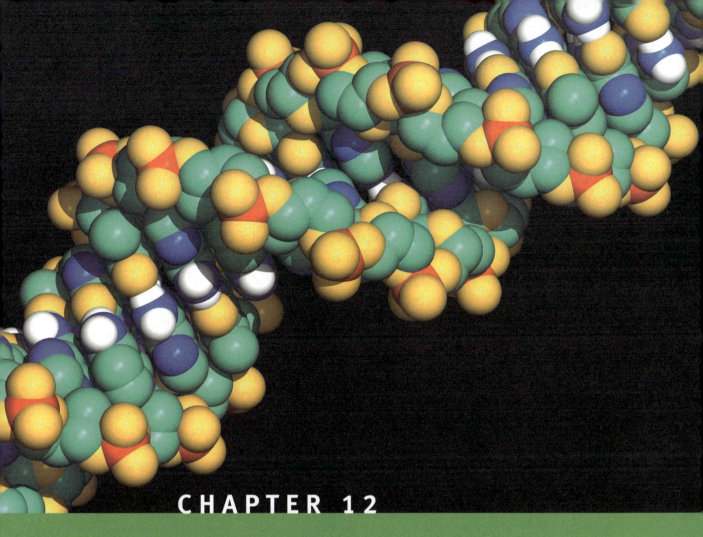

CHAPTER 12

Genes and behaviour

In this chapter

- Darwin's theory of evolution

- The biological basis of inheritance

- How genes produce proteins

- The effects of nature and nurture on behaviour

- Behavioural genetic approaches to understanding alcoholism

- Recombinant DNA and the use of transgenic animals

INTRODUCTION

A fundamental assumption of biological psychology is that the physical structure of the brain (i.e. its anatomy, physiology, neurochemistry, etc.), and its functioning (through the activity of neurons), ultimately produces behaviour. Although we have focused on examining the brain's function throughout much of this book, we must not forget that the main architects of the brain's structure are its genes. Human beings have evolved over millions of years, and during this time have developed a genome that contains 23 pairs of chromosomes, which hold around 30,000 genes. These genes provide the blueprint by which our body (and brains) are made and makes us structurally different to other animals. Obviously, the physical structure of our brain will determine the types of behaviour of which humans are capable. But, of course, we are also unique: we have differently shaped bodies (and brains) and behave individually. What, then, causes this individual variation? There are two main factors. Firstly, although we inherit a shared human genome, the bases making up the structure of its individual genes differ slightly from person to person (apart from identical twins), which means that we are all genetically unique. Secondly, we are all exposed to different environmental influences. In fact, from the moment of our conception, and especially after birth, these two factors continually interact: our genes predisposing us towards certain behaviours, and our environment affecting their expression. The question of how these factors interact, and the relative importance of each to a huge range of behaviour, such as intelligence, alcoholism or homosexuality, is of great interest to the psychologist. But there is more to understanding genes than their impact on complex forms of behaviour. Genes can also go 'wrong', causing illness and degenerative diseases. This, too, is an increasingly important area in biological psychology and has many potential benefits – not least because the development of new treatments may one day help to relieve the suffering of millions.

Darwin and the theory of evolution

The era of modern biology is often said to have begun with Charles Darwin's book *On the Origin of Species by Means of Natural Selection*, first published in 1859. Darwin was just 22 years old when he sailed from England on *HMS Beagle* in 1831. The primary mission of the voyage was to chart the South American coastline, although Darwin's task as the ship's naturalist was to collect new specimens of fauna and flora. During his journey, Darwin was impressed by the great diversity of life he encountered. For example, on the Galapagos Islands he noticed that there were 14 different types of finch, which all shared similar features, yet each bird had a beak that was uniquely adapted to its own particular habitat (and the food source it contained). It was as if all these birds had arisen from a common ancestor but had become slightly modified to enable them to adapt better to their own ecological niche.

This sounds like a perfectly reasonable theory today, but during the nineteenth century it contradicted the teachings of the Bible, which held that all species, including man, had been formed by the divine hand of God, and were unaltered since the time of creation. Darwin's theory was blasphemous as it opposed long-established religious views. Indeed, he knew that his theory would be highly controversial and, partly for that reason, Darwin spent more than 20 years compiling evidence and working on his ideas before daring to publish them (and even then he was prompted by the work of a young naturalist called Alfred Wallace, who was beginning to formulate a similar theory). Nonetheless, the impact of Darwin's work, when published, was profound as it completely changed man's conception of himself in the world. Also, just as importantly, it became widely accepted as one of the great unifying theories of biology.

The suggestion that living things change with time, which is the fundamental notion of evolution, did not originate with Darwin, but he was the first to provide a plausible mechanism by which it could occur. The theory he developed was called natural selection and was based on two simple concepts: competition and variation. The first concept was derived from Darwin's observation that all living creatures appear to provide more offspring than are needed to replace their parents, with the result that there are too many individuals for the resources that exist for them. Yet it was also clear to Darwin that animal populations remain relatively stable and do not expand beyond certain limits. Thus, the consequence of increased numbers of offspring and limited resources must be that all creatures are thrown into competition with each other.

The second aspect of natural selection is that all individuals of a species show great variation in terms of their biological characteristics. For example, as humans we all look similar, but each of us is different in terms of physique, strength, intelligence, etc. The consequence of this variability is that some individuals will be better suited to their environments than others. In turn, the individuals who are best suited will be the ones more likely to reproduce, thereby passing their 'desirable' genes on to their offspring. This became Darwin's principle of selection for which Herbert Spencer coined the term the 'survival of the fittest' (although it would have been more accurate to call it 'reproduction of the fittest'). However, Darwin's most important insight into natural selection was that, over the course of many generations, the selection process would cause great changes to develop in the body form. For example, because ancestral giraffes had a liking for feeding in tall trees, natural selection would favour the development of long necks. Following this argument to its conclusion, it was possible to predict that natural selection would eventually lead to the development of a new species.

Although Darwin described the process of evolution in great detail, he did not explain how inheritance worked. Genes had not been discovered in the nineteenth century, and the lack of knowledge concerning the mechanisms of inheritance was an obstacle to his theory. Ironically the answers to this problem had been formulated in 1865 by Gregor Mendel, a young Augustinian monk living in Bohemia, but the work had not been fully appreciated at the time and was soon forgotten until it was rediscovered around 1890. Mendel's work provided the precise rules of genetic inheritance that Darwin's theory needed to explain how natural selection worked. Sadly, Darwin died in 1882 and never knew of Mendel's research or the true legacy of his ideas to biology.

The work of Gregor Mendel

The idea that transmissible units were the means by which inheritance occurred was first proposed by Gregor Mendel in 1865. Prior to this time, most scientists believed that inheritance was a blending process in which the 'bloods' of the parents were mixed together in their offspring. But Mendel disproved this theory in a series of experiments over an eight-year period that utilised the common garden pea plant. This choice of this plant was fortuitous. Firstly, not only were peas simple to breed (e.g. pea plants have both male and female organs, and it is easy to fertilise any female flower with pollen taken from any male), but it was also possible to cross different plants or self-fertilise the same one. This meant that a variety of breeding experiments could be undertaken. Secondly, the traits that Mendel decided to examine, such as the size of the plant (i.e. tall versus dwarf), the colour of its seed (yellow versus green) or the seed texture (smooth versus wrinkled), were dichotomous – meaning that plants either had one trait or the other; that is, there was no in-between trait. Thus, Mendel avoided many of the complexities associated with animal breeding, where inherited characteristics such as size were not dichotomous. But most important of all, by using dichotomous traits it was easy to count the number of times they occurred in the offspring of selectively bred plants. Although the ratios were simple, they nevertheless enabled Mendel to gain a powerful insight into the mechanism of inheritance.

In one of his studies, Mendel crossed tall plants that were five to six feet in height with dwarfs, which were about one foot in height. The results showed that all the offspring (called the F1 or first filial generation) were tall. In other words, the dwarf plants had disappeared from the new generation. However, when Mendel self-fertilised the tall F1 plants to produce the F2 generation a different set of results were obtained. Although about three-quarters of the F2 offspring turned out to be tall, the rest were dwarf plants. In other words, whatever was responsible for causing shortness had not been lost in the F1 generation after all, but had rather been suppressed by the dominant taller plants. Mendel also obtained similar results with other traits. For example, smooth seeds were dominant over wrinkled; yellow seeds were dominant over green; and red flowers were dominant over white. Furthermore, in this type of experiment, the F1 generation always gave rise to only one type of trait, whereas the F2 generation always gave rise to both traits, but in the ratio of three to one (Figure 12.1). The consistency of these results implied that some fundamental law of inheritance was at work.

How could these findings be explained? To provide an answer, Mendel proposed that each plant contained two 'factors' (i.e. genes) which are responsible for the trait, but only one of these factors is passed on to the offspring from each parent. Thus, although each parent carried two 'genes', it only transmitted one

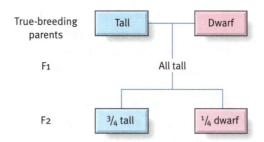

Figure 12.1   The effects of crossing true-breeding pea plants with smooth and wrinkled seeds

to its offspring. But why should some pea plants be tall and others short? To answer this, Mendel suggested that the factors controlling size in pea plants came in more than one form – or what are known today as **alleles** (an example of an allele is the gene that produces eye colour). In other words, although there was only one gene controlling size, this gene came in different forms which meant that the plant size could be either tall or short. But if this was the case then why were all pea plants in the F1 generation tall? Mendel's explanation was that the alleles could also be **dominant** or **recessive**. That is, when two different alleles came together, the allele for tallness would always dominate over the dwarf one.

To better illustrate these principles, assume that Mendel began his experiments by crossing true or **homozygous** tall plants (containing the genes TT) with homozygous dwarf plants (containing dd genes). It can be seen that the reason why all the plants in the F1 generation are tall is because they all contain the **heterozygous** allele combination Td; and because the T allele is always dominant over the d allele, all plants will be tall. But why does the F2 generation always show a mixture of traits in the ratio of 3 : 1? To help to see what happens, refer to Figure 12.2. It can be seen that when the heterozygous F1 hybrids (all containing the allele combination of Td) are crossed together, this throws up

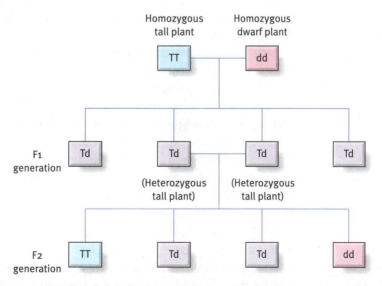

Figure 12.2   The effects of dominant and recessive alleles on the crossing of pea plants

an assortment of allele combinations. Moreover, if each plant can only pass one allele to its progeny, and if this is done in a random fashion, then such a cross will be predicted to produce three types of plants – TT, Td and dd – and in the proportions 1 : 2 : 1. Since T is the dominant allele, then both TT and Td combinations will become tall plants, whereas the dd plant will become a dwarf. In other words, as a result of breeding F1 hybrids, one would expect to obtain three tall plants and one dwarf in the F2 generation.

It should be noted that while all the traits studied by Mendel were caused by a single gene, the vast majority of human traits (although not all – see below) are controlled by many different genes. Furthermore, not all alleles operate in a dominant or recessive fashion. For example, many alleles are additive, meaning that they each contribute something to the offspring, whereas other genes may have interactive effects with each other (or may even cancel each other out). To complicate matters further, the environment can have a powerful effect on the way that many genes are expressed. Nonetheless, Mendel had shown the basic laws of inheritance, and although his work was to lay dormant for over 30 years it was to be proved fundamentally correct.

The chromosomal basis of inheritance

The results of Mendel's work were published in 1866, and his paper was sent to academic institutions throughout the world (a copy of his paper is even believed to have gone to Darwin), but his findings were overlooked and soon forgotten. Despite this, other important breakthroughs were taking place around the same time that were supporting Mendel's conception of genetic inheritance. For example, in 1875 Oskar Hertwig first observed the process of fertilisation (in sea urchin eggs), which involved the fusing together of the **gametes** (sperm and the egg) and, in 1879, Walther Flemming discovered, within the nucleus of the cell, tiny rod-like structures that were made of a material called chromatin (which were later to be called **chromosomes**). It was also shown that chromosomes existed in pairs, which was consistent with Mendel's hypothesis of two separate factors being involved in the process of genetic transmission. This idea was further supported in 1883, when Edouard van Beneden saw the separate chromosomes from sperm and egg mingle together during fertilisation. He also realised that while the cells of the body contained pairs of chromosomes, the egg and sperm were an exception as they contained only half the normal number of chromosomes. However, when the chromosomes came together in the process of fertilisation, they joined up to make new pairs. This again was in accordance with Mendelian theory, which had postulated pairs of genes coming together in fertilisation to produce new progeny.

Finally, in 1900, the importance of Mendel's work was bought to the attention of the scientific community when three scientists (de Vries, Correns and Tschernmak), after discovering the basic 3 : 1 hybrid ratios for themselves,

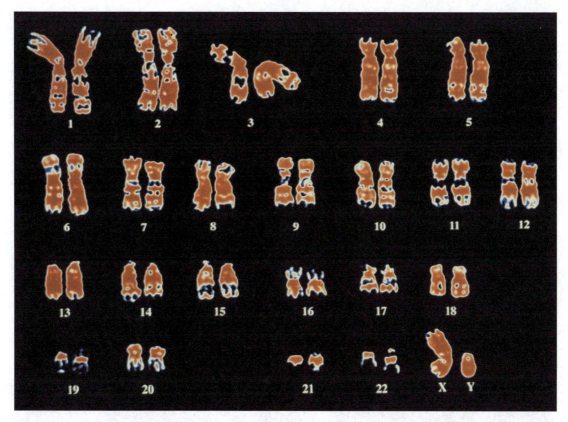

Plate 12.1   The variety of life. The 23 pairs of chromosomes. *Source*: Biophoto Associates/Science Photo Library

independently tracked down the original paper. And, in 1903, the American geneticist Walter Sutton proposed that Mendel's factors (or genes) were located on chromosomes – with inheritance being the result of individual chromosomes from each parent coming together in the fertilised egg. Thus, at long last, the ancient notion that traits were transmitted along 'bloodlines' had been disproved. Instead, it was clear that traits were transmitted by indivisible genetic particles that somehow maintained their identity while being shuffled into new combinations during fertilisation. The secret of life lay with genes.

DNA: the basis of heredity

What do genes look like? To answer this question we must first examine the structure of chromosomes. Chromosomes are long rod-like structures comprising a protein matrix that holds in place a very special chemical called **deoxyribonucleic acid** (DNA), which is coiled up in a tight twisted strand. Although DNA had first been identified by Miescher in 1869 (he had called it nuclein) and was suspected of being involved in genetic transmission, it was not until James

Plate 12.2 James Watson and Francis Crick, discoverers of DNA – probably the most important scientific advance of the twentieth century. *Source*: A. Barrington Brown/Science Photo Library

Watson and Francis Crick (see Plate 12.2) determined the structure of this molecule in 1953 that the secret of genetic transmission was finally solved. For this momentous discovery, which also initiated many new fields of scientific inquiry, Watson and Crick (along with Maurice Wilkins) were to be awarded the Nobel prize in 1962.

DNA is a large molecule made up of two chains (composed of phosphate and a sugar called deoxyribose) that wind around each other in the shape of a double helix. Linking the two strands together as they swivel around each other are pairs of molecules, like rungs of a ladder, known as **bases**. DNA contains four types of base (adenine, guanine, cytosine and thymine) and because these are held together by weak bonds, the two strands making up the DNA can easily 'unzip' and separate into two units. The bases are also very selective with which they form bonds. In fact, adenine can only bond with thymine, and cytosine with guanine. Consequently, when the two strands of DNA unwind and separate, each of the individual 'exposed' bases only acts as a magnet for its own complementary base. If the exposed bases are successful in attracting new partners, then the result will be the construction of a new strand that is identical to the old one. In this way, one molecule is able to transform itself into two molecules. Thus, DNA has the remarkable property of being able to duplicate itself – a vital prerequisite for creating new cells, and ultimately, new organisms (see Figure 12.3).

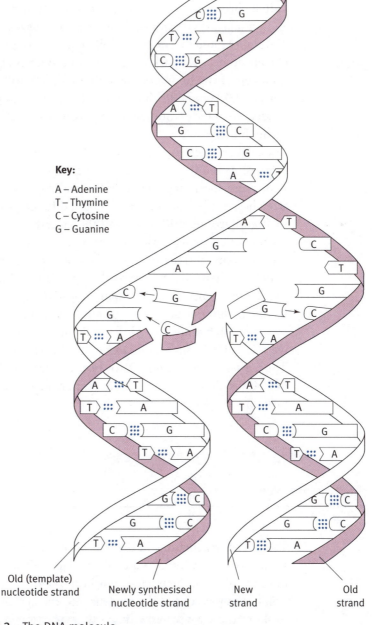

Key:

A – Adenine
T – Thymine
C – Cytosine
G – Guanine

Old (template)
nucleotide strand

Newly synthesised
nucleotide strand

New
strand

Old
strand

Figure 12.3 The DNA molecule

DNA, however, does much more than simply replicate: it also contains the genes that make proteins and enzymes – chemicals that are essential for creating and maintaining life. Genes are essentially long sequences of bases that lie between the two spiralling chains that form the backbone of DNA. As we have seen, the alphabet is very simple and consists of only four bases (which we can label A, T, G and C). Despite this small number of bases, however, there are astronomical numbers of bases on each strand of DNA (or chromosome), making the genetic code very complex. In fact, it has been estimated that the human genome (i.e. the total complement of all 23 pairs of chromosomes) contains over 3,000 million base pairs, which breaks down into approximately 65 million base pairs (A with T and C with G) for each individual chromosome. To put this figure into perspective, the 1969 edition of the *Encyclopaedia Britannica* (which also consists of 23 volumes) contains only 200 million letters – or, put another way, enough information to fill about three chromosomes. Remarkably, to enable over 3,000 million base pairs to exist, each cell of the body contains about six feet of DNA crammed into a nucleus that is 0.005 mm in diameter. This is basically the amount of information needed to build a human being from a single egg, and then to maintain it through life.

Genes are therefore stretches of DNA that contain long strings of bases. It has been estimated that our 23 pairs of chromosomes contain around 30,000 genes, with most specifying the code for making a single protein (see below). These stretches of DNA also come in many different sizes with the smallest gene consisting of around 500 bases and the largest containing over 2 million. But how do the bases provide the blueprint for making proteins? The answer is that certain combinations of bases provide a code by which to make **amino acids**, which are then constructed by the cell to make bigger molecules called proteins. In fact, our genes are only capable of making 20 types of amino acid, although from this limited pool a large number of very complex proteins can be constructed. Each amino acid is actually derived from a code of just three consecutive DNA bases (such as CGA or TGG), which are called **codons** (Table 12.1). Thus, a single gene can perhaps be more accurately described as a long sequence of codons that code for all the amino acids necessary to assemble a specific protein.

Protein synthesis

The coded instructions in the genes for making proteins are stored on chromosomes locked away in the cell's nucleus. However, protein manufacture does not take place in the nucleus but in the cell's cytoplasm. Thus, genetic information has to pass out of the nucleus into the cytoplasm. But how does this occur? In short, the answer lies with another type of nucleic acid called **ribonucleic acid** (RNA). There are three types of RNA, but the one responsible for transporting

Table 12.1   The codons (consecutive triple bases of DNA) by which amino acids are made

Amino acid*	DNA code
Alanine	CGA, CGG, CGT, CGC
Arginine	GCA, GCG, GCT, GCC, TCT, TCC
Asparagine	TTA, TTG
Aspartic acid	CTA, CTG
Cysteine	ACA, ACG
Glutamic acid	CTT, CTC
Glutamine	GTT, GTC
Glycine	CCA, CCG, CCT, CCC
Histidine	GTA, GTG
Isoleucine	TAA, TAG, TAT
Leucine	AAT, AAC, GAA, GAG, GAT, GAC
Lysine	TTT, TTC
Methionine	TAC
Phenylalanine	AAA, AAG
Proline	GGA, GGG, GGT, GGC
Serine	AGA, AGG, AGT, AGC, TCA, TCG
Threonine	TGA, TGG, TGT, TGC
Tryptophan	ACC
Tyrosine	ATA, ATG
Valine	CAA, CAG, CAT, CAC
(Stop signals)	ATT, ATC, ACT

* The 20 amino acids are organic molecules that are linked together by peptide bonds to form polypeptides, which are the building blocks of enzymes and other proteins. The particular combination of amino acids determines the shape and function of the polypeptide.

Source: From Plomin *et al.* (1997) *Behavioral Genetics, 3rd edition.*

the DNA's instructions into the cytoplasm of the cell is called **messenger RNA** (mRNA). In effect, this molecule provides a template of the gene to enable the assembly of amino acids into proteins.

Although RNA is similar to DNA in terms of its chemistry, RNA is much smaller and exists only as a single strand. This enables RNA to move freely in and out of the nucleus, and also provides a template by which transcripts of the much larger DNA molecule can be copied. Once a section of the DNA has been transcribed onto the mRNA, it leaves the nucleus and enters the cytoplasm, where it seeks out a structure called a **ribosome**, which is the site where the assembly of the protein will take place. Ribosomes are spherical structures composed of protein and a type of RNA called **ribosomal RNA** (rRNA). Put simply, rRNA acts to position the mRNA on the ribosome, and once fastened it exposes the mRNA's codons (three-base sequences) one at a time. As this happens, the exposed bases are hooked up with complementary bases, which are brought to the ribosome by yet another type of RNA called **transfer RNA** (tRNA). The tRNA molecule essentially has two components: it has a three-base

(a)

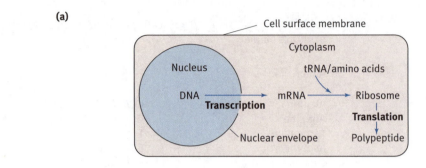

(b)

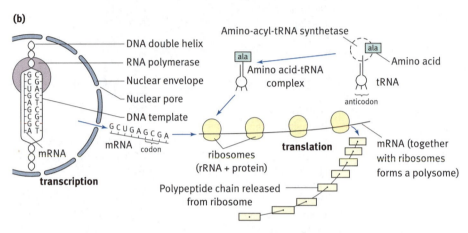

Figure 12.4 The stages of protein synthesis: (a) simplified account; (b) more complex account. *Source*: D.J. Taylor *et al.* (1997) *Biological Science 2*, p.805, fig. 23.32

sequence that allows it to zip onto the mRNA, but it also picks up (using the enzyme amino-acyl-tRNA synthetase) and carries specific amino acids which it finds in the cytoplasm. Thus, tRNA provides the mechanism by which amino acids are transported to the ribosome and fixed onto the mRNA. Once a codon has been filled up (thus adding an amino acid to the growing protein), a peptide bond is created that links the newly formed amino acid to the next one in the chain. After this, the next codon is exposed and the process is repeated until all the bases in the mRNA transcript have been filled. When all the transcripts of the mRNA have been completed and joined together, a protein is made (Figure 12.4).

The construction of a protein is a very efficient process. It has been estimated that amino acids are incorporated into the growing polypeptide chains at a rate of about 100 per second, and it takes less than a minute to make an average protein. Our bodies are continually having to manufacture proteins and it has been estimated that more than 1 million peptide bonds are made *every second* in most cells. This high rate of synthesis is required because the human body contains tens of thousands of different proteins that are continually being broken down and replaced every day.

The Human Genome Project

The Human Genome Project is undoubtedly one of the greatest feats of exploration ever undertaken and was completed in April 2003. Begun in 1990, the Human Genome Project has been an internationally organised research effort involving hundreds of laboratories around the world. Its aim was simple: to determine the complete sequence of the 3,000 million base pairs that make up the human genome (our 23 pairs of chromosomes) and to identify among these bases the exact location of all the genes that define us as human beings. The mapping of the human genome has been an arduous and mammoth task. In effect, it has decoded the famous double helix of deoxribonucleic acid (DNA) which lies embedded in our chromosomes by working out the sequence of its four chemical bases (adenine, thymine, cytosine and guanine) that form the rungs of its twisted ladder-shaped molecule. Genes are simply working stretches of base pairs, arranged in different ways and in different lengths, which are codes for making proteins. One of the most surprising findings of the project is that the number of genes in the human genome is far less than had been believed. Most estimates had previously put the number of genes at around 100,000 although there are now known to be around 30,000. Another surprising fact about our DNA is that only about 5 per cent of it is composed of genes – the rest of it consists of random base sequences which appear to be redundant.

If the DNA sequence of the human genome was ever compiled in a book (it is actually stored in computer databases) it would fill the equivalent of 13 sets of the *Encyclopaedia Britannica*. If one was to read this information from start to finish, it would take 95 years (reading at a rate of one base per second). Remarkably, almost every cell in the human body contains this information – stored in about 6 feet of DNA crammed into a nucleus that is about 0.005 mm in diameter! Also, perhaps even more astonishing – as pointed out by Steve Jones in his book *The Language of the Genes* – if all the DNA in every cell of the human body was stretched out, it would reach to the Moon and back 8,000 times!

Why then are researchers going to such trouble to map the human genome? There are many good reasons. For example, sequencing the structure of genes will enable their identification, and allow doctors to identify the most important ones that contribute to disease. Indeed, when the Human Genome Project started in 1990 scientists had discovered fewer than 100 genes that caused human disease. Today, more than 1,400 disease genes have been identified. This knowledge will help to provide new strategies to diagnose, treat and possibly even prevent human disease. The Human Genome Project is also likely to provide other health benefits. For example, in a few years time, it may be possible to take DNA from a newborn infant and analyse all the main genes that will predispose it to common illnesses such as heart disease, cancer and dementia. From this information, a lifestyle and medical regime could be drawn up that will help individuals to maximise their chances of a long, healthy life. The Human Genome Project will also lead to exciting new advances in explaining the mysteries of embryonic development, and give us important insights into our evolutionary past. Also, psychologists will undoubtedly gain a far greater appreciation of how genes act to produce behaviour, thereby allowing far greater insights into the interaction of nature and nurture. It is certain that knowledge derived from the Human Genome Project will not only dominate human biology and medicine over this millennium but will also have a huge impact on our understanding of the brain and how it produces human behaviour.

The importance of proteins

If we are to appreciate why genes are so important, we have to understand the nature of the molecules they make – namely proteins. These molecules (the word protein is derived from the Greek *proteios* meaning 'of primary importance') are vital constituents of all living things from bacteria to humans. Indeed, without them, life as we know it could not exist. Proteins are essentially large molecules that consist of amino acid chains, but they are much more than this. After the protein has left the ribosome it folds and curls into a shape that is determined by its amino acids. Part of a chain may coil into a helix, other segments lock into rigid rods, and still other parts may form clefts or flexible swivels. In short, proteins become twisted and folded to form a great variety of highly complex three-dimensional shapes. And because they can make so many shapes, they have a wide range of functions. It is estimated that a typical mammalian cell may have as many as 10,000 different proteins, each with its own unique role. Some proteins are used to make ion channels or uptake pumps in the neural membrane, which others form internal structures within the cell. Other proteins provide connective tissue and muscle, or act as carriers that are responsible for transporting chemical substances around the body (e.g. red blood cells). There are also those that form neurochemicals, hormones and antibodies.

The most important function of proteins, however, is their role as enzymes, which act as catalysts in the chemical reactions upon which life depends. Most enzymes are proteins that are folded in such a way as to form a cleft that is exactly the proper shape to bind a small molecule such as sugar. When this chemical binds to the enzyme, it results in a chemical modification (e.g. removal of an oxygen atom) that causes a chemical reaction to be accelerated. It is a simple truth that life is chemistry and in this respect there is hardly a cellular chemical reaction that does not require the presence of an enzyme. In fact, the vast majority of the proteins that are made by our genes are enzymes, which are continuously at work within our cells (and neurons) every second of our lives.

It can be difficult for a psychologist interested in behaviour to scale down to the molecular level to understand the size of proteins. To give some idea of the scale we are talking about, one of the smallest objects to the naked eye is a grain of salt, which is about half a millimetre or 500 microns (500 millionths of a metre) in size. The cell body of an average animal cell is much smaller (between 10 and 30 microns in diameter), and yet this is huge compared with a protein, which may be no more than a few nanometres in length (a nanometre is a thousand-millionth of a metre). Yet, in terms of the molecular world, proteins are large structures, and for this reason they are sometimes called macromolecules. It is interesting to contemplate the many millions of chemical reactions that must be taking place in our neurons to produce even the simplest of behaviour.

Single genes and behaviour

Over 4,000 genetic conditions that are known to affect humans can be caused by a single mutated gene (about 10 per cent of these disorders also result in mental retardation) and most have a significant impact on the person's health. These disorders are inherited in a simple Mendelian fashion and are sometimes referred to as Mendelian diseases. The major impact of many single-gene disorders occurs in the early years of a person's life, and accounts for approximately 5–10 per cent of paediatric hospital admissions and childhood mortality. Although many single-gene disorders are rare, others can be quite common. For example, familial hypercholesterolemia, with its high risk of premature heart disease, occurs in one in 500 individuals. Familial breast cancer and hereditary colon cancer both affect around one in 300, and cystic fibrosis affects around one in 2,000 white people.

Huntington's disease

One single-gene disorder that was mentioned earlier in the book (Chapter 3) is **Huntington's disease** (Figure 12.5), which causes degeneration of the brain (particularly the striatum) leading to progressive deterioration of movement, temperament and cognition. Huntington's disease is an example of **autosomal dominant inheritance**, which means that if a person inherits just one copy of the mutated gene (from either parent), that gene will become dominant and produce the faulty protein that causes the disease. If one parent carries the mutated gene there is a 50 per cent probability of inheriting Huntington's disease, and this can

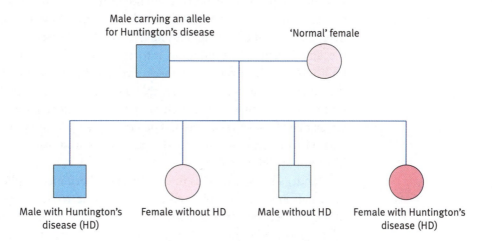

If one parent is a carrier of Huntington's disease then approximately 50 per cent of the offspring will inherit the disease

Figure 12.5   The inheritance of Huntington's disease

be explained by using knowledge of Mendel's laws (see Figure 12.2). For example, if we assume that one parent has a dominant mutated allele along with a recessive normal one (Hh), and the other parent has two normal alleles (hh), then it can be seen that their child may inherit four possible combinations of paired alleles. In short, the offspring will always inherit a normal h allele from the unaffected parent, but will have a 50 per cent chance of inheriting the H allele from the carrier parent. This means that 50 per cent of the possible gene combinations in the offspring will carry the dominant (mutated) gene.

In 1983, the gene for Huntington's disease was narrowed down to a small part of chromosome 4 (Gusella *et al.* 1983), allowing the condition to be detected with a high degree of accuracy, and 10 years later the gene was isolated and analysed (The Huntington's Disease Collaborative Research Group 1993). The cause of the mutation was found to lie with a triple repeat of the bases CAG. Normal chromosomes contain between 11 and 34 copies of this base repeat, but the Huntington's gene was found to contain more than 40 copies. Moreover, it was found that the onset of the disease was correlated with the number of repeats that the gene contained. For example, early onset of Huntington's disease was associated with genes that contained around 60 repeats, whereas later onset (after 65 years) was associated with genes that contained 40 copies of the triple repeat. It also appears that this particular triplet is unstable and can increase in subsequent generations. This phenomenon might explain a non-Mendelian process called 'genetic anticipation' in which symptoms appear at earlier ages and with greater severity in subsequent generations (Plomin *et al.* 1997).

Phenylketonuria

Another single gene defect is **phenylketonuria** (Figure 12.6), which affects about one person in every 10,000. Individuals with this condition do not produce a liver enzyme called phenylalanine hydroxylase, which is responsible for turning the amino acid phenylalanine into tyrosine. The result is that phenylalanine builds up in the liver and passes into the bloodstream. During development this can cause the brain considerable damage. Excess phenylalanine and its toxic by-products reduce brain weight, produce a deficiency of myelin and cause fewer dendrites to be formed. The consequence is a severe mental retardation, with victims generally not learning to speak and normally exhibiting an IQ of less than 20 (Hay 1985).

Mendel's laws also helps to explain the inheritance of phenylketonuria. Unlike Huntington's disease, phenylketonuria is due to an allele that is recessive. In other words, for offspring to be affected they must inherit two copies of the allele. Those who inherit only one copy of the allele are totally unaffected by the disorder, although they remain carriers and can pass it on to their offspring. In fact, about one person in 50 actually carries the phenylketonuria gene, which means that about one in 2,500 couples (50 × 50) have the potential to produce a child with phenylketonuria. However, even assuming that both parents are

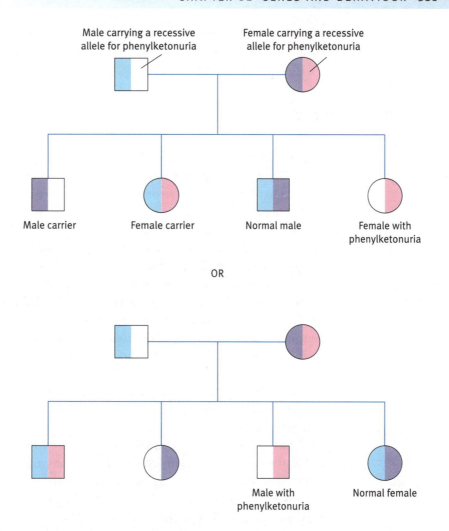

Figure 12.6 The inheritance of phenylketonuria

carriers, they nevertheless have only a 25 per cent possibility of producing a child with this disorder. To understand this point, refer again to Mendelian laws of inheritance (see Figure 12.6). For example, if each parent carries one mutant allele (P) and one normal allele (p), the only combination that will produce phenylketonuria (i.e. PP) will occur with a 1 in 4 probability.

Fortunately, phenylketonuria can be detected soon after birth by a simple blood test that has now become standard practice in hospitals. But even more important is the fact that something can be done about a positive diagnosis. Phenylalanine is one of the 10 essential amino acids that the body cannot manufacture for itself, and consequently the supply of this substance must come from the diet. Thus, by restricting its dietary intake, the build-up of phenylalanine and its metabolic products can be prevented. Indeed, providing the diet is initiated early enough in life and followed, many individuals develop normally and show

IQs of over 100. This example shows that certain human traits can result from complex and subtle interactions between genes and the environment.

X-linked inheritance

The third type of Mendelian inheritance occurs when a faulty (mutated) gene is carried on the X chromosome. As we have seen in Chapter 7, both males and females have 23 pairs of chromosomes, and differ in only one: males inheriting an XY pair of sex chromosomes, and females XX. It follows, therefore, that males always inherit their Y chromosome from the father (XY) because their mother, being XX, has no Y chromosome to pass on. Conversely, a male's X chromosome must always come from the mother. The fact that a woman has two X chromosomes is usually protective against harmful genetic effects. This is because if she has a faulty gene on one of the X chromosomes, a normal gene on the other one will normally counteract its effects. Thus, X-linked recessive conditions are only found in females if there are *two* copies of the gene (one on each X chromosome). In males, however, only one copy of an X-linked gene is required for the trait to be expressed as there will be no dominant allele to counteract its effect on the Y male chromosome. Thus, a woman can unknowingly carry a recessive gene on one of her X chromosomes and pass it on to a son who will express the trait.

X-linked conditions are much more common in boys. If a boy has inherited the X chromosome carrying the mutated gene from his mother, he will express it. In short, if the mother carries a mutation on one of her X chromosomes, the male will have a 50 per cent risk of inheriting it. If a female inherits the recessive gene on one of her X chromosomes, she will be unaffected but will be a carrier. It is possible in theory for a female to inherit an X-linked mutated gene from both her father (he will have the trait in question) and her mother, but this is very rare unless the faulty gene is common in a population. One example is the gene for deficiency of the enzyme glucose-6-phosphate dehydrogenase (G6PD), which is found in certain African-American and Mediterranean populations. But perhaps a better illustration can be seen with cats: for example, the ginger colour in cats is X-linked and most ginger cats are male, but the occasional female ginger cat can be found.

Over 100 genes are known to be X-linked in humans (and more common in males) including red–green colour blindness, Duchenne muscular dystrophy and haemophilia A (see box). Red–green blindness means that a person cannot distinguish shades of red and green, although their visual acuity is normal (see Chapter 2). Although there are no serious complications, affected individuals may be unable to hold certain jobs in transportation or the armed forces if colour recognition is required. Duchenne muscular dystrophy is a disease in which there is progressive weakening of the muscles leading to death at about 20 years. The disease occurs at a rate of 2 per 10,000 male babies. In about two-thirds of cases the gene is inherited from a carrier mother, but in the remainder it arises as a new mutation. Boys with Duchenne muscular dystrophy are never well enough to be fertile, so the gene dies out each time it is manifested in a male, although it can travel indefinitely down generations of females. The gene has been located and found to be exceptionally large, consisting of around 2 million base pairs and accounting for over 1 per cent of the X chromosome. Indeed, it is one of the longest in the human genome. The protein encoded by the gene is called dystrophin and is believed to be involved in muscle contraction. Boys with the mutant gene do not have this protein.

X-linked dominant transmission can also occur, although this type of genetic mutation is fortunately rare. One such condition is hypophosphatemic (or vitamin D-resistant) rickets, characterised by low blood and high urinary phosphate levels, short stature and body deformities. Unlike the pattern seen with the X-linked recessive inheritance, boys and girls both have a 50 per cent chance of being affected by an X-linked dominant illness from one of their parents. These conditions, however, are more common (by a ratio of 2 to 1) in females than in males, as females have an extra X chromosome.

Queen Victoria, haemophilia, Rasputin, and the fall of the Russian royal family

Haemophilia is caused by a faulty gene located on the X chromosome which results in a clotting factor of the blood being either partly or completely missing. Consequently a haemophiliac will bleed for longer than is normal after a cut or injury. The earliest descriptions of this disorder are found in Jewish legal texts from the second century AD that exempted boys from circumcision if two previous brothers had died from bleeding after the operation. After this, haemophilia appears to have been largely forgotten until 1803, when Dr John Conrad Otto, a physician from Philadelphia, described a familial bleeding disease that was inherited through the female line but only affected males. There are now known to be several types of this disease, with haemophilia A making up about 80 per cent of all cases. It has an incidence of about one in 4,000 of the UK population, although only about one in 20,000 are severely affected. Female haemophilia can exist but is extremely rare.

Haemophilia is sometimes known as 'the royal disease' because of its prevalence among the royal families of Europe. It appears to have begun with a fresh mutation in Queen Victoria of England – an event that was to dramatically alter the course of Russian and world history. In 1853, Queen Victoria gave birth to her youngest son, Leopold. The birth made medical history because Victoria received chloroform, the anaesthetic introduced by James Young Simpson only six years earlier. However, it soon became apparent that Leopold was suffering from haemophilia as he bled profusely even after small cuts and grazes. Leopold was to die at the age of 30 when he fell and suffered a brain haemorrhage. Unfortunately, two of Queen Victoria's daughters, Princess Alice and Princess Beatrice, were also carriers of haemophilia and they passed it on to several European royal families, including those of Spain and Russia. The most famous affected individual was Tsarevich Alexis (see Plate 12.3), born in 1904, who was the son of Tsar Nicholas II of Russia (who had married Alexandra, daughter of Alice). In their

Queen Victoria, haemophilia, Rasputin, and the fall of the Russian royal family continued.

Plate 12.3 A photograph of Czar Nicholas II, the Czarina Alexandra, their four daughters and their son Alexis, who suffered from haemophilia. *Source*: © Bettmann/CORBIS

desperation to treat their son, the czar and empress turned to the Siberian monk Rasputin, who had arrived in St Petersburg in 1903 claiming to have spiritual healing powers. Indeed, Rasputin appeared to have some mysterious ability to heal Alexis, which many believe was due to hypnosis. Whatever his form of treatment, Rasputin gained considerable influence at the Russian court despite tales of sexual profligacy and debauchery. His power increased so much that by 1915 he was taking a role in the selection of cabinet ministers and military decisions – an involvement that was to greatly discredit the Russian monarchy. Eventually a group of nobles assassinated Rasputin in 1916, although it was too late to save the Tsar and his family from the communist revolution, which was to destroy their lives a few months later.

Queen Victoria, haemophilia, Rasputin, and the fall of the Russian royal family continued.

Today, many people with haemophilia lead relatively normal lives. In most cases, haemophilia is managed by transfusions of fresh plasma or injections of the appropriate clotting factor. Both therapies provide relief for several days although they are relatively expensive. However, in 1984, the structure of the gene producing haemophilia A was characterised and cloned, and this has led to the availability of recombinant (genetically engineered) clotting factors, which are safer and cheaper. The great hope, nevertheless, lies with gene therapy – that is, one day, it will be possible to inject new genetic material into the individual which will correct the faulty gene, leading to proper production of the blood-clotting factors. Animal studies are currently underway to explore this possibility.

Multiple genes and behaviour

One feature of single-gene inheritance is that traits are dichotomous – that is, one either inherits the gene and exhibits the trait, or does not. However, the vast majority of human traits are the result of many different genes and do not follow this simple pattern of inheritance. Instead, polygenic traits show a continuous range of variation, and this can be seen with human height. For example, if our height was due to a single dominant gene, then only two sizes would be possible. Everyone who inherited the 'height' gene would be tall, and everyone who lacked the gene would be short (similar to Mendel's tall and dwarf pea plants). The fact that there is a great variation in human height, which may vary from under 60 cm to over 2 m, shows that it is determined by many different genes (such as those that code for growth hormone or control the rate of calcium deposition in the bones). In addition, environmental factors play an important role in determining height. Poor nutrition is one factor that can retard growth, and the absence of sunlight can result in inadequate synthesis of vitamin D, which may slow down bone development. In fact, the combined effect of genetic and environmental influences working in a given population will generally result in a trait that shows continuous variation in the form of a normal distribution or bell-shaped curve (Singer 1985).

The sum of all the intrinsic genetic information that an individual inherits at the moment of fertilisation is called the **genotype**, and this blueprint is to be found in the nucleus of just about every cell of the human body. In contrast, the appearance of an organism that results from the interaction of genes with one another and the environment is called the **phenotype**. Height produces a relatively simple phenotype, but human behaviour is much more complex, as shown by the almost endless number of ways in which we behave. But how can we tease out the interaction of genetic and environmental influences in our behaviour? Mendel was fortunate in choosing pea plants, which had simple dichotomous traits. However, this approach will not work for human behaviour, which is far too complex for this type of analysis. Fortunately, there are a number of methods that can be used, including twin and adoption studies in humans, and selective breeding and transgenic manipulation in animals, and it is to these methods that we now turn.

Twin and adoption studies

There are two types of twin: **monozygotic**, who arise from one egg, and **dizygotic**, who derive from two separate eggs. Thus, monozygotic twins develop from the same egg, which after fertilisation splits into two and results in two genetically identical individuals. In contrast, dizygotic twins arise when two eggs are released at ovulation and become fertilised by different sperms. Consequently, the genetic relationship between dizygotic twins is the same as that of other brothers and sisters – that is, they share 50 per cent of their genes. Comparing the characteristics of monozygotic and dizygotic twins provides the psychologist with an important means of assessing the relative impact of genetic influences on behaviour.

One measure used by psychologists to express the relative influence of inheritance and environment on behaviour is **concordance**. In short, twins are said to be concordant for a given trait if they both express it (or if neither does), and discordant if only one of the pair shows it. Thus, if concordance rates (which range from 0 to 100) are significantly higher in a group of identical twins compared with non-identical twins, this provides evidence that genetic influences play a more important role in the expression of that particular trait. For example, as Huntington's disease is due to a single dominant gene, the concordance rate for identical twins is 100 per cent (1.0), whereas the concordance for dizygotic twins is 50 per cent (0.5). But, of course, the same principle can be applied to other disorders with more complex genetic make-ups. Indeed, as we saw in the previous chapter, the concordance rate for schizophrenia is around 50 per cent for monozygotic twins and 15 per cent for dizygotic twins (Gottesman 1991). In contrast, bipolar illness shows a concordance rate of 69 per cent for monozygotic twins and 13 per cent for dizygotic twins (Rush *et al.* 1991). These results appear to show that genetic inheritance has a more important bearing on causing bipolar illness than for schizophrenia.

Despite this, there are problems with twin studies. For example, identical twins tend to share similar lives, and this might be one reason why they also exhibit similar patterns of behaviour. It may be, for example, that family and friends treat them as a 'pair'; or that identical twins spend more time together than dizygotic ones. In both cases, this would probably inflate the estimates of genetic influence. This problem can be resolved by studying twins who were separated early in life and then reared apart in different types of environment. Of course, this is much more difficult to do because the separation of twins is a rare event. Moreover, it also requires considerable detective skills, and luck, by researchers to find such groups of subjects! One study that is examining the effects of twins reared apart is being conducted by Thomas Bouchard and his colleagues at the University of Minnesota (e.g. Bouchard *et al.* 1990). This team of researchers, which includes psychologists, psychiatrists and medical doctors, has now managed to find 59 pairs of identical twins, and 47 pairs of fraternal twins, that were separated at an early age. Moreover, each pair has participated in a large number of personality and cognitive tests (the testing lasts approximately 50 hours and takes place over six days) and has answered around 15,000 questions including a full medical history.

The main reason for this study is to establish the extent to which identical twins reared apart are different from those bought up together and raised in the same environment. One way that Bouchard *et al.* (1990) have examined this question is to look at intelligence as measured by the Wechsler Adult Intelligent Scale. The results of this test showed that the average correlation for twins reared apart was 0.70, whereas the correlation for those reared together was 0.85. In other words, the high correlation between twin pairs showed that genetic factors were apparently the biggest influence in determining intelligence. Similar results have also been found on many other personality and cognitive tests (Bouchard 1994).

From these findings Bouchard has estimated the heritability of intelligence to be around 0.70. However, these results do not prove that intelligence is necessarily 70 per cent 'genetic'. For example, if the twins had been separately adopted by European royalty and African bushmen, then the heritability estimates would undoubtedly have been much lower. Thus, we cannot put an exact figure on the relative estimates of genetic and environmental influences. In fact, it is misleading to think of them as separate influences as genes and environment are able to interact in many subtle ways. For example, there is evidence to show that people with similar genetic endowments tend to seek out similar environments and experiences. Thus, individuals whose genetic inheritance promotes aggression are likely to become involved in aggressive activities (e.g. competitive fighting), with these experiences also contributing further to the development of aggressive tendencies. Since such individuals are likely to seek outlets for their aggressive tendencies regardless of the environment in which they are reared, then clearly one will never be able to arrive at an undisputed estimate of aggression heritability.

Inbred strains of animals

Attempts to produce different genetic strains of animals by **inbreeding** (i.e. brother–sister mating over several generations) produces another way of examining the influence of genetic inheritance on behaviour. Inbreeding is an important technique in genetic analysis because inbred lines lose much of their genetic variation, thereby making all members of an inbred strain genetically similar. The reason why this occurs is that inbreeding increases the chances of producing matching or homozygous alleles, and once two identical alleles have come together, they are not bred out of successive generations unless new genetic material is introduced. In fact, typically after 20 successive brother–sister matings all members of an inbred strain are as genetically alike as they are likely to get. Despite this, each strain will have its own unique combination of homozygous genes, which of course means that it will be genetically different from other inbred strains.

One way inbreeding has been used is to examine the effects of genetic inheritance on longevity. For example, Pearl and Parker (1922) inbred fruit flies through many generations to produce five different strains, each with its own individual average longevity, Their ages ranged from 14 days in the shortest-lived strain to 49 days in the longest-lived strain. Furthermore, once each strain had been established, the flies continued to produce generation after generation of offspring with their own average life span. These findings show the importance of genetic make-up on longevity. Despite this, the ages of all the strains obtained by Pearl and Parker were less than those in normally bred fruit flies, showing that inbreeding is not advantageous for longevity. This is because many harmful genes are often 'hidden' in normal strains because they are recessive, but with inbreeding they often find themselves matched with identical genes, which makes them become dominant.

Similar principles apply to humans with regards to intelligence. For example, it is known that children of marriages between first cousins generally show a lower IQ than for controls. In fact, it has been shown that the risk of mental retardation is more than three times greater for children of a marriage between first cousins than for unrelated controls – and the reason is the same as for the fruit flies described above, that is, inbreeding increases the chance of harmful recessive genes, which most of us carry, becoming unmasked and homozygous.

Selective breeding

Another way of studying the heritability of behavioural traits in animals is by **selective breeding** (Figure 12.7). Farmers have known for thousands of years that if a trait is inheritable then it can be selectively bred. For example, wild cattle and sheep have long legs for speed and large horns for defence, yet domestic cattle and sheep look very different with their short legs and horns accompanied by larger bodies. Similarly, dogs have been bred for a number of behavioural characteristics, including herding (sheep dogs), retrieving (labradors) and hunting (terriers). In much the same way, researchers have bred selective strains of animals in the laboratory to produce certain behaviours. The rationale is straightforward: if a behavioural trait is influenced by genetic factors then it should be possible to produce it through selective breeding.

A classic example of this approach was undertaken by Robert Tryon (1940), who selected rats for their maze-learning ability. Tryon began his study by

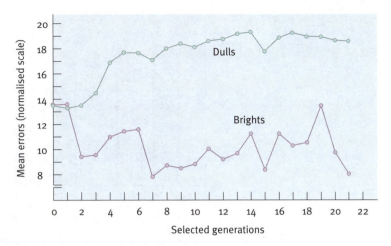

Figure 12.7   Graph showing the results of Tryon's selective breeding for maze-bright and maze-dull rats

examining the performance of a large number of rats that were trained to run through a complex 17-choice maze for food reward. Following training, Tryon mated the males and females that had shown the best performance to create a group of maze-bright rats. He also bred the males and females that had made the most errors to produce a group of maze-dull animals. When the offspring derived from these two groups matured, they were tested again in the maze, with the best 'maze-bright' and worst 'maze-dull' rats again being selected for breeding purposes. Tyron carried on this selection procedure for 21 generations, and descendants of these animals are still available today for researchers interested in rodents' learning ability.

The results of this study showed that Tryon's selection strategy produced two strains of rats that differed significantly in their ability to learn the maze. In fact, after just seven generations, the two groups were so different in their performance that the distribution of the error scores no longer overlapped. At this point, the two groups continued to maintain their behavioural differences over subsequent generations.

Another study that examined the performance of maze-bright and maze-dull rats was reported by Cooper and Zubek (1958), who reared their animals in one of three environments: (1) a standard laboratory cage; (2) an enriched environment consisting of a large cage with toys, tunnels and ramps; and (3) an impoverished environment consisting of a small grey wire-mesh cage (Figure 12.8). The results of this study showed that when the maze-bright rats reached maturity they made almost the same number of errors as the maze-dull animals reared in the enriched environment. Thus, by changing the environmental conditions in which the rats were reared, the effects of the genetic difference between the bright and dull rats was virtually eliminated. This not only shows that a genetic predisposition can be significantly influenced by environmental factors, but implies that intelligence is not fixed and can be improved with suitable learning conditions.

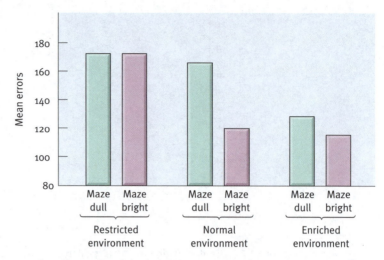

Figure 12.8 The effects of enriched and impoverished rearing on maze-bright and maze-dull rats

Selective breeding for alcohol preference

Selective breeding studies have shown that a genetic basis may exist for alcoholism. For example, it has long been known that certain strains of mice exhibit a preference for alcohol (McClearn and Rogers 1959). These researchers allowed mice a choice between drinking from a bottle that contained water and one containing a 10 per cent alcohol solution, and found that one strain of mice (called C57BL) preferred to drink most of their daily consumption from the alcohol bottle. Other strains of mice (e.g. DBA/2), however, avoided drinking the alcohol. In fact, subsequent studies have managed to selectively breed animals that exhibit even greater differences in their alcohol consumption. Indeed, one strain of rats called the P strain (preference for alcohol) consume up to five times more alcohol than the NP (no preference for alcohol) strain (Lumeng *et al.* 1977, 1993). Moreover, not only are the alcohol-preferring rats more tolerant to the effects of alcohol and show signs of withdrawal when it is unavailable, but they also have lower levels of dopamine and serotonin in their brains. This work not only implies that certain genes may predispose an individual to becoming an alcoholic but also shows that there can be neurochemical differences between individuals with varying preferences for alcohol.

As well as preference for alcohol, researchers have also selectively bred animals that exhibit differing sensitivity to alcohol. For example, McClearn and Kakihana (1981) assumed that animals who sleep more after ingesting alcohol must be more sensitive to its effects than those who sleep less. Consequently, they injected mice with alcohol and measured the amount of time they spent sleeping. Following this, they began to mate the short-sleeping mice together, as well as the long-sleeping mice, over many generations. These two lines of mice are now called the Colorado Long and Short Sleep lines and they show considerable differences in their sleep time following injections of alcohol. For example, the long-sleep animals sleep for about an average of 2 hours following an alcohol injection, while the short-sleep mice show an average sleeping time of 10 minutes! In fact, there is no overlap in sleeping times between the two strains, which indicates that a large number of genes are involved in producing this behaviour (Plomin *et al.* 1997).

The genetic basis of alcoholism in humans

Alcohol has been an integral part of human existence for thousands of years and was certainly being used long before the dawn of written history. Approximately 90 per cent of the Western population drinks alcohol at least occasionally, yet half of all the alcohol drunk is consumed by only 10 per cent of the population (Cloninger 1987). Thus, there is great variability in alcohol consumption in human populations. One possible explanation is that some people (like the strains of rats discussed above) are more genetically predisposed to drinking alcohol than others. Indeed, the idea that human drinking behaviour is inherited has a long history. For example, Aristotle declared that drunken women 'bring forth children like themselves' and Plutarch wrote that 'one drunkard begets another' (Goodwin 1980). However, it is also possible that the use of alcohol is a learned behaviour that arises as a result of environmental experience. An answer to this question has more than just theoretical significance, because it is likely to provide greater understanding of alcoholism and point ways forward to more effective intervention and treatment.

Studies of twins have provided evidence of a genetic factor in alcoholism. One of the largest studies to examine this issue was undertaken in Sweden by Kaij (1960), who compared 1,974 male twin pairs where one of each pair was known to have an alcohol problem (e.g. they had been convicted of drunkenness or involved in an alcohol-related misdemeanour). The results showed that the concordance rate of identical twins for alcoholism was 54 per cent, compared with 28 per cent for the fraternal twins. Although significant, the difference was not particularly marked, especially when considering that most of the twins had been raised in similar environments. This suggested that learning experiences also had an important role to play in this behaviour. A similar conclusion was also reached in a more recent report (Pickens *et al.* 1991) that examined alcoholism in males and females. The results of this study showed that the concordance rate for identical male twins was 76 per cent compared with 61 per cent for the fraternal twins, and the corresponding figures for female twins were 36 and 25 per cent. These researchers also estimated that alcoholism was 36 per cent inheritable for men and 26 per cent inheritable for women. In other words, the environment appeared to exert a more important influence in causing alcohol abuse.

A difficulty with these types of study (as mentioned earlier) is that twins tend to be reared in very similar environments. One way of overcoming this type of problem is to examine subjects who were born to alcoholic parents, but then adopted by non-alcoholic parents. Thus, if this group continued to show a greater incidence of alcohol problems in adulthood this would provide stronger evidence of a genetic component to drinking behaviour. One study of this sort was undertaken by Goodwin *et al.* (1973), who followed children of alcoholic parents who were adopted at, or shortly after, birth and were raised by 'normal' or non-alcoholic parents. The results showed that alcoholism was four times more likely in the sons of alcoholic fathers compared with sons of non-alcoholics. In other words, the father's genes were appearing to exert an important effect on alcohol-related behaviour in their sons.

A Swedish study conducted by Michael Bohman has confirmed and extended these findings. This study was based on a much larger sample of people (1,125 men and 1,199 women) born to single women between 1930 and 1949 and adopted at an early age. In addition, extensive information about alcohol abuse, mental illness and medical problems was available for most of these adoptees, and for their biological and adoptive parents. The results of this study showed that genetic factors played an important role in alcoholism. For example, Bohman found that the adopted sons of alcoholic fathers were three times more likely to become alcoholics than the adopted sons of non-alcoholic fathers. Similarly, adopted sons of alcoholic mothers were twice as likely to become alcoholics as those whose mothers were non-alcoholic (Bohman 1978).

Are there different types of alcoholism?

One criticism that has been made of many studies that have attempted to examine the genetic basis of alcoholism is that they assume only one form of the disorder. However, there is evidence to show that different types of alcoholism exist. For example, E.M. Jellinek, who did much to promote the idea that alcoholism was an illness in his highly influential book *The Disease Concept of Alcoholism* (1960), believed there were five different types of alcoholism. In particular, he emphasised the distinction between individuals who had persistent alcohol-seeking behaviours ('an inability to abstain entirely') and others who could abstain from alcohol for long periods but were unable to stop drinking once they had begun ('loss of control'). Similarly, the American Psychiatric Association has defined two types of alcoholism: one where the person is psychologically dependent on alcohol and engages in intermittent heavy consumption, and one where both physical and psychological dependence occur with increased tolerance and physical withdrawal symptoms when drinking ceases.

One attempt to examine different types of alcoholism from a genetic perspective was undertaken by Robert Cloninger, who was invited by Michael Bohman to re-examine the data of his Swedish adoption study described above. When Cloninger started to look more closely at the results of this study he found that individuals who had the severest alcohol problems, as shown by the number of criminal offences made under the influence of alcohol intoxication, were also those who were more likely to have had an alcoholic parent. However,

Table 12.2   Characteristics of type 1 and type 2 alcoholism as formulated by Cloninger

Type 1 ('binge type')

Has a late onset (typically after the age of 25) and is characterised by binges or loss of control (once the person starts they can't stop) punctuated by periods of abstinence

The personality is often characterised by anxiety, shyness and inhibition. In addition, there may be guilt and fear over their dependence, leading to depression

Can occur in both males and females and does not appear to have a strong genetic basis

Has been suggested that these persons are physiologically over-aroused and that alcohol serves as a depressant which acts to decrease anxiety and arousal

Type 2 ('persistent type')

Has an early onset (before the age of 25) and is characterised by persistent moderate to heavy drinking without periods of abstinence

The personality is generally characterised by impulsiveness and lack of anxiety. In addition, there is often antisocial behaviour with evidence of other forms of drug-taking and/or criminality

Occurs predominantly in males and appears to be strongly inherited from the father

Has been suggested that these persons are physiologically under-aroused and that alcohol serves as a stimulant which acts to increase arousal

as he examined this relationship further, Cloninger began to realise that a number of other features also distinguished 'severe' alcoholics from those with more moderate problems. In fact, the data revealed two types of alcoholism with different behavioural manifestations and genetic influence. These were designated as type 1 and type 2 (Table 12.2).

The most common form of alcoholism according to Cloninger is type 1. This has a late onset, normally occurrs after the age of 25, and is found in both males and females. Although individuals with this form of alcoholism may not drink for long periods of time, they cannot control or stop their drinking behaviour once they start. In terms of personality they also tend to be anxious, inhibited, cautious, shy and emotionally sensitive. Type 1 alcoholism tends to be relatively mild (it often goes untreated), and requires a genetic predisposition (there is often an alcoholic parent) along with a triggering influence from the environment. However, it is not strongly genetic and appears to depend more heavily on stressful environmental factors. In contrast, type 2 alcoholism is much more severe. It is associated with persistent and chronic drinking along with antisocial tendencies that may include a history of fighting, lying, impulsiveness and lack of remorse. It is found only in males and typically occurs before the age of 25 years. It also appears to be strongly genetic with the environment playing little part in its expression. For example, not only is the risk of alcoholism in these adoptees nine times greater than that for other adoptees, but the drinking and antisocial behaviours are likely to emerge in young adulthood regardless of the environment in which the adoptee is reared.

Not all investigators agree with Cloninger's classification, especially as it appears that some alcoholics do not fit neatly into either category. Nevertheless, there has also been support for certain aspects of the theory (e.g. Hesselbrock 1995), and it is probably the case that there are indeed different types of alcoholic with different genetic predispositions and varying susceptibility to environmental conditions. There is little doubt that Cloninger's work is a valuable contribution to our understanding of the interaction between genetics and environment in alcoholism.

Is there a gene for alcoholism?

Clearly, if alcoholism has a genetic basis then it should be possible to identify the genes that contribute to this behaviour. Several years ago a group of researchers led by Kenneth Blum generated much excitement when it was claimed that such a gene had been discovered (Blum *et al.* 1990, 1991). These investigators studied the brains of 70 deceased individuals, half of whom had been alcoholics. A sample of frontal cortex was taken from each brain and tested with nine DNA probes, each of which had been proposed as a possible alcoholism gene from previous research. Only one of these probes matched the DNA found in the brain tissues, and this matched the gene that was responsible for producing the dopamine D-2 receptor. Moreover, this gene, which is located on chromosome 11, occurs in two different forms (alleles). The majority of us have a form known as the A-2 allele, but some have the less common A-1 version, and it was the A-1 allele that was found in the tissue taken from the alcoholics' brains. In fact, this gene was present in 69 per cent of the alcoholics' brains, but absent in 80 per cent of the non-alcoholics.

This was an important finding, especially as the dopaminergic systems of the brain have been shown to play an important role in reinforcement and the pleasurable effects of drugs such as cocaine, nicotine, alcohol and heroin (see Chapter 11). Blum and his colleagues proposed that the A-1 allele might contribute to alcoholism because it manufactured fewer dopamine receptors. This would then result in neurons with fewer receptors not getting sufficient dopamine, thereby leading to craving for substances (such as alcohol) that help to stimulate the release of this neurotransmitter (Blum and Payne 1991). The discovery of the A-1 gene was also important from another perspective as it raised the possibility that a test could be developed to screen for alcoholism in the general population.

However, initial excitement has been tempered by evidence showing that the A-1 allele is also found in the brains of those suffering from a range of behavioural disorders, including attentional deficit disorder, autism, and Tourette's syndrome (Comings *et al.* 1991). It also appears that the original estimate of the A-1 allele frequency reported by Blum *et al.* (1990) was rather high. For example, Noble (1993) reviewed nine studies that compared a total of 491 alcoholics with 495 controls, and found that the A-1 allele existed in 43 per cent of the alcoholics' brains, and in 25.7 per cent of the control subjects.

Although these are positive findings, the fact that the A-1 allele is not found in the majority of alcoholics implies that it is not the primary cause of alcoholism. Indeed, even in alcoholics that are judged as 'severe' the frequency of the A-1 allele only increases to 56 per cent. Nonetheless, the A-1 gene cannot be ruled out as a possible contributor to alcoholism in at least some individuals.

Serotonin and alcoholism

Another neurotransmitter (and presumably a different genetic influence) to be implicated in alcoholism is serotonin. For example, it has been shown that the concentration of **5-HIAA** (a breakdown product of serotonin) is lower in the cerebrospinal fluid (CSF) of many alcoholics compared with non-alcoholics of the same age and general health status (Lovinger 1997). This observation suggests that alcoholics may have reduced serotonin levels in the brain. Indeed, this possibility was supported by Ballenger *et al.* (1979), who measured 5-HIAA levels in abstaining alcoholics. Although the results showed that 5-HIAA levels were relatively normal at 48 hours, they were significantly depressed at four weeks. This finding suggested that alcoholics may have naturally low levels of serotonin, which become elevated when they consume alcohol. The obvious implication is that a deficit in serotonin might be responsible for driving the alcoholic to seek and consume alcohol in order to restore the levels of this neurotransmitter in the brain.

A number of studies have confirmed that serotonergic abnormalities exist in some alcoholics, particularly those with male-limited (or type 2) alcoholism (Roy *et al.* 1987). It has also been found that many of these alcoholics show specific variations in the gene that codes for the enzyme tryptophan hydroxylase, which produces serotonin (Virkkunen *et al.* 1995). However, this relationship is not as straightforward as it first appears because low CSF levels of 5-HIAA have also been found to be linked with a variety of impulsive behaviours, including aggression, animal torture, and arson. In addition, low levels of 5-HIAA are also associated with depression and suicide (especially those that are violent and impulsive in nature). Thus, it could be that low levels of 5-HIAA are more closely associated with certain personality characteristics, such as impulsiveness and aggression, rather than with alcoholism *per se*. Indeed, many alcoholics have normal or even high levels of 5-HIAA (Roy and Linnoila 1989), showing that a serotonergic deficit does not explain all types of alcoholism.

Nonetheless, it probably remains that low serotonergic function is a contributory factor for alcoholism in at least some individuals. This is also supported from animal studies. For example, low levels of 5-HIAA in rats are associated with an enhanced preference for alcohol, whereas drug-induced stimulation of serotonergic systems (e.g. by selective serotonergic uptake inhibitors) decreases alcohol consumption (Sellers *et al.* 1992). Similar findings have also been obtained with monkeys. For example, in a long-term study, Higley *et al.* (1996) measured the CSF levels of 5-HIAA in a group of rhesus monkeys which were allowed access to alcohol. The results showed that the monkeys with the lowest levels of 5-HIAA were also the ones which had the highest rates of alcohol intake. Since the levels of 5-HIAA had remained relatively stable from infancy to adulthood in each individual monkey, this indicated that they were probably under the control of genetic factors. Despite this, alcohol consumption was also influenced by environmental factors. For example, the same investigators found that when monkeys had been deprived of maternal contact early in life, they also tended to drink more as adults. Thus, the interaction between low levels of 5-HIAA and environmental factors is likely to be a much more important determinant of drinking behaviour.

These findings also imply that serotonergic drugs may be useful for the treatment of alcoholism in humans. Indeed, certain drugs such as **fluoxetine** (Prozac) have been found to reduce drinking in some individuals. Unfortunately, the magnitude of this effect is not marked. For example, in heavy drinkers, 60 mg of fluoxetine per day (which is three times the dose used to treat depression) decreased alcohol intake from 8.7 drinks to 6.9 drinks during a four-week trial (Kranzler and Anton 1994). Furthermore, in alcoholics, the effectiveness of serotonergic drugs was even less effective in reducing alcohol intake. Nonetheless, these drugs may play an important role in the treatment of alcoholism, especially if accompanied by psychotherapy (Gallant 1993).

Recombinant DNA and genetic engineering

So far we have looked at methods that have been used to discover genes, or genetic factors, that may influence behaviour. However, in recent years more direct ways of examining the function of genes have been developed. One technique is genetic engineering, which involves taking genes from an organism, cloning them (i.e. making multiple copies), and implanting them back into another organism. In fact, genetic engineering is already taking place on a large scale. It is being used in farming to increase crop yields and make plants more resistant to disease. Animals have also been given genetically engineered products to make them grow bigger, or to increase meat and milk yields. In addition, genetically engineered cells have been commercially used to mass produce hormones, antibodies and vaccines, with a billion dollar biotechnology industry developing to take advantage of these developments. Genetically engineered cells have even been introduced into human beings to correct certain genetic diseases.

The beginning of genetic engineering, or more accurately the start of DNA recombinant technology (recombinant DNA is constructed outside the living cell by splicing two or more pieces of DNA from different sources to provide a novel combination of genes) took place in the late 1960s when scientists discovered a class of enzymes (called **restriction enzymes**) that could cut DNA with great precision at a specific base sequence. These enzymes were first found in bacteria, which used them to disable the DNA of invading viruses. However, researchers soon realised that the enzymes could also be used in the laboratory as 'molecular scissors' to cut DNA. That is, DNA could be extracted from a living organism, put into a test tube with restriction enzymes, and the result would be lots of identical DNA fragments that were all 'cut' at the same place. In fact, within a decade of their discovery, geneticists had discovered over 300 enzymes, taken from a variety of bacteria, that enabled them to cut DNA at many different places. For instance, a restriction enzyme might cut through a specific genetic sequence such as CCGTA by always severing it between the G and the T.

By themselves, lots of DNA snippets floating around in a test tube are of little value. However, a few years after the first restriction enzymes were found, geneticists also discovered that some of these chemicals also produced DNA fragments that had 'sticky ends', which allowed the snippets of DNA to be joined together. Moreover, the DNA did not even have to come from the same genome. That is, it was possible to join bits of DNA together from different organisms, or even implant new genes into foreign DNA. Again, however, this recombination was taking place outside the cell, or in the confines of a test tube (*in vitro*), but in 1972 a way of introducing new DNA into living cells was discovered (*in vivo*). This discovery was first used by Paul Berg, who took genes from a bacterium and implanted them into the DNA of a virus. A year later there was a more astonishing feat when Herbert Boyer and Stanly Cohen took DNA from a toad and placed it inside the DNA of a bacterium. In fact, each time the bacteria divided, the 'foreign' DNA was copied and passed into the new bacteria. Thus, the new foreign gene had not only been incorporated into a new host, but was there to stay for all future generations.

Being able to insert genes into rapidly dividing organisms such as bacteria allowed, for the first time, a means of cloning large numbers of identical genes. Indeed, because bacteria divide every 20 minutes, a single gene placed into a bacterial host can be multiplied many times over in a short space of time. In fact, if given adequate nutrition, bacteria could in theory grow a mass greater than that of our planet in less than two days. This new recombinant gene technology revolutionised the study of molecular biology because it allowed large amounts of new DNA to be produced. Moreover, not only did this enable investigators to more easily work out the base sequences of genes, but it also allowed them to place the cloned genes into various organisms to see what they did, or what proteins they made. This can be done, for example, by injecting the cloned DNA into an egg just after it has been fertilised. Every cell that develops from this embryonic egg will then carry the new gene. Organisms that have been manipulated in this way are known as **transgenic animals** (Figure 12.9) and they are increasingly being used in biopsychology to answer important questions about genetics and behaviour.

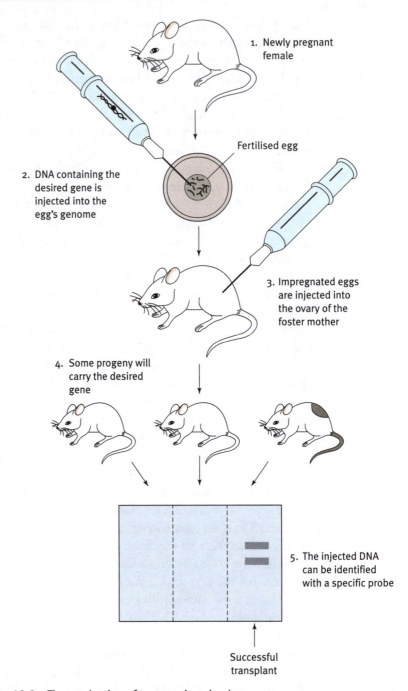

1. Newly pregnant female

Fertilised egg

2. DNA containing the desired gene is injected into the egg's genome

3. Impregnated eggs are injected into the ovary of the foster mother

4. Some progeny will carry the desired gene

5. The injected DNA can be identified with a specific probe

Successful transplant

Figure 12.9   The production of transgenic animals

The use of transgenic animals to examine behaviour

One way genetic engineering has been used to examine behaviour is by the production of transgenic animals, which have had a certain gene inactivated or 'knocked out'. The logic of this approach is compelling. For example, if a gene was knocked out that caused a mouse to have a malformed cerebellum, then one would deduce that the gene is involved in neural cerebellar development. Because we share over 99 per cent of our genes with mice, it would be likely that this gene would have a similar function in humans (Capecchi 1994). In theory, producing knockout mice (the most common type of animal used in this procedure) is straightforward. One first implants a base sequence into an egg, or early developing embryo, which aligns itself next to the gene in question and inactivates it. The animals are then reared and bred together to produce inbred strains where the knocked-out genes become homozygous (identical on both chromosomes). By using this approach it is possible to engineer virtually any desired alteration of the genome (Capecchi 1994).

Knockout mice have recently been used to help to explain why drugs such as cocaine and amphetamine can cause addiction. For example, Giros *et al.* (1996) have produced a strain of mice where the gene responsible for the uptake of dopamine has been 'knocked out' (the uptake process normally acts to remove excess dopamine from the synapse). Not only did this cause the mice to be extremely hyperactive, but they were behaviourally unaffected by the administration of cocaine and amphetamine. This finding indicates that both these drugs produce their main effects by acting on this 'transporter' protein. Also of interest was the discovery that these mice produce less dopamine than normal. In other words, the knockout of the dopamine uptake protein results in a general down-regulation of the entire dopamine system. These findings also have clinical and therapeutic implications. For example, the use of these knockout mice may help us to develop more effective blockers of the uptake pump, which will increase levels of dopamine and can be used to treat illnesses such as Parkinson's disease. Alternatively, it may be possible to design drugs that block the action of cocaine and amphetamine on the transporter protein, thus providing a means of treating stimulant abuse.

Knockout mice have also been used to examine alcohol-related behaviour. For example, it has been shown that mutant mice lacking the serotonergic 1B receptor (5-HT_{1B}) drink twice as much alcohol as normal, and will ingest solutions containing up to 20 per cent alcohol. In addition, they are less sensitive to the effects of alcohol as measured by ataxia (Crabbe *et al.* 1996). Interestingly, mice lacking the 5-HT_{1B} receptor also show a marked increase in aggressive behaviour (Saudou *et al.* 1994), which indicates that this receptor may be linked with type 2 alcoholism. Another gene, this time linked with increased alcohol sensitivity, has been identified by Miyakawa *et al.* (1997). These scientists examined mice which were mutant for a gene that produces an enzyme called Fyn kinase – a protein that had been known to influence neuronal excitability. These mice (i.e. which lacked Fyn kinase) were found to be very sensitive to the effects of alcohol. In fact, when injected with a high dose of alcohol they took twice as long to right themselves compared with normal mice. These findings lend further support to the idea that a wide range of genes underlie alcoholic-related behaviour, and it is likely that many more will be found in the future using similar knockout mice and genetic engineering.

Summary

It is believed that life on Earth has been evolving for around 3,500 million years, with *Homo sapiens* first appearing some 100,000 years ago. Human beings have evolved a genome that contains **23 pairs** of **chromosomes**, which hold around **30,000 genes**. These not only provide the blueprint by which the body (and brain) are made, but they also govern the internal working of our cells. The laws of genetic inheritance were first established by **Gregor Mendel** in 1865 working with pea plants. He showed that each individual plant contained two 'factors' (now recognised as genes) that came in different forms (**alleles**) and controlled a certain trait (e.g. height, colour). Each allele could also be **dominant** or **recessive**, although only one of these was passed on from each parent to offspring. Thus, if a plant inherited both a dominant and a recessive gene, it always expressed the dominant trait, although the recessive trait would be exhibited if two recessive genes were inherited. Genes are passed to offspring by **gametes** (in animals this is the **sperm** and **egg**), which contain unpaired chromosomes, which become paired 'again' during **fertilisation**. Chromosomes are made from **deoxyribonucleic acid** (DNA), and its chemical structure was established in 1954 by **James Watson** and **Francis Crick** in what was probably the most important scientific advance of the twentieth century. They showed that DNA is made up of two chains of deoxyribose that swivel around each other in the shape of a double helix. Between the two chains are pairs of **bases** (**adenine, guanine, cytosine** and **thymine**) that are like rungs of a ladder. Genes are essentially long sequences of paired bases (the largest human gene contains over 2 million bases) that contain **codons** (special triple bases) that code for single **amino acids**, which are the 'building blocks' of **proteins** – a class of molecule with a wide variety of functions vital for life. Put simply, protein synthesis occurs when **messenger ribonucleic acid** (mRNA) carries a transcript from the DNA (in the **nucleus**) to a **ribosome** located in the **cytoplasm**. Here, amino acids are bought to the transcript by **transfer ribonucleic acid** (tRNA), forming a chained molecule which becomes a protein.

Some genetic conditions are caused by a **single dominant allele** whereby if a person inherits the gene, that person will develop the disorder. One such condition is **Huntington's disease**, which is caused by a **mutation** occurring on chromosome 4. Other conditions such as **phenylketonuria** are caused by **recessive alleles**, where two copies of the gene have to be inherited for the illness to develop. A third type of single-gene disorder may occur through **X-linked inheritance**, where the mutation is carried on the X chromosome. These conditions (e.g. **haemophilia**) usually manifest themselves in **males** (XY), as **females** (XX) typically have a 'good' X chromosome to counteract the one carrying the mutation. However, most behaviours of interest to the psychologist are caused by **multiple genes**, whose expression also depends on environmental influences. The sum of all genetic information that a person inherits is called the **genotype**, but the totality of genes and environmental influences expressed is called the **phenotype**. One way of measuring the relative influence of gene and environmental influences on human behaviour is by measuring the rate of **concordance** in identical (**monozygotic**) and non-identical (**dizygotic**) twins. In short, the higher the concordance in identical twins, the more likely is the condition to be determined by genetic factors. Experimental strategies can also be used to measure the impact of genetic influences on behaviour, including **inbreeding** to produce different strains of animals and **selective breeding** to produce a certain trait (e.g. for alcohol preference). Over the last decade or so, the use of **transgenic animals** in which the genome has been modified in some way (e.g. a certain gene is '**knocked out**' or another added) has begun to revolutionise our genetic understanding of behaviour – and this is certain to continue long into the future.

Essay questions

1. 'DNA makes RNA, and RNA makes protein'. Discuss.

   Helpful Internet search terms: *Central dogma of genetics. Structure of DNA. Protein synthesis. Introduction to nucleic acids. RNA. Codons and amino acids.*

2. Discuss some of the methodological approaches that can be used to examine the influence of multiple genes on behaviour.

   Helpful Internet search terms: *Twin and adoption studies. Inbreeding. Selective breeding. Genetic analysis of complex behaviour. Multiple genes and behaviour. Behavioural genetics.*

3. Is alcoholism a disease? To what extent can alcoholism be considered a genetic disorder?

   Helpful Internet search terms: *Is alcoholism a disease? Medical model of alcoholism. Genetics of alcoholism. Type 1 and type 2 alcoholics. Causes of alcoholism.*

4. What are transgenic animals and how are they produced? In what ways have they contributed to our understanding of brain and behaviour?

   Helpful Internet search terms: *Transgenic animals. Genetic engineering. Receptor knockout mice. Knockout mice in neurobiology. Transgenic animals and degenerative disease.*

Further reading

Begleiter, H. and Kissin, B. (eds) (1995) *The Genetics of Alcoholism*. Oxford: Oxford University Press. A series of articles written by various experts that looks at the genetic and biological factors that predispose a given individual to alcoholism.

Bodner, W. and McKie, R. (1994) *The Book of Man*. London: Abacus. Written for the non-specialist reader, this is a highly readable account that discusses the many varied implications of genetic research for understanding human nature.

Crawley, J.N. (2000) *What's Wrong with My Mouse? Behavioral Phenotyping of Transgenic and Knockout Mice*. New York: John Wiley. A useful overview of mutant mouse technology and its use in behavioural neuroscience.

Gershon, E.S. and Cloninger, C.R. (1994) *New Genetic Approaches to Mental Disorders*. Washington: American Psychiatric Press. A book that shows how new genetic technology is being used to provide new insights into mental disorders.

Goodsell, D.S. (1996) *Our Molecular Nature: The Body's Motors, Machines and Messages*. New York: Copernicus. A beautifully illustrated book that will help any student learn more about the molecular nature of the body, including a vivid account of protein synthesis, and a chapter on molecules and the mind.

Jones, S. (1994) *The Language of the Genes*. London: Flamingo. An absorbing and enlightening book that helps to show what geneticists can and cannot tell us about ourselves.

Plomin, R., DeFries, J.C., McClearn, G.E. and Rutter, M. (2000) *Behavioral Genetics*. New York: Freeman. A superb textbook, now in its fourth edition, that is simply the best introduction to behavioural genetics for undergraduate students.

Plomin, R., DeFries, J.C., Craig, I.W. and McGuffin, P. (eds) (2003) *Behavioral Genetics in the Postgenomic Era*. Washington: American Psychological Association. Excellent comprehensive textbook that not only covers new methodological developments but also examines the behavioural genetics of cognitive abilities, clinical disorders (including schizophrenia and depression) and personality.

Steen, R.G. (1996) *DNA and Destiny: Nature and Nurture in Human Behavior*. New York: Plenum Press. A lucid and interesting account which attempts to show the impact of genetic influences on controversial and complex behaviour such as intelligence, aggression, homosexuality and drug addiction.

Watson, J. (2003) *DNA: The Secret of Life*. London: Arrow Books. The remarkable story of DNA from its discovery over 50 years ago to the present day. Contains chapters on genetic fingerprinting, disease and nature/nurture.

Wexler, A. (1995) *Mapping Fate*. Berkeley, CA: University of California Press. A personal and moving account of the search for the gene responsible for Huntington's disease.

See website at www.pearsoned.co.uk/wickens for further resources including multiple choice questions.

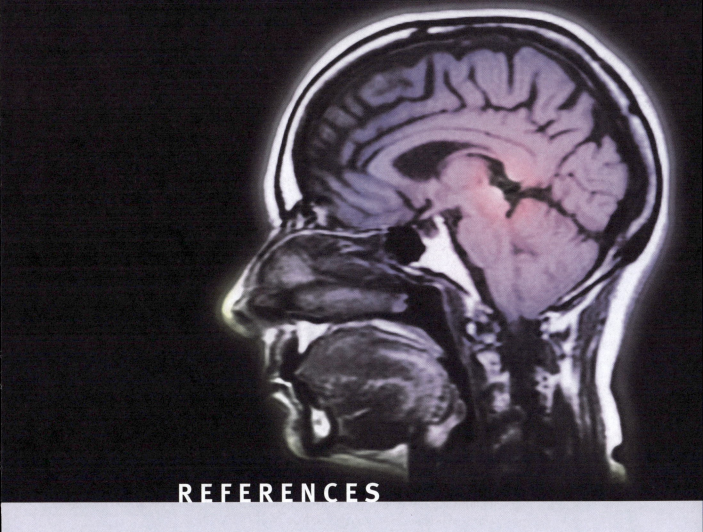

REFERENCES

A

Adam, K. and Oswald, I. (1977) Sleep for tissue restoration. *Journal of the Royal College of Physicians*, **11**, 376–88.

Adkins-Regan, E. (1989) Sex hormones and sexual orientation in animals. *Psychobiology*, **16**, 335–47.

Aggleton, J.P., Bland, J.M., Kentridge, R.W. and Neave, N.J. (1994) Handedness and longevity: Archival study of cricketers. *British Medical Journal*, **309**, 1681–4.

Agosta, W.C. (1992) *Chemical Communication: The Language of Pheromones*. New York: Scientific American Library.

Alexander, G.E., DeLong, M.R. and Strick, P.L. (1986) Parallel organization of functionally segregated circuits linking basal ganglia and cortex. *Annual Review of Neuroscience*, **9**, 357–82.

Allee, W.C., Collias, N.E. and Lutherman, C.Z. (1939) Modification of the social order in flocks of hens by the injection of testosterone propionate. *Physiological Zoology*, **12**, 412–40.

Allen, L.S. and Gorski, R.A. (1992) Sexual orientation and the size of the anterior commissure in the human brain. *Proceedings of the National Academy of Sciences*, **89**, 7199–202.

Allen, L.S., Hines, M., Shryne, J.E. and Gorski, R.A. (1989) Two sexually dimorphic cell groups in the human brain. *Journal of Neuroscience*, **9**, 497–506.

Anand, B.K. and Brobeck, J.R. (1951) Hypothalamic control of food intake. *Yale Journal of Biological Medicine*, **24**, 123–40.

Anden, N.E., Carlsson, A., Dahlstrom, A. *et al.* (1964) Demonstration and mapping of nigro-neostriatal dopamine neurons. *Life Sciences*, **3**, 523–30.

Andreasen, N.C. (1985) Positive vs negative schizophrenia: A critical evaluation. *Schizophrenia Bulletin*, **11**, 380–9.

Andreasen, N.C. (1988) Brain imaging: Applications in psychiatry. *Science*, **239**, 1381–8.

Anisfeld, M. (1996) Only tongue protrusion modelling is matched by neonates. *Developmental Review*, **16**, 149–61.

Antelman, S.M., Szechtman, H., Chin, P. and Fischer, A.E. (1975) Tail pinch-induced eating, gnawing and licking behaviour in rats: Dependence on the nigrostriatal dopamine system. *Brain Research*, **99**, 319–37.

Arendt, J., Aldhous, M., Marks, M. *et al.* (1987) Some effects of jet-lag and their alleviation by melatonin. *Ergonomics*, **30**, 1379–93.

Archer, J. (1994) Testosterone and aggression. *Journal of Offender Rehabilitation*, **21**, 3–26.

Aserinsky, E. and Kleitman, N. (1953) Regularly occurring periods of eye motility and concomitant phenomena. *Science*, **118**, 273–4.

Asberg, M., Schalling, D., Traskman-Bendz, L. *et al.* (1987) Psychobiology of suicide, impulsivity, and related phenomena. In Meltzer, H.M. (ed.) *Psychopharmacology. The Third Generation of Progress*. New York: Raven Press.

Ashton, H. (1992) *Brain Function and Psychotropic Drugs*. Oxford: Oxford University Press.

Ashton, R. (2002) *This is Heroin*. London: Sanctuary House.

Avery, D.H., Eder, D.N., Bolte, M.A. *et al.* (2001) Dawn stimulation and bright light in the treatment of SAD: A controlled study. *Biological Psychiatry*, **50**, 205–16.

Ax, A. (1953) The physiological differentiation between fear and anger in humans. *Psychomatic Medicine*, **15**, 433–42.

B

Backlund, E.-O., Granberg, P.-O., Hamberger, B. *et al.* (1985) Transplantation of adrenal medullary tissue to striatum in Parkinsonism: First clinical trials. *Journal of Neurosurgery*, **62**, 169–73.

Baily, C.H. and Chen, M. (1983) Morphological basis of long-term habituation and sensitisation in Aplysia. *Science*, **220**, 91–3.

Bailey, J.M. and Pillard, R.C. (1991) A genetic study of male sexual orientation. *Archives of General Psychiatry*, **48**, 1089–96.

Bailey, J.M., Pillard, R.C., Neale, M.C. and Agyei, Y. (1993) Heritable factors influencing sexual orientation in women. *Archives of General Psychiatry*, **50**, 217–23.

Ballantine, H.T., Bouckoms, A.J., Thomas, E.K. *et al.* (1987) Treatment of psychiatric illness by stereotactic cingulotomy. *Biological Psychiatry*, **22**, 807–19.

Ballenger, J.C., Goodwin, F.K., Major, L.F. and Brown, G.L. (1979) Alcohol and central serotonin metabolism in man. *Archives of General Psychiatry*, **36**, 224–7.

Balon, R. (1997) Selective serotonergic reuptake inhibitors and sexual dysfunction. *Primary Psychiatry*, Sept., 28–33.

Bard, P. (1934) On emotional expression after decortication with some remarks on certain theoretical views. *Psychological Review*, **41**, 309–29.

Bard, P. and Mountcastle, V.B. (1948) Some forebrain mechanisms involved in the expression of rage with special reference to suppression of angry behaviour. *Association of Research into Nervous and Mental Disorders*, **27**, 362–404.

Barlow, H.B. (1982) David Hubel and Torten Wiesel: Their contributions towards understanding the primary visual cortex. *Trends in Neurosciences*, **5**, 145–52.

Barr, C.E., Mednick, S.A. and Munk-Jorgensen, P. (1990) Exposure to influenza epidemics during gestation and adult schizophrenia. *Archives of General Psychiatry*, **47**, 869–74.

Baxter, L.R. (1995) Neuroimaging studies of human anxiety disorders. In Bloom, F. and Kupfer, J.R. (eds) *Psychopharmacology: The Fourth Generation of Progress*. New York: Raven Press.

Baylor, D.A. (1970) Photoreceptor signals and vision: Proctor Lecture. *Investigations in Opthalmology and Visual Science*, **28**, 34–49.

Beach, F.A. (1940) Effects of cortical lesions upon the copulatory behavior of male rats. *Journal of Comparative Psychology*, **29**, 193–239.

Beal, M.F., Kowall, N.W., Ellison, D.W. *et al.* (1986) Replication of neurochemical characteristics of Huntington's disease by quinolinic acid. *Nature*, **321**, 168–71.

Beaumont, G. (1991) The use of benzodiazepines in general practice. In Hindmarch, I. *et al.* (eds), *Benzodiazepines: Current Concepts*. Chichester: John Wiley.

Becker, J.B., Breedlove, S.M. and Crews, D. (1993) *Behavioral Endocrinology*. Cambridge, MA: MIT Press.

Berger, S.P. *et al.* (1996) Haloperidol antagonism of cue-elicited cocaine craving. *Lancet*, **347**, 504–8.

Bielajew, C. and Shizgal, P. (1986) Evidence implicating descending fibers in self-stimulation of the medial forebrain bundle. *Journal of Neuroscience*, **6**, 919–29.

Bjorklund, L.M., Pernaute, R.S., Chung, S. *et al.* (2002) Embryonic stem cells develop into functional dopaminergic neurons after transplantation in a Parkinson rat model. *Proceedings of the National Academy of Sciences, USA*, **99**, 2344–9.

Bliss, T.V.P. and Lomo, T. (1973) Long-lasting potentiation of synaptic transmission in the dentate area of the anaethetized rabbit following stimulation of the perforant path. *Journal of Physiology (London)*, **232**, 331–56.

Blum, K., Noble, E.P., Sheridan, P.J. *et al.* (1990) Allele association of human dopamine D2 receptor gene in alcoholism. *Journal of American Medical Association*, **263**, 2055–60.

Blum, K., Noble, E.P. and Sheridan, P.J. (1991) Association of the A1 allele of the D2 dopamine receptor gene with severe alcoholism. *Alcohol*, **8**, 409–16.

Blum, K. and Payne, J.E. (1991) *Alcohol and the Addictive Brain*. New York: Free Press.

Bohman, M. (1978) Some genetic aspects of alcoholism and criminality. *Archives of General Psychiatry*, **35**, 269–76.

Borbely, A. (1986) *Secrets of Sleep*. London: Penguin.

Bos, N.P.A. and Mirmiram, M. (1990) Circadian rhythms in spontaneous neuronal discharges of the cultured suprachiasmatic nucleus. *Brain Research*, **511**, 158–62.

Bouchard, C. (1994) Genetics of obesity: Overview and research directions. In Bouchard, C. (ed.) *The Genetics of Obesity*. Boca Raton, FL: CRC Press.

Bouchard, C. (1995) The genetics of obesity: From genetic epidemiology to molecular markers. *Molecular Medicine Today*, **1**, 45–50.

Bouchard, C., Tremblay, A., Despres, *et al.* (1990) The response to long-term overfeeding in identical twins. *New England Journal of Medicine*, **322**, 1477–82.

Bouchard, T.J., Jr (1994) Genes, environment and personality. *Science*, **264**, 1700–1.

Bouchard, T.J., Jr *et al.* (1990) Sources of human psychological differences: The Minnesota study of twins reared apart. *Science*, **250**, 223–8.

Bozarth, M.A. (1986) Neural basis of psychomotor stimulant and opiate reward: Evidence suggesting the involvement of a common dopaminergic system. *Behavioral Brain Research*, **22**, 107–16.

Bozarth, M.A. (1987) Ventral tegmental reward system. In Engel, J. and Oreland, L. (eds) *Brain Reward Systems and Abuse*. New York: Raven Press.

Bradley, P.B. (1989) *Introduction to Neuropharmacology*. London: Wright.

Bradshaw, J.L. and Mattingley, J.B. (1995) *Clinical Neuropsychology: Behavioral and Brain Science*. San Diego: Academic Press.

Breedlove, S.M. (1994) Sexual differentiation of the human nervous system. *Annual Review of Psychology*, **45**, 465–88.

Bregin, P. (1993) *Toxic Psychiatry*. London: HarperCollins.

Bremer, G. (1937) L'activité cérébrale au cours du sommeil et de la narcose. *Bulletin de l'Academie Royale de Belgique*, 4, 68–86.

Bruning, J.C., Gautam, D., Burks. D.J. *et al.* (2000) Role of brain insulin receptor in control of body weight and reproduction. *Science*, **289**, 2243–6.

Butters, N. (1984) Alcoholic Korsakoff syndrome: An update. *Seminars in Neurology*, **4**, 226–44.

Byne, W. (1994) The biological evidence challenged. *Scientific American*, May, 26–31.

Byne, W., Bleier, R. and Houston, L. (1988) Variations in human corpus callosum do not predict gender: A study using magnetic resonance imaging. *Behavioral Neuroscience*, **102**, 222–7.

Byne, W., Tobet, S., Mattiace, L. *et al.* (2001) The interstitial nuclei of the human anterior hypothalamus. An investigation of variation within sex, sexual orientation, and HIV status. *Hormones and Behavior*, **40**, 86–92.

C

Campion, J., Latto, R. and Smith, Y.M. (1983) Is blindsight an effect of scattered light, spared cortex and near threshold vision? *Behavioral and Brain Sciences*, 6, 423–86.

Cannon, W.B. (1927) The James–Lange theory of emotions: A critical examination and an alternative theory. *American Journal of Psychology*, **39**, 106–24.

Cannon, W.B. and Washburn, A.L. (1912) An explanation of hunger. *American Journal of Physiology*, 29, 441–54.

Capecchi, M.R. (1994) Targeted gene replacement. *Scientific American*, March, 52–59.

Carlson, A.J. (1912) The relation between the contractions of the empty stomach and the sensation of hunger. *American Journal of Physiology*, **31**, 175–92.

Carlson, N.R., Martin, G.N. and Buskist, W. (2004) *Psychology*. Harlow: Prentice Hall.

Carlsson, A. and Lindqvist, M. (1963) Effect of chlorpromazine or haloperidol on the formation of 3-methoxytyramine and normetanephrine in mouse brain. *Acta Pharmacology and Toxicology*, **20**, 140–4.

Castellucci, V.F. and Kandel, E.R. (1974) A quantal analysis of the synaptic depression underlying habituation of the gill-withdrawal reflex in Aplysia. *Proceedings of the National Academy of Sciences*, USA, **71**, 5004–8.

Chemelli, R.M., Wilioe, J.T. and Sinton, C.M. (1999) Narcolepsy in orexin knockout mice: Molecular genetics of sleep regulation. *Cell*, **98**, 437–51.

Chen, W.R., Lee, S.H., Kato, K. *et al.* (1996) Long-term modification of synaptic efficacy in the human inferior and middle temporal cortex. *Proceedings of the National Academy of Sciences, USA*, **93**, 8011–15.

Cheng, J.J., de Bruin, J.P.C. and Feenstra, M.G.P. (2003) Dopamine reflux in nucleus accumbens shell and core in response to appetitive classical conditioning. *European Journal of Neuroscience*, **18**, 1314.

Cheyette, S.R. and Cummings, J.L. (1995) Encephalitus lethargica: Lessons for contemporary neuropsychiatry. *Journal of Neuropsychiatry*, 7, 125–34.

Chi, J.G., Dooling, E.C., Grant, J.L. *et al.* (1977) Gyri development and the human brain. *Annals of Neurology*, 1, 86–93.

Clarke, J. (1990) Interhemispheric function in humans: Relationships between anatomical measures of the corpus callosum, behavioral laterality effect and cognitive profiles. Unpublished doctoral dissertation, University of California, Los Angeles.

Clavier, R.M. and Routtenberg, A. (1975) Brainstem self-stimulation attenuated by lesions of the medial forebrain bundle but not by lesions of locus coeruleus or the caudal ventral norepinephrine bundle. *Brain Research*, **101**, 251–71.

Cloninger, C.R. (1987) Neurogenetic adaptive mechanisms in alcoholism. *Science*, **236**, 410–16.

Cohen, N.J. and Corkin, S. (1981) The amnesic patient H.M.: Learning and retention of a cognitive skill. *Society for Neuroscience Abstracts*, 7, 235.

Cohen, N.J. and Squire, L.R. (1980) Preserved learning and retention of pattern-analysing skill in amnesia: Dissociation of knowing how and knowing that. *Science*, **210**, 207–10.

Coleman, D.L. (1973) Effects of parabiosis of obese with diabetes and normal mice. *Diabetologia*, **9**, 294–8.

Colle, L.M. and Wise, R.A. (1987) Opposite effects of unilateral forebrain ablations on ipsilateral and contralateral hypothalamic self-stimulation. *Brain Research*, **407**, 285–93.

Comings, D.E., Comings, B.G., Muhleman, D. *et al.* (1991) Dopamine D2 receptor locus as a modifying gene in neuropsychiatric disorders. *Journal of the American Medical Association*, October, 1793–1800.

Connell, P.H. (1958) *Amphetamine Psychosis*. London: Maudsley Monographs No. 5.

Cooper, R.M. and Zubek, J.P. (1958) Effects of enriched and restricted early environments on the learning ability of bright and dull rats. *Canadian Journal of Psychology*, **12**, 159–64.

Corbett, D., Laferriere, A. and Milner, P.M. (1982) Elimination of medial prefrontal cortex self-stimulation following transection of efferents to the sulcal cortex in the rat. *Physiology and Behavior*, **29**, 425–31.

Corbett, D. and Wise, R. (1979) Intracranial self-stimulation in relation to the ascending noradrenergic fiber systems of the pontine tegmentum and caudal midbrain: A moveable electrode mapping study. *Brain Research*, **177**, 423–36.

Corkin, S. (1984) Lasting consequences of bilateral medial temporal lobectomy: Clinical course and experimental findings. *Seminars in Neurology*, **4**, 249–59.

Cotzias, G.C., Van Woert, M.H. and Schiffer, L.M. (1967) Aromatic acid, amino acids and modification of Parkinsonism. *New England Journal of Medicine*, **276**, 374–9.

Crabbe, J.C. *et al.* (1996) Elevated alcohol consumption in null mutant mice lacking 5-HT$_{1B}$ serotonin receptors. *Nature Genetics*, **14**, 98–101.

Creese, I. *et al.* (1976) Dopamine receptor binding predicts clinical and pharmacological properties of antischizophrenic drugs. *Science*, **194**, 481–3.

Crow, T.J. (1980) Molecular pathology of schizophrenia: More than one disease process? *British Medical Journal*, **280**, 66–8.

Crow, T.J. (1985) The two-syndrome concept: Origins and current status. *Schizophrenia Bulletin*, **11**, 471–85.

Culliton, B.J. (1976) Psychosurgery: National commission issues surprisingly favorable report. *Science*, **194**, 299–301.

D

Dabbs, J.M. and Morris, R. (1990) Testosterone, social class, and antisocial behavior in a sample of 4,462 men. *Psychological Science*, **1**, 209–11.

Daly, J.W. and Fredholm, B.B. (1998) Caffeine – an atypical drug of dependence. *Drug and Alcohol Dependence*, **51**, 199–206.

Damasio, A.R. (1994) *Descartes' Error*. New York: Picador.

Damasio, H., Grabowski, T., Frank. *et al.* (1994) The return of Phineas Gage: Clues about the brain from the skull of a famous person. *Science*, **264**, 1102–5.

Damasio, A.R., Tranel, D. and Damasio, H. (1990) Face agnosia and the neural substrates of memory. *Annual Review of Neuroscience*, **13**, 89–109.

Davidson, J.M. (1980) The psychobiology of sexual experience. In Davidson, J.M. and Davidson, R.J. (eds) *The Psychobiology of Consciousness*. New York: Plenum Press.

Davidson, J.M., Camargo, C.A. and Smith, E.R. (1979) Effects of androgens on sexual behavior of hypogonadal men. *Journal of Clinical Endocrinology and Metabolism*, **48**, 955–8.

Davis, H.P., Rosenweig M.R., Becker, L.A. and Sather, K.J. (1988) Biological psychology's relationships to psychology and neuroscience. *American Psychologist*, **43**, 359–71.

Davis, J.D., Gallagher, R.J., Ladove, R.F. and Turausky, A.J. (1969) Inhibition of food intake by a humoral factor. *Journal of Comparative and Physiological Psychology*, **67**, 407–14.

Deakin, J.F.W. (1988) The neurochemistry of schizophrenia. In Bebbington, P. and McGuffin, P. (eds) *Schizophrenia: The Major Issues*. Oxford: Heinemann.

Delgado, J.M.R. and Anand, B.K. (1953) Increase of food intake induced by electrical stimulation of the lateral hypothalamus. *American Journal of Physiology*, **172**, 743–50.

DeLong, M.R. (1974) Motor functions of the basal ganglia: Single unit activity during movement. In Schmitt, F.O. and Worden, F.G. (eds) *The Neurosciences: Third Study Program*. Cambridge, MA: MIT Press.

Dement, W.C. (1976) *Some Must Watch While Some Must Sleep*. San Francisco: San Francisco Book Company.

Dement, W. and Kleitman, N. (1957) Cyclic variations in EEG during sleep and their relation to eye movements, body motility and dreaming. *Electroencephalography and Clinical Neuropsychology*, **9**, 673–90.

Deneau, G., Yanagita, T. and Seevers, M.H. (1969) Self-administration of psychoactive substances by the monkey. *Psychopharmacologia*, **16**, 30–48.

DeValois, R.L. and DeValois, K.K. (1988) *Spatial Vision*. New York: Oxford University Press.

Devane, W.A., Hanus, L., Breuer, A. *et al*. (1992) Isolation and structure of a brain constituent that binds to the cannabinoid receptor. *Science*, **258**, 1946–9.

Dewsbury, D.A. (1991) 'Psychobiology'. *American Psychologist*, **46**, 198–205.

Diamond, M.C., Scheibel, A.B., Murphy, G.M. and Harvey, T. (1985) On the brain of a scientist. *Experimental Neurology*, **88**, 198–204.

Di Chiarra, G. and Imperato, A. (1988) Drugs abused by humans preferentially increase synaptic dopamine concentrations in the mesolimbic system of freely moving rats. *Proceedings of the National Academy of Sciences*, **85**, 5274–84.

Dorociak, Y. (1990) Aspects of sleep. *Nursing Times*, **86**, 38–40.

Doty, R.L. (2001) Olfaction. *Annual Review of Psychology*, **52**, 423–53.

Douglas, R.J. (1967) The hippocampus and behavior. *Psychological Bulletin*, **67**, 416–42.

Dudel, J. (1978) Excitation of nerve and muscle. In Schmidt, R.F. (ed.) *Fundamentals of Neurophysiology*. New York: Springer-Verlag.

E

Eastman, C.L., Boulos, Z., Terman, O. *et al*. (1995) Light treatment for sleep disorders: Consensus report VI. Shift work. *Journal of Biological Rhythms*, **10**, 157–65.

Egaas, B., Courchesne, E. and Saitoh, O. (1995) Reduced size of the corpus callosum in autism. *Archives of Neurology*, **52**, 794–801.

Ehringer, H. and Hornykiewicz, O. (1960) Verteilung von Noradrenalin und Dopamin (3-hydroxytyramin) in Gerhirn des Menschen und verhalten bei Erkrankungen des Extrapyramidalensystems. *Klin. Wochenscher.*, **38**, 1236–9.

Eichebly, M., Payette, P., Michalisyn, E. *et al*. (1999) Increased insulin sensitivity and obesity resistance in mice lacking the protein tyrosine phosphatase-1B gene. *Science*, **283**, 1544–8.

Einstein, A. (1954) In Seelig *et al*. (eds) *Ideas and Opinions*. New York: Bonanza.

Ekman, P. and Friesen, W.V. (1978) *The Facial Action Coding System*. Palo Alto, CA: Consulting Psychologists Press.

Ekman, P., Levenson, R.W. and Frieson, W.V. (1983) Autonomic nervous system activity distinguishes among emotions. *Science*, **221**, 1208–10.

Ellis, H.H. and Ames, M.A. (1987) Neurohormonal functioning and sexual orientation: A theory of homosexuality–heterosexuality. *Psychological Bulletin*, **101**, 233–58.

Emery, A.E.H. and Mueller, R.F. (1992) *Elements of Medical Genetics*. Edinburgh: Churchill Livingstone.

Empson, J. (1993) *Sleep and Dreaming*. New York: Harvester Wheatsheaf.

Epstein, A.N., Nicolaidis, S. and Miselis, R. (1975) The glucoprivic control of food intake and the glucostatic theory of feeding behavior. In Mogenson, G.J. and Calarasu, F.R. (eds) *Neural Integration of Physiological Mechanisms and Behavior*. Toronto: Toronto University Press.

Eslinger, P.J. and Damasio, A.R. (1985) Severe disturbance of higher cognitive function after bilateral frontal lobe ablation: Patient EVR. *Neurology*, **35**, 1731–41.

Ettenberg, A., Pettit, H.O., Bloom, F.E. and Koob, G.F. (1982) Heroin and cocaine intravenous self-administration in rats: Mediation by separate neural systems. *Psychopharmacology*, **78**, 204–9.

Evarts, E.V., Shinoda, Y. and Wise, S.P. (1984) *Neurophysiological Approaches to Higher Brain Functions*. New York: John Wiley.

Evarts, E.V., Wise, S.P. and Bousfield, D. (1985) *The Motor System in Neurobiology*. New York: Elsevier.

F

Fadiga, L., Fogassi, L., Pavesi, G. *et al*. (1995) Motor facilitation during observation: A magnetic stimulation study. *Journal of Neurophysiology*, **73**, 2608–11.

Farde, L., Wiesel, F.A., Stone-Edwards, S. *et al*. (1990) D2 dopamine receptors in neuroleptic free naive schizophrenic patients. *Archives of General Psychiatry*, **47**, 213–19.

Feldman, R.S., Meyer, J.S. and Quenzer, L.F. (1997) *Principles of Neuropsycho-pharmacology*. Sunderland, MA: Sinauer.

Fibiger, H.C. and Philips, A.G. (1987) Role of catecholamine transmitters in brain reward systems: Implications for the neurobiology of affect. In Engel, J. and Oreland, L. (eds) *Brain Reward Systems and Abuse*. New York: Raven Press.

Fibiger, H.C. *et al.* (1992) The neurobiology of cocaine-induced reinforcement. In Ciba Foundation Symposium 166. *Cocaine: Scientific and Social Dimensions*. Chichester: John Wiley.

Fielden, J., Lutter, C. and Dabbs, J. (1994) *Basking in glory: Testosterone changes in world cup soccer fans*. Psychology Department, Georgia State University.

Finger, S. (1994) *Origins of Neuroscience*. New York: Oxford University Press.

Foote, S.L. (1987) Locus coeruleus. In Adelman, G. (ed.) *Encyclopedia of Neuroscience*. Boston: Birkhauser.

Forger, N.G. and Breedlove, S.M. (1986) Sexual dimorphism in human and canine spinal cord: Role of early androgen. *Proceedings of the National Academy of Sciences*, USA, **83**, 7257–531.

Fried, I., Wilson, C.L., McDonald, K.A. and Behnke, E.J. (1998) Electric current stimulates laughter. *Nature*, **391**, 650.

Friedman, M.I., Tordoff, M.G. and Ramirez, I. (1986) Integrated metabolic control of food intake. *Brain Research Bulletin*, **17**, 855–9.

Funkenstein, D. (1955) The physiology of fear and anger. *Scientific American*, **192**, 74–80.

G Galaburda, A.M. (1993) Neurology of developmental dyslexia. *Current Opinion in Neurobiology*, **3**, 237–42.

Galaburda, A.M. and Livingstone, M. (1993) Evidence for a magnocellular deficit in developmental dyslexia. *Annals of the New York Academy of Sciences*, **682**, 70–82.

Galaburda, A.M. and Kemper, T.L. (1979) Cytoarchitectonic abnormalities in developmental dyslexia. *Annals of Neurology*, **6**, 94–100.

Galaburda, A.M., Sherman, G.F., Rosen, G.D. *et al.* (1985) Developmental dyslexia: Four consecutive patients with cortical abnormalities. *Annals of Neurology*, **18**, 222–33.

Gallant, D. (1993) Amethystic agents and adjunct behavioral therapy and psychotherapy. *Alcoholism: Clinical and Experimental Research*, **17**, 197–8.

Gallistel, C.R., Gomita, Y., Yadin, E. *et al.* (1985) Forebrain origins and terminations of the medial forebrain bundle metabolically activated by rewarding stimulation or by reward blocking doses of pimozide. *Journal of Neuroscience*, **5**, 1246–61.

Gardner, E.L. and Vorel, R.S. (1998) Cannabinoid transmission and reward-related events. *Neurobiology of Disease*, **5**, 502–33.

Garrett, B.E. and Griffiths, R.R. (1997) The role of dopamine in the behavioral effects of caffeine in animals and man. *Pharmacology, Biochemistry and Behavior*, **57**, 533–41.

Gazzaniga, M.S. (1970) *The Bisected Brain*. New York: Appleton-Century.

Gellar, I. (1962) Use of approach avoidance behavior (conflict) for evaluating depressant drugs. In Nodine, J.H. and Moyer, J.H. (eds) *Psychosomatic Medicine*. Philadelphia: Lea & Febiger.

Geschwind, N. (1972) Language and the brain. *Scientific American*, **226** (April), 76–83.

Geschwind, N. and Levitsky, W. (1968) Human brain: Left–right a symmetries in temporal speech region. *Science*, **161**, 186–7.

Geschwind, N. and Behan, P. (1982) Left handedness: Association with immune disease, migraine and developmental learning disorders. *Proceedings of the National Academy of Sciences*, **79**, 5097–100.

Gilling, D. and Brightwell, R. (1982) *The Human Brain*. London: Orbis.

Giros, B., Jaber, M., Jones, S.R. *et al.* (1996) Hyperlocomotion and indifference to cocaine and amphetamine in mice lacking the dopamine receptor. *Nature*, **379**, 606–12.

Gloor, P. (1990) Experimental phenomena of temporal lobe epilepsy. Facts and hypotheses. *Brain*, **113**, 1673–94.

Goeders, N.E. and Smith, J.E. (1983) Cortical dopaminergic involvement in cocaine reinforcement. *Science*, **221**, 773–5.

Golbe, L.I., Dilorio, G., Bonavita, V. *et al.* (1990) A large kindred with autosomal dominant Parkinson's disease. *Annals of Neurology*, **27**, 276–82.

Goldstein, K. (1952) The effect of brain damage on personality. *Psychiatry*, **15**, 41–5.

Goodnick, P.J. and Goldstein, B.J. (1998) Selective serotonin reuptake inhibitors in affective disorders: 1. Basic pharmacology. *Journal of Psychopharmacology*, **12**, S5–S20.

Goodwin, D.W. (1980) Genetic factors in alcoholism. In Mello, N.K. (ed.) *Advances in Substance Abuse*, Vol. 1. Greenwich, CT: JAI Press Inc.

Goodwin, D.W., Schulsinger, F., Hermansen, L. *et al.* (1973) Alcohol problems in adoptees raised apart from alcoholic biologic parents. *Archives of General Psychiatry*, **28**, 238–43.

Goodwin, F.K. and Jamison, K.R. (1990) *Manic Depressive Illness*. New York: Oxford University Press.

Gorski, R.A., Gordon, J.M., Shryne, J.E. and Southam, A.M. (1978) Evidence for a morphological sex difference within the medial preoptic area of the rat brain. *Brain Research*, **148**, 333–46.

Gossop, M. (2000) *Living With Drugs*. Aldershot: Ashgate.

Gottesman, I.I. (1991) *Schizophrenia Genesis*. New York: Freeman.

Goy, R.W., Bercovitch, F.B. and McBrair, M.C. (1988) Behavioral masculinisation is independent of genital masculinisation in prenatally androgenised female rhesus monkeys. *Hormones and Behavior*, **22**, 552–71.

Graham, R.B. (1990) *Physiological Psychology*. Belmont: Wadsworth.

Gregory, R.L. (1981) *Mind in Science*. London: Penguin.

Gregory, R. (ed.) (1987) *The Oxford Companion to the Mind*. Oxford: Oxford University Press.

Griffiths, R.R., Bigelow, G.E. and Henningfield, J.E. (1980) Similarities in animal and human drug-taking behavior. In Meool, N.K. (ed.) *Advances in Substance Abuse*, Vol 1. Greenwich, CT: JAI Press.

Grigorenko, E.L., Wood, F.B., Meyer, M.S. *et al*. (1997) Susceptibility loci for distinct components of developmental dyslexia on chromosomes 6 and 15. *American Journal of Human Genetics*, **60**, 27–39.

Grillner, S. (1996) Neural networks for vertebrate locomotion. *Scientific American*, **271**, 48–53.

Groves, P.M. and Rebec, G.V. (1992) *Biological Psychology*. Dubuque: William Brown.

Gurevich, E.V., Bordelon, Y., Shapiro, R.M. *et al*. (1997) Mesolimbic dopamine D3 receptors and use of antipsychotics in patients with schizophrenia: A post-mortem study. *Archives of General Psychiatry*, **54**, 225–32.

Gusella, J.F., Wexler, N.S., Conneally, P.M. *et al*. (1983) A polymorphic DNA marker genetically linked to Huntington's disease. *Nature*, **306**, 234–8.

H

Haas, K. and Haas, A. (1993) *Understanding Sexuality*. St Louis: Mosby.

Halaas, J.L., Gajiwada, K.S., Maffei, M. *et al*. (1995) Weight-reducing effects of the plasma protein encoded by the obese gene. *Science*, **269**, 543–6.

Halpern, D.F. and Coren, S. (1988) Do right handers live longer? *Nature*, **333**, 213.

Harper, P.S. (ed.) (1991) *Huntington's Disease*. London: Saunders.

Hart, B.L. (1967) Testosterone regulation of sexual reflexes in spinal male rats. *Science*, **155**, 1283–4.

Hay, D.A. (1985) *Essentials of Behaviour Genetics*. Melbourne: Blackwell.

Hebb, D.O. (1949) *The Organisation of Behavior*. New York: John Wiley.

Heimer, L. and Larsson, K. (1967) Impairment of mating behavior in male rats following lesions in the preoptic–anterior hypothalamic continuum. *Brain Research*, **3**, 248–63.

Hepper, P.G., Shahidullah, S. and White, R. (1991) Handedness in the human fetus. *Neuropsychologia*, **29**, 1107–11.

Heriot, A. (1955) *The Castrati in Opera*. London: Secker & Warburg.

Herkenham, M., Lynn, A.B., Johnson, M.R. *et al*. (1991) Characterization and localization of cannabinoid receptors in rat brain: A quantatitive *in vivo* autoradiographic study. *Journal of Neuroscience*, **11**, 563–83.

Hesselbrock, M.N. (1995) Genetic determinants of alcoholic subtypes. In Begleter, H. and Kissin, B. (eds) *The Genetics of Alcoholism*. Oxford: Oxford University Press.

Heymsfeld, S.N., Greenberg, A.S., Fujioka, K. *et al*. (1999) Recombinant leptin for weight loss in obese and lean adults. *Journal of the American Medical Association*, **282**, 1568–75.

Higley, J.D., Mehlman, P.T., Poland, R.E. *et al*. (1996) CSF testosterone and 5-HIAA correlate with different types of aggressive behaviors. *Biological Psychiatry*, **40**, 1067–82.

Hobson, J.A. (1988) *The Dreaming Brain*. London: Penguin.

Hobson, J.A. (1989) *Sleep*. New York: Scientific American Library.

Hobson, J.A., McCarley, R.W. and Wyzinsky, P.W. (1975) Sleep cycle oscillation: Reciprocal discharge by two brainstem neuronal groups. *Science*, **189**, 55–8.

Hodgson, L. (1991) Why do we need sleep? Relating theory to nursing practice. *Journal of Advanced Nursing*, **16**, 1503–10.

Hoffman, I.S. and Cubeddu, L.X. (1982) Presynaptic effects of tetrahydropapaveroline on striatal dopaminergic neurons. *Journal of Pharmacology and Experimental Therapeutics*, **220**, 16–22.

Holmes, D. (1991) *Abnormal Psychology*. New York: HarperCollins.

Holtzman, S.G. (1990) Caffeine as a model drug of abuse. *Trends in Neurosciences*, **11**, 355–6.

Hopkins, A. (1993) *Clinical Neurology*. Oxford: Oxford University Press.

Horne, J. (1978) A review of the biological effects of total sleep deprivation in man. *Biological Psychology*, **7**, 55–102.

Horne, J. (1988) *Why We Sleep*. Oxford: Oxford University Press.

Hubel, D.H. (1982) Exploration of the primary visual cortex. *Nature*, **299**, 515–24.

Hubel, D.H. (1988) *Eye, Brain and Vision*. New York: Scientific American Library.

Hughes, J. (1991) *An Outline of Modern Psychiatry*. Chichester: John Wiley.

Hughes, J.T., Smith, T., Kosterlitz, H.W. *et al.* (1975) Identification of two related pentapeptides from the brain with potent opiate agonist activity. *Nature*, **258**, 577–9.

Hunt, D.M., Dulai, K.S., Bowmaker, J.K. and Mollon, J.D. (1995) The chemistry of John Dalton's color blindness. *Science*, **267**, 984–8.

Huntington's Disease Collaborative Research Group (1993) A novel gene containing a trinucleotide repeat that is expanded and unstable on Huntington's disease chromosomes. *Cell*, **72**, 971–83.

Huppert, F.A. and Piercy, M. (1979) Normal and abnormal forgetting in organic amnesia: Effect of locus of lesion. *Cortex*, **15**, 385–90.

Huston, J.P. and Borbely, A.A. (1973) Operant conditioning in forebrain ablated rats by use of rewarding hypothalamic stimulation. *Brain Research*, **50**, 467–72.

Hyde, T.M., Stacey, M.E., Coppola, R. *et al.* (1995) Cerebral morphometric abnormalities in Tourette's syndrome: A quantitative MRI study of monozygotic twins. *Neurology*, **45**, 1176–82.

Imperato, A. and Di Chiarra, G. (1986) Preferential stimulation of dopamine release in the nucleus accumbens of freely moving rats by ethanol. *Journal of Pharmacology and Experimental Therapeutics*, **239**, 219–28.

Institute for the Study of Drug Dependence (1996) *Heroin: Drug Notes*. London: ISDD.

J

Jablensky, A., Sartorius, N., Emberg, G. *et al.* (1992) Schizophrenia: Manifestations, incidence and course in different cultures. A World Health Organisation 10 country study. *Psychological Medicine Monograph*, Suppl. 20.

Jacobs, L.F., Gaulin, S.J.C., Sherry, D.F. and Hoffman, G.E. (1990) Evolution of spatial cognition: Sex-specific patterns of spatial behavior predict hippocampal size. *Proceedings of the New York Academy of Sciences*, **87**, 6349–52.

James, W. (1890) *The Principles of Psychology*. New York: Holt.

Jaskiw, G. and Kleinman, J. (1988) Postmortem neurochemistry studies in schizophrenia. In Schulz, S.C. and Tamminga, C.A. (eds) *Schizophrenia: A Scientific Focus*. New York: Oxford University Press.

Jellinek, E.M. (1960) *The Disease Concept of Alcoholism*. New Haven, CT: Hillhouse.

Jimerson, D.C., Lesem, W.H., Kaye, W.H. and Brewerton, T.D. (1992) Low serotonin and dopamine metabolite concentrations in CSF from bulimic patients with frequent binge episodes. *Archives of General Psychiatry*, **49**, 132–8.

Johnson, P.L. and Stellar, J.R. (1994) N-methyl-D-aspartate acid-induced lesions of the nucleus accumbens and/or ventral palidum fail to attenuate lateral hypothalamic self-stimulation reward. *Brain Research*, **546**, 73–84.

Johnson, W.G., Hodge, S.E. and Duvosin, R. (1990) Twin studies and the genetics of Parkinson's disease: A reappraisal. *Movement Disorders*, **5**, 187–94.

Johnstone. E.C., Crow, T.J., Frith, C.D. *et al.* (1978) The dementia of dementia praecox. *Acta Psychiatrica Scandinavica*, **57**, 305–24.

Jones, H.S. and Oswald, I. (1968) Two cases of health insomnia. *Electroencephalography and Clinical Neurophysiology*, **24**, 378–80.

Jones, S. (1993) *The Language of the Genes*. London: Flamingo.

Joslyn, W.D. (1973) Androgen-induced dominance in infant female rhesus monkeys. *Journal of Child Psychology and Psychiatry*, **14**, 137–45.

Jouvet, M. and Renault, J. (1966) Insomnie persistante aprés lesions des noyaux du raphe chez le chat. *C.R. Soc. Biol. (Paris)*, **160**, 1461–5.

Jouvet, M. (1967) Neurophysiology and the states of sleep. *Science*, **163**, 32–41.

K

Kaij, L. (1960) *Studies on the Etiology and Sequels of Abuse of Alcohol*. University of Lund: Department of Psychiatry.

Kandel, E.R. (1979) Small systems of neurons. *Scientific American*, **241** (Sept.), 67–76.

Kandel, E.R. and Hawkins, R.D. (1992) The biological basis of learning and individuality. *Scientific American*, Sept., 53–60.

Kandel, E.R., Schwartz, J.H. and Jessell, T.M. (1995) *Essentials of Neural Science and Behaviour*. Stamford: Appleton & Lange.

Kane, J.M. (1992) Clinical efficacy of clozapine in treatment of refractory schizophrenia: An overview. *British Journal of Psychiatry*, **160** (Suppl. 17), 41–5.

Kapp, B.S., Frysinger, R.C., Gallagher, M. *et al.* (1979) Amygdala central neuclus lesions: Effects on heart rate conditioning in the rabbit. *Physiology and Behaviour*, **23**, 1109–17.

Kapp, B.S., Pascoe, J.P. and Bixler, M.A. (1984) The amygdala: A neuroanatomical systems approach to its contributions to aversive conditioning. In Butters, N. and Squire, L.R. (eds) *The Neuropsychology of Memory*. New York: Guilford Press.

Kebbian, J.W. and Calne, D.B. (1979) Multiple receptors for dopamine. *Nature*, **277**, 93–6.

Keele, S.W. and Ivry, R. (1991) Does the cerebellum provide a common computation for diverse tasks? A timing hypothesis. *Annals of the New York Academy of Sciences*, **608**, 197–211.

Kendell, R.E. and Adams, W. (1991) Unexplained fluctuations in the risk of schizophrenia by month and year of birth. *British Journal of Psychiatry*, **158**, 758–63.

Kendrick, K.M. and Baldwin, B.A. (1987) Cells in temporal cortex of conscious sheep can respond preferentially to the sight of faces. *Science*, **236**, 448–50.

Kertesz, A. (1979) *Aphasia and Associated Disorders*. New York: Grune & Stratton.

Kety, S.S., Rosenthal, D., Wender, P.H. and Schulsinger, F. (1968) The types and prevalence of mental illness in the biological and adoptive families of adopted schizophrenics. In Rosenthal, D. and Kety, S.S. (eds) *The Transmission of Schizophrenia*. Elmsford: Pergamon Press.

Keynes, R.D. (1979) Ion channels in the nerve-cell membrane. *Scientific American*, **240**, 126–35.

Kimura, D. (1992) Sex differences in the brain. *Scientific American*, **267**, 80–7.

Kimura, D. and Harshman, R.A. (1984) Sex differences in brain organisation for verbal and non-verbal functions. *Progress in Brain Research*, **61**, 423–41.

Kinsey, A.C., Pomeroy, W.B. and Martin, C.E. (1948) *Sexual Behavior in the Human Male*. Philadelphia: Saunders.

Kluver, H. and Bucy, P.C. (1938) An analysis of certain effects of bilateral temporal lobectomy in the rhesus monkey with special reference to 'psychic blindness'. *Journal of Psychology*, **5**, 33–54.

Kolb, B. and Whishaw, I.Q. (1985) *Fundamentals of Human Neuropsychology*. New York: Freeman.

Kondo, Y., Sachs, B.D. and Sakuma, Y. (1997) Importance of the medial amygdala in rat penile erection evoked by remote stimuli from estrous females. *Behavioral Brain Research*, **88**, 153–60.

Koob, G.F. (1999) Drug Reward and Addiction. In Zigmand, M.J. *et al.* (eds) *Fundamental Neuroscience*. San Diego: Academic Press.

Koob, G.F. and Bloom, F.E. (1988) Cellular and molecular mechanisms of drug dependence. *Science*, **242**, 715–23.

Koob, G.F., Maldonado, R. and Stinus, L. (1992) Neural substrates of opiate withdrawal. *Trends in Neurosciences*, **15**, 186–91.

Kranzler, H.R. and Anton, R.F. (1994), Implications of recent neuropsychological research for understanding the etiology and development of alcoholism, in the *Journal of Consulting and Clinical Psychology*, **62**, 1116–26.

Kuffler, S.W. (1953) Discharge patterns and functional organization of the mammalian retina. *Journal of Neurophysiology*, **16**, 37–68.

Kuhar, M.J., Ritz, M.C. and Boja, J.W. (1991) The dopamine hypothesis of the reinforcing properties of cocaine. *Trends in Neurosciences*, **14**, 299–302.

Kuhn, R. (1958) The treatment of depressive states with G22355 (imipramine hydrochloride). *American Journal of Psychiatry*, **115**, 459–64.

L

Lacoste-Utamsing, M.C. and Holloway, R.L. (1982) Sexual dimorphism in the human corpus callosum. *Science*, **216**, 1431–2.

Lader, M. and Herrington, R. (1990) *Biological Treatments in Psychiatry*. Oxford: Oxford University Press.

Langston, J.W., Irwin, I., Langston, E.B. and Forno, L.S. (1984) Pargyline prevents MPTP-induced Parkinsonism in primates. *Science*, **225**, 1480–8.

Langston, J.W. (1990) Predicting Parkinson's disease. *Neurology*, **40**, 7–74.

Larsen, B., Shinhoj, E. and Lassen, N.A. (1978) Variations in regional cortical blood flow in the right and left hemispheres during autonomic speech. *Brain*, **101**, 193–209.

Larsen, J., Hoien, T., Lundberg, I. *et al.* (1990) MRI evaluation of the size and symmetry of the planum temporale in adolescents with developmental dyslexia. *Brain and Language*, **39**, 289–301.

Laurelle, M., Abi-Dargham, A., Van Dyck, C.H. *et al.* (1996) Single photon emission computerized tomography imaging of amphetamine-induced dopamine release in drug-free schizophrenic subjects. *Proceedings of the National Academy of Sciences, USA*, **93**, 9235–40.

Lashley, K.S. (1950) In search of the engram. *Symposium for the Society of Experimental Biology*, **4**, 454–82.

Lassen, N.A., Ingvar, D.H. and Skinhoj, E. (1978) Brain function and blood flow. *Scientific American*, **239** (4), 50–9.

Lavie, P. (1996) *The Enchanted World of Sleep*. New Haven, CT: Yale University Press.

Lavie, P., Pratt, H., Scharf, B. *et al.* (1984) Localised pontine lesion: Nearly total absence of REM sleep. *Neurology*, **34**, 118–20.

Lawrence, D. and Kuypers, H. (1968) The functional organisation of the motor system in the monkey. *Brain*, **91**, 1–36.

Le, A.D., Poulos, C.X. and Cappell, H. (1979) Conditioned tolerance to the hypothermic effect of alcohol. *Science*, **206**, 1109.

Leake, C.D. (1958) *The Amphetamines: Their Actions and their Uses*. Springfield, IL: Charles C. Thomas.

LeDoux, J.E. (1994) Emotion, memory and the brain. *Scientific American*, June, 32–9.

LeDoux, J.E. (1998) *The Emotional Brain*. London: Weidenfeld & Nicolson.

Lenneberg, E.H. (1967) *Biological Foundations of Language*. New York: John Wiley.

LeVay, S. (1991) A difference in hypothalamic structure between heterosexual and homosexual men. *Science*, **253**, 1034–7.

LeVay, S. (1993) *The Sexual Brain*. Cambridge, MA: MIT Press.

Levenson, W.R., Ekman, P., Heider, K. and Frieson, W.V. (1992) Emotion and autonomic nervous system activity in the Minangkabu of west Sumatra. *Journal of Personality and Social Psychology*, **62**, 972–88.

Lewy, A.J. (1980) Light suppresses melatonin secretion in humans. *Science*, **210**, 1267–9.

Lewy, A.J., Sack, R.L., Singer, C.M. *et al.* (1989) Winter depression: The phase between sleep and other circadian rhythms may be critical. In Thompson, C. and Silverstone, T. (eds) *Seasonal Affective Disorder*. London: Clinical Neuroscience Publishers.

Lickey, M.E. and Gordon, B. (1991) *Medicine and Mental Illness*. New York: Freeman.

Lin, L., Faraco, J., Kadotani, H. *et al.* (1999) The sleep disorder canine narcolepsy is caused by a mutation on the hypocretin (orexin) receptor 2 gene. *Cell*, **98**, 365–76.

Lindsley, D.B., Bowden, J. and Magoun, H.W. (1949) Effect upon the EEG of acute injury to the brainstem activating system. *Clinical Neurophysiology*, **1**, 475–86.

Lindvall, O. (1991) Prospects of transplantation in human neurodegenerative diseases. *Trends in Neurosciences*, **14**, 376–84.

Lindvall, O., Backlund, E.-O., Farde, L. *et al.* (1987) Transplantation in Parkinson's disease: Two cases of adrenal medullary grafts in the putamen. *Annals of Neurology*, **22**, 457–68.

Livingstone, M.S. and Hubel, D.S. (1988) Segregation of form, colour, movement and depth: Anatomy, physiology and perception. *Science*, **240**, 740–9.

Leonard, C.T. (1998) *The Neuroscience of Human Movement*. St Louis: Mosby.

Logue, A.W. (1986) *The Psychology of Eating and Drinking*. New York: Freeman.

Lorens, S.A. (1966) Effect of lesions in the central nervous system on lateral hypothalamic self-stimulation in the rat. *Journal of Comparative and Physiological Psychology*, **62**, 256–62.

Lovinger, D.M. (1997) Serotonin's role in alcohol's effects on the brain. *Alcohol World: Health and Research*, **21**, 114–19.

Low, L. (1999) Diabetes. In *Research Directions in Diabetes: Welcome News Supplements*. London: Wellcome Trust.

Lugaresi, E., Medori, R., Montagna, P. *et al.* (1986) Fatal familial insomnia and dysautonomia with selective degeneration of the thalamic nuclei. *New England Journal of Medicine*, **315**, 997–1003.

Lumeng, L., Hawkins, T.D. and Li, T.K. (1977) New strains of rats with alcohol preference and non-preference. In Thurman, J.R. *et al.* (eds) *Alcohol and Aldehyde Metabolizing Systems*. New York: Academic Press.

Lumeng, L., Murphy, J.M., McBride, W.J. and Li, T.K. (1993) Genetic influences on alcohol preference in animals. In Begleter, H. and Kissin, B. (eds) *The Genetics of Alcoholism*. Oxford: Oxford University Press.

M   MacLean, P.D. (1955) The limbic system ('visceral brain') and emotional behaviour. *Archives of Neurology and Psychiatry*, **73**, 130–4.

Macmillan, M. (1996) Phineas Gage: A case for all reasons. In Code, C. *et al.* (eds) *Classic Cases in Neuropsychology*. Hove: Psychology Press.

Mahut, H.S., Zola-Morgan, S. and Moss, M. (1982) Hippocampal resections impair associative learning and recognition memory in the monkey. *Journal of Neuroscience*, **2**, 1214–29.

Magni, F., Moruzzi, G., Rossi, G.F. and Zanchetti, A. (1959) EEG arousal following inactivation of the lower brain stem by selective injection of barbiturate into the ventribal circulation. *Archives Italiennes de Biologie*, **95**, 33–46.

Maguire, E.A., Frackowiak, R.S.J. and Frith, C.D. (1997) Recalling routes around London: Activation of the right hippocampus in taxi drivers. *Journal of Neuroscience*, **17**, 7103–10.

Maguire, E.A., Gadian, D.G., Johnsrude, I.S. *et al.* (2000) Navigation-related structural change in the hippocampi of taxi drivers. *Proceedings of the National Academy of Sciences, USA*, **97**, 4398–403.

Magnusson, A. and Axelrod, J. (1993) The prevalence of seasonal affective disorder is low among descendants of Icelandic emigrants in Canada. *Archives of General Psychiatry*, **50**, 947–51.

Malamut, B.L., Graff-Radford, N., Chawluk, J. *et al.* (1992) Memory in a case of bilateral thalamic infarction. *Neurology*, **42**, 163–9.

Malaspina, D., Harlap, S., Fenning, S. *et al.* (2001) Advancing paternal age and the risk of schizophrenia. *Archives of General Psychiatry*, **58**, 361–7.

Maldonado, R., Stinus, L., Gold, L.H. and Koob, G.F. (1992) Role of different brain structures in the expression of the physical morphine withdrawal syndrome. *Journal of Pharmacology and Experimental Therapeutics*, **261**, 669–77.

Manning, J.T. (2002) *Digit ratio: A Pointer to Fertility, Behavior and Health*. New Jersey: Rutgers University Press.

Mark, V.H. and Ervin, F.R. (1970) *Violence and the Brain*. New York: Harper & Row.

Martin, R.A. (2001) Humor, laughter, and physical health: Methodological issues and research findings. *Psychological Bulletin*, **127**, 504–19.

Martin-Iversen, M.T., Szostak, C. and Fibiger, H.C. (1986) 6-Hydroxydopamine lesions of the medial prefrontal cortex fail to influence intravenous self-administration of cocaine. *Psychopharmacology*, **88**, 310–14.

Masters, W.H. and Johnson, V.E. (1966) *Human Sexual Response*. Boston: Little, Brown.

Masters, W.H., Johnson, V.E. and Kolodny, R.C. (1995) *Human Sexuality*. New York: HarperCollins.

Matsuda, L., Lolait, S.J., Brownstein, M.J., Young, A.C. and Bonner, T.I. (1990) Structure of a cannabinoid receptor and functional expression of the cloned cDNA. *Nature*, **346**, 561–4.

Mayer, J. and Marshall, N.B. (1956) Specificity of goldthioglucose for ventromedial hypothalamic lesions and hyperphagia. *Nature*, **178**, 1399–1400.

Mazur, A. and Booth, A. (1998) Testosterone and dominance in men. *Behavioral and Brain Sciences*, **21**, 353–97.

Mazzolini, R.G. (1991) In Corsi, P. (ed.) *The Enchanted Loom: Chapters in the History of Neuroscience*. New York: Oxford University Press.

McCarley, R.W. (1995) Sleep, dreams, and states of consciousness. In Conn, P.M. (ed.) *Neuroscience in Medicine*. Philadelphia: Lippincott.

McCarley, R.W., Greene, R.W., Rainnie, D. *et al.* (1995) Brainstem modulation and REM sleep. *Seminars in the Neurosciences*, **7**, 341–54.

McCarley, R.W. and Hobson, J.A. (1975) Neuronal excitability modulations over the sleep cycle: A structured and mathematical model. *Science*, **189**, 58–60.

McClearn, G.E. and Kakihana, R. (1981) Selective breeding for ethanol sensitivity: SS and LS mice. In McClearn, G.E. *et al.* (eds) *The Development of Animal Models as Pharmacogenetic Tools*. Washington: NIAAA Monograph.

McClearn, G.E. and Rodgers, D.A. (1959) Differences in alcohol preference among inbred strains of mice. *Quarterly Journal of Studies on Alcohol*, **52**, 62–7.

McGinty, D.J. and Sterman, M.B. (1968) Sleep suppression after basal forebrain lesion in the cat. *Science*, **160**, 1253–5.

McKenna, P.J. and Bailey, P.E. (1993) The strange story of clozapine. *British Journal of Psychiatry*, **162**, 32–7.

McKim, W.A. (2003) *Drugs and Behaviour*. Englewood Cliffs, NJ: Prentice Hall.

McLean, D., Forsythe, R.G. and Kapkin, I.A. (1983) Unusual side effects of clomipramine associated with yawning. *Canadian Journal of Psychiatry*, **28**, 569–70.

McMacken, D., Cockburn, J., Anslow, P. and Gaffin, D. (1993) Correlation of fornix damage with memory impairment in six cases of colloid cyst removal. *Acta Neurochic (Wein)*, **135**, 12–18.

McManus, C. (2002) *Right Hand, Left Hand*. London: Weidenfeld & Nicolson.

Mecacci, L. (1991) Pathways of perception. In Corsi, P. (ed.) *The Enchanted Loom: Chapters in the History of Neuroscience*. New York: Oxford University Press.

Meddis, R. (1977) *The Sleep Instinct*. London: Routledge.

Michael, C.R. (1969) Retinal processing of visual images. *Scientific American*, **220**, 104–14.

Michael, R.P. (1980) Hormones and sexual behaviour in the female. In Krieger, D.T. and Hughes, J.C. (eds) *Neuroendocrinology*. Sunderland, MA: Sinauer.

Milner, B. (1970) Memory and the medial temporal regions of the brain. In Pribram, D.H. and Broadbent, D.E. (eds) *Biology of Memory*. New York: Academic Press.

Milner, B., Corkin, S. and Teuber, H.-L. (1968) Further analysis of the hippocampal amnesic syndrome: 14 year follow-up study of HM. *Neuropsychologia*, **6**, 317–38.

Mink, J.W. (1999) Basal ganglia. In Zigmond, M.J. *et al.* (eds) *Fundamental Neuroscience*. San Diego: Academic Press.

Mirmiran, M. (1986) The importance of fetal/neonatal REM sleep. *European Journal of Obstetrics, Gynecology and Reproductive Biology*, **21**, 283–91.

Mirsky, A.F., Bieliauskas, L.A., French, L.M. *et al.* (2000) A 39-year followup of the Genain quadruplets. *Schizophrenia Bulletin*, **26**, 699–708.

Mishkin, M. (1978) Memory in monkeys severely impaired by combined but not separate removal of the amygdala and hippocampus. *Nature*, **273**, 297–8.

Miyakawa, T., Yagi, T. Kitazawa, H. *et al.* (1997) Fyn-kinase as a determinant of ethanol sensitivity: Relation to NMDA-receptor function. *Science*, **278**, 698–701.

Mobbs, D., Greicius, M.D., Abdel-Azin, E. *et al.* (2003) Humor modulates the mesolimbic reward centres. *Neuron*, **40**, 1041–8.

Monaghan, E. and Glickman, S. (1992) Hormones and aggressive behavior. In Becker, J., Breedlove, S. and Crews, D. (eds) *Behavioral Endocrinology*. Cambridge, MA: MIT Press.

Money, J. (1960) Phantom orgasm in the dreams of paraplegic men and women. *Archives of General Psychiatry*, **3**, 373–82.

Money, J. and Ehrhardt, A.E. (1996) *Man and Woman, Boy and Girl. Gender Identity from Conception to Maturity*. Baltimore: Johns Hopkins University Press.

Money, J., Schwartz, M. and Lewis, V.G. (1984) Adult erotosexual status and fetal hormonal masculinization and demasculinization. *Psychoendocrinology*, **9**, 405–14.

Moore, R.Y. and Eichler, V.B. (1972) Loss of circadian adrenal corticosterone rhythm following suprachiasmatic lesions in the rat. *Brain Research*, **42**, 201–6.

Morgan, C.T. and Morgan, J.D. (1940) Studies in hunger: The relation of gastric denervation and dietary sugar to the effect of insulin upon food intake. *Journal of General Psychology*, **57**, 153–63.

Morin, C.L. and Eckel, R.H. (1997) Transgenic and knockout rodents: Novel insights into mechanisms of body weight regulation. *Nutritional Biochemistry*, **8**, 702–6.

Morris, R.G., Garrud, P., Rawlins, J.N.P. and O'Keefe, J. (1982) Place navigation impaired in rats with hippocampal lesions. *Nature*, **297**, 681–3.

Moruzzi, G. and Magoun, H.W. (1949) Brain stem reticular formation and activation in the EEG. *Electroencephalography and Clinical Neurophysiology*, **1**, 455–73.

Murray, A.M., Hyde, T.M., Knabe, M.B. *et al.* (1995) Distribution of putative D4 receptors in post-mortem striatum from patients with schizophrenia. *Journal of Neuroscience*, **15**, 2186–91.

N

Nauta, W.J.H. (1946) Hypothalamic regulation of sleep in rats: Experimental study. *Journal of Neurophysiology*, **9**, 285–316.

Navarro, M., Carrera, M.R.A., Fratta, W. *et al.* (2001) Functional interaction between opioid and cannabinoid receptors in drug self-administration. *Journal of Neuroscience*, **21**, 5344–50.

Nehlig, A. (1999) Are we dependent upon coffe and caffeine? A review on human and animal data. *Neuroscience and Biobehavioral Reviews*, **23**, 563–76.

Noble, E.P. (1993) The D2 dopamine receptor gene: A review of association studies in alcoholism. *Behavioral Genetics*, **23**, 119–29.

Nolte, J. (1999) *The Human Brain: An Introduction to its Functional Anatomy*. St Louis: Mosby.

O

Olds, J. (1958) Satiation effects in self-stimulation of the brain. *Journal of Comparative and Physiological Psychology*, **51**, 675–8.

Olds, J. and Milner, P. (1954) Positive reinforcement produced by electrical stimulation of septal area and other regions of the rat brain. *Journal of Comparative and Physiological Psychology*, **47**, 419–27.

Olds, M.E. and Forbes, J.L. (1981) The central basis of motivation: Intracranial self-stimulation studies. *Annual Review of Psychology*, **32**, 523–74.

Olds, M.E. and Olds, J. (1963) Approach-avoidance analysis of rat diencephalon. *Journal of Comparative Neurology*, **120**, 259–95.

Ogden, J.A. and Corkin, S. (1991) Memories of H.M. In Abraham, W.C. *et al.* (eds) *Memory Mechanisms: A tribute to G.V. Goddard*. Hillsdale, NJ: Lawrence Erlbaum.

Ojemann, G.A. (1975) The thalamus and language. *Brain and Language*, **2**, 1–120.

Ojemann, G.A. (1983) Brain organisation for language from the perspective of electrical stimulation mapping. *The Behavioral and Brain Sciences*, **2**, 189–230.

O'Keefe, J. and Conway, D.H. (1978) Hippocampal place units in the freely moving rat: Why they fire when they fire. *Experimental Brain Research*, **31**, 573–90.

O'Keefe, J. and Nadel, L. (1978) *The Hippocampus as a Cognitive Map*. Oxford: Oxford University Press.

Olton, D.S., Becker, J.T. and Handelmann, G.E. (1979) Hippocampus, space and memory. *Behavioral and Brain Sciences*, **2**, 313–65.

Olton, D.S. and Papas, B.C. (1979) Spatial memory and hippocampal function. *Neuropsychologia*, **17**, 669–82.

Olton, D.S. and Samuelson, R.J. (1976) Remembrance of places passed: Spatial memory in rats. *Journal of Experimental Psychology: Animal Behavior Processes*, **2**, 97–115.

Ornstein, R. (1988) *Psychology*. San Diego: Harcourt Brace Jovanovich.

Oswald, I. and Adam, K. (1980) The man who had not slept for 10 years. *British Medical Journal*, **2**, 1684–5.

Owen, F., Cross, A.J., Crow, T.J. *et al.* (1978) Increased dopamine receptor sensitivity in schizophrenia. *Lancet*, **ii**, 223–5.

P

Palmer, J.D. (1975) Biological clocks of the tidal zone. *Scientific American*, **232**, 70–9.

Papez, J. (1937) A proposed mechanism of emotion. *Archives of Neurology and Psychiatry*, **38**, 725–43.

Pasick, A. (2000) The yawning orgasm and other antidepressant side effects. Reported in www.contac.org/contaclibrary/medications6.htm

Pearl, R. and Parker, S.L. (1922) Experimental studies on the duration of life. II. Hereditary differences in duration of life in live-breed strains of Drosophila. *American Naturalist*, **56**, 5–19.

Penfield, W. and Rasmussen, T. (1950) *The Cerebral Cortex of Man*. New York: Macmillan.

Penfield, W. and Roberts, L. (1959) *Speech and Brain Mechanisms*. Princeton, NJ: Princeton University Press.

Pert, C.B. and Snyder, S.H. (1973) Properties of opiate-receptor binding in rat brain. *Proceedings of the National Academy of Sciences*, **70**, 2243–7.

Pettit, H.O., Ettenberg, A., Bloom, F.E. and Koob, G.F. (1984) Destruction of dopamine in the nucleus accumbens selectively attenuates cocaine but not heroin self-administration in rats. *Psychopharmacology*, **84**, 167–73.

Pfohl, B. and Winokur, G. (1983) The micropsychopathology of hebephrenic/catatonic schizophrenia. *Journal of Nervous and Mental Disease*, **171**, 296–300.

Philips, A.G. and Broekkamp, C.L.E. (1980) Inhibition of intravenous cocaine self-administration by rats after micro-injection of spiroperidol into the nucleus accumbens. *Society for Neuroscience Abstracts*, **6**, 105.

Philips, A.G. and Fibiger, H.C. (1978) The role of dopamine in maintaining intracranial self-stimulation in the ventral tegmentum, nucleus accumbens and medial prefrontal cortex. *Canadian Journal of Psychology*, **32**, 58–66.

Philips, A.G. and Fibiger, H.C. (1989) Neuroanatomical basis of intracranial self-stimulation: Untangling the Gordian knot. In Liebman, J.M. and Cooper, S.J. (eds) *The Neuropharmacological Basis of Reward*. Oxford: Clarendon Press.

Philips, R.G. and LeDoux, J.E. (1992) Differential contribution of amygdala and hippocampus to cued and contextual fear conditioning. *Behavioural Neuroscience*, **106**, 274–85.

Phoenix, C.H., Goy, R.W., Gerall, A.A. *et al.* (1959) Organising action of prenatally administered testosterone propionate on the tissues mediating mating behaviour in the female guinea pig. *Endocrinology*, **65**, 269–382.

Piccolino, M. (1997) Luigi Galvani and animal electricity: Two centuries after the foundation of electrophysiology. *Trends in Neurosciences*, **20**, 443–8.

Pierce, K., Muller, R.-A., Ambrose, G. *et al.* (2001) Face processing occurs outside the fusiform 'face area' in autism: Evidence from functional MRI. *Brain*, **124**, 2059–73.

Pickens, R.W., Svikis, D.S., McGrue, M. *et al.* (1991) Heterogeneity in the inheritance of alcoholism: A study of male and female twins. *Archives of General Psychiatry*, **48**, 19–28.

Pilowsky, L.S., Costa, D.C., Ell, P.J. *et al.* (1994) D2 dopamine receptor binding in the basal ganglia of antipsychotic-free schizophrenic patients. *British Journal of Psychiatry*, **164**, 16–26.

Piven, J. (1997) The biological basis of autism. *Current Opinion in Neurobiology*, **7**, 708–12.

Plomin, R., DeFries, J.C., McClean, G.E. and Rutter, M. (1997) *Behavioral Genetics* (3rd edn). New York: Freeman.

Pomp, D. (1999) Animal models of obesity. *Molecular Medicine Today*, **5**, 459–60.

Porac, C. and Coren, S. (1981) *Lateral Preferences and Human Behavior*. New York: Springer-Verlag.

Posner, M.I. and Raichle, M.E. (1994) *Images of Mind*. New York: Scientific American Library.

Post, R.M., Fink, E., Carpenter, W.T. and Goodwin, F.K. (1975) Cerebrospinal fluid amine metabolites in acute schizophrenia. *Archives of General Psychiatry*, **32**, 1063–9.

Prange, A.J., Wilson, I.C., Lynn, C.W. *et al.* (1974) L-Tryptophan in mania: Contribution to a permissive hypothesis of affective disorders. *Archives of General Psychiatry*, 30, 56–62.

Prisko, L. (1963) Short term memory in cerebral damage. Unpublished PhD dissertation, McGill University.

Provine, R.R. (1989) Contagious yawning and infant imitation. *Bulletin of the Psychnomic Society*, **27**, 125–6.

Provine, R.R., Tate, B.C. and Geldmacher, L.L. (1987) Yawning: No effect of 3–5 per cent CO_2, and exercise. *Behavioral and Neural Biology*, **48**, 382–93.

R

Raisman, G. and Field, P.M. (1973) Sexual dimorphism in the neuropil of the pre-optic area of the rat and its dependence on neonatal androgen. *Brain Research*, **54**, 1–29.

Rapoport, J. (1989) *The Boy Who Couldn't Stop Washing*. London: Fontana.

Rasmussen, K., Beiter-Johnson, D.B., Krystal, J.H. *et al.* (1990) Opiate withdrawal and the rat locus coeruleus: Behavioral, electrophysiological and biochemical correlates. *Journal of Neuroscience*, **10**, 2308–17.

Rasmussen, T. and Milner, B. (1977) The role of early left brain damage in determining lateralization of cerebral speech functions. *Annals of the New York Academy of Sciences*, **299**, 355–69.

Rechtschaffen, A., Gilliland, M.A., Bergmann, B.M. and Winter, J.B. (1983) Physiological correlates of prolonged sleep deprivation in rats. *Science*, **221**, 182–4.

Reul, J.M.H.M., Labeur, M.S., Grigoriadis, D.E. *et al.* (1994) Hypothalamic–pituitary–adrenocortical axis changes in the rat after long-term treatment with the reversible monoamine oxidase-A inhibitor Moclobemide. *Neuroendocrinology*, **60**, 509–19.

Reul, J.M.H.M., Stec, I., Soder, M. and Holsboer, F. (1993) Chronic treatment of rats with the antidepressant amitriptyline attenuates the activity of the hypothalamic–pituitary–adrenocortical system. *Endocrinology*, **133**, 312–20.

Reynolds, G.P. (1983) Increased concentrations and lateral asymmetry of amygdala dopamine in schizophrenia. *Nature*, **305**, 527–9.

Rickels, K., Schweizer, E., Csanalosi, I. *et al.* (1988) Long term treatment of anxiety and risk of withdrawal. *Archives of General Psychiatry*, **45**, 444–50.

Rizzolatti, G., Fadiga, L., Gallese, V. and Fogassi, L. (1996) Premotor cortex and the recognition of motor action. *Cognitive Brain Research*, **3**, 131–41.

Rizzolatti, G., Fogassi, L. and Gallese, V. (2001) Neurophysiological mechanisms underlying the understanding and imitation of action. *Nature Reviews: Neuroscience*, **2**, 661–70.

Roberts, D.C.S., Corocoran, M.E. and Fibiger, H.C. (1977) On the role of the ascending catecholaminergic systems in intravenous self-administration of cocaine. *Pharmacology, Biochemistry and Behavior*, **6**, 615–20.

Roberts, D.C.S. and Koob, G. (1982) Disruption of cocaine self-administration following 6-hydroxydopamine lesions of the ventral tegmental area in rats. *Pharmacology, Biochemistry and Behavior*, **17**, 901–4.

Robins, L.N. (1979) Vietnam veterans three years after Vietnam. In Brill, L. and Winick, C. (eds) *Yearbook of Substance Abuse*. New York: Human Science Press.

Robson, P. (1999) *Forbidden Drugs*. Oxford: Oxford University Press.

Rochford, G. (1974) Are jargon aphasics dysphasic? *British Journal of Disorders of Communication*, **9**, 35.

Rodier, P.M. (2000) The early origins of autism. *Scientific American*, February, 38–45.

Roffwarg, H.P., Muzio, J.N. and Dement, W.C. (1966) Ontogenetic development of the human sleep–dream cycle. *Science*, **152**, 604–19.

Rogers, P.J. and Blundell, J.E. (1980) Investigation of food selection and meal parameters during the development of dietary induced obesity. *Appetite*, **1**, 85.

Roland, P.E. (1984) Organisation of motor control by the normal human brain. *Human Neurobiology*, **2**, 205–16.

Roland, P.E., Larsen, B., Lassen, N.A. *et al.* (1980) Supplementary motor area and other cortical areas in the organisation of voluntary movements in man. *Neurophysiology*, **43**, 118–36.

Roll, S.K. (1970) Intracranial self-stimulation and wakefulness: Effects of manipulating ambient catecholamines. *Science*, **168**, 1370–2.

Rolls, B.J., Rolls, E.T., Rowe, E.A. and Sweeney, K. (1981) Sensory specific satiety in man. *Physiology and Behavior*, **27**, 137–42.

Rolls, E.T., Sanghera, M.K. and Roper-Hall, A. (1979) The latency of activation of neurones in the lateral hypothalamus and substantia inomminata during feeding in the monkey. *Brain Research*, **164**, 121–35.

Rolls, E.T. (1994) Neural processing related to feeding in primates. In Legg, C. and Booth, D. (Eds) *Appetite: Neural and Behavioural Basis*. Oxford: Oxford University Press.

Rose, R.M., Bernstein, I.S. and Gordon, T.P. (1975) Consequences of social conflict on plasma testosterone levels in rhesus monkeys. *Psychosomatic Medicine*, **37**, 50–62.

Rosenthal, D. (1963) *The Genain Quadruplets*. New York: Basic Books.

Rosenthal, N.E., Sack, D.A., Carpenter, C.J. *et al.* (1985) Antidepressant effect of light in seasonal affective disorder. *American Journal of Psychiatry*, **141**, 163–70.

Rosenzweig, M.R., Bennett, E.L. and Diamond, M.C. (1972) Brain changes in response to experience. *Scientific American*, February, 22–9.

Ross, E.D. (1984) Right hemisphere's language, affective behavior and emotion. *Trends in Neurosciences*, **7**, 342–6.

Rossetti, Z.L., Hmaidan, Y. and Gessa, G.L. (1992) Marked inhibition of mesolimbic dopamine release: A common feature of ethanol, morphine, cocaine and amphetamine abstinence in rats. *European Journal of Pharmacology*, **221**, 227–34.

Rosvold, H.E., Mirsky, A.F. and Pribram, K.H. (1954) Influence of amygdalectomy on social behaviour in monkeys. *Journal of Comparative and Physiological Psychology*, **47**, 173–8.

Roy, A. and Linnoila, M. (1989) CSF studies on alcoholism and related disorders. *Progress in Neuropsychopharmacology and Biological Psychiatry*, **13**, 505–11.

Roy, A., Virkkunen, M. and Linnoila, M. (1987) Reduced central serotonin turnover in a group of alcoholics? *Progress in Neuropsychopharmacology and Biological Psychiatry*, **11**, 173–7.

Royal College of Physicians Committee on Geriatrics (1981) Organic mental impairment in the elderly. *Journal of the Royal College of Physicians*, **15**, 142–67.

Rumsey, J.M., Horwitz, B., Donohue, B.C. *et al.* (1999) A functional lesion in developmental dyslexia: Left angular gyral blood flow predicts severity. *Brain and Language*, **70**, 187–204.

Rusak, B. (1977) Involvement of the primary optic tracts in mediation of light efferents on hamster circadian rhythms. *Journal of Comparative Physiology*, **118**, 165–72.

Rush, A.J., Cain, J.W., Raese, J. *et al.* (1991) Neurological basis for psychiatric disorders. In Rosenberg, R.N. (ed.) *Comprehensive Neurology*. New York: Raven Press.

Russek, M. (1971) Hepatic receptors and the neurophysiological mechanisms controlling feeding behaviour. In Ehrenpreis, S. (ed.) *Neurosciences Research*, Vol. 4. New York: Academic Press.

Russell, M.J., Switz, G.M. and Thompson, K. (1980) Olfactory influences on the human menstrual cycle. *Pharmacology, Biochemistry and Behavior*, **13**, 737–8.

Rutlidge, L.L. and Hupka, R.B. (1985) The facial feedback hypothesis: Methodological concerns and new supporting evidence. *Motivation and Emotion*, **9**, 219–40.

S

Sacks, O. (1985) *The Man who Mistook his Wife for a Hat*. London: Picador.

Sacks, O. (1990) *Awakenings*. London: Picador.

Salldou, F., Amara, D., Dierich, A. *et al.* (1994) Enhanced aggressive behaviour in mice lacking 5-HT$_{1B}$ receptor. *Science*, **265**, 1875–8.

Sartorius, N., Jablensky, A., Korten, A. *et al.* (1986) Early manifestations and first-contact incidence of schizophrenia in different cultures. *Psychological Medicine*, **16**, 909–28.

Schachter, S. and Singer, J.E. (1962) Cognitive, social and physiological determinants of emotional state. *Psychological Review*, **69**, 379–99.

Schildkraut, J.J. (1965) The catecholamine hypothesis of affective disorders: A review of supporting evidence. *American Journal of Psychiatry*, **122**, 509–22.

Schneider, G.E. (1967) Contrasting visuomotor functions of tectum and cortex in the golden hamster. *Psychologische Forschung*, **31**, 52–62.

Schwartz, M.W. and Seeley, R.J. (1997) The new biology of body weight regulation. *Journal of the American Dietetic Association*, **97**, 54–8.

Schwartz, W.J. and Gainer, H. (1977) Suprachiasmatic nucleus: Use of 14-C labelled deoxyglucose uptake as a functional marker. *Science*, **197**, 1089–91.

Scoville, W.B. and Milner, B. (1957) Loss of recent memory after bilateral hippocampal lesions. *Journal of Neurology, Neurosurgery and Psychiatry*, **20**, 11–21.

Seeman, P. (1995) Dopamine receptors and psychosis. *Scientific American Science and Medicine*, September, 28–37.

Sellers, E.M., Higgins, G.A. and Sobell, M.B. (1992) 5-HT and alcohol abuse. *Trends in Pharmacological Sciences*, **13**, 69–75.

Sham, P.C., O'Callaghan, E., Takei, N. *et al.* (1992) Schizophrenia following prenatal exposure to influenza epidemics between 1939 and 1960. *British Journal of Psychiatry*, **160**, 461–6.

Shepherd, G. (1991) *Foundations of the Neuron Doctrine*. New York: Oxford University Press.

Sherer, M.A., Kumor, J.M. and Jaffe, J.H. (1989) Effects of intravenous cocaine are partially attenuated by haloperidol. *Psychiatry Research*, **27**, 117–25.

Sherry, D.F., Jacobs, L.F. and Gaulin, S.J.C. (1992) Spatial memory and adaptive specialization of the hippocampus. *Trends in Neurosciences*, **15**, 298–303.

Shimizu, N., Oomura, Y., Novin, D. *et al.* (1983) Functional correlations between lateral hypothalamic glucose-sensitive neurons and hepatic portal glucose-sensitive units in the rat. *Brain Research*, **265**, 49–54.

Shoulson, I.E. and the Parkinson Study Group (1989) Effect of deprenyl on the progression of disability in early Parkinson's disease. *New England Journal of Medicine*, **321**, 1364–71.

Sidman, M., Stoddard, L.T. and Moore, J.P. (1968) Some additional quantitative observations of immediate memory in a patient with bilateral hippocampal lesions. *Neuropsychologia*, **6**, 245–54.

Siegel, J.M., Moore, R., Thannickal, T. *et al.* (2001) A brief history of hypocretin/orexin and narcolepsy. *Neuropsychopharmacology*, **25**, 14–20.

Siegel, S. (1976) Morphine analgesic tolerance: Its situation specificity supports a Pavlovian conditioning model. *Science*, **193**, 323–5.

Siegel, S. (1984) Pavlovian conditioning and heroin overdose: Reports by overdose victims, *Bulletin of the Psychonomic Society*, **22**, 428–30.

Siffre, M. (1975) Six months alone in a cave. *National Geographic*, **147**, 426–35.

Singer, H.S., Hahn, I.H. and Moran, T.H. (1991) Abnormal dopamine uptake sites in postmortem striatum from patients with Tourette's syndrome. *Annals of Neurology*, **30**, 558–62.

Singer, S. (1985) *Human Genetics*. New York: Freeman.

Singer, T.P. and Ramsey, R.R. (1990) Mechanism of neurotoxicity of MPTP. *FEBS Letters*, **274**, 1–8.

Skene, D.J., Lockley, S.W. and Arendt, J. (1999) Melatonin in circadian sleep disorders in the blind. *Biological Signals and Receptors*, **8**, 90–5.

Slaby, A.E. (1995) Suicide as an indicum of biologically-based brain disease. *Archives of Suicide Research*, **1**, 59–73.

Smith, A. and Sugar, O. (1975) Development of above normal language and intelligence 21 years after hemispherectomy. *Neurology*, **25**, 813–18.

Smith, G.P. and Gibbs, J. (1994) Satiating effect of cholecystokinin. *Annals of the New York Academy of Sciences*, **713**, 236–40.

Smith, O.A. (1956) Stimulation of lateral and medial hypothalamus and food intake in the rat. *Anatomical Record*, **124**, 363–4.

Snowdon, D. (2001) *Aging With Grace*. London: Fourth Estate.

Snyder, S.H. (1986) *Drugs and the Brain*. New York: Scientific American Library.

Snyder, S.H. and D'Amato, R.J. (1986) MPTP: A neurotoxin relevant to the pathophysiology of Parkinson's disease. *Neurology*, **36**, 250–8.

Sodhi, M.S., Arranz, M.J., Curtis, D. *et al.* (1995) Association between clozapine response and allelic variation in the 5-HT$_{2C}$ gene. *NeuroReport*, **7**, 169–72.

Spence, M.A., Flodman, P.L., Sadovnick, A.D. *et al.* (1995) Bipolar disorder: evidence for a major locus. *American Journal of Medical Genetics*, **60**, 370–476.

Spencer, D. and Corbett, J.R. (1986) Accumbens infusion of amphetamine increases and picrotoxin decreases reward from hypothalamic stimulation. *Society for Neuroscience Abstracts*, **12**, 1142.

Sperry, R.W. (1964) The great cerebral commissure. *Scientific American*.

Sperry, R.W. (1974) Lateral specialisation in the surgically separated hemispheres. In Schmidt, F.O. and Worden, F.G. (eds) *The Neurosciences: Third Study Program*. Cambridge, MA: MIT Press.

Springer, S.P. and Deutsch, G. (1989) *Left Brain, Right Brain*. New York: Freeman.

Squire, L.R., Amaral, D.G., Zola-Morgan, S. and Kritchevsky, M.P.G. (1989) Description of brain injury in amnesic patient N.A. based on magnetic resonance imaging. *Experimental Neurology*, **105**, 23–5.

Squire, L.R. and Zola-Morgan, S. (1985) Neuropsychology of Memory: New links between humans and experimental animals. In Olton, D., Corkin, S. and Gamzu, E. (eds) *Memory Dysfunction*. New York: New York Academy of Sciences.

Squires, R.F. and Braestrup, C. (1977) Benzodiazepine receptors in the rat brain. *Nature*, **266**, 732–4.

Stahl, S.M. (1996) *Essential Psychopharmacology: Neuroscientific Basis and Applications*. Cambridge: Cambridge University Press.

Stahl, S.M. (1998) Mechanism of action of serotonin selective reuptake inhibitors: Serotonin receptors and pathways mediate therapeutic effects and side effects. *Journal of Affective Disorders*, **51**, 215–35.

Steele, K.M., Bass, K.E. and Crook, M.D. (1999) The mystery of the Mozart effect: Failure to replicate. *Psychological Science*, **10**, 366–9.

Stein, L. and Wise, C.D. (1969) Release of norepinephrine from hypothalamus and amygdala by rewarding medial forebrain bundle stimulation and amphetamine. *Journal of Comparative and Physiological Psychology*, **67**, 189–98.

Stein, L. and Wise, C.D. (1971) Possible etiology of schizophrenia: Progressive damage to the noradrenergic reward system by 6-hydroxydopamine. *Science*, **171**, 1032–6.

Stellar, E. (1954) The physiology of motivation. *Psychological Review*, **61**, 5–22.

Stellar, J.R. and Corbett, D. (1989) Effects of regional neuroleptic infusion suggest a role for nucleus accumbens in lateral hypothalamic self-stimulation. *Brain Research*, **477**, 126–43.

Stephan, F.K. and Zucker, I. (1972) Circadian rhythms in drinking behaviour and locomotor activity of rats are eliminated by hypothalamic lesions. *Proceedings of the National Academy of Sciences, USA*, **60**, 1583–6.

Stern, E., Silbersweig, D.A., Chee, K.-Y. *et al.* (2000) A functional neuroanatomy of tics in Tourette syndrome. *Archives of General Psychiatry*, **57**, 741–8.

Stevens, C.F. (1979) The neuron, in *The Brain: A Scientific American Book*. San Francisco: Freeman and Co.

Stoudemire, A. (1998) *Clinical Psychiatry for Medical Students*. Philadelphia, Lippincott-Raven.

Strack, F., Martin, L.L. and Stepper, S. (1988) Inhibiting and facilitating conditions of the human smile: A non-obtrusive test of the facial feedback hypothesis. *Journal of Personality and Social Psychology*, **54**, 768–77.

Stricker, E.M., Rowland, N., Saller, C.F. and Friedman, M.I. (1977) Homeostasis during hypoglycemia: Central control of adrenal secretion and peripheral control of feeding. *Science*, **196**, 79–81.

Stunkard, A.J., Foch, T.T. and Hrubec, Z. (1986) A twin study of human obesity. *Journal of the American Medical Association*, **256**, 51–4.

Swaab, D.F. and Hofman, M.A. (1990) An enlarged suprachiasmatic nucleus in homosexual men. *Brain Research*, **537**, 141–8.

Szabo, B., Siemes, S. and Wallmichrath, I. (2002) Inhibition of GABAergic neurotransmission in the ventral tegmental area by cannabinoids. *European Journal of Neuroscience*, **15**, 2057–61.

Szasz, T.S. (1960) The myth of mental illness. *American Psychology*, **15**, 113–18.

T

Tetrud, J.W. and Langston, J.W. (1989) The effect of deprenyl (selegrine) on the natural history of Parkinson's disease. *Science*, **245**, 519–22.

Thannickal, T.C., Moore, R.Y., Niehuis, R. *et al.* (2000) Reduced number of hypocretin neurons in human narcolepsy. *Neuron*, **27**, 469–74.

Thomas, L. (1981) The problem of dementia. *Discovery*, August, 34–6.

Thompson, R.F. (1993) *The Brain: A Neuroscience Primer*. New York: W.H. Freeman.

Tranel, D., Damasio, A.R. and Damasio, H. (1988) Intact recognition of facial expression, gender, and age in patients with impaired recognition of face identity. *Neurology*, **38**, 690–6.

Tryon, R.C. (1940) Genetic differences in maze-learning ability in rats. *Yearbook of the National Society of Student Education*, **39** (1), 111–19.

Turner, A.M. and Greenough, W.T. (1983) Synapses per neuron and synaptic dimensions in occipital cortex of rats reared in complex, social or isolation housing. *Acta Stereologica*, **2** (Suppl. 1), 239–44.

Turner, A.M. and Greenough, W.T. (1985) Differential rearing effects on rat visual cortex synapses. 1. Synaptic and neuronal density and synapses per neuron. *Brain Research*, **329**, 195–203.

Tyler, A. (1986) *Street Drugs*. London: Hodder & Stoughton.

U

Ungerleider, L.G. and Mishkin, M. (1982) Two cortical visual systems. In Ingle, D.M. (ed.) *Analysis of Visual Behavior*. Cambridge, MA: MIT Press.

Ungerstedt, U. (1971) Adipsia and aphagia after 6-hydroxydopamine induced degeneration of the nigrostriatal dopamine system. *Acta Physiologica Scandinavica*, **367**, 95–122.

V

Valenstein, E.S. and Campbell, J.F. (1966) Medial forebrain bundle–lateral hypothalamic area and reinforcing brain stimulation. *American Journal of Physiology*, **210**, 270–4.

Van Essen, D.C., Anderson, C.H. and Felleman, D.J. (1992) Information processing in the primate visual system: An integrated systems perspective. *Science*, **255**, 419–23.

Victor, M., Adams, R.D. and Collins, G.H. (1971) *The Wernicke–Korsakoff Syndrome*. Oxford: Blackwell.

Virkkunen, M., Goldman, D., Nielson, D.A. and Linnoila, M. (1995) Low brain serotonin turnover (low CSF 5-HIAA) and impulsive violence. *Journal of Psychiatry and Neuroscience*, **20**, 271–5.

W

Wangensteen, O.H. and Carlson, H.A. (1931) Hunger sensations in a patient after total gastrectomy. *Proceedings of the Society of Experimental and Biological Medicine*, **28**, 545–7.

Watson, J.B. (1913) Psychology as the behaviorist views it. *Psychological Review*, **20**, 158–77.

Wedekind, C., Seebeck, T., Bettens, F. and Paepke, A.J. (1995) MHC-dependent male preferences in humans. *Proceedings of the Royal Society of London B*, **260**, 245–9.

Weeks, J.R. (1962) Experimental morphine addiction: Method for autonomic intravenous injections in unrestrained rats. *Science*, **138**, 143–4.

Weinberger, D.R., Bigelow, L.B., Kleinman, J.E. *et al.* (1980) Cerebral ventricular enlargement in chronic schizophrenia: An association with poor response to treatment. *Archives of General Psychiatry*, **37**, 11–13.

Weinberger, D.R. and Wyatt, R.J. (1982) Brain morphology in schizophrenia: *In vivo* studies. In Henn, F.A. and Nasrallah, H.A. (eds) *Schizophrenia as a Brain Disease*. New York: Oxford University Press.

Weingarten, H.P. (1983) Conditioned cues elicit feeding in sated rats: A role for learning in meal initiation. *Science*, **220**, 431–3.

Weinsier, R.L., Hunter, G.R., Heini, A.F. *et al.* (1998) The etiology of obesity: Relative contribution of metabolic factors, diet, and physical activity. *The American Journal of Medicine*, **105**, 145–58.

Weiskrantz, L., Warrington, E.K., Sanders, M.D. and Marshall, J. (1974) Visual capacity in the hemianoptic field following a restricted occipital ablation. *Brain*, **97**, 709–28.

Wenger, J.R., Tiffany, T.M., Bombardier, C. *et al.* (1981) Ethanol tolerance in the rat is learned. *Science*, **213**, 575–6.

Wiesel, T.N. (1982) Postnatal development of the visual cortex and the influence of the environment. *Nature*, **299**, 583–91.

Wilner, P. (1985) *Depression: A Psychobiological Synthesis*. New York: John Wiley.

Winn, P., Tarbuck, A.E. and Dunnett, S.B. (1984) Ibotenic acid lesions of the lateral hypothalamus: Comparison with the electrolytic lesion syndrome. *Neuroscience*, **12**, 225–40.

Wise, R.A. and Bozarth, M.A. (1984) Brain reward circuitry: Four circuit elements 'wired' in apparent series. *Brain Research Bulletin*, **12**, 203–8.

Witelson, S.F. (1985) The brain connection: The corpus callosum is larger in left handers. *Science*, **229**, 665–8.

Witelson, S.E. (1989) Hand and sex differences in the isthmus and genu of the human corpus callosum. *Brain*, **112**, 799–646.

Witelson, S.F., Kigar, D.L. and Harvey, T. (1999) The exceptional brain of Albert Einstein. *Lancet*, **353**, 2149–53.

Woods, S.C., Seeley, R.J., Porte, D. and Schwartz, M.W. (1998) Signals that regulate food intake and energy homeostasis. *Science*, **280**, 1378–83.

Y

Yanagita, T. (1987) Prediction of drug abuse liability from animal studies. In Bozarth, M.A. (ed.) *Methods for Assessing the Reinforcing Properties of Abused Drugs*. New York: Springer-Verlag.

Youdin, M.B.H. and Riederer, P. (1997) Understanding Parkinson's disease. *Scientific American*, January, 38–45.

Young, A.B. *et al.* (1988) NMDA receptor losses in putamen from patients with Huntington's disease. *Science*, **241**, 981–3.

Z

Zaidel, E. (1985) Language and the right hemisphere. In Benson, D.F. and Zaidel, E. (eds) *The Dual Brain: Hemispheric Specialization in Humans*. New York: Guilford Press.

Zellar, E.A., Barsky, J., Fouts, J.R. *et al.* (1952) Influence of isonicotinic acid hydrazide (INH) and 1-isonicotinyl-2-isopropyl hydrazine (IIH) on bacterial and mammalian enzymes. *Experimentia*, **8**, 349–50.

Zhang, Y., Proenca, R., Maffei, M. *et al.* (1994) Positional cloning of the mouse obese gene and its human homologue. *Nature*, 372, 425–32.

Zhou, J.-N., Hofman, M.A., Gooren, L.J.G. and Swaab, D.F. (1995) A sex difference in the human brain and its relation to transexuality. *Nature*, 378, 68–70.

Zinberg, N.E. (1984) *Drug, Set, and Setting*. New Haven, CT: Yale University Press.

Zola-Morgan, S. and Squire, L.R. (1985) Amnesia in monkeys following lesions of the mediodorsal nucleus of the thalamus. *Annals of Neurology*, 17, 558–64.

Zola-Morgan, S. *et al.* (1989) Lesions of the perirhinal and parahippocampal cortex that spare the amygdala and the hippocampal formation produce severe memory impairment. *Journal of Neuroscience*, 9, 4355–70.

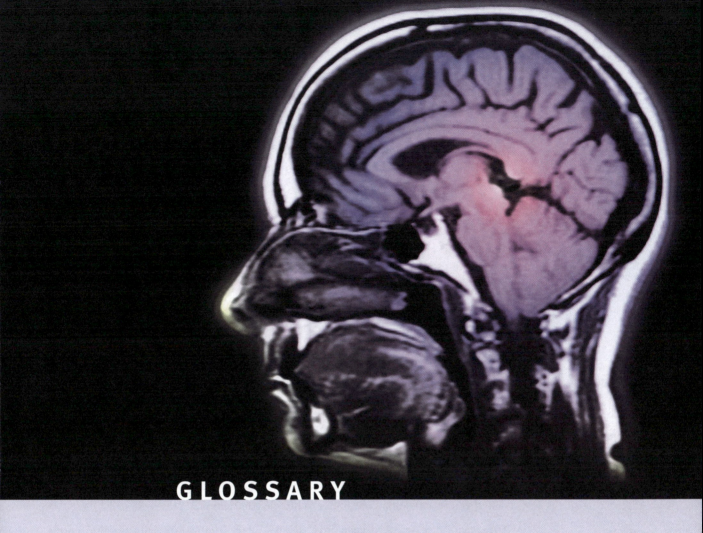

GLOSSARY

A

Absorptive phase The phase of metabolism that occurs during and immediately after a meal in which insulin is released by the pancreas gland. It contrasts with the post-absorptive phase, where glucagon is secreted by the pancreas gland.

Acetylcholine (Ach) An excitatory neurotransmitter that is used at the neuromuscular junction, in the autonomic nervous system, and throughout the brain.

Acetlycholinesterase (AchE) An enzyme found in the synapse that inactivates acetylcholine.

Actin A protein which acts along with myosin to produce contraction of muscle fibres.

Action potential The electrical signal or nerve impulse generated by the neuron, and conducted along axons (leading to transmitter release), which allows information to be passed from place to place in the nervous system.

Adenosine A nucleotide (a nitrogen-containing molecule) which has a variety of roles in the nervous system including that of an inhibitory neurotransmitter at some sites.

Adenosine triphosphate (ATP) A molecule which is the main source of energy in the cells of all living organisms.

Adenylate cyclase A membrane-bound enzyme that in some neurons is activated by G proteins to catalyse the synthesis of cAMP (a second messenger) from ATP.

Adipocyte A fat or lipid cell.

Adrenal hyperplasia   A condition where the adrenal glands secrete excess amounts of male sex hormones or androgens. This can masculinise the foetus if it occurs in early development.

Adrenaline   Also known as epinephrine. A substance that acts both as a hormone (released from the adrenal glands) and as a neurotransmitter in certain regions of the brain.

Agnosia   A partial or complete inability to perceive sensory information which is not explainable by deficits in basic sensory processing such as blindness.

Agonist   An agonistic drug is one which mimics or facilitates the action of a given neurotransmitter – normally by acting on its receptor.

Agraphia   A difficulty or inability to write, although reading (alexia) is generally unimpaired.

Akathisia   A condition of motor restlessness which can range from inner disquiet to an inability to remain stationary or sit still.

Akinesia   Absence or poverty of movement.

Alcohol dehydrogenase   An enzyme found in the liver that metabolises alcohol.

Alexia   An inability to read although the person has no visual deficits.

Allele   An individual has two alleles for each gene, one on each of their two chromosomes. The alleles can be identical or different, and dominant or recessive.

Alpha motor neuron   A neuron which arises from the ventral horn of the spinal cord and whose activation contributes to muscle contraction.

Alzheimer's disease   A degenerative disease of the brain, especially cerebral cortex and hippocampal regions, that affects about 20 per cent of people over the age of 80 years.

Amacrine cell   A specialised neuron in the retina that interconnects adjacent bipolar and ganglion cells.

Amino acids   A group of simple compounds (around 20 are made by cells) that can be linked together by peptide bonds to make larger and more complex molecules called proteins.

Amnesia   An incomplete or total loss of memory.

Amphetamine   A stimulant drug which 'works' by facilitating the release of catecholamines – especially dopamine – from nerve endings.

Amygdala   A group of nuclei located in the front of the medial temporal lobe which forms an important part of the limbic system.

Androgen   A steroid male sex hormone, which includes testosterone.

Angular gyrus   A region of the posterior parietal lobe, bordering the primary visual cortex, where strokes can lead to reading problems and word blindness.

Anomia   A difficulty in finding the 'right' word especially when naming objects. It is associated with Broca's aphasia.

Anorexia nervosa   A condition where the individual suffers loss of appetite, or refuses to eat sufficient amounts of food in pursuit of thinness.

Antagonist A drug which opposes or inhibits the effects of a particular neurotransmitter on the postsynaptic cell – normally by competing at a receptor site.

Anterior thalamus A group of nuclei at the front of the thalamus which forms an important link in the circuitry of the limbic system. It receives input from the hippocampus (via the fornix) and mammillary bodies, and sends its output to the cingulate gyrus.

Aphagia Cessation of eating. Most notably known to be one consequence of damage to the lateral hypothalamus.

Aphasia An inability to produce or comprehend language.

Aplysia A large marine snail that has provided a simple animal model by which to examine the synaptic basis of learning and memory.

Apraxia An inability to make voluntary movement in the absence of paralysis or other peripheral motor impairment.

Arcuate fasciculus A neural pathway that connects Wernicke's area with Broca's area, with damage to this structure causing conduction aphasia.

Ataxia An impairment of muscle coordination which is often associated with damage to the cerebellum and basal ganglia.

Attentional deficit hyperactivity disorder A developmental disorder associated with hyperactivity, impulsiveness and inability to concentrate.

Auditory cortex Located in the temporal cortex adjacent to the planum temporale and receives input from the medial geniculate body of the thalamus.

Autism A developmental disorder characterised by social withdrawal, language and communication deficits, and stereotypical behaviour.

Autonomic nervous system The part of the peripheral nervous system that controls the autonomic functions of the body, primarily though its action on glands and the smooth muscles of internal organs. It has two divisions – the sympathetic and parasympathetic – which act in opposite fashion.

Autoradiography A histological technique that shows the distribution of radioactive chemicals in the CNS, normally undertaken by mounting brain tissue on a slide of photographic emulsion, which is then developed.

Autoreceptors Receptors located on the presynaptic neuron whose main function is to regulate the amount of neurotransmitter that is released.

Autosomal dominant inheritance Essentially means if one inherits the gene, then one will inherit the characteristic. A prime example of this type of inheritance is Huntington's disease.

Axon A long thin extension that arises from the nerve cell body and which carries the nerve impulse to the axon terminal, where neurochemicals are released.

Axon hillock A cone-shaped area where the axon joins the cell body, and the critical site where depolarisation needs to take place for the action potential to be formed.

B

Balint's syndrome A disorder associated with bilateral damage of the parietal lobes consisting of three main features: optic ataxia (difficulty in accurately reaching for objects under visual guidance), paralysis of eye fixation, and simultanagnosia (difficulty in perceiving more than one object at a time).

Basal forebrain   A region of the brain that lies anterior and lateral to the hypothalamus and forms part of the circuitry of the limbic system.

Basal ganglia   A group of subcortical nuclei and interconnected pathways which are important for movement and contains the caudate nucleus, putamen and globus pallidus.

Bases   Simple nitrogenous molecules (adenine, guanine, cytosine and thymine) that form pairs and make up the rungs in the double helix of DNA.

Benzodiazepines   A class of drug which are used for their anxiolytic and sleep-inducing properties, including Valium, Librium and Temazapam.

Beta-adrenergic receptor   A class of noradrenergic (NA) receptor that is linked to the cAMP second messenger system.

Biochemistry   Is the study of the chemical processes and reactions in living organisms, many of which involve enzymes.

Bipolar cells   Interneurons found in the retina that have axon-like processes at both ends of their cell body.

Bipolar depression   A psychiatric disorder characterised by periods of depression and euphoria – sometimes known as manic depression.

Blindsight   The ability of subjects with damage of their primary visual cortex to accurately point towards, or track objects, in their 'blind' visual field.

Blood–brain barrier   A barrier formed by tightly packed cells in the capillaries, and their covering by astrocytes (glia cells), that prevents the passage of many harmful substances into the brain.

Bradykinesia   Slowness and poverty of movement and speech.

Brainstem   The old part of the brain that extends from the spinal cord and includes the medulla oblongata, pons and midbrain. This region of the brain also has many different nuclei (e.g. locus coeruleus and raphe) and contains the reticular formation, which controls electrical activity in the forebrain.

Broca's aphasia   Sometimes called expressive or non-fluent aphasia characterised by poor speech articulation, difficulty in finding the right word (anomia), and lacking the intonation and inflection of normal language (dysprosody).

Broca'a area   A region of the left posterior frontal cortex, located close to the face area of the primary motor cortex, that is involved in the production of speech.

Bulimia   Bouts of excessive eating and purging that is often seen in people with anorexia nervosa.

C

Cannon–Bard theory   A theory of emotion proposed by Walter Cannon and Philip Bard that argues that a stimulus first elicits an emotion, which is then followed by physiological changes.

Cataplexy   A symptom of narcolepsy, often triggered by an emotional event, that includes complete loss of muscle tone and paralysis which occurs during waking.

Catastrophic-dysphoric reaction   Feelings of despair, hopelessness and anger that are sometimes observed in people with damage to the left hemisphere.

Catecholamines   A class of monoamines that contain a catechol nucleus which includes noradrenaline and dopamine.

Caudate nucleus   An important part of the basal ganglia which along with the putamen makes up the striatum.

Central nucleus of the amygdala   The predominant output of the amygdala with projections to the brainstem and hypothalamus.

Cerebellum   A major structure meaning 'little brain' located at the back of the brainstem (near the pons) and importantly involved in motor coordination.

Cerebral cortex   Six-layered covering of the cerebral hemispheres, with an outer appearance of various distinct gyri and fissures, composed of neurons and their synaptic connections.

Cerebrospinal fluid (CSF)   The fluid that fills the ventricles of the brain and the subarachnoid space surrounding the brain and spinal cord. Its main function is to protect the CNS from mechanical injury, and to absorb and remove waste products of neuronal metabolic activity.

Cholecystokinin (CCK)   A hormone secreted by the duodenum that regulates gastric mobility and may be involved in the satiation of hunger. It is also found in neurons of the brain, where it may have a neurotransmitter function.

Chromosome   A long strand of DNA, coupled with protein, that acts as a carrier for genetic information. Human beings have 23 pairs of chromosomes, which are found in the nucleus of nearly every cell in the body.

Cillary muscles   The muscles that control the lens of the eye which allow visual images to be focused on the retina. They also give the eyes their distinctive colour.

Cingulate cortex   A large arc of 'old' limbic cortex that lies above and spans the corpus callosum.

Classical conditioning   A form of learning first demonstrated by Pavlov in which a neutral stimulus is paired with a stimulus that evokes behaviour (*unconditioned stimulus*). With repeated trials the neutral stimulus becomes a *conditioned stimulus* that is able to evoke the behaviour by itself.

Codon   A sequence of three bases in DNA which provides a code for making an amino acid.

Cognitive-arousal theory   A theory proposed by Stanley Schachter and Jerome Singer that maintains that in order to experience an emotion an individual has to experience physiological arousal *and* attribute the arousal to an appropriate stimulus.

Commissurotomy   Another name for the surgical operation in which the corpus callosum is severed thereby disconnecting the two cerebral hemispheres.

Complex cell   A type of neuron found in the visual cortex that responds (i.e. fires) when a line is presented in its visual field that is positioned, or moves, in a highly specific orientation.

Computerised axial tomography (CAT)   A non-invasive scanning technique that takes detailed three-dimensional pictures of brain structure by computer analysis of X-rays taken at different points and planes around the head.

Conditioned compensatory response   A conditioned (learned) response that acts to reduce a drug's impact on the body, and a proposed important contributor to drug tolerance.

Conduction aphasia   Caused by damage to the arcuate fasciculus, which connects Wernicke's area with Broca's area, and characterised by an inability to fluently repeat words, especially if they are abstract or non-meaningful.

Cone   A photoreceptor found in the retina which is responsible for fine-detailed vision and colour. There are three main types of cone with sensitivities to wavelengths of light roughly corresponding to blue, green and red.

Cornea   The transparent outer surface or 'window' of the eye whose curvature also gives it a role in focusing.

Corpus callosum   A broad thick band of around 20 million axon fibres that provides a channel for communication between the two cerebral hemispheres.

Cortical module   In the primary visual system a module is a self-contained unit which consists of two ocular dominance columns, a full range of orientation columns, and two cylindrical blobs that code for colour. Other types of module probably exist throughout the cerebral cortex.

Corticospinal pathway   The motor pathway originating in the motor cortex (and surrounding areas) of the cerebral cortex, and terminating in the grey matter of the spinal cord. The majority (85 per cent) of its axons (the lateral corticospinal tract) cross in the medulla to influence the opposite (contralateral) side of the body, whilst the remainder (ventral corticospinal tract) pass down to the same side (ipsilateral) part of the spinal cord.

Cortisol   A glucocorticoid hormone released by the adrenal glands, vital for life, and secreted in higher amounts during times of stress.

Cyclic AMP   A chemical that is involved in many biochemical reactions of the body, including an important role as a second messenger that causes the opening of ion channels following certain types of receptor activation.

Cytochrome blobs   Peg-like structures found in the primary visual cortex that are stained by the enzyme cytochrome oxidase and have an important role in colour processing.

D

Declarative memory   A type of memory that can be voluntarily 'declared' to consciousness and verbally expressed. In effect, it refers to an ability to recount what one knows. The ability to form new declarative memories is disrupted by damage to the hippocampus.

Deep cerebellar nuclei   A group of three nuclei (fastigial, interposed and dentate) within the cerebellum that receive input from the Purkinje neurons of the cerebellar cortex, and which send input out of the cerebellum.

Delayed non-matching to sample test   A test used to measure short-term memory in primates where the animal has to choose a different object from a tray to the one previously chosen after a given delay.

Delta-9-tetrahydrocannabinol   The main psychoactive ingredient in marijuana.

Dendrite   A treelike extension of the neuron's body that contains neurotransmitter receptors which receives chemical input from other nerve cells.

2-deoxyglucose A sugar that enters cells, including neurons, but is not metabolised. It can be combined with a radioactive isotope to enable the most active regions of the brain to be identified by autoradiography.

Deoxyribonucleic acid (DNA) A long nucleic acid composed of two helical strands (made from the sugar deoxyribose and phosphate) and four bases (adenine, thymine, cytosine and guanine) that provides the code for hereditary information.

Depression A psychiatric condition characterised by unhappiness, lethargy, sleep disturbances and negative thoughts. Sometimes referred to as unipolar depression to distinguish it from bipolar depression, where bouts of mania are also present.

Deuteranopia An inherited from of colour blindness in which red and green cannot be discriminated.

Diabetes mellitus A disease caused by the pancreas gland secreting insufficient amounts of insulin, which is a hormone that allows the uptake of glucose into cells. Consequently, untreated diabetics have high levels of blood sugar.

Diencephalon The part of the forebrain that contains the thalamus and hypothalamus.

Dizygotic twins Twins that develop from two different eggs (and thus two different sperms) and who are 50% genetically different. Sometimes called fraternal twins.

Dopamine A catecholamine neurotransmitter that is predominantly found in the striatum, nucleus accumbens, amygdala and frontal cortex.

Dopamine theory of schizophrenia The idea that schizophrenia is due to increased dopaminergic activity in the brain. The theory is supported, in part, by the finding that several effective antipsychotic drugs work by blocking dopamine receptors.

Dorsal An anatomical term that refers to structures towards the back of the body, or the top of the brain (e.g. a dorsal fin of a fish is located on its back or upper surface).

Dorsal lateral geniculate nucleus See lateral geniculate nucleus.

Dorsal raphe A structure found in the upper brainstem that, along with the medial raphe, provides the forebrain with its serotonergic innervation.

Dorsolateral area of frontal cortex Area of the prefrontal cortex lying above the orbital frontal region that receives input from the dorsomedial thalamus.

Dorsomedial thalamus An important relay of information from the limbic system (particularly the amygdala and entorhinal cortex) to the cortex of the frontal lobe.

Dual-centre set-point theory of hunger A theory developed in the 1950s that viewed the lateral hypothalamus as being the initiator of hunger and feeding, and the ventromedial hypothalamus as the satiety centre.

Duodenum The first 25 cm of the small intestine, which also include the pancreatic duct.

Dyskinesia Any impairment in the ability to initiate voluntary movement.

Dyslexia A term that refers to a group of reading disorders of varying severity.

Dystonia Lack of muscle tone.

E

Edinger–Westphal nucleus A small nucleus in the midbrain that sends fibres into the parasympathetic nervous system, which controls contraction of the pupil.

Electroencephalogram (EEG)   An apparatus that enables the gross electrical activity of the brain to be recorded from electrodes placed on the scalp.

Encephale isole preparation   A surgical preparation in which the brain is disconnected from the rest of the nervous system by a complete transection of the lower brainstem.

Encephalitus lethargica   An influenza-like illness that first appeared in 1916 and disappeared mysteriously in 1927, which caused many of its victims to fall into a prolonged stupor. Many of those who recovered went on to develop Parkinson's disease.

Endocrinology   The study of how hormones influence the functioning of the body. Behavioural endocrinology refers more specifically to how hormones influence brain and behaviour.

Engram   Another term for the anatomical, biochemical and/or physiological site of memory.

Entorhinal cortex   A form of transitional cortex found on the medial surface of the temporal lobes that provides the main neural gateway to the hippocampus.

Epinephrine   An American term for adrenaline.

Equipotentiality   The idea that all parts of the association cerebral cortex play an equal role in the storage of memories. This view contrasts with the theory that different parts of the cerebral association cortex have highly specialised functions.

Ethanol   Another term for ethyl alcohol, which is the type of alcohol found in alcoholic beverages.

Excitatory postsynaptic potential   A small change in the electrical potential of a neuron towards a positive direction, produced by excitatory neurotransmitters, that increases the likelihood of an action potential.

Exocytosis   The secretion of substances by the cell (e.g. neurotransmitters) caused by the fusion of organelles or vesicles with the plasma membrane.

Extrapyramidal system   The motor system of the brain whose output fibres to the spinal cord do not cross in the pyramidal region of the medulla. The term is commonly used to refer to the basal ganglia and an array of brainstem nuclei to which they are connected.

F

Flight or fight response   A pattern of physiological responses (e.g. increased heart rate, faster respiration, pupil dilation) produced by the sympathetic nervous system that helps to mobilise the body's resources to threat or the presence of danger.

Follicle-stimulating hormone   A hormone released by the anterior pituitary gland that causes maturation of the ovarian follicle and the secretion of oestrogen and progesterone.

Forebrain   A term that refers to all of the brain tissue lying above the midbrain, including the hypothalamus, thalamus, basal ganglia, limbic system and neocortex.

Fornix   A long arching fibre tract containing in the region of 1.2 million axons, that extends from the hippocampus to the mammillary bodies, anterior nucleus of the thalamus and hypothalamus.

Fovea   A pit in the centre of the retina containing colour-sensitive cones, and where visual acuity is at its greatest.

Free radicals Highly reactive and short-lasting breakdown products of oxygen which contain an unpaired outer electron. They are believed to be involved in ageing and certain types of degenerative disease.

Frontal cortex The front portion of the cerebral cortex that contains several important anatomical areas including the orbitofrontal and dorsolateral regions, Broca's area, and primary motor cortex.

G

GABA The abbreviation for gamma-aminobutyric acid – an amino acid neurotransmitter that is probably the most common inhibitory substance in the central nervous system.

Gamete A reproductive cell – namely the sperm or ovum – that contains 23 individual (not paired) chromosomes.

Gamma motor neuron A nerve cell located in the ventral horn of the spinal cord that innervates muscle spindles.

Ganglion cells Neurons whose cell bodies are found in the retina and whose axons give rise to the optic nerve.

Gene A long sequence of paired bases found in DNA that contains various codons, and which acts as a functional unit to make one or more proteins.

Genetic engineering A group of techniques, including the formation of transgenic animals, that involve altering the natural state of an organism's genome.

Gigantocellular tegmental field An area of the medullary reticular formation which contains large neurons and whose axons innervate the thalamus and cerebral cortex.

Glial cells The supporting cells of the central nervous system that also help to maintain the functioning of neurons. In the brain these consist of astrocytes, oligodendrocytes and microglial cells.

Globus pallidus Part of the basal ganglia which receives input from the striatum and whose main output goes to the ventral lateral nucleus of the thalamus.

Glucagon A hormone released by the pancreas gland which acts on the liver to convert glycogen into glucose.

Glutamate An amino acid which is the major excitatory neurotransmitter in the central nervous system.

Glycogen A stored form of sugar, found mainly in the liver, which can be converted into glucose by the pancreatic hormone glucagon.

Gonadotropin-releasing hormone A releasing factor secreted by the hypothalamus which acts on the anterior pituitary gland to help to secrete luteinising hormone and follicle stimulating hormone.

Gonads The primary reproductive organs – namely the ovaries or testes.

G-protein A type of protein, found attached to metabotropic receptors, which activates a cascade of proteins inside the cell including the formation of cAMP (a second messenger) in some neurons.

Growth hormone A hormone produced by the anterior pituitary which stimulates growth during development. It is also secreted in adults, reaching its peak about an hour after falling asleep.

Gyri   The raised ridges of the cerebral cortex (the fissures between the gyri are called sulci) which can also provide helpful landmarks in the identification of various cortical areas.

Hebbian synapse   A hypothetical synapse that is strengthened every time a presynaptic and postsynaptic neuron fire together, and believed to be a important mechanism in the neural basis of learning and memory.

Hemiplegia   Paralysis or loss of muscle tone of one half of the body.

5-HIAA   A breakdown product of the neurotransmitter serotonin.

Hippocampus   An important part of the limbic system located in the medial part of the temporal lobe consisting of folded primitive three-layered cortical tissue. The hippocampal formation consists of the subiculum, the hippocampus proper (Ammon's horn) and dentate gyrus, and is crucially involved in memory and cognitive mapping.

Histofluorescence technique   A type of histological technique which uses fluorescence to localise a wide variety of chemical substances in the central nervous system.

Homeostasis   The requirement of the body to maintain a consistent internal environment, despite exposure to various chemical changes and external fluctuations.

Homovanilic acid (HVA)   A breakdown (metabolite) product of dopamine that is found in the cerbrospinal fluid.

Horizontal cell   A type of neuron found in the retina that makes lateral connections between photoreceptors (i.e. rods and cones) and bipolar cells.

Hormone   A term generally used to refer to substances synthesised and secreted by endocrine glands, and transported in the blood to their target of action.

Human Genome Project   An international research project begun in 1990 and completed in 2003 which mapped the 3,000 million base pairs, or so, that make up the human genome (i.e. our 23 pairs of chromosomes).

Huntingtin   The protein produced by the gene that is responsible for causing Huntington's disease.

Huntington's disease   An autosomal dominant disorder (if one inherits the faulty gene one will inherit the disorder) which typically leads to degeneration of the basal ganglia in middle age. It is now known to be caused by an excessive number of the triple base CAG repeats on a small part of chromosome 4.

6-hydroxydopamine   A chemical neurotoxin that is selective for destroying catecholamine (dopamine and noradrenaline) containing neurons.

Hypercolumn   A cubic region of the primary visual cortex that is comprised of both orientation dominance columns and all possible orientation columns for a particular portion of the visual field.

Hypercomplex cell   A type of neuron found in the visual cortex that has functional properties similar to a complex cell (i.e. it fires when a line is presented in its visual field that is positioned in a highly specific orientation) except the stimulus has to be of a certain length.

Hyperphagia   Excessive eating and weight gain. As seen, for example, following lesions of the ventromedial hypothalamus.

Hypothalamic–pituitary–adrenal axis   The system in which the hypothalamus releases corticotrophin-releasing factor (CRF) into the anterior pituitary gland, which in turn secretes adrenocorticotropic hormone (ACTH) into the blood, which stimulates the adrenal cortex to release glucocorticoids such as cortisol.

Hypothalamus   A small collection of various nuclei lying just below the thalamus, which governs a wide range of homeostatic processes and species-typical behaviours. The hypothalamus is also involved in the regulation of the autonomic nervous system, and exerts control over the secretion of hormones from the pituitary gland.

I

Implicit memory   A type of memory which involves no explicit or conscious intention to learn or memorise.

Inbreeding   A way of producing different strains of animals, usually by brother–sister matings over several generations. This tends to produce genetically stable strains as it increases the chances of developing homozygous (identical) alleles.

Inferior colliculi   Small protrusions found near the upper surface of the midbrain that relay auditory information to the medial geniculate nucleus.

Inhibitory postsynaptic potential   A small change in the electrical potential of a neuron towards a negative direction, produced by inhibitory neurotransmitters, that decreases the likelihood of an action potential.

Insulin   A hormone released by the pancreas gland that enables glucose (and amino acids) to enter the cells of the body. It plays a particularly important role in allowing nutrients to be quickly stored immediately following a meal.

Interneuron   Typically a neuron with a short axonal process that is located within a given nucleus or structure.

Interstitial nuclei of the anterior hypothalamus   Four small cell groups (INAH 1–4) located in the anterior hypothalamus which are believe to be involved in sexual behaviour. In particular, INAH 2 and 3 have been shown to be larger in the male.

Inverse agonist   A drug that produces a neurochemical or behavioural effect opposite to that of a normal agonist.

Ion channel   A specialised protein complex in the plasma membrane of neurons that allows certain ions (most notably sodium, potassium and calcium) to pass into the cell. Ion channels can be *voltage-dependent* (i.e. they open when the membrane potential reaches a certain level), or *neurotransmitter-dependent* (i.e. they open when a neurotransmitter activates the cell).

Ionotropic receptor   A receptor complex where the binding site for a neurotransmitter and the ion channel form part of the same unit (e.g. the GABA receptor). Thus, activation of the receptor leads directly to a configurational change in the shape of the channel that allows ions to pass through. This contrasts with metabotropic receptors, which require the mediation of second messengers to open ion channels.

Iris   The ring of muscles that control the opening of the pupil and which gives the eyes their colour.

K

Klinefelter's syndrome   A genetic condition where males inherit an extra X chromosome (YXX) resulting in increased feminisation.

Korsakoff's syndrome   A syndrome whose main feature is anterograde amnesia, due to thiamine deficiency bought on by chronic alcoholism. It appears to be associated with damage to the mammillary bodies and dorsomedial thalamus.

L

Lateral geniculate nucleus   A region within the thalamus that receives fibres from the optic nerve and projects to the primary visual cortex.

Lateral hypothalamus   A region of the hypothalamus that has been implicated in a wide range of behaviours including eating, drinking, aggression, movement, sexual behaviour and attention.

L-dopa   A dopamine precursor that is able to cross the blood–brain barrier and provide a successful drug treatment for Parkinson's disease, which is due to degeneration of the nigral-striatal pathway and dopamine deficiency in the striatum.

Lens   A transparent structure in the eye, just behind the pupil, which helps to focus visual images onto the retina.

Leptin   A substance manufactured and secreted by adipocytes that communicates to the brain how much fat is being stored. It also appears to suppress food intake.

Lesioning technique   A surgical technique, often involving a *stereotaxic apparatus*, where parts of the central nervous system are either removed or destroyed using electrical or chemicals means.

Leydig cells   The cells in the testes that produce testosterone.

Limbic system   A group of interconnected brain regions that includes an arc of phylogenetically old cortex on the basal surface of the neocortex, and several other regions including the hippocampus, amygdala, fornix, mammillary bodies hypothalamus and anterior thalamus.

Lithium   An element that contains only three electrons, which means that it normally exists in the form of a positive ion (i.e. it easily loses its outer electron). It is used in psychiatry as a treatment for bipolar illness.

Locus coeruleus   A dark blue pigmented nucleus in the pons region of the brainstem which is the main origin of noradrenaline-containing neurons in the forebrain.

Long-term potentiation   A stable and enduring increase in the excitability of a neuron due to its repeated activation by high-frequency stimulation. It is believed to underlie the neural basis of learning and memory.

Lordosis   A female reproductive posture, observed in many four-legged mammals, in which the hindquarters are wriggled and raised, and tail turned to one side, thereby facilitating the act of copulation.

Luteinising hormone   A hormone released by the anterior pituitary gland that in females causes ovulation (the release of the egg from the ovary) and the development of the follicle into a corpus luteum. In males, luteinising hormone stimulates the Leydig cells to produce testosterone.

M

Magnetic resonance imaging (MRI)   A non-invasive scanning technique that measures the magnetic resonance of hydrogen atoms in the brain (induced by a strong magnetic field and radio waves) to build up a detailed three-dimensional image of brain structure.

Magnocellular cells   Large neurons found in the bottom two layers of the lateral geniculate nucleus that process information about form, spatial relationships and motion.

Mammillary bodies   Two nuclei located in the posterior region of the hypothalamus which receive a large input from the hippocampus via the fornix.

Mass action   A term used by Karl Lashley to refer to the capacity of the cerebral cortex to store memories throughout its structure.

Medial forebrain bundle   A large bundle of fibres that courses through the hypothalamus and interconnects regions of the forebrain with the midbrain.

Medial frontal cortex   The region of the prefrontal cortex that lies adjacent to the cingulate gyrus.

Medial geniculate body   A region of the thalamus that receives information from the inferior colliculus and sends output to the auditory cortex located in the temporal lobe.

Medial hypothalamus   The central area of the hypothalamus, which contains several important regions including ventromedial, dorsolateral and arcuate (infundular) nuclei. This part of the hypothalamus appears to be importantly involved in feeding, emotion and aggression.

Medial preoptic area   An area of the anterior hypothalamus implicated in many behaviours including sexual behaviour, temperature regulation and sleep.

Medial temporal lobes   Includes the amygdala and adjacent cortex (the uncus), the hippocampus and adjacent cortex (subiculum, entorhinal cortex and perirhinal cortex), and the fusiform gyrus.

Medulla oblongata   The part of the brainstem which emerges from the spinal cord. It is the origin of several cranial nerves, and contains centres for vital functions such as respiration, sneezing, vomiting and swallowing.

Melatonin   The hormone released by the pineal gland and believed to be important in the regulation of the body's circadian rhythms.

Mesofrontal dopamine pathway   The dopamine projection arising predominantly from the ventral tegmental area that goes to the frontal cortex.

Mesolimbic dopamine pathway   The dopamine projection arising predominantly from the ventral tegmental area that goes to the limbic system including the nucleus accumbens.

Mesostriatal dopamine pathway   Another name for the nigrial-striatal pathway, which passes from the substantia nigra to the striatum.

Messenger RNA   A single-stranded nucleic acid that transcribes the genetic message from DNA and transports it into the cytoplasm for protein synthesis.

Metabotropic receptor   A receptor linked to a G-protein just inside the cell, which in turn sets into motion a number of chemical events (including the activation of second messengers) leading to protein phosphorylation (i.e. opening) of certain ion channels.

MHPG   The main breakdown (metabolite) product of noradrenaline found in the cerebrospinal fluid. Otherwise known as 3-methoxy-4-hydroxphenylglycol.

Microglia   Glia cells that act as phagocytes (part of the immune system) in the central nervous system.

Millisecond   One thousandth of a second.

Millivolt   One thousandth of a volt.

Mitochondria   Organelles in the cytoplasm of the cell responsible for generating adenosine triphosphate (ATP), which is used as energy to drive a wide variety of chemical reactions.

Molecular biology   The branch of biology concerned with the synthesis, structure and function of molecules necessary for life.

Monoamine   A group of neurotransmitters that contain an amine in their chemical structure which includes serotonin, dopamine and noradrenaline.

Monoamine oxidase (MAO)   An enzyme found in neurons and glial cells that breaks down and inactivates monoamine neurotransmitters.

Monoamine oxidase inhibitors   Substances that inhibit the action of monoamine oxidase, thereby increasing the amount of monoamines in the synapse. These drugs have been shown to be effective antidepressants.

Monoamine theory of depression   The hypothesis that depression is due to a synaptic deficiency or under-activity of monoamines in the brain (especially noradrenaline and/or serotonin).

Monozygotic twins   Genetically identical twins who derive from the same egg.

Morris water maze   A large tank of water, filled with an opaque substance, containing a small platform hidden just below the surface. Since the platform cannot be directly observed, animals placed into the water have to use spatial knowledge to locate its whereabouts. Rats with hippocampal lesions are poor at performing this task.

Motor aphasia   A disorder in which the person is unable to make the correct movements of the mouth and tongue to articulate words. This type of deficit is associated with Broca's aphasia.

Motor cortex   The region of the cerebral cortex, located in the precentral gyrus of the posterior frontal cortex, which is topographically organised and sends its fibres into the corticospinal tracts to produce voluntary muscle movement.

Motor endplate   The specialised site on a muscle fibre which receives input from a motor nerve ending.

Müllerian duct   A primitive duct in the embryo that has the potential to develop into the female reproductive organs (fallopian tubes, uterus and upper vagina).

Muscle fibres   A collection of individual long cylindrical muscle cells, enclosed by an outer membrane called the sarcolemma, that make up skeletal muscle.

Muscle spindles   Long thin fibrous capsules that lie embedded between muscle cells, which provide information about stretching to neurons located in the spinal cord.

Myelin   The fatty sheath that covers and insulates the axon produced by the extensions of certain glial cells (oligodendroglia in the central nervous system, and Schwann cells in the peripheral nervous system).

Myofibrils   Small thin fibres within individual muscle cells, made up of short segments called sarcomeres, which contain fine filaments of *actin* and *myosin*.

Myosin   A protein found in the myofibrils of muscle cells that slides over actin to cause muscle contraction.

N

Narcolepsy   A condition where the person is overcome by sudden bouts of intense sleep typically accompanied by loss of muscle tone (cataplexy) that can last between 5 and 30 minutes.

Natural selection   The driving force behind evolution, sometimes referred as the 'survival of the fittest', where the strongest organisms most adapted to their habitat will be the ones most likely to pass on genes to their offspring.

Negative feedback   An important mechanism in homeostasis and many hormone systems. It refers to the process by which a physiological variable (e.g. body temperature) or hormone release reaches a sufficient level to turn off further activity (e.g. shivering) or secretion in that system.

Neocortex   The most recently evolved part of the brain consisting of six layers that form the 'crumpled' outer surface of the cerebral cortex.

Neuroanatomy   The study of the anatomical structure of the nervous system including its neural pathways and connections.

Neuromodulator   A chemical that alters the reactivity of the cell to a neurotransmitter.

Neuromuscular junction   The synapse that exists between the alpha motor neuron and the motor endplate which uses acetylcholine as its neurotransmitter.

Neuron   Essentially a specialised cell for generating and conducting electrical information which forms the fundamental unit of the nervous system. Also called a nerve cell.

Neuroscience   A discipline which encompasses a broad range of fields concerned with the structure and functioning of neurons including molecular and cell biology, anatomy, biochemistry, physiology and behaviour.

Neurotransmitter   A chemical that is released by an axon terminal into a synapse following the arrival of an action potential, and which typically crosses the synapse to bind (attach itself) to receptors on a postsynaptic cell.

Neuropeptide Y   A peptide believed to act as a neurotransmitter in the hypothalamus and involved in the regulation of feeding behaviour.

Neurophysiology   The scientific discipline that attempts to understand the electrical properties of neurons.

Neuropsychology   The discipline that attempts to localise functions to different regions of the human brain. Traditionally this pursuit has been undertaken with brain-damaged individuals, although non-invasive scanning techniques are now being used to address similar questions.

Nigral-striatal pathway   Dopaminergic pathway that extends from the substantia nigra to the striatum which shows marked degeneration in Parkinson's disease.

Nodes of Ranvier   A small gap in the myelin sheath surrounding the axon, where the action potential is renewed by the process of saltatory conduction.

Noradrenaline (NA)   A catecholaminergic neurotransmitter, also known as norepinephrine, found in the brain and the sympathetic division of the autonomic nervous system.

Nucleus accumbens   An area of the brain sometimes called the ventral striatum that receives a dopaminergic projection from the ventral tegmental area which is importantly involved in reward and feelings of pleasure.

Nucleus of the solitary tract   An area located in the medulla which receives information from the stomach, duodenum, liver and taste buds. Curiously, electrical stimulation of this area produces brain waves resembling those of slow-wave sleep.

O

Obsessive–compulsive disorder   An anxiety disorder where the person is afflicted with uncontrollable thoughts (obsessions) and engages in seemingly senseless rituals (compulsions).

Occipital cortex   The most posterior part of the cerebral cortex, which is also sometimes called the visual cortex.

Ocular apraxia   An inability to voluntarily shift attention to a new visual stimulus. It is one of the main features of Balint's syndrome and is associated with damage to the occipital-parietal regions of the brain.

Oligodendroglia   A type of glia cell which may have dozen of branches (*oligodendro* is Greek for 'tree with few branches') that wrap around axons to form the myelin sheath.

Opiate   A drug with similar properties to opium including morphine and heroin. The central nervous system also produces opiate-like peptides sometimes called endogenous endorphins.

Optic ataxia   The inability to accurately point to a target under visual guidance. Along with ocular apraxia and simultanagnosia it is also a feature of Balint's syndrome.

Optic chiasm   The point on the underside of the brain, just anterior to the pituitary gland, where the two optic nerves join, and where the majority of fibres cross to the opposite side of the brain.

Optic radiations   The axon fibres that project from the dorsal lateral geniculate region of the thalamus to the primary visual cortex.

Orbitofrontal region   The part of the prefrontal cortex that lies above the eyes which receives information from the dorsomedial thalamus.

Orexins   A group of proteins formed in the hypothalamus known to be involved in feeding, and also found in projections to the brainstem, where they have been implicated in sleep and narcolepsy.

Ovulation   The monthly process in which a mature ovum (egg) is released by the ovaries into the upper fallopian tubes. At this point fertilisation can occur if the ovum is impregnated by a sperm cell.

P

Pancreas gland   An endocrine gland located below the stomach, with its head tucked into the curve of the duodenum, which releases insulin and glucagon.

Papez circuit   A brain circuit connecting the hippocampus with the hypothalamus, thalamus and cingulate gyrus, first described by James Papez in 1937. Believed to be important in memory formation and emotional behaviour.

Parahippocampal gyrus   A region of the limbic cortex adjacent to the hippocampus which is essentially a continuation of the cingulate gyrus.

Parasympathetic nervous system   A major branch of the autonomic nervous system (along with the sympathetic nervous system) whose main function is to conserve and restore the body's resources (i.e. reduce arousal).

Parietal lobe   The part of the cerebral cortex posterior to the central fissure and above the Sylvian fissure.

Parkinson's disease   A brain disorder caused by degeneration of cells in the substantia nigra and reduced dopamine release in the striatum, leading to poverty of movement, tremor and rigidity.

Parvocellular cells   Neurons found in the top four layers of the lateral geniculate nucleus that process information about colour and fine detail for object recognition.

Patellar tendon reflex   A diagnostic reflex in which the tapping of the patellar tendon produces contraction of the quadriceps femoris muscle.

Periaqueductal grey area   The area that surrounds the cerebral aqueduct in the mid-brain. It is the major centre through which the hypothalamus enacts behaviours critical to the survival of the self and species.

Peripheral nervous system   All the nerves and neurons beyond the brain and spinal cord including the autonomic nervous system and somatic nervous system.

Perirhinal cortex   A region of the limbic cortex adjacent to the hippocampus.

PGO waves   An abbreviation for pons–geniculate–occipital waves – a distinctive burst of electrical activity originating in the pons and passing to the visual cortex via the thalamus, which is a characteristic of REM sleep.

Pharmacology   The study of how drugs work on the body.

Phenylketonuria   A hereditary disorder that can lead to brain damage caused by a recessive gene which causes the absence of phenylalanine hydroxylase (an enzyme that converts phenylalanine into tyrosine).

Physiology   The study of how the body and its parts function.

Pineal gland   A small gland situated in the epithalamus, once thought by Descartes to be the seat of the soul, but now known to secrete the hormone melatonin, which is involved in the regulation of circadian rhythms.

Pituitary gland   An endocrine gland connected to the hypothalamus consisting of two lobes – the adrenhypophysis containing many secretory cells, and the posterior neuro-hypophysis containing many nerve endings.

Place cells   Neurons found in the hippocampus that become highly active when the animal is in a particular location. They appear to be important for spatial navigation and forming a cognitive map of the environment.

Planum temporale   A region of the temporal lobe that is part of Wernicke's area lying adjacent to the primary auditory cortex, which is generally found to be larger on the left side of the brain. Abnormalities in this region has been found in some people with dyslexia.

Pons   The region of the brainstem above the medulla and lying below the midbrain. It contains a number of important nuclei including the locus coeruleus and the raphe.

Pontine nucleus   A large nucleus found in the pons which receives motor input from the cerebral cortex, and sends projections to the cerebellum.

Positron emission tomography (PET)   A non-invasive technique for examining brain function in humans that measures the brain's metabolic activity by use of short-lasting radioactive substances (usually 2-deoxyglucose) which emit subatomic particles called positrons.

Prefrontal cortex The most anterior region of the frontal lobes consisting of the association cortex which receives input from the mediodorsal thalamus.

Premotor area An area of the cerebral cortex located just in front of the primary motor cortex involved in the selection of movements.

Preoptic-basal forebrain A region of the brain lying just anterior to the optic chiasm. It is normally considered part of the hypothalamus although embryologically it is derived from different tissue.

Primary auditory cortex The first region of the cerebral cortex, located in the temporal lobes, which receives auditory information (via projections from the medial geniculate body of the thalamus).

Primary motor cortex A band of tissue located in the precentral gyrus of the frontal lobe that sends fibres into the corticospinal tracts and is important for voluntary movement.

Primary somatosensory cortex A band of tissue in the parietal lobes, adjacent to the primary motor cortex, which receives touch, pain and temperature information. It is particularly important for receiving motor feedback from the body.

Primary visual cortex The first region of the cerebral cortex, located in the occipital lobes, which receives visual information (via projections from the lateral geniculate body of the thalamus).

Procedural memory A type of implicit memory that is 'remembered' when an individual performs an action (sometimes described as 'knowing how' memory). Unlike declarative memory, it appears to be unaffected by damage to the hippocampus.

Prosopagnosia The inability to identify people by the sight of their faces, although other features such as their voice can be recognised.

Protanopia Ah inherited form of colour blindness in which red and green are confused. This is due to the cones coding for red frequencies of light being filled with green opsin.

Proteins A class of large molecules composed of smaller chains of amino acids that have a wide range of functions in the body and are vital for life. The DNA in a cell determines what proteins will be synthesised.

Psychiatry The branch of medicine concerned with the understanding and treatment of mental illness.

Psychosurgery The use of brain surgery to remedy mental health problems such as depression or compulsive behaviours in the absence of any identifiable brain damage.

Pulvinar region A large thalamic nucleus overhanging the superior colliculus and geniculate bodies. It is believed to have a role in vision and also possibly speech.

Pupil The aperture that controls the amount of light entering the eye.

Putamen A large nucleus that along with the caudate forms the neostriatum. It is an important component of the basal ganglia, receiving dopaminergic input from the substantia nigra, and glutamatic input from the cerebral cortex.

Pyramidal system A large system of fibres originating in the motor regions of the cerebral cortex which forms the pyramidal tracts that project to the spinal cord. Also known as the corticospinal tract.

R

Radioligand binding   A technique that is able to identify and count the number of neurochemical receptors. A ligand (i.e. a chemical known to bind to the receptor in question) is radioactively labelled and incubated with the tissue. The unbound ligand is then washed away, and the radioactivity from the bound ligand left in the tissue is measured.

Raphe nuclei   A group of nuclei located in the reticular formation of the medulla, pons and midbrain. Of particular importance are the dorsal and medial raphe, which together account for about 80 per cent of the serotonin found in the forebrain.

Rapid eye movement (REM) sleep   A stage of sleep characterised by small-amplitude, fast EEG waves, lack of muscle tone, and rapid eye movements. It is also the stage of sleep in which we normally dream.

Receptive field   The region where a stimulus causes the maximal response of a cell in a sensory system. In vision, this area is part of the visual field, whereas in touch this area may be mechanical pressure on a receptor or nerve ending.

Receptor   In this book, a receptor refers to a specialised protein molecule found in the membrane of a neuron that is sensitive to a specific neurochemical. In turn, the binding of a substance at a postsynaptic cell typically causes small changes in its electrical potential. There are two types of receptor: *ionotropic* and *metabotropic*.

Recessive gene   A gene that does not express its characteristics unless it is present in 'double dose', that is, a copy inherited from both parents.

Recombinant DNA   Genetic material made outside the living cell by splicing two or more pieces of DNA from different sources to create a combination of genes not normally found in nature.

Red nucleus   A large nucleus located in the midbrain tegmentum that receives inputs from the cerebellum and motor areas of the cerebral cortex, and which in turn sends axons to the spinal cord via the rubrospinal tract.

Reflex   A stereotyped, predictable and involuntary movement to a stimulus.

Refractory period   A period of a few milliseconds during and after a nerve impulse in which the responsiveness of a neuron is reduced and unable to generate another impulse.

Regional blood flow (RBF)   A technique which measures the flow of blood to various areas of the brain (e.g. by monitoring radioactive water or xenon-133). It is based on the assumption that the greater the rate of blood flow to an area, the more active that region will be.

Resting potential   The membrane potential of a neuron when it is at rest, and not being altered by excitatory or inhibitory postsynaptic potentials. The resting potential inside a neuron is generally around −70 mV compared with its outside.

Restriction enzymes   A group of enzymes that can cut strands of DNA at specific points or base sequences. They can be likened to molecular scissors.

Reticular activating system   A diverse group of cells in the reticular formation that project to the thalamus, which in turn project to widespread areas of the cerebral cortex. It is believed that this system is responsible for keeping us awake and regulating sleep–wake cycles.

Reticular formation   A highly complex network of dispersed nuclei and fibre tracts which extends throughout the core of the brainstem to the thalamus. It is involved in a wide range of functions including those that are vital for life.

Retina   A layer of cells located at the back of the eye that contains the photoreceptors (rods and cones) which transduce light into neural information.

Retrograde amnesia   An impairment of memory for information that was acquired prior to the onset of amnesia. This contrasts with *anterograde amnesia*, which is abnormal memory loss that occurs after the onset of amnesia.

Re-uptake pump   A special transporter protein generally found in the membrane of presynaptic neurons that rapidly removes neurotransmitter from the synapse.

Ribonucleic acid (RNA)   A single-stranded nucleic acid that contains the sugar ribose. There are three main types of RNA (messenger, transfer and ribosomal), all of which are involved in protein synthesis.

Ribosomes   Spherical structures found in the cytoplasm of the cell, sometimes likened to work benches, where the production of proteins takes place.

Rods   The most common type of photoreceptor found in the retina, which are very sensitive to changes in light intensity.

Rubrospinal tract   The pathway from the red nucleus to the spinal cord, which has an important role in the movement of the limbs.

S

Saccadic eye movements   Involuntary, rapid and small movements of the eyes that are used to monitor our visual surroundings.

Saltatory conduction   The means by which the action potential is propagated down the axon. In effect, this occurs by the action potential 'jumping' from one node of Ranvier to the next (i.e. small gaps in the myelin), where it is amplified back to its original intensity.

Schizophrenia   A severe mental illness (or psychosis) which is typically characterised by hallucinations, delusions, incoherent thought, paranoia and emotional withdrawal.

Sclera   The outer tough white material that covers most of the eyeball.

Seasonal affective disorder   A disorder in which the individual regularly becomes depressed during the winter months. It is also characterised by lethargy, sleep disturbances and carbohydrate cravings.

Second messenger   A chemical (such as cAMP) found in the cytoplasm that is activated when a neurotransmitter binds to a G protein-linked receptor (i.e. metabotropic receptor), which then causes protein phosphorylation (i.e. the opening) of ion channels.

Selective breeding   The breeding of animals that have been selected for a particular trait (e.g. alcohol consumption). The successive breeding of such animals over several generations can produce strains with distinct behavioural characteristics.

Sensory-specific satiety   The tendency to get bored eating one type of food if consumed over a long period.

Septum   A structure in the limbic system which has reciprocal connections with the hippocampus, amygdala and hypothalamus.

Serotonin   A monoamine neurotransmitter, also called 5-hydroxytryptamine (5-HT), which is implicated in a wide range of functions.

Serotonin uptake blocker   A class of drug that includes fluoxetine (Prozac), which selectively blocks the re-uptake of serotonin from the synaptic cleft.

Sexually dimorphic nucleus   A nucleus found in the preoptic area (i.e. anterior hypothalamus) that is much larger in males than in females.

Simultanagnosia   An inability to perceive different aspects of a visual scene. Although individual elements may be identified, the person will not be able to perceive the scene as a whole. This is one of the main symptoms of Balint's syndrome.

Sleep apnoea   A disorder where breathing is frequently and temporarily suspended during sleep, which results in the person waking.

Sleep cycle   A cycle of four slow-wave sleep stages (SWS 1-4) that progresses from predominantly theta activity (4–7 Hz) to delta activity (1–4 Hz), followed by a period of REM sleep. Each sleep cycle lasts approximately 90 minutes.

Slow-wave sleep   Sleep that is characterised by slower EEG brain waves (e.g. 1-7 Hz) than is found in waking, where beta (13-30 Hz) and alpha activity (8-12 Hz) predominate.

Sodium/potassium pump   A transport mechanism within the plasma membrane of a neuron that regulates the concentration of sodium and potassium ions inside and outside the neuron. It removes approximately three sodium ions from the neuron for every two potassium ions it takes back in.

Soma   Another term for the cell body (from the Greek for body).

Somatic nervous system   A division of the peripheral nervous system that controls skeletal muscles. It also sends sensory input from skin, muscle, tendons, joints etc. to the spinal cord and brain.

Splenium   The rear part of the corpus callosum which transfers visual information between the hemispheres.

Split-brain procedure   A surgical operation called a commissurotomy in which the corpus callosum is cut, thereby severing direct communication between the two hemispheres of the brain. This procedure has shown that the left hemisphere tends to be dominant for language, and the right hemisphere more dominant for emotion and spatial reasoning.

Stem cells   Embryologically early and undifferentiated cells, from which other types of cell, including neurons, can be derived.

Striate cortex   Another term for the primary visual cortex, so called because it has a striped (i.e. striated) appearance

Striated muscle   Another term for skeletal muscle that moves the skeleton.

Striatum   Part of the basal ganglia that is composed of the caudate nucleus and putamen, so called because of its stripped appearance in sections.

Subiculum   The area of limbic cortex in the parahippocampus gyrus that is in direct contact with the hippocampus.

Substantia nigra   A dark-pigmented nucleus found in the midbrain tegmentum which sends dopaminergic fibres to the striatum, and is known to show marked degeneration in Parkinson's disease.

Subthalamus A nucleus involved in motor behaviour that lies below the thalamus. It receives input from the striatum, and sends fibres to the globus palladus and substantia nigra.

Summation The combined accumulation of excitatory and inhibitory inputs impinging on a neuron. If the summation of inputs is sufficient to shift the resting potential of a neuron by about +15 mV at the axon hillock, an action potential will be formed.

Superior cervical ganglion A large branch of the sympathetic nervous system that includes input from the suprachiasmatic nucleus and projects to the pineal gland.

Superior colliculi Bump-like protrusions in the roof of the midbrain which receive a projection from the optic nerve, and are important in orientating the head and eyes.

Supplementary motor cortex Area of the frontal cortex that lies anterior and adjacent to the upper part of the primary motor cortex, and is important for the sequencing of goal-directed movements.

Suprachiasmatic nucleus A tiny nucleus lying just above the optic chiasm in the medial hypothalamus which acts as a biological clock and is important in the regulation of circadian rhythms.

Sympathetic nervous system A major branch of the autonomic nervous system (along with the parasympathetic nervous system) whose main function is to mobilise the body's resources for flight or fight (i.e. increase arousal).

Synapse A tiny gap or junction that most commonly lies between an axon terminal and the postsynaptic cell. There are billions of synapses in the human brain and they are important sites of information processing.

Synaptic vesicles Protective sacs that store molecules of neurotransmitter in the endings of axons. These become bound with the membrane, leading to neurotransmitter release, through the process of exocytosis.

T

Tardive dyskinesia A disorder characterised by involuntary or tic-like movements, especially of the face, mouth and lips, associated with long-term use of antipsychotic medication.

Tectum The roof or most dorsal area of the midbrain that includes the inferior and superior colliculi.

Tegmentum The part of the midbrain (or upper brainstem) located beneath the tectum that contains ascending and descending tracts, the nuclei of various cranial nerves, and structures such as the red nucleus and substantia nigra.

Temporal lobe The area of the cerebral cortex lying below and lateral to the Sylvian fissure and parietal lobe.

Testicular feminisation syndrome Another term for androgen insensitivity syndrome, a disorder in which the body is insensitive to male sex hormones such as testosterone. Consequently, during foetal growth, genetic males with XY chromosomes develop as females.

Testis-determining factor A protein that binds to undifferentiated gonad tissue in the foetus, beginning at around six weeks, which causes them to become testes.

Testosterone   The main sex hormone produced by the male gonads or testes. It has organisational effects on the body and central nervous system during foetal and pubertal development, and activational effects on certain types of behavior in adulthood.

Tetrahydroisoquinolines   Opiate-like substances that are formed by the metabolites of alcohol interacting with catecholamines in the brain.

Thalamus   A symmetrical pair of ovoid structures located above the hypothalamus (separated by the third ventricle), made up of a large number of nuclei. The thalamus functions as the principal relay station for sensory information going to the cerebral cortex and is crucially involved in regulating its electrical activity.

Threshold potential   The increase in voltage (normally around +15 mV) that needs to be reached at the axon hillock for an action potential to be formed.

Tolerance   Drug tolerance occurs when the repeated use of a substance leads to that agent producing less of an effect than it did originally – and may lead the individual to increase the dosage, resulting in addiction. The reasons for drug tolerance are complex and include biological causes (pharmacokinetic and pharmacodynamic), as well as behavioural or learned causes.

Tourette's syndrome   A disorder normally beginning in late childhood characterised by complex tic-like movements of the body and involuntary utterances of sounds and noises.

Transfer RNA   The single-stranded nucleic acid that is responsible for bringing amino acids found in the cytoplasm to the ribosome for protein synthesis.

Transgenic animals   Animals that have been genetically engineered or modified using DNA from another organism. These include, for example, knockout mice, which have had genes inactivated or 'knocked out'.

Tricyclic antidepressants   A class of antidepressant drug, which includes imipramine, that contains a three-ring chain in its molecular structure.

Turner's syndrome   A genetic condition in which the female inherits only one X chromosome and does not develop functional ovaries.

Tyramine   An amino acid found in many foodstuffs and potentially a powerful elevator of blood pressure if not metabolised by monoamine oxidase.

U

Unipolar depression   Chronic or acute major depression that does not alternate with periods of mania.

V

Vagus nerve   The longest cranial nerve in the body, consisting of both sensory and motor divisions, innervating structures of the head, neck, thorax and abdomen.

Ventral tegmental area   An area of the tegmentum which receives input from the medial forebrain bundle and is the main source of dopaminergic neurons to the forebrain, believed to be particularly important for arousal and reinforcement.

Ventricles   The hollow spaces in the brain that contain cerebrospinal fluid.

Ventromedial hypothalamus   A large nucleus in the hypothalamus which has been shown to be important in feeding and female sexual behaviour.

Viscera   Another term for the main internal organs of the body.

Visual cortex   Another name for the cortex found in the occipital lobes.

Vitreous humor   A clear gelatinous substance found in the chamber of the eyeball behind the lens.

Vomeronasal organ   A sensory organ found in reptiles and most mammals (including humans) that responds to certain types of olfactory (smell) information including pheromones.

Wada test   A test invented by Juan Wada in the 1940s that anaesthetises one of the cerebral hemispheres by an injection of sodium amytal into the carotid artery (in the neck) leading to one side of the brain. This test shows that language tends to be lateralised to the left hemisphere, especially in people who are right-handed.

Wernicke–Geschwind model   A highly influential model of language which emphasises the passage of information through Wernicke's area, the arcuate fasciculus and Broca's area in the comprehension and production of language.

Wernicke's aphasia   A language impairment characterised by fluent and meaningless speech, and poor language comprehension.

Wernicke's area   A region of the auditory association cortex (temporal cortex) that is involved in language comprehension and the production of meaningful speech.

Wolffian duct   A primitive duct in the embryo that has the potential to develop into the male reproductive organs (epididymis, vas deferens and seminal vesicles).

Working memory   A form of short-term memory that is able to concurrently hold information whilst other information is processed or other tasks are performed.

Yakovlev circuit   A brain circuit that includes the amygdala, dorsomedial thalamus and orbitofrontal cortex.

Zeitgeber   An environmental cue such as light that helps to reset a free-running circadian rhythm.

INDEX

Page numbers in **bold** denote glossary definition.

B

T

U